日本生物武器作战调查资料

〔日〕近藤昭二　王　选／主编

第一册

社会科学文献出版社
SOCIAL SCIENCES ACADEMIC PRESS (CHINA)

图书在版编目(CIP)数据

日本生物武器作战调查资料：全六册 / (日) 近藤昭二, 王选主编. -- 北京：社会科学文献出版社, 2019.7（2025.10重印）

ISBN 978-7-5201-4722-4

Ⅰ. ①日… Ⅱ. ①近… ②王… Ⅲ. ①第二次世界大战－生物战－史料－日本 Ⅳ. ①E313.9

中国版本图书馆CIP数据核字（2019）第075886号

日本生物武器作战调查资料（全六册）

主　　编 / ［日］近藤昭二　王　选

出 版 人 / 冀祥德
责任编辑 / 邵璐璐
责任印制 / 岳　阳

出　　版 / 社会科学文献出版社 · 历史学分社（010）59367256
地址：北京市北三环中路甲29号院华龙大厦　邮编：100029
网址：www.ssap.com.cn
发　　行 / 社会科学文献出版社（010）59367028
印　　装 / 河北虎彩印刷有限公司

规　　格 / 开　本：787mm×1092mm 1/16
印　张：218.75　幅　数：3500幅
版　　次 / 2019年7月第1版　2025年10月第3次印刷
书　　号 / ISBN 978-7-5201-4722-4
定　　价 / 4980. 00元（全六册）

读者服务电话：4008918866

教育部哲学社会科学研究重大课题攻关项目
“日本侵华史料整理与研究”（项目号：09JZD0013）
子课题“日军对华生物战”成果

上海市大华公益基金会资助出版

主编简介

〔日〕近藤昭二

日本NPO法人「731部隊·細菌戦資料センター」共同代表之一。主编『731部隊·細菌戦資料集成』（光盘版，柏書房，2003）。

王　选

日本NPO法人「731部隊·細菌戦資料センター」共同代表之一，浙江省义乌市二战细菌战问题研究中心法人代表、主任。主编《大贱年：1943年卫河流域战争灾难口述史》（中国文史出版社，2017），合著《1944衡阳会战亲历记》（西苑出版社，2012）。

资料解说（一）

王　选

1. 创设——细菌战研究的开始

第一次世界大战中，德军使用化学武器，造成极大的伤亡。为此，1925 年 6 月 17 日，44 个国家在日内瓦裁军会议上通过协议，签署了禁止毒气战、细菌战的国际条约——《关于禁止使用窒息性瓦斯、毒性瓦斯与同类瓦斯以及细菌学战争手段议定书》（简称《日内瓦条约》）。日本也派代表参加会议，参与了条约的起草和签署（当时日本国内未予核准）。

《日内瓦条约》对化学、生物武器的禁止，仅限于使用，并未包括化学、生物武器的开发、制造、保存、移动等方面。注意到这一问题的，是后来成为关东军防疫部部长（731 部队长）的石井四郎，当时他还是京都大学研究生院一名从事细菌学、血清学、病理学研究的学生。他看到了出席日内瓦会议的原田丰二等军医的会议报告。石井毕业后，在大学导师清野谦次的建议下，从 1928 年 4 月起，在两年时间内，游历了 25 个欧美国家，途中所见所闻，使他痛感日本细菌战研究的落后。

回到日本 4 个月后，石井四郎就任日本陆军军医学校教官。对于缺乏矿产资源的日本来说，生物武器价廉，生产成本低，自动传播杀伤力大，其有效性及研究的空间使石井决定倾心投入。于是他开始游说陆军中央，提议设立开发生物武器的军事机关。当时在日本参谋本部作战课任职的远藤三郎在 1932 年 1 月 20 日的日记中记载："那时候，老是看到石井跑到参谋本部来，向各位参谋游说细菌战的重要性。"

1932 年 8 月，在小泉亲彦教官的支持下，在已经有防疫部的日本陆军军医学校，又设立了以石井四郎为首的防疫研究室（资料 1.1.2）。

石井长女春海在日本的英文报纸 *The Japan Times*（1982 年 8 月 29 日）上说："如果没有战争，如果父亲没有选择医学，以父亲的天分，在医学以外的领域，在政治领域，也很可能会有所成就。"据美国国家档案馆所藏文献中日本某微生物学者所言："石井极为聪明，对事业很投入，可他不是一个学者型的人，野心很大，喜欢做大事情。"[①] 如此野心旺盛、组织能力强的石井，在日本入侵中

① National Archives of the United States，331，1434，13.

国东北后不久，即跑到当地，推行大规模细菌战研究，包括人体实验（资料 1.1.3、1.1.4）。

战后，1955 年 12 月 28 日为其教官清野谦次守灵的那天夜里，石井即席发言："政府确立了国家百年大计：保护官兵健康，减少死亡率和患病率……于是，先在陆军军医学校里设了研究室，满洲哈尔滨（以洛克菲勒研究所为中心），然后在南支的中山大学，一个一个的把研究所建了起来，一共建了 324 个研究所……哈尔滨建的研究所有丸楼 14 倍半那么大，里头有火车、飞机，是一个所有设施全面具备的综合型研究所（指哈尔滨平房 731 部队的设施——引者注），在那里专心做研究……已看到目标的实现，最后将在整个大东亚，首次完成这个民族阵线的全面防御。""最盛时期，范围之广从哈尔滨到荷属东印度，从北海道到西里伯斯（Celebes）。"（资料 6.1.11 附录）

石井刚到满洲时，用的是化名"东乡太郎"，初期在哈尔滨东南约 70 公里的一个村落背荫河建了一个守备队式的设施，开始进行人体实验。1932 年远藤三郎任关东军作战主任时，曾到"东乡部队"视察，其著述《日中十五年战争与我》中描述如下：

（是由）一个相当大的酱油作坊改建的，四周围着高垒的土墙，里面出勤的军医全部用的化名，管得很严格，不许与外部通信。部队名称"东乡部队"。被实验者一个一个被监禁在坚固的铁格子里，对人体接种各种病原菌，观察病情的变化。用于这些实验的是哈尔滨监狱的死囚犯，说起来是死囚犯又是为了国防，但是其残酷令人惨不忍睹。死了的，用高压电气炉焚毁一尽，不留痕迹。①

由于国际法的禁止，出于实战的考虑及人伦上的忌讳，"东乡部队"为使其研究保持高度机密，建立了严密的警备体制。令人意外的是，1934 年农历八月十五中秋节，16 名被囚禁的中国人越狱后成功逃脱。"东乡部队"难以继续保持机密。

越狱的 16 名中国人中 12 名投奔了东北抗日联军第三军，第三军得知情况后，袭击了背荫河"东乡部队"，资料 1.1.3 、1.1.4 记述的是当时遭到袭击后，日军的部分伤亡情况。越狱事件发生后，"东乡部队"为防止内部机密败露，关闭了背荫河的设施，一度撤回日本东京陆军军医学校，后又搬回哈尔滨南岗。

1936 年 5 月 30 日，石井四郎所率"东乡部队"（又称"加茂部队"）获天皇的"军令陆甲第七号"（"军令陆甲"为日本陆军军事机密事项，参见资料 1.2.3），成为正式的部队，不再是陆军军医学校防疫研究室的派出机构，归属关东军，在平房建立一大型基地，名称为关东军防疫部。有关该部队据日本陆军中央命令的正式组编与改编，参见资料 1.2。

此后，日军设立的防疫给水部队 / 细菌部队、有关机构如下：

1937 年　东京　登户陆军研究所

① 日中書林、1974、162 頁。

1938 年　北京　华北派遣军防疫给水部队 / 1855 细菌部队

1939 年　南京　华中派遣军防疫给水部队 / 1644 细菌部队

　　　　　广州　华南派遣军防疫给水部队 / 8604 细菌部队

1942 年　新加坡　南方军防疫给水部队 / 9620 细菌部队

当时，日本陆军内部称这些与石井细菌战有关的部队，包括陆军军医学校防疫研究室为“石井机关”，防疫研究室为其研究中枢。防疫研究室统筹军内外研究人员，以“委托研究”制度、“共同研究”、“论文指导”等形式，组织动员日本医学界、民间研究机构参与军事医学、防疫学，包括细菌战相关研究。

据日本研究者常石敬一《731 部队——生物武器犯罪的真相》（講談社、1995）一书，“石井机关”人员编制超过 10000 名，其中满洲“新京”（长春）100 部队、南京 1644 部队和哈尔滨 731 部队一样，日常性地进行人体实验。

作为“中枢”，防疫研究室编辑发行《陆军军医学校防疫研究报告》（以下简称《防疫报告》），刊载“石井机关”研究人员的相关研究纪要和成果。本资料集第 4 章收入的 731 部队核心研究人员金子顺一、高桥正彦的博士论文集，均为战时《防疫报告》刊载的论文。

2. 警觉——细菌战的动向

资料 2.1 中那位支持石井四郎的细菌战研究与准备的“石光技师”，全名石光熏，毕业于东京帝国大学医学部，关东军防疫部正式编成两年后的 1938 年即服役于该部队，直到战争结束，是一名老资格的细菌部队高级军官。

资料 2.2 显示，日本陆军军医学校的有关人员对黄热病毒非常感兴趣，竭力想法从美国研究机构把病毒株弄到手，为美军军医总部以及 G-2（参谋二部，即情报部门）察觉，开始对轴心国的细菌战动向有所警觉。

美国未能及时掌握日本的情况，其实当时日军以陆军军医学校防疫研究室为据点开始细菌战研究已达 9 年，哈尔滨平房规模巨大的细菌战专门设施也基本完成，编制人员多达 3000 名以上。第 3 章、第 4 章、第 9 章等的资料显示，这支细菌部队 1940 年即在当时为中国军队占领的要地——浙江省衢县、宁波、金华实施大规模的细菌武器攻击。

资料 2.3 中的 Dr. Ryoichi Naito 是石井四郎京都帝国大学的后辈内藤良一，其战后出版的杂文集《老 SL 的噪音》中如此记述：“陆军省派我去美国费城学习当时刚开始开发的冻结真空干燥技术。4 月回国后，就在陆军军医学校负责搞疫苗、血清。”[①] 据资料 3.26 1943 年 1 月 8 日美国联邦安全局情报，1942 年 3 月 8 日，另有一日本人 Dr. Hayakawa 试图从巴西一实验室获取黄热病毒。

① 綠十字株式会社、1980、55 頁。

当时，内藤在陆军军医学校防疫研究室担任“细菌学”和“要务”的教官。内藤1931年于京都帝国大学医学部医学科毕业，同年成为军医中尉，1934年又进入母校的研究生院学习，当时微生物学教室的前辈即增田知贞，后来也成为陆军军医学校防疫研究室的干部，并接替石井四郎担任日军驻南京1644部队第二任部队长（参见第6章、第9章、第10章资料）。

内藤良一以编辑、发行细菌部队成员、委托学者的研究纪要《陆军军医学校防疫研究报告》①，从事真空干燥技术的研究，在“石井机关”中占有重要地位。在战后美国四任调查官赴日的细菌战调查中，内藤也扮演了重要角色，斡旋期间，拖延美方掌握日本细菌战研究人体实验、实施细菌武器攻击的真相（参见第6章、第9章资料）。

朝鲜战争期间，内藤与“石井机关”同僚成立了企业“日本血库”，此后发展为“绿十字株式会社”，内藤为首任会长。20世纪90年代，“绿十字”将已知晓有HIV病毒污染嫌疑的美国进口血制品在日本市场销售，致超过2000名日本人感染HIV病毒，制造了战后日本最大的“药害”事件。

资料2.3中的Dr. Miyakawa即东京帝国大学传染病研究所所长宫川米次博士（1934年2月起担任所长，1940年1月20日由三田村笃志接任）。美国方面在调查中，曾一度把他当作日本细菌战研究的重要人物予以关注。

3. 情报——在中国实施的细菌战

第3章所收资料为美国国家档案馆（National Archives of the United States）所藏美国战时有关日本实施细菌战的情报资料，自1941年至1945年战争结束，内容基本上与日军在华细菌战有关。这些资料中大部分为近年检索发现，目前尚未见诸研究发表，其中有些内容与中国战时情报内容一致（参见中央档案馆等编《细菌战与毒气战》，中华书局，1989），有的资料来自中国方面。

此章所收资料较多，主要内容如下。

第一，1940年浙江省宁波、金华、衢州，1941年湖南常德遭受日军鼠疫菌攻击后，中国政府搜集证据，展开调查，组织中外专家鉴定后，由中央卫生署总长发布，同时通过各种途径——报纸、电报、广播、医学杂志、年鉴、外交使领馆等向国际社会呼吁。例如，所收美国国家新闻检阅处情报1942年10月19日墨西哥报纸报道的中国政府声明，题目即为《日本人在中国实施细菌战》（资料3.24）。

当时搜集的证据后来成为远东国际军事法庭国际检察局备案证据材料（参见第5章、第9章）。资料3.20英文论文《常德鼠疫及其防治措施》现藏于中国第二历史档案馆。作者王诗恒（S. H. Wang）当时为贵阳医学院1944级学生，1942年赴湖南实习公共卫生。在当时正在常德指导鼠疫防疫的国际红十字会防疫专家R. Pollitzer博士（资料3.8）的指导下完成的这篇论文，是当时最完整的常德遭受日军细菌武器——鼠疫跳蚤攻击后，爆发鼠疫的流行病观察报告。此前，1940年浙江各地遭

① 王选：《“石井机关”与研究报告》，解学诗、〔日〕松村高夫等：《战争与恶疫——日军对华细菌战》，人民出版社，2014。

受日军鼠疫菌攻击后鼠疫流行，R. Pollitzer 博士也曾作为中国国民政府派遣的鼠疫防疫专家，赴各地现场指导鼠疫防疫，对此浙江省包括县级国民政府战时鼠疫防疫档案中均有记载（参见中共浙江省委党史研究室、浙江省档案局编《日军侵浙细菌战档案资料汇编》，浙江人民出版社，2015、2017）。

当时国际学术界关于常德的鼠疫流行是否由日军投放物质引起有不同意见（资料 3.8、3.9）。1993 年发现的日军中国派遣军司令部作战参谋井本熊男日记（『井本日誌』）中具体记载了日军 731 等部队对于常德实施鼠疫跳蚤攻击，使之尘埃落定。井本的日记为日本防卫厅图书馆所藏，1993 年由日本历史学者吉见义明、伊香俊哉发现，将相关内容予以整理发表。[①] 2011 年新发现的“石井机关”核心研究人员金子顺一论文《PX 效果略算法》（参见资料 4.1）记录了日军在中国战场使用鼠疫跳蚤的 6 次攻击，其中也包括常德，印证了井本日记中的相关记载。

从第 3 章资料来看，当时美军情报部门对于 1941 年湖南常德的细菌战鼠疫菌攻击也通过多种渠道做了调查，如当地的美国宗教团体和人士、教会医院人员等。

第二，关于日军炭疽攻击的关联性资料，列举部分如下。

资料 3.26 美国的轴心国细菌战方面情报中提及德国和日本的炭疽攻击准备。资料 3.47、3.48 1945 年 1 月美军情报报告中提及在菲律宾莱特缴获的日军文件显示日军部队注射炭疽疫苗，分析有可能使用炭疽攻击。

资料 6.3.5 美国第三任赴日细菌战调查官 Norbert H. Fell 博士（参见表 2）1947 年 4 月 22 日对增田知贞的讯问记录，增田承认：“在中支那地区（中国中部地区——引者注）对中国军队实施了试验性的细菌炸弹攻击，细菌炸弹有强有力的攻击性效果，特别是如果填装的是炭疽的话，见效很快。”

资料 6.2.8 美国第二任调查官 Arvo T. Thompson 中校提交的日期为 1946 年 5 月 31 日的《日本细菌战活动报告（1946 年 1 月 11 日至 3 月 11 日）》（参见表 2）第八部分：攻击性细菌战活动中列举了日军设计制作的各种型号细菌炸弹，其中包括炭疽炸弹 Ha 弹（附有设计图），填充 1500 颗外涂防腐剂带炭疽孢子的钢制弹丸。据以上调查报告，1938 年，Ha 弹生产量达 500 枚。另一种细菌炸弹 Uji（宇治）50 型也曾用于炭疽孢子菌液投放试验，1940~1941 年产量达 500 枚，1940~1942 年间，进行了大规模范围内的野外投放试验，先期使用染料和非病原菌填充炸弹，后期使用炭疽孢子悬浮液填充炸弹（称炭疽炸弹投放试验用的是大型牲畜，比如马、牛、羊）。

据资料 6.3.6，1947 年 4 月 27 日增田知贞向美国调查官 Fell 提供了以下有关情报：在细菌战研究的早期阶段，他们即确信炭疽为最有效的细菌武器。经过各种实验，包括人体实验可知，引发人体炭疽感染可以使用下列手段：a. 口入，或掺入食物中；b. 吸入；c. 皮肤破口感染；d. 注射（参见资料 7.1）。根据实验结果，炭疽可以三种方式投放：a. 攻击个体的人，用隐蔽的方式，以特工、间谍撒播，不留痕迹，看似是自然原因引起感染；b. 填充炭疽的炸弹，炸弹碎

① 『戦争責任研究』（季刊）第 2 号、1993 年 2 月。参见李力《浙赣细菌战（1940~1944 年）》，解学诗、〔日〕松村高夫等:《战争与恶疫——日军对华细菌战》，第四章。

片造成人体伤口，随后引起感染死亡；c. 飞机空中投放细菌，污染水源或者区域。

资料 10.24 中，增田（知贞）称：1945 年 8 月，平房销毁了尚存的 400 公斤干燥炭疽菌（参见资料 6.3.7、9.32）。以上说明，当时，日军已经具备干燥炭疽菌的技术，这项技术关联日军炭疽的储备能力、攻击的方式和手段，包括上述增田知贞向美国调查官提供的三种投放方式。

资料 6.3.11 美国调查官对石井四郎的讯问记录中，石井也称：关于炭疽，我认为是最佳细菌（武器），因为可以大量生产，抗性强，毒性持久，致死率可达 80%~90%。最佳流行病病菌则为鼠疫，最佳媒介物引发疾病病菌为流行性脑炎。

资料 6.3.17 美国第三任细菌战调查官 Fell 的调查报告《日本细菌战活动新情报简要总结》（参见表 2）中提到石井等提供一份以人为攻击对象的细菌战活动的报告，共 60 页，并列举了相关的作为细菌武器的细菌，予以简述，第一类即为炭疽，第二类鼠疫，第三类伤寒、副伤寒 A 型 & B 型、痢疾，第四类霍乱，第五类鼻疽，第六类流行性出血热（“孙吴热”），同时说明所有的有关实验均为用人体的实验。

关于炭疽的简介，列出 a. 感染、致命剂量；b. 直接感染；c. 疫苗实验；d. 投弹试验；e. 污染草地；f. 喷洒试验；g. 稳定性；h. 事故性和实验室内感染。“投弹试验”中提到用 Uji（宇治）弹的投放人体试验。“稳定性”中提到，添加 0.5% 苯酚可维持炭疽孢子在干燥蛋清、土壤等里 10 年的稳定性，其他如黄油、奶酪、牛奶、奶油里可维持 5 年的稳定性。“事故性和实验室内感染”中日军实验发现人与人之间感染的例子：三名劳工未穿防护服进入炭疽污染的草地后均出现皮肤症状，用血清治愈，但是两名与他们居住一起的劳工被感染，其中一人死亡。也有实验室人员戴着防护面罩，仍然被感染。

第三，日军攻击使用的细菌除鼠疫、霍乱、伤寒、副伤寒、痢疾外，还可能有白喉、肺结核，甚至脑炎（资料 3.61、6.3.12）。浙江战时，特别是浙赣战役期间，地方志有关疾病流行的记载中，有相当数量的白喉、脑炎病例集中性发生（参见《日军侵浙细菌战档案资料汇编》）。

第四，除日军细菌部队实施细菌武器攻击外，日本特工、宪兵，甚至一般部队，也作为“谋略手段”散布细菌（资料 3.41、3.57、3.66）。中国各地的战时档案文献中有关于日本特工、汉奸撒播细菌的情报文献（参见《细菌战与毒气战》）。

第五，资料 3. 53、3.54、3.55、3.56、3.61、3.62 美军有关日军细菌战情报中接连提到上海市内数地、浙江嘉兴、江西九江的日军细菌战相关活动，涉及日本医生组织（同仁会）、科研机构、地方医院的参与。中国战时档案文献中也有相关记载（参见《细菌战与毒气战》）。

第六，资料 3.23、3.40、3.49、3.52、3.59、3.60 有关日军在河南、福建、江西、云南（滇缅地区）实施细菌武器攻击的情报，尚期待相关案例的调查研究。

4. 证据——731 部队金子顺一、高桥正彦论文集

金子顺一、高桥正彦均为日军细菌部队核心研究人员。

资料 4.1《金子顺一论文集》为金子顺一（参见资料 6.3.7）于 1944 年 12 月向东京帝国大学申请医学博士学位时提交的论文集。2011 年，由日本 NPO 法人 731 部队・细菌战资料中心理事奈须重雄于日本国会图书馆关西馆发现。

1937 年 7 月，金子顺一被分配至 731 部队，1943 年 3 月调任日本陆军军医学校部员，兼职于陆军第九技术研究所，从事秘密武器的开发，特别是承载细菌武器的“风船炸弹”的研究。

《金子顺一论文集》由 8 篇战时细菌战研究论文组成，其中 7 篇发表于日本陆军军医学校防疫研究报告第一部。《防疫报告》分第一、第二部两大类，第二部的论文机密度低，共发行 900 号，其中 800 多号已于 2005 年由日本不二出版社根据美国国会图书馆所藏原件影印出版，其余尚缺。据其编者常石敬一，第一部为“军事秘密”，机密度高，用誊写版印刷，限制发行部数，一版至多印百来册。第一部与第二部的区别主要在于内容，第一部的研究非常具实际性，比如有关实战的论文。常石敬一提及有关者证言：1945 年 8 月 14 日，日本陆军省次官向全军发布命令，“烧毁重要文件”，防疫研究室也不例外，全烧毁了。《防疫报告》第一部发表的论文除了《金子顺一论文集》的 7 篇被集中发现以外，目前在日本仅有数篇被发现。

金子 8 篇论文中的主论文为资料 4.1.1《雨下散布的基础考察》，“雨下”为空中散布细菌等物质的一种方式。限于篇幅，本专题仅收入 8 篇中《PX 效果略算法》（见资料 4.1.3）一文全文。

《PX 效果略算法》中的“PX”为带鼠疫菌跳蚤印度客蚤的代号，论文中金子以日军 6 次对中国各地 PX 攻击的相关基本数据，参照石井四郎关于细菌战的“ABDEO”（外因、媒介、病原、内因、运用）理论，[①] 推算 PX 作为武器的“效果”，即一定量的 PX 散布后，因之感染鼠疫死亡的人数。6 次 PX 攻击具体参见论文中表 1。

表 1　日军对中国各地的 6 次 PX 攻击

攻击时间	目标	PX(千克)	效果（人）	
			一次	二次
1940 年 6 月 4 日	农安	0.005	8	607
1940 年 6 月 4~7 日	农安、大赉	0.010	12	2424
1940 年 10 月 4 日	衢县	8.0	219	9060
1940 年 10 月 27 日	宁波	2.0	104	1450
1941 年 11 月 4 日	常德	1.6	310	2500
1942 年 8 月 19~21 日	广信、广丰、玉山	0.131	42	9210

注：1. P 为鼠疫，X 为印度客蚤，是跳蚤的一种，为传播鼠疫的主要媒介；

2. 效果一栏中的“一次”指 PX 散布后第一次感染鼠疫死亡人数；“二次”指第二次感染死亡人数。论文中并没有说明死亡人数的统计方法和具体来源。

金子论文中的日军 6 次 PX 攻击证实了第 3 章和第 5 章资料中中国方面对于日军实施细菌武器攻击——散布鼠疫菌的指控。资料 6.3.6 美国第三任调查官 Fell 对亀井贯一郎的讯问记录中，亀井

① 〔日〕波多野澄雄：《细菌战研究进入新阶段：〈金子顺一论文集〉中的“ホ号作战”》，解学诗、〔日〕松村高夫等：《战争与恶疫——日军对华细菌战》。

提到："金子了解对中国人的试验性攻击的效果，其中包括用鼠疫菌的攻击。"（参见资料 6.3.7）

自 1993 年日本历史学者吉见义明、伊香俊哉于井本熊男日记中发现有关日军在中国战场实施细菌武器攻击的内容记载以来，《金子顺一论文集》为日本国内所发现的另一日本军方重大的细菌战证据材料。日本历史学者波多野澄雄撰文《细菌战研究进入新阶段：〈金子顺一论文集〉中的"ホ号作战"真相》，根据以上金子论文的内容以及井本日记的相关记载，对日军在华细菌战做了梳理。[①] 据日本"十五年战争与日本医学研究会"西山胜夫（滋贺医科大学）的研究，1944 年末，金子向东京帝国大学提出博士学位申请，实际审查战后 1948 年 11 月 10 日才开始，时值远东国际军事法庭结束两周前，当时金子在生物理化学研究所新潟支所任制造课长。金子论文的研究显而易见与细菌武器的攻击性使用有关，但是 27 名审查员无一提出异议。1949 年 1 月，金子以战时日本军队细菌战研究的成果，被授予东京帝国大学医学博士学位。[②]

资料 4.2 为 731 部队第一部鼠疫班班长高桥正彦关于 1940 年农安、"新京"鼠疫的调查研究报告，2000 年 9 月由日本历史学者松村高夫（庆应义塾大学）在庆应大学医学部仓库里发现。高桥的论文也是为申请医学博士学位提交，日本国立国会图书馆关西馆博士论文库有收藏。

2003 年，松村高夫与江田泉为吉林省档案馆藏《731 部队特别移送・防疫档案选编》撰写的《"新京"・农安鼠疫流行解说》[③] 首次披露以上高桥的报告，并对解学诗提出的 1940 年"'新京'、农安鼠疫"为 731 部队细菌谋略的疑问做了讨论。[④]

2011 年发现的金子论文《PX 效果略算法》确证了 1940 年日军对农安的鼠疫攻击：6 月 4 日农安一次，6 月 4 ~ 7 日农安、大赉一次，均为历年该地区自然鼠疫将开始流行的时期。6 月 17 日，农安出现首例鼠疫感染病例，高桥在论文中列举了各项理由，"断定"此后 9 月 27 日起，"新京"（长春）开始发生的鼠疫流行，为农安传播而至。据资料 4.2.6 高桥报告第四编《关于流行中分离的鼠疫菌》，1940 年鼠疫流行的农安、"新京"以及周边各县分离的 110 株鼠疫菌，形状、特性相同。

高桥报告中有关 1940 年农安、"新京"鼠疫的观察和研究，涉及各个领域，内容详尽。据资料 4.2 附录，当时向小县城农安派遣了至少由 1000 名专业人员组成的防疫队伍。

金子顺一的论文和高桥正彦报告的内容显示，两者的"成果"均得之于有组织的专业性团队的调查研究。

5. 远东国际军事法庭国际检察局的调查

根据日本政府接受的《波茨坦公告》第十条，盟军最高司令官麦克阿瑟主持设立远东国际军事

① 〔日〕波多野澄雄：《细菌战研究进入新阶段：〈金子顺一论文集〉中的"ホ号作战"》，解学诗、〔日〕松村高夫等：《战争与恶疫——日军对华细菌战》。

② 西山勝夫『戦争と医学 Ⅱ』文理閣、2014。

③ 吉林省档案馆、日本日中近现代史研究会、日本 ABC 企划委员会编《吉林省档案馆藏七三一部队罪行铁证：特别移送・防疫档案选编》，吉林人民出版社，2003。

④ 解学诗：《"新京"鼠疫谋略（1940 年）》，解学诗等：《战争与恶疫：七三一部队罪行考》，人民出版社，1998，第三章。

法庭，制定法庭宪章及程序。美国国家的有关对日方针政策由美国国务院—陆军—海军三部协调委员会（SWNCC）决定，提交总统杜鲁门批准后，由美军最高权力机构——总参谋部传达给麦克阿瑟。

1945 年 12 月 7 日第一批到达东京的美国法务官 Robert Donihi 于 2002 年 6 月在美国家中接受日本媒体（本资料集主编之一近藤昭二）采访时说，在他往东京的飞机上，首席检察官 Joseph H. Keenan 就打招呼了："不起诉天皇裕仁，别往那方面去想。""不追究裕仁的责任，为了盟军治理日本，加以利用。"

1946 年 2 月 2 日，英国检察团到达东京之前，法庭国际检察局大部分是美国检察官，苏联检察团 47 人直到距离开庭 20 天的 4 月 13 日才到达。中国检察团接着英国检察团于 1946 年 2 月初到达，代表中国的检察官为向哲浚，国际检察局分工负责第二组日本对中国军事侵略的为美国检察官 Thomas H. Morrow 上校。

据资料 5.3.1，向哲浚等到达大约三星期后的 3 月 2 日，Morrow 即向首席检察官 Keenan 提交书面报告，提出日军违反国际法，在中国战场实施化学战和细菌战，已于 2 月 27 日向调查部门提出要求安排讯问石井将军。并提及美军报纸 *Pacific Stars and Stripes* 1946 年 2 月 27 日刊载的 UP 特派员 Peter Kalisher 的报道：以石井为首的日本研究机构用美国和中国战俘做鼠疫人体实验，实施细菌战实验（参见资料 6.2.7）。Morrow 报告在最后提出，生化武器使用的问题很重要，因为是国际法禁止的；并提出日军实施被禁止战争手段是东京的政府，不是战场指挥官的决策。

资料 5.3.2 为 3 月 8 日 Morrow 再次向 Keenan 提交的报告，提及曾就有关细菌战和石井中将活动的陈述，与美国第二任赴日细菌战调查官 Thompson 中校（资料 6.2）会面；美军报纸 *Pacific Stars and Stripes* 的报道与 *China Handbook* 中对于日军细菌战的指控（参见资料 3.35，该书第十七章"公共卫生和医疗"提及日军在中国的细菌武器攻击）相应。Morrow 称："有关谈话，结果被否。但是 Thompson 让我们去找盟军总司令部化学战部队长官 Marshall 上校。"（参见资料 5.3.6、5.3.7）根据上下文，"有关谈话"应该指与"石井中将"的"谈话"，为取得其有关细菌战活动的"陈述"。

资料 5.3.3 为 3 月 12 日中国检察官向哲浚与 Morrow 检察官等赴中国调查，取得关于日军化学战、细菌战第一手证据材料，4 月 12 日回到东京后，向 Keenan 提交的中国调查报告。资料 5.3.4 为随同向哲浚与 Morrow 赴中国调查的国际检察局第二组美国助理检察官 David N. Sutton 撰写的细菌战调查报告。这次调查中，Sutton 具体负责日军细菌战调查，Morrow 具体负责日军化学战调查。美国国家档案馆藏有相当数量中国检方提交的有关日军化学战的证据材料。

资料 5.3.4 Sutton 的中国细菌战调查报告共有 37 页，具体列举了日军 1940 年 10 月 4 日在浙江省衢县、27 日在浙江省宁波、1941 年 11 月 4 日在常德空中撒播谷物等物质，随后当地的鼠疫爆发流行，以及相关证据，包括临床记录、流行病学专家的分析报告。报告最后提出，决定对细菌战进行审判，建议以下为出庭证人：医学博士金宝善、陈文贵、Dr. Robert Pollitzer、容启荣。据第 3 章资料，金宝善为当时国民政府行政院中央卫生署总长，负责编辑 *China Handbook* 中有关战时防疫及日军细菌战的部分；陈文贵为国民政府派赴常德调查鼠疫的调查队负责人、《常德鼠疫调查报告书，1941 年 12 月 12 日》的作者，时任国民政府军政部战时卫生人员训练总所检验学组主任、中国红十字会总会救护队部检验医学指导员；Dr. Robert Pollitzer 为常德鼠疫调查队国际红十字会流行病防疫专家，国际联盟援助中国专家雇员；容启荣为国民政府中央卫生署防疫处处长、《防治湘西鼠疫经过报告书》的作者。

报告第 18 页有一份浙江省卫生厅的数据，列举了 1940 ~ 1944 年浙江省一些与日军"散布带腺鼠疫菌物质"有关的鼠疫流行时间与地点——宁波、衢县、义乌、东阳，并说明义乌、东阳的鼠疫是由衢县传播而来的。

1997 年 8 月，浙江宁波、衢州、义乌、东阳与湖南常德的日军细菌战鼠疫受害者，在社会各界的支持下，联合日本及国际社会和平力量，经过数年的调查后，在东京地方法院起诉日本政府。中国原告方向日本法庭提交了共 450 件事实证据，其中包括上述 Sutton 报告中建议出庭作证的四位中外医学专家的报告书、鉴定书等（参见第 3 章资料）。

细菌战诉讼中国原告方出庭证人中村明子，原日本国立预防病研究所研究员，在东京地方法院法庭上对本资料中金宝善、陈文贵、Dr. Robert Pollitzer、王诗恒等当时有关常德细菌战的调查报告书、鉴定书、医学论文等评价如下：即使以今天的流行病专业标准来看，这些文献也是具备科学性和客观性的。

2002 年 8 月，中国原告方提出的日本在中国以上地区实施细菌战鼠疫攻击，造成鼠疫蔓延，大量平民感染死亡，以及井本日记中记载的浙江省江山县日军撒播霍乱菌，造成当地民众感染死亡的指控，获得东京地方法院判决的全面认定，判决并认定日本细菌战违反国际法，日本对此犯罪负有国家责任。2005 年东京高等法院的判决、2007 年日本最高法院的决定维持了以上判决结果。

资料 5.1 为国际检察局有关日军在华细菌战的证据材料 No.1895 下落不明的相关文件，证据文件上有中国检察官向哲浚秘书高文彬的英文签名（William Kaw）。文件中提到另一份细菌战证据材料 No.1896，即资料 5.2。No.1896 是中国在押日军战俘榛叶修的讯问记录及本人亲笔供述，其中包括一份用日文手写的《日军罪行证明书》，日期为"民国三十五年四月十七日"，附有一张其手绘的位于南京中山东路的 1644 部队建筑分布图，日期为"三十五年四月十九日"。榛叶修为日军 1644 细菌部队九江支队卫生兵，1944 年 3 月于九江脱离日军部队，为当地游击队俘获。资料 5.2 附战时美军对榛叶修（俘虏番号 229）反复讯问的记录及相关情报报告。榛叶修的供述证实日军配备专业细菌部队，并在中国战场实施了细菌武器攻击。

榛叶修日语读音为 Shinba Osamu，以上资料中"Chimba Isamu""Chin You Shu 椿叶修"或是日文汉字读音错误，或是中文汉字读音，指的是同一人。榛叶修是目前所知日军细菌部队约 1 万名人员中唯一一名在战时被盟军俘获的。

据 Sutton 检察官文献记录（美国 Richmond 大学法学图书馆 Sutton Collection, Working and Personal Series），1946 年 5 月 9 日，Sutton 发现他桌子上有一张中国检察官向哲浚留下的字条，还有一份榛叶修《日军罪业证明书》的英文译文，4 月 17~19 日在日本静冈对榛叶修讯问的记录。向检察官还留下了一份日军在中国战场使用各种化学武器的报告：事例、武器的种类及所造成的中国军队伤亡。并在另一段落里提及1940~1941 年日军对中国各地的鼠疫攻击（参见资料 3.16），日军人员、机构的细菌战相关活动。①

资料 5.3.6、5.3.7 为盟军总司令部化学战部队长官 Geoffrey Marshall 上校向美军化学战部队长官

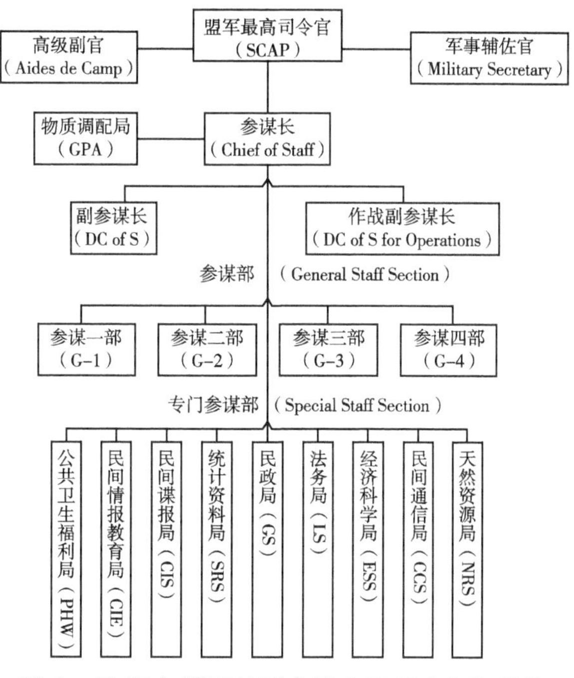

图 1　1947 年盟军总司令部（GHQ）组织结构

资料来源：参考 Charles A. Willoughby『GHQ 知られざる諜報戦』（延禎監修、平塚柾緒編、山川出版社、2011）。

提交的报告，内容有关日本在中国使用化学武器和细菌武器。资料 5.3.6 为资料 5.3.3 Morrow 中国调查报告摘要。资料 5.3.7 文件内容关于日军细菌战，其附录尚未发现。

资料 5.3.9 为 1946 年 6 月 4 日首席检察官 Keenan 予国际检察局成员的通报：中央讯问中心成立，在日本，任何日本和外国国籍人士的讯问均由盟军占领军总司令部 G-2 副参谋长（C. A. Willoughby）直接掌管和指导。手续必须经过 G-2 审批与安排，并须向 G-2 提交一式三份讯问记录。

资料 5.3.10 为 1946 年 12 月 13 日国际检察局代理休假的首席检察官 Keenan 主管事务的美国检察官 Frank S. Tavenner, Jr. 予苏联检察官 A. N. Vasiliev 少将的照会，题目：细菌战。称数位检察官仔细审阅了少佐 Karazawa（柄泽）、少将 Kawashima（川岛）有关石井部队攻击性细菌武器实验活动的证词（参见资料 9.37、9.38）。已有一名具有经验的美国调查官派遣日本调查日本细菌战 7 周，未发现任何证据表明这些实验来自东京参谋本部的命令，也未曾接收到有关此类实验的报告。法庭认为当前的证据不足以立罪。关于该资料的历史背景，参见表 2。

1946 年 5 月 3 日开庭至 1948 年 11 月 12 日结束的远东国际军事法庭（东京审判），最终并未审判违反国际法的日本细菌战战争犯罪。资料 9.37、9.38、10.28、10.30 有关国际检察局代理主管、美国检察官 Frank S. Tavenner, Jr. 涉及的日本细菌战战争犯罪责任追究的关系。

① Jeanne Guillemin, *Hidden Atrocities: Japanese Germ Warfare and American Obstruction of Justice at the Tokyo Trial*, Columbia University Press, New York, 2017, pp.194–195.

表 2　远东国际军事法庭国际检察局、美国四任赴日调查官、盟军占领军总司令部法务局的日军细菌战调查

年	月	日	远东国际军事法庭国际检察局调查	美国四任调查官赴日调查	动态、法务局调查
1945	8	9			苏军出兵中国东北
		10			大本营作战参谋朝枝繁春从东京飞抵“新京”（长春），告731部队长石井四郎参谋总长的命令：“关于贵部队今后的处置，贵部队一切的证据，从地球上永远、彻底地隐灭。”
		15	天皇发布投降诏书		陆军省军务局军事课课员新妻清一书面指示掩盖731等部队证据；日军南京1644细菌部队（多摩部队）开始销毁证据
		26			日本政府在外务省设立战后联络中央事务局，第一部主管战争犯罪事务
		28		美国军事科学调查团到达日本，其成员调查官M. Sanders开始调查日本细菌战研究（资料6.1）	
		29	同盟国战争犯罪委员会发布设立远东国际军事法庭公告		
	9	11	盟国占领军总司令部指控原日本首相东条英机等39名战争罪犯，予以逮捕		
		24	太平洋地区美陆军总司令部发布《战犯审判规定》（乙、丙级）		
		27			盟国占领军总司令麦克阿瑟会见天皇
	11	1		•《Sanders报告》（资料6.1.11）提交	
		9		•《Sanders报告·补遗》（资料6.1.12）提交	1644细菌部队长增田知贞给新妻清一有关掩盖证据的书信，称“唯人体实验与细菌作战绝不能漏口”
		19	盟军总司令部第二次指控11名战犯		
	12	2	盟军总司令部第三次指控59名战犯		

续表

年	月	日	远东国际军事法庭国际检察局调查	美国四任调查官赴日调查	动态、法务局调查
1945	12	6	盟军总司令部第四次指控9名战犯，下令逮捕		
		14			盟军占领军总司令部存档日本共产党告发石井防疫给水部队信函，提及细菌实验和攻击准备等（资料9.1）
		21			盟军占领军总司令部存档今地节告发陆军军医学校秘密研究室石井细菌战人体实验（资料9.2）
1946	1	1		调查官 Arvo T. Thompson 到达日本	天皇神格否定宣言
		9		9日，731部队长北野政次被美国军用飞机从上海接回东京，接受美国调查官调查。即赴对盟军陆军联络委员会报到，委员长有末精三告知：已与美军方说定，不会成为战犯	9~11日，新妻清一所藏《与731部队长北野政次联络事项》（作者不详）称：人体实验与细菌作战无论如何不能泄露
		17		美方确知石井四郎下落	
		19	麦克阿瑟公布《远东国际法庭宪章》，命令设立法庭		
	3	2	国际检察局美国检察官 Morrow 向首席检察官 Keenan 提交书面报告，提及日军在中国战场的化学战和细菌战，并指出实施这些被禁止的战争手段的指令来自东京政府，并非战地指挥官；要求讯问石井四郎（资料5.3.1）		
		8	Morrow 向 Keenan 提交书面报告：会见美国调查官 Arvo T. Thompson 等，就细菌战听取石井中将活动陈述一事，遭否（资料5.3.2）		
		12	Morrow 与国际检察局助理检察官 D. N. Sutton、中国检察官向哲浚及其秘书赴中国调查取证，获得日军化学战、细菌战第一手证据材料。数日后，首席检察官 Keenan 一行也到达上海，与 Morrow 等会面，商定在中国的调查活动方针		
	4	12	Morrow、向哲浚一行回到东京		
		16	Morrow 向 Keenan 提交中国调查总结报告（资料5.3.3）		

续表

年	月	日	远东国际军事法庭国际检察局调查	美国四任调查官赴日调查	动态、法务局调查
1946	4	23	D. N. Sutton 提交日军细菌战调查报告（资料 5.3.4）		
		29	国际检察局向远东国际军事法庭提交 28 名甲级战犯起诉状		
	5	3	远东国际军事法庭开庭		
		31		●《Thompson 报告》（资料 6.2.8）提交	
	6	4	首席检察官 Keenan 通告国际检察局：中央讯问中心成立，任何日本和外国国籍人士的讯问均由盟军占领军最高司令部 G-2 副参谋长直接掌管并指导（资料 5.3.9）		
		24	接受国际检察局搜查科科长 R. L. Morgan 讯问时，陆军上将田中隆吉提到日军在“满洲国”境内用中国人做毒气实验		
		26			法务局调查官讯问 100 部队队员纪野猛记录（资料 9.3）
		28			法务局调查官讯问 100 部队山口本治记录（资料 9.4）
	8	6	Morrow 就日本对中国的侵略战争与违反国际法犯罪行为出庭陈述		
		8			法务局调查科提交编号 330 细菌战调查报告：西村告发 100 部队信函（资料 9.8）
		12	Morrow 被召回美国（资料 5.3.11）		
		23			盟军占领军总司令部存档西村武等告发细菌战战争犯罪信函（资料 9.9）
		29	Sutton 在法庭陈述证据材料 1703 号：南京地方法院检察处首席检察长陈光虞《首都地方法院检察处奉令调查敌人罪行报告书》中提到日军“多摩部队”（荣字 1644 部队）向中国俘虏注射各种有毒细菌，用来做医药实验。		
	9	4			法务局调查科提交编号 330 调查报告：100 部队（资料 9.10）
	10	14			法务局调查科提交编号330 调查报告：100部队（资料 9.11）

续表

年	月	日	远东国际军事法庭国际检察局调查	美国四任调查官赴日调查	动态、法务局调查
1946	11	5			法务局调查科提交编号330调查报告：京都上木宽告发石井在哈尔滨大型人体实验设施用战俘做实验（资料9.12）
		8			法务局调查科提交编号330调查报告：告发石井四郎人体实验匿名信函（资料9.13）
		12			法务局调查科提交330调查报告（资料9.14）
		20			法务局调查科提交330调查报告，题目：中将石井四郎（资料9.16）
		27			法务局调查科提交330调查报告：100部队（资料9.17）
	12	3			法务局调查科提交330调查报告：100部队部队长若松有次郎讯问内容等（资料9.20）
		13	美国代理Kennan主管检察官Frank S. Tavenner, Jr. 予苏联检察官Vasiliev少将备忘录：审阅了日本战俘柄泽十三夫、川岛清关于石井部队进行细菌武器实验的证词，目前证据尚不足以立案。将继续调查，目前没有必要请苏联方面出示证人（资料5.3.10）		
1947	1	7	苏联检察官Vasiliev少将通过国际检察局调查部门向盟军占领军总司令部G–2提出：要求讯问石井四郎等三名731部队干部，讯问目的是向法庭提交有关关东军细菌战证据材料（资料10.1）		
		15	G–2安排McQuail中校与苏检察官Smirnov上校一行会面，苏方告知苏联在押日本战俘731部队生产部部长川岛清、课长柄泽十三夫有关人体实验、实施细菌武器攻击的供述，要求讯问石井等三人。称日本的细菌战资料不仅对于苏联，对于美国也具有价值。提出讯问以上三位日本人时，不要告知他们有可能成为战争罪犯，并且要求他们发誓不得向任何人透露讯问（资料10.1）		

续表

年	月	日	远东国际军事法庭国际检察局调查	美国四任调查官赴日调查	动态、法务局调查
1947	1	24			法务局调查科提交 330 调查报告：100 部队西村武讯问记录（资料 9.21）
		28			法务局调查科提交编号 330 调查报告：讯问陆军军医学校防疫研究室主任内藤良一记录：开始供认石井细菌战人体实验（资料 9.23）
	2	6			法务局调查科提交编号330调查报告（资料9.24）
		25			法务局调查科提交编号 330 调查报告（资料 9.25）
		27	苏联检察官 Vasiliev 赴 G-2，打听石井等人在日本的下落（资料 10.6）		
	3	6			法务局调查科提交编号 330 调查报告：100 部队纪野猛讯问记录（资料 9.26）
		7	盟军日本委员会苏联代表 K. Derenvyanko 少将提交占领军总司令部备忘录 1087：要求将石井等人移交苏联方面（资料 10.22）		
		11			法务局调查科提交编号 330 调查报告，包括纪野猛再讯问记录（资料 9.27）
		17			法务局调查科提交编号 330 调查报告，包括增田知贞讯问记录（资料 9.28）
					法务局调查科提交编号330调查报告，包括大内守、町田时男讯问记录，称目前的调查结果显示为相当于一大规模计划的战略性细菌战（资料 9.29）
		20	盟军总司令部获美军总参谋部允许苏联检察官在盟军最高司令部掌控下讯问石井四郎等，讯问中不得提及美国的相关讯问（资料 10.15）		
	4	1		美国政府选派 N. H. Fell 为第三任调查官（资料 6.3）	

续表

年	月	日	远东国际军事法庭国际检察局调查	美国四任调查官赴日调查	动态、法务局调查
1947	4	4			法务局调查科提交编号 330 调查报告，为阶段性报告，称法务局的调查是为追究用盟军人员进行违法人体实验的战争犯罪者，提交法庭审判。关东军军马防疫厂与关东军防疫给水部进行的战俘人体实验显示实施战略性细菌战的大规模计划（资料 9.30）
		10	盟军总司令部回复苏联代表 Derenvyanko 少将备忘录 1087：不能移交石井四郎等人，对作为战争犯罪的讯问要求不予准许（资料 10.22）		
		16		Fell 到达日本（资料 6.3）	
		18			法务局调查科提交 330 号调查报告：17 日 G–2 回函：今后细菌战调查将在 ATIS 中央讯问中心监管下，在东京办事处进行。案件定性为机密。由美军总参谋部直接命令，G–2 监管（资料 9.31）
	5	6			麦克阿瑟向美国陆军部报告如果书面承诺免责，石井将提供全部细菌战资料（资料 9.32）
		8~9		讯问中，石井四郎提出，书面文件保证免责，可以提供所有资料（资料 6.3.11）	
		13	苏联检察官Smirnov讯问村上隆（资料 6.3.12），监督：Fell 调查官、McQuail中校（资料 10.26）		
		16	苏联检察官Smirnov讯问大田澄（资料 6.3.13），监督：Fell 调查官、McQuail中校（资料 10.26）		
	6	3			美国陆军部发送法务局长官 Carpenter 电文：石井示意上面了解并授权细菌战项目，如给予书面保证不追究，可详告项目。要求 Carpenter 提交可能构成石井等战争犯罪证据和指控的情报（资料 9.32）
		6			法务局 Carpenter 报告美国陆军部：国际检察局备案苏联在押日本战俘细菌战供述等材料，涉及细菌实验、攻击（资料 9.33）

续表

年	月	日	远东国际军事法庭国际检察局调查	美国四任调查官赴日调查	动态、法务局调查
1947	6	9			法务局接到G-2长官C. A. W（Willoughby）与美军化学战部队司令电话纪要：调查发现情报极其重要，不用于战争犯罪审判。情报必须保密（资料9.34）
		13	苏联检察官Smirnov讯问石井四郎，主持：McQuail中校（资料10.26）		
		20		•《Fell报告》（资料6.3.17）提交	
		22	美国检察官Tavenner与法务局Carpterner会谈，报告苏联在押战俘川岛清、柄泽十三夫供述内容。国际检察局认为，根据目前所掌握的，石井等确实违反了陆战法规。表明此意见，并非建议起诉和审判石井四郎等。建议将川岛、柄泽证词提交华盛顿（资料9.36）		美国陆军部电告法务局Carpenter：弄清国际检察局是否掌握证据，掌握何等证据，支持其追究石井等战争犯罪（资料9.35）
		27			法务局Carpenter电文告陆军部：22日与检察官Tavenner再次会谈，对方报告柄泽、川岛有关细菌战证词，再次提出石井等违反陆战法规（资料9.36）
		30	国际检察局检察官Tavenner发送法务局Carpenter电文：提供川岛清、柄泽十三夫供述，建议提交华盛顿（资料9.37）		法务局Carpenter向华盛顿提交苏联提供在押日本战俘川岛清、柄泽十三夫供述英文译文（资料9.38）
	7	17			法务局调查科Smith少尉提交调查科主任细菌战调查经过总结：G-2接手后，从技术角度进行调查，法律追究被中止，G-2授权方可完成对暴行的调查；石井等被指控战争犯罪，违反陆战法规，用战俘做实验（资料9.39）
	8	1		美国政府三部协调委员会远东小委员会明确：石井等人提供的细菌战资料保留于情报渠道，不作为“战争犯罪”的证据。对于国家安全，日本细菌战资料远比追究战争犯罪重要（资料10.31）	
		30			盟军总司令部G-2就有关细菌战调查，直接联络美国陆军部（资料9.40）

续表

年	月	日	远东国际军事法庭国际检察局调查	美国四任调查官赴日调查	动态、法务局调查
1947	10	10	首席检察官 Keenan 表明：天皇与实业界不负有战争责任		
		28		美国第四任调查官 E. V. Hill 等到达日本（资料 6.4）	
	12	5			法务局调查科提交报告，题目：哈尔滨实验室有关调查，由盟军总司令部 G–2 实行，调查科不再进行该案调查（资料 9.41）
		12		•《Hill 报告》（资料 6.4.1）提交	
		31	首席检察官 Keenan 审讯东条英机，天皇的战争责任问题浮出水面		
1948	11	12	远东国际军事法庭判决 25 名被告有罪		
	12	23	对东条英机等 7 名被告执行绞刑		
1949	12	25~30			苏联在伯力举行对 12 名日本军人细菌战罪行的审判，其中包括川岛清、柄泽十三夫
1950	2				莫斯科外文出版局多国语言发行伯力审判法庭记录
					苏联驻美大使照会美国务卿 Dean G. Acheson，告知伯力审判结果，证据证明天皇与石井等负有责任，提议举行特别军事法庭予以审判（资料 10.37）
	5	31			苏联驻美大使再次就前次问题照会美国务卿 Acheson，称中国政府表示赞同（资料 10.37）
1950	12	15			苏联驻美大使 A. Panyushkin 第三次照会美国国务卿 Acheson，要求予以答复（资料 10.38）
1951	3	1			第七次日本国会众议院外务委员会上，众议员听涛克已就（日共）731 部队细菌战问题向政府提出质疑
	9	8	《旧金山和约》签订		

资料来源：常石敬一『医学者たちの組織犯罪：関東軍七三一部隊』朝日新聞社、1994；太田昌克『731免責の系譜：細菌戦部隊と秘蔵のファイル』日本評論社、1999；Sheldon H. Harris, *Factories of Death: Japanese Biological Warfare, 1932-45, and the American Cover-up,* Routledge, 1994; Jeanne Guillemin, *Hidden Atrocities: Japanese Germ Warfare and American Obstruction of Justice at the Tokyo Trial,* Columbia University Press, New York, 2017。

6. 美国四任调查官赴日细菌战调查

如表 2 所示，战争一结束，美国为到手日军细菌战研究资料，接连派遣四任调查官赴日调查日军细菌战。在远东国际军事法庭，苏联检察官一再向国际检察局提交苏联在押日军 731 部队战俘关于人体实验的供述，要求 G-2 准予其讯问石井四郎等日军细菌战有有人员，追究细菌战战争犯罪。此时，石井四郎等以免于追究其细菌战战争犯罪责任为交换条件，将日军细菌战研究包括人体实验的技术资料提供于美方（第 9 章、第 10 章资料）。

（1）Murray Sanders 调查

第一任赴日调查官 Murray Sanders 中校为美国化学战部队（CWS）特别项目部所属 Camp Detrick（生物武器研究基地）人员。战争结束时，美国从马尼拉派遣美军太平洋部队科学技术顾问团，由麻省理工大学校长 Karl T. Compton 博士率领，赴日本调查日本科学研究，Sanders 中校作为该团成员，调查日本的生物战 / 细菌战研究实况。

Sanders 从马尼拉坐船到横滨港登陆时，手拿着照片去接应他的即为内藤良一（参见资料 2.3）。Sanders 此前仅听取过 G-2 与科学情报部的简单介绍，并不了解详情。内藤英语娴熟，深知日本细菌战，成为“石井机关”方面应对美国调查的前台人物。

调查官 Sanders 中校待遇特殊，他的办公室位于距盟军总司令部不远的日本最大保险公司——第一生命的大楼里。调查从与石井四郎同样被美军注意的宫川米次入手，内藤在一旁为他做翻译，把握情况。每天的调查讯问结束后，内藤就穿梭于原日军各部门人员之中，互通消息，攻守同盟，准备第二天向 Sanders 吐露的内容。

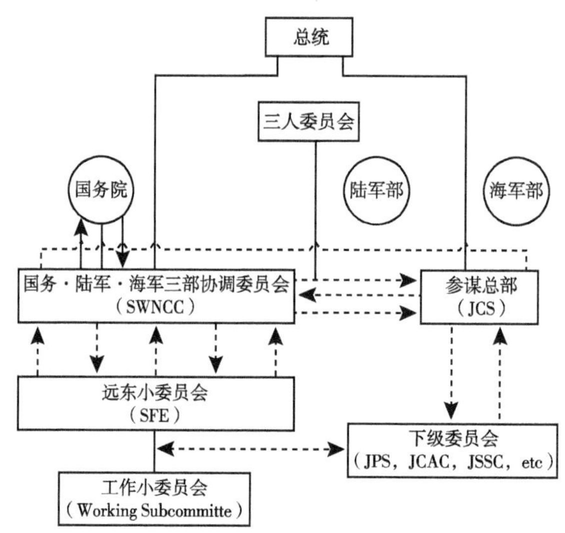

图 2　美国对日占领决策机构

资料来源：参考五百旗頭真『米国の日本占領政策——戦後日本の設計図（下）』（中央公論社、1985）。

Sanders 的调查还遇到来自另一方面的难以逾越的困境。资料 6.1.5 中 Sanders 写道：曾准备前往哈尔滨实地调查，未能成行。资料 6.1.11 Sanders 提交的调查报告（《Sanders 报告》）中平房 731

部队所在地与配置图是在日本国内调查所获。

资料 6.1.6 为 Sanders 所属美军太平洋部队科学技术顾问团领队 Compton 博士归国后关于日本调查情况的说明，称日本人否认曾实行进攻性细菌战的准备，他对此表示怀疑，并认为他们可能在隐瞒。他提到日本科学家们在谈话中说道："这个，我们是不可以说的。"

20 世纪 80 年代，日本陆军省某技术部门负责人新妻清一中佐在接受英国的电视台编导 David Wallace① 采访时称："当明白 Sanders 手中掌握的调查依据就是这么些的时候，我真是放下了心。我知道陆军的那些机密文件并没有交到他的手里。"

资料 6.1.11《Sanders 报告》中有一个显而易见的自相矛盾的内容：在讯问中，出月三郎大佐、井上隆朝大佐、神林浩军医中将等均称，日本的细菌战研究仅限于防御方面；而内藤良一的供述是："平房的研究所的任务，从一开始，就是将生物武器作为实用性武器进行开发。"

资料 6.1.12 的 Sanders 调查补充报告中，应日本陆军省的要求，Sanders 听取了日军、政府高官关于日本细菌战研究的说明，其内容虚假。其中提到的一些人名如下。

① Tadakasu 正确的拼写应为 Tadakazu，为最后一任日本陆军省次官若松只一。

② Torashiro KAWABE 为参谋次长河边虎四郎。

③ Yoshijiro UMEZU 为参谋总长梅津美治郎，1939 年 9 月至 1944 年 9 月任关东军司令官，其间 731 部队细菌战活动相关的命令由他签发。梅津为远东国际军事法庭被告之一，未因细菌战战争犯罪被追究责任。

④ S. SHIMOMURA 为陆军大臣下村定。

《Sanders 报告》中特别写道，从东京疏散转移到新潟支所的陆军军医学校防疫研究室的生物战研究记录，在调查的最后一天全部到手。所谓"生物战研究记录"估计是内藤良一等编辑发行的《陆军军医学校防疫研究报告》。

1945 年 11 月，Sanders 因病回美国。

（2）Arvo T. Thompson 调查

Sanders 回美国后，美国对日本细菌战的调查仍然继续，次任调查官 Thompson 中校到达日本前，对日本相关人员的讯问由 S. E. Whitesides 上校、A. H. Schwichtemberg 上校进行，讯问人员中有美军用飞机从上海带回东京的 731 部队第二任部队长北野政次，一直潜伏在日本国内、第一次露面的石井四郎，731 部队航空班班长、药剂少校增田美保，731 部队老资格干部、担任过 731 部队孙吴支队长的佐佐木义孝。资料 6.2.1 中的 Kanbayashi 应为 Hiroshi KANBAYASHI，日本陆军省医务局长神林浩。

资料 6.2.2 对石井四郎的讯问记录内容，对照 1947 年以后暴露的事实真相，几乎全是伪证。

资料 6.2.4 中，Thompson 根据美方掌握的常德鼠疫菌投放，以及资料 2.3 中有关日本试图从美

① 参见 Peter Williams and David Wallace, *Unit 731: The Japanese Army's Secret of Secrets,* Hodder and Stoughton, 1989。

国研究机构入手黄热病毒株的事件，追问石井四郎，石井一副毫不知晓的样子，未做正面回答，并始终强调一点：在未得到陆军中央正式认可的情况下，持续进行着预防医学与水质净化的研究。Thompson 也并未轻易上当，资料 6.2.8 的调查报告中如此记述：讯问中，情报提供者的回答如此一致，似乎是根据指示提供有关情报的量和性质，所有的情报好像均来自记忆，但是一些情报，比如提供的炮弹图如此具体详尽，文件证据有可能并未全部销毁。

资料 6.2.5 中的 731 部队航空班班长增田美保曾于 1941 年 11 月 4 日驾机实施常德鼠疫攻击（参见第 3 章、第 6 章资料），他曾对近藤昭二说："（常德攻击）那是实验性的。"增田美保供述记录中提及"负伤者"，应该是指 731 部队航空班队员铃木，因一次机内管道出问题，伤寒菌泄漏到飞机内部而感染身亡。另外提到的平泽正欣班长也在执行任务中因飞机坠落死亡。

资料 6.2.7 美军报纸 *Pacific Stars and Stripes* 1946 年 2 月 27 日刊载的 UP 特派员 Peter Kalisher 报道中提到此前 1 月 6 日报道中的内容：（日本）共产党告发"石井在满洲实施腺鼠疫人体实验，用美国、中国俘虏做实验对象"。文中说，石井是一位果断但几乎无情的人物，1941 年为中校，1945 年晋升为中将。这篇文章在远东国际军事法庭国际检察局美国检察官 Morrow 上校 1946 年 3 月 2 日向首席检察官 Keenan 提交的有关日军在中国的战争犯罪调查报告中也有提到（参见资料 5.3.1）。

资料 6.2.8 为对 731 部队背荫河创建时期以来的资深干部大田澄的讯问记录，大田曾担任 731 部队第二部、第四部、总务部部长，华中派遣军防疫给水部队（1644 部队）部队长，为浙江、湖南细菌武器攻击现场指挥官。战败时，大田指挥了 731 部队的设施破坏和证据销毁。第 10 章资料中，苏联一再提出要求审讯的日本细菌战战犯三人之一即为大田澄。战后，大田家乡岛根县曾上演过一出话剧《冬之旅》，剧中的主人公即以他为原型。此后，大田自杀。

（3）Norbert H. Fell 调查

据资料 10.1，1947 年 1 月初，远东国际军事法庭国际检察局苏联检察官 Vasiliev 少将通过国际检察局调查部门向 G-2 长官 Willoughby 提出，要求讯问 731 部队干部石井、菊池、大田，有关细菌武器攻击和人体实验。1 月 15 日，G-2 安排 McQuail 中校与苏联检察官 Smirnov 上校一行会面，苏方摊牌苏联在押日本战俘 731 部队生产部部长川岛清、课长柄泽十三夫有关人体实验、实施细菌武器攻击的供述，要求讯问石井等三人。此时，美国非常被动，派遣的两任调查官已经结束调查回国，尚未获得日方关于人体实验、细菌武器攻击的供述。为应对苏联检察官讯问在日本的日军细菌部队有关人员的要求，1947 年 4 月 6 日，美国派遣生化武器研究基地 Camp Detrick 的部门主任 Norbert H. Fell 博士赴日再度调查细菌战（参见第 10 章资料）。

4 月 16 日 Fell 到达日本后，先开始审阅盟军总司令部 G-2 与法务局的调查文件，此后 Fell 在日本持续调查了两个月（参见表 2）。

Fell 讯问的日本 731 等细菌部队主要人员如下。

①资料 6.3.5 增田知贞——日军驻南京 1644 细菌部队第二任部队长。第一任部队长由石井四郎兼任。

②资料 6.3.7 金子顺一——731 部队核心研究人员。资料 4.1 金子顺一博士论文集是他从事的细菌战专门领域研究成果。金子也负责“风船炸弹”（“风船”为气球等空中漂浮物）研究。

③资料 6.3.8 菊池齐——731 部队第一部（研究部）部长。

④资料 6.3.11 为石井四郎讯问记录，其中值得注意的是，石井开口向美方提交易的条件：“如果能以书面文件保证我本人、上司与部下免于追究责任，可以向你们提供所有的资料。”

⑤资料 6.3.12 村上隆历任 731 部队总务部、第二部（实战研究、野外实验部）部长。

⑥资料 6.3.13 大田澄与资料 6.3.5 中的增田知贞、资料 6.3.7 中的金子顺一均为日本细菌战最知情者。

⑦资料 6.3.14 碇常重为 731 部队第二部部长。

⑧资料 6.3.15 若松有次郎为位于“满洲国”“新京”的关东军军马防疫厂（100 部队）部队长，也是盟军总司令部法务局、苏联方面的追踪对象（参见第 9 章资料）。

资料 6.3.6 龟井贯一郎谈话记录中，龟井提及日本细菌战情报完全地提供给德国，一个大型的德国实验室已经完好无损地落人苏联人手中，因此，苏联人有可能已经把握了日军细菌战的活动。（参见资料 3.48）

资料 6.3.18 为 Fell 通过美军 Camp Detrick 长官与 G–2 副参谋长的有关事项联络：有关日本细菌战调查资料收集、运送美国的情况等，其中提到所有调查所获资料由情报系统掌握，不用于“战争犯罪”的程序。资料 6.3.17 为 Fell 的调查总结报告《Fell 报告》。根据该报告，美军终于拿到了日本细菌战的重要研究资料、证据材料，并运回了美国。

《Fell 报告》2 中提到“有影响力的日本人政治家”“非常愿意与美国方面全面合作”，这里指的是协助 Fell 调查并担任翻译的龟井贯一郎，他是日本外交官、大政翼赞会成员，当时已被撤销公职（参见资料 6.3.4）。

报告 2 的 b 中提到的“植物学者与植物生理学者”分别为毕业于北海道大学的八木泽行正技术少佐与毕业于京都大学的军队文职研究人员滨田稔。

报告 2 中提到有一份由 19 名日本细菌战研究主要人员集中花了一个月时间准备的 60 页以人为攻击对象的英文报告，并列有这份报告的分类目录。在目前美国国家档案馆等解密公开的相关资料中，尚未发现这份报告。

报告 2 的 c 中提到日军细菌战研究人员提交的对中国军队和平民实施的 12 次野战实验性攻击的效果总结，其中包括实验性攻击目标村庄、乡镇的地图。这份地图在目前美国国家档案馆等解密公开的相关资料中尚未发现。报告 5 是关于这 12 次野战实验性攻击的概述（参见第 3 章、第 4 章资料）。

报告 2 的 i 中提到日本方面 8 月底准备完毕由细菌攻击引起疾病流行的 200 名感染者的约 8000 枚病理幻灯片（slides）。这批病理幻灯片（参见资料 9.14）目前在美国国家档案馆等解密公开的相关资料中也尚未发现。

（4）Edwin V. Hill 与 Joseph Victor 调查

继 Fell 后，美军 Camp Detrick 又派遣了两名研究人员 Edwin V. Hill 博士与 Joseph Victor 博士赴日调查，当时与日本石井等方面以免于追究战争犯罪责任作为条件的交换已经成立，两位赴日的目的是进一步收集情报，以确认日本方面提供的专业技术资料，包括人体实验的各种报告、标本等。

Hill 博士在总结报告中称，调查得到盟军占领军总司令部 G–2 副长官 Charles A. Willoughby 全力协助；所讯问人员是自愿提供情报，讯问中也未提出要保证其免于追究战争犯罪责任。G–2 副长官 Charles A. Willoughby 是美国做出对日本细菌战战犯“免责”决定的关键人物（参见第 9 章、第 10 章资料）。

Hill 与 Victor 讯问的日本细菌部队有关人员来自 731 部队、东京大学传染病研究所、1644 部队、陆军军医学校，并有关东军总参谋长等高级指挥官。

值得注意的是，当时远东国际军事法庭仍然在进行中，但是在“交易”的前提下，讯问中日本方面有关人员已不回避人体实验的内容，如 731 部队结核班二木秀雄的讯问记录中的某种人体实验：“(菌）注入体内后，即出现伴随热度的剧烈症状，一个月后死亡。”731 部队田部井和讯问记录中的肠伤寒实验：“3 名实验对象自杀。”还有将实验对象暴露于 10 克泥土与 10 毫克细菌混合的散弹爆炸。

7. 日本细菌部队人员向美国提供的人体实验解剖报告

第 7 章收入的三种日本细菌部队人体实验解剖报告（包括彩色人体解剖图）分别为“A”报告（炭疽报告）、“G”报告（鼻疽报告）、“Q”报告（鼠疫报告）。原藏于美国陆军 Dugway Proving Ground 图书馆，据美国历史学者、日本细菌战历史专著《死亡工厂：美国掩盖的日本细菌战犯罪》作者 Sheldon Harris 教授，为 1978 年解密。1992 年，Harris 教授与日本 NHK 联名向位于美国犹他州的 Fort Dugway Proving Ground 提出要求其公开后，被准许阅览和复制。

据美军 Fort Detrick 历史研究者 Norman Covert，三种报告原来为 Camp Detrick 所藏，后来随一部分研究成果转移到 Dugway Proving Ground。

资料 6.3.17《Fell 报告》简单介绍石井等提供的 60 页以人为攻击对象的细菌武器研究中几种作为武器的细菌，其中包括了“炭疽”、“鼠疫”和“鼻疽”，均为人畜共通的烈性传染病菌。

资料 7.1“A”报告为炭疽人体实验解剖报告。731 部队中研究炭疽的主要为大田澄大佐及肥野藤信三、野口圭一、植村肇少佐。

根据“A”报告中实验对象的号码，一共 33 名，经皮下注射感染 1 例、口入感染 6 例、口腔散布感染 12 例、鼻腔感染 4 例。报告为实验对象感染后，内脏器官病理变化的记录。全体均有睾丸解剖，为 25~37 岁男性。感染至死亡时间：2~4 日。

关于炭疽，如上所述，见资料 6.3.6；增田知贞在细菌战研究的初期阶段，即确信炭疽是最有效的细菌武器。据资料 6.3.11，1947 年 5 月 8 日、9 日 Fell 调查官对石井四郎的讯问记录中，石井也供称，炭疽是最佳细菌武器，因为可以大量生产，抗性强，毒性持久，致死率可达 80%~90%。最佳流行病是鼠疫，最佳媒介传播疫病是脑炎。石井的如此“结论”，当然是通过各种实验，包括人体实验所获得的结果。资料 9.40 显示，1947 年 8 月底，美国军方仍在通过盟军总司令部 G–2，要求增田知贞用地图详细标示安达实验场炭疽实验具体地点。

资料 7.2“G”报告为鼻疽人体实验解剖报告。731 部队中主要由石井四郎、石川太刀雄丸研究鼻疽。与“A”报告一样，报告中实验对象以号码标示。这些报告显然是在大量的实验研究资料，包括病理记录、标本、照片、图片、论文等的基础上制作的，这些相关的资料目前还未发现。“G”报告中共 21 例实验对象，皮肤感染 16 例，鼻腔感染 5 例。感染后，4~45 日内死亡。

日军细菌部队中另一研究炭疽、鼻疽的部队为 100 部队——关东军军马防疫厂，部队长为若松有次郎（参见资料 6.3.15、第 9 章资料），该部队与 731 部队互相协作，大规模的露天细菌人体实验使用的是 731 部队安达野外实验场。

上述资料 6.3.17 中，《Fell 报告》列举并简介的第五类细菌即为鼻疽。Fell 称日本人鼻疽研究不多，他们显然害怕这种微生物。发生过 7 例实验室内感染，2 例死亡，2 例截肢，3 例血清疫苗治愈。

资料 7.3“Q”报告为石井所称细菌武器中“最佳流行病”鼠疫的人体实验解剖报告，以“Q”命名的理由尚不明。

“Q”报告收入 57 名鼠疫患者人体解剖报告，其中农安 39 人，“新京”18 人。解学诗对照 1940 年满铁“新京”工事事务所《鼠疫防疫作业报告书》（吉林省档案馆藏）中的 1940 年“新京”市鼠疫患者表，发现其中 8 名死者的名字缩写（罗马字）、年龄、性别、发病时间，与“Q”报告中“新京”被解剖鼠疫死者的相同，另有 4 人只是发病期间有些差异。以上共 12 人，其中 7 人为当时居住在“新京”的日本人。①

“Q”报告制作者在前言中自称“I”，没有具体姓名。战后日本病理学会会刊上发表的文章称：“昭和十五年，满洲国农安地区鼠疫流行之际，发表者中一名（石川）解剖了 57 具鼠疫死者尸体。这个数字是世界纪录。”“石川”应为 731 部队病理班班长石川太刀雄丸（参见资料 6.4.2），文中的 57 具鼠疫死者人体解剖的数字与“Q”报告所收人体解剖报告数字一致。

“Q”报告前言中也提到，作者当时与高桥等一起在农安与“新京”进行流行病与细菌学调查，“高桥”应为资料 4.2《关于农安、新京鼠疫流行报告》的作者高桥正彦，731 部队鼠疫班班长。前言中所称“1943”年农安地区鼠疫流行的年份有误，应为 1940 年。

常石敬一认为，PX 即鼠疫跳蚤，也许是日军 15 年细菌战研究的最大“成果”。增田知贞称，731 部队投入细菌武器攻击的大部分预算都用于 PX（带鼠疫菌印度客蚤）的研究（参见资料 4.1）。“Q”报告是三种报告中篇幅最大的，共 747 页（其中第 444 页缺失）。

资料 6.3.17 Fell 调查官在他提及美军化学战部队司令的《日本细菌战活动新情报简要总结》

① 解学诗：《“新京”鼠疫谋略（1940 年）》，解学诗、〔日〕松村高夫等：《战争与恶疫——日军在华细菌战》，第三章。

（《Fell 报告》）中，列举日本用于人的生物武器内容中包括了这项技术，并称日本研究的最有效的两种细菌武器，一为炭疽，主要用于牲畜，二是带鼠疫菌的跳蚤。《Fell 报告》中还提到石井四郎等向其提供了一份对中国军队和平民的 12 次细菌武器试验性攻击的效果总结和标示攻击地点的地图。12 次试验性攻击中，2 次空中撒播鼠疫跳蚤，取得成功；3 次地面人工撒播鼠疫跳蚤；2 次人工地面或饮水系统中撒播霍乱，2 次人工地面或饮水系统中撒播伤寒，均取得有效的结果。

12 次试验性细菌武器攻击中，5 次为鼠疫跳蚤攻击，2 次霍乱，2 次伤寒，尚余 3 次攻击使用的细菌，《Fell 报告》中没有说明，需要参照上文提及的 12 次试验性攻击效果总结和标示地点的地图。这份资料，目前美国国家档案馆公开的相关文献中尚未发现。

资料 6.3.5 1947 年 4 月 22 日 Fell 对曾任华中派遣军防疫给水部部长，即 1644 部队部队长的增田知贞的讯问记录中，增田称在中国中部地区（“中支那”），对中国军队实施了试验性的细菌炸弹攻击，包括填充炭疽菌的炸弹。由此《Fell 报告》中未具体说明使用细菌的 3 次攻击，有可能包括炭疽的攻击。战后井本日记、高桥报告（资料 4.2）、金子论文（资料 4.1）的发现，使得日本在中国战场使用 PX 实施的鼠疫攻击，有了一定程度的把握，资料 4.1.3 金子的论文《PX 效果略算法》中列举的在中国各地的鼠疫跳蚤攻击，空中撒播为 3 次，地面撒播为 3 次。

作为最有效细菌武器的 PX 鼠疫跳蚤也有一个致命的技术性缺陷：混同投放的物质，比如谷物、豆子、棉絮、布条等，人的肉眼可以观察到，因此攻击的同时，易为被攻击方察觉，并留下证据。关于日军在中国战场使用炭疽攻击的具体时间、地点、散布手段及其“效果”，目前还了解甚少，这应是今后研究不可忽略的课题。

8. 美国海军情报局技术情报中心报告

资料 8 为美国海军技术情报局关于日本细菌战的报告，由局长 T. B. Inglis 提交（《Ingris 报告》）。报告中的 60 页关于“人体实验情报”的简要，为资料 6.3.17 美国第三任赴日调查官 Fell 的调查报告内容的一部分。如上所述，这份重要的资料 Fell 到手后上交送达美国，但是在目前美国国家档案馆公开的 Fell 调查相关资料中尚未发现。《Ingris 报告》的最后部分“关于日本生物战计划评价”的内容明显不如《Fell 报告》。

9. 指控——盟军总司令部法务局调查

根据 1945 年 10 月 2 日盟军最高司令官麦克阿瑟命令，盟军总司令部法务局（Legal Section, LS，参见图 1）的部门职能为：向盟军最高司令官就法律问题及战争犯罪有关的政策提出意见，追究战争犯罪。12 月 8 日，远东国际军事法庭国际检察局（International Prosecution Section, IPS）成立后，与侵略战争相关的具有国际性质的问题转由国际检察局主管，法务局的职能限定为一般性的战时违反国际法的战犯的搜查、起诉，犯罪嫌疑人的登记等手续履行，下设部门有起诉科、调查科、战争犯罪人登记科、法律科。

1946 年 3 月 10 日，法务局有 39 名军官（其中 16 名在马尼拉），69 名下士官，60 名军队文职人员；此外，澳大利亚部 11 人，英国部 8 人，加拿大部 6 人，中国部 3 人。

盟军总司令部法务局原来是与日本各地美国占领军法务部、对敌谍报部队（CIC）、搜查部（CID）联合行动，先进行与盟军俘虏有关的日本国内调查，盟军一登陆，日本人告发细菌战战争犯罪的信函即从日本各地纷至沓来，这些来信都转到法务局存档，由法务局调查科（Investigation Division）立案调查。第 9 章收入了当时法务局调查科对有关石井四郎等细菌战案件调查的记录，编号 #330。调查遍布日本各地。来自美国印第安纳的 Neil R. Smith 少尉是有关细菌战调查的中心人物，调查开始时的主要对象为东京大学传染病研究所。原日军驻长春细菌部队 100 部队（关东军军马防疫厂）队员西村武与纪野猛的告发信函中人体实验负责人的姓名一致，于是 100 部队最先进入法务局调查范围。

资料 9.1、9.2、9.3、9.4、9.8、9.9 为日本人投书盟军占领军各部门告发日本细菌战的信函及英文译文，以及对告发人的讯问记录。其中最早告发石井防疫给水部队细菌战活动的为 1945 年 12 月 14 日日共的信函英文译文，其次是 12 月 21 日来自东京今地节的告发信函。资料 9.3、9.4 为 100 部队纪野猛、山口本治的告发及讯问记录。资料 9.8 为 1946 年 8 月 8 日，法务局调查科启动编号 330 的细菌战调查报告，内容包括 100 部队西村武告发信函。资料 9.10、9.11 为编号 330 有关 100 部队的调查报告。

1946 年 11 月 5 日，法务局调查科提交编号 330 调查报告，有关京都上木宽告发石井四郎在哈尔滨大型设施用战俘做人体实验。三天后，11 月 8 日，法务局调查科又提交编号 330 调查报告，有关来自福岛县的告发石井四郎的匿名信及译文，称曾在石井的部队服役，知晓其“恶虐无道”的行为和一切秘密。当时，美国军方另一系统作为高度机密的第二任赴日细菌战调查 Arvo T. Thompson 中校的调查（参见资料 6.2）已经结束数月（参见表 2）。此后，法务局调查科开始石井四郎的调查，11 月 20 日，法务局调查科即提交编号 330 调查报告，题目：中将石井四郎。同时 100 部队的调查仍在继续（资料 9.17、9.20、9.21、9.26、9.27）。

资料 9.23 1947 年 1 月 28 日法务局对内藤良一讯问记录中，内藤开始吐露石井用战俘做细菌战实验。法务局调查科调查官 Neal R. Smith 中尉在调查报告中称，这是内藤第一次做此供述。但是当时中国科的资料中未有关于哈尔滨实验站的暴行材料，中国政府已经开展调查，调查报告将尽快送调查科。

1 月 7 日，苏联检察官已经通过国际检察局向 G–2 提出要求讯问石井四郎等三名日军细菌部队将校，1 月 15 日，苏方与美方会谈，苏方向美方摊牌其已获得在押日军 731 部队战俘关于细菌战人体实验的供述（参见表 2、资料 5.3.10、9.37、9.38、10.1）。

资料 9.29 1947 年 3 月 17 日法务局调查科提交的编号 330 调查报告指出：目前为止的调查结果显示相关于一项大规模计划的战略性细菌战。

资料 9.30 为 1947 年 4 月 4 日法务局调查科 Smith 少尉应盟军总司令部 G–2 要求提交的细菌战调查阶段性总结报告，其中提到调查始于收到一封自称“NISHIMURA”（西村）的来信，告发战俘人体鼻疽实验（参见资料 7.2）。报告说明，法务局的日军细菌战调查是为追究用盟军人员进行违法人体实验的战争犯罪者，送交法庭审判；调查发现，作为发动大规模计划的战略性细菌战的一部分，关东军防疫给水部、关东军军马防疫厂均对鼠疫、鼻疽、炭疽进行了研究（参见资料 7.1、7.2、7.3）。

据资料 9.31，以上报告提交两周后，4 月 18 日，即美国第三任调查官 Fell 博士到达日本两天后，Smith 少尉即报告法务局接到 G–2 回复：细菌战调查将作为秘密案件在 ATIS（盟军翻译部）掌控下实施，列为秘密案件。该调查由美军总参谋部直接命令，G–2 监管；每一步骤、讯问或者联络都必须与该部协调；需保持高度机密，以保护美国国家利益，防止复杂事态发生。

资料 9.32 为 1947 年 6 月 3 日美国陆军部发送法务局长官 Carperter 执行的电文，先是转告 5 月 6 日 CINCFE 发来电文 C–52423 的摘要，提及三名日本人已经供述人体实验，并经石井明确确认，至少对中国军队实施了三次试验性实战攻击。石井的意思是上面了解并授权了细菌战项目。如果给予书面文件保证不追究战争犯罪责任，关于该项目，他可以详告。接着陆军部要求 Carpenter 提交任何可能构成对于石井以及其他人的战争犯罪证据和指控的详细情报。

据资料 9.33，1947 年 6 月 6 日 Carperter 即报告陆军部，国际检察局美国检察官 Frank S. Tavenner, Jr.（参见资料 5.3.10）告知：苏联在押的石井下属川岛清少将、柄泽十三夫少佐、秦彦三郎中佐的供述，以及中国中央卫生署总长 P. Z. King 博士证词已在国际检察局备案，证词内容涉及细菌实验、攻击等。但 1946 年 12 月，当时即代理首席检察官 Keenan 主管事务的 Tavenner 曾决定，鉴于目前证据还不充分，不作为证据提交法庭。Carpenter 认为，苏联检察官将争取要求讯问日本细菌战有关人员，以作为指控石井等细菌战犯罪的证据（参见第 10 章资料）。资料 9.33 附国际检察局备案证据材料文件 9307：原关东军军医部长梶塚隆二讯问记录；文件 9308：原关东军总参谋长秦彦三郎中将证词；1946 年 4 月 4 日中国中央卫生署代理总长 J. C. Fang（方颐积）证明下列 Dr. P. Z. King（金宝善）1942 年 3 月 31 日陈述为中华民国卫生总署的正式公文（参见资料 5.3.5）。川岛清供述为文件 9305、9309，柄泽十三夫的供述为文件 9306。

6 月 9 日，法务局即接到 G–2 长官 C.A.W.（Willoughby）与美军化学战部队司令的电话纪要，其中提到调查发现的情报极为重要，必须保持高度机密，不得用于对战争犯罪的审判（资料 9.34）。6 月 20 日，美国第三任调查官 Fell 向化学战部队司令提交日本细菌战活动“新情报”的调查报告（参见资料 6.3.17）。两天后，6 月 22 日，陆军部即电告法务局 Carpenter，要求其搞清国际检察局是否掌握证据及掌握何等证据，支持其石井为首的日军细菌战人员违反陆战法规的主张（资料 9.35）。据资料 6.3.18，6 月 24 日，Fell 给 G–2 发来联络函（附 6 月 20 日的调查报告，资料 6.3.17），明确调查所获全部资料由情报系统掌握，不用于“战争犯罪”审判程序。称目前为止所获的资料非常重要，对其项目将来的发展会具有巨大价值。

据资料 9.36，6 月 27 日法务局长官 Carpenter 向陆军部发送电文称，5 天前，即 6 月 22 日，Carpenter 又与国际检察局 Tavenner 会谈，对方再次提及：石井等违反了陆战法规；1940 年 10 月 27 日日军飞机在宁波撒播麦谷，29 日腺鼠疫爆发，有充分证据表明，日军对衢县、金华、常德实施了细菌战（参见资料 5.3.10）；川岛、柄泽的供述证实了石井部队的实验。

据资料 9.37，6 月 30 日，国际检察局代理主管 Frank S. Tavenner, Jr. 发送法务局长官 Carpenter 上校电文：BW Group，建议将有关证人证词提交华盛顿，附 KAWASHIMA, Kiyoshil（川岛清）少将证词两份、KARAZAWA, Tomio（柄泽十三夫）少佐证词一份（资料文件中没有附件）。据资料 9.38，同日，Carpenter 将国际检察局备案的苏联在押日军战俘 731 部队第四部部长川岛清少将（两份）及其下属柄泽十三夫少佐的证词发往华盛顿 Civil Affairs Division, War Crimes Branch。

Tavenner 6 月 30 日电文中也提及，1946 年 12 月，国际检察局曾就川岛清、柄泽十三夫、秦彦三郎、金宝善的证词使用达成一致意见，认为证据尚不足以立案（参见资料 5.3.10）。苏联检察官可能会争取讯问被指控者，将以上证词及他们的独自调查发现作为证据。

7 月 17 日，法务局调查科 Smith 少尉将编号 330（Motoji YAMAGUCHI, et al.）的细菌战调查总结报告提交调查科主任，回顾了调查的经过，直到为 G–2 接手从技术角度进行调查，此案法律追究被中止，处于停滞状态，待 G–2 授权方能完成对战争暴行的调查。石井等被指控战争犯罪，违反陆战法规用俘虏做实验（资料 9.39）。

据资料 9.40, 此后，1947 年 8 月 30 日，就细菌战调查事项，美国陆军部直接发电文 W85347 联络美军远东军司令部，称以上电文回复 C–55493 为 G–2 执行长官上校 C. S. Myers 所发，并非法务局长官 Carpenter。电文有关增田知贞的调查中，提及增田提交的“A Compilation of BW Agents”已送达美国；美国陆军部索要的有关进行过炭疽实验的安达实验场的详细情报将于 9 月 16 日从日本航空送往美国。这两份电文被列为“最高机密”。增田提交的“A Compilation of BW Agents”在目前美国国家档案馆解密公开的日军细菌战有关文献中也还未发现。

资料 9.41 1947 年 12 月 5 日 Smith 少尉的报告显示，法务局调查科已不再进行有关细菌战的调查，Motoji YAMAGUCHI, et al. 案的调查已由盟军总司令部 G–2 主持。一周之后，1947 年 12 月 12 日，美国第四任赴日调查官 Edwin V. Hill 向上级提交了细菌战调查报告（参见资料 6.4）。

当时，在日本，远东国际军事法庭国际检察局、盟军总司令部法务局、美军从美国派遣的四任调查官，共三个渠道，一开始是各自、分别地对日军细菌战进行调查，最终归于盟军总司令部 G–2 掌控之下，为美国对日占领决策机构左右（参见图 1、图 2）。其间苏联持有其国内在押日军战俘，继续进行着“独自的调查”。美、苏两大国以是否在远东国际军事法庭追究日本细菌战战争犯罪为焦点，开始了关于日军细菌战证据材料的争斗。

10. 苏联的追究与美国的对策

1947 年 1 月 7 日，远东国际军事法庭国际检察局苏联检方通过国际检察局调查部门向盟军总司令部 G-2 提出，要求讯问日军细菌部队石井四郎等三名将校（参见资料 5.3.9）。资料 10.1 为 1947 年 1 月 9 日，盟军总司令部 McQuail 中校提交 G-2 长官 Willoughby 少将来自苏联助理检察官 Vasiliev 少将的公函，说明讯问的目的是向法庭提交有关关东军细菌战的证据材料。另一份资料为 1947 年 1 月 15 日，G-2 安排 McQuail 中校与苏联检察官 Smirnov 上校一行会谈后，McQuail 提交的报告。会谈中，苏联检方说明讯问的理由是依据苏联在押日军战俘 731 部队第四部部长川岛清及其下属柄泽十三夫提供的情报，石井四郎中将、菊池齐大佐（731 部队第一部部长）、大田澄大佐（731 部队总务部部长）牵涉以下犯罪嫌疑：囚徒人体实验、跳蚤与细菌的大量生产、跳蚤的生产方法、安达的露天实验、平房的证据销毁等（参见资料 9.38）。苏方称，日本细菌战的技术不仅对苏联有价值，对美国也是有价值的。提出讯问以上三位日本人时，不要告知他们有可能成为战争罪犯，并且要求他们发誓不得向任何人透露讯问。

1947 年 1 月 7 日苏联检方通过国际检察局向 G-2 提出要求讯问石井等人前，据资料 5.3.10，1946 年 12 月 13 日，代理休假的首席检察官 Keenan 主管事务的美国检察官 Tavenner 已回复苏联检察官 A. N. VASILYEV 少将的照会，称数位检察官已经仔细审阅了苏方提供的 KARAZAWA（柄泽）少佐、KAWASHIMA（川岛）少将有关石井部队攻击性细菌武器实验活动的证词，认为尚不足以立案。

另一方面，1947 年 1 月 28 日，内藤良一在接受法务局的调查时，开始开口承认石井四郎在哈尔滨的实验设施用俘虏做细菌战研究人体实验（参见资料 9.23）。日军 731 等细菌部队人员一直对美国调查官钳口不吐的人体实验真相开始败露。此时，美国两任赴日调查官已经结束细菌战调查回国，调查中已向日军细菌部队相关人员承诺“系科学调查，与战争犯罪无关”，但是并没有从他们口中获得以上人体实验、细菌武器攻击的供述。资料 10.1 1947 年 1 月 15 日 G-2 McQuail 中校在与苏联检察官 Smirnov 上校一行会谈报告中也列举了两任美国调查官的调查报告。

苏联的披露和追究显然使美国方面陷于被动。一方面，美国需要对苏联检察官的要求做出适当的回应，另一方面要继续进行美国单方面对日本细菌部队人员的讯问，掌控尚未到手的日军细菌战特别是人体实验的资料。第 10 章收入的主要是华盛顿与东京之间，有关苏联检察官提出的讯问石井等日本细菌战有关人员的要求，在对美国国家利益种种角度的考虑的基础上，形成最终政策的来往公文。

苏联检方的不懈要求使盟军总司令部面临极大的压力，2 月初以来，其接二连三向本国发送电文，就苏联方面提出的讯问细菌战部队人员的要求，征求上级各部门的意见。电文中提及苏联方面是为战争犯罪的指控收集证据材料，并打算在远东国际军事法庭举行追加审判，认为美国肯定会同意（资料 10.2、10.3、10.4）。

据资料 10.5，2 月 26 日，为答复东京，美国国务院—陆军—海军三部协调委员会（SWNCC）工作小组发布一份内部讨论摘要，提及 1946 年 7 月 24 日，盟军总司令部已向参谋总部报告：苏联检察官提出要求讯问石井、菊池与大田，苏联人认为东京审判有第二期，届时苏联也将参加。当时美国方面还认为让苏联人讯问对美国没什么坏处。据资料 10.6，第二天，1947 年 2 月 27 日，远东国际法庭苏联检察官 Vasiliev（原文拼写错误）将军携翻译向日本美军总司令部情报部门催促，打听其要求讯问的石井等人在日本的下落，并再次强调，苏联方面只是要得到与战争犯罪有关的情报。可是，美国在第一任调查官开始对日本细菌部队人员进行调查时，要求对方供出真相的前提条件就是，该调查以科学调查为目的，与战争犯罪无关（参见资料 6.1）。次日，G–2 长官向本国电文报告：苏联检察官每天提出要求准许讯问日军有关细菌人员（资料 10.7）。3 月 7 日，盟军日本委员会苏联代表 K. Derenvyanko 少将提交盟军占领军总司令部备忘录 1087：要求将石井等人移交苏联方面（资料 10.22）。3 月 20 日，华盛顿终于告知东京，有条件地准许苏联方面讯问石井等人（资料 10.15、10.16、10.17）。3 月 29 日，华盛顿决定选派第三任调查官 Fell 博士赴日继续调查（参见资料 6.3.1、6.3.2）。4 月初，Fell 到达日本。19 日，盟军总司令部法务局向 Fell 博士提供石井等日本细菌战有关人员名单（参见资料 6.3.3）。目前的资料中，Fell 最早的讯问记录为 4 月 21 日（参见资料 6.3.4）。

Fell 到达日本后的 4 月 10 日，盟军总司令部 John B. Cooley 上校即就苏联方面 3 月 7 日提出的备忘录 1087 号回复盟军日本委员会苏联代表 K. Derevyanko 少将，将很快安排其与要求单独会面的对象会面；但拒绝将石井将军和大田大佐移交苏方，因为苏联方面指控的日本人与在中国或满洲的战争犯罪并未明确相关；已在考虑对提出的对象由国际检察局、盟军总司令部及苏联检察官实行共同讯问。必须指出的是，共同讯问的许可不以战争犯罪调查为由，也并不开此先例（资料 10.22）。

据资料 10.24 1947 年 5 月 6 日的电文内容，G–2 已通过在日本的相关渠道确认了苏联人手中的重要证据材料川岛清、柄泽十三夫的供述（参见资料 9.37、9.38）。

资料 10.26 是资料 10.22 中所提及的“共同讯问”的一份记录：1947 年 5 月 13 日远东国际法庭苏联检察次官 Smirnov 上校对 731 部队第二部部长村上隆的讯问记录（参见资料 6.3.12），讯问监督为 Fell 调查官、G–2 McQuail 中校（参见资料 10.1）；1947 年 5 月 16 日 Smirnov 上校对 731 部队主要干部大田澄的讯问记录（参见资料 6.3.13），讯问监督为 Fell 调查官、McQuail 中校；1947 年 6 月 13 日 Smirnov 上校对石井四郎的讯问记录，讯问主持为 McQuail 中校。在美国调查官面前倚仗手中的技术资料讨价还价的石井，在这份苏联检察官的讯问记录中，又是另一番态度。接受苏联检察官讯问的石井等，事先均被告知，不得向苏方透露美国方面的调查讯问，也不得向苏方提供向美方提供的细菌战资料。

资料 10.28、10.30 为 G–2 副长官 Willoughby 给国际检察局代理主管美国检察官 Tavenner 的信：感谢提供信息，并感谢对 G – 2 McQuail 中校的大力协助，一再重申有关信息保密的重要性。

资料 10.29、10.31、10.32、10.33 为针对三部协调远东小委员会工作小组提出的有关苏联检察官讯问某些日本人的意见报告，各部门提出的反馈。从中可以看出，行政部门和军队虽然因角度有所不同，有些技术性的不同意见，但均以美国国家利益的考虑为前提。

资料 10.31 1947 年 8 月 1 日三部协调委员会远东小委员会文件 SFE188/2 中明确：石井等所提供的日本细菌战资料保留于情报渠道，不作为“战争犯罪”的证据。对于国家安全来说，日本细菌战资料的重要性远远超过战争犯罪的追究。据资料 10.32，SFE188/3 国务院的意见基本意见一致，只是提出没有必要如此承诺，资料也有可能获得；承诺的话，今后有可能使美国陷入严重的尴尬局面。

资料 10.34 1948 年 3 月 11 日美国国务院—陆军—海军—空军四部协调委员会（SWNACC）在送交总参谋部发送麦克阿瑟的回复电文中，明确告知美国所要的情报和科学数据已经到手，达到预期。

远东国际军事法庭结束后，没有达到在该法庭审讯日军细菌战战争犯罪目的的苏联，于 1949 年 12 月 25 日在伯力举行了“原日本陆军军人因准备和使用细菌武器被控案”审判，简称“伯力审判”，12 名苏联在押日本战俘被起诉和判刑，其中包括从关东军司令到饲养细菌战研究实验用老鼠的士兵，还有证词在远东国际军事法庭国际检察局备案的 731 部队川岛清和柄泽十三夫。伯力审判日语翻译人员称，为准备诉讼，苏联曾对约 1000 名在押日本战俘进行调查，确定了 100 名相关人员，从中选定 12 名作为被告。

1950 年，苏联出版了伯力审判材料，以多国语言发行。资料 10.35、10.36、10.37、10.38 显示，伯力审判后，苏联继续通过外交、政治途径，呼吁设立特别国际军事法庭，审判日本天皇与石井四郎，追究日本的细菌战战争犯罪责任。中国政府表示赞同，远东国际军事法庭中国法官梅汝璈也在媒体上声明支持。

苏联以对日本细菌战战争犯罪的追究，追及昭和天皇的战争犯罪责任，与美国对日占领的基本政策对立。资料 10.35 为驻各国美国大使馆向美国国务卿发送的有关电文：据 1950 年 2 月 10 日美国驻伦敦大使馆的电文，有英国外交官估计，苏联对天皇的指控得到中国支持，说明两个国家不可能同意与以天皇为名义首脑的日本谈和。

资料 10.37、10.38 有关苏联大使三次照会美国国务卿 Dean G. Acheson，告知伯力审判结果：证据表明日本天皇和石井等负有战争犯罪责任，提议举行特别军事法庭予以审判。

1956 年 11 月，得知被释放、即将归国的消息后，吐露日军 731 部队细菌战人体实验真相的柄泽十三夫在苏联日军战俘集中营自杀身亡。

1969 年，美国总统尼克松声明废弃生物武器，终结了美国进攻性武器研制项目。1972 年，151 个国家，包括美国，签订了《禁止生物武器公约》，该条约规定范围超过了《日内瓦条约》，禁止发展、生产和拥有生物武器。美国国家档案馆等所藏相关资料页面上的档案印章表明，美国从 70 年代前后开始解密日军细菌战相关资料，但如第 6 章美国四任调查官赴日细菌战调查的报告显示，尚有重大相关资料未予公开。原苏联伯力审判的档案资料也待全面公开，特别是调查阶段的资料，包括 1000 名日本战俘的调查报告，以及其中 100 人，包括 12 名原告和出庭证人的调查记录。

本资料集收入的战后美国调查官对日本细菌部队人员的讯问记录，有些原文字迹难以辨认，附有打字复原的 transcription。

资料解说（二） 美军接收的日本资料的下落

〔日〕近藤昭二　王　选

从太平洋战争开始到美军占领日本时期，美军战地缴获或没收、接收了大量的日军有关文件、印刷物，总计达50万件以上。其中下落未明、作为绝密文件隐藏至今的，就是731部队·细菌战的相关资料。这些资料是在美国呢，还是归还了日本？

（一）日本议员在国会上向政府提出质疑

1997年12月17日，在日本国会参议院决算委员会上，议员栗原君子（社民党）就上述问题向政府提出质疑，相关部门负责人、防卫厅防卫局局长佐藤应答如下：

> 防卫厅于昭和33年接收了美国归还的原陆军的资料，防卫研究所保存了4万件，作为战史调查研究的参考。这些资料中，据我所知，不存在有关731部队——正式名称为关东军防疫给水部——的活动情况，及该部队与细菌战的关系之类内容的资料。但是，在这些归还的资料里关于关东军部队编制等的资料中，确认有4件提及关东军防疫给水部，其内容并非有关该部队的活动状况以及与细菌战的关联。

1998年4月2日栗原议员、1999年2月18日田中甲议员（民主党）再次分别在国会提出相关质疑，政府方面维持了上述回答。

1958年防卫厅战史研究室接收了美国归还的4万件资料后，1960年2月，美国陆军技术部队告知将归还日本曾经用于研究的接收资料，6月24日，约95立方英尺的资料运抵日本；11月，约650立方英尺水路学有关的美国接收资料运抵日本，归还到日本海上保安厅。

（二）日本国立国会图书馆与美方的交涉

1967年，日本国立国会图书馆馆长河野义夫赴美与美国国会图书馆馆长L. Quincy Mumford会面，要求美国归还接收的日本图书，特别是当时日本国内禁止发行的书籍。Mumford的回答是：需通过外交途径和美国国务院交涉。河野回到日本后，收到了美国国会图书馆寄来的战时日本内务省禁止发行的单行本的3册目录。此后，日本国会图书馆收书部部长外垣丰重开始赴美国国会图书馆调查美军接收图书的下落。副馆长铃木平八郎也曾造访美国国会图书馆进行交涉。1974年11月20

日双方达成协议：美国国会图书馆将完成缩微胶卷拍摄的日本图书原本，分数次归还日本。

一年零八个月后，日本国会图书馆收到了美国寄来的第一批完成胶卷拍摄的日本图书 190 册。这些图书均为发行前未通过日本内务省审查，被没收的禁书，当时被美军接收，日本国内没有复本，是日本国会图书馆特别向美国提出要求归还的。这些从美国归还的图书中没有有关 731 部队・细菌战的图书。

（三）日本政府与美方的交涉

1972 年 12 月，日本政府开始出面，就原日军的资料、图书的归还与美方交涉。

1958 年美国将一批原日军资料归还日本防卫厅后，日本学术会议向总理大臣提出劝告书，建议设立向一般公众开放的国立公文图书馆，以防止公文书散佚。此后，日本政府成立“公文书制度调查联络会议”，经过多方讨论，于 1971 年 7 月设立日本国会图书馆，作为总理府附属机构。整理美国归还的资料后，发现大量的资料尚未归还日本。由此日本学界成立“归还・公开美国没收资料公开会”。此后，众议院外务委员会上，议员寺前严（共产党）向大平外相提出资料归还问题，媒体也开始不断报道、关注此问题。

1972 年 12 月 7 日，总理府召集有关接收公文书等归还问题的各相关省厅会议，商讨决定：截至 1973 年 1 月底，各相关省厅完成关于美国接收公文书的情况、公文书的种类与数量等的调查报告，送交总理府。

那么多资料在战争刚结束的一片混乱中被美国接收，又过去那么多年，对于各省厅何时何地何种资料被接收，要理出头绪难度很大。但是，1974 年 3 月 13 日，总理府总务副长官宫崎还是根据各省厅的调查报告，向美国方面提出了调查并归还接收的资料的要求。

8 个月后，1974 年 11 月 11 日，在美国的巴尔的摩港，三井大阪商船的黑部丸装载着美国国会图书馆运送来的约 150 盒，相当于 66 个纸箱的日本接收资料，起航返回日本。这些公文资料总数为 2730 件，其中原日军资料约 1000 件，内阁及各省厅资料约 350 件，警察资料约 500 件，其他资料约 350 件。

日本国内要求公开这批资料的呼声很高，1975 年 7 月 10 日，日本国立公文书馆第一批公开了 1272 件陆海军相关资料（目录 9 册）。据福岛铸郎的调查（『出版研究』6 号，1975 年 10 月），这批资料里，陆军军司令部、师团、部队的调查、情报收集等的记录，作战计划等军事行动有关的文件资料有很多，包括军用地图。武器和军需工厂的文件资料、陆军直辖技术部门各种武器的试验研究报告，以及兵工厂的生产报告、武器使用说明等也有很多。

但是以上美国归还的资料中，并没有本资料集第 6 章美国调查官调查报告中日军细菌部队人员提供的细菌战相关资料——文件、显微镜标本、照片、病理标本等。1958 年以来美国四次归还日本的接收资料中，未有一件是美国第三、第四任细菌战调查官调查报告中的资料。

（四）美国国内对 731 部队・细菌战资料的追索

1981 年，美国记者 John Powell，Jr.（其父 John Powell 为东京审判南京大屠杀一案日军暴行出庭证人）于美国杂志 *Bulletin of Atomic Scientists* 1981 年 10 月号上发表论文《历史上被掩盖的一章：日本的生物武器（1930~1945）》（日文版，『創』，1982 年 1 月），长久以来掩藏在历史阴影中的日军细菌战问题被揭开。曾被日军俘虏的盟军军人也开始指控在关押期间曾遭受 731 部队人体实验。被关押于满洲奉天俘虏集中营的美军军人——退伍军人会奉天老兵团体，向社会舆论呼吁，引起社会关注，相关书籍的出版和电视报道将美军俘虏的人体实验受害问题推上了国会。美国蒙塔纳州民主党代表 Pat Williams 议员听取了奉天老兵团体的申诉后，采取了行动，于 1982 年 6 月 10 日众议院退伍军人问题小委员会上召开听证会，让原奉天战俘营老兵及其他有关团体人员在国会公开作证。但是当时老兵的证词中未能举出充足的证据，也掺杂了情感和主观推测，最终未能推动调查，形成报告。

三年后，英国电视纪录片《731 部队：天皇知道吗？》触及日军用盟军俘虏进行人体实验一事，战后美国第一任赴日细菌战调查官 Sanders 中校则在采访镜头中披露美方与日军细菌部队石井四郎等的秘密“交易”。这部纪录片在西方社会造成冲击性的效应。

Pat Williams 议员和原战俘老兵们不断呼吁，游说国会。1986 年，第 97 届议会，Douglas Applegate（民主党）议员担任众议院议长时，再次在众议院退伍军人问题小委员会举行了听证会。听证会上，美国陆军部档案管理官 John Henry Hatcher 博士作为美军相关部门代表出席作证（Hatcher 1971 年以中校军衔从美国空军退役，1982 年起担任该职务）。

据 Hatcher 的证言，在陆军档案保管系统内的有关部分，对听证会提出申诉的相关证据资料进行了很长时间的检索，发现约 200 页的二手资料，这应该是陆军所藏资料中的全部相关资料。没有找到本听证会申诉的相关证据材料。盟军占领日本期间所接收的敌方资料，可能有与缴获的纳粹资料那样的一手资料。但是日本的资料由于语言上的障碍，20 世纪 50 年代后半期，并未像德国资料那样复制保存，就归还了日本。归还日本的资料中也许有我们现在手头没有的一手资料。资料不复制就这么归还日本是国防部和国务院的决定。

Hatcher 的证言中有以下三点非常明确：①资料归还日本政府的时间是 20 世纪 50 年代后半期或 60 年代初；②二手资料存放在美国陆军部档案保管部门；③关于已经归还的资料可以向日本政府问询。不过 Hatcher 在证言中露了这么一句：也有可能是陆军其他部门在保管，或者移送到国家档案馆了，尚未确认。

此次听证会后，小委员会未采取任何行动，也未制作报告书，提议立法救助相关老兵。

直到 1998 年，美国制定纳粹战争犯罪情报公开法，继而于 2000 年制定日本帝国政府情报公开法。根据该法规，The Interagency Working Group（IWG）得以设立，着手审查日本战争犯罪有关档案资料。审查 800 万页档案资料后，IWG 于 2007 年 1 月公布了其中解密的 10 万页日本战争犯罪档案资料及其目录，包括本资料集收入的美国四任赴日调查官的调查报告（参见第 6 章）。但是第三任调查官的《Fell 报告》和第四任调查官的《Hill 报告》中提及的日本细菌战一手资料，尚未在这些被解密公开的美国国家档案资料中被发现。

（五）日本国内追索 731 部队・细菌战资料的新动向

2009 年 10 月，日本国内 12 名历史研究者成立了“731 部队・细菌战真相究明会”（简称“究明会”），于 2010 年 1 月 7 日向日本政府提交了“要望书”。22 日，取得与当时执政党民主党的副干事长生方幸夫面谈的机会，请求其就要求公开 731 部队・细菌战资料一事，与防卫省协调。2 月 9 日，究明会又向防卫省提交了“要请书”。

2 月 24 日，防卫省防卫政策局防卫政策课总括班班长、防卫政策课课员、防卫研究所图书馆史料室室长等与究明会人士举行了一次意见交换会。45 分钟的交流会上，防卫省方面提供了一份已得到确认的相关资料目录，共 29 件资料，其中 12 件为美军归还资料，内容基本上为有关部队的编制（本资料集收入其中的 3 件，参见资料 1.2）。其余 17 件为移送厚生省保管的职员表，以及一些细菌部队成员个人赠送的研究报告。29 件资料中新公开的只有一件，其他 28 件均为 2002 年 8 月 28 日中国细菌战受害索赔诉讼一审判决次日，于众议院议员会馆由国会议员召集的细菌战诉讼原告团、日本律师团、中日两国诉讼支援团体与人士与防卫省、外务省、厚生省相关部门的意见交换会上公开的资料。意见交换会上，究明会方面提出《Fell 报告》《Hill 报告》中未公开的资料，向防卫省追问美国归还资料的接收部门、保管机构等。

此后两年，究明会与防卫省继续交涉了 5 次，要求公开《卫生学校纪事》《化学学校纪事》等相关资料，对方一直回复无法找到。2011 年，究明会成员依据情报公开法，要求日本防卫省公开资料，并于 2013 年起诉日本政府。2014 年 9 月 19 日，防卫省向媒体公开称找到了一册原告提出要求公开的《卫生学校纪事》，表示向原告道歉，并将继续寻找资料，予以公开。目前日本国内关于 731 部队细菌战的情报（《化学学校纪事》《卫生学校纪事》）公开的两起诉讼尚在日本东京地方法院进行。

2011 年，本资料集编者近藤昭二、王选、奈须重雄与日本民间研究者同仁正式注册成立 NPO 日本 731 部队・细菌战资料中心，理事会由国际人士，包括中国国籍持有者组成，以民间合力，继续推动日本 731 部队・细菌战资料的全面公开。迄今，已经数次协助中国国内细菌战受害者访问日本，在日本社会作证，向日本政府部门请愿，要求就日本 731 部队・细菌战历史真相进行调查，包括日本国内、国际。

同年，编者奈须重雄于日本国会图书馆关西博士论文库中，发现 731 部队核心研究人员金子顺一博士论文集（参见资料 4.1），内容为战时细菌战相关研究。“日本十五年战争与日本医学研究会”研究者也在持续关注战时、战后日本细菌战部队和机构有关人员的相关论文发表，包括博士学位论文，追究战时日本医学界的战争责任。

这段历史真相的全面揭开，有待日、美两国及各国各方有志者，与日本细菌战的受害者一起，发出呼吁，追索到底。

目　录

1　创设——细菌战研究的开始

2　警觉——细菌武器的使用

3 情报——在中国实施的细菌战

1　创设——细菌战研究的开始

1.1 《陆军军医学校五十年史》

1.1.1 防疫研究室、防疫研究室作業の一部

资料出处：北島規矩朗編『陸軍軍医学校五十年史』陸軍軍医学校、1936。

内容点评：1932 年 8 月，以石井四郎为首的防疫研究室在日本陆军军医学校内设立。本资料为《陆军军医学校五十年史》中防疫研究室初成立时的照片。

昭和十一年十一月

陸軍軍醫學校五十年史

陸軍軍醫學校

防疫研究室

防疫研究室作業ノ一部

1.1.2　其三　防疫研究室設立

资料出处： 北島規矩朗編『陸軍軍医学校五十年史』陸軍軍医学校、1936、184 頁。

内容点评： 本资料为《陆军军医学校五十年史》第四篇“陆军军医学校时代　满洲事变中有关陆军军医事务”第九章“建筑、给水等设施改善”中“其三 防疫研究室设立”。

ルモノノ魁ナリ。教室建物ハ當時臨時建造物トシテ獨立セシガ昭和八年四月軍醫學校建造物中ニ編入セラル。

其三　防疫研究室設立

設立ノ主旨　防疫研究室ハ國軍防疫上作戰業務ニ關スル研究機關トシテ陸軍軍醫學校内ニ新設セラレタルモノナリ。此新設ニ關シテハ昭和三年海外研究員トシテ滯歐中ナリシ陸軍一等軍醫石井四郎ガ各國ノ情勢ヲ察知シ我國ニ之ガ對應施設ナク、國防上一大缺陷アル事ヲ痛感シ、昭和五年歐米視察ヲ終ヘ歸朝スルヤ、前記國防上ノ缺陷ヲ指摘シ之ガ研究整備ノ急ヲ要スル件ヲ上司ニ意見具申セリ。爾來陸軍軍醫學校教官トシテ學生指導ノ傍ラ餘暇ヲ割キ日夜實驗研究ヲ重ネツツアリシガ、昭和七年小泉教官ノ絶大ナル支援ノ下ニ上司ノ認ムル處トナリ、軍醫學校内ニ同軍醫正ヲ首班トスル研究室ノ新設ヲ見ルニ至リシモノナリ。

防疫研究室開設　昭和七年八月陸軍軍醫學校ニ石井軍醫正以下五名ノ軍醫ヲ新ニ配屬セラレ防疫研究室ヲ開設ス。當時防疫部ノ地下教室ヲ改造シ基礎的研究ニ向ヒ日夜營々作業ニ從事ス。

防疫研究室ノ作業進展ニ伴ヒ防疫部地下室ニ於ケル研究室ハ狹隘ヲ感ズルニ至レリ、依テ石井軍醫正ハ上司ニ意見具申ノ結果、軍醫學校ニ隣接セル近衞騎兵聯隊敷地五千餘坪ヲ小泉近衞師團軍醫部長支援ノ下ニ軍醫學校ニ讓與セシメ防疫研究室ノ新築ニ着手シ、昭和八年四月工費約二〇萬圓ヲ以テ起工、同年十月竣工セリ。

新研究室ハ鐵筋コンクリート造二層建七九七平方米、延一、七九五平方米トシ、附屬建物トシテ動物舍木造三九七平方米、事務室八六三平方米、變電室及機關室、倉庫等ヲ附ス。

滿洲防疫機關設立　防疫研究ノ基礎進ムニ隨ヒ、防疫ノ實地應用ニ關シ石井軍醫正ハ萬難ヲ排シ挺身滿洲ニ赴キ、防疫機關ノ建設ニ關シテ盡瘁セリ。而シテ該研究ノ實績擧ルヤ、内地ト不可分ノ關係ニ在ル在滿各部隊ノ防疫上皇軍作戰ノ要求ヲ滿タス必要上、昭和十一年遂ニ防疫機關ノ新設ヲ見ルニ至レリ。

同機關ハ内地防疫研究室ト相呼應シテ皇軍防疫ノ中樞トナルハ勿論、防疫ニ關シ駐屯地作戰上重要ナル使命ヲ達成セン事ニ邁進シツツアリ。（詳細別記）

1.1.3　本年中本校職員ニシテ戦死竝殉職セシ者左記四名アリ

资料出处：北島規矩朗編『陸軍軍医学校五十年史』陸軍軍医学校、1936、209～210 頁。

内容点评：1930 年代初期，石井四郎在哈尔滨东南约 70 公里处的背荫河建立了一个守备队式的设施，开始人体实验，并实行了严密的戒备。1934 年中秋，16 名被囚禁的中国人越狱成功，其中 12 人投奔了东北抗日联军第三军。此后，第三军袭击了背荫河。本资料为《陆军军医学校五十年史》第四篇“陆军军医学校时代　昭和十年　陆军军医学校教则（昭和十年三月九日改定）”第四章“成绩报告”中关于当时遭受该袭击后，陆军军医学校人员战死的内容。

为防止人体实验败露，此后，该设施遭关闭。

基本動作、應用動作ニ關スル學術ヲ教育シ剛健ナル氣力、體力ヲ養成シ白兵ノ使用ニ習熟セシム

第四章 成績報告

第二十五條 本教則第八條ニ據リ教官ハ甲種、乙種竝丙種學生ニ就キ試驗ヲ實施シ其成績ハ點數ヲ以テ之ヲ示シ擔任課目教育終了後二週間以内（最終教育課目ニ在リテハ教育終了三週間前）ニ關係教育主任（教官）ヨリ又甲種學生ノ專攻成績ハ各擔任教官ヨリ教育終了三週間前ニ校長ニ提出スルモノトス

校長ハ前項ノ成績ヲ點檢綜合シ列序ヲ附ス

第二十六條 學生ノ教育狀況ハ教育終了後直ニ教育主任（教官）ヨリ之ヲ校長ニ提出シ校長ハ教育終了後一ヶ月以内ニ教育實施ノ概況ヲ醫務局長ヲ經テ陸軍大臣ニ報告ス

内科學教室ニ於テハ前年一月軍陣内科ノ大使命トシテ軍隊結核ニ關スル各種ノ研究ヲ課セラレ、之ガ早期發見、豫防ヲ急務トシテ研究實施ニ移リ、教官中村軍醫監主宰ノ下ニ東京第一衛戍病院看護兵ニ就キ調査研究ヲ實施セシガ、之ガ研究ハ現下ニ於ケル國軍衛生上ノ焦眉ノ急務タルニ鑑ミ、更ニ本年三月改メテ三木軍醫監主宰ノ下ニ内科學教室職員全員ハ東京第一衛戍病院内科病室及兵舍關係職員ノ熱心ナル協力ヲ得テ同病院看護兵ニ就キ精細ナル檢査ヲ實施シ、更ニ十月伊吹軍醫正ヲ主任トシテ近衛師團兵ニ就キ同樣ノ研究調査ヲ果セリ。

昭和六年乃至九年事變ニ於ケル滿洲事變ノ功績ニ關シテハ昭和九年三月三十一日ヲ以テ功績調査ノ締切日ト定メラレシヲ以テ、各關係者ニ就キ調査ヲ了ヘ功績上申中ノ處、本校高等官職員ニシテ昭和七年九月十六日ヨリ同十一年八月三十一日ニ至ル間ニ於テ行賞發令セラレタル者學校長以下七十九名アリ。行賞ノ發令ハ昭和九年四月二十九日附ニシテ敍賜ト同日附ヲ以テ夫々昭和六年乃至九年事變從軍記章ヲ授與セラレタリ。

本年中本校職員ニシテ戰死竝殉職セシ者左記四名アリ。

左　記

囑託　田下五郎

本籍　千葉縣山武郡千代田村大里加茂一四五一

明治四十二年四月一日生

昭和十年七月十八日滿洲國濱江省雙城縣藍棋子溝（背陰河東南方約四粁）ニ於テ匪賊討伐中左胸部穿透性貫通銃創ヲ受ケ戰死。

囑託　田下丑之助

本籍　千葉縣山武郡千代田村大里加茂一四五一

大正二年九月十一日生

昭和十年六月五日滿洲國濱江省雙城縣李家瓦房（背陰河東南方三粁）ニ於テ匪賊討伐中頭部貫通銃創ヲ受ケ戰死。

雇員　萩原豐

本籍　千葉縣山武郡千代田村大里一二一五

大正八年三月二十四日生

昭和十年六月二十五日腸チフス」ニ罹リ同月二十九日東京第二衛戍病院ニ入院同年七月二十九日死亡。

雇員　渡邊綱吉

本籍　秋田縣南秋田郡土崎港町清水町六〇

明治四十一年一月二十八日生

昭和十年六月二十四日腸チフス」ニ罹リ同日東京第二衛戍病院ニ入院同年七月二十六日死亡。

十二月二十七日午後二時ヨリ築地本願寺ニ於テ壯嚴裡ニ葬儀竝慰靈祭ヲ執行セリ。

昭和十一年

1.1.4　昭和十年二月五日兼学校一等軍医石井要ハ満州ニ於テ関東軍特殊任務ヲ帯ビ匪賊討伐ニ参加シ

资料出处： 北島規矩朗編『陸軍軍医学校五十年史』陸軍軍医学校、1936、216 頁。

内容点评： 本资料为《陆军军医学校五十年史》第四篇“陆军军医学校时代 昭和十一年 陆军军医学校令（昭和十一年七月二十八日改正）附则”中关于当时陆军军医学校附一等军医石井要在遭到东北抗日联军第三军袭击后负伤死亡的内容。

八月以來從來陸軍省醫務局內陸軍軍醫團ニ於テ編纂發行シアリタル軍醫團雜誌ノ編纂業務ヲ陸軍軍醫學校ニ移管セラレタルヲ以テ、學校幹事三木軍醫監ヲ編纂委員長トシ、副委員長、委員ヲ任命シ陣容ヲ整ヘ益々其堅實ナル發展ノ爲盡瘁スルコトトナレリ。

本年六月十一日靜岡縣濱松市ニ於テ二千六百名ノ患者發生シテ死亡者四十三名ヲ出シ、陸軍側ハ飛行第七聯隊、高射砲聯隊、濱松陸軍飛行學校等合計四十二名ノ患者發生セリ。濱松衛戍病院長安倍軍醫正ノ急報ニ依リ、醫務局長ハ病原ノ究明及研究員ノ現地派遣ヲ軍醫學校長ニ命ジ、軍醫學校長ハ北野教官以下數名ヲ現地ニ急行セシムルト共ニ、病原ト認メラルル大福餅及患者ノ糞便、吐瀉物ヲ學校ニ取寄セ防疫教室ニテ檢索セシメシガ、現地及教室共ニ病原ハゲルトネル氏菌ナルコトヲ確認シ、同月十四日之ヲ公表シテ濱松市ヲ始メ全國ノ非常ナル不安ヲ一掃セリ。十一日患者發生以來流言蜚語百出シテ一般ニ人心恟々タルモノアリ、靜岡縣衛生課、名古屋醫科大學、內務省衛生技師、傳染病研究所技師、警視廳衛生技師、其他各方面ノ細菌學、法醫學ノ權威者續々濱松市ニ集リ、晝夜兼行ニテ病原ノ究明ニ努メタルモ、混沌トシテ眞因不明ノ間ニ、我ガ陸軍軍醫學校ニテ速ニゲルトネル氏菌ヲ糞便中ヨリ發見シ、玆ニ世人ハ始メテ我ガ陸軍醫學ガ現代日本ノ醫學ヲ凌駕シ居ル實狀ヲ認識シテ驚嘆ノ聲ヲ發セリ。

陸軍軍醫學校診療部ハ昭和四年現在地ニ移轉セシガ、爾來學生ノ增加ニ伴ヒ漸次狹隘ヲ告グルニ到リシヲ以テ、小泉醫務局長ハ東京第一衛戍病院靈室及軍醫學校自動車庫ヲ他ニ移轉シテ此地ニ建築費豫算二十萬圓ヲ以テ八十ノ病牀ヲ有スル新病棟ヲ新築スルコトニ決定シ、本年九月上旬工ヲ起シ、十月一日寺師學校長以下關係學校職員、大藏省關係職員竝西村組工事關係者參列ノ下ニ壯嚴ナル地鎭祭ヲ行ヒ、昭和十一年三月下旬竣工ノ豫定ヲ以テ目下着々工事進捗中ナリ。因ニ新病棟ハ地下道ニ依リテ舊病棟ト連絡セシムル計畫ナリ。

昭和十年十二月五日兼學校附一等軍醫石井要ハ滿洲ニ於テ關東軍特種任務ヲ帶ビ匪賊討伐ニ參加シ、常崗（拉濱線山河屯東南方約三千粁）附近ノ戰鬪ニ於テ左頸部ニ敵彈ヲ受ケ哈爾賓衛戍病院ニ入院シ、後東京第一衛戍病院ニ還送セラレ加療中ノ處、本年二月一日卒去ス。依テ二月七日午後三時ヨリ築地本願寺ニ於テ學校葬ヲ營ミ其位靈慰ムル所アリタリ。

1.2 关东军防疫部文献

1.2.1 在満兵備充実に対する意見の件（1936 年 4 月 22 日）（节选）

资料出处： アジア歴史資料センター（https://www.jacar.go.jp/）、C01003179100。

内容点评： 本资料为 1936 年 4 月 22 日日本关东军参谋长签发“关参一发第九三八号”《充实在满兵备意见书》。此处节选该文件第三部分第二十三、二十四有关设立关东军防疫部、关东军军兽防疫部的内容。

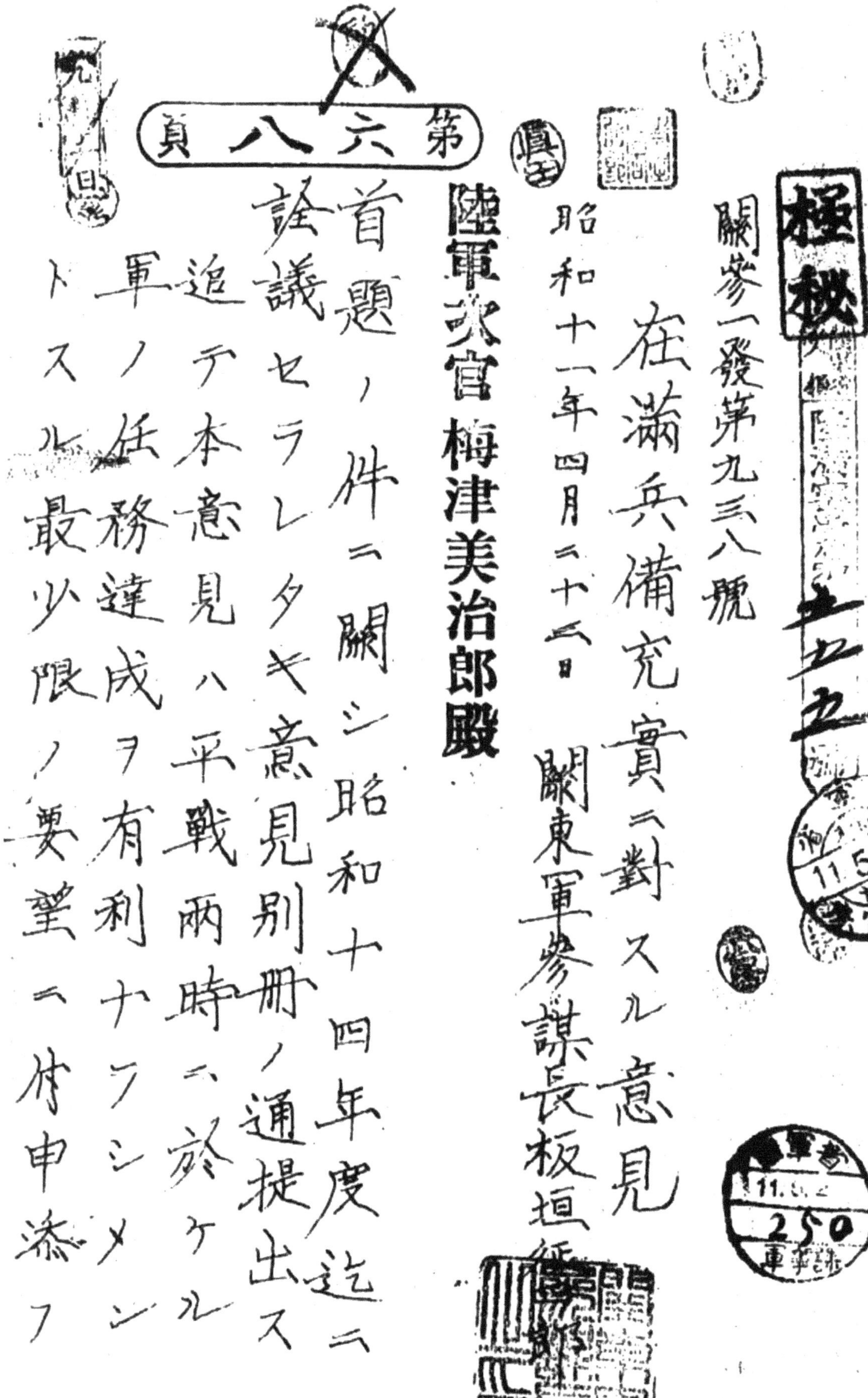

極秘

關參一發第九三八號

在滿兵備充實ニ對スル意見

昭和十一年四月二十三日

關東軍參謀長板垣征四郎

陸軍次官梅津美治郎殿

第六八頁

首題ノ件ニ關シ昭和十四年度迄ニ詮議セラレタキ意見別冊ノ通提出ス

追テ本意見ハ平戰両時ニ於ケル軍ノ任務達成ヲ有利ナラシメンヲトスル最少限ノ要望ニ付申添フ

尚細部又ハ具體的意見ニ關シテ

ハ後日提出致度

極秘

拾部ノ内第五號

在滿兵備充實ニ關スル意見

昭和十二年四月二十三日
關東軍司令部

目次

第六、騎兵集（旅）團ノ増強

第七、砲兵部隊ノ増設及改編

第八、高射砲部隊ノ増強及新設

第九、國境築城守備部隊ノ増強

第十、獨立混成第一旅團ノ増強改編

第十一、中戰車聯隊及混成戰車聯隊ノ新設

第十二、獨立混成第十一旅團ノ増強

第十三、自動車部隊ノ増強改編

第十四、工兵部隊ノ増設

第十五、通信部隊ノ増強改編

第十六、鐵道部隊ノ増強改編

第十七、關東軍鐵道線區司令部ノ増強改編

第十八、關東憲兵隊ノ擴充

第十九、關東衛戍病院ノ擴充

第二十、關東軍測量隊ノ増強

第二十一、關東軍教育隊ノ新設、改編

第二十二、關東軍兵事々務取扱機關ノ増設

第二十三、關東軍防疫部ノ新設増強

第二十四、關東軍軍獸防疫廠ノ新設増強

第二十五、關東軍補充馬廠ノ新設増強

第二十六、關東軍野戰兵器廠ノ擴充

第二十七、關東軍野戰航空廠ノ擴充

第二十八、關東陸軍倉庫ノ擴充

第二十九、關東軍自動車廠ノ新設増強

第二十關東軍技術實驗部ノ化學戰
部隊ノ新設

其四、諸施設ノ整備增強ニ就テ

其五、滿洲國陸軍ノ整備ニ就テ

第二十三　關東軍防疫部ノ新設增強

豫定計畫ノ如ク昭和十一年度ニ於テ急性傳染病ノ防疫對策實施及流行スル不明疾患其他特種ノ調查研究並細菌戰準備ノ爲關東軍防疫部ヲ新設ス

又在滿部隊ノ增加等ニ伴ヒ昭和十三年度以降其ノ一部ヲ擴充ス

關東軍防疫部ノ駐屯地ハ哈爾賓附

四六

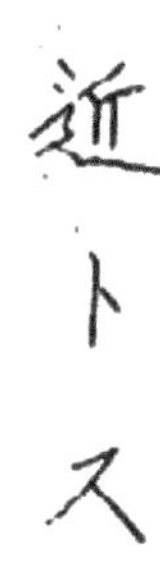
近
ト
ス

第二十四、關東軍軍獸防疫廠ノ新設增強

豫定計畫ノ如ク昭和十一年度ニ於テ關東軍ニテ臨時編成シアル病馬廠ヲ改編シテ傷病馬收療、防疫、細菌戰對策ノ研究機關タラシムル如ク關東軍軍獸防疫廠ヲ新設ス

又在滿部隊ノ增加等ニ伴ヒ昭和十三年度以降其一部ヲ擴充ス

關東軍軍獸防疫廠ノ駐屯地ハ寬城

四七

予附近トス

附表

在滿兵備充實案一覧表

昭和十一年四月二十三日 關東軍司令部

部隊(事項)	要領	着手順序 昭和十二年度	昭和十三年度	昭和十四年度	昭和十五年度	昭和十六年度	摘要
關東軍司令部ノ増強改編	平戰兩時ニ於ケル關東軍ノ現行任務ニ於テモ關東軍司令部ハ昭和十二、十三年度ニ於テ作戰、謀略、教育関係諸機關ヲ主トシ共他所要ノ増強改編ヲ要ス 又兼テ関東軍ノ任務ノ擴大セラルル場合ニ於テハ関東軍司令部ハ根本的ニ改編セラルノ要アリ	一部ノ増強	一部ノ増強 根本的改編				
飛行集團ノ増強 偵、戰、軽、重、直協 所要數 八 一八 一六 一四 八 既存數 四 六 二 四 増加數 四 一二 一四 一〇 八 四十八中隊ト八小	第二次航空兵備充實計畫ヲ繰上ケ昭和十三年度以降之ヲ實行ニ移シ昭和十四年度迄ニ次ノ如ク之ヲ充實ス但シ国有編制ノ飛行團一箇ハ昭和十五年度ニ於テ内地ヨリ満洲ニ移駐ス 飛行集團司令部 一箇 国有編制ノ飛行團(偵四十、戰二十、軽爆四十、重爆二十)四箇 戰闘飛行團(戰六十、軽爆八十) 一箇 直協小隊 八箇		一、集團司令部ノ新設 [illegible]	一、第六飛行團ノ一部 二、第五飛行團ノ半部 三、第六飛行團ノ二部 四、第七飛行團ノ編成 [illegible] 五、直協小隊ノ一部新設	一、第六飛行團ノ一部 二、第七飛行團ノ半部 三、直協小隊ノ二部新設	一、飛行團ノ一部移駐 (編制ニ充タザル部隊ハ之ニ充テ其大部ヲ完成シ真ニ[illegible]ルモノトス)	一、第六飛行團ハ北安鎮、孫呉附近ノ間ニ位置ス 一、第五飛行團ハ勃利、佳木斯附近ノ間ニ位置ス 三、第四飛行團ハ牡丹江、東京城、延吉附近ノ間ニ位置ス 四、内地ヨリ移駐スル飛行團ハ斉々哈爾、海拉爾附近ノ間ニ位置ス 五、第七飛行團(新編飛行團)ハ新京、奉天附近ノ間ニ位置ス 六、直協小隊ハ師團司令部所在地附近ノ飛行隊ニ附設ス
在滿師團ノ増設	第二、第九、第十六師團ノ外ニ昭和十四年度迄ニ新ニ現交代制師團ノ編制ノ三箇師團ヲ滿洲ニ派遣増加ス 但シ第九師團ハ昭和十二年度ニ於テ第一、第十二師團ハ昭和十三年度ニ於テ内地ニ歸還セシメ之ニ交ルヘキ内地ヨリノ師團ヲ滿洲ニ派遣ス 又新ニ増加セラルヘキ師團二箇及現在滿師團ニ代ルヘキ師團二箇計六箇ノ内少クモ四箇師團ハ成ルヘク速ニ常駐制トシ高定員タラシムルモノトス	一、一箇師團ノ派遣増加	一、二箇師團ノ派遣 [illegible]	一、四箇師團ノ歸還及之ニ交ル師團ノ派遣	一、一箇師團ノ派遣増加		一、昭和十二年度ニ於テ増加セラルヘキ一箇師團ハ概ネ[illegible]ニ配置ス 一、昭和十二年度ニ於テ増加セラルヘキ一箇師團ハ概ネ間島ニ配置ス從テ現ニ東部防衛地區ヲ擔任シアル師團配置ノ一部ヲ変更ス 三、昭和十四年度ニ増加セラルヘキ一箇師團ハ[illegible]

事項	要領	配置
飛行集團ノ増強 偵、戦、軽、重、直協 所要数 八 一八 一五 一五 八 現在数 四 六 三 四 増加数 四 一二 一二 一一 八 四十八中隊トナル	第一次航空兵備充実計畫ヲ繰上昭和十五年度以降之ヲ實行ニ移シ昭和十四年度迄ニ次ノ如ク之ヲ實施ス但シ固有編制ノ飛行團一箇ハ昭和十五年度ニ於テ内地ヨリ満洲ニ移駐ス 飛行集團司令部 一箇 固有編制ノ飛行團(偵一中戦五中[illegible]) 四箇 戦闘飛行團(戦六中[illegible]) 一箇 直協小隊 八箇	一、第六飛行團ハ公主嶺、鎮東附近ノ間ニ位置ス 二、第五飛行團ハ勃利、佳木斯附近ノ間ニ位置ス 三、第四飛行團ハ牡丹江、東京城、延吉附近ノ間ニ位置ス 四、内地ヨリ移駐スル飛行團ハ斉々哈爾、海拉爾附近ノ間ニ位置ス 五、第七飛行團(戦闘飛行團)ハ斉々哈爾、新京、奉天附近ノ間ニ位置ス 六、直協小隊ハ師團司令部所在地附近ノ飛行隊ノ所在地ニ配置ス
在満師團ノ増設	第八、第九、第十二師團ノ外ニ昭和十四年度迄ニ新ニ現戰時編制ヲ以テ編制ノ四箇師團ヲ満洲ニ派遣増加ス 但シ第九師團ハ昭和十二年度ニ於テ第十二師團ハ昭和十二年度ニ於テ内地ヘ歸還セシメ之ニ交ルヘキ内地ヨリノ師團ヲ満洲ニ派遣ス 又新ニ増加セラルヘキ師團二箇及現在満師團ニ代ルヘキ師團二箇計六箇ノ内少クモ四箇師團ハ成ルヘク速ニ常駐制トシ高定員タラシムルモノトス	一、昭和十一年度ニ於テ増加セラルヘキ一箇師團ハ穆棱附近ニ配置ス 二、昭和十二年度ニ於テ増加セラルヘキ一箇師團ハ龍江省ニ配置スルモ現ニ東部國境地區ヲ擔任シアル師團ノ一部ヲ變更ス 三、昭和十四年度迄ニ増加セラルヘキ一箇師團ハ東部國境附近ニ位置セシメ[illegible] [illegible]
獨立混成旅團ノ新設	獨立混成第十一旅團ノ編制ト同一ノ獨立混成旅團一箇ヲ昭和十二年度ニ新設シ之ヲ三江省方面ニ配置シ鐵道守備及防衛ニ任セシムル外對蘇戰略的態勢ヲ有利ナラシム	一、昭和十二年度ニ於テ獨立混成旅團新設後三江省ノ防衛ヲ擔任シ得ル如ク配置ヲ完成ス
獨立守備隊ノ改編	獨立守備隊ハ之ヲ數箇大隊ヲ以テ編成シ得ル如ク昭和十四年度迄ニ改編スルモノトシ其要領左ノ如シ 第一、第二獨立守備隊ハ現制ノ如シ 第三、第四、第五獨立守備隊ハ之ヲ各歩兵二大隊ヨリ成ル一隊ニ分割シ二箇ノ現獨立守備隊ヲ以テ六箇ノ獨立守備隊ヲ編成ス 但シ第五獨立守備隊ハ各大隊ノ二中隊ヲ昭和十三年三月迄ニ増設セシメタル後前項ノ如ク改編スルモノトス	一、第一獨立守備隊ハ概ネ現在ノ如ク奉天、安東兩省ニ於ケル治安維持及鐵道守備ヲ擔任ス 二、第二獨立守備隊ハ概ネ現在ノ如ク吉林省ニ於ケル治安維持及鐵道守備ヲ擔任ス 三、[illegible]

騎兵集(旅)團ノ増強	昭和十一年度ニ於テ騎兵第一、第四旅團ノ騎砲兵中隊及裝甲自動車隊ヲ合シテ集團騎砲兵大隊及裝甲自動車隊トナス外昭和十五年度ニ於テ更ニ騎兵集團ハ騎砲兵大隊一箇ヲ増加シ両旅團ニ各一箇ヲ附スルト共ニ騎兵第三旅團ノ騎砲兵中隊ヲ騎砲兵大隊ニ擴充ス 又騎兵集(旅)團内各部隊ノ編制ヲ戰時(新裝)編制ニ應スル如ク昭和十二年度ニ於テ増強ス 昭和十四年度ニ於テ騎兵集團ノ主力ヲ兆南ニ一旅團ヲハイラルニ移駐ス	一、騎兵集團ノ騎砲兵中隊及裝甲自動車隊ノ合併		一、集團内騎砲兵大隊ヲ増加シ [illegible]	一、集團ノ移駐	一、騎兵集團ハ昭和十四年度ニ於テ其一旅團ヲ以テハイラルニ、其主力ヲ以テ兆南ニ移駐シ概ネ兆南附近衛戍地區内ノ防衛ヲ擔任ス
砲兵部隊ノ増強 砲兵集團司令部 獨立重砲兵聯隊一箇 十加聯隊一箇 ノ新設 十五榴聯隊一箇 迫撃砲聯隊一箇 ノ新設 野戰重砲兵聯隊ノ増強	獨立野砲兵聯隊一箇ヲ昭和十一、十二年度ニ於テ新設スル外昭和十一年度ニ十五榴聯隊一箇ヲ昭和十三年度ニ十加聯隊一箇ヲ昭和十二年度ニ大(新裝)編制ニ應スル如ク編成シ之ヲ滿洲ニ移駐ス、又新ニ十加聯隊及十加聯隊ヨリ成ル聯隊一箇ヲ昭和十四年度ニ新設ス 又昭和十五年度ニ於テ野戰重砲兵第九聯隊ヲ戰時(新裝)編制ニ應スル如ク増強シ昭和十五年度ニ於テ新設ス(?)聯隊ト共ニ一旅團内ニ編合ス 右増強ニ伴ヒ砲兵集團司令部ヲ昭和十二年度ニ新設ス	一、獨立野砲兵聯隊ノ大部	一、獨立野砲兵聯隊ノ [illegible] 新設 二、十加聯隊ノ [illegible] 三、砲兵集團司令部 [illegible] 四、野戰重砲兵聯隊ノ新設	一、十五榴聯隊ノ新設 二、砲兵集團司令部ノ [illegible] 三、野戰重砲兵 [illegible]	一、十加、十五榴聯隊ノ新設	一、砲兵集團司令部ハ新京ニ位置ス 二、獨立野砲兵聯隊ハ興凱鎭ニ位置ス 三、十加聯隊ハ公主嶺ニ位置ス 四、十五榴聯隊ハ延吉附近ニ位置ス 五、野戰重砲兵聯隊ハ海拉爾ニ位置ス
高射砲部隊ノ増強 高射砲第七大隊ノ聯隊ニ改編 高射砲聯隊一箇ノ新設 在滿師團ニ高射砲中隊附設 要地防空施設ノ完成	高射砲第七大隊ハ概定ノ如ク昭和十一、十二年度ニ於テ聯隊トシ又人員ヲ増加シ高射砲第七聯隊ニ改編ス 昭和十五年度ニ於テ高射砲聯隊一箇ヲ新設スル外在滿師團ノ高射砲隊ヲ同編制ニ改メ野砲兵聯隊内ニ高射砲(一中隊)ヲ増強ス 又昭和十二年度ヨリ昭和十四年度迄ニ要地特ニ國境附近ノ要地ノ防空施設ヲ完成ス	一、高射砲第七聯隊ノ大部	一、高射砲第七聯隊ノ [illegible] 二、高射砲 [illegible] ノ大部 三、師團高射砲隊 [illegible] 四、要地防空施設	一、高射砲聯隊新設 二、師團高射砲隊ノ新設 三、要地防空施設	一、要地防空施設	一、高射砲第七聯隊ハ公主嶺ニ位置ス 二、新設高射砲聯隊ハ牡丹江附近ニ位置ス
國境築城守備部隊ノ増強	第一次竣成築城ニ應スル守備部隊(築城部ニ屬スル歩兵大隊及第二次築城守備ニ要スル獨立歩兵四大隊並砲兵部隊)ヲ昭和十二年度ニ増設ス 第二次築城守備部隊(大大隊)ノ半部ヲ昭和十三年度ニ於テ増設ス 又各地區築城守備隊内ニ工兵小部隊ヲ昭和十二、十三年度ニ於テ増設スル外對空視設ヲ増強ス		一、第一次ノ [illegible] 二、[illegible] 三、[illegible] 四、[illegible] 設増強	一、第二次ノ [illegible] 二、各地區ノ [illegible] 三、對空施設ノ増強		

獨立混成第一旅團ノ增強 戰車第三聯隊ノ獨立編制增強	豫定ノ新京ニ一部ヲ更ヘテ昭和十二年度ニ於テ獨歩第一聯隊ニ速射砲一中隊ヲ新設シ戰車第三大隊ノ裝甲自動車中隊ヲ獨立戰車中隊ニ改變シ該大隊ヲ戰車第四聯隊トナシ、昭和十三年度ニ於テ獨立野砲兵第一大隊ニ對空機關銃隊ヲ新設スル外、戰車第三大隊ニ中戰車一中隊ヲ增設シテ戰車第三聯隊トナシ旅團内ノ編合ヲ解キ北滿某地ニ移駐セシム 又昭和十四年度迄ニ旅團内各部隊ノ編制、裝備ヲ改善スル外修理機關ヲ附設增強ス	一、豫備隊ノ增設	一、歩兵[illegible] [illegible]	一、[illegible] [illegible]	一、[illegible] [illegible]		一、獨立混成第一旅團ハ公主嶺ニ位置ス 二、戰車第三聯隊ハ齊々哈爾ニ位置ス
中戰車聯隊一箇ノ新設 混成戰車聯隊一箇ノ新設	昭和十四年度ニ於テ戰車第五聯隊ヲ獨立戰車第四聯隊ニ增強スル外昭和十五、十六年度ニ於テ戰車第四聯隊ト概ネ同編制ノ戰車一箇聯隊ヲ新設シ北滿ニ駐屯セシム 又別ニ昭和十七年度ニ於テ戰車一中隊基幹ノ混成戰車一箇聯隊ヲ新設シ海拉爾ニ駐屯セシム				一、中戰車聯隊本部ノ新設 二、混成戰車聯隊本部ノ新設	一、中戰車聯隊[illegible]ノ新設 二、混成戰車聯隊[illegible]ノ新設	一、新設中戰車聯隊ハ寧安附近ニ位置ス 二、新設混成戰車聯隊ハ海拉爾ニ位置ス
獨立混成第十一旅團ノ增強	豫定計畫ノ如ク昭和十六、十七年度ニ亙リ人員約千五百增加シ旅團ノ定員ヲ約六千トナシ各歩兵聯隊ニ歩兵一大隊、歩兵砲一隊ヲ、野山砲兵大隊ニ一中隊ヲ增加スル外旅團ニ裝甲車ノ裝備ヲ增加ス	一部	殘部				
自動車部隊ノ增強 自動車第一、第二大隊ノ增強改編 自動車二箇大隊ノ新設	自動車第一隊及材料廠一箇ヲ昭和十六、十七年度ニ於テ增設シ從來ノ關東軍自動車隊ヲ二箇大隊(各大隊本部、四中、一材料廠)ニ分割ス 別ニ昭和十六、十四年度ニ於テ自動車二箇大隊(各大隊本部、四中、一材料廠)ヲ新設ス	一、第二大隊ノ半部(分離ス)	一、第二大隊ノ殘半部	一、自動車一箇大隊	一、自動車一箇大隊		一、第一大隊ハ新京、第二大隊ハ牡丹江トス 二、新設大隊ノ一箇ハ齊々哈爾、他ノ一箇ハ齊々哈爾ニ配置ス 但シ當分ノ間各大隊ノ一部ヲ海拉爾ニ分駐セシム
工兵部隊ノ增強 築城工兵一大隊 陸上交通工兵一大隊 渡河(鐵舟)工兵一大隊 ノ新設	昭和十二年度ニ於テ國境築城工事實施ノ爲築城工兵一箇大隊(築城作業隊)ヲ、昭和十三年度ニ於テ陸上交通工兵一箇大隊及渡河(鐵舟)工兵大隊一箇ヲ新設ス 右工兵力ノ增加ニ伴ヒ軍司令部ニ工兵幕僚機關ヲ增設ス		一、築城工兵一大隊	一、陸上交通工兵一大隊 一、渡河(鐵舟)工兵一大隊			一、築城工兵一大隊ハ興凱湖附近ニ、陸上交通工兵一大隊ハ新利附近ニ位置ス 二、渡河(鐵舟)工兵一大隊ハ哈爾濱附近ニ位置ス

通信部隊ノ増強 電信第一大隊ノ増強及編[illegible] [illegible] 騎兵集団 [illegible] 通信隊新設 満洲通信機関ノ編制装備ノ増強	昭和十一年度ニ於テ確定計画ノ如ク電信第一大隊ノ固定無線隊ニ力ヲ満洲ニ移駐シ電信第[illegible]大隊ヲ[illegible]一大隊(四中隊)、無線一大隊(一中隊)ノ電信第[illegible]大隊ト為ス外昭和十三年度ニ於テ無線一中隊及無線情報隊一隊ヲ増設ス 昭和十二年度ニ独立混成第[illegible]旅団、騎兵集団及第一、第二独立守備隊ノ通信隊ヲ新設ス 昭和十二年度ヨリ昭和十四年度ニ亘リ状態通信機関ノ編制装備ヲ増強ス	一、電信第[illegible]大隊ノ増強及改変	一、[illegible] 二、[illegible] 通信隊 [illegible] 四、通信機関ノ増強	一、電信第二大隊ニ無線中隊、無線情報隊一隊増設 三、通信機関ノ増強	一、通信機関ノ増強		
鉄道部隊ノ増強 鉄道第三聯隊ノ増強 鉄道第四聯隊ノ新設 装甲列車隊ノ新設	昭和十一、十二年度ニ於テ確定計画ノ如ク鉄道第三聯隊ニ一大隊ヲ増設シテ鉄道第四聯隊ヲ分離改編スル外昭和十三、十四年度ニ於テ鉄道第四聯隊ニ一大隊ヲ増設シ両聯隊共戦時(動員)編制ニ概ネ近キ如ク編制装備ヲ増強ス 昭和十二年度ヨリ昭和十四年度ニ亘リ本部、歩兵一大隊(不齊、歩兵二中隊、機関銃一中隊)、砲兵隊(二中隊)、軌道車一中隊、通信一中隊、鉄道一中隊、材料廠ヨリ成ル装甲列車隊ヲ新設ス	一、鉄道第三聯隊ノ一部増強	一、鉄道第三聯隊ノ増強並ニ鉄道第四聯隊ヲ分離改編ス 二、装甲列車隊一部ノ新設	一、鉄道第三聯隊ニ一大隊ノ増設 二、両聯隊ノ編制装備ノ増強 三、装甲列車隊ニ一部	一、鉄道第四聯隊ニ一大隊ノ増設 二、両聯隊ノ編制装備ノ増強 三、装甲列車隊ニ一部		一、鉄道第三聯隊ハ哈爾浜、鉄道第四聯隊ハ海林ニ位置ス 二、装甲列車隊ハ哈爾浜附近ニ位置セシメ所要ニ應シ各一部ヲ牡丹江及北安鎮、佳木斯ニ分駐セシム
関東軍鉄道線区司令部ノ増強	研究中						
関東憲兵隊ノ拡充	在満部隊及駐屯地ノ増加ニ伴ヒ所要ノ兵力ヲ増加ス 而シテ軍令憲兵トシテノ運用及其能率化ヲ図ル為在満憲兵隊ノ制度、編制、装備等ヲ改善ス	一、一部	一、一部 二、制度、編制、装備ノ改善	一、一部 二、編制装備改善	一、一部 二、編制装備ノ改善		
関東軍陸軍病院ノ拡充	在満部隊ノ増加、改編ニ伴ヒ之ニ應スル如ク所要ノ増加ヲ行フ	一、一部	一、一部	一、一部	一、一部		
関東軍測量隊ノ増強	確定計画ノ如ク昭和十一年度ニ於テ陸地測量部ヨリ出張人員中所要部分ヲ移駐シ関東軍測量隊ニ編合ス 而シテ爾後測量隊ノ増強ハ一部ニ止メ他ノ測量業務ハ大部ハ満洲国ノ事業タラシム	一、全部					一、関東軍測量隊ハ新京ニ位置ス

関東軍教育隊ノ新設改編	予定計画ノ如ク昭和十八、十九年度ニ於テ独立守備隊、独立歩兵聯隊、独立歩兵大隊ノ下士官候補者ノ教育ヲ現地ニ於テ実施シ得ル如ク教育隊ヲ新設ス 又在満部隊ノ増強ニ伴ヒ昭和十六、十七年度ニ関東軍教育隊ヲ改編シ在満将校特ニ主トシテ歩兵将校ノ本科専門事項ニ関シ識能ヲ向上シ得ル如ク施設ス	一、下士官候補者教育隊ノ新設約半部	一、同上新設ノ約半部	一、軍教育隊ヲ改編シ主トシテ在満歩兵将校ノ実施教育施設ノ大部	一、同上一部ノ増設		一、軍教育隊ハ旅順ニ位置ス
関東軍兵事々務取扱機関ノ増設	在満在郷軍人ノ増加ニ伴ヒ満洲国内ヲ数区ニ区分シ之ニ兵事々務取扱機関ヲ設ケ之カ召集、服役等ニ資セシムルト共ニ徴募及民間諸団体ノ指導ニ任セシム		一、半部	一、半部			
関東軍防疫部ノ新設	予定計画ノ如ク昭和十一年度ニ於テ悪性伝染病ノ防疫対策ノ実施及流行スル不明疾患其他特種ノ調査研究並細菌戦準備ノ為防疫部ヲ新設ス 在満部隊ノ増加等ニ伴ヒ昭和十五年度以降其一部ヲ拡充ス	一、全部新設		一、一部ノ拡充	一、一部ノ拡充		一、関東軍防疫部ハ哈爾賓附近ニ位置ス
関東軍軍馬防疫廠新設	予定計画ノ如ク昭和十一年度ニ於テ関東軍ニ臨時編成シアル病馬廠ヲ改編シ之ヲ以テ病馬ノ収療、防疫、細菌戦対策ノ研究機関タラシムル如ク軍馬防疫廠ヲ新設ス 在満部隊ノ増加等ニ伴ヒ昭和十五年度以降其一部ヲ拡充ス	一、全部		一、一部ノ拡充	一、一部ノ拡充		一、軍馬防疫廠ハ寛城子附近ニ位置ス
関東軍補充馬廠ノ新設	予定計画ノ如ク昭和十三年度ニ於テ在満部隊ニ対スル満洲馬及一部本邦馬ノ調教補充機関タラシムル如ク軍補充馬廠ヲ新設ス 在満部隊ノ増加等ニ伴ヒ昭和十四年度ニ其一部ヲ拡充ス			一、全部			一、補充馬廠ハ寛城子附近ニ位置ス
関東軍野戦兵器廠ノ拡充	予定計画ノ如ク昭和十六、十七年度ニ於テ北満各要地ニ支廠及出張所ヲ設置スル如ク拡充ス 在満部隊ノ増加、作戦準備等ニヨリ昭和十四年度ニ於テ其ノ一部ヲ増設ス		一、支廠 哈爾濱 出張所 牡丹江 [illegible]	一、出張所 海拉爾、北安鎮、新京	一、一部ノ出張所増設		

項目	内容	(一)	(二)	(三)	(四)	(五)	
関東軍野戦航空廠擴充	豫定計畫ノ如ク昭和十一年度ヨリ昭和十四年度迄ニ奉天航空廠ヲ充實スル外別ニ哈爾濱ニ支廠ヲ新設ス 又在満航空隊ノ増加ニ伴ヒ支廠ヲ昭和十四年度迄ニ別ニ新設スルト共ニ前項諸施設ヲ増強ス	一、一部	一、一部	一、一部	一、一部		
関東陸軍倉庫擴充	豫定計畫ノ如ク昭和十一年度ヨリ昭和十四年度ニ亘リ各要地ニ支庫、出張所ヲ設置スル如ク擴充ス 在満部隊ノ増加及作戦準備等ヨリ昭和十四年度ニ一部ノ支庫、出張所ヲ増設擴大ス	一、一部	一、一部	一、一部	一、一部		
関東軍自動車廠新設	豫定計畫ノ如ク昭和十三年度ニ於テ野戦兵器廠内ノ自動車関係ヲ分離シ在満自動車部隊ニ即應スル如ク此等ヲ統合シテ関東軍自動車廠ヲ新設ス 又昭和十四年度ニ於テ其ノ一部ヲ増設スルト共ニ若干ノ出張所ヲ新設ス			一、本部	一、一部ノ増設 二、若干ノ出張所新設		一、自動車廠ハ新京ニ位置ス
関東軍技術審査部（化學戦部隊）ノ新設	昭和十一年六月晋所関参一發第一〇八號関東軍司令部編制ニ對スル意見ニ添付セル之カ新設意見ニ概ネ同様ナルモ特ニ化學戦関係部門ヲ強化シ所要ノ教導隊ヲ附設スルカ又ハ別ニ化學戦部隊ヲ満洲ニ新設ス		一、大部	一、一部			
飛行場ノ整備	昭和十一年度ニ引續キ飛行場ノ新設及既設飛行場ノ補修ヲ行フ 但シ一部満洲國ヲシテ負擔セシム	一、一部	一、一部	一、一部	一、一部	一、残部	
人馬其他物件ノ收容施設	在満部隊ノ増加ニ伴ヒ之ヲ増設ス	一、一部	一、一部	一、一部	一、一部	一、一部	
在満教育施設		一、一部	一、一部	一、一部	一、一部	一、一部	

備考

一、着手順序ハ全般的兵力充實ノ關係ニ依リ變更ヲ要スルモノアリ

二、部隊ノ順序ハ緩急順序ニアラス

三、満洲國陸軍指導要綱ニ準據シ在満日本軍兵力ノ増強ト共ニ満洲國陸軍ノ整備ヲ昭和十四年度迄ニ概成ス

1.2.2　関東軍防疫部工事実施の件（1936 年 7 月 29 日）

资料出处：アジア歴史資料センター（https://www.jacar.go.jp/）、C01003176500。

内容点评：1936 年 5 月 30 日，根据天皇命令“陆甲第 7 号”，石井四郎所率“东乡部队”不再是陆军军医学校研究室的派出机关，成为隶属于关东军的正式部队，名称为“关东军防疫部”。本文件编号为“陆满三二六”，为陆军省发布的关于关东军防疫部工程建筑的规定。

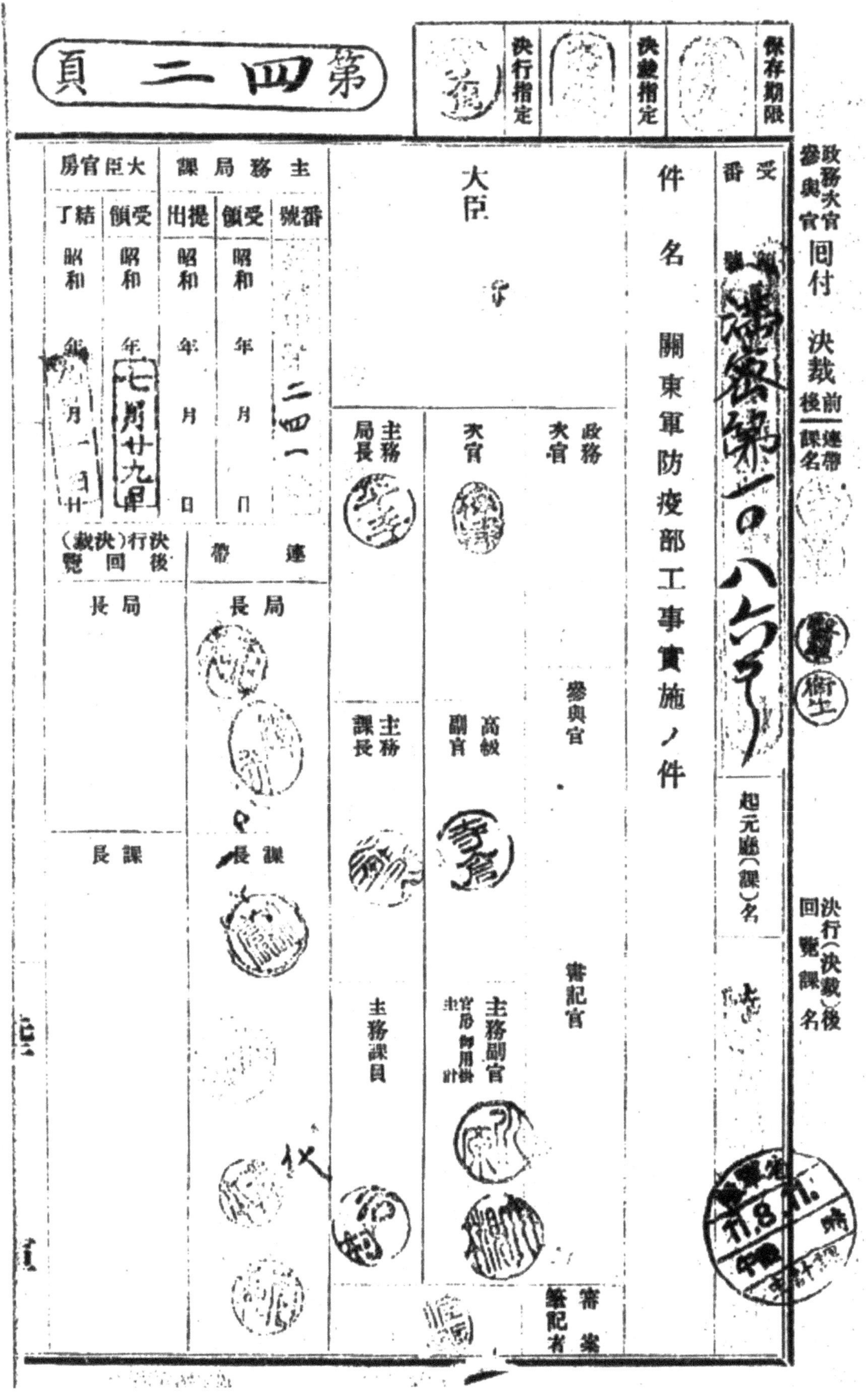
第四二頁

保存期限　決裁指定　決行指定

受番號　陸普第一〇八六七號
件名　關東軍防疫部工事實施ノ件
起元廳（課）名

大臣

政務次官　次官　局長　主務局長　參與官　高級副官　主務課長　書記官　主務副官　主務課員

主務課　番號　二四一　受領　昭和　年　月　日　提出　昭和　年　月　日
大臣官房　受領　昭和七月廿九日　結了　昭和　年　月　日

連帶　局長　課長
決行（決裁）後回覽　局長　課長

審案　筆記者

政務次官　參與官　回付　決裁前後　連帶課名
決行（決裁）後回覽課名

衛生

陸軍省　11.8.11.

關東軍經理部長ヘ連案（暗電）

首題工事ハ哈爾賓衛戍病院分研究室ヲ含ミ昭和十一年度滿洲事件費築造費金百拾萬圓ヲ目途トシテ實施スヘシ

陸滿第二六

昭和十一年七月廿九日

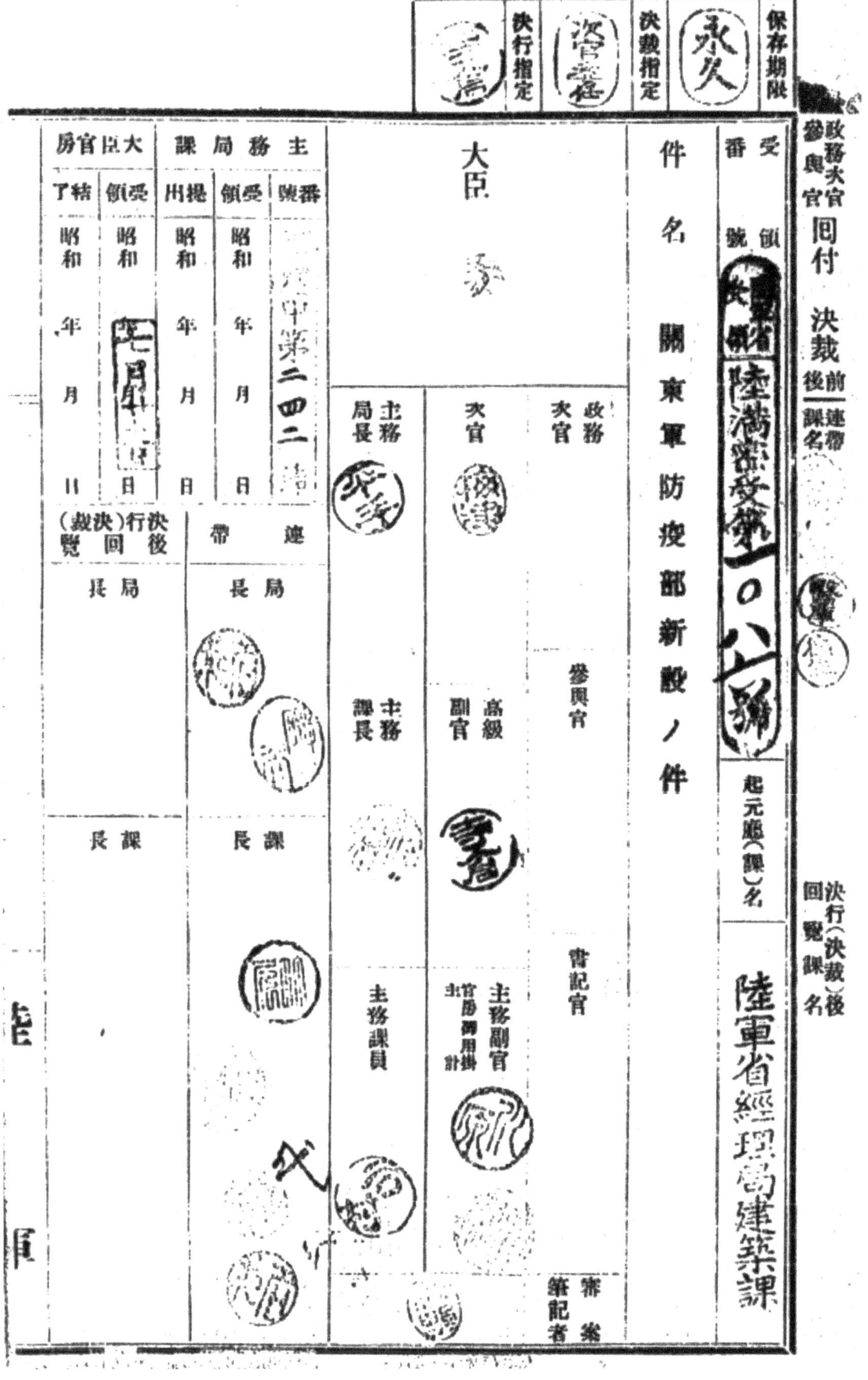

保存期限 永久
決裁指定
決行指定

受領番號 陸満密受第一〇八八號
件名 關東軍防疫部新設ノ件
起元庁（課）名 陸軍省經理局建築課

大臣
政務次官
次官
參與官
高級副官
書記官
主務局長
主務課長
主務課員
主務副官
審案筆記者

主務局課：番號 陸中第二四二號；受領 昭和 年 月 日；提出 昭和 年 月 日
大臣官房：受領 昭和 年 月 日；結了 昭和 年 月 日

連帶：局長、課長
決行（決裁）後回覽：局長、課長

政務次官 參與官 回付 決裁前後
連帶課名
決行（決裁）後回覽課名

次官ヨリ關東軍經理部長ヘ通牒案

首題工事ハ別紙ノ通概算決定セラレシニ付依命通牒ス

追而建築方針及建築要領ハ概ネ昭和十年十二月十九日陸滿普第

一一五四號ニ準スル儀ニ付申添フ

陸滿普第六九五號　昭和十一年七月廿九日

（部局長）

1.2.3　防疫部傭人補充に関する件（1936 年 8 月 22 日）

资料出处: アジア歴史資料センター（https://www.jacar.go.jp/）、C01003183100。

内容点评: 本文件编号为“陆满密三二七”，为陆军省发布的陆军军医学校向关东军防疫部派送专业技术人员的命令。

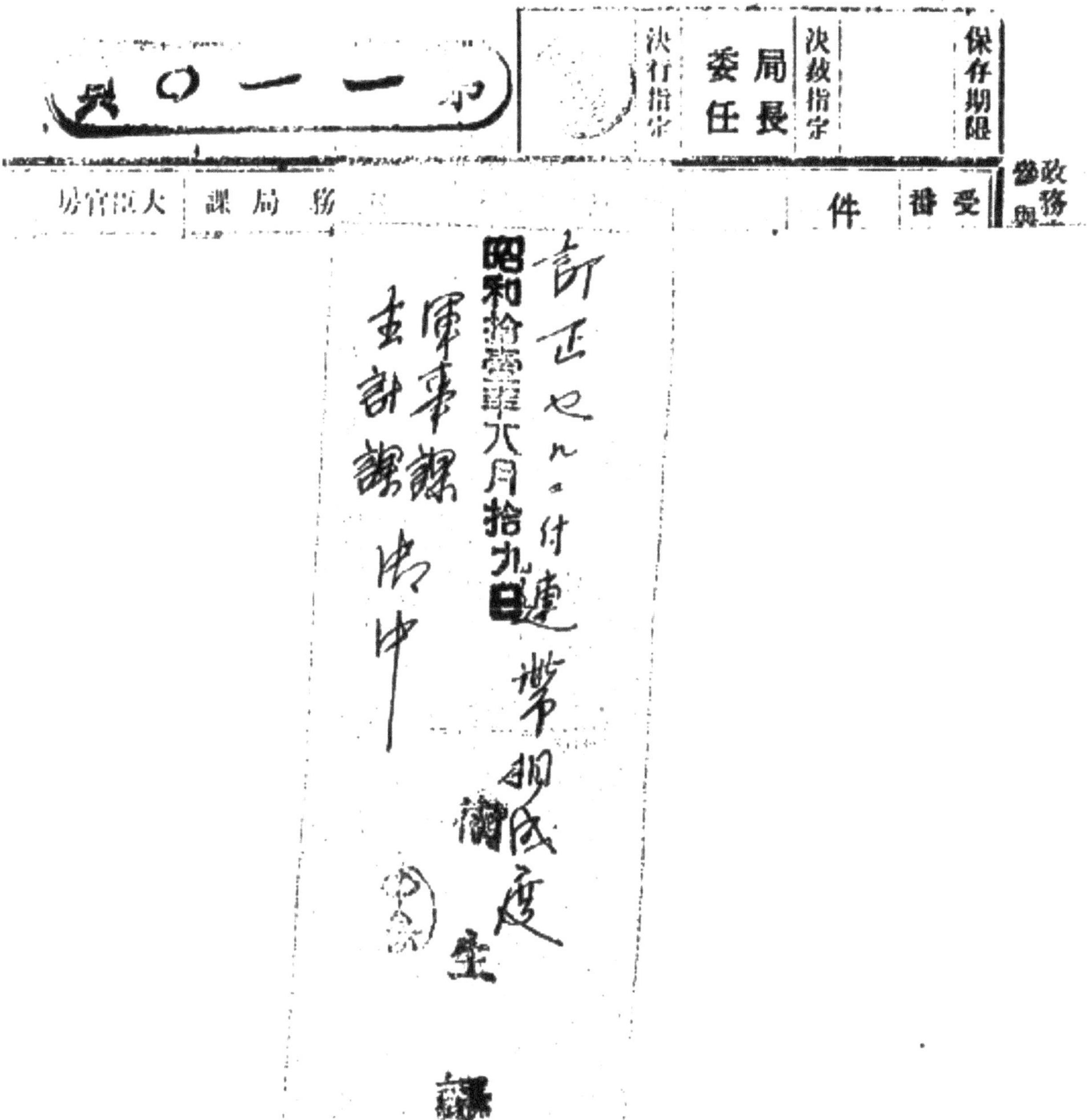

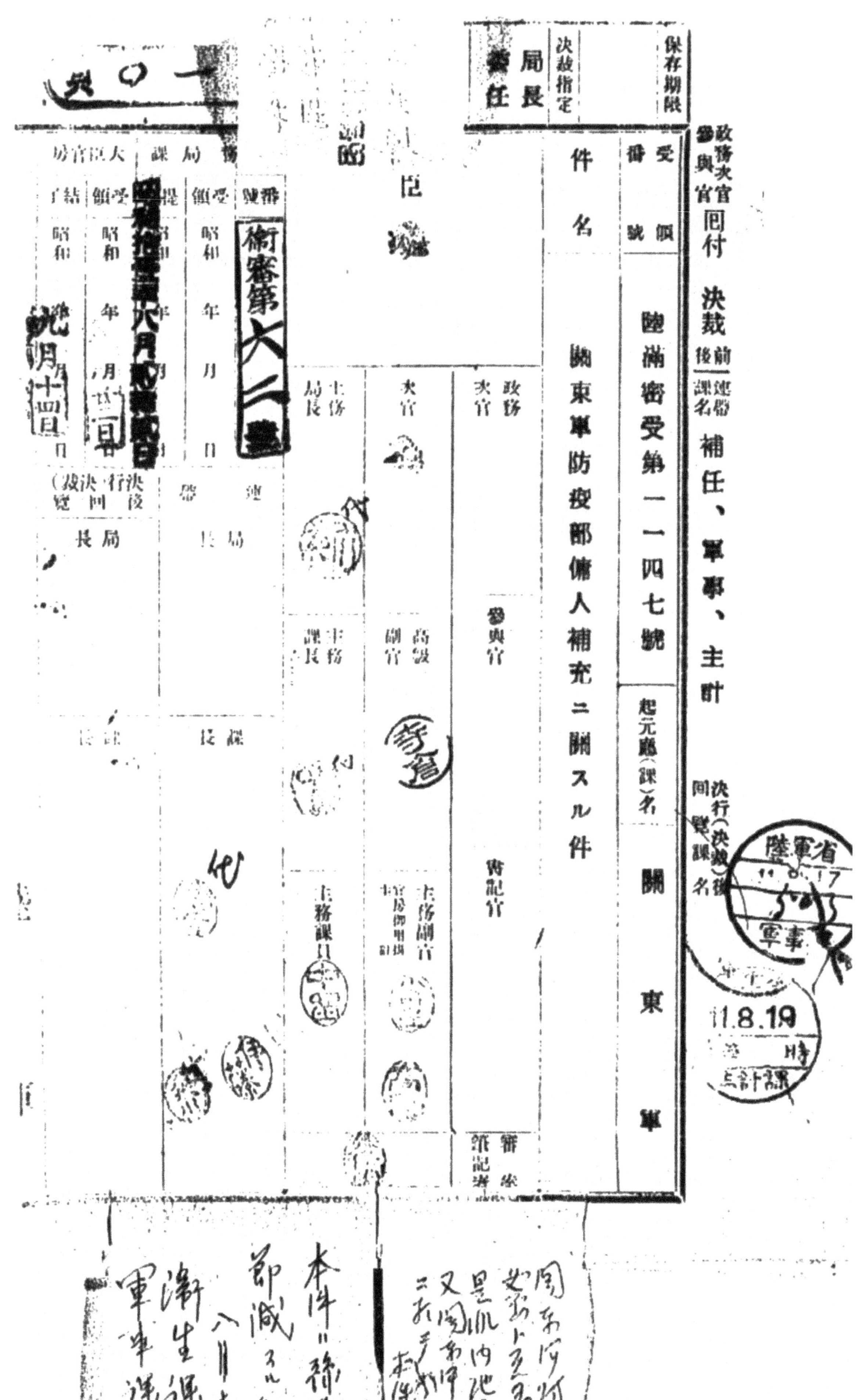
保存期限
決裁指定 局長委任
政務次官 參與官 回付
決裁 前後 連帶課名 補任、軍事、主計
受領番號 陸滿密受第一一四七號
件名 關東軍防疫部傭人補充ニ關スル件
起元廳（課）名 關東軍
決行（決裁）後回覽課名
衛密第六八二號
陸軍省 11.8.19

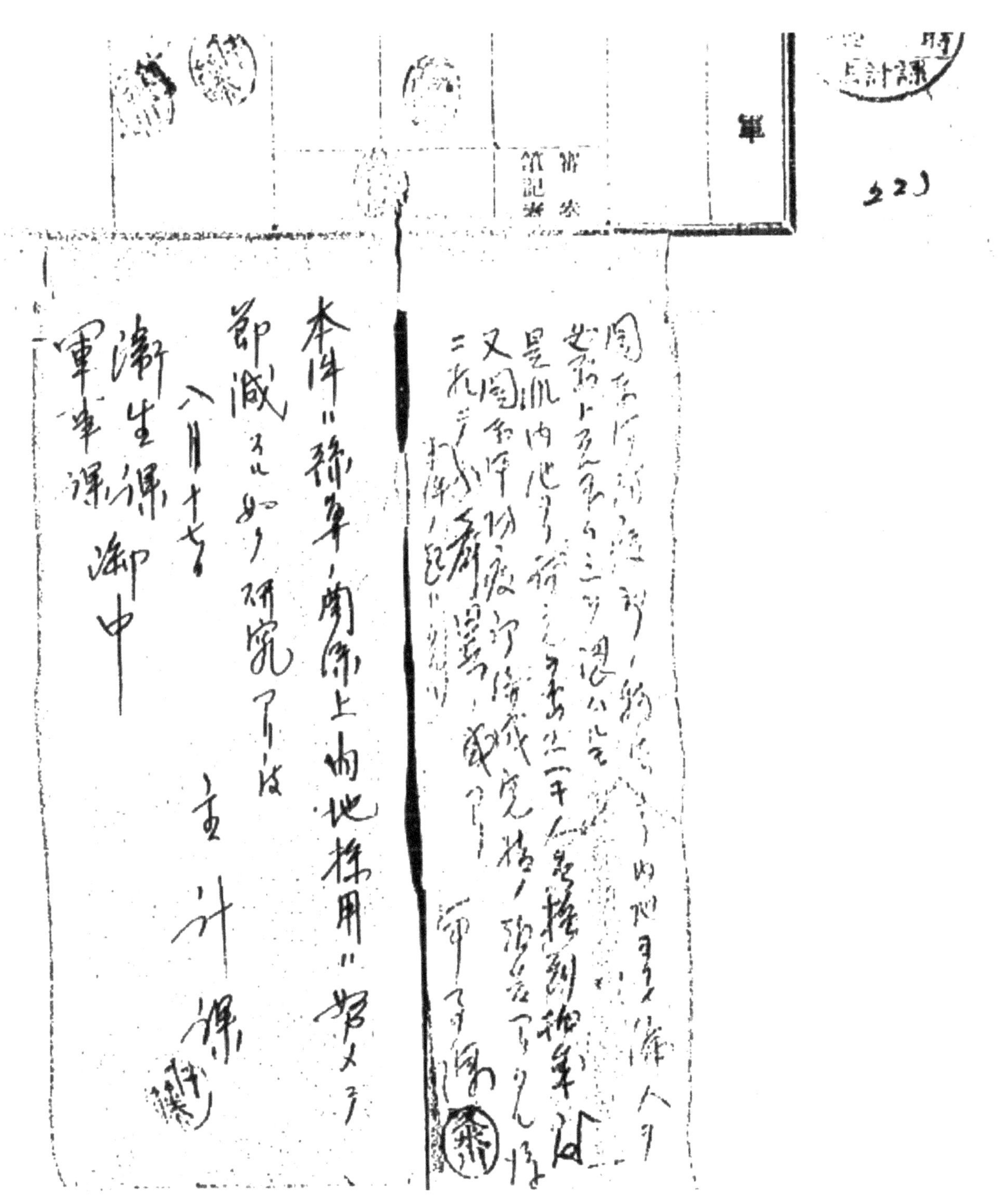

本件ハ孫呉ノ関係上内地採用ハ認メラ
節減スル如ク研究アリ度
八月十七日　主計課
衛生課
軍事課　御中

陸満密

陸軍軍醫學校長へ達案

其ノ校ヨリ關東軍防疫部編成[illegible]へ左記人員ヲ配属スヘシ

但到着日時場所ニ關シテハ關東軍司令官ト協議スヘシ

左記　陸満密第三一七號　昭和十一年八月廿二日

雇傭人　五十名　四十　昭和十一年八月[illegible]

雇傭人　三十八名　昭和十一年十二月配属

陸満密

次官ヨリ關東軍參謀長へ通牒案

關東軍防疫部編成要員トシテ左記ノ通陸軍軍醫學校ヨリ配屬セシ

メラルヽニ付承知セラレ度

追テ到着日時場所ニ關シテ直接同校ヘ連繫セラレ度

左　記

陸滿密第三二七號　昭和十一年八月廿一日

雇傭人　五十名（四十）　昭和十一年八月配屬

雇傭人　三十八名　昭和十一年十二月配屬

陸軍

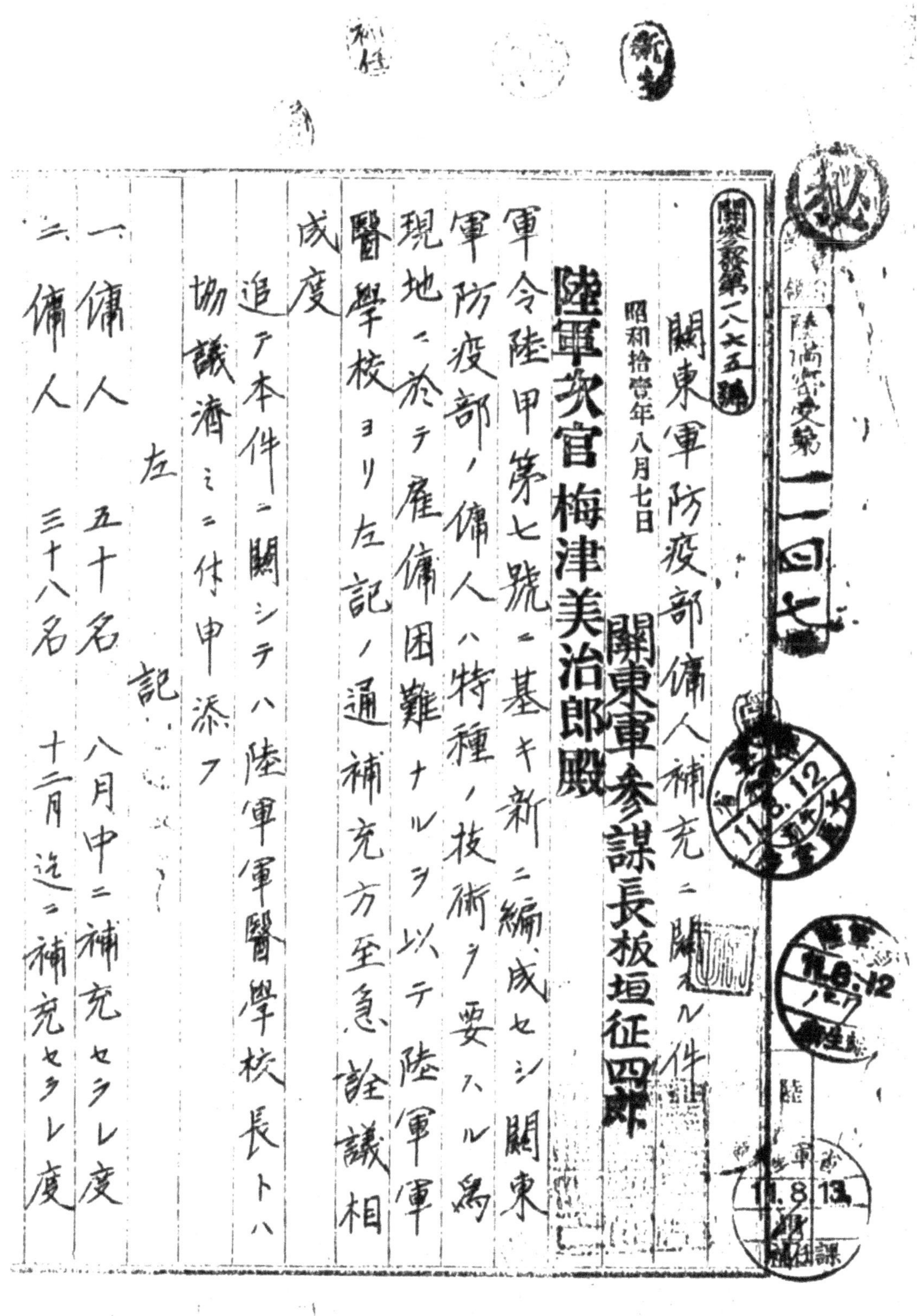

秘

陸満密受第一二四七號

關參一發第一八六五號

關東軍防疫部傭人補充ニ關スル件

昭和拾壹年八月七日

關東軍參謀長板垣征四郎

陸軍次官梅津美治郎殿

軍令陸甲第七號ニ基キ新ニ編成セシ關東軍防疫部ノ傭人ハ特種ノ技術ヲ要スル爲現地ニ於テ雇傭困難ナルヲ以テ陸軍軍醫學校ヨリ左記ノ通補充方至急詮議相成度

追テ本件ニ關シテハ陸軍軍醫學校長トハ協議濟ミニ付申添フ

左記

一、傭人　五十名　八月中ニ補充セラレ度

二、傭人　三十八名　十二月迄ニ補充セラレ度

貴諒ニ於テ書

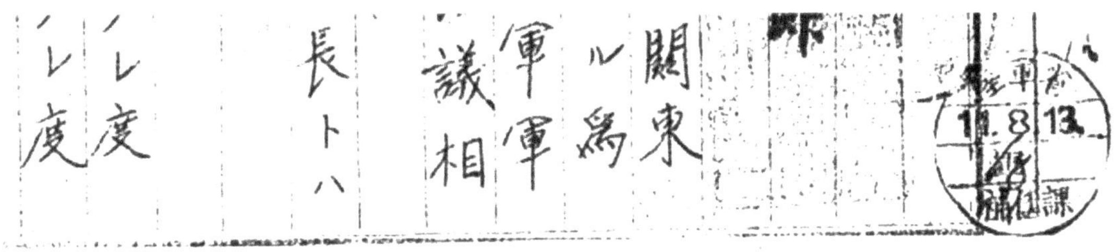

關東
ル爲
軍軍
議相
長ト八
レ度
レ度

貴課ニ於テ處理相成度

2　警觉——细菌武器的使用

2.1　極メテ有力ナル兵器トシテノ黄熱病毒（1939年3月）

资料出处：陸軍中央兵器生產、日本防衛研究所所藏。

内容点评：本资料为1939年3月石井部队技师石光撰写的报告:《作为极有力武器的黄热病毒》第1章（编者按：第2、3章省略）。“石光”全名“石光熏”，毕业于东京帝国大学，关东军防疫部正式编成两年后的1938年即服役于该部队，至战争结束。

極メテ有力ナル兵器トシテノ黄熱病毒

石井部隊

石光技師

昭和十四年三月

1-7

緒言

黄熱ニ關スル纏ツタ記載トシテハHabana ノ Finlay 研究所ノ Hoffmann ガ Kolle － Kraus － Uhlenhuth ノ Handbuch（一九三〇）ニ書イタモノトMense ノ熱帶病學Handbuch（一九二九）ヲ擧ゲ得ルガ之等ハ何レモ約十年以前ノ出版デアル

従テ最近十年間ニ大ナル進歩ヲ遂ゲタ黄熱ニ關スル知見、特ニ病毒及豫防接種、動物試驗ニ關スル其レニ就テハ殆ンド記載ガ無イ、私ハ各種文獻ヲ渉獵シテ主トシテ最近十年間ノ研究ニ關シ些カ纏メル所ガアツタノデ以下ニ綜説トシテ印刷ニ附シ諸官ノ御參考ニ供スル事ニシタ

黄熱病毒

黄熱ノ系統的研究ハ一八八一年ニ溯ル。Finlay ハコノ年 Habana ニ於テ黄熱傳播ハ Aedes Aegypti ナル蚊ニヨツテ行ハレル事ヲ發見シタ。然シ乍ラ當時ハコノ説ニ對シテ否認スル學者モ相當ニアツタ。所ガ一九〇一年ニ Reed.Carroll .Agramonte 等ノ米國黄熱研究隊ハコノ説ニ就テ科學的確證ヲ與ヘタ。

又黄熱病原体ハ濾過性デアル事ヲ記載シタ。然ルニコノ意義極メテ大ナル病原体ノ濾過性ナリト云フ大發見モ當時尚一般ノ承認ヲ得ルニ至ラズ、約三十年ノ後ニ初メテ氏等ノ大業績ガ確認セラレタノデアル

即チ漸ク一九二八年ニ Stokes Bauer Hudson ハ印度赤毛猿(Macacus

Rhesus）ニ黄熱ヲ感染セシメル事ニ成功シタ、コノ事ハ黄熱研究ニ取ツテハ劃期的發見デアル。

カクシテ罹患猿血液ヲ更ニ次ノ健康猿ニ注射シ継代シ得タノデアル

又氏等ハ病原体ノ濾過性ナル事ヲ確證シタ。

因ニ其後ノ研究者ニヨリ黄熱病原体ハ一八〜二七mmト測定サレタ

顧ミルニReed等ノ時代（一九〇一）トStokes等ノ時代（一九二八）トノ間ニハ實ハ可視微生物コソガ黄熱病原体ナリトシテ研究ヲ其方向ニ進メタ學者ガ多数アル、就中野口英世博士ノLeptospira，Icteroides説、Kuczynski ノHepatodistrophicans菌説等著名デアル。

初テStokes等ノ動物實驗ガ成功シテ以來ハ俄然トシテ黄熱ノ研究ガ進步シタ、何故ナラバ從前ハ感染可能ナル實驗動物ヲ見出シ得ズ從テ研究室作業ガ極メテ困難デアツタノデアル。

又猿ハ罹患血液ノ注射ニヨルノミデナク人間ト同様ニ蚊ニヨツテモ感染シ其上人間ト同様ノ臨床的及病理解剖學的所見ヲ呈スルトイフ都合ノヨイ動物デアル。

カカル猿ニ對シ黄熱免疫血清ノ極メテ少量ヲ以テ感染防禦ヲナシ得ルト云フ觀察ハ時ニ人類ニ對スル實際豫防及治療問題ニ取ツテ重要ナル所見ト云ハネバナラナイ。

一九三〇年Theilerハマウス腦感染ニ成功シタ。

即チ猿ニ適應シテ來タ病毒ヲ以テマウス腦接種ヲ繼代シタ

1—10

マウスハ脳接種後急性ニ經過スル脳炎ニ罹ッテ四肢ノ麻痺ヲ主症候トシテ斃レル、卽チ本病毒ハマウスニ取ッテハ特ニ神經親和性ガ強イカ、ル病毒ニ於テハマウスニ對スル內臟親和性ハ證明サレナイ。

マウス脳通過ノ代ヲ重ネル中ニコノ病毒ハ對猿病原性ノ一部ヲ徐々ニ失ヒマウスニ對シテノ固定毒トナル。

マウス体內ニ於テハ病毒ヲ脳ト脊髓ノ外ニ尙坐骨神經及副腎中ニ證明出來ル、反之、一般ニ血液中及脾肝腎ニハ證明出來ナイ。

次ニ海猽モ亦マウス病毒ヲ脳內接種スル事ニヨッテ感染セシメ得ルコノ際海猽モ同樣ニ定型的ナ致死的脳炎ニ罹ル。

以上三種動物ノ他ニ猬（Erinaceus europaeus）モ亦黄熱ノ內臟親和性病毒接種デ罹患シ四日乃至七日デ死スル　人間及猿ト同樣ノ病理組

織学的変化ヲ呈シ又病毒ヲ血液、肝、腎カラ証明セレルトイフ。満洲猬（E.europ.amurensis）及朝鮮猬、ウスリー猬ガ吾人ノ手近ニ存在スル事ハ注目ニ價スル。

以上四種ノ動物ノ外ニ馬モ亦或ル意味ニ於テ黄熱病毒ノ感受性ガアル。即チPetit及Stephanopouloハ馬ニ本病毒ヲ接種シテ強力ナル抗体生産ヲ馬血清ニ證明シタ

之ハ人間ガ黄熱罹患後ニ生スル抗体ヨリモ強クサヘアルトイフ。

上述ノ記載デモ解ル通リ單一黄熱病毒モ動物継代接種ニヨツテ臓器親和性ヲ異ニスル二群ノ病毒株ガ徐々ニ分レテ來ル。即チ一ハ主トシテ内臓親和性デアリ他ハ神経親和性デアル。前者ハ主ニ腹部臓器（肝、脾、腎）ヲ人間及猿、猬ニ於テ犯シ、後者ハ、反之、マウス及海猽ニ

1-11

於テ脳症状ヲ呈セシメル。

コノ場合前者ハ皮下接種、後者ハ脳内接種ニヨル繼代デアル事ヲ申添ヘル。

之ハ明ニ両病毒株共ニ元来ハ両方（内臓親和ト神経親和）ノ性質ヲ有スルノデアルガ感染方法ノ相違（皮下接種ト脳内接種）ニヨッテ一方ノ性質ヲ徐々ニ失ヒ同時ニ他方ノ性質ヲ徐々ニ強メルモノデアラウ

人間ニ於テモ内臓親和性ノ他ニ神経親和性ガ明ニ出得ル事ハStephanopoulo等ガ観察シテ居ル。即チ黄熱ニ罹ッタ二三ノ人デ脳炎症状ヲ證明シテ居ル。

黄熱病毒ヲ長期間保存スル最適ノ方法ハ罹患動物ノ肝ヲ磨リ砕イタモノノ少量ヲ眞空乾燥シ、コノ乾燥粉末ヲデシケーターニ保管スルノデアル。

又若シ肝ヲ氷結セシメルト二乃至三週間ハ毒力ヲ保ツ、Sellards and Hindle（一九二八）ガ西アフリカカラロンドンヘ送ッテ成功シタ方法デアル。

本病毒ハ五五度ニ五分間加熱スルト毒力ハ消滅スル。

黄熱豫防接種

黄熱病毒ハ他ノ多クノ病毒ト同様ニ無生活培地ニハ培養出來ナイ。組織培養ニヨル方法ヲ以テ既ニ痘瘡、口蹄疫、ペルペス病毒等ヲ培養スル事ガ出來ル様ニナッタノデアルカラ之等ノ方法ガ黄熱病毒培養ニ應用サレルノハ當然デアル。

一九三二年Haagen, Theiler ハ協同シテマウス腦通過繼代黄熱病毒即チ神経親和性病毒ヲ in vitro ニ培養スル事ニ成功シタ、一九三三年ニハ既ニ百代以上ヲ培養継代サセテ居ル。

コノ培養ハ眞正滴状組織培養ニ於テモ亦緻培養ニ於テモ液状培地ニ於テ可能デアル。後者ガ特ニ實際上ノ意義ヲ有スル。病毒ハ in vitro デハ只生活細胞ノ存在ノ下ニノミ生存シ培殖スル。培地ニ生活細胞ガ無ク又ハ滅殺細胞トナル時ハ黄熱病毒ハ速ニ死滅スルノデアル。

Haagen ノ今日迄ノ経験デハ黄熱病毒ハ次ノ培地ニ最モ良ク培養サレルト云フ。

一〇％健常猿血清加 Tyrode 氏液ニ新鮮ナル鶏胎児組織小片ノ少量ヲ加ヘ pH ヲ七、六トス。

コノ培地ニ於テハ本病毒ハ毒力及其他ノ生物学的性質ヲ永ク保ツ。

コノ培養ノ毒力試驗トシテマウスノ脳内接種ヲ行ッタ所マウスハ六日間ニ全部脳炎症候ノ下ニ斃レタ。

Berkefeld ニテ濾過シタ病毒モ亦培養ノ出發材料ニ適當デアル。

コノ培養神經親和性病毒ハ之ヲ凍結狀態デ乾燥スルト試驗管中ニ於テ少クトモ半年ハ毒力減少スル事ナク保存セラレル。

Haagen ト Theiler ニヨリ初メテ成功シタ。コノ黄熱病毒ノ in Vitro 培養法ハ漸次追試證明サレタ、ソレニハ先ヅ Lloyd 、Theiler 、Ricci ノ發表ヲ擧ゲ得ル。

氏等ハ神經親和性病毒ノ代リニ汎親和性病毒ヲ用ヒタ、卽チ神經親和デアリ且又內臟親和ノ性質ヲ有スル病毒デアル。之ヲ自然病毒ト名ケテ居ル。何故ナラバコノ病毒ハ普通一般ニ見ラレルモノデアッテ、

1－13

マウス腦繼代通過ニヨリテ一方ノ性質（神經親和）ノミ強力トナッテ居ル固定毒ニハ猶ナッテ居ラナイモノデアル。

コノ病毒ハ既知ノマウス腦病毒ノ如クニハ、勿論、強イ神經親和性ヲ示サナイ。

一九三一年ニSawyerハ黄熱免疫ノ證明方法トシテ黄熱ヲ經過シタ人間ノ血清ニヨル黄熱病毒中和試驗（マウス腦内接種ヲ應用シテ）ニ成功シタ。

コノ方法ガ成功シテカラ黄熱ノEpidemiologieハ大ナル進歩ヲ來シタ、即チ流行地ハ勿論從前非流行地ト思ハレタル地方ニ於テ無症候感染經過者ガ多數アルガ之等ノ人々カラ血清ヲトッテ試驗スレバ容易ニ黄熱經過者タル事ヲ確メ得ル。

Sawyer 及ビ Findlay ガコノ方面ノ研究ニ貢献シテ居ル。

近年南米及アフリカノ總一七一例中其二〇%ニ於テ血清中ニ免疫物質ヲ證明シタ、カクシテ次ノ問題ニ直面スルニ至ッタ、即チ黄熱ハ野生動物間ノ流行性疾患デアッテ其レガ特別ノ場合ニ於テ人間ニ地方病的及流行病的ニ襲ヒ來ルノデハアルマイカ。

實ニカヽル考察ハ Hoffmann ガ Handbuch（一九三〇）ニ黄熱ヲ記載シタモノヽ中ニハ決シテ見出シ得ナイ所デアル。

一九三二年ニハ Sawyer 及協同研究者ハマウス脳病毒ト免疫人血清トヲ以テ黄熱豫防注射ニ成功シタ。コノ研究ヲ基礎トシテ所謂 Sero-Vaccination ガ諸學者ニヨッテ行ハレタ、英國デハ Hindle Findlay、ニヨリ佛國デハ Petit ニヨリ、南米デハ Aragao ニヨリ實施セラレタ

1-14

然シ乍ラコノ方法ハ免疫人血清ヲ要スルノデ多人数ニ注射スル事ハ實行困難デアル。

然ルニ一九三四年佛領西アフリカデ三千人以上ノ希望者ニ行ハレタLaigret, Beilarde ノマウス脳ヲ材料トセル乾燥生活病毒接種法ハ極メテ實際的デアル。本法ノ實験的研究ハ既ニ一九三一年Tunis ノPasteur研究所デ麻痺狂患者ヲ以テスル人体實験トシテ行ヒ其實行性ヲ確メテ居ルノデアル。

一九三六年ノ報告デハ一萬二千名ニ接種シタト云フ。

只惜ムラルハ稀ニデハアルガ接種後脳炎症状ヲ呈スル人ガ出ルノデ未ダ理想的方法トハ云ヒ得ナイ。

一九三六年ニナッテ培養病毒ヲ以テスル能動免疫ガ行ハレタ。

一九三七年Theiler, Smith ハ黄熱豫防接種材料トシテハ理想ニ近イ病毒ヲ組織培養ニヨッテ得ルヤウニナッテ居ルガ之ガ廣ク應用ニ適スルニ至ルニハ今後吾人ハ特別實驗的研究ヲ重ネテ判定スヘキデアルト信ズル。

Theiler, Smith ノ方法ハ腦脊髓ヲ除去シタ鷄胎兒ヲ含ム培地ニ長期間培養サレタ病毒ヲ用フルノデアッテカヽル病毒ハ内臓親和性及神經親和性ガ甚ダ低下シテ居ル、從テ本培養病毒ヲ赤毛猿ノ皮下ニ接種スルモ病毒ハ血中カラ證明セラレ難ク（内臓親和性ノ低下）死亡スルモノハナイ。

ロノTheiler, Smith 法ノ他ニ尚黄熱ノ汎親和性病毒（自然病毒）ヲ組織培養ニ永代ニ繼イデ徐々ニ變化サセ、之ヲ接種材料トスル事トカ能

1-15

働的ニ成長スル移植可能性ノマウス癌ニ本病毒ヲ培養スル事ニヨツテ變化セシメラレタルモノヲ材料トスル事等多大ノ期待ガ持タレル。

黄熱ノ能働免疫ハ接種後六週間デ初メテ有効トナル又Findlay ガ一九三八年一〇月ニ述ベタ所ニヨルト血清検査法ニヨリ免疫ハ二乃至三年間持續スル、尚組織免疫ノ持續期間ハ其レヨリモ尚長カルヘシト説イテ居ル。

因ニ免疫血清ニヨル豫防効果ハ十乃至十四日間デアル、但シ注射後間モナク効力ヲ發生スル

昨一九三八年十月ロンドン熱帯病學會デBoperガ講演シタ所ニヨルト南米ニ於テハ黄熱豫防接種ヲ一九三八年ノ九ケ月間ニ八十萬人以上ニ行ツタトイフ事デアル。

此際ニ一言述ベテオク事ハ黄熱病毒ハ人間及猿ニ於テハ内臓細胞デアル、從テ研究竝作業者ニハ時ニ危險デアル、然ルニマウス病毒ヲ以テ研究スル場合ハ比較的安全デアル。

黄熱傳播竝及其防禦對策

吾人ノ今日ノ知識ニヨレバ感染及傳播ハ殆ンド全ク…………只一ツノ除外例ハブラジルノ發林黄熱デアッテ、コノ感染ハ尚不明デアルガ多分近縁ノ蚊ニヨルモノデアラウ…………Aedes Aegypti（ネッタイシマカ）ニヨル、之ハ最モ廣ク瀰ッテ居ル蚊デアッテ全地球ノ熱帶亞熱帶ニ住ミ又温暖時季ニハ南北緯四二－四三度（札幌、浦鹽、新京、赤峰、内蒙北部、イリー、アルマアタ、コーカサス山脈北方）迄ハ存在スルノデアル。

1－16

コノ蚊ハ吾ガ國ニ於テハ琉球、小笠原父島、台灣、澎湖島、南洋サイパン、ヤルート島ニ分布スルノヲ知ラレテ居ル。

細谷ハ昭和六年琉球デ四七九匹ノ蚊（主トシテ塗蚊）ヲ分類シ（山田信一郎理博ニヨル）三一九匹（六六、六%）ノネツタイシマカヲ見出シテ居ル。

黄熱羅患印度赤毛猿ニコノ蚊ヲツケテ吸血セシメルト約十二乃至十六日後ニ蚊ハ傳染能力ヲ獲得シ爾後ハ全生存期間ヲ通ジテ其能力ヲ保有シテ居ル。

黄熱感染猿ノ病毒血ヲ攝取シタ蚊ハ大体吸血後数日ハ病毒量ノ減少ヲ來シ最初ノ一週間ニ於テ其含有病毒量ハ最少トナルモ其後短時日内ニ蚊体内ニ於ケル病毒ハ急速ニ増殖シテ感染原ノ猿血清内ノ病毒量以

ヒニ増殖スル事ガアル。

自然界ニ於テハネッタイシマカノミガ傳播者トナッテ居ルガ最近ノ實驗的研究デハ多クノ蚊ガ傳播可能デアル事ハ吾人ノ注目スヘキ點デアル。例ヘバオランダノ學者ハA.Albopiotus（ヒトスジシマカ）ヲ以テ傳播試驗ニ成功シテ居ル。

コノ蚊ハ本州、四國、九州、台灣一帶ニ普通ナル種類デアル。又Whitman（一九三七）ハAedes soapularis.Aedes Flu.Viatilis ハ確ニ有力ナ黄熱傳播者デアルトシテ居ル。

Harvard醫科大學ハNew Jersey州ノ普通ノ蚊デアル處ノAedes triseriatusガ黄熱ヲ傳播シ得ル事ヲ一九三八年ニ論ジテ居ル。

佛國學者ガ一九三七年ニ發表シタ所ニヨルト舊北區（沖繩以北ノ日

本本土、朝鮮、シベリア、中央アジア、トルコ、歐洲各國ハ舊北區ニ入ル）ノ蚊デ巴里ニモ普ネク見ラレル Aedes geniculatus ガ黄熱傳播能力ヲ有スルト云フ、之等ノ業蹟ハ吾人ニ取リ極メテ重要デアル。

ネツタイシカマハ今日ニ於テハ全世界ノ溫暖地方ニ棲息シテ居ル、然ルニ黄熱ノ分布區域ハコノ蚊ノ分布區域ニ達シテ居ラナイ。特ニ本病ガ人口稠密ナル南部アジア及極東ニ浸入シテ居ラナイ、之等ノ地方トアフリカ及南米トノ間ノ交通ハ活潑ニ行ハレテ居ルニモ拘ラズ本病ノ浸入シナイ事ハ不思議デアル。

コノ現象ヲ Habana ノ Hoffmann ハ次ノ樣ニ説明シテ居ル、

即チネツタイシマカハ以前ハコノ地方ニ棲息シテ居ナカツタノデ黄熱ガ浸入シテ居ナイモノデアラウ、比較的近年ニコノ蚊ガ西アフリカカラアジア地方ニ擴ツタモノデアラウト云ツテ居ル。

米國デハ南米トノ間ニ航空ガ盛トナルニツレテ黄熱ガ飛行機ニヨツテ侵入シ來ル事ヲ常ニ警戒シテ居ルガ米國衛生當局ハ試驗デハ蚊ニ色ヲツケタモノヲ飛行機ニトマラセテ出發セシメタ所、最高四二〇〇米、一乃至四日間ノ航空旅行ニ堪ヘタト云フ。

又ベルギー領コンゴーデハ黄熱ハ既ニ一九三二年迄ニ二回襲ツテ居ルノデ、ココデモ種々ノ研究ヲシテ居ルガ其中ニ次ノ實驗ガアル、特別ニ作ツタ籠ニ五三九四匹ノ蚊ヲ Leopoldville カラ Coquilhatville ニ飛行機デ送ツタ。二三八四匹（四四％）ハ生キテ着イタ。コノ間ニ一七〇〇粁ヲ飛ビ最高度ハ二〇〇〇米デ二・三日カヽツテ居ル。

昨一九三八年ニハ吾人ノ見逃スベカラザル研究ガ Whitfield ニヨツテ

1-18

ナサレテ居ル。

黄熱病患極期（患ガ最初ニ四〇度ノ熱ヲ出シタ時）患ノ血液ト食塩水トノ等量混合液中ニ蚊ノ「ボーフラ」ヲ入レ蛹トシ、其蛹ヲ取リ出シテ水中ニ飼育シテ成虫トシタ。其ノ雌蚊二九匹ヲ以テ健康猿ヲ吸血セシメタ所ガ猿ハ黄熱ニ罹ッタ。

次イデ蚊ノ卵ヲ病毒血液ニ浸シ翌日孵化シタ「ボーフラ」ヲ洗滌シ成虫トシ毒力ヲ検査シタガ卵ヲ浸シタ液ノ弱毒ノ場合三回ハ陰性、強毒ノ場合一回ハ陽性デアッタト云フ。

蚊卵ノ實驗ハ極メテ重要デアルト信ズル。時ニ蚊卵ハ封筒ニ入レテ郵送シテモ十分生命ヲ保ッテ居ルノデアル。

ネッタイシマカニ對スル適温ハ二六―三二度デ一七度ニナルト刺ス

要ヲシナクナル、交卵ハ二〇度以上ノ時ニ孵化スル。

蚊ヲ永ク生カスニハ夜間二十二度以下ニナラヌ事、日中ハ二十五度以上ナル事ヲ要スル。

コノ蚊ハ人家ノ比較的近クニ棲息スル、動物ヨリモ人間ヲ好ンデ刺ス。

感染蚊ヲ数日間一六度ニ保ツ時ハ病ヲ感染セシメル能力ヲ失フ。コノ温度関係ハ吾人ニ取ッテハ重大ナル點デアッテ比較的低温ニ堪ヘ得ル蚊ヲ養成スル様ナ必要ガ生ズルカモ知レナイ。

ドイツノ Eysell ハ Habana ノ Hoffmann カラ送ラレタ乾燥卵ヲ七ケ月後ニ Kassel ニ於テ孵化サセテ居ル。

× × ×

1-17

黄熱防疫ニ於テハ蚊ガ主要對象トナル。蚊ハ成虫時期ヨリモ幼虫時期ニ撲滅スル方ガ容易デアル。

然シ乍ラ今日各國ガ最モ怖レテ居ル事ハ飛行機ニヨル黄熱成虫蚊ノ搬入デアル、從テ航空檢疫ニ關シテハ一見神經過敏ト思ハレル位ニ取締ガ嚴重デアル。

一九三七年汎アメリカ衛生會議ハ汎アメリカ航空會社ト協定ヲ結ンデ全航空關係者ハ黄熱ワクチン豫防注射ヲナス事、凡テノ旅客ハ乘リ込ミ前ノ六日間（黄熱ノ潜伏期）ヲ何所ニ過シタカヲ記述スル事ヲ要求サレル事ニナツタ。

米國衛生局醫官ハクリストバル、運河地帯、リマ、ベルー、マイアミ、ブラウンスピル等ニ派遣サレテ居ル。

コノ注射用ワクチンハ紐育及リオノロックフエラー研究所ガ供給スル所ニナッテ居ル。

又附加注意トシテ飛行機ハ空間殺虫劑（主トシテ除虫菊エキス製劑）デ燻シ、又朝ハ完全ニ通風シテ旅客ノ入ルヲ待ツト云フ協定ガナサレタ。

又アフリカ、イラク、印度ノ各空港ハ特ニ黄熱ニ對スル衛生警察ヲ組織シ其ノ防禦ニ專念シテ居ル。

英國ノ Impeisal airways 會社ハ飛行機ガ黄熱汚染地ヲ飛出スヤ否ヤ航空中ニ於テ蚊ヲ撲滅スル裝置ヲ一九三八年ニ考案シ將ニ之ヲ採用セントシテ居ル、殺虫劑ハ蚊ニハ高度ニ有害デアルガ、旅客ニハ不快ノ感ジヲ與ヘズ又可燃性デナイ。

1-20

黄熱ニ感染可能ナル猿ニ就テ

印度赤毛猿（Macacus rhesus）ガ最モ感受性強ク、次デM,Cynomolgus（南洋尾長猿）、M,inuus（無尾猿）ノ類ニ感受性ガアル。又ジヤバノNemestrinusモ罹ル。

猿ヲ黄熱ニカケル場合、ネツタイシマカデ刺サセルト三—四日ノ潜伏期後突然四〇度ノ高熱ヲ出シ之ガ約三六乃至四八時間續ク。次デ熱ハ平温以下トナリ虚脱ガ來リ死ハ殆ンド常ニ第五日又ハ第六日ニ來ル

人間ノ場合（發病後最初ノ三日間ノミ血液中ニ病毒ガアル）ト異リ印度赤毛猿ニ於テハ血液ハ死ノ瞬間迄傳染力ヲ有スル、コノ點ハ吾人ノ特ニ重視セネバナラヌ所デアル。

但シ血液毒力ハ最初ノ發熱ニ於テ四〇度以上ニ上ツタ時ガ一番強イ事

ハ確デアル、然シ乍ラ一部分ノ印度赤毛猿ニハ純粋ナ發熱ガナイ事ガアルシ又不顯感染ヲナスモノガアル。

次ニ神經親和性病毒（マウス腦ヲ一四〇代通過シタモノ）ヲ印度赤毛猿ニ注射スルト、コノ病毒ノ場合ハ第十九時間目カラ第十二日ニ亙リ病毒ガ血液中ニ證明サレタト云フ實驗モアル。

又Asibi株（之ハ今迄知ラレテ居ル黄熱病毒デハ最強デアル）ノ黄熱病毒ヲ猿ノ皮下ニ注射スルト九五%ノ猿ニ四－七日デ死ヲ致サセルト云フ實驗ガアル　從テロ、ハ、ノ▲トシテ猿ヲ用フル場合致死期日ヲナルベク延バシ、其上ニ高度ノ病毒ヲ血液中ニ有セシメル樣ニ工夫スル必要ガアル。

都合ノ良イ事ニハコノ際猿体トシテ本病毒ヲ最モ多量ニ含ムモノハ血

液デアル。

兵器トシテノ黄熱病毒

一、攻撃法

(イ)雌蚊ヲ感染後吸血ニヨリ病毒保有蚊トシ、コノ多数ヲ村落、都市ニ撒布ス、撒布方法ハ飛行機其他ニヨル、島嶼攻撃ノ場合ハ艦艇ニヨル。

(ロ)蚊卵ヲシテ病毒保有卵トセシメ之ヲ飛行機、艇舟、又ハ謀略ニヨリ敵地(水ヒ、水邊、水中)ニ撒布ス。

(ハ)感染後又ハ猬ヲ敵地(ナルヘク黄熱傳播可能ナル蚊ノ多数存在スル地及時季ヲ撰ビ)ニ放ツ。飛行機又ハ挺身隊ニヨル。

(ニ)要塞戰ハ敵陣攻撃ニ於テハ友軍敵防接觸完了後、戰車、裝甲自動[illegible]等ニヨリ細菌兵器ヲ敵軍ニ對シ應用ス。

六、防禦法

(イ) Laigret ノマウス脳固定病毒ニヨル豫防接種

本法ハ稀ニ脳炎症状ノ副作用ヲ惹起スル事アル故コノ點除去ニ關シ尚研究ヲ要ス。但シ大量製産ハ最モ容易ナリ。

(ロ) 組織培養病毒ニヨル豫防接種、特ニ Theiler, Smith（一九三七）法

本法ハ稍理想ニ近シ、當隊ハ本法實施ニツキ急速研究ヲ要ス。

(ハ) 黄熱豫防注射効力ハ注射後六週間目ヨリ効アリテ少クトモ三四年間ハ持續スルモノナル故、汚染地ニ入ル友軍ハ進出豫定期日ノ九十日前迄ニハ豫防接種ヲ完了シ置クヲ要ス。

1-22

(二)防蚊法ノ實施（防蚊マスク、かとり線香等）

幼虫殺滅法ノ實施（水面ヘノ諸藥物撒布）

三、ロンドン（五二度）ケベック、ニユーヨーク、ボストン等ノ如キ高緯度ノ大都市ガ過去ニ於テ黄熱ニ侵襲セラレテ居ル事ハ吾人ニカヽル高緯度地方ニ於ケル本兵器ノ活用ヲ示唆ス。

四、黄熱ハ流行後暫時トシテ地方病トシテ殘存スル事アルモ一般ニハ數ケ月續ク所ノ流行病トシテ終ル（自然流行ノ場合ニ於テスラ）故ニ黄熱ニ汚染セラレタル敵地占領後ハ比較的容易ニ之ヲ撲滅シ得。

五、世界大戰ドイツ野戰軍ニ於ケル罹患率ハ毎千人ニツキ

マラリア…………十六人

腸チフス…………十二人

コレラ…………八人

發疹チフス。。。。。。。。。。。。。。。　六人

ト大略算定サレル。

蚊（Anopheles）ニヨツテ傳播サレルマラリアノ罹患率最大ナル事ハ同ジク蚊ニヨツテ傳播サレル黄熱ノ將來ニ於ケル傳播ニ關シ一ノ示唆ヲ與ヘル。

六、南部アジア、極東、南洋諸島ニ今日迄黄熱ガ發生シテ居ナイノハ正ニ一ノ奇蹟デアル。

之等諸地方ニハネツタイシマカヲ初メトシヒトスジシマカノ如キ黄熱病媒蚊ガ繁居シテ居ル、又南洋尾長猿（Macacus cynomolgus）ハ南部アジア到ル所ニ分布シテ居ルシ、ジヤバノNemestrinus猿

1—23

ガ感染可能デアル事カラ考ヘルト印度赤毛猿ヲ蓄スル印度ヲ初メトシ、ジャバ、アジア一帯ニ黄熱病豫ハ準備萬端正ニ完了セリト云フ所デアル。

Megaw。ハ印度ノネッタイシマカガ黄熱傳播可能ナル事ヲ實驗的ニ説明シタ。從テ東洋（印度モ含ム）ニ黄熱ガ蔓延シタ事ガ無イノニ就テ一部學者ノ稱ヘル「東洋地方ノネッタイシマカハ生物學的ニ異ッテ居リ黄熱感染ニ抵抗スルモノデアル」トノ見解ニハ反對スルト云ッテ居ル。

尚英、佛、米、南米、獨ニハ黄熱専攻學者ガ多数アル、顧テ吾ガ日本ニ於テハ今日迄黄熱ヲ研究シタ學者ハ皆無デアル。

（野口英世博士ハ残念乍ラスピロヘータニ病原ヲ求メテ居ラレタ）

ロ・ハニ於テ吾ガ國ノ最弱點デアル。

パリパストール研究所ノ、Stophanopoulo ハ一九三四年夏予ニ向テ「若シ台灣渉リニ黄熱ガ起ッタラ是非傳研等カラ自分ヲ呼ブ樣招電ヲ發シテ欲シイ、旅費滞在費等ハ凡テロックフエラー研究所ガ出シテ呉レル事ニナッテ居ルカラ」ト語ッタ。

彼ハロックフエラー研究所カラ研究費ヲ貰ッテ佛領西アフリカトパリノ間ヲ往復シテ研究シテ居ル黄熱專門家デアル。

海南島ハ佛領印度支那ト指呼ノ間ニアル事ヲ吾人ハ牢記スル必要ガアル。

ハ、對ソロ・ハ作戰ニ於テハ寒冷ニ對スル考慮ト同時ニ熱帶病ニ對スル作戰準備ヲ要ス。

1-24

既ニ一九三四年ニ於テソ滿ニ於ケル「マラリア防遏診療所」ガ三九〇ケ所ニ配置セラレ、マラリア時季ニハ其他ニ三二〇ノ移動診療班ガ組織セラレテ居ル事ヲ吾人ハ記憶セネバナラヌ。

九 黃熱病毒ハ極メテ有力ナル兵器デアル、當隊ハ至急黃熱研究班ヲ編成シ攻擊及防禦ニ關スル實驗室研究及野外演習ヲ實施スルヲ要ス。

編成要員トシテハ病毒學者（Virologs）及蚊ヲ專攻スル衞生昆虫學者ヲ以テス。

時ニ後者ハソ滿國境及軍管轄地區ニ於ケル蚊屬ノ分布ヲ至急調査スルヲ要ス。

2.2 16 Jan. 1941: Possible Use of Yellow Fever by the Axis in Bacterial Warfare, MEMORANDUM FOR THE CHIEF OF STAFF, from SHERMAN MILES, Brigadier General, U. S. Army, Acting Assistant Chief of Staff, G-2; Received at the War Department 13:57 15 Jan. 1941: Paraphrase of Code Radiogram

资料出处： National Archives of the United States, R112, E295A, B11.

内容点评： 本资料为1941年1月16日美国陆军准将Sherman Miles向总参谋长提交的报告，题目：轴心国可能在细菌战中使用黄热病毒。提及日本陆军军医学校的有关人员对黄热病毒非常感兴趣，竭力想把病毒弄到手，美军军医总部以及G-2（参谋二部，即情报部门）察觉后，开始对轴心国的细菌战动向有所警觉。附1941年1月15日美国陆军省收到的英军方面关于Angle-Egyptian Sudan地区黄热病流行情况的报告。

1/16/41

G-2/10568-40

G-2
CHM/TJB

January 16, 1941.

MEMORANDUM FOR THE CHIEF OF STAFF:

Subject: Possible use of Yellow Fever by the Axis in Bacterial Warfare.

Reference my previous memorandum, January 11, 1941 which pointed out the possibility that the Axis was employing Yellow Fever as a bacterial weapon in the Sudan, there is attached a paraphrase of a cablegram from London which presents a less alarming picture of the situation.

SHERMAN MILES,
Brigadier General, U. S. Army,
Acting Assistant Chief of Staff, G-2.

Enclosure
td

Copy to Surgeon General
Secretary of War

JAN 16 1941 

Paraphrase of Code Radiogram Received
at the War Department 13:57 Jan. 15, 1941

London, filed 18:45, January 15, 1941.

1. In connection with your cabled request of January 11 concerning the location, extent, character and source of the present yellow fever epidemic in the Anglo-Egyptian Sudan, we are informed that in the Sudan, particularly in the region of Malakal and the Nuba Mountains in the southern part, there has been an epidemic of yellow fever for many years.

2. Neither the airplane nor the automobile is thought to have played any part in the present epidemic.

3. All British military personnel have been immunized against the disease and there are no cases among the British troops. Only the natives are being immunized at the present time.

4. There have been 1,500 deaths and 15,000 cases during the present yellow fever epidemic. The report of the Surgeon General indicates a definite improvement in conditions. His report is summarized in the following tabulation:

Yellow Fever in the Anglo-Egyptian Sudan

Week	Cases	Deaths
November 3-9, 1940	733	75
November 10-16, 1940	300	29
November 17-23, 1940	87	10
November 24-30, 1940	34	4
December 1-7, 1940	22	6

Week	Cases	Deaths
December 8-14, 1940	29	9
December 15-21, 1940	15	3
December 22-28, 1940	11	2

5. A total of 3,000 doses of serum per week is being produced for the purpose of immunizing military personnel by the Welcome Bureau of Scientific Research (laboratory believed to be at Khartum, - G-2). This is the maximum production for the Welcome Bureau.

6. It is suggested that the Rockefeller Institution be contacted in connection with this matter.

SCANLON

Distribution:

Chief of Staff
WPD
G-1
SG
PHS

-2-

2.3 27 Jan. 1941: Letter from J. H. Bauer, Laboratories of the International Health Division at the Rockefeller Institute of Medical Research, to Colonel James S. Simmons, Office of the Surgeon General, War Department

资料出处：National Archives of the United States, R112, E295A, B11.

内容点评：本资料为1941年1月27日洛克菲勒医学研究所国际卫生部实验室主任J. H. Bauer予美国陆军部军医总长办公室James S. Simmons上校的信函。其中的Dr. Ryoichi Naito是指石井四郎京都帝国大学的后辈内藤良一，他当时在陆军军医学校防疫研究室担任"细菌学"和"要务"的教官；Dr. Miyakawa是指东京帝国大学传染病研究所所长宫川米次。

COPY
mee

THE ROCKEFELLER FOUNDATION

International Health Division
Wilbur A. Sawyer, M.D., Director

Laboratories of the International
Health Division at the Rockefeller
Institute for Medical Research
York Avenue and 66th Street, N. Y.

January 27, 1941

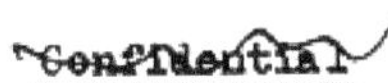

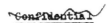

Dear Colonel Simmons:

I received your confidential letter of January 24 and think that Colonel Fox must have misunderstood me. During the past years we have received only two requests for virulent yellow fever virus. One of them came from Dr. M. V. Hargett of the U. S. Public Health Service in Hamilton, Montana. This request was complied with. The other was from Dr. G. J. Stefanopoulo, Pasteur Institute, Paris, which was refused.

What I mentioned in my conversation with Colonel Fox were the following requests and an incident which occurred two years ago. For your information I am having a statement, which I prepared at the time for Mr. Fosdick, copied in this letter as follows:

"On February 23 Dr. Ryoichi Naito, who said that he was an Assistant Professor at the Army Medical College, Tokio, visited the laboratory, bring a letter of introduction from the Military Attache of the Japanese Embassy in Washington. The letter stated that a cable had been received from the Superintendent of the Institute of Infectious Diseases of the Tokio Imperial University asking Dr. Naito to secure strains of yellow fever virus for that institute. When I inquired of Dr. Naito which strains he wished to have, the reply was that he would like to have the strain now used for vaccination and also a virulent, unmodified Asibi strain. I telephoned to Dr. Sawyer and asked for instructions in this matter and suggested that Dr. Sawyer see Dr. Naito personally, which he agreed to do. I asked Dr. Naito to present the letter of introduction from the Japanese Embassy to Dr. Sawyer.

"Later Dr. Sawyer telephoned to inform me that he had declined to furnish the virus, basing his refusal on the resolution passed by the Far Eastern Bureau of the Health Section of the League of Nations and also by the Far Eastern Congress of Tropical Medicine in which the governments of India, Netherlands, Siam, and others agreed to prohibit indefinitely the introduction of yellow fever virus for any purpose whatever into the Asiatic countries. After visiting Dr. Sawyer Dr. Naito returned to the Institute and asked a number of questions dealing mostly with yellow fever vaccine. He particularly wanted to know where the vaccine used in Brazil is prepared. I told him that it was prepared in our laboratory in Rio de Janeiro, and that that used in Columbia and Central America was shipped from this laboratory.

~~CONFIDENTIAL~~ SECRET

CONFIDENTIAL

Colonel Simmons 2 January 27, 1941

"I introduced Dr. Naito to Dr. Theiler. The others had already gone to lunch. Dr. Naito said that he had spent the last year and a half at the Robert Koch Institute in Berlin working with Dr. Schulzberger on the leptospiras and that upon his return to Japan now he thought he would probably be sent to actual field service in Manchuria."

* * * *

"Three days later, i.e., on Sunday February 26, 1939, Mr. Glasounoff, a technician in our laboratory, arrived at my apartment about 2:00 p.m. and reported the following: In the morning when Glasounoff arrived at work in his car about 8:30, he was signaled to stop by a person unknown to him on the corner of York Avenue and 68th Street just as he was turning into 68th Street. The man was about 25, inconspicuous in appearance, of medium height, with no trace of foreign accent. The man looked at his license number and asked if his name was Glasounoff, and receiving an affirmative reply, said he knew someone who would like to meet him and who had some matters to discuss with him which would be very much to the latter's interest. Glasounoff asked the person's name and was told that he would learn that later when they met. Glasounoff's curiosity was aroused considerably and he thought that this person referred to might have some interesting news regarding his family, and therefore agreed to an appointment. Some time ago a person unexpectedly called at the Rockefeller Institute and brought news from his sister in France from whom he had not heard in several years. Accordingly Glasounoff and the person who stopped his car agreed on meeting the unknown person after Glasounoff had finished his work. The time was set at one o'clock, and the place selected was on Exterior Street (Madame Curie Avenue) on the East River where the Institute wall facing the river begins, or approximately the block between 67th and 68th.

"After finishing his work, which consisted of feeding the animals and taking the temperature of the infected monkeys, at one o'clock Glasounoff proceeded to the appointed place in his car by way of 70th Street. He stopped opposite the Institute animal house wall which is a blind wall and without windows. He parked his car just behind another car which he says bore a New York license number ending in 4848, but he cannot remember the letter section. As soon as he arrived another car drove up and parked behind his car. It was then raining very hard and the car windows were steamed so he could not see clearly through his back window the outline of the other car but thinks it was a 1939 Buick and is sure it was a four-door sedan. As soon as this car stopped, a man got out, looked into Glasounoff's car, opened the

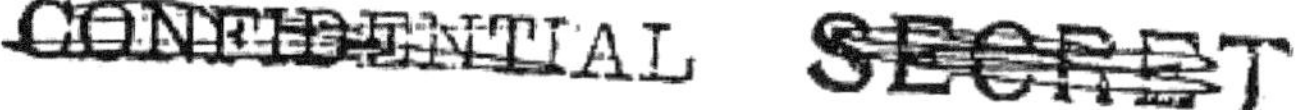
CONFIDENTIAL SECRET

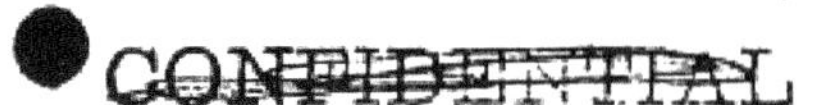

Colonel Simmons 3 January 27, 1941

door, and asked whether it was Mr. Glasounoff. Upon receiving an affirmative answer, he entered Glasounoff's car and sat beside him on the front seat. The stranger began the conversation by talking in a general way about Glasounoff's work and then stated that he also was engaged in research work, that he and another person, whose name he did not mention but stated he was a very famous scientist, were working together, but that they were handicapped for the lack of proper material and said that he thought Glasounoff was the proper person to help him in securing this material. When Glasounoff stated that he was not in a position to furnish any material, the man answered that the material specifically needed was yellow fever virus, Asibi strain. He said that he knew definitely that Glasounoff would have no difficulty in securing it. When Glasounoff suggested that the man or the person for whom he was anxious to secure this material approach Dr. Sawyer, the man answered that he preferred not to attempt to secure it through official channels. The answer was that since they are planning to do work similar to that carried out in our laboratory, there might be jealousy in letting him have it. When Glasounoff refused to comply with the request, the man offered to pay him for it; in fact he offered him a check for $1,000 and asked Glasounoff to sign a paper, the exact nature of which Glasounoff did not know. Upon further refusal from Glasounoff, the man increased the sum to a total of $3000, promising $1000 immediately and an additional $2000 when the material is delivered to him. When Glasounoff told him that he could not get the virus because all virus is locked in the icebox, the man suggested that he bleed an infected monkey, desiccate the virus, and deliver it to him, which he assured Glasounoff he could do while working on Sundays without difficulty. Following Glasounoff's repeated refusals, the man stated that he had better think it over thoroughly before giving his final answer as it would be good for Glasounoff to comply with this request. In the course of their conversation Glasounoff made a move to reach into the back of the car. The man grabbed his arm, told him to stay where he was without moving, and removed the ignition key to the car, putting it into his pocket and repeating that it would be for Glasounoff's good to comply with the request. Upon receiving the final refusal, he slammed the car door, returned to his own car, which had the motor running, and drove off immediately in a southern direction past Glasounoff's car. Being somewhat frightened and excited, Glasounoff did not notice the license number of the car. After the disappearance of the car he returned to the laboratory, walking through very heavy rain, and telephoned Dr. Theiler in Hastings, reporting briefly what had occurred, and asked his advice about the next move. Dr. Theiler recommended reporting the affair to me.

CONFIDENTIAL 

CONFIDENTIAL

Colonel Simmons 4 January 27, 1941

"After listening to Glasounoff's story, I telephoned Dr. Sawyer and asked his opinion regarding the advisability of reporting it to the police. He pointed out that there was a possibility that if reported to the police, a certain amount of newspaper publicity would follow involving the name of the Rockefeller Institute and suggested that I consult Dr. Gasser and Dr. Rivers first. Upon calling Dr. Gasser I learned that he was out of town and was not expected back before Tuesday. Dr. Rivers agreed that it was better not to report to the police but suggested talking the matter over in detail with Mr. Smith Monday and then decide upon further steps. When I reported the results of my calls to Dr. Gasser and Dr. Rivers, Dr. Sawyer suggested calling Mr. Smith, which I did. He too agreed that in informing the police the newspapers would get hold of the matter, and it was his opinion that inasmuch as Glasounoff did not get the license number, the police would have nothing to go on, and that better plans could be made on Monday.

"After this conversation I advised Glasounoff to return home, get his duplicate key for his car, and come into the laboratory Monday morning.

"Glasounoff described the man who met him at one o'clock as being about 40 with a slight mustache. He wore a brown coat, brown hat, and blue suit with a red stripe. On the whole he got the impression that the man was educated, well dressed, and that he had a trace of foreign accent."

Whether there was any connection between the request from Dr. Naito and the episode reported by Mr. Glasounoff we are unable to say. Nevertheless the episode was investigated in detail by Mr. Fosdick himself, and he reported it to the State Department. Mr. Glasounoff was followed by a private detective for several weeks, but nothing more of a suspicious nature was reported.

Six months later, i.e., in August 1939, Dr. Sawyer received a letter from Dr. Miyagawa, Director of the Government Institute for Infectious Diseases at Tokyo, stating that Professor Kobayashi would attend the Third International Congress for Microbiology in September 1939 and requested that we furnish him with yellow fever virus of the strain used for yellow fever vaccine. This request was likewise refused on the basis of the resolution passed by the Far Eastern Bureau of the Health Section of the League of Nations.

CONFIDENTIAL 

CONFIDENTIAL

Colonel Simmons 5 January 27, 1941

Before the present war started, virulent strains of yellow fever virus, to our knowledge, were used for experimental studies in the following institutions:

1. Paris, France - Pasteur Institute by Dr. G. J. Stefanopoulo, whose work for a number of years was subsidized by The Rockefeller Foundation.

2. Amsterdam, Holland - Institute of Tropical Medicine by Dr. Schuffner and his co-workers.

3. Antwerp, Belgium - Department of Tropical Medicine at the University of Antwerp by Dr. Louis van den Bergh.

4. London, England - Wellcome Bureau of Scientific Research by Dr. G. M. Findlay.

5. Boston - Harvard University Medical School by Dr. A. W. Sellards.

6. Rockefeller Foundation Laboratories in:

New York
Rio de Janeiro, Brazil
Bogota, Columbia
Entebbe, Uganda.

We have received no information about what happened to the material in Amsterdam and Antwerp. In Paris we presume it must have been destroyed for otherwise Dr. Stefanopoulo would not have asked for fresh material.

Sincerely yours

/S/ J. H. Bauer

J. H. BAUER

Colonel James S. Simmons
Office of the Surgeon General
War Department
Washington, D. C.

JHB:MJH

SECRET

CONFIDENTIAL

2.4　3 Feb. 1941: MEMORANDUM FOR COL. SIMMONS, OFFICE OF THE SURGEON GENERAL: Japanese attempts to secure virulent strains of yellow fever virus, from Ralph C. Smith, Lieut. Col., General Staff, Executive Officer, G-2

资料出处： National Archives of the United States, R112, E295A, B11.

内容点评： 本资料为 1941 年 2 月 3 日美军 G-2 执行长官参谋 Ralph C. Smith 提交美陆军部军医总长办公室 James S. Simmons 上校的备忘录，题目：日本人试图入手剧毒黄热病毒株。

C O P Y

G-2/10568-40

G-2
RSB

WAR DEPARTMENT
War Department General Staff
Military Intelligence Division G-2
Washington

February 3, 1941

MEMORANDUM FOR COL. SIMMONS, OFFICE OF THE SURGEON GENERAL:

Subject: Japanese attempts to secure virulent strains of yellow fever virus.

1. Correspondence with Dr. Bauer returned herewith.

2. G-2 concurs in your belief that the Japanese are endeavoring to obtain virulent strains of yellow fever virus for the purpose of waging bacterial warfare.

3. Steps are being taken to prevent any of the American or British supplies of this virus from falling into Japanese or other Axis hands, through undercover activities or theft.

4. Information is requested as to whether the Surgeon General, through the Rockefeller Foundation, can take similar steps to guard the Brazilian and Colombian supplies of this virus.

For the Acting A.C. of S., G-2:

(Sg) Ralph C. Smith

RALPH C. SMITH,
Lieut. Colonel, General Staff,
Executive Officer, G-2.

Enclosure

mis

SECRET

2.5 19 Feb. 1941: Yellow Fever Vaccine, MEMORANDUM for Chief, Planning and Training Division, from James S. Simmons, Lieut. Col., Medical Corps (Thru. Chief, Professional Service Division)

资料出处：National Archives of the United States, R112, E295A, B11.

内容点评：本资料为 1941 年 2 月 19 日美军卫生部队 James S. Simmons 中校提交美军 Planning and Training Division 主任的备忘录，题目：黄热病疫苗。

CONFIDENTIAL

jss:ve

February 19, 1941

MEMORANDUM for Chief, Planning and Training Division (Thru: Chief, Professional Service Division).

Subject: Yellow fever vaccine.

1. In view of the confidential information which has recently been made available, indicating the possibility that yellow fever might be used for offensive warfare in the Far East, it would seem advisable for the Medical Department to give consideration to certain precautionary measures at this time. With this in view, it is recommended that sufficient yellow fever vaccine be obtained from the Rockefeller Foundation to protect our garrisons in Hiwaii and the Philippines, if required. Sufficient vaccine for use in each of these departments could be sent in a single lot, and properly stored for use only in case the need for it should become evident. It is believed that the shipment, receipt and storage of this vaccine could be arranged informally between this office and the respective department surgeons.

2. It is, of course, to be hoped that no occasion will arise making it necessary to use the vaccine, and in this case the stored material could be discarded with only an insignificant financial loss.

3. On the other hand, should an emergency arise requiring its use, the arrangements suggested above would eliminate the serious delay incident to shipment of vaccine from the United States to these distant garrisons.

James S. Simmons,
Lieut. Col., Medical Corps.

SECRET

CONFIDENTIAL

2.6 18 Mar. 1941: Yellow Fever Vaccination, To: Assistant Chief of Staff, G-1, from Larry B. McAfee, Colonel, Medical Corps, Executive Officer

资料出处： National Archives of the United States, R112, E295A, B11.

内容点评： 本资料为 1941 年 3 月 18 日美军卫生部队执行长官 Larry B. McAfee 上校提交美军 G-1 参谋长助理的报告，题目：黄热病疫苗。

March 18, 1941

Subject: Yellow fever vaccination.

To: Assistant Chief of Staff, G-1.

1. Letter of the Adjutant General (AG 720.3 (1-10-41) M-A-M) ordered the vaccination of all military personnel in the "tropical regions of the Western Hemisphere." It was not the intention of the Surgeon General's Office to include the territory of Hawaii in this first directive.

2. In view of the information received on the subject of Japanese Bacteriological and Parachute Troops, it is recommended that the provisions of War Department directive (AG 720.3 (1-10-41) M-A-M) requiring vaccination against yellow fever for troops in the tropical regions of the Western Hemisphere, be amended to include United States troops in all tropical regions.

For The Surgeon General:

Larry B. McAfee,
Colonel, Medical Corps,
Executive Officer.

Jss:ve

3　情报——在中国实施的细菌战

3.1 25 Feb. 1941: G-2/2667-H-519, I.B.59, MEMORANDUM FOR THE ASSISTANT CHIEF OF STAFF, WPD: Japanese Bacteriological and Parachute Troops, FROM: SHERMAN MILES, Brigadier General, U.S. Army, Acting Assistant Chief of Staff, G-2

资料出处： National Archives of the United States, R112, E295A, B11.

内容点评： 本资料为 1941 年 2 月 25 日美军情报部参谋长执行助理、陆军准将 Sherman Miles 向陆军部参谋长助理提交的报告，题目：日本细菌战部队和伞兵部队。

CONFIDENTIAL

G-2
CHM/RSB

G-2/2657-H-519 I.B. 59

February 25, 1941.

MEMORANDUM FOR THE ASSISTANT CHIEF OF STAFF, WPD:

Subject: Japanese Bacteriological and Parachute Troops.

1. This Division has information from the Commanding General Philippine Department, considered by the latter as highly reliable, to the effect that:

a. A bacteriological warfare battalion is attached to each of the 5th and 6th Chemical Warfare Regiments Japanese Army;

b. Two hundred fully trained Japanese parachute troops arrived at Taiping Cheung airdrome (in Southeast China) on December 16, 1940.

2. Although no such units as the 5th and 6th Chemical Warfare Regiments, Japanese Army, have as yet been identified by G-2, the Division is inclined to concur in General Grunert's evaluation of the information contained in 1 a. above. In this connection see I.B. 29, Memorandum for the Assistant Chief of Staff, WPD, February 3, 1941, subject Japanese Attempts to Secure Virulent Strains of Yellow Fever Virus.

3. The information contained in 1 b. above is in all probability factual, as G-2 has reliable information from a number of other sources to the effect that parachute training is being conducted in the Japanese Army. It is estimated that from 1,500 to 2,000 troops have been so trained to date.

4. As the defense plans of our overseas possessions are your staff responsibility, your recommendations are requested as to what use should be made of the information outlined above in connection with those defense plans and the training and equipment of the

troops involved.

SHERMAN MILES,
Brigadier General, U. S. Army,
Acting Assistant Chief of Staff, G-2.

CC:
Deputy Chief of Staff
G-3
Surgeon General
Chief, Chemical Warfare Service

emb

3.2　13 Mar. 1941: MEMORANDUM for The Assistant Chief of Staff WPD: Japanese Bacteriological and Parachute Troops, FROM: Larry B. McAfee, Colonel, Medical Corps, Executive Officer

资料出处： National Archives of the United States, R112, E295A, B06.

内容点评： 本资料为 1941 年 3 月 13 日美军卫生部队执行长官 Larry B. McAfee 上校向总参谋长助理提交的备忘录，题目：日本细菌战部队和伞兵部队。

~~CONFIDENTIAL~~

March 13, 1941

MEMORANDUM for The Assistant Chief of Staff WPD.

Subject: Japanese Bacteriological and Parachute Troops.

1. Reference informal action sheet dated March 12, 1941, subject Japanese Bacteriological and Parachute Troops. In view of the information contained in paragraph 1a and 2 of the attached memorandum for the Assistant Chief of Staff WPD, February 25, 1941, and in memorandum dated February 3, 1941, it is recommended that the provisions of War Department directive (AG 720.3 (1-10-41) M-A-M) requiring vaccination against yellow fever for troops in the tropical regions of the Western Hemisphere be amended to include United States troops in all tropical regions.

2. Attention is also invited to the fact that radiogram (86 WTJ PR 32 WD - Manila PI 112P Mar 13 1941) has just been received in this office from The Surgeon, Philippine Department, requesting "information relative to advisability of routine toxoid immunization against tetanus for all troops this Dept. subject to field service in event of an emergency stop tetanus toxoid can be produced locally." The above radiogram has been forwarded to the Adjutant General by first indorsement, March 13, 1941, with recommendation that immediate steps be taken to initiate the immunization of all troops in the Philippine Islands with tetanus toxoid, the toxoid to be obtained from the Medical Supply Officer, New York General Depot, Brooklyn, N. Y., and shipped by aeroplane to the Philippine Islands.

3. It is believed that similar provisions should be made for the immunization of troops against tetanus in ~~all~~ other overseas possessions and bases.

4. In this connection it is desired to again invite attention to the fact that this office has repeatedly recommended active immunization against tetanus with tetanus toxoid for the entire Army. It is believed that this procedure should be authorized at once in order to start immunization which requires a period of six weeks for its completion.

For The Surgeon General:

Larry B. McAfee,
Colonel, Medical Corps,
Executive Officer.

~~SECRET~~

3.3 12 Dec. 1941: REPORT ON PLAGUE IN CHANGTEH, HUNAN (Dec. 12th, 1941), W. K. Chen, M.D. Head, Dept. of Laboratory Medicine Central E.M.S.T.S., Consultant, Chinese Red Cross Medical Relief Corps, TO: Dr. R. K. S. Lim, Director, Central E.M.S.T.S., and C.R.C.M.R.C. KWUIYANG

资料出处： National Archives of the United States, R112, E295A, B11.

内容点评： 本资料为 1941 年 12 月 12 日，贵阳图云关中国红十字会总会医疗救护总队指导、军政部战时卫生人员训练总所检验学组主任、医学博士陈文贵（W. K. Chen）提交总所主任、总队长林可胜（R. K. S. Lim）医师报告，题目:《湖南常德鼠疫调查报告》。

Central Emergency Medical Service Training School
Department of Laboratory Medicine
Tuyunkuan, Kweiyang
Dec. 12th, 1941.

Dr. R. K. S. Lim
Director, Central E.M.S.T.S., and C.R.C.M.R.C.
KWEIYANG

Dear Sir,

I have the honour of submitting to you the attached report on the results of our investigation of the recent plague epidemic in Changteh, Hun.

By your order, an Investigation Unit consisting of Dr. B. Liu, Dr. Y. K. Hsueh (C.R.C.M.R.C.) and myself and Technicians, C. L. Chu and C. L. Ting (E.M.S.T.S.) with field laboratory equipment, test animals, sulfathiazole and plague vaccine left Kweiyang on November 20th, arriving at Changteh on November 24th. The same night we started working on a human case just dead from plague-like infection. Autopsy findings, together with bacteriological and animal tests, leave no doubt that we were dealing with a genuine case of bubonic plague with septicemia.

The investigation was completed on November 30th. The handling of the outbreak was discussed with the local authorities in charge of anti-epidemic measures. Vaccine and sufficient drugs were left in the hands of the medical units. As no fresh cases appeared, we left Changteh on December 2nd and returned to Kweiyang on December 6th. We brought back with us, the stained smears, pure cultures of P. pestis which were isolated during this study and a sample of the grain dropped from the enemy plane.

Yours respectfully,

W. K. Chen, M.D.
Head, Dept. of Laboratory Medicine
Central E.M.S.T.S.
Consultant, Chinese Red Cross Medical Relief Corps.

Dr. Chen's report and his material have been examined by us and we have no hesitation in endorsing the conclusions arrived at in his report.

T. S. Sze, M.B., B.S., D.T.M&H., D.P.H. (Lond.) Dr.P.H.
Head, Dept. of Preventive Medicine,
Central E.M.S.T.S.
Consultant, Chinese Red Cross Medical Relief Corps.

F. C. Lin, M.D., B.S.
Senior Instructor, Dept. of Lab. Medicine
Central E.M.S.T.S.
Consultant Bacteriologist, C.R.C.M.R.C.

REPORT ON PLAGUE IN CHANGTEH, HUNAN

(Dec. 12th, 1941.)

Contents

\- - - - - -

Note: The "tables" referred to in this report merely summarize in chart form the information given in the Appendices and have, therefore, not been mimeographed.

(I) PREAMBLE - CIRCUMSTANCES LEADING TO THE SUSPICION OF PLAGUE

On November 4th, 1941, at about 5 a.m. a single enemy plane appeared over Changteh, flying very low, the morning being rather misty. Instead of bombs, wheat and rice grains, pieces of paper, cotton wadding and some unidentified particles were dropped. These materials fell chiefly in the Chi-ya-hsiang (雞鴨巷) and Kwan-miao Street (關廟街) (Area "A" in map) and around the East Gate district (Area "B" in map) of the city. After the all clear signal (5 p.m.), specimens of rice grains were collected and sent by the police to the Kwangteh Hospital (廣德醫院) for examination, which revealed the presence of micro-organisms reported to resemble P.pestis. (This was, however, shown to be erroneous by Dr. Chen Wen-kwei later). Although the finding was by no means conclusive, suspicion that the enemy had scattered plague-infective material was in the mind of the medical workers who saw the incident on the spot.

(II) REPORT OF SUSPECTED AND PROVEN CASES OF BUBONIC PLAGUE:

Nothing happened until November 11th, seven days after the "aerial incident" when the first suspicious case of plague came to notice. This was a girl of eleven years old, living in Kwan-miao Street (Area "A" in map), complaining of high fever (105.7° F.) since November 11th. She She was admitted to the Kwangteh Hospital. No other positive clinical finding was recorded but direct blood smear examination was said to have revealed the presence of P.pestis like organisms. She died on the 13th of November and post-mortem examination showed highly suspicious evidences of plague, smears from internal organs exhibiting similar organisms to those found in the blood (Case No. 1 Table).

On November 13th another case was found dead. On enquiry the patient had high fever on November 11th and died on November 13th. Liver puncture was performed. Direct smear examination showed the presence of micro-organisms resembling plague bacilli. This patient was living on Chang-ching Street (長清街) in the East Gate District (Area "B" in map) (Case No. 2, Table).

Two more cases came to notice, both with high fever and enlargement of glands in the groin ("buboes") beginning on November 12th. Smear examination of gland puncture fluid showed the presence of plague-like micro-organisms in both cases. One died on the 13th and the other on the 14th. Both lived in the East Gate district (Area "B" in map) (Case Nos. 3 and 4, Table).

The fifth case, admitted to the Isolation Hospital on November 19th, had fallen ill with fever and delirium (and buboes) on November 18th. He died on the day of admission. Autopsy revealed apparently negative findings. (Case No. 5, Table).

The sixth case, a man of 28, living in Kwan-miao Street (Area "A" in map) came down with fever, malaise and buboes on November 23rd and died the next day. This case was proved by Dr. Chen Wen-kwei, Head of the Dept. of Laboratory Medicine, Central Training School, who had just arrived from Kweiyang with an investigation unit, to be genuine bubonic plague by post-mortem findings, confirmed by culture and animal tests. (Case No. 6, Table and Appendix).

All these cases were natives of Hunan and had lived in Changteh or in its immediate environs for years.

Since then to date no fresh cases of plague have come to notice.

CONCLUSION:

The last case seen was proved to be bubonic plague. The clinical history and smears from five other cases leave little doubt that they were also cases of plague.

(III) INFORMATION GATHERED FROM INVESTIGATION AND ENQUIRY:

a. General Information

Changteh is a city situated on the western shore of the Tung Ting Lake, directly on the northern bank of the Yuan River. Formerly, highway connections were available between this city and Hupeh Province in the north, Changsha in the east and Taoyuan and other cities in south west Hunan. At present all the highway communications have been cut and the nearest highway is at Chengchiayi (60 km.) to the southwest by river. River traffic to Changsha via the Tung Ting Lake, and to Yuanling and Chihchiang via the Yuan River is still open. At present, therefore, communication with Changteh is only possible by boat or by footpaths.

Changteh has hot summers and cold winters which begin early in November. At the time of enquiry, atmospheric temperature ranged between 40°- 50° F.

Changteh was an important business centre in Northern Hunan but since the war its prosperity has been much reduced due to frequent enemy air-raids and the cutting off of highway communications.

b. Medical Institutions at Changteh

Kwang-Teh Hospital - a missionary hospital of 100 beds.
Hsien Health Centre (Wei-Sheng-Yuan) holds out-patient clinics.
An Isolation Hospital of 50 beds was established after the outbreak of plague.

c. Medical Statistics:

Changteh has now a population of about 50,000. No mortality statistics are available. It is known to be an endemic centre of cholera, and cholera epidemics have arisen from year to year.

There has been no noticeable increase in human deaths prior to the "aerial incident".

Since the first suspicious death from plague, records were kept of deaths in the city by the Hsien Health Centre, information being obtained from the police and coffin dealers. From November 12th - 24th, seventeen deaths were reported in all, including those suspected of plague. No information was available about the causes of the other deaths.

d. Environmental Sanitation:

General sanitation of the city is rather poor. Frequent air-raids have destroyed many houses. Most new houses are built of wood and provide easy access to rats.

Area "A". - Kwan-miao Street and Chi-ya-hsiang region (see map).

This district is almost in the heart of the city and habitations are overcrowded. Streets are narrow and dirty. Several of the houses in which plague deaths had occurred were visited and found to have dark and poorly ventilated rooms with no floors. Garbage accumulations were commonly seen in the corner of the rooms. Rat holes were found everywhere. Other houses did not differ in general appearance from those described.

Area "B". - East Gate region (see map).

Although less crowded, this district was even less impressive, being the living quarters of the poorer class. Environmental sanitation did not differ materially from Area "A".

On enquiry it was elicited that no conspicuous increase of dead rats was found either prior to or during the present outbreak. An Indian wandering rat-trap was set in one of the plague-death houses for three successive nights but no rats were caught. Some 200 rats were "bought" from the people and dissected but none of them showed any evidence of plague infection. These rats could not be traced to their place of origin. Many tangle-foot flea traps were also set in the houses in which plague death had occurred, but failed to catch any fleas.

(IV) DISCUSSION AND CONCLUSIONS:

(1) Was plague present in Changteh?

a. That plague was present in Changteh was proved by the case of bubonic plague investigated by Dr. Chen Wen-kwei who had had special training in plague work in India. This case, a man of 28 years old, was seen sick with high fever and "buboes" on November 24th and died the same evening. He came to stay in the "infected" area on November 19th and fell sick on November 23rd. On post-mortem examination he was found to have died of bubonic plague. Direct smear, culture and guinea-pig inoculation tests of material taken from groin lymph-nodes, spleen, liver and heart's blood all confirmed the diagnosis. (For detail protocol see Appendix I)

b. That an epidemic outbreak of plague has taken place between November 11th and 24th was also evident from the discovery of five suspicious cases referred to above. It may be argued that none of these cases were bacteriologically confirmed by animal inoculation tests, but the clinical history with high fever, enlarged lymph-glands in the groin ("buboes") and smears from either lymph-glands, liver or spleen being positive for P. pestis morphologically and their rapidly fatal course (death within 24-48 hours of the onset of the disease), leaves little or no doubt about their being actual cases of plague. Moreover most of the cases occurred at about the same time. Hence an epidemic outbreak of bubonic plague did exist beginning from November 11th, seven days after the "aerial incident".

All smears were re-examined by Dr. Chen Wen-kwei who confirmed the finding of plague-like bacilli.

(2) How did the plague outbreak arise? Could any connection be established between the outbreak and the alleged infective material scattered by the enemy plane on November 4th, 1941?

Three possibilities may be enquired into, namely

I. Did plague exist prior to the "aerial incident"?

II. Did plague come to Changteh from contiguous districts known to be plague stricken?

III. Was the plague due to the scattering of infective material from the enemy plane on November 4th, 1941?

I. That the present outbreak of plague may be due to a local disease having suddenly broken out into epidemic proportions is out of the question because Changteh has never been, as far as is known, afflicted by plague. During previous pandemics and severe epidemics elsewhere in China, this part of Hunan, nay this part of Central China in general has never been known to come under the scourge of the disease. Spontaneous plague is not known

II. That the present outbreak may have been due to direct contiguous spread from neighbouring districts known to be plague stricken is also untenable on epidemiological grounds. Epidemiologically, plague spreads along transport routes for grain on which the rats feed. Ships form good carriers of rats because they contain cargo and form good harbourages for these animals. Hence the coastal towns in Fukien and Kwangtung Provinces were usually the first to become infected by plague from other plague-stricken ports, the disease gradually spreading inland later. Epidemic foci now exist in certain districts of Fukien and Chekiang and a few cities of Kiangsi bordering the former two provinces. The nearest city to Changteh, where plague is now severely epidemic, is Chuhsien in Chekiang about 2,000 km. away by land or river communication. Incidentally it may be noted that the plague in Chuhsien is also attributed to infective material dropped by enemy planes in 1940. With the existing state of communication, it is not possible for plague to spread from Chuhsien to Changteh. Besides, all the cases occurring in Changteh were native inhabitants of that city and as far as can be ascertained, were not known to have been away from the city or its immediate environs at all. Changteh, being a rice producing district, furthermore supplies rice to other districts and does not receive rice from other cities. It is clear, therefore, that the present outbreak of bubonic plague in Changteh is native in origin.

III. That enemy scattered plague infective material from the plane on November 4th, 1941 at 5 a.m. and caused the epidemic outbreak of plague beginning on November 11th, is probable for the following reasons:

1. All the cases came from the areas where the grain, etc., dropped by enemy plane was found.

2. Among the wheat and rice grains and rags of cotton and paper scattered there were most probably included infective vectors, probably fleas. The latter was not found by those who swept and burned the material, because:-

   a. Lay people did not know the possibility of dangerous and infective fleas being scattered down and therefore did not look for them.

   b. The air-raid alarm on November 4th lasted from 5 a.m. to 5 p.m. with the result that the fleas must have in the meantime escaped from the rags and grains and hid themselves in nearby houses of more equable temperature and humidity long before the grains and rags were swept and burnt after the all-clear signal.

3. Plague might be caused by infective material in one of three ways:

   a. Grains thrown down may be infected with plague organisms which when eaten by local rats cause infection among them. Later, the infection is transmitted from the diseased rats to the rat-fleas and these in turn infect men through their bites.

   This was unlikely or unsuccessful for two reasons:

   i. Grains collected and submitted to cultural and animal inoculation tests have to date been found negative for plague organisms (Appendix [illegible])

   ii. There was apparently no evidence of any excessive rat mortality since the "aerial incident".

- 5 -

b. Infected fleas may have been thrown down together with the grain and rags. The grain attract the local rats which offer refuge to the infective fleas and thereby become infected. Local fleas then become infected and further infect rats and men.

Apparently this did not take place since:-

i. All the human cases of plague were infected within 15 days after the "aerial incident". Normally human plague cases begin to appear at least two weeks after the rat epizootic which also takes time (say two weeks) to develop.
ii. There was no apparent rat epizootic preceding or during the human outbreak as already referred to.

If infected fleas were released from the plane, what prevented them from starting an epidemic among the local rats? In order that a rat epizootic may take place, it is necessary that the flea population or rat-flea (Xenopsylla cheopis) index should be high. Although no data is available concerning the normal rat-flea index in Changteh, it is probable in view of the cold weather, that it was not high enough to cause rapid spread of the disease among the rats. It is not yet known whether the rats of Changteh have become infected with plague, Further research is necessary and only time can tell.

c. Infected fleas thrown down with the grain, etc., may have bitten human individuals directly and caused the outbreak of plague.

The evidence of this mode of transmission seems complete:

i. The normal incubation period of bubonic plague, i.e. the interval between the bite of the infective flea and the onset of disease, is 3 - 7 days but may occasionally be prolonged to 8 or even 14 days. Most of the cases seen had an incubation period of 7 - 8 days, which would indicate that these individuals were bitten by the infective fleas very soon after they were released, probably on November 4th or 5th. Thus, the first case had its onset on November 11th, seven days after the "aerial incident". Similarly with the second case. The third and fourth cases fell ill on the 12th eight days after the "incident". The fifth case, about which the diagnosis was more doubtful than any other fell sick on November 18th (?). The proven case had been working in a nearby village (陬家嘴) and came into the city to live in one of the infected areas on November 19th. On November 23rd, five days after entering the infected area, and 15 days after the "aerial incident", he fell ill. Assuming he was bitten on the 19th, the question arises as to whether the infective fleas could have survived from November 4th to November 19th. The answer is in the affirmative, for it is known that infected fleas can live under suitable conditions for weeks without feeding.

ii. All the human cases were inhabitants of the area where grain, etc. dropped by the enemy plane were found.

From the evidence presented the following conclusions may be drawn:

1. <u>That plague was epidemic in Changteh from November 11th to 24th, 1941</u>.

2. <u>That the cause of the epidemic was due to the scattering of plague infective material, probably infective fleas, by an enemy plane on November 4th, 1941</u>

APPENDIX I

Clinical and Autopsy Notes of the Proven Case of Bubonic Plague

Case No. 6:

Name of Patient: Kung Tsao-sheng (龔操勝)
Date of Autopsy: November 25th, 1941
Place: Isolation Hospital, Changteh

Operator: Dr. W. K. Chen
1st Assistant: Dr. Y. K. Hsueh
2nd Assistant: Dr. B. Liu
Recorder: Dr. C. C. Lee

Clinical History of the Patient:

The patient, a male of 28, lived in a small lane in front of the Kwan-Miao Temple, and used to work in a village outside Changteh. He returned to the City on November 19th, 1941, on account of the death of his mother six or seven days before. The cause of her death was not definitely known (? tuberculosis -- long standing illness with severe emaciation). He felt unwell in the evening of November 23rd, and experienced feverishness and headache with malaise at about 11 p.m. The next morning he complained of pain and tenderness in the right groin for which a Chinese plaster was applied. He vomited once during the afternoon, and from then on his condition grew rapidly worse. Dr. C. C. Lee of the 4th Emergency Medical Service Training School and the 4th Sanitary Corps, was called at 7 p.m. to see the patient, and found him to be dying. Important findings on examination were high fever, and enlarged and tender glands in the right inguinal region. Plague was strongly suspected. The patient was to have been sent to the Isolation Hospital, but he died at 8 p.m. before he could be removed. With the aid of the police, the body was brought to the Wei-Sheng-Yuan by 10 p.m. where disinfection of clothing and bedding was carried out in order to kill fleas. The plaster covering the groin was removed; cardiac puncture and aspiration of the right inguinal gland were performed for culture under sterile technique; and, since the light was inadequate, autopsy was postponed until the next morning. The body was laid in a coffin with the lid nailed down.

Autopsy Findings:

1. General Appearance: The cadaver was medium-sized and appeared very thin.

2. Skin: Face was slightly blue, and lips cyanotic. No petechial spots or flea-bite wounds were seen. Lesions resembling scabies in the right popliteal region.

3. Lymph Glands: The right inguinal glands were enlarged. Mesenteric lymph nodes also slightly enlarged.

4. Chest Findings: Lungs normal in gross appearance. There was fluid estimated at 20 c.c. approximately in each pleural cavity. Pericardial effusion of about 20 c.c. also present. Heart very flabby but not enlarged. Cardiac puncture through the right auricle performed under sterile technique and a few c.c. of blood were obtained and inoculated on blood agar slant.

5. Abdominal Findings: Liver firm. Spleen enlarged to twice its normal size. Kidneys normal. Haemorrhagic spots seen on the surface of liver spleen, and intestine. No free fluid in the abdomen.

Bacteriological Findings:

Specimen of right inguinal glands, liver, spleen and blood were taken for direct smears, culture and animal tests.

1. Direct Smears: Carbol-thionin blue and Gram's method of staining were employed for all the smears. 50% ether in absolute alcohol was used for fixation. Under the microscope many oval-shaped Gram negative bacilli with their bipolar regions deeply stained were found.

2. Cultivation: Under sterile technique, specimens of cardiac blood, inguinal glands, liver and spleen of the patient were inoculated on blood agar slant of pH 7.6 and incubated in a wide-mouth thermos bottle. Temperature was regulated

at 37° centigrade. Twenty-four hours later, many minute greyish-white opaque colonies were found on the surface of the media. All were pure cultures. Smear examination showed Gram negative bipolar staining organisms.

3. Animal Inoculation Test:

A. Guinea-pig No. 1. The animal was artificially infected by smearing splenic substance of the cadaver on its right flank which was newly shaven at 3 p.m. on November 25th, 1942. (The splenic substance was found to have contained many Gram negative bipolar staining bacilli). The animal began to develop symptoms at 8 p.m. on November 26th, and was found dead in the early morning of November 28th. Thus the incubation period was not more than 29 hours and the whole course of the disease ran at most 32 hours.

Autopsy Findings:

1. Skin:	Swolling and redness at the site of inoculation.
2. Gland:	Bi-lateral enlargement of inguinal glands, more marked on the right side with congestion.
3. Subcutaneous Tissues:	Edematous and congested. Haemorrhage at the site of inoculation.
4. Chest Findings:	Not remarkable.
5. Abdominal Findings:	Spleen enlarged and congested. Liver, kidneys and G.I. tract also congested.

Specimens of heart blood, liver, spleen and inguinal lymph glands were taken for smears and culture.

Microscopic examination of the stained smears (Carbol-thionin blue and Gram's stains) revealed Gram negative bipolar staining bacilli similar to those seen in the direct smears made of autopsy material from the patient.

Culture of these specimens on blood agar slants at pH 7.6 was made. Twenty-four hours later, pure cultures of similar organisms were found.

B. Guinea-pig No. 2. This animal was similarly treated as Guinea-pig No. 1 at 9 a.m. on November 26th, but the inguinal gland of the cadaver was used instead. Symptoms were first noticed at 8 a.m. on November 28th, an incubation period of 47 hours. Death of the animal occurred 44 hours later (in the morning of November 30th).

Autopsy of the animal showed essentially the same gross pathological changes as those of guinea-pig No. 1. Direct smears of lymph glands liver, and spleen showed similar findings.

C. Guinea-pig No. 3. This time a pure culture of the organisms was used to smear on the newly shaven left flank of the guinea pig. (The culture was obtained by growing the cadaver's heart blood on blood agar slant at pH 7.6 for 24 hours). The animal appeared to have become ill 45 hours later and was found dead in the early morning of November 30th. The course of the disease of the animal was, therefore, not more than 40 hours.

On autopsy, gross pathological changes were found to be similar to those of guinea-pigs No. 1 and No. 2 except that changes of lymph-glands and spleen were more pronounced.

Smear examination of heart blood, lymph-gland, liver, and spleen yielded similar results.

Conclusion:

Clinical history, autopsy findings and bacteriological findings prove the patient to be a case of bubonic plague, dying from septicaemic infection from Pasteurella pestis.

APPENDIX II

Clinical Notes of Cases Suspected to be Plague

Case No. 1. (Tsai Tao-erh)

This patient, a girl of eleven living in Tsai Hung Shen Charcoal Dealer Shop (關廟街蔡鴻勝炭號), Kwan Miao Street, was said to have fallen ill on November 11th, 1941 and was sent by the police to the Kwangteh Hospital at 7 a.m. the next day for treatment. On admission she was seen by Dr. H. H. Tan and was found delirious. Temperature 105.7° F. Eczema of the right ear. No glandular enlargement or tenderness. Few rales were heard in the chest. Abdominal findings were said to be normal. Blood smears (Wright and Gram's stains) showed organisms resembling P.pestis morphologically. Patient was then isolated and sulfanilamide treatment given. Her general condition turned from bad to worse in the morning of November 13th, when petechial spots of skin were noted. Blood smear examination was repeated and revealed the same result as before. At about 8 a.m. she died.

Essential features of autopsy were enlarged left infra-auricular lymph nodes. No sign of pneumonia; liver and spleen enlarged with hemorrhagic spots on their surfaces. Kidneys were also hemorrhagic. Splenic smear showed similar findings as the blood smear. Culture of the splenic substances was done in the Kwangteh Hospital but no definite report was obtained.

Case No. 2. (Tsai Yü-chen)

This was a woman of 27, living in Chang Ching Chieh (長清街), East Gate district; she was said to have had an abrupt onset of fever on November 11th and died on the 13th. While her cortege was passing Tehshan, Dr. Kent of Red Cross Medical Relief Corps met it and made enquiry of the cause of her death. The above information led him to suspect plague. Post mortem liver puncture was done and smear examination showed organisms resembled P. pestis morphologically.

Case No. 3. (Nieh Shu-sheng)

This was a man of 58 living in No. 1, 3rd Chia, 4th Pao, Chi Ming Cheng (啟明鎮四保三甲一户) East Gate district. Developed high fever in the evening of November 12th, complained of pain and tenderness in the groin on November 13th. Aspiration of the enlarged groin gland was done by Dr. P. K. Chien of Red Cross Medical Relief Corps and smear examination (Wright Stain) showed P.pestis like organisms. The patient died in the same evening.

Case No. 4. (Hsu Lao-san)

The patient was a man of 25, living in No. 5, 5th Chia, 5th Pao, Yun An Hsiang, Yang Chia Hsiang, East Gate district (東門楊家巷永安鄉五保五甲五户). Became ill, with fever and headache since November 12th. Seen by Dr. H. H. Tan and Dr. T. C. Fang, and found to have tender and enlarged groin lymph glands the next day. Aspiration of the gland was done in the Kwangteh Hospital and smear examination (Wright's Stain) showed P.pestis like organisms.

Case No. 5 (Hu Chung-fa)

A man living in Chung Fa Hospital, Kwan Miao Street (關廟街鍾發醫院). In the morning of November 19th, he went to the Wei Sheng Yuan complaining of being infected with plague and demanding treatment. He appeared, at that time, quite irritable and spoke somewhat incoherently. His pulse rate was rapid, but fever was not high. Groin glands were enlarged. Other findings were not recorded. He was immediately admitted to the Isolation Hospital. In the evening his temperature went up and he died.

Autopsy by Drs. H. H. Tan and M. N. Shih showed bluish discoloration of the skin, more marked over the chest and abdomen. No enlargement of lymph glands were noticed. Spleen was found to be slightly enlarged and other abdominal findings were not remarkable. Smear and culture of splenic material showed only Gram positive cocci and bacilli. It should be noted that Dr. Tan was working with inadequate culture media.

APPENDIX III

Notes on Examination of Grain Dropped by Enemy Plane

Examination of a sample of the grain dropped by the enemy plane over Changteh City on November 4th, 5 a.m., 1941 and collected from the ground next morning and examined after an interval of fully 34 days.

Gross Examination. The sample consists of barley, rice and unidentified plant seeds.

Culture Examination. The sample was put into a sterile mortar and ground with 5 c.c. sterile saline. This mixture was cultivated on blood agar slants and copper sulphate agar slants. (all pH 7.6). After incubation at 37° C. for 24 - 48 hours, only contaminating organisms of staphylococci, B. coli and unidentified Gram positive bacilli with central spores were found; no P. pestis like organisms were found.

Animal Inoculation. Two c.c. of the above mixture were injected subcutaneously into a guinea pig on Dec. 8th, 1941 at 9 a.m. The testing animal died in the evening of Dec. 11th after showing no sign of illness.

Autopsy Findings. On the morning of December 12th, autopsy of the dead animal was performed. Local inflammation, general congestion of subcutaneous tissue, inguinal lymph glands not enlarged, liver and spleen normal and not enlarged. Heart and lungs normal. Smears made from lymph gland, spleen and liver showed no P. pestis like organisms. Only Gram positive bacilli and some Gram negative bacilli were present.

Culture of heart blood of the dead animal showed unidentified Gram positive bacilli with central spores. P. pestis not found. Culture from the lymph nodes, spleen and liver showed pure culture of B. coli only. P. pestis also not found.

Conclusions: By culture and animal inoculation tests, P. pestis is not present in the sample.

3.4 19 Dec. 1941: Letter to Col. William Mayer, Embassy of the U.S., Chungking, China, from /s/ E. Torvaldson, Changteh, Hunan, CHRISTIAN AND MISSIONARY ALLIANCE

资料出处：National Archives of the United States, R112, E295A, B11.

内容点评：本资料为 1941 年 12 月 19 日湖南常德基督教传教士同盟的 E.Torvaldson 予重庆美国驻华使馆武官 William Mayer 上校询问湖南常德鼠疫爆发情况信函的回复。

CONFIDENTIAL

C-O-P-Y

CHRISTIAN AND MISSIONARY ALLIANCE

Changteh, Hunan
December 19th, 1941

Colonel William Mayer,
Embassy of the United States of America,
Chungking, China.

Dear Sir:

Your letter of Dec. 8th, asking for information regarding the Bubonic Plague here in Changteh, came to hand on the 17th.

On the morning of November 4th, before daylight, and with quite a fog prevailing, the Alarm went, and one plane arrived over the city, flying very low, passing over the city and our own compound three times and then flew away.

It was discovered right afterwards that it had dropped small packages of unhulled rice, also gauze etc. Samples of this rice was brought to the Presbyterian Hospital for examination bacteriologically, and was found to contain bacillus resembling that of plague. Without further investigation and experimentation it was impossible to make a definite statement on the matter.

The culture obtained was injected into two rabbits, but the reaction was slight. However, within a few days from the time the unhulled rice was dropped, a young girl was carried to the Hospital, showing all the symptoms of plague. Smears taken both before and after death, confirmed the diagnosis of the Hospital Doctor.

Since then other cases have been treated and Chinese Government experts have proved by experimentation with Guinea pigs and further laboratory tests, that plague conditions prevail here.

A Foreign Red Cross Doctor and his Chinese staff have been here for several weeks. This Doctor told us personally, that there has been between 20 and 25 registered deaths, how many that were not registered is hard to know. Just the other day one man died. So far it has not reached the epidemic stage, but the concensus of opinion among medical men here is, that it is likely to spread.

Plague has been unknown to the oldest inhabitants here, being practically unheard of until the arrival of the plane. There can be little doubt that the unhulled grain was distributed by the Japanese plane on the early morning of the 8th (?) of November.

CONFIDENTIAL

CONFIDENTIAL

This is all the information I am able to give at this time, and we certainly hope this evil plague will not spread much more.

Respectfully yours,

/s/ E. Torvaldson.

CONFIDENTIAL

3.5　20 Dec. 1941: Letter to Col. William Mayer, Military Attache, Embassy of the U. S., Chungking, Szechuan, from /s/ W. W. Pettus, M.D., YALE-IN-CHINA ASSOCIATION, Changsha, China

资料出处：National Archives of the United States, R112, E295A, B11.

内容点评：本资料为 1941 年 12 月 20 日湖南长沙耶鲁中华会医学博士 W. W. Pettus 予重庆美国驻华使馆武官 William Mayer 上校询问湖南常德鼠疫流行情况信函的回复。

CONFIDENTIAL

C-O-P-Y

YALE-IN-CHINA ASSOCIATION

American Headquarters
905-A Yale Station, New Haven, Conn.

Changsha, China,
December 20, 1941

Colonel William Mayer, U.S.A.,
Military Attache,
Embassy of the United States of America,
Chungking, Szechuan

S.G.O. 710.-1 (China)F

Dear Colonel Mayer:

Your letter of December 6, 1941 requesting information on the plague epidemic in Changteh, Hunan has been received. Fortunately the day it arrived, Dr. Politzer was visiting me en route to Changteh to investigate the plague. As you probably know, he is an expert epidemiologist, formerly employed by the League of Nations, now working for the National Health Administration. At present he is spending all his time on plague study and control and has an international reputation in this field. He generously offered to give me all the information which he obtains on this case to be forwarded to you, with the one stipulation that you will not mention the source, since his official report must go through the National Health Administration.

There is no doubt that the disease is plague. This has been confirmed both by Dr. Politzer and by the bacteriology department of our Hsiang-Ya Hospital here in Changsha. In all thirty cases have been reported to the Hunan Provincial Health Department. There have been no new cases in the past ten days and there is a good chance that the epidemic is under control.

Dr. Politzer states that he can see no way in which the plague could have been introduced to Changteh by natural means. It is now endemic in Chekiang and Fukien; but it is practically impossible for it to have jumped across Kiangsi and Eastern Hunan (the travel route would go through Hengyang and Changsha before reaching Changteh from the East).

A Presbyterian missionary in Changteh saw the Japanese plane which dropped several loads of rice and other material. Eight days later the first case of plague appeared. Bacteria, which morphologically resemble the plague bacillus were recovered from the material dropped. This is strong evidence, but not absolutely conclusive because animal injection is necessary to absolutely prove the identity of the organism.

CONFIDENTIAL

- 1 -

CONFIDENTIAL

So, at the present time, it seems that case against the Japanese is exceedingly strong, but it is not absolutely "in-the-bag." When I receive the results of the investigation now in progress, I shall let you know.

Sincerely yours,

/s/ W. W. Pettus, M.D.

- 2 -

3.6 20 Dec. 1941: Letter to Dr. Co Tui, The American Bureau for Medical Aid to China, from R. K. Lim, E.M.S.T.S.

资料出处： National Archives of the United States, R112, E295A, B11.

内容点评： 本资料为 1941 年 12 月 20 日，军政部战时卫生人员训练总所 R. K. S. Lim（林可胜）呈纽约美国对华医疗援助局 Co Tui 博士《湖南常德鼠疫调查报告》的相关文件（参见 3.3，1941 年 12 月 12 日陈文贵《湖南常德鼠疫调查报告》）。

CORRESPONDENCE AND REPORT ON BACTERIOLOGICAL WARFARE
RECEIVED BY THE AMERICAN BUREAU FOR MEDICAL AID TO CHINA ON MAY 6

EMERGENCY MEDICAL SERVICE TRAINING SCHOOL
(In Co-operation with the Chinese Red Cross)

December 20th, 1941

Dr. Co Tui,
The American Bureau for Medical Aid to China,
1790 Broadway,
New York, N. Y.
U.S.A.

Dear Dr. Co Tui,

I am herewith forwarding you a Report on Plague in Changteh (December 12th, 1941) by our Investigation Unit which was sent specially to investigate into the plague alleged to be caused by the scattering of plague infective material by an enemy plane on November 4th, 1941. That the enemy is waging bacterial warfare against us is established beyond any doubt.

Yours sincerely,

R.K.S. Lim

JW:

3.7　29 Dec. 1941: No. 260, Transmission of Report on the Plague Situation in 1941, to the Secretary of the State, from C. E. Gauss, Embassy of the U. S., Chungking

资料出处： National Archives of the United States, R112, E295A, B11.

内容点评： 本资料为 1941 年 12 月 29 日重庆美国驻华使馆 C. E. Gauss 向美国国务卿转送的国民政府中央卫生署关于 1941 年鼠疫流行情况的报告。

(COPY)　　　　　　　　　　　　　　　　　　　　　　　　　　　　/Y

~~CONFIDENTIAL~~

EMBASSY OF THE UNITED STATES
OF AMERICA

No. 260　　　　　　　　　　　　　　　　Chungking, December 29, 1941

Subject: Transmission of Report on the Plague Situation in 1941.

The Honorable

The Secretary of State,

Washington, D. C.

Sir:

I have the honor to transmit herewith a copy of a report on the plague situation in unoccupied China during 1941 which the Embassy has received from the National Health Administration in Chungking.

Respectfully yours,

C. E. GAUSS

C. E. Gauss

Enclosure:

1. Copy of report, as stated

Original and two copies to the Department

812.1

BCHjr:MCL

Enclosure no. 1 to despatch no. 260 dated December 29, 1941 from American Embassy at Chungking.

(COPY)

THE PLAGUE SITUATION DURING WINTER 1941

For many years plague had been more or less a local problem in a few semi-isolated areas. Owing to blockade of the maritime traffic by the Japanese and to improvement of means of communications in the interior, the disease in 1940 and 1941 has begun to show a tendency of migrating toward the hinterland. From Fukien it has spread to Chekiang and Kiangsi; and more recently in November an outbreak has occurred in Hunan.

The startling report of plague breaking out in Changteh, Hunan was received on November 11. From that date to November 25, 6 cases were confirmed by bacteriological examination and animal inoculation test. Efforts were made immediately to control this outbreak by means of isolation, quarantine measures, preventive inoculations, disinfection and disinfestation, rat eradication, and house cleaning under the joint auspices of the National Health Administration, the Chinese Red Cross Medical Relief Corps, and the Army Medical Administration. There were no cases occurring from November 25 to December 13; but a new case was reported on December 14. In view of the possibility of its further spread inland, the medical colleges and institutions were requested to reserve the drug sulfathiazole for plague control work as far as possible and to be aware of the possibility of bacteriological warfare on the part of the enemy.

In Chekiang, plague broke out for the first time this winter in I-wu, about 200 kilometers northeast of Chuhsien. From October 2 to end of November, there were 113 cases, of whom 94 died and 8 recovered. The remaining cases were under treatment. From December 1 to 6, 10 human cases were reported. Control measures were initiated by senior members dispatched by the National Health Administration, including Dr. R. Pollitzer, formerly League of Nations expert detailed to China, and are being carried on by the provincial health authorities.

As plague was found towards the end of November to be enzootic among rats in Kinhwa, an important town situated between I-wu and Chuhsien, members of the National Health Administration also took the lead in organizing the Kinhwa Plague Control Committee to take precautionary measures against the spread of this disease to Kinhwa.

Two additional plague cases occurred in Chuhsien, Chekiang during November, where it may be remembered plague had occurred for the first time last winter. A special unit was detailed by the National Health Administration to that locality to take effective control measures. No new human or rat cases were found from December 1 to 8.

In Fukien plague has been endemic since 1894, and 31 hsiens have since then been known to be infected at one time or another. In 1940 plague occurred in 15 hsiens with a total of 257 cases. At the present time, there is an outbreak of the disease in Lungchi and Loyuen, while Chienyang, Chengwo, Yungan, Sungki, Shunchang and Yungchi are already under control.

Chungking, December 17, 1941.

3.8 30 Dec. 1941: Appendix 2: Letter to Dr. P. Z. King, Director-General, National Health Administration, Chungking, from Dr. R. Politzer, Epidemiologist, National Health Administration

资料出处： National Archives of the United States, R112, E295A, B11.

内容点评： 本资料为 1941 年 12 月 30 日，湖南常德卫生署第十四防疫大队中央卫生署流行病专家 R. Politzer 医师予重庆中央卫生署总长金宝善（P. Z. King）信函，报告常德鼠疫流行情况，判断鼠疫爆发由 11 月 4 日晨日机空中投下谷物等混杂物引起。

Appendix 2

COPY

Weishengshu Anti-Epidemic Unit No. 14
Changteh, Hunan, December 30, 1941

Dr. P. Z. King
Director-General
National Health Administration
Chungking

Dear Sir:

I have the honour to report on the plague situation in Changteh as follows:

1) As unanimously stated by the inhabitants of Changteh, an enemy airplane, appearing in the morning of November 4th, 1941 and flying unusually low, scattered over certain parts of the city fairly large amounts of grain admixed to which were other materials as discussed below.

2) On November 12th a girl, 12 years of age, was admitted to the local Missionary Hospital in a most serious condition with high fever and delirium. She died the next day. Post mortem examination revealed the presence of swollen lymphatic glands on the left side of the neck but since eczema was present in this region, a local infection of the skin might have been the cause of the gland swelling. Be this as it may, it is certain that numerous gram-negative bacilli, showing the microscopic appearance of plague bacilli, were found in her blood during life and in smears made after death from the sleen.

3) This initial case was followed by six further plague cases confirmed by microscopical examination and in one instance also by culture and animal experiment, the last case being recorded on December 20th. Of these six patients five had infuinal buboes whilst the sixth presumably had septicaemic plague. All the above mentioned seven patients succumbed to the infection. They were all residents of Changteh.

4) In addition a number of suspicious cases was recorded but subsequent investigations made it probable that only one of these patients, dying on November 19th, might have actually suffered from (? septicaemic) plague.

5) Examination of small quantities of the grain dropped from the plane (the bulk of the grain had been collected and burnt as soon as possible) did not lead to definite results. I personally was shown on December 23rd two bouillon cultures made with this material. In smears from these cultures as well as from the subcultures made under my supervision, gram-positive bacilli and cocci preponderated whilst the minority of gram-negative bacilli present did not show appearances characteristic for P. pestis. A guinea-pig infected on December 23rd with the combined material from these cultures and subcultures, remained well to date.

6)

- 2 -

6) It might be emphasized, however, that those negative findings do by no means exclude a causal connection between the aerial attack on November 4th and the subsequent plague outbreak in Changteh. It should be noted in this connection that:

(a) Plague bacilli are not fit to subsist for appreciable length of time on inanimate objects or to grow and survive when cultivated together with such microorganisms as found in the present instance. The fact that we failed to find plague bacilli in the cultures in question does therefore not exclude that they were orginally present on the grain.

(b) It must moreover be kept in mind that the question whether or not the grain dropped from the plane was originally contaminated with plague bacilli, is not of such paramount importance as it would seem at first glance. The Indian Plague Commission and other investigators after them had little or even no success when truing to infect highly susceptible rodents including guinea-pigs under optimal laboratory conditions through prolonged contact with plague-contaminated inanimate objects or by feeding such animals with materials containing plentiful plague bacilli. That it would be possible to obtain better results when trying to utilise such methods in the case of human beings by throwing plague-contaminated materials from a plane, seems not likely.

On the other hand, it must be admitted that human infections would be likely to occur if the material dropped from the plane would serve as a vehicle for plague-infected fleas. Hence there is no doubt that the latter procedure would recommend itself to experts who think it fit to participate in bacterial warfare and I for one am led to assume that this method was used in the present instance. Support for this assumption is furnished by the statement made by several witnesses that the plane dropped besides grain also some other material or materials variously described as peices of cotton or cloth, paper or pasteboard. Such materials, expecially the first two, would offer good protecti n for fleas.

7) Further support for the assumption that the recent plague outbreak was due to enemy action is furnished by the following considerations:

(a) Observations as to the time and the place of the outbreak are well compatible with such assumption:

We have seen that the first victim was admitted to hospital on November 12th, i.e. 8 days after the aerial attack -- a period of reasonable length, expecially if infected fleas were involved which first had to seek for individuals to feed upon. It is known on the other hand that plague fleas may remain infective for weeks or even months.

The

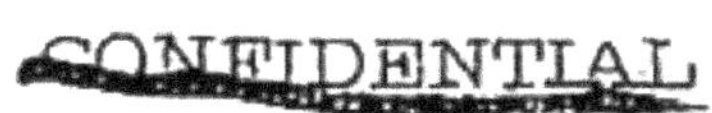

The first six of the confirmed plague cases developed in persons living in two areas which had been copiously sprinkled with the materials dropped from the plane and only the seventh patient lived at some distance from one of these areas.

(b) If we temporarily dismiss for the sake of argument the assumption that the recent plague outbreak in Changteh was due to enemy action, we would be rather at loss to say how it could have originated. It must be noted in this connection that

(i) No previous outbreak of plague in Hunan is on record in modern times and the very intensive anti-epidemic work done in this province since the end of 1937 has shown no evidence whatsoever suggestive of plague.

(ii) The nearest foci from which plague infection could have been derived, are in Eastern Chekiang and Southern Kiangsi. It takes at least about 10 days to reach Changteh from either of these areas so that a person contracting plague infection in one of them and then starting on his journey to Changteh would be likely to fall ill before arrival. Such travellers have repeatedly to change from one transport vehicle to another and to stay overnight in the various stations en route; they have to use their own bedding during part of the journey at least. That they would carry along infected fleas on their persons or in their effects in therefore unlikely.

(iii) Changteh is sutuated on a river system entirely different from those in Chekiang or Southern Kiangsi so that direct traffic by boat which might lead to the transport of infected rat and or fleas, is out of question.

(iv) The Changteh re icn produces rice and cotton so that it would be absurd to assume that such commodities, infested with plague rat and or fleas would have been imported from elsewhere.

(c) As recently confirmed by our observations in Chekiang and Kiangsi, bubonic plague outbreaks in China are in most, if not in all, instances ushered in by a very considerable mortality of the local rats. No such rat falls have been observed in Changteh and we have not been able thus far to get any definite evidence that the local rats have become infected.

8) All the observations and considerations recorded above leave little if any room for doubt that the recent

plague

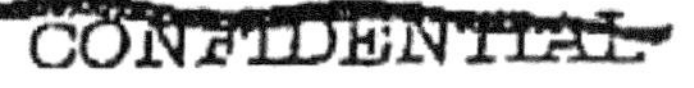

CONFIDENTIAL

- 4 -

plague outbreak in Changteh was in causal connection with the aerial attack of November 4th.

9) It is reassuring that no further human case was reported during the last ten days but this does not exclude the possibility that further cases might occur.

10) It is impossible to decide at present whether or not the rats have become involved in the outbreak. As mentioned, so far no definite evidence of rat plague was found and it appears that the "Indian" rat fleas (X.cheopis) are infrequent at present. It must be kept in mind on the other hand that (a) Instances of rat plague, if existing, would be infrequent at the present junction and (b) Owing to untoward conditions (Inclement weather and constant air alarms) we have been able so far to examine only limited numbers of rats. Prolonged observation will be necessary to decide this most important point.

Respectfully submitted by

(Signed) Dr. R. Politzer

Epidemiologist,
NATIONAL HEALTH ADMINISTRATION

3.9 23 Mar. 1942: The Alleged B.W. Incident at Changteh, Biology Section, Experimental Station, Porton

资料出处： National Archives of the United States, R112, E295A, B11.

内容点评： 本资料为 1942 年 3 月 23 日英国 Porton 实验所生物部报告，题目：指控的常德细菌战事件。报告对湖南常德鼠疫爆发流行是由日军投放物质引起的说法提出质疑。

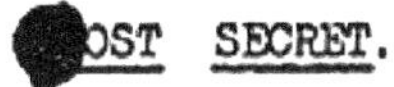

MOST SECRET.

The alleged B.W. incident at Changteh.

A number of non-technical reports have been received since Dec. 27th 1941, stating that a Japanese aircraft dropped sundry materials on Changteh, Hunan, China, a city of 50,000 inhabitants, on November 4th 1941. Shortly after this incident several cases of bubonic plague occurred, and it was concluded by Chinese medical workers on the spot that the outbreak was due to the materials dropped from the aircraft.

I asked for a technical report on January 10th 1942. This arrived on March 21st 1942. It consists of a report by Dr. W.E. Chen, consultant to the Chinese Red Cross Medical Relief Corps, who led an investigation unit of the Central Emergency Medical Service Training School, Kweiyang. This unit arrived at Changteh on November 24th. The report was forwarded on Dec. 12th to Dr. R.K.S. Lim, Director E.M.S.T.S., who in turn forwarded it on Dec. 20th to Dr. John B. Grant, All India Institute of Hygiene and Public Health, Calcutta.

This report is attached without appendices and map.

Comment.

1. There is no reason to doubt that an aircraft passed over Changteh without dropping bombs and that it did drop something.

   (a) The incident took place at 5 a.m. on a misty cold morning when presumably few observers would be about, and when according to meteorological evidence it would be dark and visibility would be nil.

   (b) It is not specifically claimed that the eye of the observer followed the objects dropped in their passage from the aircraft to the ground.

   (c) These objects (cereal grains, bits of paper and "cotton wadding" or "rags of cotton") were picked up 12 hours after the passage of the aircraft in streets (dscribed as "narrow and dirty") of houses ("many" of which had been demolished by bombing) in which "garbage accumulations were commonly seen".

   (d) The only objects examined bacteriologically were rice grains picked up next morning but not examined until 34 days later when the commission had left Changteh. No plague bacilli were found.

   Thus there is certainly a probability that the materials picked up did not fall from the aircraft, and even if they did there is no direct evidence that they were harmful.

2. That one case of plague occurred after an interval of 7 days after passage of the aircraft is proved. It may reasonably be agreed that the other cases were also plague.

   This outbreak was remarkable because plague did not occur in Changteh. It is, however, a question whether this statement is decisive. It is qualified by the remark "as far as is known". It is true that there is in Changteh a missionary hospital with 100 beds, but "no mortality statistics are available". This suggests an ill-developed condition of the medical services and opens up a possibility that sporadic cases of plague had occurred before.

3. However, the Commission accepted the statement that plague was unknown, and on reasonable evidence concluded that it could not have been imported. They were thus faced with the problem of finding an explanation. They were, of course, familiar with the aircraft incident and "noted that the plague in Chuhsien is also attributed to infective material dropped by enemy planes in 1940". They came to the conclusion that the material dropped "probably included infective vectors, probably fleas" which escaped into nearby houses during the 12-hour period of the air raid alarm. Flea traps set in the affected houses failed to catch any fleas; 200 rats contained no plague bacilli.

The final conclusion of the Commission is that "the epidemic was due to the scattering of plague infective material, probably infective fleas, by an enemy plane on November 4th 1941".

In his covering letter to Dr. John B. Grant, Calcutta, Dr. Lim writes:- "That the enemy is waging bacteriological warfare against us is established beyond any doubt".

4. From a survey of this evidence there is no reason to doubt that something was dropped from the aircraft and that cases of plague occurred, but since no plague bacilli were found on the materials alleged, but not proved, to have been dropped, nor in local rats, and since no fleas were found, there is clearly no proved connection between the aircraft and cases of plague. Furthermore, the evidence does not seem convincing that natural plague in the neighbourhood could be excluded. Thus, while admitting the possibility of the account and its value for propaganda (cf. Dr. Lim's exaggeration), an impartial reader can hardly admit that it constitutes a case on which action can be based.

Biology Section,
Experimental Station,
Porton.
23. 3. 42.

Insert new paragraph 4 in place of paragraph 4 in original:-

4. From a survey of this evidence there is every reason to doubt whether anything was seen to drop from the aircraft. Certainly no plague bacilli were found in materials alleged to have been dropped. There is thus no proved, or even reasonably suspected, connection between the aircraft and the cases of plague, nor is the evidence convincing that the district was normally free from plague.

For these reasons, this incident cannot be accepted as a proved instance of B.W.

(Paragraph added for BW Intelligence Summary No. 1 - vide BW 5260 of 2-9-44).

3.10 31 Mar. 1942: REPORT GIVES MEDICAL EVIDENCE OF BUBONIC PLAGUE CAUSED BY JAPAN'S BACTERIAL BOMBS, Dr. Wang Shih-chieh, Minister of Information and Government spokesman; JAPANESE ATTEMPT AT BACTERIAL WARFARE IN CHINA, P. Z. King, Director-General, NATIONAL HEALTH ADMINISTRATION

资料出处： National Archives of the United States, R112, E295A, B11.

内容点评： 本资料为 1942 年 3 月 31 日，中国政府发言人王世杰（Wang Shih-chieh）在新闻发布会上发表的日本细菌弹引发腺鼠疫的医学证据，以及同日中央卫生署总长金宝善（Dr. P. Z. King）报告：日本在中国实施细菌战的企图。

Chungking 1940

CONFIDENTIAL

REPORT GIVES MEDICAL EVIDENCE OF BUBONIC PLAGUE CAUSED BY JAPAN'S BACTERIAL BOMBS

CHUNGKING, March 31 (CNS)....Dr. Wang Shih-chich, Minister of Information and government spokesman at today's press conference, disclosed details of a lengthy report on Japan's bacteriological warfare in China submitted to the Chinese Government by foreign and Chinese medical experts. The investigators were Dr. R. Pollitzer, epidomiologist of the National Health Administration and formerly of the League of Nations Anti-Epidemic Commission; Dr. Robert K. S. Lim, Director of the National Red Cross Society of China; and Dr. Chen Wen-kwei who had had special training in plague work in India and is now head of the Department of Laboratory Medicine, Central Emergency Medical Training School.

Dr. Wang's statement follows:

"It may be recalled that in October and November 1940 suspicion of Japan's resort to bacterial warfare was already aroused when Japanese planes, raiding Ningpo, Chuhsion and Kinghwa, all in Chekiang Province, scattered considerable quantities of infected grains. But because of inadequate laboratory facilities in those localities our Health Administration authorities hositated then to draw positive conclusions establishing Japan's guilt. Thorough investigation of the more recent case at Changteh in Hunan on Nov. 4, 1941, however, has proved Japan's crime beyond any doubt.

"As in the previous cases a lone Japanese plane flew over Changteh early in the morning dropping no bombs but large quantities of wheat and rice grains, pieces of paper, cotton wadding and some other unidentified particles. Unlike the previous cases, however, there was the Changteh Red Cross laboratory unit which made an examination of the grains and rags scattered by the enemy plane. Dr. Chen Wen-kwei was sent to investigate fully the matter on the spot. As Dr. Chen discovered cumulative evidences of the Japanese plane having dropped bacteriological bombs, Dr. Robert K. S. Lim and Dr. R. Pollitzer were asked to conduct a thorough-going investigation of the matter. The findings of these doctors are unanimous: (1) That either direct blood smear examination or post mortem examination of the six victims of bubonic plague who died between Nov. 11 and 24 revealed that they died of precisely the same plague bacilli found from the particles dropped from the Japanese planes on Nov. 4. (2) That the normal incubation of the plague bacilli found from the particles dropped by the enemy plane ranges normally from three to seven days and sometimes to fourteen days which period coincided with the dates on which death claimed the six victims. (3) That all the six victims were residents in the east gate district of Changteh where the enemy plane unloaded the infected particles. (4) That these six victims could not have died of plague caused by other factors than the visit of the Japanese plane on Nov. 4 inasmuch as Changteh has never been inflicted by bubonic plague since the nearest city inflicted by bubonic plague was Chuhsien in Chekiang which is 2,000 kilometers away and inasmuch as Changteh being a rice-producing center does not receive rice from other districts.

"The Chinese Government has been taking stringent measures so as to put the consequences of such inhuman warfare on the part of Japan under effective control. It is also going to pass on the full information to the Allied Governments calling their serious attention to such criminal war conduct of Japan. I shall not be surprised that Japan would deny that she had resorted to bacterial warfare just as she denied her guilt of raping, maltreatment of civilians, use of poisonous gas and other atrocities in the past. But it is our belief that truth cannot be suppressed. All I would like to add is to stress once again that in addition to state responsibility the principle of individual criminal responsibility of those officers and men who ordered or carried out such inhuman methods of warfare should be given effect to by the United Nations when the day of reckoning comes."

JAPANESE ATTEMPT AT BACTERIAL WARFARE IN CHINA.

Up to the present time the practicability of bacterial warfare is little known to the public, because applicable experimental results, if available, are usually kept as a military secret. In the past, the artificial dissemination of diseased germs had been done for military purposes. The pollution of drinking water supplies by the introduction of diseased animals or other infected materials into the wells had been practised by retreating armies with the intention of causing epidemics of gastro-intestinal infections among the opposing troops in pursuit. Fortunately, such water-borne infections can be controlled with relative ease by boiling of all drinking water and disinfection by chemical means. Whether or not other infectious diseases could be intentionally spread by artificial means with deadly results in a wide area had not been demonstrated prior to the outbreak of the present Sino-Japanese War. However, in the last two years sufficient circumstantial evidence has been gathered to show that the Japanese have tried to use our people as guinea pigs for experimentation on the practicability of bacterial warfare. They have tried to produce epidemics of plague in the Free China by scattering plague-infected materials with aeroplanes. The facts thus far collected are as follows:-

1. On the 29th October, 1940, bubonic plague for the first time occurred in Ningpo of Chekiang Province. The epidemic lasted a period of thirty-four days and claimed a total of ninety-nine victims. It was reported that on the 27th October, 1940, Japanese planes raided Ningpo and scattered a considerable quantity of wheat grains over the port city. Although it was a curious fact to find "grains from heaven", yet no one at the time seemed to appreciate the enemy's intention and no thorough examination of the grains was made. All the plague victims were local residents. The diagnosis of plague was definitely confirmed by laboratory test. There was no excessive mortality among rats noticed before the epidemic outbreak; and despite careful investigation no exogenous sources of infection could be discovered.

2. On the 4th October, 1940, a Japanese plane visited Chü-hsien of Chekiang. After circling over the city for a short while, it scattered rice and wheat grains mixed with fleas over the western section of the city. There were many eye-witnesses, among whom was a man named Hsü, who collected some grains and dead fleas from the street outside of his own house and sent them to the local Air-raid Precautionary Corps for transmission to the Provincial Hygienic Laboratory for examination. The laboratory examination result was "that there were no pathogenic organisms found by bacteriological culture methods". However, on the 12th November, thirty-eight days after the Japanese plane's visit, bubonic plague occurred in the same area where the grains and fleas were found in abundance. The epidemic in Chü-hsien lasted twenty-four days resulting in twenty-one deaths. As far as available records show, plague never occurred in Chü-hsien before. After careful investigation of the situation it was believed that the strange visit of the enemy plane was the cause of the epidemic and the transmitting agent was the rat fleas, presumably infected with plague and definitely dropped by the enemy plane. As plague is primarily a disease of the rodents, the grains were probably used to attract the rats and expose them to the infected fleas mixed therein. It was regrettable that the fleas collected were not properly examined. Owing to the deficient laboratory facilities, an animal inoculation test was not performed; otherwise it would have been possible to show whether or not the fleas were plague-infected, and a positive result would have been an irrefutable evidence against Japan.

3. On the 28th November, 1940, when the plague epidemic in Ningpo and Chü-hsien was still in progress, three Japanese planes came to Kinghwa, an important commercial centre situated between Ningpo and Chu-hsien, and there they dropped a large quantity of small granules, about the size of shrimp-eggs. These strange objects were collected and examined in a local hospital. The granules were more or less round, about 1 mm. in diameter, of whitish-yellow tinge, somewhat translucent with a certain amount of glistening reflection from the surface. When brought into contact with a drop of water on a glass-slide, the granule began to swell to about twice its original size. In a small amount of water in a test-tube, with some agitation it would break up into whitish flakes and later form a milky suspension. Microscopic examination of these granules revealed the presence of

numerous gram-negative bacilli, with distinct bipolar staining in some of them and an abundance of involution forms, thus possessing the morphological characteristics of P. pestis, the causative organism of plague. When cultured in agar medium these gram-negative bacilli showed no growth; and because of inadequacy of laboratory facilities animal inoculation test could not be performed. Upon the receipt of such startling report from Kinghwa, the National Health Administration despatched Dr. W.W. Yung, Director of the Department of Epidemic Prevention, Dr. H.M. Jettmar, epidemiologist, formerly of the League of Nations' Epidemic Commission, and other technical experts to investigate the situation. When arriving in Kinghwa early in January 1941, they examined twenty-six of these granules and confirmed the previous observations, but inoculation test performed on guinea pigs by Dr. Jettmar gave negative results. It is difficult to say whether or not the lapse of time and the method of preservation of the granules had something to do with the negative results from the animal inoculation test, which is a crucial test for P. pestis. At all events no plague occurred in Kinghwa and it indicated that this particular Japanese experiment on bacterial warfare ended in failure.

4. On the 4th November, 1941, at about 5 a.m. a lone enemy plane appeared over Changteh of Hunan Province, flying very low, the morning being rather misty. Instead of bombs, wheat and rice grains, pieces of paper, cotton wadding and some unidentified particles were dropped. There were many eye-witnesses, including Mrs. E.J. Bannon, R.N., Superintendent of the local Presbyterian Hospital and other foreign residents in Changteh. After the "all clear" signal had been sounded at 5 p.m., some of these strange gifts from the enemy were collected and sent by the police to the local Presbyterian Hospital for examination, which revealed the presence of micro-organisms reported to resemble P. pestis. On the 11th November, seven days later, the first clinical case of plague came to notice, then followed by five cases within the same month, two cases in December, and the last case to date on the 13th January 1942. The diagnosis of bubonic plague was definitely confirmed in one of the six cases in November by bacteriological culture method and animal inoculation test. According to the investigation of Dr. W.K. Chen. bacteriologist who had had special training in plague work in India, and Dr. R. Pollitzer, epidemiologist of the National Health Administration and formerly of the League of Nations' epidemic Commission, the Changteh plague epidemic was caused by enemy action because of the following strong circumstantial evidences:

a) That Changteh has never been as far as is known afflicted by plague. During previous pandemics and severe epidemics elsewhere in China, this part of Hunan, nay this part of Central China in general, has never been known to come under the scourge of the disease.

b) That the present outbreak may have been due to direct contiguous spread from neighbouring plague-infected districts is also untenable on epidemiological grounds. Epidemiologically, plague spreads along transport routes for grain on which the rats feed. The nearest epidemic centre to Chü-hsien in Chekiang, about 2000 kilometers away by land or river communication. Furthermore, Changteh, being a rice producing district, supplies rice to other districts and does not receive rice from other cities. Besides, all the cases occurring in Changteh were native inhabitants who had not been away from the city or its immediate environs at all.

c) That all the cases came from the areas within the city where the strange objects dropped by enemy plane were found, and that among the wheat and rice grains and cotton rags there were most probably included infective vectors, probably fleas. The fleas were not noticed on the spot because they were not looked for and because the air raid alarm lasted some twelve hours with the result that the fleas must have in the meantime escaped to other hiding places.

d) That there was no apparent evidence of any excessive rat mortality before and for some time after the "aerial incident". About two hundred rats were caught and examined during the months of November and December, but no evidence of plague was found. However, toward the end of January and the firs part of February this year, among seventy eight rats examined there were eighteen with definite plague infections. As plague is primarily a disease of the rodents, the usual sequence of events is that than an epizootic precedes an epidemic; but that did not take place in the present case. The infected fleas from the enemy plane must have first attacked men and a little later the rats.

- 3 -

e) That all the first six human cases were infected within fifteen days after the "aerial incident" and that infected fleas are known to be able to survive under suitable conditions for weeks without feeding. The normal incubation period of bubonic plague is 3 to 7 days and may occasionally be prolonged to 8 or even 14 days. The time factor is certainly also a strong circumstantial evidence.

5. A serious epidemic of plague occurring in Suiyuan, Ningsha and Shensi Provinces has been recently reported. From the last week of January this year to date there have been some six hundred cases. According to a recent communique from the local military in the north-western frontier, "a large number of sick rodents had been set free by the enemy in the epidemic area". However, considering the fact that plague is known to be epizootic among the native rodents in the Ordos region in Suiyuan, one must wait for confirmation of this report. Technical experts, including Dr. Y.H. Yang, Director of the "eishengshu North-West Epidemic Prevention Bureau", have been sent there to investigate and help to control the epidemic.

The enumeration of facts thus far collected leads to the conclusion that the Japanese Army has attempted at bacterial warfare in China. In Chekiang and Hunan they had scattered from the air infective materials and succeeded in causing epidemic outbreaks of plague. Aside from temporary terrorization of the general population in the afflicted areas, the inhuman act of our enemy is most condemnable when one realises that once the disease has taken root in the local rat population, it will continue to infect men for many years to come. Fortunately, the mode of infection and the method of control of plague are known and it is possible to keep the disease in check by vigorous control measures. Our difficulty at present is the shortage of the anti-epidemic supplies required. The recent advance in chemotherapy has given us new drugs that are more or less effective for the treatment of plague cases, and they are sulfathiazole and allied sulphonomide compounds which China cannot as yet produce herself. For prevention, plague vaccine can be produced in considerable quantities by the Central Epidemic Prevention Bureau in Kunming and the North-west Epidemic Prevention Bureau in Lanchow, provided the raw material required for vaccine production such as peptone and agar-agar are available. Rat-proofing of all buildings and eradication of rats are fundamental control measures, but under war conditions they cannot be satisfactorily carried out. If rat poisons such as cyanogas and barium carbonate can be obtained from abroad in large quantities, deratization campaigns may be launched in cities where rats are a menace.

P.Z. King, Director-General,

NATIONAL HEALTH ADMINISTRATION.

March 31, 1942.

3.11 6 Apr. 1942: EPIDEMIOLOGICAL REPORT NO. 1, presented to the American Bureau for Medical Aid to China, NATIONAL HEALTH ADMINISTRATION, Jan. 24, 1942: The Plague Situation

资料出处：National Archives of the United States, R112, E295A, B11.

内容点评：本资料为 1942 年 4 月 6 日，中国中央卫生署提交美国对华医疗援助局的《流行病报告第 1 号：鼠疫流行情况》（1942 年 1 月 24 日）。

CONFIDENTIAL

EPIDEMIOLOGICAL REPORT NO. I

Presented to the American Bureau for Medical Aid to China - Received April 6, 1942

NATIONAL HEALTH ADMINISTRATION

The Plague Situation

Hunan. As far as available records show, plague for the first time broke out in Changteh, Hunan, on November 11, 1941. It was reported that seven days prior to the outbreak, Japanese planes came over to Changteh and scattered grains and rags. And it was over the same area where these strange materials were found that the first few plague cases occurred. In November, there were six cases with definite clinical signs and symptoms of bubonic plague and one of these cases was confirmed by bacteriological examination and animal inoculation test. Two other cases occurred on December 14 and 20 respectively; and the last case to date was reported on January 13. Examinations of about two hundred rats in November and December revealed no evidence of plague among them. Anit-epidemic units of the National Health Administration, the Army Medical Administration, the Chinese Red Cross Medical Relief Corps, and the Hunan Provincial Health Department, were despatched to Changteh to help to check the epidemic. By means of isolation of cases, quarantine of contacts, disinfection and disinfestation, and other measures, the situation has been more or less put under control. It is feared, however, that the disease may have worked its way into the rat population and established a focus of infection among the rodents. The following telegram from Changteh dated December 29, 1941, was received from Dr. R. Pollitzer, epidemiologist of the National Health Administration:

> "Circumstantial evidence strongly suggests that plague outbreak in Changteh was caused by enemy action. Last human case on December 20th, So far no infected rats found but this needs further investigation — Pollitzer"

Chekiang. In Chuhsien, plague occurred for the first time in November 1940, claiming 21 victims in twenty-four days. It was reported that thirty-eight days before the outbreak of plague, Japanese planes dropped grains mixed with fleas over Chuhsien; and it was believed that that was the cause of the epidemic, although there was still a possibility of the disease being imported from Fukien, via Chingyuan. The disease has unfortunately become enzootic among rats and reappeared in epidemic form in the spring of 1941. From March to July, 1941, there were 157 human cases with 148 deaths. After a quiescence of three months, a human case was again reported on November 13, but none since. The Weishengshu Anti-epidemic Corps has established its 4th Divisional Headquarters in Chuhsien and is now responsible for the technical part of the control program in that area. On account of shortage of experienced personnel for plague work, a systematic and practical training course is now being offered in Chuhsien under the auspices of the Weishengshu Anti-epidemic Corps.

On October 2, 1941, bubonic plague appeared in I-wu, about 131 kilometers from Chuhsien by rail. It was probably a direct extension of the infection

from Chuhsien. During the three months, October-December, there were 130 cases, of whom 102 ended fatally. The cases were distributed as follows:

	No. of Cases	No. of Deaths	No. of Infected Rats
October	31	28	40
November	77	60	37
December	22	14	23
Total	130	102	100

According to the report of the Weishengshu Anti-epidemic Corps, the epidemic in I-wu seems to be on the decline, as there was only one case during the ten-day period, January 1-10, 1942. Of these human cases, only two showed signs of pneumonic involvement, while all the others were bubonic. It is with deep regret that we record here the death of Dr. Liu Chung-hsin, leader of one of Chinese Red Cross Medical Relief Corps Anti-epidemic Units, from pneumonic plague in I-wu on December 30, 1940.

Plague continued to spread from I-wu southeasterly to Tung-yang, 18.2 kilometers apart, in January this year, where for the first ten days there were nine cases reported. No further details have so far been received.

Fukien. Plague is endemic in Fukien province. For the ten months, January to October, 1941, there were 425 cases with 280 deaths occurring in twenty-one hsiens, namely: Yung-chi, Sien-yu, Cheng-hwo, Nan-an, Chang-pu, Lung-hsi, Chang-tai, Pu-tien, Yung-chun, Teh-wa, Chang-ting, Yung-an, Lo-yuan, Lien-kong, Sung-ki, Nan-ping, Chien-yang, Chien-ow, Shao-wu, Shun-chang, and Ping-hwo. The disease continued to appear in small numbers in the last three months, but detailed reports have not arrived.

Kwangtung. Plague occurred from February to May, 1941 in the Lien-chiang district where it is also known to be endemic. There were sixty cases during these four months, and none later until the end of November when two deaths from plague were reported. No further report has been received since.

Chungking
January 24, 1942

3.12 7 Apr. 1942: Telegram received from the Ministry of Foreign Affairs, dated Apr. 6, 1942, Chungking, Chinese Embassy, Washington

资料出处：National Archives of the United States, R112, E295A, B11.

内容点评：本资料为 1942 年 4 月 7 日华盛顿中国驻美使馆收到的重庆中国外交部 4 月 6 日电文：中央卫生署总长金宝善（Dr. P. Z. King）声明及中外医学专家调查报告，证实日本在中国至少 5 次实施细菌战的企图。

C
O
P
Y

CONFIDENTIAL

Inc. 2
1 - 1

Following is the text of a telegram received from the Ministry of Foreign Affairs, dated April 6, 1942, Chungking:

"National Health Administration Director-General Dr. P. Z. King's statement on Japanese attempt at bacterial warfare against China and reports submitted by Chinese and foreign medical experts definitely prove that at least on five occasions Japan has resorted to ruthless bacterial warfare in China.

"In the first instance, a quantity of wheat grains was dropped by Japanese planes over Ningpo on October 27th, 1940. An epidemic broke out soon after and lasted thirty-four days claiming ninety-nine victims. Diagnosis of plague was definitely confirmed in laboratory test. On October 4th, 1940, a Japanese plane scattered rice and wheat grains and fleas over Chusien, Chekiang. Bubonic plague appeared thirty-eight days later causing twenty-one deaths. Kinghwa was attacked by three Japanese planes on November 18th, 1940, dropping a large quantity of translucent granules like shrimp-eggs. Microscopic examination revealed the presence of plague bacilli though no epidemic resulted. On November 4, 1941, a Japanese plane visited Changteh, Hunan, dropping rice, paper and cotton wads on which bacilli were found. Later nine cases of plague were reported. Numerous circumstantial evidences including infected rats proved beyond doubt the origin of the epidemic. Lastly, a serious attack of plague has broken out in Suiyuan, Ninghsia, and Shensi. Six hundred cases were reported. A recent communique from local military authorities stated that a large number of sick rodents was set free by the enemy there."

MDC Sa 384 China (4-13-42)
(18) M.I.D. 730 Bacteriology, Japan 4-13-42 (2-19-42)

Chinese Embassy,
Washington, April 7, 1942

3.13　9 Apr. 1942: Voice of China, Government Statements: CHINESE GOVERNMENT FINDS EVIDENCE OF FIVE ENEMY ATTEMPTS AT BACTERIOLOGICAL WARFARE

资料出处：National Archives of the United States, R112, E295A, B11.

内容点评：本资料为 1942 年 4 月 9 日 Voice of China 广播报道中国政府声明：中国政府发现敌人 5 次细菌战攻击企图的证据。

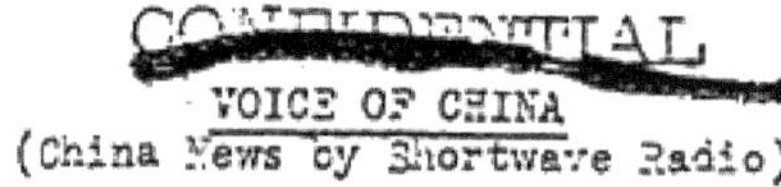

CONFIDENTIAL
VOICE OF CHINA
(China News by Shortwave Radio)

919288
(Extract from ...)

Government Statements

CHINESE GOVERNMENT FINDS EVIDENCE OF FIVE
ENEMY ATTEMPTS AT BACTERIOLOGICAL WARFARE

9 Apr 1942

NEW YORK, April 9 (CNS)....Following is the text of a telegram received by the Chinese Embassy in Washington from the Ministry of Foreign Affairs, dated April 6, 1942, Chungking:

"National Health Administration Director-General Dr. P. Z. King's statement on Japanese attempt at bacterial warfare against China and reports submitted by Chinese and foreign medical experts definitely prove that at least on five occasions Japan has resorted to ruthless bacterial warfare in China.

"In the first instance, a quantity of wheat grains was dropped by Japanese planes over Ningpo on October 27, 1940. An epidemic broke out soon after and lasted thirty-four days claiming ninety-nine victims. Diagnosis of plague was definitely confirmed in laboratory test. On October 4, 1940, a Japanese plane scattered rice and wheat grains and fleas over Chusion, Chekiang. Bubonic plague appeared thirty-eight days later causing twenty-one deaths. Kinghwa was attacked by three Japanese planes on November 18, 1940, dropping a large quantity of translucent granules like shrimp-eggs. Microscopic examination revealed the presence of plague bacilli though no epidemic resulted. On November 4, 1941, a Japanese plane visited Changteh, Hunan, dropping rice, paper and cotton wads on which bacilli were found. Later nine cases of plague were reported. Numerous circumstantial evidences including infected rats proved beyond doubt the origin of the epidemic. Lastly, a serious attack of plague has broken out in Suiyuan, Ninghsia, and Shensi. Six hundred cases were reported. A recent communique from local military authorities stated that a large number of sick rodents was set free by the enemy there."

1942
areas infected by
air drops in China

3.14　9 Apr. 1942: Telegram received from the Foreign Office, Chungking, dated April 6, 1942, Chinese Embassy, London

资料出处： National Archives of the United States, R112, E295A, B11.

内容点评： 本资料为 1942 年 4 月 6 日伦敦中国驻英使馆所获重庆外交部 4 月 6 日发来的电文：中国卫生署总长金宝善（Dr. P. Z. King）声明，公布中外专家调查报告，证实日本在中国实施细菌战攻击至少 5 次。

COPY.

The following telegram has been received from the Foreign Office, Chungking, dated April 6, 1942.

A statement by Dr. P.Z. King, Director General of the National Health Administration, on the Japanese attempt at bacteriological warfare in China, together with reports submitted by Chinese and foreign medical experts, definitely prove that on at least five occasions Japan has resorted to ruthless bacteriological warfare in China.

In the first instance a quantity of wheat grains were dropped by Japanese planes over Ningpo on October 27th, 1940. An epidemic broke out soon after and lasted thirty-four days, claiming ninety-nine victims. The diagnosis of plague was definitely confirmed by a laboratory test.

On October 4th 1940 a Japanese plane scattered rice and wheat grains and fleas over Chusieh in Chekiang. Bubonic plague appeared thirty-eight days later causing twenty-one deaths.

On 18th November 1940, Kinghwai was attacked by three Japanese planes. They dropped a large quantity of translucent granules like shrimp eggs. Microscopic examination revealed the presence of plague bacilli, though no epidemic resulted.

On November 4th 1941 a Japanese plane visited Changteh in Hunan, dropping wheat, rice paper and cotton wads on which bacilli were found. Later nine cases of plague were reported. Numerous items of circumstantial evidence, including infected rats, proved beyond doubt the origin of the epidemic.

Lastly, a serious attack of plague has broken out in Suiyuan, Ninghsia and Shensi. Six hundred cases have been reported. A recent communique from the local military authorities stated that a large number of sick rodents had been set free by the enemy there.

A Note with the full text of Dr. King's statement and of the reports has been sent to the local foreign diplomatic representatives with a view to calling their attention to the above. The full text will follow by air mail.

Chinese Embassy, London. April 9, 1942.

3.15 16 Apr. 1942: MI 000.76 4-16-42, Newspapers: Transmitted herewith are copies of a newspaper article by Fletcher Pratt captioned "Japs Try Out Germ War; May Be Their Ace in Hole to Avert Defeat by U. S.", To: Chief, MIS, WD, From: J. Edgar Hoover, Director, FBI

资料出处：National Archives of the United States, R112, E295A, B11.

内容点评：本资料为 1942 年 4 月 16 日美国联邦调查局局长 J. Edgar Hoover 呈美国陆军部军事情报局局长 1942 年 2 月 28 日 *Philadelphia Record* 的一篇报道剪报，作者为 Fletcher Pratt，题目:《日本人发动细菌战；这也许是他们避免被美国打败的最后一张王牌》。

MI 000.76 4-16-42 copy
Newspapers

~~CONFIDENTIAL~~

Federal Bureau of Investigation
United States Department of Justice
Washington, D. C.

Date: April 16, 1942

To: Chief
Military Intelligence Service
War Department
Washington, D. C.

From: J. Edgar Hoover - Director, Federal Bureau of Investigation

Subject:

Transmitted herewith are copies of a newspaper article by Fletcher Pratt captioned "Japs Try Out Germ War; May Be Their Ace in Hole To Avert Defeat by U. S."

The clipping was made available by an outside source who suggests that in view of the newspaper article and the recent reported flight of enemy aircraft over Los Angeles, that the terrain by examined with the thought that diseased germs might have been spread.

Previouc Distribution:
FBI
ONI

G2/CI Distribution:
Psych. Warfare Br.
SGO
IG
File

Source: Undetermined
Inform: Undetermined

FMH:rs
5-1-42

~~CONFIDENTIAL~~

Fletcher Pratt Says:

Japs Try Out Germ War; May Be Their Ace in Hole To Avert Defeat by U. S.

By FLETCHER PRATT
Philadelphia Record Military Critic

The Japs already are using that ultimate horror, bacteriological warfare, and it is probably their ace in the hole against us.

They are experimenting, as they always do with new and deadly tricks of war, against those ideal subjects, the Chinese—ideal because the news from China gets through to America only with difficulty and often remains unbelievable after it gets here.

It started last November 4. A single Japanese plane appeared over Changteh, northwest of Changsha in Honan province, flew over the city for about an hour and disappeared. No bombs were dropped, but after the all-clear sounded streets and compounds were found liberally sprinkled with rice-grains embedded in little tufts of cotton.

Plague Cases Follow

Laboratory examination showed both rice and cotton to contain cultures of bubonic plague; within a week there were cases of bubonic at Changteh, which had not had a case of the disease since the founding of the Chinese Republic.

In December, just after the attack on Pearl Harbor, Japanese planes appeared over Chinhau, Chin and Chiu, in Chekiang province, again dropping no bombs, but trailed behind them what appeared to be white fumes. This time the white fumes proved to be living fleas, infected with cultures of bubonic and typhus, and fish eggs with the same. The reason for both the fish eggs and the rice is to make contact with the local rats; rats are the best spreaders of bubonic plague, the "Black Death" of the Middle Ages.

Chinese sources remark rather bitterly that it probably will be a long time before the

4, Column 5.

Western World will believe this sort of thing. Unfortunately, this is probably true, despite the fact that the report comes from thoroughly reliable sources.

It was first discussed in a short wave broadcast from Chungking by Dr. Robert [illegible] head of the Chinese Red Cross. Its authenticity is verified by Dr. Lin [illegible], head of [illegible] News Service in Rockefeller Center.

And it is the subject of a memorandum written by the military attache of the Chinese Embassy in Washington.

Moreover, it should be kept in mind that every prediction, every indication furnished by the Chinese intelligence service thus far has proved 100 percent accurate. It is the only Allied espionage service that has a real fifth column of considerable dimensions working behind the enemy lines.

Accounts for Confidence.

The thing also fits perfectly with the strategical necessities confronting Japan, and accounts perfectly for the confidence with which they are measuring their strength against the ultimately superior resources of the U. S.

Take the long view on the war. Suppose the Japs do conquer all the area of the Southwest Pacific, even including Australia. What then? They must know that they would in the long run have to face American armies immensely superior in numbers, supported by production capacities in ships, planes and weapons beside which their own production would be of the pipsqueak order.

Plan for Eventualities.

It is inconceivable that their military men would not have a plan for such an eventuality. It is equally inconceivable that the plan would be based on anything so nebulous as their own possibility of withstanding the attack of the superior forces to which they had already shown the technique of making such attacks.

Well, here's one answer. Another is probably furnished by the fact that the Japanese several times have used the two deadliest of the war gases, mustard and lewisite, against the Chinese. In other words, they are planning, coolly and deliberately, to cut us down with disease.

From the Japanese point of view such a program has the rare advantage of being almost foolproof. One of the main [illegible]

Japs Try Out Germ War; May Be Their Ace in Hole To Avert Defeat by U. S.

By FLETCHER PRATT
Philadelphia Record Military Critic

The Japs already are using that ultimata horror, bacteriological warfare, and it is probably their ace in the hole against us.

They are experimenting, as they always do with new and deadly tricks of war, against those ideal subjects, the Chinese —ideal because the news from China gets through to America only with difficulty and often remains unbelievable after it gets here.

It started last November 4. A single Japanese plane appeared over Changteh, northwest of Changsha in Honan province, flew over the city for about an hour and disappeared. No bombs were dropped, but after the all-clear sounded streets and compounds were found liberally sprinkled with rice-grains embedded in little tufts of cotton.

Plague Cases Follow

Laboratory examination showed both rice and cotton to contain cultures of bubonic plague; within a week there were cases of bubonic at Changteh, which had not had a case of the disease since the founding of the Chinese Republic.

In December, just after the attack on Pearl Harbor, Japanese planes appeared over Chinhau, Chin and Chiu, in Chekiang province, again dropping no bombs, but trailed behind them what appeared to be white fumes. This time the white fumes proved to be living fleas, infected with cultures of bubonic and typhus, and fish eggs with the same. The reason for both the fish eggs and the rice is to make contact with the local rats; rats are the best spreaders of bubonic plague, the "Black Death" of the Middle Ages.

Chinese [illegible] remark rather bitterly that it probably will be a long time before the

4, Column 5.

Western World will believe this sort of thing. Unfortunately, this is probably true, despite the fact that the report comes from thoroughly reliable sources.

It was first discussed in a short wave broadcast from Chungking by Dr. Robert [illegible] head of the Chinese Red Cross. Its authenticity is verified by Dr. [illegible] head of [illegible] News Service in Rockefeller Center.

And it is the subject of a memorandum written by the military attache of the Chinese Embassy in Washington.

Moreover, it should be kept in mind that every prediction, every indication furnished by the Chinese intelligence service thus far has proved 100 percent accurate. It is the only Allied espionage service that has a real fifth column of considerable dimensions working behind the enemy lines.

Accounts for Confidence.

The thing also fits perfectly with the strategical necessities confronting Japan, and accounts perfectly for the confidence with which they are measuring their strength against the ultimately superior resources of the U. S.

Take the long view on the war. Suppose the Japs do conquer all the area of the Southwest Pacific, even including Australia. What then? They must know that they would in the long run have to face American armies immensely superior in numbers, supported by production capacities in ships, planes and weapons beside which their own production would be of the pipsqueak order.

Plan for Eventualities.

It is inconceivable that their military men would not have a plan for such an eventuality. It is equally inconceivable that the plan would be based on anything so nebulous as their own possibility of withstanding the attack of the superior forces to which they had already shown the technique of making such attacks.

Well, here's one answer. Another is probably furnished by the fact that the Japanese several times have used the two deadliest of the war gases, mustard and lewisite, against the Chinese. In other words, they are planning, coolly and deliberately, to cut us down with disease.

From the Japanese point of view such a program has the rare advantage of being almost foolproof. One of the main objections against germ warfare is that it's hard to stop the spread of a plague once started. This does not hold in the case of Japan versus the U. S. There is no connection, no communication across the Pacific.

We have been warned.

3.16 1 May 1942: No.38, Chinese Press Reports on Bacterial and Chemical Warfare, To: Chief, MIS, WD, from DAVID D. BARRETT, Lt. Col., CWS (Inf), Assistant Military Attache

资料出处：National Archives of the United States, R112, E295A, B11.

内容点评：本资料为 1942 年 5 月 1 日重庆美驻华大使馆武官助理、化学战部队中校 David D. Barrett 向美国陆军部军事情报局长官提交的报告，题目：中国媒体关于细菌战和化学战的报道。

EMBASSY OF THE UNITED STATES OF AMERICA
Office of the Military Attache
Chungking

COPY

May 1, 1942

No. 38

Subject: Chinese Press Reports on Bacterial and Chemical Warfare.

To : Chief, Military Intelligence Service, War Department, Washington, D. C.

1. There is attached herewith a translation of two dispatches in the Hsin Hua Jih Pao relating to Japanese activities in the use of bacteria and chemicals.

2. The evidence submitted appears far from conclusive.

For and in the absence of the Military Attache.

DAVID D. BARRETT
Lieutenant Colonel, CWS (Inf).
Assistant Military Attache

Extracts from Chinese Press April 25, 1942

Japanese Attempts to Create Plague in North China

1. (Special to Hsin Hua Jih Pao) According to an intelligence circular from the Military Authorities of Hopei-Shansi-Chahar area, during their latest mopping up actions in Wuchi-Shentze area in Central Hopei, the Japanese troops released along their route of action a large number of plague carrying mice. These mice are not afraid of mankind and move slothfully. The dead ones have red pox dotted all over their bodies. Experiments indicate that they carry plague germs of the blood letting and blood poisoning kind. This virulent plot was, however, luckily checkmated by timely preventive measures by the Chinese troops.

2. (Special to Hsin Hua Jih Pao) During their latest mopping up operations in Taihangshan (mountain range bordering Shansi-Hopei, the Japanese made use of vesicant chemicals in large quantities. These chemicals are liquid solutions, which were to be smeared on furniture or anything which the Chinese soldiers might easily touch when these things were within their reach. The chemical-smeared articles were left, when the Japanese retreated, in a tidy and orderly manner in order to invite touching by the Chinese troops. A number of cases of poisoning were reported along both banks of the lower valley of the Chingchang River and in areas to the east of Wusiang, north of Changchih in Shansi. In more serious cases the affected persons become swollen all over their bodies, followed by blisters. The Japanese also left behind poisoned rice, meats, canned goods, weapons, uniforms, shoes, stockings, et cetera. A villager in the vicinity of Shehsien, northwest of Changte in Honan, picked up a pair of leather shoes on the way and put them on. His feet became swollen and later developed blisters. Other villagers on the east bank of the river suffered from similar intrigues.

Note: Members of the Chinese staff of this office who were in Peiping during the winter and spring of 1940-41 report that the Japanese authorities, through the Chinese police, engaged to purchase mice from the city population at ten cents each. The ten cents was not tempting to the people and such transactions were never seriously considered. At the time, the Japanese announced that they needed mice for laboratory purposes.

3.17 1 Mar. & 15 Jun. 1942: New York Times articles on Japanese germ warfare in China; April 9, 1942, Broadcast from Chungking, China: "Japanese attempt at bacterial warfare in China" by Dr. P. Z. King, director of the national health administration

资料出处： National Archives of the United States, R112, E295A, B11.

内容点评： 本资料包括两份文件，分别是《纽约时报》1942 年 3 月 1 日 Harrison Forman 报道、6月15日报道；1942年4月9日重庆广播：中央卫生署总长金宝善（Dr. P. Z. King）文章，题目:《日本企图在中国实施细菌战》。

Chungking Fears Attack With Gas Airplanes Said to Spread Plague

All in Chinese Capital Urged to Get Masks—Bubonic Cases in Changteh Laid to Flier Who Dropped Infected Fleas Last Nov. 4

Why not heat the ... to prevent ...

By HARRISON FORMAN

CHUNGKING, China, March 1—Thousands of gas masks have been distributed to government workers in Chungking during the past several weeks while the public has been urged to buy an expensive type of mask like those carried in Britain.

The precautions are being taken in the belief that the Japanese no longer care what the world will think of methods employed in a desperate effort to win in China. Gas has already been used in a number of forms at the front.

A new terror weapon in the hands of the ruthless Japanese looms closer with the report of bubonic plague in Changteh in Hunan Province. Dr. R. Pollitzer, former League of Nations epidemologist, stationed now in Changteh, announced that he had dissected five rats infected with bubonic plague.

"Circumstantial evidence strongly suggests the plague outbreak in Changteh was caused by enemy action," reads a telegram to Chungking from Dr. Pollitzer, who has had sixteen years' experience in fighting plagues and cholera in Harbin, Shanghai and elsewhere in China before his present connection as epidemologist of the National Health Administration.

Dr. Pollitzer concludes that while no new human case has turned up since his Jan. 13 discovery of infected rats, Changteh is now an infected area, with eradication complicated by war conditions. Authorities, however, are killing rats in the hope of stamping out the hibernating disease, which breaks out with the coming of warm weather.

Traced to Nov. 4 Raid

The plague is traced to Nov. 4, when Changteh, a city of 50,000, was raided by a single Japanese plane. The plane flew just over the roofs instead of at an altitude of 20,000 feet. It circled for twenty minutes and then flew off, not dropping a single bomb.

The returning residents were further puzzled when they observed scattered rice grains mixed with wisps of cotton rags, most of them near the two main gates. The police cleaned up and burned whatever was in sight, saving samples for analysis. These were found contaminated with bubonic plague baccili. Less than a week later six cases of plague were reported. All victims died within thirty-six hours.

Dr. Robert Lim, head of the Chinese Red Cross and the army medical training services, rushed to Changteh, arriving in time to perform autopsies that confirmed the presence of bubonic plague. There were two more cases Dec. 14 and 20. The last case was on Jan. 13.

There had been no plague reported in Changteh for more than ten generations. The nearest epidemic region is more than 500 miles distant. The victims were not transients or refugees who might have brought in the disease but were residents who had not traveled more than a few miles from Changteh. All lived near the two main gates.

The plague is usually transmitted through bites from fleas that have lived on infected rats, which soon die. The absence of dead rats and the short time that elapsed since the visit of the mysterious raider supported the argument that infected fleas were dropped from the Japanese plane.

The fact that the plague did not spread is attributed to the cold spell, which set in shortly thereafter. It is feared there will be an outbreak in the Spring.

Similar Raid in Chekiang

Bubonic plague was reported after a similar mysterious raid in Chekiang Province in November, 1940, under almost identical circumstances, low-flying planes dropping fleas in packets of grain or rice to attract rats. The outbreaks occurred about a week later. As in Changteh no dead rats were seen, leading to the belief that the plague was directly transmitted by infected fleas.

At Chuhsien in Chekiang province there were twenty-one victims twenty-four days after the mysterious Japanese raid. Though the cold weather checked the plague the disease spread among rats and remained dormant until the Spring of 1941, when it appeared. Between March and July there were 157 cases and 148 deaths.

The National Health Administration and the War Ministry are co-operating in burning homes that are believed to be infected and disinfecting river boats that enter or leave suspected areas. Air raid precautions workers throughout the country have been warned to destroy all articles dropped from Japanese planes and to disinfect sweeping implements afterward.

The National Health Administration has instructed all local health authorities to prepare anti-epidemic equipment. Anti-epidemic bureaus have been ordered to prepare ample quantities of anti-bubonic plague vaccine for public sale.

Dr. Lim, discussing the plague peril, said:

"I do not expect Americans, British and others to believe stories that the Japs are resorting to bacteriological warfare today as they did not believe for a long time the stories that the Japs were using gas in China. I realize that the idea of a widespread scattering of the plague appears at first somewhat in the realm of fantasy.

"It is my belief that the Japs thus far have been experimenting in China and it is my firm conviction that Japan is planning large-scale bacteriological warfare, not only here but elsewhere, especially when things start going wrong for her."

June 15, 1942

Germ Warfare From Air Laid To Foe in China

Relief Official Back With Documents Telling How Bubonic Plague Broke Out

First-hand evidence that the Japanese have been using germ warfare to spread bubonic plague in China for the last year and a half was presented yesterday by Robert Barnett, former Rhodes Scholar and Rockefeller Foundation fellow, who returned to New York recently from a six-week trip to China as a representative of United China Relief.

The evidence, made public by Mr. Barnett in an interview at the office of United China Relief, 1790 Broadway, is in the form of documents from P. Z. King, director-general of the Chinese National Health Administration in Chungking; Miss E. J. Bannan, a registered nurse at the Presbyterian Hospital, Changteh, Hunan Province; Dr. R. Pollitzer, former epidemiologist of the League of Nations and at present holding the same post with the Chinese National Health Administration, and Dr. W. K. Chen, consultant with the Chinese Red Cross Medical Relief Corps, at Kweiyang, China.

Scatter Germs From Air

Statements by these persons to the effect that the Japanese have tried to produce epidemics of bubonic plague in China by scattering grain and other matter mixed with plague-infested fleas from airplanes were released by Mr. Barnett and corroborated as authentic by Dr. Donald D. Van Slyke, of the Rockefeller Institute, who is president of the American Bureau of Medical Aid To China.

"These statements are documentary proo fthat the Japanese are engaging in germ warfare," Mr. Barnett said.

Dr. Van Slyke commented: "I have read the documents and my impression is that they are entirely authentic."

The statements, which were forwarded recently by Dr. King to Dr. T. V. Soong, Chinese Ambassador to the United States, reported four specific instances of Japanese planes dropping plague-infected fleas on the soil of Free China. These took place in Chu-hsian, Chekiang Province, on Oct. 4, 1940; Ningpo, Chekiang, Oct. 29, 1940; Kinghwa, Chekiang, Nov. 28, 1941, and Changteh, Hunan, Nov. 4, 1941.

Mr. Barnett, who was born in Shanghai, the son of an official of the Young Men's Christian Association, and attended the University of North Carolina, Yale University and Oxford University, said there were also other instances of Japanese germ warfare which had not yet been completely authenticated.

Methods Experimental

Dr. King, in his report to Dr. Soong, said "sufficient circumstantial evidence has been gathered to show that the Japanese have tried to use our people as guinea pigs for experimentation on the practicability of bacterial warfare."

The Japanese methods were clearly experimental, Dr. King reported, but caused many deaths from bubonic plague. Lone planes would fly over Chinese cities and drop grain mixed with plague-infected fleas. The grain would attract rats, who would become infected, and in turn would infect men, women and children. Rats are the classic carriers and transmitter of bubonic plague, he pointed out, and wherever the plague strikes the mortality among rats is even greater than among people.

Miss Bennan, in a report to Dr. King from the Presbyterian Hospital, Changteh, Hunan Province, on Dec. 18, 1941, on an outbreak of plague in that city, stated that it "followed the visit of an enemy plane on the morning of Nov. 4."

"The unhulled wheat and grain found on the streets and roofs of houses in Changteh was dropped from that plane," Miss Bannan reported. "I might say in this connection that I watched the flight of the plane closely that morning. In appearance it was somewhat like a hydroplane and flew low over the city—lower than any plane has yet flown in the more than twenty bombings I have witnessed here."

Miss Bannan said some of the grain was collected and brought to the hospital for examination, and that a laboratory test was made which "showed bacillus closely resembling that of plague."

Patients Brought In

About ten days after the grain was dropped a young girl was brought to the hospital seriously ill with plague, Miss Bannan reported, and on succeeding days other patients were brought in and treated for plague.

"Finally I might add that this is the first occasion during my long residence here—almost thirty years—that there has been an outbreak of plague in this area," Miss Bannan stated. "If the facts be true, as I believe they are, there can be only one conclusion drawn and that is that the enemy is now carrying on a ruthless and inhuman warfare against combatants and non-combatants alike. Truly a new way of spreading Japanese 'culture.'"

Dr. Pollitzer, who has passed many years studying plagues, went to Changteh to investigate, and in a report to Dr. King on Dec. 30, 1941, stated that examination of small quantities of the grain dropped from the plane "did not lead to definite results," but that he assumed the Japanese had dropped plague-infected fleas with the grain. Several witnesses stated the plane also dropped pieces of cloth or paper he reported, "and such material would offer good protection for fleas."

Dr. Pollitzer pointed out that no previous outbreak of plague in Hunan Province is on record. "All my observations and considerations leave little, if any, room for doubt that the recent plague outbreak in Changteh was in casual connection with the aerial attack," he stated.

Dr. Chen, who accompanied Dr. Pollitzer to Changteh, reported that autopsy findings, together with bacteriological and animal tests, "left no doubt that we were dealing with a genuine case of bubonic plague."

Serious Epidemic Reported

Dr. King, in his report to Dr Soong, stated that a serious epidemic of plague has broken out recently in Suiyuan, Ningsha and Shensi Provinces. "Fortunately the mode of infection and the method of control of plague are known," he statede, "and it is possible to keep the disease in check by vigorous control measures. Our difficulty at present is the shortage of the anti-epidemic supplies required. In view of the fact that China will be an important base of the United Nations for counter-offensive actions against the Japanese I am sure you will agree with me as to the importance of exercising vigorous plague-control measures."

Mr. Barnett revealed that doctors in China are now using improvised surgical scissors and forceps, hand-hammered out of automobile scrap. This is typical of the new self-sufficiency arising in China, he said.

"The attack on Tokio was a shot in the arm for Chinese morale,' he declared. "While the need for relief is great, the people feel real relief can come only with victory. And victory is possible only if military supplies come through. They therefore no longer expect relief supplies. They know precious transport space must be used for military supplies."

Broadcast from Chungking, China.

Radio Station XGOY - 9635 K. C.

April 9, 1942 - 7.30 A.M., P.W.T.

Note: The following article is for the editors of China at war for use as they may see fit. The title of the article is "Japanese attempt at bacterial warfare in China" - By Dr. P. Z. King director of the national health administration.

****

Up to the present time the prabticability of bacterial warfare is little known to the public because applicable experimental results, if available, are usually kept as a military secret. In the past the artificial dissemination of disease germs has been done for military purposes. The pollution of drinking water supplies by the introduction of diseased animals or other infected materials into the wells had been practiced by retreating armies with the intention of causing epidemics gastrointestinal infections among the opposing troops in pursuit. Fortunately such water born infections can be controlled with relative ease by boiling of all drinking water and disinfection by chemical means.

Whether or not other infectious diseases could be widely and intentionally spread by artificial means with deadly results had not been demonstrated prior to the outbreak of the present Sino-Japanese War. However, in the last two years sufficient circumstantial evidence has been gathered to show that the Japanese have been using our people guinea pigs for experimentation on the practicability of bactetial warfare. They have tried to produce epidemics of plague in free China by scattering plague infected materials with airplanes.

-2-

The Facts Thus Far Collected are as Follows:

1 - On October 29, 1940 Bubonic Plague for the first time occurred in Ningpo of Chekiang province. The epidemic lasted a period of thirty four days and claimed a total of ninety nine victims.

It was reported that on October 27, 1940 Japanese planes raided Ningpo and scattered a considerable quantity of wheat grains over the port city. Although it was a curious fact to find "Grains from Heaven" yet no one at the time seemed to appreciate the enemy's intention and no thorough examination of the grains was made. All the plague victims were local residents. The diagnosis of plague was definitley confirmed by laboratory tests. There was no excessive mortality among rats noticed before the epidemic and despite careful examination no exogenous sources of infection could be discovered.

2 - On October 4, 1940 a Japanese plane visited Chuhsien of Chekiang province. After circling over the city for a short while it scattered rice and wheat grains mixed with fleas over the western district of the city. There were many eye witnesses among whom was a non named HSU who collected some grains and dead fleas from the street outside of his own house and sent them to the local air raid precautionary corps for transmission to the provincial hygienic laboratory for examination. The laboratory examination result was that "There were no pathogenic organisms found by bacteriological culture methods." However, on November 12th, thirty eight days after the Japanese plane's visit, Bubonic plague appeared in the same area where the grains and fleas were found in abundance. The epidemic in Chuhsien lasted twenty four days resulting in twenty one deaths.

As far as avilable, records show plague never occurred in Chuhsien before. After careful investigation of the situation it was believed that the strange visit of the enemy plane was the cause of the epidemic and the transmitting

-3-

agent was the rat fleas presumably infected with plague and definitely dropped by the enemy plane.

As plague is primarily a disease of rodents, the grains were probably used to attract the rats and expose them to the infected fleas mixed therein. It was regretable that the fleas collected were not properly examined. Owing to deficient laboratory facilities and animal inoculation test was not performed otherwise it would have been possible to show whether or not the fleas were plague infected and positive result would have been an irrefutable evidence against Japan.

3 - On November 28, 1940 when the plague epidemic in Ningpo and Chuhsien was still in progress three Japanese planes come to Kinhwa, and important commercial city situated between Ningpo and Chuhsien, and there they dropped a large quantity of small granules about the size of shrimp eggs. These strange objects were collected and examined in a local hospital. The granules were more or less round, about one millimeter in diameter, or whitish-yellow, somewhat translucent with a certain amoung of glistening reflection from the surface. When brought into contact with a drop of water on a glass slide the granule began to swell to about twice its original size. In a small amount of water in a test tube with some agitation it would break up into whitish flakes and later form a milky suspension. Microscopic examination of these granules revealed the presence of numberous gram-negative bacilli with distinct bipolar staining in some of them and an abundance of involution forms thus possessing the morphological characteristics of B. Pestis, the positive organism of plague. When cultured in agar medium these gram-negative bacilli showed no growth and because of inadequacy of laboratory facilities animal inoculation best could not be performed.

Upon the receipt of such a startling report from Kinhwa the national health administration dispatched Dr. W.W. Yung, director of the Department

-4-

of epidemic prevention; Dr. H. M. Jettmar, epidemiologist formerly of the League of Nation's epidemic commission, and other technical experts to investigate the situation. When arriving in Kinhwa early in January 1941 they examined twenty six of these granules and confirmed the previous observations, but inoculation tests performed on guinea pigs by Dr. Jettmar gave negative results. It is difficult to say whether or not the lapse of time and the method of preservation of the granules had something to do with the negative results from the animal inoculation test which is a crucial test for B. Pestis. At all events no plague occured in Kinhwa and it indicated that this particular Japanese experiment on bacterial warfare ended in failure.

4 - On November 4, 1941 at about five A.M. a lone enemy plane appeared over Changteh in Hunan province flying very low; the morning being rather misty. Instead of bombs, wheat and rice grains, pieces of paper, cotton wadding and some unidentified particles were dropped. After the all clear signal had been sounded some of these strange gifts from the enemy were collected and sent by the police to a local missionary hospital for examination which revealed the presence of microorganisms reported to resemble B. Pestis.

On November 11th, seven days later, the first clinical case of Plague came to notice, then followed by five more cases by January 13, 1942. The diagnosis of Bubonic plague was definitely confirmed in one of the six cases in November by bacteriological culture method and animal inoculation test.

According to the investigation of Dr. W.W. Chen, bacteriologist, who had had special training in plague work in India, and Dr. R. Pollitzer, epidemiologist of the national health administration and formerly of the League of Nation's epidemic commission, the Changteh Plague epidemic was caused by enemy action because of the following strong circumstantial evidences:

-5-

A - That Changteh has never been, as far as is known, is afflicted by plague. During previous pandemics and severe epidemics elsewhere in China thi part of Hunan, as a matter of fact this part of central China in general, has never been known to come under the scourge of the disease.

B - That the present outbreak may have been due to direct contiguous spread from neighboring plague infected districts is also untenable on epidemiological grounds. Epidemiologically plague spreads along transport routes for grain on which the rats feed. The nearest epidemic center to Changteh is Chuhsie in Chekiang about two thousand kilometers away by land or river communication. Furthermore Changtehh, being a rice producing district, supplies rice to other districts and does not receive rice from other cities. Besides all the cases occurring in Changteh were native inhabitants who had not been away from the city or it immediate environs at all.

C - That all the cases came from the areas within the city where the strange objects dropped by enemy planes were found, and that among the wheat and rice grains and cotton rags were the most probably included infective vectors, probably fleas. The fleas were not noticed on the spot because they were not looked for and because the air raid alarm lasted some twelve hours with the result that the fleas must have in the meantime escaped to other hiding places.

D - That there was no apparent evidence of any excessive rat mortality before and for sometime after the "Aerial incident." About two hundred rats were caught and examined during the months of November and December but no evidence of Plague was found. However, toward the end of January and the first part of February this year among seventy eight rats examined there were eighteen with definite plague infection. As plague is primarily a disease of rodents the did not take place in the present case. The infected flease from the enemy plane must have first attacked mena and a little later the rats.

E - That all the first six human cases were infected within fifteen days after the "Aerial Incident" and that infected fleas are known to be able to survive under suitable conditions for weeks without feeding. The normal incubation period of Bubonic Plague is three to seven days and may occasionally be prolonged to eight or even fourteen days. The time factor is certainly also a strong circumstantial evidence.

5 - A serious epidemic of plague occurring in Suiyuan, Ningsia and Shensi provinces has recently been reported. From the last week of January this year to date there have been some six hundred cases. These cases were reported in a recent communique from the local military in the northwestern part of the epidemic area. However, considering the fact that Plague is known to be enzootic among the native rodents in the ordos region in Suuiyuan one must wait for confirmation of the reports that probably the plague was caused there by enemy action.

The technical experts including Dr. Y. N. Yang, director of the National Health Administration's northwest epidemic prevention bureau, has been sent there to investigate and help control the epidemic.

The innummbration of facts thus far collected leads to the conclusion that the Japanese army has attempted at bacterial warfare in China. In Chekiang and Hunan they had scattered from the air infective materials and succeeded in causing epidemic outbreaks of plague. Aside from temporary terrorisation of the General Population in the afflicted areas this inhuman act of our ememy is most condemnable when one realizes that once the disease has taken root in the local rat population it will continue to infect men for many years to come. Fortunately the mode of infection and the method of control

-7-

of plague are known and it is possible to keep the disease in check by vigorous control measures. Our difficulty at present is the shortage of antiepidemic supplies required. The recent advance in Chemotherapy has given us new drugs that are more or less effective for the treatment of plague cases. These are sulfathiazole and allied sulphonanide compounds which China cannot as yet produce herself.

For prevention, plague vaccine can be produced in considerable quantities by the central epidemic prevention bureau in Kunking and the northwest epidemic prevention bureau in Lanchow, provided the raw materials required for vaccine production such as peptone and agar are available.

Rat proofing of all buildings and eradication of rats are fundamental control measures but under war conditions they cannot be satisfactorily carried out.

If rat poisons such as Cyanogas and Barium carbonate can be obtained from abroad in large quantities deratization campaigns may be launched in cities where aats are a menace.

****

(The above article is by Dr. P. Z. King director of the national health administration.)

3.18 5 May 1942: No. 396, Transmission of report concerning plague situation in unoccupied China, to the Secretary of State, from C. E. Gauss, Embassy of the U. S.

资料出处： National Archives of the United States, R112, E295A, B11.

内容点评： 本资料为1942年5月5日重庆美国驻华大使馆官员C. E. Gauss呈送美国国务卿报告，题目：关于中国未沦陷地区鼠疫流行情况报告。

CONFIDENTIAL

2400.1-5
5 May 1942 MIS

EMBASSY OF THE
UNITED STATES OF AMERICA

No. 396 Chungking, May 5, 1942

SUBJECT: Transmission of report concerning plague situation in unoccupied China.

The Honorable,
The Secretary of State,
Washington, D. C.

Sir:

I have the honor to refer to my despatch no. 323 of March 17, 1942 and to previous despatches concerning outbreaks of bubonic plague in China and to transmit herewith a copy of Epidemological Report no. 4 of the National Health Administration concerning Bubonic Plague in Hunan, the northwestern provinces, Chekiang and Fukien.

The report describes a marked increase during the past two months in the increase in rat plague in Changteh, Hunan, where the original infection is believed by the Chinese authorities to have been the result of Japanese bacteriological warfare. It is stated that there is considerable danger of plague spreading from Changteh owing to that city's position as a rice exporting center and to the shortage of sulfathiazol.

The epidemic of plague in the northwestern provinces appears to have subsided and the situation in Chekiang appears to be under control.

Respectfully yours,

C. E. GAUSS

C. E. Gause

Enclosure:
Copy of a report as stated.

Original and 2 copies by pouch to the Department
812.1
BCHjr/hgd

8419 7

CONFIDENTIAL

no. 1 to despatch no. 396 dated May 5, 1942
American Embassy at Chungking.

(COPY)

EPIDEMIOLOGICAL REPORT NO. 4

National Health Administration

1. Plague in Hunan

Plague appeared for the first time in Changteh, Hunan in the winter of 1941, most probably as a result of Japanese attempt at bacterial warfare, according to the investigation of Dr. R. Pollitzer, epidemiologist of the National Health Administration. From Nov. 11, 1941 to January 13, 1942, there occurred a total of 9 cases. After a period of quiescence for about two months, new cases began to appear as follows:

Number of Plague Cases in Changteh in 1942

Date	No. of Cases	Type of Disease
Jan. 13	1	Bubonic
Mar. 24	1	"
Mar. 28	1	"
April 2	1	"
April 3	1	"
April 7	1	"
April 8	1	"
April 10	1	Pneumonic
April 13	1	Bubonic
April 14	1	"
April 15	1	"
April 17	5	Bubonic 4; Pneumonical
April 18	2	Bubonic

A recent communique from Dr. Pollitzer, dated April 7, states that there is an alarming increase of rat plague as evidenced by the following figures:

Date	No. of Rats Examined	No. of Rats Found infected	Per cent of Infected rats.
Feb. 16-28	114	19	16.7
Mar. 1-15	385	74	19.2
Mar. 16-31	425	107	25.2
April 1-7	145	61	42.1

As plague has already established a foothold among the rat population in Changteh, it is not at all surprising that this second epidemic outbreak was

8419 8

- 2 -

preceded by an epizootic.

The danger of plague invading Szechuen, Hupeh and Kweichow is great, because Changteh is a well-known rice-producing district and because plague is a disease generally spread along rice transportion routes. As a control measure, a "sanitary cordon" has been established around the infected area by setting up quarantine stations at all important traffic junctions. The greatest difficulty encountered is that there is now only a limited quantity of sulfathiazole available for the treatment of cases, and practically no cyanogas at hand to deal with the infected rats and fleas. Preventive inoculations, compulsory isolation and strict quarantine are measures taken at present for control of the situation.

II. Plague in Northwestern Provinces

The most serious epidemic of plague this year occurred in Suiyuan, Ningsha, Shensi and Shansi. It was probably a flaring up of an old infection, as the disease is known to be endemic in those areas. Most of the cases were of the pneumonic type and the mortality rate was high. It was reported at one time that the disease has claimed over 600 victims in two months; but subsequent investigation revealed the following figures:

Province	No. of Plague Cases January 1-April 4, 1942
Suiyuan (Wu-yuan, Lin-ho, Tung-sheng and Chun-ko-erh-chi)	387
Ningsha (Teng-kow)	24
Shensi (Fu-Ku)	30
Shansi (Ho-chu)	13

According to reports received here, the epidemic is now over as there have been no new cases since the first week of April.

III. Plague in Chekiang

To avoid a lengthy description, the plague situation in Chekiang this year may be best shown as follows:

Date	No. of Plague Cases		
	Chu-hsien	I-wu	Tung-yang
Jan. 1-10	0	1	10
11-20	0	5	8
21-31	0	4	

8419 1 9

(Continued)

Date	No. of Plague Cases		
	Chu-hsien	I-wu	Tung-yang
Feb. 1-10	0	1	0
11-20	0	4	0
21-28	0	0	0
Mar. 1-10	0	0	0
11-20	0	3	0
21-31	0	4	4
Apr. 1-10	0	2	4
11	1	?	?

IV. Plague in Fukien

In Fukien where plague has been endemic for many years, the disease has from January 1 to April 5 appeared in 11 hsiens, namely: Yung-an, Tung-an, Lung-hsi, Pu-tien, Chin-men, Yuan-shiao, Ping-tan, Chang-pu, Ku-tien, Nan-an, and Chien-yang. No details have thus far been received.

/s/ W.W. Yung

W.W. Yung, M.D., M.P.H.
Director, Dept. Of Epidemic Prevention

April 23, 1942

3.19 16 May 1942: Letter to Dr. Whayne, Division of Medical Intelligence, Office of the Surgeon-General, WD, from Roger S. Greene

资料出处： National Archives of the United States, R112, E295A, B11.

内容点评： 本资料为 1942 年 5 月 16 日美国国务院 Roger S. Greene 予陆军部军医总长办公室医学情报科 Dr. T. F. Whayne 信函：1942 年 3 月 10 日 Dr. Robert Lim（林可胜）关于常德鼠疫情况来信摘要。

ADDRESS OFFICIAL COMMUNICATIONS TO
THE SECRETARY OF STATE
WASHINGTON, D. C.

DEPARTMENT OF STATE
WASHINGTON

Personal

May 16, 1942.

Dear Dr. Whayne:

Referring to our telephone conversation yesterday, I enclose an extract from a letter from Dr. Robert Lim, dated March 10, 1942, in regard to the plague situation at Changteh. This should be considered in connection with the report dated December 12, 1941, which I believe you have received from the American Bureau for Medical Aid to China.

With regard to the persons who signed the Pathological Report, dated December 12, 1941, I learn that Dr. W. K. Chen has had considerable training in Bacteriology in the Peping Union Medical College, though there seem some doubt about the soundness of his medical education. He had papers on some of his studies in Typhus, Cholera, and Tetanus in the proceedings of the Society for Experimental Biology and Medicine in 1931, 28, 784-86; 1932, 29, 1160-62; 1933, 30, 887-891; 1933, 31, 334-36.

Dr. F. C. Lin who testifies to having examined the material is known to me and I believe is quite competent for routine diagnosis.

Sincerely yours,

Roger S. Greene

Roger S. Greene

Enclosure:
Extract from letter.

Dr. T. F. Whayne,
Division of Medical Intelligence,
Office of the Surgeon-General,
War Department,
1818 H Street, N. W.,
Washington, D. C.

China #1

EXCERPTS ON PLAGUE FROM A LETTER OF DR. LIM'S FROM CHUNGKING, dated March 10th, 1942

"At the western end of the line in this South-Central area (western shore of the Tung Ting lake) plague has broken out at Changteh. Evidence points strongly to the spreading of plague through the dropping of plague infected fleas with grain from an enemy plane. Plague is unknown in this region (no history for 200 years at least), and Changteh is not in communication with other plague areas in Chekiang and Fukien. A report has been sent to you and the Rockefeller Foundation. The date of the dropping of plague infected materials by a plane was Nov. 4, 1941. Less than a dozen cases (proved by autopsy, clinical history, bacteriological culture and animal passage) have occurred between November and February this year, but the latest report is that of a small number of rats examined recently, 40% were proved to have died of plague. This augurs ill for the coming summer, when the rat flea will multiply. I refer again to the need for sulfathiazole, cyanogas dust, and pumps. We are going ahead, along with the Government Laboratories to produce plague vaccine, and are sending a man to the Haffkine Institute, India to learn the latest technique. The Weishengshu is also sending a man; both men are being supported by the Rockefeller Foundation (arranged by Dr. Balfour).

"Central East - (Eastern Kiangsi, Southern Anhuei, Kinagsu, Chekiang & Fukien). Here the line remains unchanged, running north of the Poyang lake along the Yangtze river to just below Wuhu, and then straight across country to Hangchow. The blockade against small traffic from Shanghai is not strict, and numbers of people and a small amount of local goods are coming through Hangchow, and the Chekiang coast.

"The main trouble here is plague, which is alleged to have started from the dropping of plague infected materials in Chekiang. About this we are not certain, as plague is endemic in Fukien and might have spread north to Chekiang and westward to adjacent parts of Kiangsi, because the sea blockade has driven trade along inland highways. However, in view of the outbreak at Changteh, it is possible that the origin of plague in Chekiang is also due to enemy planes. The epidemic is spreading and is affecting a good many places in Chekiang and along the borders of Chekiang, Kiangsi, and Fukien. We lost a unit leader (doctor) from plague at the end of last year. We have sent all the ABMAC sulfathiazole we could spare. The ARC shipped vaccine, cyanogas and pumps by plane from Hongkong to Nanhsiung at our request last year and our trucks brought these supplies to Chekiang.

"We are now organizing training in combatting plague, and hope to tighten up anti-epidemic measures against this disease throughout the country."

RECEIVED BY THE AMERICAN BUREAU FOR MEDICAL AID TO CHINA on May 8, 1942

3.20 REPORT ON PLAGUE IN CHANGTEH AND MEASURES FOR ITS CONTROL BY WANG SZE HENG

资料出处：中国第二历史档案馆藏，档案号：372（2）–16。

内容点评：本资料为 1942 年 7 月 20 日王诗恒（S. H. Wang）英文论文《常德鼠疫及其防治措施》。王诗恒当时为贵阳医学院 1944 级学生，1942 年赴湖南进行公共卫生方面的实习。这篇论文由当时在常德指导鼠疫防疫的国际红十字会防疫专家伯力士（R. Pollitzer）指导，是当时最完整的关于常德细菌战鼠疫的流行病观察报告。

REPORT ON PLAGUE IN CHINGTEH AND MEASURES FOR ITS CONTROL

BY WANG SZE HING (王詩恒)

00498

ACKNOWLEDGMENT

I must express my sincerest gratitude to Dr.R.Pollitzer for his invaluable encouragement and advices in this work and his kindness in giving me permission to use his data.I am also much indebted to Dr.C.J.Chen for his constant encouragement and suggestions made on this paper.

S.H.Wang
July 20th,1942.

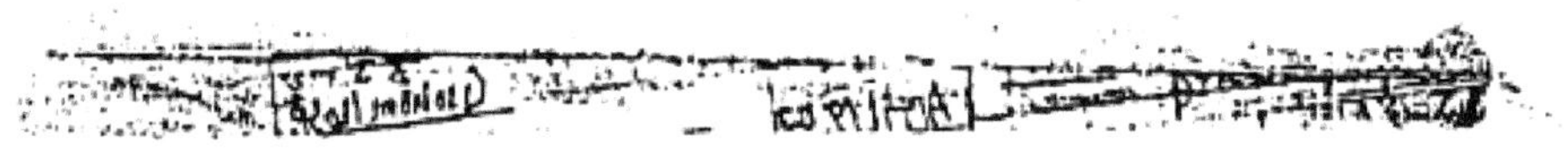

00..!0

CONTENTS:

PART ONE—
Study of Rats, Fleas, and Human Cases of Plague in Changteh.
A. History of the Outbreak.
B. Study of Human Plague.
C. Study of Rodents.
D. Study of Fleas.
E. Discussion of Study.

PART TWO--
Detailed Duscussion of Measures for the Control of Plague.
A. Measures in Plague-infected Districts.
B. Measures around Foci of Infection.

SUMMARY--

· 馆址

REPORT ON PLAGUE IN CHANGTEH AND MEASURES FOR ITS CONTROL
PART ONE
Study of Rats. Fleas and Human Cases of Plague
A. History of the outbreak:
We are engaged in the fithting of a bacteriological warfare, the terrible pest first introfuced into this province of Human by the enemy. In the early morning of November the 4th,1941 one Japanese airplane flew very low over the city of Changteh and dropped some unshunked rice and cotten pieces at Kwan-mia Street (関廟街) and Chi-n lane (鶏鵝巷)which are near the center of the city. These things were collected and sent to the local mission hospital (Kangteh Hospital) for analysis.Smear from them showed some Gram-negative bipolar-stained bacillivery suggest of B.pestis together with some Sort of Gram positive bacilli.Culture also done and the same sort of Gram-negative bacilli were found.But animal experiment with rabbits failed to show any result while white mice and guinea pigs were inobtainab at that time.On November the 11th it was said among the people that many dead rats were found at Kwan-mia Street and Chi-n lane and several people there died of acute illness in one or two days.Unfortunately no rats were sent to the hospital for examinationand no such sick people came to the hospital until the morning of November the12th 1941 when a girl from Kwan-mia Street,acutelyill,was brought to the Kwangteh hospital by her mother. Blood smear from Her showed the presence of bipolar-stained bacilli She died in the next morning,only thirty six hours from the onset of for illness.Post-mortem examination was done and revealed the case to be even more suspicious of plague. Three more case, one dead bodyand two patients, were examined and found to be positive for the same sort of bacilli on Nov.13th and 14th. It was not until Nov. 24th when the fourth patient who came into our hands gave us a chance to prove the exitence of plague by successful animal inoculation of guunea pigs. No doubt the first four case must be plague and probably also some of those who died of acute illness shortly before Nov. the 12th . The existence of plague was scientifically proved. As there is no written record of plague infection ever existed in Human and the sudden appearance of many dead rats and rapidly dying patient at places where suspicious plague-infected rice and cotton were dropped and exactly at an interval of time quite consistent with the incubation period of plague undoubtedly confirmed the enemy as the introductory agent of this plague epi[illegible] in Changteh .
A study of the 18 human case and 23 dead bodies of plague, of the 1879 examined rats and of the 3536 fleas collected form the examined rats during the period of Nov.12,1941-June 30,1942
B.Study on Human Plague:
The first case we encountered was a 12 year old girl from Kwan-mia Street sent to the Kwangteh hospital on Nov.the 12th.

0042

was presented a typical clical picture of septicemic plague and plague bacilli were demonstrated in number-right the peripheral blood on first day of admission and numerous in number right before death. Two more case of plague (Tab.1 case No. 2+3). both of typical of the both bubonic type, were seen on Nov.13th and 14th and both died soon afterwards. In the morning of Nov. 14th a doctor in the Red Cross Unit stopped a coffin on the way and seen the dead body for post mortem examination as soon as he found the history suspicious. B.pestis was again demonstrated in smears taken from liver and spleen (Tab,1case No. 4). On Nov. 24th a bubonic case of plague was reported and examined and the diagnosis of plague was made both clinically and bacteriologically. Dr, W.K.Chen(陈文贵) was then in Changteh and he performed guinea pig inoculations which after wards proved to be positive. The existence of plague was then definitely confirmed. Orders and therefore sent out that all sick and dead must be reported and examined. In this way we obtained our case on recors in Table 1. Patients who are sus-picious or definitely proved to be suffering from plague are immediately sent to the Isolation H-ospital out side of East Gate and contacts segregated for close watch. Partial post-mortem examination was done with the dead bodies instead of a complete one as the latter was more dangerous and are sed more general resentment of the peoole. Those cadavers suspicious or definitely positive for plague were at first burned but later this method was abandoned because of the strong objection of the people. Such dead bodies were then buried in public cemetery espaciously for this purpose instead of being bruned, Of course there must be many case which we missed since no quarantine station or guards were installed during the first few months and intelligence service was porly organized. The people also tried every means to hide the sick and the dead in order to avoid of being quarentined or examined post mortem. There are only 2 case in December (Tab. I + III), one in Jannary none inFebruary and two in the last third of march. InApril the incidence of human plague suddenly short up. 20 out of the total 39 case examinad in April were found to be definitely positive and three suspicious Among the positive case there was one 5-year old boy (Tab.Icase No.II)who had sudden onset of high fever with rigidity of neck and soon fell into comatous condition. Cerebro-spinal fluid withdrawn was clear but slightly under preddure and microscopically no definite organisms were fpund, while his blood smear was definitely positive for B. pestis. This might be case of plague meningitis. There are two female case (Tab,I Case No.16+17) from one Chen family. one was of the bubonic type with septicemia, and another had tender glands at groin and later developed secondary pneumonic plague. They bothdied soon after admission. For the rest of the cases refer to Tab.I

The first patient was treaded with sulfanilamide together with general symptomatictreatments, while the other cases during the early months were mostly seen too late to allow any treatment. Since March we had got sulfathiazole and began to treat pat ents with it, a new treatment first tried in India. Up to then all the pateints who came into the hospital died and this

00161
place where the infected rice cotton were dropped
place where plague-positive rats were found
plague-positive patients or dead body was found

[illegible] of Human Plague in Changteh Nov. 12, 1941 – June 30, 1942

Date of Death	Discharged Well	Total Time of [illegible]	Chief Symptoms & Signs	Laboratory Findings: Specimens from Patients	Laboratory Findings: Specimens from Dead Bodies	Diagnosis	Inoculations of Plague Vac. 1st	2nd	3rd	Remarks
Nov. 13, 41	—	1½ days	Sudden chill, high fever, headache	Blood smear [illegible]	Liver, spleen smears B. pestis +	Plague septicemic	—	—	—	Rabbits inoculated with patient's blood culture to prove the experiment
[illegible] 14, 41	—	½ day	[illegible] gland enlarged	Juice fr. bubo: B. pestis +	—	Plague bubonic	—	—	—	
[illegible] 13, 41	—	[illegible]	[illegible] gland enlarged	Juice fr. bubo: B. pestis +	—	Plague bubonic	—	—	—	
[illegible] 24, 41	—	[illegible]	Sudden high fever	—	Liver smear B. pestis +	Plague septicemic	—	—	—	
[illegible] 24, 41	—	[illegible]	Sudden high fever, [illegible] inguinal gland enlarged	[illegible]	Spleen [illegible] B. pestis +	Plague bubonic	—	—	—	Guinea pig inoculation [illegible]
[illegible] 14, 41	—	[illegible]	Sudden [illegible] fever, [illegible]	Blood smear [illegible] B. pestis +	Spleen [illegible] B. pestis +	Plague bubonic	—	—	—	
[illegible] 20, 41	—	[illegible]		—	Spleen, liver [illegible] B. pestis +	Plague bubonic	—	—	—	
[illegible] 13, 42	—	[illegible]		—	Spleen [illegible] B. pestis +	Plague bubonic	—	—	—	
[illegible] 24, 42	—	[illegible]	[illegible] and abdomen	—	Spleen [illegible] B. pestis +	Plague septicemic	—	—	—	[illegible]
[illegible] 20, 42	—	[illegible]	Inguinal gland enlarged	Bubo B. pestis +	—	Plague bubonic	—	—	—	Sulfathiazole taken: [illegible] tablets
[illegible] 5, 42	—	[illegible]	[illegible]	[illegible] B. pestis +	—	[illegible]	—	—	—	Sulfathiazole taken: [illegible] tab.
[illegible] 2, 42	—	[illegible]	[illegible]	—	Spleen [illegible] B. pestis +	Plague bubonic	—	—	—	
[illegible] 12, 42	—	[illegible]	[illegible] inguinal gland enlarged	Juice from bubo: B. pestis +	—	Plague bubonic	—	—	—	Sulfathiazole taken: 56 tab.
[illegible] 6, 42	—	[illegible]	[illegible] gland enlarged, [illegible] body	—	Liver smear [illegible]	Plague bubonic	—	—	—	
[illegible] 6, 42	—	[illegible]	Cough & bloody sputum	—	Spleen [illegible] B. pestis +	Plague pneumonic	—	—	—	
[illegible] 11, 42	—	[illegible]	[illegible] inguinal [illegible] enlarged	Sputum B. pestis +	—	Plague pneumonic (secondary)	—	—	—	Sulfathiazole taken: 22 tab.
[illegible] 11, 42	—	[illegible]	Cervical gland enlarged	Blood smear B. pestis +	—	Plague bubonic & septicemic	—	—	—	Sulfathiazole taken 24 tab.
—	May 19, 42	38 [illegible]	Fever, cough, bloody sputum	Sputum (April 15) B. pestis +	—	Plague pneumonic	April 7.	—	—	Sulfathiazole taken: 242 tab.
[illegible] 12, 42	—	[illegible]	Cough & bloody sputum	—	Spleen [illegible] B. pestis +	Plague pneumonic	—	—	—	
[illegible] 12, 42	—	[illegible]	[illegible]	—	Spleen & liver [illegible] B. pestis +	Plague septicemic	—	—	—	
[illegible] 14, 42	—	[illegible]	[illegible]	—	Spleen B. pestis +	Plague septicemic	—	—	—	
[illegible] 17, 42	—	[illegible]	[illegible] cervical gland enlarged.	—	Spleen & liver B. pestis	Plague bubonic	—	—	—	
—	May 14, 42	[illegible]	[illegible] inguinal gland enlarged [illegible]	Juice fr. bubo: B. pestis +	—	Plague bubonic.	April 3	April 10	—	Sulfathiazole taken: 40 tab.
—	May 18, 42	[illegible]	[illegible] inguinal gland enlarged [illegible]	Juice fr. bubo: B. pestis +	—	Plague bubonic	April 3	April 10	—	Sulfathiazole taken: [illegible] tab.
[illegible] 17, 42	—	[illegible]	Cough & bloody sputum	—	Spleen [illegible]	Plague pneumonic	—	—	—	
[illegible] 1, 42	—	[illegible]	[illegible]	—	Spleen B. pestis +	Plague pneumonic	—	—	—	Said to have [illegible]
—	May 21, 42	[illegible]	[illegible] inguinal gland enlarged	Bubo juice B. pestis +	—	Plague bubonic	April 7.	April 14	—	Sulfathiazole taken: 234 tab.
[illegible] 19, 42	—	[illegible]	Cough & bloody sputum	—	Spleen & liver [illegible]	Plague pneumonic	—	—	—	
[illegible]	—	[illegible]	Cough, aching [illegible]	—	Liver: B. pestis +	Plague septicemic	—	—	—	Date of [illegible] the family [illegible]
[illegible]	[illegible]	[illegible]	[illegible]	[illegible]	Spleen [illegible]	Plague septicemic	—	—	—	
[illegible]	May 16, 42	[illegible]	Rt. inguinal gland enlarged.	Juice fr. bubo: B. pestis +	—	Plague bubonic	April 1	April 8	April 15	Sulfathiazole taken: [illegible] tab.
[illegible] 24, 42	[illegible]	[illegible]	[illegible]	[illegible]	Spleen & liver [illegible]	Plague septicemic	—	—	—	
[illegible] 24, 42	[illegible]	[illegible]	Fever & delirium.	[illegible]	Spleen B. pestis +	Plague septicemic	—	—	—	
[illegible] 2, 42	[illegible]	[illegible]	[illegible] axillary gland enlarged.	Blood smear [illegible]	—	Plague bubonic	—	—	—	Sulfathiazole taken: [illegible] tab.
[illegible] 4, 42	[illegible]	[illegible]	Cough and hemoptysis.	[illegible]	Spleen B. pestis +	Plague septicemic	March 2	—	—	
[illegible] 11, 42	[illegible]	[illegible]	[illegible]	[illegible]	Spleen & liver B. pestis +	Plague septicemic	—	—	—	
May 7, 42	[illegible]	[illegible]	[illegible]	—	Liver B. pestis +	Plague septicemic	—	—	—	
May 7, 42	[illegible]	[illegible]	[illegible] gland enlarged, [illegible]	—	Liver B. pestis +	Plague septicemic	—	—	—	
[illegible]	[illegible]	[illegible]	Lt. inguinal gland [illegible]	Juice from bubo: B. pestis + +	Spleen & liver: B. pestis +	Plague bubonic	—	—	—	
[illegible]	[illegible]	[illegible]	[illegible] on chest.	[illegible]	—	Plague septicemic	—	—	—	
[illegible]	[illegible]	[illegible]	High fever, [illegible]	Blood smear: B. pestis + +	—	Plague bubonic	—	—	—	

TABLE I Detailed Record of Hu[illegible]

No.	Name	Sex	Age	Occupation	Locality	Date of Reporting	Date Onset of Illness	Date Admitted to Hospital	Date Occurrence of Death	Date Discharged Well	Total Time of Isolation
1.	蔡桃兒	♀	12	[illegible]	關廟街蔡洪盛號	Nov.12.41.	Nov.11.41.	Nov.12.41.	Nov.13.41.	—	1 12/24 days (Kwangteh Hos)
2.	徐老三	♂	25	Workman	北門內常德 [illegible]	Nov.14.41.	Nov.12.41.	Nov.14.41.	Nov.14.41.	—	1/2 day (Kwangteh Hos)
3.	聶述生	♂	58	Merchant	啟明鎮 [illegible]	Nov.13.41.	Nov.12.41.	—	Nov.13.41.	—	—
4.	蔡玉珍	♀	27	Housewife	東門內常清街	Nov.14.41.	Nov.11.41.	—	Nov.24.41.	—	—
5.	龔超勝	♂	28	Servant	關廟前街 18號	Nov.24.41.	Nov.23.41.	—	Dec.2.41.	—	—
6.	王瑞生	♂	38	Coppersmith	東門內永安街 [illegible]	Dec.14.41.	Dec.13.41.	Dec.14.41.	Dec.14.41.	—	3/24 (Isolation Hos)
7.	王貴秀	♀	15	Peddler	三板橋 [illegible]	Dec.19.41.	Dec.18.41.	Dec.19.41.	Dec.20.41.	—	[illegible] (Isolation Hos)
8.	胡嫂	♀	30	Servant	關廟街楊家巷	Jan.13.42.	Jan.11.42.	—	Jan.13.42.	—	—
9.	向玉新	♂	50	Peddler	三華嚴巷 52號	March 24.42.	March 20.42.	—	March 24.42.	—	—
10.	陳孔紀	♂	52	Pao-chang	(His home is in [illegible])	March 24.42.	March 21.42.	March 24.42.	March 28.42.	—	4/24 (Isolation Hos)
11.	陳桃???	♂	5		[illegible]	April 2.42.	March 30.42.	April 2.42.	April 5.42.	—	[illegible] (Kwangteh Hos)
12.	蔣???	♂	45	Peddler	北門內 [illegible]	April 3.42.	April 1.42.	—	April 2.42.	—	—
13.	鄧???	♂	32	Reporter	[illegible]	April 6.42.	April 5.42.	April 6.42.	April 12.42.	—	6 (Isolation Hos)
14.	[illegible]	♂	[illegible]	Student	[illegible]	April 7.42.	April 1.42.	—	April 6.42.	—	—
15.	張金?	♂	15	Servant	[illegible]	April 7.42.	April 1.42.	—	April 6.42.	—	—
16.	陳???	♀	[illegible]	Housewife	法院西街 [illegible]	April 9.42.	April 6.42.	April 9.42.	April 11.42.	—	2 (Isolation Hos)
17.	陳???	♀	[illegible]	[illegible]	法院西街 [illegible]	April 9.42.	April 6.42.	April 9.42.	April 11.42.	—	2 (Isolation Hos)
18.	[illegible]	♂	27	Reporter	[illegible]	April 11.42.	April 9.42.	April 11.42.	—	May 19.42.	38 (Isolation Hos)
19.	[illegible]	♀	26	Housewife	三板橋 [illegible]	April 13.42.	April 10.42.	—	April 12.42.	—	—
20.	毛仁山	♂	60	[illegible]	五鋪街 [illegible]	April 14.42.	April 11.42.	—	April 12.42.	—	—
21.	[illegible]	♀	[illegible]	Housewife	法院西街 [illegible]	April 15.42.	April 11.42.	—	April 14.42.	—	—
22.	[illegible]	♂	[illegible]	Mason	五鋪街 [illegible]	April 17.42.	April 15.42.	—	April 17.42.	—	—
23.	楊???	♂	[illegible]	Student	五鋪街 [illegible]	April 17.42.	April 13.42.	April 17.42.	—	May 14.42.	27 (Kwangteh Hos)
24.	楊???	♀	[illegible]	Student	五鋪街 [illegible]	April 17.42.	April 15.42.	April 17.42.	—	May 18.42.	31 (Kwangteh Hos)
25.	陳???	♂	5[illegible]	Merchant	五鋪街 [illegible]	April 17.42.	April 14.42.	—	April 17.42.	—	—
26.	[illegible]	♀	[illegible]	Housewife	[illegible]	April 18.42.	Jan.30.42.	—	April 18.42.	—	—
27.	[illegible]	♂	32	Reporter	[illegible]	April 15.42.	April 16.42.	April 15.42.	—	May 21.42.	33 (Guandam Hos)
28.	[illegible]	♀	[illegible]	Servant	北門 [illegible]	April 17.42.	April 13.42.	—	April 17.42.	—	—
29.	[illegible]	♀	68	Housewife	[illegible]	April 17.42.	Jan.30.42.	—	April 18.42.	—	—
30.	[illegible]	♀	[illegible]	Housewife	[illegible]	April 20.42.	April 13.42.	—	April 17.42.	—	—
31.	[illegible]	♂	2[illegible]	Merchant	[illegible]	April 25.42.	April 24.42.	April 25.42.	—	May 16.42.	2[illegible] (Isolation Hos)
32.	[illegible]	♀	49	Housewife	[illegible]	April 25.42.	April 17.42.	—	April 24.42.	—	—
33.	[illegible]	♀	53	Farmer	五鋪街 [illegible]	April 30.42.	April 21.42.	—	April 24.42.	—	—
34.	[illegible]	♀	37	Housewife	五鋪街 [illegible]	May 2.42.	April 10.42.	May 2.4[illegible]	May 3.42.	—	18/24 (Isolation Hos)
35.	[illegible]	♂	4[illegible]	Carpenter	五鋪街 [illegible]	May 2.42.	April 21.42.	—	May 2.42.	—	—
36.	王???	♂	[illegible]	Peddler	[illegible]	May 7.42.	May 5.42.	—	May 7.42.	—	—
37.	李???	♀	26	Housewife	[illegible]	May 9.42.	May 5.42.	—	May 7.42.	—	—
38.	[illegible]	♀	5[illegible]	Housewife	[illegible]	May 10.42.	May 4.42.	—	May 7.42.	—	—
39.	[illegible]	♀	33	Housewife	五鋪街 [illegible]	May 17.42.	May 15.42.	May 17.4[illegible]	May 18.42.	—	7 (Kwangteh Hos)
40.	龍???	♂	51	Merchant	[illegible]	June 3.42.	May 22.42.	—	June 2.42.	—	—
41.	趙丁生	♂	13	Apprentice of a Shop	[illegible]	June 15.42.	June 13.42.	June 15.4[illegible]	June 15.42.	—	3/24 (Isolation Hos)

Patients (underlined with red pencil) altogether 18 Dead bodies altogether 23

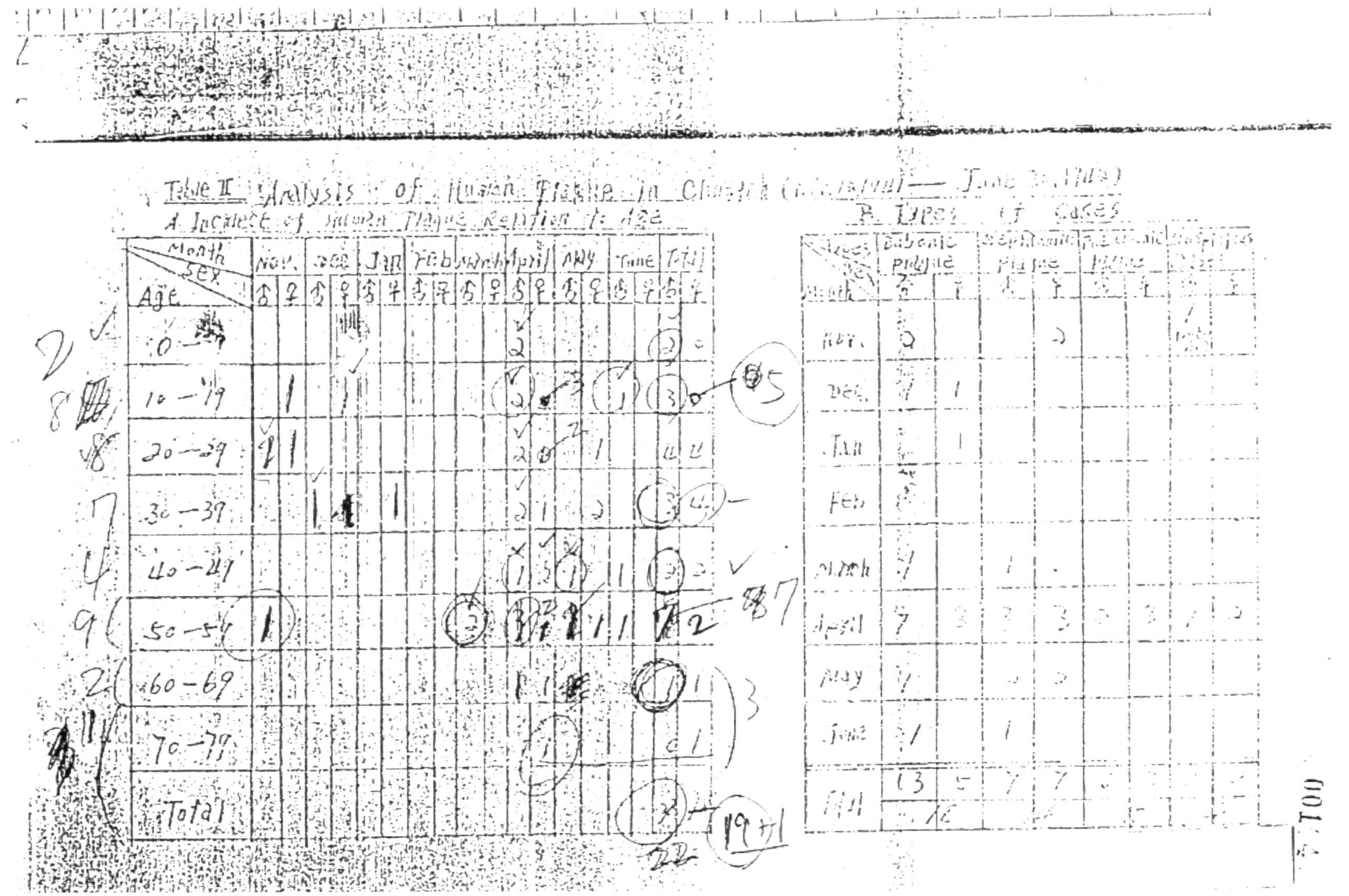

001[illegible]

Table II. Analysis of Human Plague in Changteh ([illegible] — June [illegible])

A. Incidence of Human Plague Relation to Age

Month / Sex / Age	Nov. ♂	Nov. ♀	Dec. ♂	Dec. ♀	Jan ♂	Jan ♀	Feb ♂	Feb ♀	March ♂	March ♀	April ♂	April ♀	May ♂	May ♀	June ♂	June ♀	Total ♂	Total ♀
0—9											2						2	[illegible]
10—19		1		1							2				1		3	
20—29	2	1									2	0		1			4	4
30—39			1	1		1					2	1		2			3	4
40—49											1	5	1		1		3	2
50—59	1								3		3	1	1	1	1		1	2
60—69											1	1	[illegible]				1	1
70—79												1					2	1
Total																	[illegible]	

B. Types of Cases

Types / Month	Bubonic plague ♂	Bubonic plague ♀	Septicemic plague ♂	Septicemic plague ♀	Pneumonic plague ♂	Pneumonic plague ♀	[illegible] ♂	[illegible] ♀
Nov.	2			2			1	
Dec.	2	1						
Jan	2	1						
Feb	2							
March	4		1	.				
April	7	2	2	3	2	3	1	2
May	2		2	2				
June	1		1					
All	13	5	7	7	[illegible]			[illegible]
	16							

00105

Table II C. Incidence of human Plague in Relation to Locality

District	Street Name \ Month / Sex	Nov. ♂	Nov. ♀	Dec. ♂	Dec. ♀	Jan. ♂	Jan. ♀	Feb ♂	Feb ♀	March ♂	March ♀	April ♂	April ♀	May ♂	May ♀	June ♂	June ♀	Total ♂	Total ♀
城區中心部	関廟街	1	1				1			1								2	3
	長清街		1															0	1
	華嚴巷									1								1	0
	府坪街											1						1	0
	洗脚西街												3					0	3
	衛門口											1						1	0
城東區	府前街	1																1	0
	永安街				1													1	0
	五鋪街											6	1	1	2			7	3
	米市橋												1					0	1
	三鋪街															1		1	0
	西園巷															1		1	0
城南區	大河街												1					0	1
	下南門											1						1	0
	双忠街													1	1			0	1
城北區	呂角湾	1																1	0
	三板橋				1								1					0	2
	長老子											1						1	0
	神象子												(1)	2				0	1
	北正街												(1)					0	1
	孫祖祠													0	1			0	1
	隆慶橋												0	1				1	0
郊鄉	呂南樹											1						1	0
	山閣廟											2						2	0
	清平鄉												1					0	1
Total																		23	18

Time	Patients			Dead Bodies			Total Cases of Plague	
	Total Examd	Positive	Suspicious	Total Examd	Positive	Suspicious	Positive	Suspicious
Nov. 12-30th		2	1		2	0	4	1
Dec 1-15th		1	0		0	[illegible]	[illegible]	[illegible]
Dec 16-31th		1	0		0	0	1	[illegible]
Total for Dec		2	0		0	0	2	0
Jan 1-15th		0	0		1	0	1	[illegible]
Jan 16-31th		0	0		0	0	0	0
Total for Jan		0	0		1	0	1	0
Feb 1-15th	1	0	0	0	0	0	0	0
Feb 16-30th	0	0	0		0	0	0	0
Total for Feb	1	0	0	0	0	0	0	0
March 1-15th	0	0	0	0	0	0	0	[illegible]
March 16-31th	1	1	0	3	1	0	2	[illegible]
Total For March	1	1	0	3	1	0	2	0
April 1-15th	9	5	0	6	6	0	11	[illegible]
April 16-30th	10	4	0	14	5	3	9	3
Total For April	19	9	0	20	11	3	20	3
May 1-15th	2	1	0	4	4	0	5	0
May 16-31th	1	1	0	0	0	0	1	0
Total For May	3	2	0	4	4	0	6	0
June 1-15th	3	1	0	[illegible]	1	0	1	0
June 16-30th	5	0	0	3	0	0	0	0
Total For June	8	1	0	6	1	0	2	0
Total For Period Nov. 12 1941—June 30, 42		17	1		20	3	37	4

Table III Record of Human Plague examined in Changteh

001?6

mad the people even more reluctant to be sent there when they got sick. Since April 11th we had five cases who finally did recover and left the hospital in good condition through sulfathiazole treatment. Among these five there was one pneumonic patient 'Tab. I Case No. 18' and four bouhonic patients9(Case No. 23 24 27 31) of which two came from one family (Case No. 23 24). that patient suffering from primary pneumonic plague is a single man who serves as a reporter in the local newspaper. He was admitted on the third day after onset of disease. Fortunately no more pneumonic patients appeared in the same place. No case of septicemic has so far been cured. There has been no bad effect of sulfathiazole in our trial except slight and passing hematuria in few instances, and some patients even tolerated more than 200 tablets.

There were 5 case sinces in May, 2 in first half of Junly and no case sice then. A detailed record of the human cases and analysis of the cases with regard to age and sex locality and types of the cases can be seen in Table II A, B, C. and the map.

G. Study on rodents:

Some of the rodents notably rats, are well-known reserviors of plague infection for men. The study of rats is therefore absolutly necessary during a plague epidemic In Chang'teh no rats were examined until December 1941 when Dr. R. Pollitzer, the plague sepicialist, arrived at the city. Since then the rats have been properly studied by him. It has been so arranged that every Pao had to furnish weekly three rats, dead or alive one dollar fien for the every one rat. But of course short of the difficulty for the rat collection was great and often there were not enough rats for study. Therefore the figures we have got for the percentages of the infected rident was not absolutly accurate, but anyhow they can give us rough idea of the epizootic condition and it does seem to, correspond with the epidemic. There were altogether 1879 rats examined during the peroid of December 24th 1941 to June 30th, 1942, (Tab. IV) of whih 415 were found to be positive and 139 suspicioue. The average percentages for the months Junuary February and March were and 20 percent but in April it shot up to 44.40 percent, while from May it again declined. For detailed data please refer to Table IV and Chart I A.B. THe daily percentages of infected rats together with the number of the same in April are plotted in Chart II. The distribution of the infective ratsis roughly spotted on the map and tabulated on Table V.

It should be state that the microscopic findings do not correspond persistently to the microscopic findings in the rats. Sometime rats proved to be positive microscopically do show gross pathological changes of the organs such as subcutaneous congestion enlargement and congestion of spleen and liver and enlarge gland often oven with the typical sign of effusion of pleural cavity. But others are positive only microscopically wethout any visible changes seen in the dissedting room. It is usually during the active phase of the epizootic that we often find gross changes in the rats

8.100

Table IV Record of Rodents Examined in Changteh (Dec. 20, 1941 — June 30, 1942)

Time	Number of Rodents Examined				Number found positive				Number found Suspicious				Percentage of Rodents Infected			
	Rattus Norvegicus	Rattus Rattus	Mice	Total	Rattus Norvegicus	Rattus Rattus	Mice	Total	Rattus Norvegicus	Rattus Rattus	Mice	Total	Rattus Norvegicus	Rattus Rattus	Mice	Total
Dec. 20–Jan. 3 / Jan 30–31th	28	30	1	59				5								8.45%
Feb 1–15th	15	37	2	54	7	6	0	13	1	3	0	4	46.66%	16.21%	0	[illegible]
Feb 16–28th	53	52	9	114	2	15	2	17	4	1	1	6	3.77%	28.84%	[illegible]	[illegible]
Total For Feb	68	89	11	168	9	21	2	32	5	4	1	10	13.24%	23.60%	18.00%	19.04%
March 1–15th	100	237	48	385	4	68	2	[illegible]	12	16	7	35	4.00%	[illegible]	[illegible]	[illegible]
March 16th–31	94	[illegible]	37	425	15	89	3	[illegible]	10	23	8	[illegible]	13.95%	30.27%	8.10%	[illegible]
Total For March	194	531	85	810	19	157	5	181	22	39	15	76	9.80%	29.56%	5.90%	22.35%
April 1–15th	52	187	22	261	17	98	3	118	4	13	2	17	32.7[illegible]%	[illegible]	[illegible]	[illegible]
April 16–30	20	69	9	98	3	36	2	41	0	[illegible]	0	2	15.00%	52.17%	22.22%	[illegible]
Total for April	72	256	31	359	20	134	5	159	4	15	2	21	27.77%	52.34%	16.13%	44.40%
May 1–15th	10	40	10	60	2	8	3	13	2	3	2	7	20.00%	20.00%	30.00%	[illegible]
May 16–31	14	79	59	152	1	7	8	16	1	10	6	17	7.14%	8.86%	13.56%	[illegible]
Total for May	24	119	69	212	3	15	11	29	3	13	8	24	12.50%	12.60%	15.94%	13.65%
June 1–15th	12	50	66	128	2	2	1	5	0	1	2	3	16.66%	4.00%	1.51%	[illegible]
June 16–30	18	87	38	143	0	3	1	4	4	1	4	5	0.00%	3.44%	2.63%	[illegible]
Total for June	30	137	104	271	2	5	2	9	0	2	6	8	6.00%	3.65%	1.92%	3.32%
Total for above months	416	1162	301	1877				415				139				22.0[illegible]%

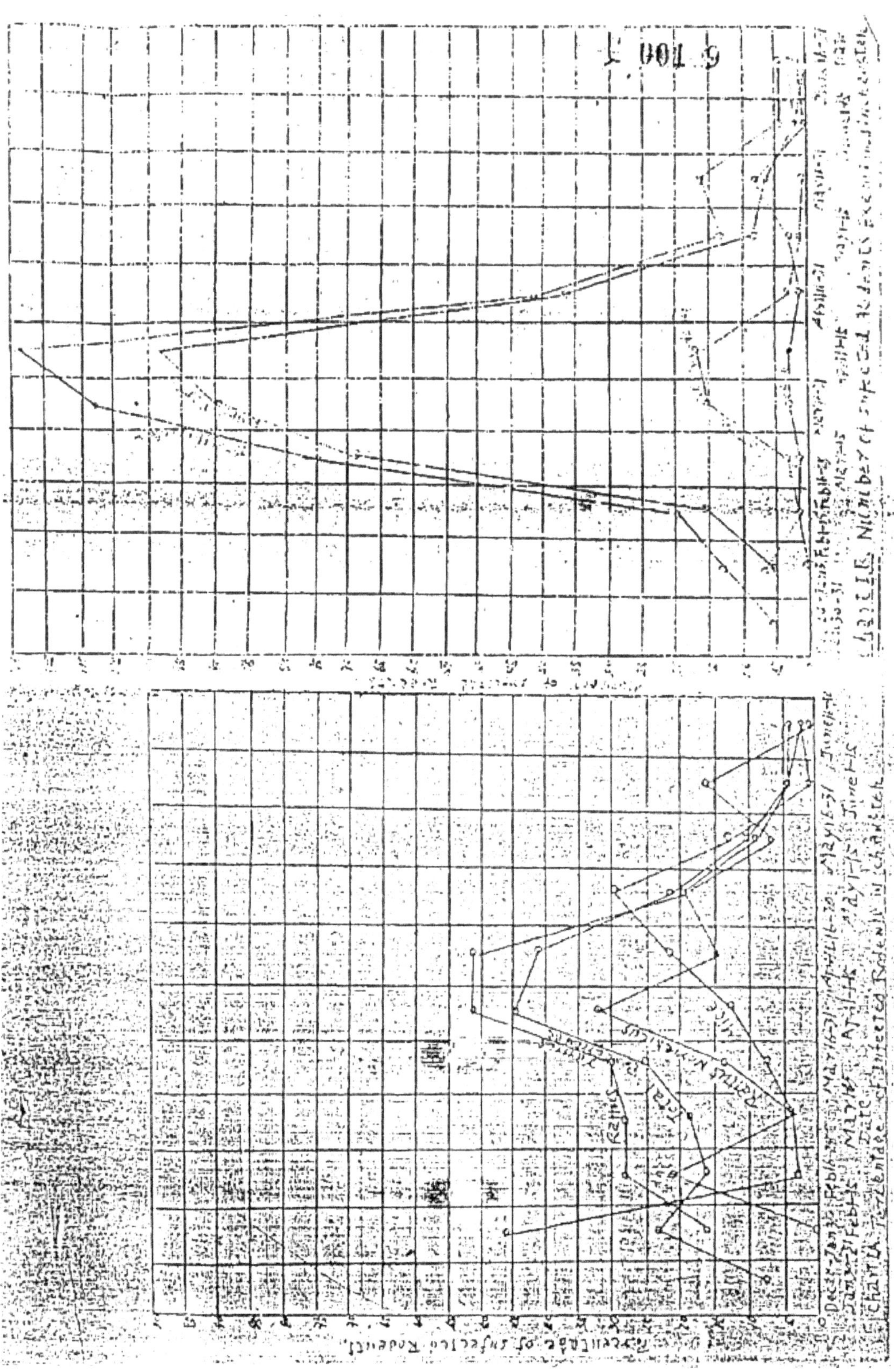

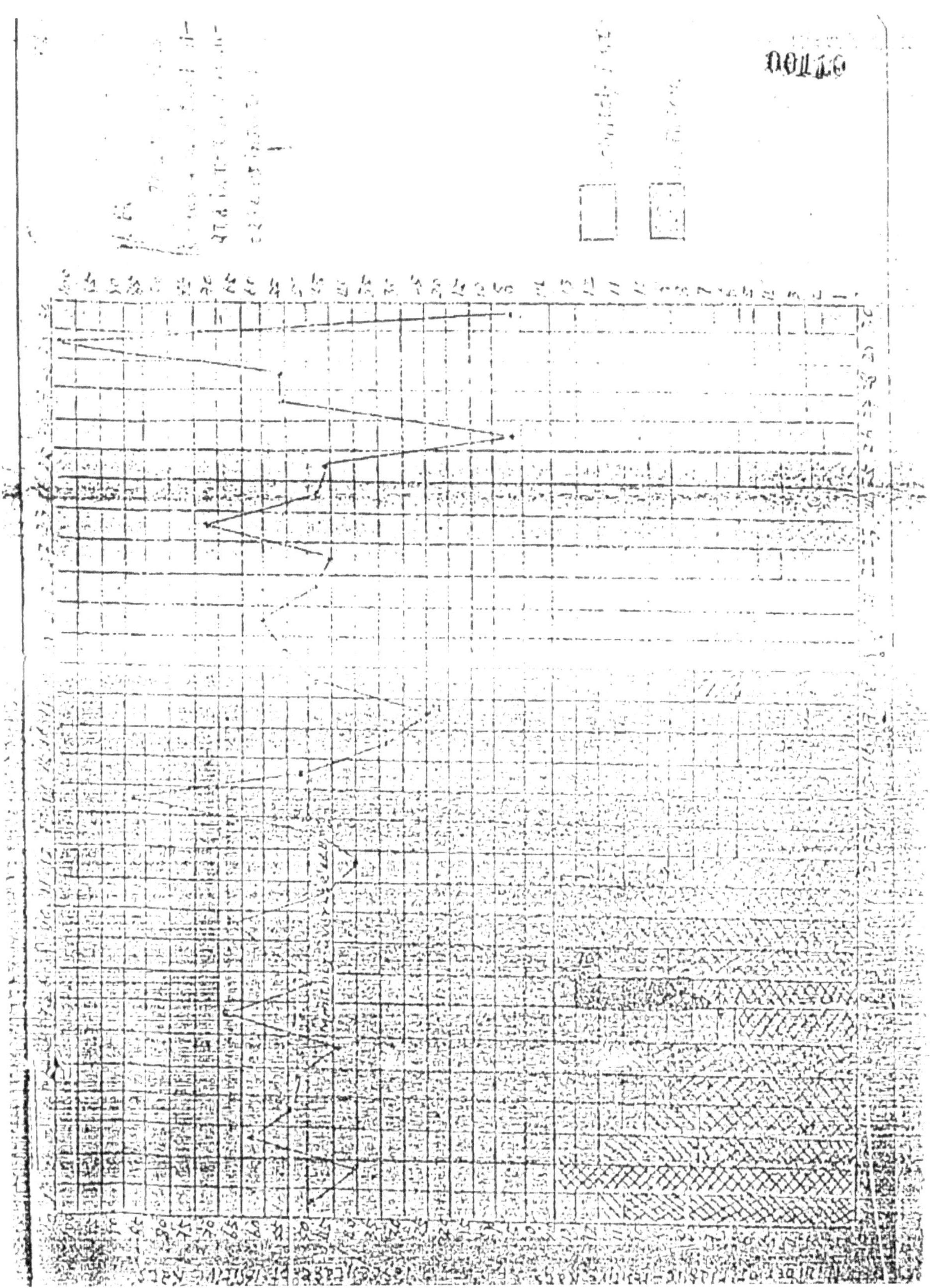

DISTRICTS	No. Infected	First-Infected Rats found on
關廟街及雞鵝巷	22	Jan. 30
大河街[illegible]	1	Feb. 20
救急院(鐵路西)	2	Feb. 26
北門	2	Feb. 27
廣德醫院附近(?)	1	Feb. 27
[illegible]門	2	Feb. 28
Total	32	

February 1942

Districts	No. Examined	Found Positive
關廟街雞鵝巷	375	16
廣德醫院附近	95	21
大河街	116	23
救急院	115	14
西門	12	1
北門	105	26
城外	2	—
Total	810	181

March 1942

Table V Distribution of Plague-Positive Rodents in Changteh

00111

D. Study on Fleas:

Fleas is the most important vector among the insects in the spread of plague infection. It is even more dangerous than the rats because it seldom dies of plague itself and the period for its infectivity is rather long. During an plague epidemic it is essential that we make a thorough study of the fleas as to their infectiousness, the percentage and indicies of different species of fleas especially of the cheopes index and percentage for the fleas (Xenopsylla cheopis) of Indian are especially dangerous epidemiologically in two respects firstly is that the stomachs of the Indian fleas are more liable to the tendency of producing blockage at the jumction the ante-stomach and the stomach proper when infected with B. pestis because there are more teeth at the inner wall along the junction: secondly is because the larvae of this flea species do not feed in blood but on rice so X. cheopis are usually more abundant in the rice shops and store houses and by this means the infection of plague is easily spread from one place to another along with the transportarion of rice.

The collection of fleas from dead rodents is by combing the hair of the rodints with anatomical forceps when the animals are placed in a basin of water and then remove the fleas to a petri-dish or glass jar containing alcohol. From live rodents the fleas are collected by placing the cloth bags containg the entrapped rodents into an air-tight container in to which some chloroform is poured to anesthetize both the animals and the fleas. Take out bags after about ten minutes and pickout the fleas carefully with forceps. This may enable the calculation of cheopis indicies. A tray half filled with oil placed a little below the ground or floor level at night time with a dim light nearly recommended for the collection of fleas in the house hold especially in the household of infected area, for study. With facilities at hand animal experimentation by rubbing a mixture of crushed fleas to the skin of guinea pigs should be done in order to dect if the fleas are infected for the infective of fleas may often be the herald of pest before the infection among the rodints are discovered. Even when the infection in rodents apparently subsides the infection among the fleas may still lags behind for months.

In our data the number of fleas collecod is very small. This is mostly due to the fact that most of the rodent examined are dead ones and some even much decomposed so that many of the fleas must have already made their escape when the animals came in to our hands. Although the campaign for trapping live rats has been tried, stilln no very satisfactory result were obtain from figures on Table VI and curves of chart III we observe the rarity of Inian fleas and the predominences of the Euopean fleas mainly (Ceratophyllus anisus). It was only in the second half of June when we get a relatively high percentage of the Indian fleas. In fact these 10 Indian fleas were collected from one live Rattus norvegicous at east end of the city. The number of human flea and cat fleas (Pulex irritans and Ctenocephalides felis respectively) collected from the rodents are too small to be of any significance. The cheopis indix cannot be calculated with our insufficient data.

Table VI Record of Fleas Studied in Changteh ([illegible] — June [illegible])

Time	Number of Different Species of Fleas Collected: Xenopsylla cheopis	Ceratophyllus anisus sp.	Leptopsylla musculi	Pulex irritans	Ctenocephalides felis	Total	Percentage of Different Species of Fleas: Xenopsylla cheopis	Ceratophyllus anisus sp.	Leptopsylla musculi	Pulex irritans	Ctenocephalides felis
Dec.–Jan.	7	47	52	[illegible]	0	[illegible]	[illegible]	[illegible]	[illegible]		
Feb. 1–5th	2	[illegible]	30	[illegible]	1	[illegible]	1.51%	[illegible]	[illegible]		
Feb. 6–[illegible]	2	142	142	[illegible]	0	[illegible]	1.38%	[illegible]	[illegible]		
Total for Feb.	6	271	61	0	1	339	1.77%	79.94%	17.99%	0	0.29%
March 1–5th	[illegible]	[illegible]	70	[illegible]	[illegible]	[illegible]	[illegible]	[illegible]	[illegible]		
March 6–[illegible]	[illegible]	60	[illegible]	[illegible]	[illegible]		[illegible]	[illegible]	[illegible]	[illegible]	
Total for Mar.	37	1442	212	1	0	1722	2.15%	83.74%	12.35%	0.06%	0
April 1–15th	0	607	226	[illegible]	[illegible]	[illegible]	0	[illegible]	[illegible]		
April 16–30th	1	137	128	2	[illegible]	[illegible]	[illegible]	[illegible]	[illegible]	[illegible]	
Total for April	1	744	352	2	0	1099	0.09%	66.70%	32.03%	0.18%	0
May 1–14th	0	[illegible]	11	[illegible]	[illegible]	[illegible]	0	[illegible]	[illegible]		
May 15–31th	[illegible]	[illegible]	66	[illegible]	[illegible]		[illegible]	[illegible]	[illegible]		
Total for May	1	133	85	0	0	219	0.45%	60.73%	38.81%	0	0
June 1–[illegible]	0	[illegible]	15	[illegible]	0		[illegible]	[illegible]	[illegible]		
June [illegible]	[illegible]	[illegible]	19	[illegible]	0		[illegible]	[illegible]	[illegible]		
Total for June	10	16	25	0	0	51	19.60%	31.37%	49.03%	0	0
Total [illegible]	[illegible]	[illegible]	[illegible]	[illegible]	[illegible]	[illegible]	[illegible]	[illegible]	[illegible]		

0011

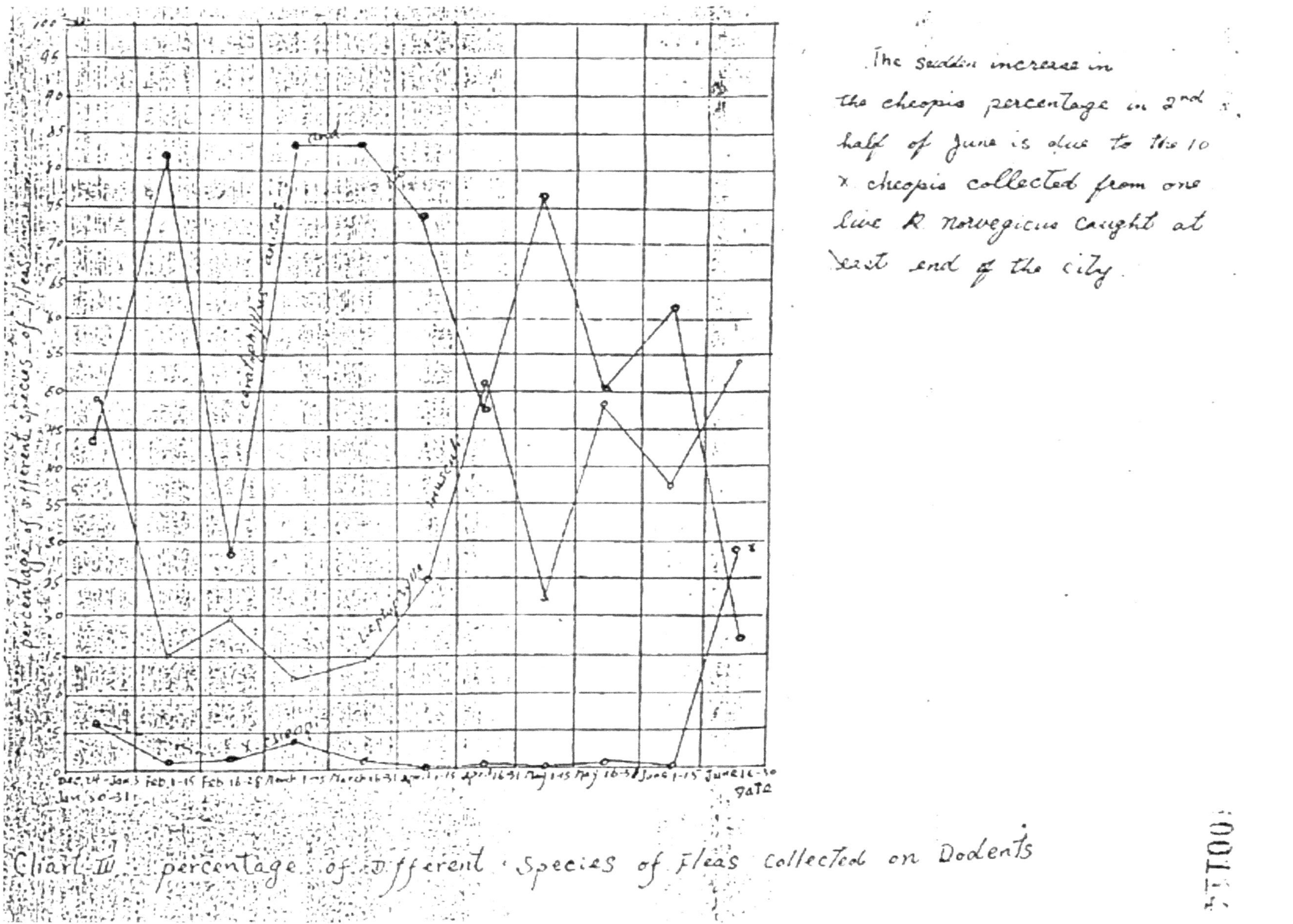
The sudden increase in the cheopis percentage in 2nd half of June is due to the 10 x cheopis collected from one live R norvegicus caught at East end of the city
00114
Chart IV percentage of Different Species of Fleas collected on Rodents
percentage of different species of fleas
DATE

-5-

00115

E. Discussion :

Plague as an infective disease in men is not so simple a process of direct transmission of the causative agent to the victom. The factots involved in the whole process may be diagramatically repreesinted as such:

Plague bacilli(the causative agent)
↓
rats and other Rodents(reservior of infection for men)
↓
fleas (Vector of transmitting plague infection from rats to rats and rats to men)
↓
Men (the Victim)

2. Primary septicemic plague | 3. Primary skin plague

1. Bubonic plague

Secondry pneumonic plague

↓

Man---(Primary pneumonic plague)

It is evident that the rice and cotton pieces dropped down by the Japanese airplane must contain infected fleas of plague. Rice is a favorable food for the rats and naturally they come to contract the disease easily. From the first infected rats more rats are infected through the fleas vectors. As a result more fleas are infected. Rats die of the plague, but fleas usually not so the latter come to bite men when they cannot find enough rat hosts and thus the epedemic is started. So epidemic in human being always follows an epizootic in rodents.

Of the rodents we studied a greater percentage of the infected rats is of the Rattus rattus species. As R. rattus usually live in the houses and come into easy contacts with human being, the situation must be considered more serious. Chart IV and V show the relation of human cases with number and percentage of infected rats respectively. It will be seen that epidemic sets in when the percentage of infection in rodents is above 20 percent. Since May the epidemic and epizootic both began to come down. In first half of still get sporadic of June case although already the weather was rather hot This indicated the rat plague must be more serious than our findings, as only insufficient number of animals were examined. In second half of June the low incidence of rat pest and human cases encountered showed the expected off-season has really set in. Variousfactors are responsible for the spontaneous decline of plague in summer. Mult important among them is that the fleas are less infective during the hot season than under the condition of temperature and humidity prevailing in spring and autumn. The number and humidity-pre species of fleas prevailing on the rodents is also of great importance

At the beginning of an epizootic the rodents have no immunity

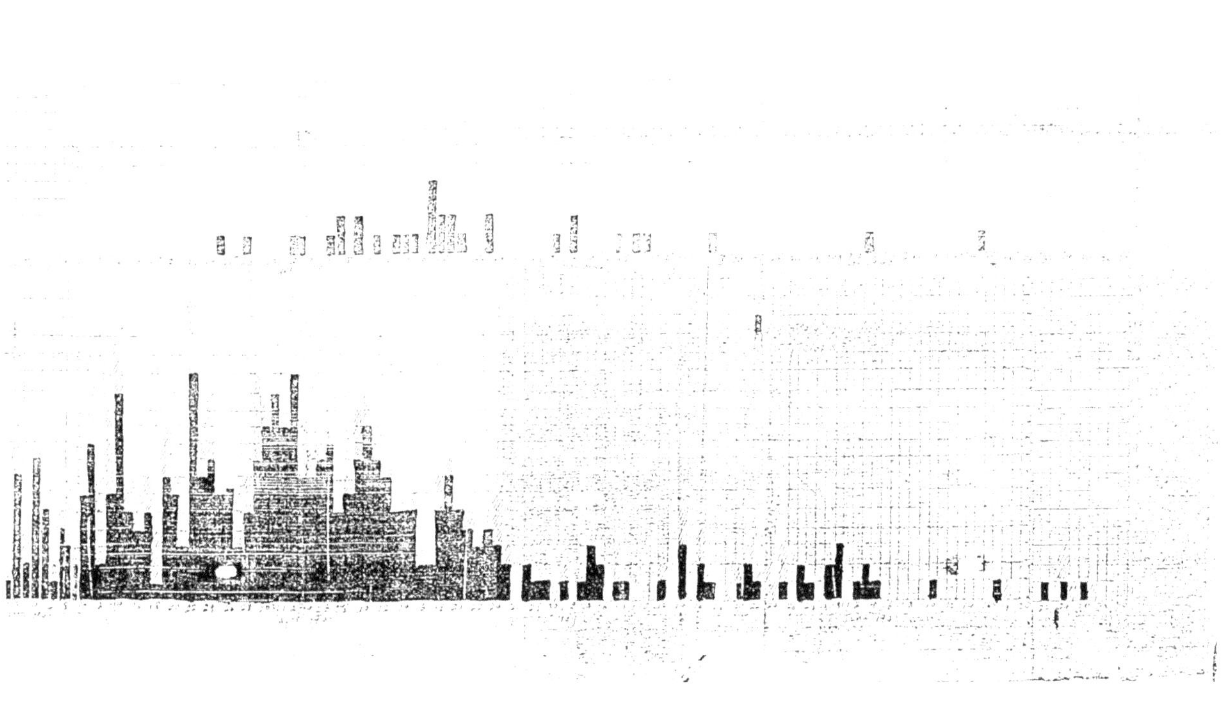

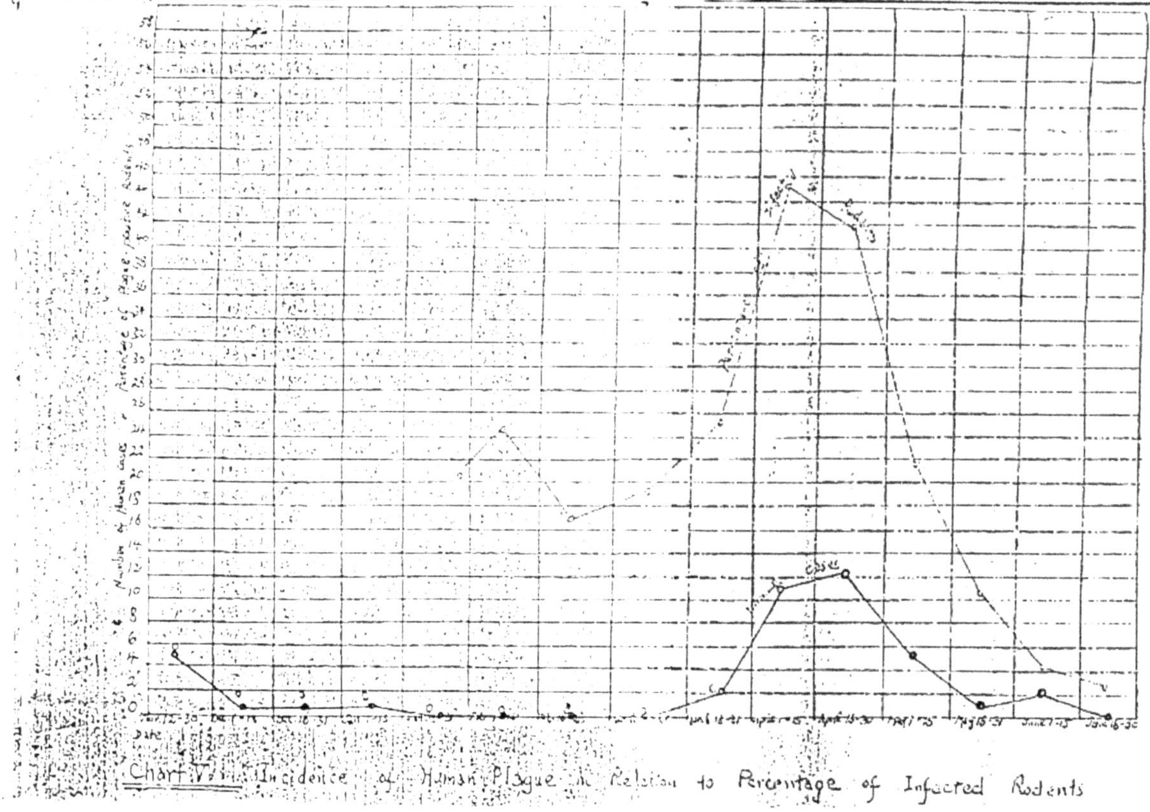

Chart V. Incidence of Human Plague in Relation to Percentage of Infected Rodents

001157

001-3

toward the infection and so are very susceptible. As time goes on they gradually develop immunity and such immunity can pass on to their young. How long can this immunity last is not yet clear but it is usually lost when the epizootic ends. In the spot map we can see the distribution of the infected rats in Changteh is rather wide. This must be due to the travelling of the infected rats in the city and the travelling of people and patient carrying infected fleas with them. New rats may also be brought to the place by ships and trains and this why susceptible rodents can be constantly present during an epizootic.

Our data on fleas show the marked rarity lf the Indian fleas. This must not mean that we have really very few Indian fleas in Changteh. The failure to get more X.cheopics must be due to the fact that we have not succeeded to get rats from every corner of the city sspeecially in the rice shops and store houses. The fact that one sewer rat gave us 10 X.cheopis can prove this conjecture to be no without ground. The increase in cheopis index often foretells a coming outbreak of plague.

The demonstration of B. pestis in the bubonic juice of bubonic patients and in the bloody sputum of patients of pneumonic is usually very easy, but it is not so easy to demonstrate the bacilli in the peripheral blood of septicemic patients unless not long before death. So the early diagnosis of septicemic plague should be made with more close observation and wisdom. It is always wiser to suspect a case earlier than diagnose a case of plague too late.

It must be emphasized here that the five cases which recovered under treatment are those that have been inoculated with plague vaccine. Though it is a pity that antiplague vaccinat on connot absolutely protect men against the disease, still it can render the patient to be more resistant the infection and make mild the gravity of the disease so there will be enough time for treatment.

From Table II we see that sex and age plays no special role in the infection of plague. But no children under five years of age are the victims of plague in our record on Table I.

The new chemotherapy with sulfathiazole is preferred to anti plague serum is because the former is more convenient to use and with less untoward effects. During an epidemic the demand for the serum great and often it is not possible to get enough amount of serum because the manufacture and transportation are difficult. especially during this wartime China. And serum has it is time limit for effectiveness. But sulfathiazole tablets can be compactly packed up for transportation and ifk kept well will not deteriorate. When that during is along with sodium bicarbonate precautions as to an egg-free and low-protein(animal protein) diet and force fluid are observed, the toxic effects such as the production of sulphohemoglobinemia and renal damage can be avoided. The results of treatment with sulfathiazole in our patients is quite encouraging. Sulfathiazole itself is not bacteriolgicidal, but it renders the body more resistant toward the infection. It has 69-70% chances of cure especially with early diagnosed bubonic patients With the septicemic type the chances for cure is doubtful. Now we give 2-4 Gm. (4-8 tablets) for initial dose to be followed by 1 Gm. every 2-4 hours according to the gravity case. The treatment is continued as lng long as the patient is in a serious condition unless appearance of a hematuria makes it necessary to reduce the dosage or to stop the treatment. Sodium bicarbonate 1.gm. is given twice daily

The hearts of the plague patients are especially weakened by the toxin so care must be taken not to let the patient overexert his or her heart At least one weeks rest in bed is absolutely necessary when he or she recovers.. Duing illness cardiac stimulants or tonic are often recommended. This will make the chance for recovery even greater.

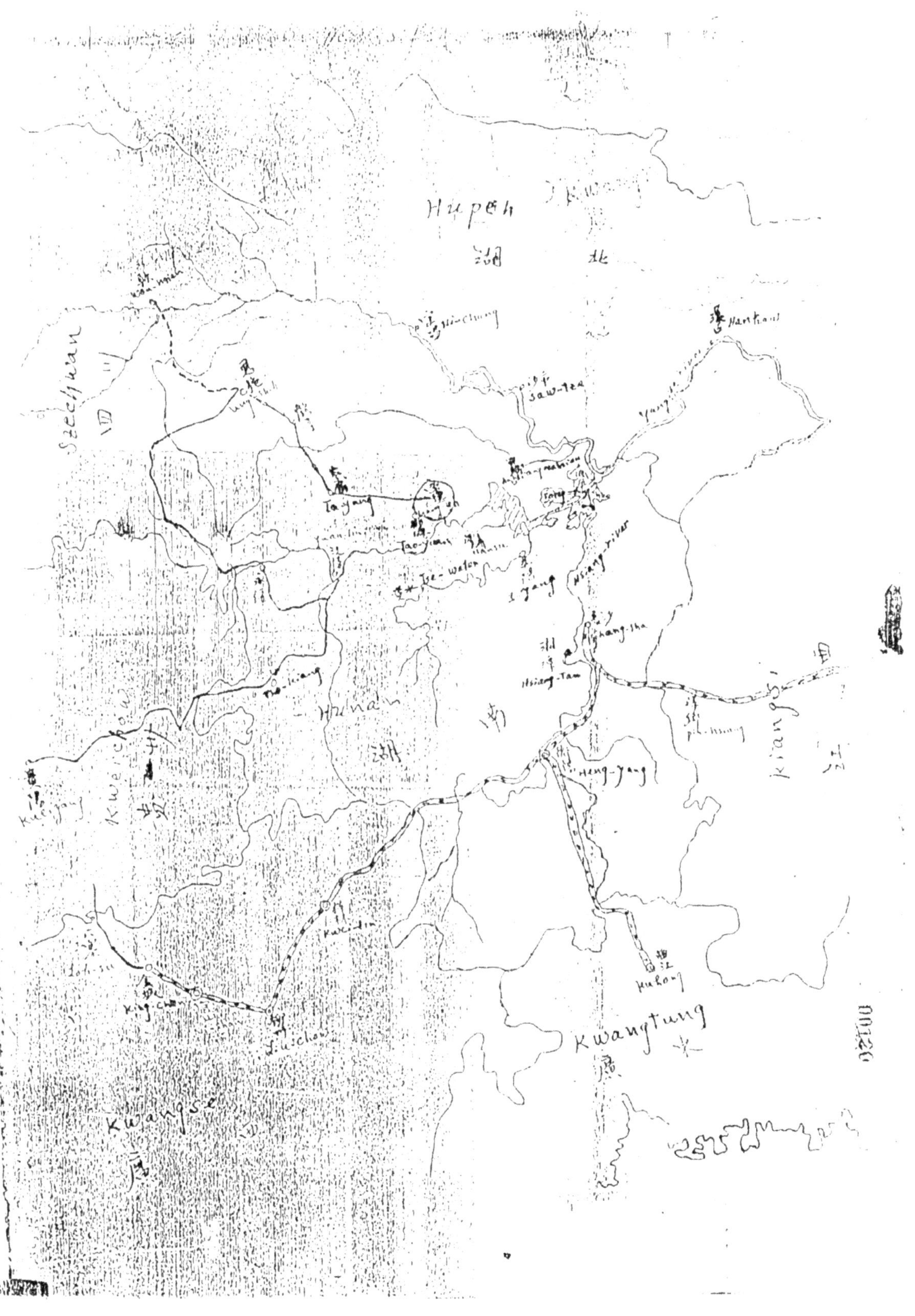

00123

SECOND PART

Measures for the Control of Plague.

Hunan is a rather important province in nowaday China. It is not only aKey to the southwestern provinces of China through its river ways, highways and railways, but is also a province Well-Known for its production of rice and cotton, especially those districts around Dong Ting Lake (洞庭湖) such as Anhsiang (安乡), I-Yang (益阳), Hansu (汉寿), Nahsien (南县) and Changteh. Though Changteh itself is not the most important hsien for the rice and cotton production, it nevertheless serves as a strategic way in the transportation of such goods into the other provinces, as this city is well communicated with others by several ways:

A. Westward to Ta-Yung (大庸) and Ho-fu (鹤峰) and Ung-shih (恩施) in Hupeh then to Wan-hsein in Szechwan.
B. By water through the Yuan-river (沅水) to Yuan-ling (沅陵) and then by highway to Yong-Seu (永绥), Ung-Shih and Wan-hsien (万县).
C. From Yuan-ling by highway westward to Kweichow (贵州) through Tse-Kiang (芷江).
D. Through Tong-ting Lake there are three important ways:
   1. Southeastwards through the Hsiang-river to Changsha.
   2. Northeastwards through Yangtze down to Hankow.
   3. Northwestwards through Yangtze up to Sha-Sze (沙市) and then to Yi-chang (宜昌) and Wan-hsien.
   From Changsha connections can easily be made through railways to Kwangtung, Kiangse.

As mentioned above, fleas, especially the Indian fleas, can be easily carried along with the transportation of cotton and rice. And with such facilities in communciaction, rits and patients can easily escape from the infected districts. It is therefore manifest that the seriousness of the plague epidemic in Changteh lies not alone in the condition inside that city but in the great danger of its spread into the other districts and provinces nearby. So measures for its control must be strictl carried out. The writer tries to discuss in detail all the measures which should be carried out in order to control the spread of the disease, some of which measures have already been put into practice in Changteh. The general scheme of the whole work is based on Dr. pollitzer's plan:

Scheme of the preventive work of plague:

I. In plague-infected districts
   A. General measures:
      1. Public health propaganda.
      2. Mass inoculation.
      3. Campaign against rats
         a. Destruction
            i.) ... laying. iii) Poisoning
            ii.) Trapping iV) Fumigating
         b. Major rat-proofing.

4

P 00

c. Minor rat-proofing.
d. Food protection.
e. Cleanness (Disposal of rubbish).
4. Intelligence and laboratory services.
5. Administrative measures.
a. Epidemic-preventive committee and the technical committee.
b. Regulation for shops, store houses and places of public assemblies, etc.

B. Measures in infected foci:
1. Hospitalization of patients.
2. Contact isolation.
3. Destruction of fleas and rats followed by rat-proofing.
4. Disposal of the dead.
5. Evacuation (closing of houses).
6. Burning of houses.

II. Measures round foci of infection:

A. Quarantine measures.
1. Control of passengers and their luggage.
2. Control of rice and cotton.
3. Control of thorough-going traffic.
4. control of boats and ships.

B. Preventive measures in adjacent cities.
1. Propaganda.
2. Anti-rat measures based upon survey of rats and fleas.
3. Laboratory and intelligence services.
4. Preparations for
a. Inoculation campaign.
b. Staff, supplies and buildings for anti-plague work.
5. Committees.
6. Quarantine measures for incoming passengers and goods, especially those from the infected districts.

These measures are to be discussed fully one by one :

A. General Measures for Infected Districts:
1. Public health propaganda:-
The importance of public health propaganda need not be mentioned here. It is only with the understanding and cooperation of the people that we can hope to achieve the measures to be carried out. As plague is a disease chiefly in the poor people, the ordinary way of propaganda by means of newspaper, posters, pamphlets and speeches in public assemblies is not sufficient as the poor often can not read or are too busy for work to have any leisure time in reading or attending meetings. House to house propaganda done at a convenient time to the people is best recommended for this purpose. Attention must be paid to the building of the houses as regards rat-proofing, presence of double partitions, celings and floors and the way the people keep their food. See and inquire if any dead or sick rats are around. Make a brief note of each house inspected and classify them. Give advices as to rat-proofing, rat-destruction and food protection and other general indeas of plague and its preventive measures. Explain everything as simple as

00__3

possible and in sincere manner. These houses should be reinspected after one week to see if any improvement has been made. If not readvise them and inspect for the third time few days later. If still nothing has been done, then the sanitary engineers must carry out compulsary measures for the shops and the store houses.

2. Mass Inoculation:

As discussed above in the first part, anti-plague vaccination cannot absolutely protect the people from getting the disease. But before any better preparation for immunization is available, this vaccination is still recommended on a large scale as it can lessen the chance for infection and alter the gravity of the disease even if the person unfortunately contracts the disease. From immunological point of view, oneinjection of the vaccine is not enough to produce good protection of the body against the germs, another injection should be given to serve as a stimulus to the first one so will enhance the immunity.

The way of inoculating people at the strategic ways of the city is not very convenient for people would not come for the second injection. House to house inoculation is the only way we may expect good result and is strongly recommended. This must again be done at a convenient time for the family members, usually at eveningtides or noon-time. The Pao-chang ( ) and Kia-chang ( ) should be asked to help in this campaign. Very care must be taken as to the asepsis of the technic so that people will have no pretext to escape the inoculation and no rumor of whatever soft will be spread out. The people ought to be told of the possible reactions to occur. Certificates are to be given at end of the second or third injections with date of injection care-fully written on it.

Strictly speaking no people should be excluded from the mass inoculation. But in the hope of lessening resistance from the people, three groups of people may be excluded:

(a) Small children under age of two years old,
(b) the seriously ill, especially such with chronic diseases, like tuberculosis, heart and kidney troubles, etc. Person with acute diseases should be inoculated after they have recovered.
(c) The pregnant women.

The pregnant women must unfortunately also be listed in the three groups of people as the native people usually havegreat traditional prejudice against inoculating the pregnant. If anything is happened to that woman, which is most likely that abortion or miscarriage be resulted due to causes other than the injection, then the people will blame us. Ift there is no objection of the family toward inoculating the preganant, we must try every means to inoculate her.

The immunity obtained by vaccination does not last long usually not longer than three to six months. It is therefore necessary to repeat the inoculation at the end of that period if plague is still persisting in that place. In Changteh so far such inoculations have been carried

[illegible]

Table VI　Preventive Inoculation of Plague Vaccine In Changteh

Month / No. of Inoculations	Nov. 2–Dec. 31	January	February	March	April	May	June	Total
First Inoculation	[illegible]	2,37[illegible]	1,150	[illegible]	6,[illegible]	[illegible]		[illegible]
Second Inoculation	1,353	77[illegible]	1,18[illegible]	[illegible]	[illegible]	[illegible]		[illegible]
Total Inoculations	4,30[illegible]	3,15[illegible]	2,3[illegible]	[illegible]	1,126	1,66[illegible]		[illegible]

Population of Changteh city	Civilian	62,41[illegible]
	Army	4,000
	Total	66,51[illegible]
Number of people inoculated (Civilian & Army)		17,[illegible]
Percentage of Population Inoculated		26.[illegible]%

out at all the medical institutions in the city and at all the quarantine stations established at the six city gate ways and at Loh-lou-kow and Hwang-mo-kan of the river ways. Up to May only 28.6 percent of the population, includingon the army, has been inoculated (Table VII). This figure shows but a very small fraction of the population is protected. Hous to house inoculation is to be started in early August in anticipating an Autumn outbreak.

It is clear that inoculation will only confer a passing protection but will not eradicate plague. Consequently it must be combined with an energetic anti-rat campaign.

3. Campaign against Rats:

a. Destruction of rats-- This can be achieved through four different ways. namely, slaying, trapping, poisoning and fumigating. Slaying is very simple but rather dangerous with infected ones. Trapping, needs specialtechnic. Thetrap and the biscuit or meat placed inside must all be free from any smell of the human hand, for the rats are very clever animals. Flame the trap each time before use and the hands of the one in handling this business must be dusted with earth before he holds the trap or place in the f food piece. the house members must be told to keep their food away from the rats in the nights when the traps are set ant to place the trap with the entrapped victim into the cloth bag given to them when any rat is trapped . They should not touch or move the trap otherwise.

Poisoning is best achieved by barium carbonate, for this is very poisonous to rats but innocuous to men and other domestic animals. Mix barium carbonate with flour in the proportion of one to four parts. Water is added into the mixture to make into small balls of one inch diameter. Theballs must then be dipped in melted paraffin or candle wax or must be quicked fried in animal or vegetabl-e oil. Afterwards they must be handles and distributed w with the aid of chopsticks but must not be touched with the fingers. For first two or threenights better try with non-poisonous flour balls in order to have an idea of how mu much barium carbonate is needed in that house hold and whether rats will come to eat them or not. Theadvantage in using barium carbonate is that when the rats ingest it, some sort of gastroenteritis is developed which will cause them to feel extremely thirsty and so go out of the houses to search for water. Consequently they die outside. This method is again not very good during active phase of the epidemic.

For fumigating the best chemical is calcium cyanide powder, called cyanogen commercially. This will liberate hydrocyanic acid slowly in moist air so is more safer than the use of gas of hydrocyanic acid directly. It can ever kill fleas. This is the best way for rat-destruction du during epidemics but is rather expensive for practical no. nozzle the powder is put into a specially designed pump the nozzle of which is inserted into the rat holes carefully sought out. Seal the hole around the nozzle so that no

I2- £00..C

leakage of the liberated gas will result. while one person is pumping, the other worker must look around the house in order to detect any leakage from other holes which may communicate with the one being handled. Block any leakage as soon as discovered and if necessary spread tear-gas, 50cc. for I,000 cubic foot of space, to prevent the people from going into the house when there is leakage. For solidly built houses this method is very safe and ective, and people may come back after one or two days. Even no evacuatio-n of the people is needed if they be intelligent enough to beward of any danger. For house less solidly built and with too many rat holes; this method is more dangerous and less effective. For the haythatched mud houses this method is absolutely inapplicable. Only experts are allowed to handle this method.

b. Major Rat-proofing:-- Rat destruction should be considered only a temporary measure against rats. This must be follo-wed by rat-proofing, From experience we know that rats usually multiply more rapidly after a massive rat-destruction action due to a better living conditionfig for those that survive the action, because they have more food and more comfortable place to live in. So the houses must be so built that no rats can hide and live in them. Thesanitary engineers should make designs for the new houses. Before the building of any new house, the owner must report the police which in turn will report the Epidemic Prevention Bureau for orders.

c. Minor Rat-proofing:--Thepoor class of people cannot afford to rebuild new houses. In order to attain rat-proofing aims, these houses should be altered such as the removal of double partitions, floors and ceilings and the blockage of rat holes. In this way the rats wi-ll have no more hiding places, Here again the sanitary engineers should look after such matter.

d. Food Protection:-- Protection of food against rats is the most efficacious way to extinguish rats from the households. Foods can be easily well-kept in the native kongs if tin cans or other secure containers are not available, the most important point which usually is neglected by the people is to clean up the table right after the evening meal insted of letting it stand uncleaned throughout the night. If this precaution is not taken, then rats will have a heatty meal in the night and of course they would like to come again. On the other hand if they can find no food they will naturally disappear from the household.

e. Cleanness:-- Cleanness of the houses and streets must be observed. Broken furniture must not be kept in the corners or attics so that rats will have no places for hiding. In fact such furniture will never be used again, so better persuade the people to use them as fire wood. Things to be piled up such as firewood, boxes etc. should be placed on platforms some distance from the wall. Rubbish must be poured into the public rubbish boxes

I

well-covered up before dark . Sanitary parades in regular intervals, elg. every one or two months, may be organized.

Those above five measures against rats in fact are the most important of all the anti-plague measures listed above. During this quiescent season it is the best time for carrying out a massive rat destruction and proofing movement so that there isyet hope to avoid the expected coming outbreak in Autumn.

4. Intelligence and Laboratory Sefvices:

The police, the Paochang and Kia-chang should be asked to coorperate in getting the intelligence reports. The sick and dead must be reported as early aspossible and examined by the medical men. We should also try our best to get the understanding and sincere cooperation of other practitioners and the native Chinese odoctors so that they will report us any case coming into their hands. Itis only by such well-organized intellignece service that we can get hodd of most of the cases, if not all. Emphasis is again laid on the importance of early reporting of the sick so that there will betime for the sick to recover under treatment and for the prevention of the spread of the disease of any acture case exists. Each practitioner should have a diagnostic book recording the name , addvess,date of onset of disease and other significant dates and the chief symptoms and signs of the patients. Inspectors should be sent out at regular intervals to see their record book and if any suspicious case is present further findings regarding the case must be done.

A simple laboratory where diagnosis of cases by microscopic studies can be made and a nearby room or shed where rodents can be examined together with some experimental animals is enough to meet the need. A post-mortem room for the examination of human dead bodies must be also available.

5. Administrative Measures:

The Epidemic Prevention Committee should consist of some local chiefs together with other men doing the administrative side of work, while the technical committee consists only of the medical staff and the sanitary engineering men. Itis the technical men who must diregt the whole planning and carrying out of the work, not the men doing administrative work. The technical men must be prompt, emergetic, honest and strong-minded. Drastic measures and due punishments must be strictly carried out, especially at the beginning, so that the people will give in.

Regulations should be made for shops and stores houses regarding rat-proofing and the proper way of food storage. During pneumonic outbreaks all public assemblies ought to be stopped.

B. Measures in the Infected Foci:

I. Hospitalization of the Patients ~~on one hand as~~

Hospitalization is good for the patient on one hand as he can get good nursing care, proper diet, absolute rest in bed and immediate specific treatments, and on the other hand chances for spreading the infection will be stopped.

2.Contact Isolation:

The contacts of pneumonic patients must be segregated for watch for one week. Their temperature, pulse rates and respiratory rates are taken twice daily. Any slight elevation in temperature or quickened pulse rate should be taken as suspicious and must be at once isolated from the restof the contacts and treatment started immediately when condition gets worse. The contacts of the bubonic plague patients have no absolute need for isolation, but still it is better for them to evacuate temporarily as they may contract the disease if they stay in the same house longer for chances of being bitten by infected f fleas are great . Care must be taken not to let any contact escape, especially those of the pneumonic contacts.

3. Destruction of rats and fleas:

ngDestruction of rats must be carried out along with the killi ng of fleas, for if rats alone are killed while the fleas left behind, the latter will come to bite men instead. The homes of the bubonic patients should be sprayed with kerosene oil emulsion to kill the fleas and the rats should n also be searched and killed. For the home of the pneumonic patients there is no need to disinfect the room by formalin and sulphur, but the floor and the bed soiled by the bloody s sputum which is very infectious should be washed with boiling water (IOO℃.) and then sprayed with lime. Beds are bestly burnt away. Sheets and beddings should either be burnt or boiled. Alcohol is the best disinfectant here but too expenive. After disinfectionthe room are closed till the contacts come back after one wiik. Rat-proofing measures are to be followed. The isolation hospital and the contact isolation camps must be freed from rats and insects such as fleas, lice and bed-bugs. Before admission to the ward or camp, the patients and the contacts must be deflead. Perform delousing if necessary.

4. Desposal of the Dead:

The dead should be burnt which is the safest way. But because of the strong objection of the people toward cremation, we now provide a special cemetery for burying the suspicious or positive cases. The coffin ought to be made of solid material, and lime is spread inside. The ground level of the cemetery ought to be higher, for the dead must be buried to the depth of si six feet. When after one hot season, the coffin may be transferred to other places for burial if the family members wish to.

5. Evacuation of the neighboring Houses:

Evacuate people in the houses adjacent to those where patient are discovered. Better move the people to a public building specially prepared for this purpose. During evacuation, the houses should all be freed from rats and fleas or improvedd through saintary engineering measures when necessary. Peroid for those people to come back is judged accoring to the active spreading of the infection. If possiblethe evacuated people should stay away from their houses until the plague season is over.

6. Burning of Houses:

This method is best applied at the beginning of the epidem-ic when only few of the houses are infected. All windows and doors must be closed and any hole or ditch communicating the house with outside must be blocked before the houses are set on fire. Such precaution is necessary in order not to let a single rat escape from the focus. When epidemic has reached its full swing, the burning of houses is not applicable as too many houses have to be burnt since theyare built very close together. The burning of the whole city must be care-fully considered, it should not be done unless absolutely necessary, that is when quarantine measures cannot be carried out and the neighboring districts are in great danger to be infected. A secure wall enclosing the whole city must be first built before the city can be safely burnt.

II. Measures Round Foci of Infection:

A. Quarantine Measures:

Quarantine itself cannot extinguish epidemic, but is a meas-ure to prevent the spread of the infection into neighooring districts. This is a very troublesome measure but must be strictly carried out.

I. Control of Passengers and their luggage:

It is hard to detect patients in the incubation period. If such people, especially of the pneumonic type, are allowed to travel to other place, a new epidemic will be resulted. One instance is the moo-ling-hsiang ( ), lung pest epidemic at end of May I942 introduces by oneman who had came to Changteh shortly before that epidemic for some business transaction and unfortunately contracted plague infection. He went back to that country, a subdistrict of Taoyuan when he was yet in the incubation period. The result is that all five in the family, including himself, died and also eleven others who came into contact with them. It is luck-ky that this outbreak of lung pest is different ~~from~~ ~~[illegible]~~ ordinary lung plague by the absence of the usual vehicle of infection, namely bloody-sputum and cough in the latter cases. So finally the epidemic is checked by itself spont-aneously.

Contacts of the bubonic patients when let loose is not so dangerous, but their luggage must be deflead.

It is a rule that every patient suffering from pneumonic plague and every contact with them must be carefully sought out and isolated. During a pneumonic outbreak no passenger is allowed to pass unless after seven days of quarantine. Even the trains and ships and buses must be stopped when necessary.

2. Control of Rice and Cotton:

No grains or cotton produced. or stored in the infected districts are allowed to export. Such goods passing the infected districts during transportation from one place to ~~[illegible]~~ ~~be detained for quarantine.~~

-16-

another must not be allowed to disload there and have to leave there before night fall, otherwise the goods will be detained for quarantine.

3. Control of Boats and Ships:

This is very important as boats usually serve as a means of carrying rats from one place to another. Boats are not allowed to come near to the banks of the infected cities after dusk and before dawn. They should be ordered to anchor at a distance at least twenty feet away from the bank during night times, the deck communicating the boat with the bank must be taken away. Any communication with the land after dark is achieved by small junks.

B. Measures in Adjacent Cities:

These will not be discussed here. They are to be carried out more or less according to those discussed. above

SUMMARY

I. The plague outbreak in Changteh, Hunan, was introduced by the Japanese by dropping plague-infected rice and cotton on Nov. 4th, 1941 from an airplane.

2. Study of human plague during the period of Nov. 12, 1941 to June 30, 1942 is presented and discussed. Five out of the 17 positive and one suspicious patients recovered. 20 dead bodies were found to be positive and 3 suspicious. The following points are noted:

a. The diagnosis of bubonic and primary pneumonic plague is comparatively easy during the epidemic but in septicemic cases B. pestis is often not demonstrable in the peripheral ~~b. Early treatment with large doses of~~ blood in early stage of the disease.

b. early treatment with large doses of sulfathiazole if such treatment is combined with good general treatment and adequate nursing, 60-70 percent of the bubonic patients may be cured and it will even be possible to save some patients with primary pneumonic plague. So far no confirmed case of septicemic plague has been cured. We have not met with serious toxic affiects when giving sulfathiazole.

c. Immunity resulting from anti-plague vaccination does not always give complete protection but is apt to modify the disease into a milder form and reduce the mortality of people who contracted plague after having been inoculated.

3. 1879 rats and mice were examined with the maximum percentage of infection reaching 44.40 in April. When the infection in rodents is above 20 percent an epidemic in humans is apt to set in.

4. 3536 fleas collected from the examined rodents are studied and rarity of x. cheopis was observed.

5. Measures for the control of plague are fully discussed.

3.21 Reported Japanese Warfare in China in late 1941 or 1942, Ray F. CHESLEY, Capt, Sn, C.

资料出处： National Archives of the United States, R112, E295A, B11.

内容点评： 本资料为美军上尉 Ray F. Chesley 报告：关于 1941 年底或 1942 年日本人在中国的细菌作战。

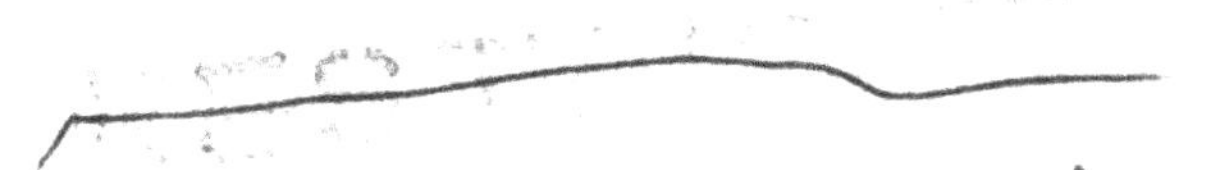

Reported Japanese Warfare in China in late 1941 or 1942

The Chinese reported that a plague epidemic had been started in one of their towns by the Japanese who were reported to have spread the disease by flying over the town and dropping wastepaper, cotton, newspapers, and rags. Six cases of plague with three deaths were reported at the time the news reached our headquarters.

I was sent to the town to try to pick up any information about the epidemic which might be available. The Chinese report stated that plague had never occurred nearer than several hundred (500 as I remember) miles from this town. They also reported that the strain of B. pestis from all cases was the same as demonstrated by blood smears. They also reported that since this area was self-sufficient no grain was imported.

The small amount of waste cotton and rags exhibited certainly showed no evidence that B. pestis was spread by that means and appeared rather to be surgical dressings.

Rice had been imported into the town from Burma and was stored in the vicinity of the area where the plague occurred--all cases occurred within an area of 1/4 mile--and only one piece of "infected cotton" had fallen in this area and that at the very outside edge of it.

In my opinion there not only was inconclusive evidence of bacterial warfare being employed by the Japanese but there were no grounds to suggest that it had been employed.

RAY F. CHESLEY
Captain, Sn. C.

Dictated by Capt Chesley about 14 May '45 & typed after his departure.
GWA
24 May '45

3.22 13 May 1942: U.S. NATIONAL CENSORSHIP Record No. LA 2190-42: CHUNG SAI YAT PO, 5-9-42: ENEMY EMPLOYS DISEASE-GERM WARFARE

资料出处： National Archives of the United States, R112, E295A, B11.

内容点评： 本资料为 1942 年 5 月 13 日美国国家新闻审查处存档的 1942 年 5 月 9 日旧金山中文报纸《中西日报》(*CHUNG SAI YAT PO*) 报道，题目：敌军实施了细菌战。

Photo. No. CONFIDENTIAL Records No. LA 2190-42

UNITED STATES OF AMERICA
NATIONAL CENSORSHIP

SURFACE Mail No.

For use in the case of Registered Letters (If unregistered, insert "NONE")

Registered No.

Serial No. NONE

FROM—

CHUNG SAI YAT PO

716 SACRAMENTO ST.
SAN FRANCISCO, CALIF.

To—

NAMPING KUNGSOW

PO. BOX. 31
MEXICALI, B.C.

Date of letter (or postmark if letter undated) PUBLICATION: 5-9-42
NO POSTMARK

PREVIOUS RECORDS, IF RELEVANT

Nos.

For interoffice use by A. C. or D. A. C. only.

Allocation of this comment sheet:

C.P.C.
C.D.R.

G.O.

Whether to be photographed— NO

If so, to whom photograph is to be sent—

DISPOSAL OF ORIGINAL LETTER—
Released, held, condemned or sent with comment to— RELEASED

710.-1 (China) F

COMMENT

CHINESE
NOT PREVIOUSLY CENSORED

AIR & MILITARY

In the above mentioned Chinese newspaper, CHUNG SAI YET PO, on page 8 the following article appears in Chinese: The heading was "ENEMY EMPLOYS DISEASE-GERM WARFARE". The content of the article is translated thus:

"On May 6th, (1942) our (China's) Board of Health issued the report that our enemy force (Japan's) is not heeding the law of humanity. It is now actually using airplanes to scatter BUBONIC PLAGUE GERMS all over China from North to South. In Central China, in HUNAN PROVINCE, all along SHAN-TEH, last winter, nine types of epidemics resulted. Since Feb. 19 1942, several more kinds developed. Upon examination, 24.4% of these cases contained these BUBONIC PLAGUE germs. In the three provinces of KWEICHOW, HUPEI, and TSECHUAN, the epidemic danger is very grave. According to the Head of the Epidemic Disease Dept. of the Board of Health, the ensuing quotation was given: "This type of epidemic is especially prevalent in the rice-producing district. SHAN-TEH is a rice-producing district." Anti-toxin for such is sorely lacking in these places. In the Northern part of China which consisted of the SHANSI, SHENSI, SINYUAN & NINGSIA provinces, this desease is also extremely widespread. Once, within a 3-months' period, the death rate was over 600 people. From Janauary 5, to April 4, 1942, there were 387 cases reported: NINGSIA had 24, SHENSI had 30, & SHANSI had 13. In CHEKIANG, since Dec. 1940, the enemy scattered these "disease-seeds" in CHU-YUAN IN FUKIEN, this epidemic has become a prevalent disease, spreading over 11 cities & towns, including WING-OH."

WD DIST.
5-30-42
1-SOS (MD)
1-IG
1-EB
1-PWB
3-CB
1-G-2 RS
gps/ah

dmb 5-13-42

Division (or section)	TABLE	EXAMINER	D. A. C.	DATE
PRINTS & PUB'S	15	2358	2318	5-12-42

CONFIDENTIAL

NC Form No. 8
December 12, 1941

16—25396-1 U. S. GOVERNMENT PRINTING OFFICE

3.23 25 Sep. 1942: 2400.1-3, CHUNGKING Sep. 25 (Chinese News Service) by wire

资料出处： National Archives of the United States, R112, E295A, B11.

内容点评： 本资料为 1942 年 9 月 25 日美国纽约中国新闻社重庆电讯：中国航空委员会报告，8 月 30 日有三架日军飞机在河南南阳投下带鼠疫菌的高粱和玉米粒。

RESTRICTED

2400.1-3
25 September 1942

CHUNGKING Sept. 25 (Chinese News Service)....by wire.....

Three Japanese planes dropped a large quantity of "kaoliang" and corn grains in Nanyang, Hoan Province, on the morning of Aug. 30th, reported, the Aeronautical Commission of the Chinese Government. According to the report, the grains were analyzed by local medical officers and found to contain bubonic plague bacteria.

(Editor's note "Kaoliang", grown in North China, comes of a group of grain sorghums. At least on five previous occasions the Japanese have attempted bacterial warfare against China by dropping infected grains and other substance. They were: over Ningpo on Oct. 27, 1940; over Chuhsien, Oct. 4, 1940; over Kinhwa, Nov. 8, 1940, all in Chekiang province; and over Changteh, Hunan Province, on Nov, 4, 1941. Except in Kinhwa, plague epidemics broke out at each locale following the attack claiming a number of victims. In all cases laboratory tests definitely established the fact that droppings from the enemy planes contain plague bacilli. A full report on these cases of Japanese biological warfare was made public on April 9,1942, by Dr. P.Z. King, Director-General of the National Health Administration, and attracted wide attention. Text of the report was released by CHINESE NEWS SERVICE on April 9 and was reprinted in CHINA AT WAR of August, 1942.)

Transmitted by Mrs. Price, Foreign Broadcast Monitoring Service, F.C.C.
9-29-42 Chinese News Service is located at 1250 6th Ave., New York City.

RESTRICTED

3.24 24 Oct. 1942: CENSORSHIP, Record No. 8A 82558, FROM: MEXICO, D.F.: JAPS CHARGED WITH GERM WARFARE

资料出处： National Archives of the United States, R112, E295A, B11.

内容点评： 本资料为1942年10月19日美国国家新闻审查处存档墨西哥新闻报道摘要：据中国政府声明，日本人实施了细菌战。

CENSORSHIP
AMERICA

TYPE OF CENSORSHIP

Record No. SA 82558

Mail No. | Sea (S). Air (A). Land (L). A | Mail (M) M | Cable | Tel | Registered No. NONE | Serial No. | Page 1 of 2 pages.

FROM:
MEXICO, D.F.
(NO RETURN ADDRESS)

LIST: NONE

TO:
MEDICAL ECONOMICS INC.
WILLIAM ALAN RICHARDSON,
MANAGING EDITOR,
RUTHERFORD, N.J.

WAR DEPT - S.G.O
IN

NOV 20 AM 9:09

LIST: NONE

Date of letter (or postmark if undated): OCT. 19, 1942	To be photographed: NO	To whom photograph is to be sent:	DISPOSAL OF ORIGINAL COMMUNICATION:
Previous relevant records: NONE	For interoffice use by A. C. or D. C. only:	Station distribution: DR	Held (H). Released (R). R Condemned (C). Returned to sender (RS) Or sent with comment to:
	Language: ENGLISH	Previously censored by: NONE	

DR use only	Division (or Section)	Table	Examiner (Censor-Cable)	D. A. C.	Exam. date	Typing date
	PRESS	2	12142	A/2188	OCT. 22, 1942	om 10-24-42

COMMENT

ADB
AG
BEW -4
BF
BR
BP
CAA
CAN
CCC
CIAA -1
COI
COM
CPC
DL
ED -1
FBI -1
FCC
FR
FSA
FTC
IMM
INT
JSM
LC
MC
MEW 5
MID -8
ONI -1
OPA
PO
RFC
SC
SD -2
T -1
WPB

POLITICAL - ECONOMIC - MILITARY

I. MEXICO PHYSICIANS LAUNCH PROPAGANDA AGAINST U.S. CLINIC
II. MEXICAN HOSPITALS MAY TRY LOTTERIES
III. MEDICAL STUDENTS PROTEST FORCED RURAL DUTY
IV. JAPS CHARGED WITH GERM WARFARE

Cover contains news correspondence.

I. Mexican Physicians Launch Propaganda against U.S. Clinic.
In article titled "Mexico Vs The Mayos" writer states that group of Mexico physicians led by Dr. Conrado Zuckerman have launched a bitter propaganda campaign against the Mayo Clinic in Rochester, Minn. Zuckerman says Mexicans go to the Mayos because of the attraction of distance, because it is fashionable, or because, knowing they are going to die they are willing to try anything. At Mayos the sufferer virtually lacks a doctor, and the multiplication of hands has harmful results. It appears that 90% of trips to Rochester are fatal.

II. Mexican Hospitals may Try Lotteries.
In article titled "Lauds Hospital Lottery" writer states Hospital heads harassed by shringking endowments are studying Mexico's Loteria Nacional as possible salution. Latest authority to report favorably on the lottery is Eusebio Delfin of Cuba.

III. Medical Students Protest Forced Rural Duty.
In article titled "Back to the Farm Draft" writer states that protest of medical students to serving in rural districts is the first serious challenge to the law.

Dr. Gustavo Argil, Director of National Faculty of Medicine denies this resentment will lead to laws repeal.

IV. Japs Charged With Germ Warfare.
In article titled "Bacillus Blitzkreig," writer states that according to an official announcement by the Chinese Government that examination of grain dropped by Japanese planes disclosed that it was impregnated

From MTS

ORSHIP
AMERICA

CONFIDENTIAL

TYPE OF CENSORSHIP

RECORD No. SA 82558

Mail No. | Sea (S). Air (A). Land (L). A | Mail (M) M | C XXXXX | T XXXXXXXX
Registered No. NONE | Serial No. | Page 2 of 2 pages.

FROM:
MEXICO, D.F.
(NO RETURN ADDRESS)

LIST: NONE

TO:
MEDICAL ECONOMICS INC.
WILLIAM ALAN RICHARDSON,
MANAGING EDITOR,
RUTHERFORD, N.J.

LIST: NONE

Date of XXXXXX postmark if XXXXX undated): OCT. 19, 1942	To be photographed: NO	To whom photograph is to be sent:	DISPOSAL OF ORIGINAL COMMUNICATION:
Previous relevant records: NONE	For interoffice use by A. C. or D. C. only:	Station distribution: DR	Held (H). Released (R). R Condemned (C). Returned to sender (RS)
	Language: ENGLISH	Previously censored by: NONE	Or sent with comment to:

DR use only	Division (or Section)	Table	Examiner (Censor Cable)	D. A. C.	Exam. date	Typing date
	PRESS	1	12142	A/2188	OCT. 22, 1942	omm 10-24-42

COMMENT

POLITICAL - ECONOMIC - MILITARY

ADB
AG
BEW
BF
BR
BP
CAA
CAN
CCC
CIAA
COI
COM
CPC
DL
ED
FBI
FCC
FR
FSA
FTC
IMM
INT
JSM
LC
MC
MEW
MID
ONI
OPA
PO
RFC
SC
SD
T
WPB

with Bubonic Plauge.

EXAMINER'S NOTE: News copy is labeled "News Vane" indicating writer may be Eric Vane.

ENCLOSURES: No letter of transmittal.
6 news articles.

CH
A/AC/12091
10-23-42

From MIS

3.25 3 Dec. 1942: 2400.1-2, FCCL A 289, Chungking in English at 12:01 PM to Europe

资料出处：National Archives of the United States, R112, E295A, B11.

内容点评：本资料为 1942 年 12 月 3 日重庆发往欧洲的英文电文，提及传染病防疫部门负责人的湘西常德调查，认为当地鼠疫爆发流行肯定由敌人攻击引起。

RESTRICTED

2400.1-2
3 December 1942.

FCCL A289

Chungking in English at 12:01 PM to Europe:

(Text) "When the head of the Epidemic Prevention Department retunned to Changsha from a detailed investigation of the plague situation in (Changteh), Western Hunan, he said that there was every reason to believe that the outbreak was due to enemy action.

"The Plague first broke out on November 11, 1941, a week after enemy raiders had dropped bombs.

"In December infected rats were found, but as there is no communication with the town except by water from other towns whence rats might have brought disease, it was decided that the fleas must have bred locally, as the surrounding district is a cotton and rice producing area.

"The first case was traced to grain and rice which must have been contaminated by infected fleas, and all the first batch of cases occurred seven or eight days after the raid-and that is also the length of the incubation period of the bacteria before the disease is apparent."

(Reception was poor, and several other reasons advanced to support the belief that bacteriological warfare was being employed by the Japanese were not sufficiently audible to be transcribed-ed).

RESTRICTED

3.26 8 Jan. 1943: Letter to Col. Bayne-Jones, from John P. Marquand, FEDERAL SECURITY AGENCY: Digest of Information Regarding Axis Activities in the Field of Bacteriological Warfare

资料出处：National Archives of the United States, R112, E295A, B11.

内容点评：本资料为 1943 年 1 月 8 日美国联邦安全局 John P. Marquand 提交 S. Bayne-Jones 上校的报告，题目：轴心国细菌战方面活动情报汇编。内容包括日军在湖南常德实施的鼠疫攻击。

FEDERAL SECURITY AGENCY
WASHINGTON

OFFICE OF
THE ADMINISTRATOR

Room 308
2101 Constitution Avenue
Washington, D.C.
January 8, 1943

JAN 11 1943

Colonel S. Bayne-Jones
Room 1209
1818 H Street, N.W.
Washington, D.C.

Dear Colonel Bayne-Jones:

Please find enclosed a summary of intelligence of which I spoke to you and Colonel Simmons. I have tried to collect all information on the subject which is available in case it may be eventually needed as a partial explanation of any of our activities.

This has been quite a job because the bits and pieces of this intelligence have been widely distributed. If you, or Colonel Simmons, can think of anything to add, or find any inaccuracies, I should be immensely grateful if you would point them out.

Also I rather imagine this document should have some sort of conclusions based on the evaluation of this information. This seems a little beyond me in my civilian capacity, and I should greatly appreciate it if you and Colonel Simmons have any suggestions, if you have, please forward them to me here.

With many thanks for your kindness in letting me see your files, I am

Sincerely yours,

John P. Marquand

DECLASSIFIED
E.O. 12065, Sec. 3-402
NND 579-5
WG Lewis NARS 2/1/80

Dictated but not read
JPM:ref

Enclosure

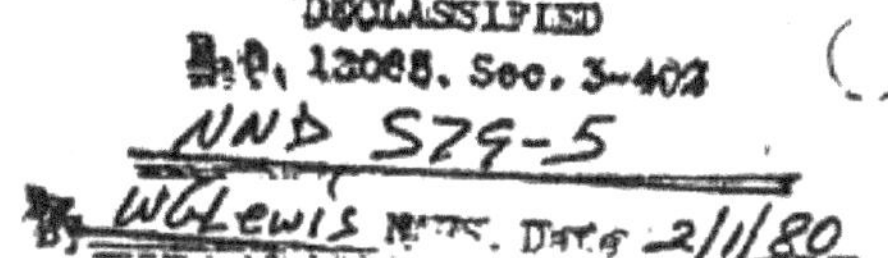

~~Copy #~~ 7

January 8, 1943

~~SECRET~~

Digest of Information
Regarding
Axis Activities in the Field of Bacteriological
Warfare

German use? Nov 1917

Purpose

The purpose of this digest is to summarize all intelligence collected by various branches of the government, indicating enemy activity in bacteriological warfare and the use of poisons, so that this evidence may be used to explain, if necessary, such measures as may be taken by our authorities in this field.

Introduction

Due to the extra-legal position of bacteriological warfare and the use of poisons, even under the present lax rules of warfare, all initiative and preparations are concealed by the enemy governments involved under the veil of utmost secrecy which doubtless accounts for the brevity and scarcity of this intelligence. For the purpose of convenience, it is arranged here in three categories:

1. Intelligence of the years 1917-1939.
2. Intelligence beginning with the present war--from sources considered reliable.
3. Rumors and information from less reliable sources.

Intelligence of the years 1917-1939.

1. Certain discoveries were made in the German legation at Bucharest in the last war tending to show that a virus in considerable quantity was imported by

~~SECRET~~

2 1/8/43

SECRET

German agents for the purpose of inoculating cavalry horses in the Rumanian army with glanders. Further details of this will be found in the confidential M.I.S. Report, March 20, 1930, paraphrasing a speech by Dr. L. Georges of France. Also in C.W.S. Bibliography and in C.W.S. - BW History.

2. There are also reports that similar activities were attempted during the last war in the remount services of France and the United States. Details may be found in the C.W.S. Bibliography.

3. At intervals since the great Spanish influenza epidemic of 1918, there have been reports from various sources that the germs of this epidemic were deliberately spread by German agents. For details see files and bibliography of the C.W.S.

4. A letter from the Surgeon General of the United States Army in 1918 notes that German troops were inoculated against cholera. This step caused anxiety as it was considered a possible basis for a malicious attempt to spread the disease. There was a general belief among well-informed officers at the time that the Germans had poisoned wells with cholera germs.

5. Wickham Steed, a British journalist, reported in 1934 that German agents were working in the Paris Metro and the London Underground on experiments dealing with the introduction of bacteria through ventilating systems. This report is allegely based on German documents, examined by Mr. Steed. In an M.I.S. report of

SECRET

3 1/8/43 SECRET

February 2, 1942, a Dr. Helmuth Simmons, alleges that these German documents, and more, are in his possession. The Steed disclosure created a very considerable sensation at the time and is the basis for much of the literature on bacteriological warfare.

6. In C.W.S. Intelligence, February 13, 1942, is a report from Dr. Maurice Wolf and Mr. Robert Wiel, offering proof that the Germans were experimenting with BW as far back as 1929.

Intelligence beginning with the present war--from sources considered reliable.

1. In February 1939, an effort was made by the Japanese to obtain Yellow Fever Virus from the Rockefeller Institute of New York. A Japanese doctor, from a Japanese laboratory, with an introduction from the Japanese Military Attache in Washington, made a direct request to the Institute for this virus but was refused. Shortly after the refusal, an attempt was made to obtain this same virus by offering a bribe of three thousand dollars to an employee of the Rockefeller Institute. The full details of this affair are contained in a report made by Dr. Wilbur A. Sawyer, Director, International Health Division of the Institute, and transmitted in a letter to Colonel Simmons of the Surgeon General's Office. In this same connection, it is

reported by M.I.S., March 8, 1942, that a Doctor Hayakawa endeavored to obtain Yellow Fever Virus from a laboratory in Brazil.

2. February 25, 1941, A.C. of S., G-2, to A.C. of S. in W.P.D., stated that reliable information indicates that Japanese have a bacteriological warfare battalion attached to each of two chemical warfare regiments and have trained over 2000 parachute troops.

3. From the British Air Attache, Bern, May 1941, came a report, G-2, #3887, dealing in very considerable detail with the activities of a Professor Menk of Hamburg who was said to have moved after the occupation of France to the Foch Institute near Paris. There, it is reported, he was busying himself with experiments on botulinus as a war weapon, planning to spread this poison in bombs. His method is reported in considerable detail. The Surgeon General's Office has commented: "While this report is obviously inaccurate in many details, it contains certain points which may be of significance."

4. There are several detailed reports of Japanese efforts to affect Chinese areas with Bubonic Plague by dropping objects from airplanes--Changteh and Chekiang Province. These efforts are summarized in an M.I.S. Report, December 27, 1941; a report from Science Service, paraphrased by C.W.S. Intelligence, November 27, 1941;

1/8/43 SECRET

5

Laboratory reports of Medical Aid to China, C.W.S. Intelligence, December 12, 1941; Eye-witness accounts and C.W.S. Intelligence Reports, December 18, 1941; Missionaries accounts of same, December 19, 1941; Medical Reports from Yale-in-China; and reports of autopsies, December 20 and 30, 1941. Also report of Red Cross and report of United States Military Attache and of Chinese Minister of Foreign Affairs. All these tend to confirm Japanese use of Bubonic organisms in attacks at Changteh.

Rumors and information from less reliable sources.

1. April 15, 1940, in a secret British document on BW, the French tell of an insident of sabotage in Africa where, during the inoculations, of natives with anti-meningococcal vaccine, 49 deaths from tetanus poison occurred. The French believe that one ampoule was removed in transit between Dakar and the inoculation station and one containing tetanus toxin was substituted.
2. January 11, 1941, M.I.S. Report, suspicion that yellow fever among British forces in Sudan--never before known in this portion of Africa--may have been deliberately transmitted by enemy.
3. November 3, 1941, M.I.S. reports that the German Dye Trust will spread influenza in its United States plants in the event of war.

SECRET

6 1/8/43

4. November 8, 1941, M.I.S., British have encountered typhus (sic) bacteria in water supply of ships at sea.

5. January 30, 1942, J. Edgar Hoover in a letter to O.N.I. quotes a confidential informant, long a resident in Tokyo as hearing a German doctor there, while under the influence of liquor, state that certain German doctors were in Japan for the sole purpose of teaching Japanese bacterial warfare and someday Germany would get its revenge on the United States by the use of such a weapon. The doctor referred particularly to anthrax baccili and typhus germs.

6. February 2, 1942, O.N.I. gives the report of a Dr. Helmuth Simmons (seeking entry into this country) on German preparations for bacteriological warfare. The Germans, Dr. Simmons says, will make bacterial attacks in powder and not in liquid form. Tests have already been made on sheep on an island near Spain. (Also on young Jews, C.W.S. Intelligence.) Anthrax was discovered to be particularly efficient. A bacterial projector has already been perfected called the Himmler Bomb. German experts and French scientists are making further investigations at the Pasteur Institute in Paris. Several factories in France,

7 1/8/43 

particularly sugar factories, are now in production for BW. He speaks of a product, a few kilos of which are sufficient to kill the inhabitants of a large town, but he says that such a town can be repentered safely a few hours later. He claims to possess the documents, and more, which form the basis of the Wickham Steed articles.

7. Late February, 1942, F.B.I. memorandum states that a telephone call was received in Los Angeles from an informant, saying he was Japanese, warning that Jap saboteurs had in possession five or six cans of jelly-like substance, reported to be a mixture of typhoid and bubonic bacteria to be placed in Los Angeles water system. Later, a similar call advised that plague and typhoid containers would be taken to Owens Valley by Japanese evacuees. Caller stated his father was a Japanese Army Officer from Superior supposedly located in Brazil. No such containers were ever found, among Japanese household effects.

8. Letter dated April 13, 1942, Switzerland to a British address, submitted by M.I.D. Counter-Intelligence Group, Censorship Branch, "I am confirmed they (Germans) are going to use bacteria of every description....I have heard that in Germany they seem to be vaccinating <u>everybody</u>

8

1/8/43

SECRET

for diphtheria, and so forth....They seem so cock-sure of victory and what they have in the background in the way of surprises, who knows?"

9. August 3, 1942, M.I.S.--Account of "Hitler Bacteria Waffe", from an informant in United States who received facts from brother-in-law, a government employee in Germany--a bacterial poison so deadly that not even blood plasma will cure it. This is now stored in long glass tubes in strategic places throughout Europe to be used by Hitler only as a last resort. Will be pumped by diesel engines into water and filteration plants. Informant seeking citizenship, and little credence is placed in this report.

10. August 22, 1942, M.I.S.--Reports and rumors of sabotage mentioning eye diseases early in year among shipyard workers on Pacific Coast, with the reputed origin in Japan. See letter to Dr. Parran from J. Edgar Hoover, giving report of an individual of unknown reliability, that Japanese were collecting these bacteria--August 11, 1942. Jaundice in Army as a result of yellow fever inoculations, vaccine being possibly contaminated by enemy agents. Steel filings and glass discovered in meat products in a Chicago packing house.

11. August 30, 1942, a report from J. Edgar Hoover to A. A. Berle, Jr., tells of German scientists in Brazil owning laboratories on farms where they are actively engaged in experiments with bacteria and poisons. The principal objective of these agents is to study and prepare the way for spreading, when the moment is opportune, germs capable of altering public health in such a manner as to create a calamity uncontrollable by the government. It is said that a large number of germ-affected food products have already been put into circulation and a second, more violent dose, can be given that will cause fatalities and contaminate large numbers of the population. It is asserted that a recent outbreak of typhoid in the Brazilian Capitol was in line with these experiments.

12. November 5, 1942, F.B.I. report on an investigation by Military Intelligence, a jar of poisoned tomatoes contained a large quantity of bichloride of mercury found near mess tables at Fort Schafter, Hawaii.

13. November 27, 1942, O.N.I. received a report from Polish sources that Hitler and Himmler had conferred on November 11, on the subject of bacteriological warfare, and concluded to employ this, and also chemical warfare when it appears the tide is definitely turning against them. Britain was specified as the point of attack.

SECRET

16

14. December 17, 1942, O.N.I. calls attention to a Berlin trans-ocean broadcast in English, December 14, announcing new methods of combating spotted fever of typhus. In this connection, Germans state they have succeeded in producing bacteria in tins for prophylactic vaccinations. These bacteria which are kept alive in the tins are now being mass-produced under new technical procedure.

15. December 28, 1942, memorandum from F.B.I. summarizing an anonymous letter from Florida addressed to Attorney General. Writer indicates that he heard a Nazi state: "When Hitler sees himself losing ground, if and when the United States gets into the war, he will use his secret weapon, bacteria, which he has stored and prepared in all quarters of the globe. That is why I do not want to see the United States get into this war." Writer mentions influenza epidemic of the last war, and a German woman bacteriologist, Tillie Spiecker Karn, who now has a laboratory in Forest Hills and whose German butler recently died of convulsions. Investigation of letter is now underway.

3.27 14 Dec. 1942: CHINESE CHOLERA EPIDEMIC NOW MAMMOTH etc.

资料出处：National Archives of the United States, R112, E295A, B11.

内容点评：本资料为美国收集的中国疫情情报汇编，包括重庆、广东、上海、浙江、绥远、北平、天津。

14 December 1942

CHINESE CHOLERA EPIDEMIC NOW MAMMOTH

Tokyo reports (Dec. 14, 2:00 a.m. EWT) in English to the western U.S., Central and South America: "The cholera epidemic which has from the beginning of the year ravaged the areas under the Chungking regime has reached mammoth proportions according to latest reports from Chiang's capital.

11,964 Cases--"For the first 9 months of the year more than 11,964 cases have broken out, resulting in 4,570 deaths in the 11 provinces including Chungking. The cause of the epidemic is believed to be from local insanitary conditions and the bringing in of cholera germs from Burma by the Chinese soldiers.)

FCC 12/14/42

None of the reports emanating from Japanese sources have been confirmed either by Chinese or neutral sources. Neither can this Office add any information in confirmation of the Chingking broadcast, telling of the outbreak of a Bubonic Plague in southwestern Chekiang.

The information concerning the flowering of the bamboo in the Arakan (northwestern Burma) area and the accompanying plague of rats is believed to be the most reliable of all information on the six enclosed pages.

It may be added that, as far as this Office knows, none of the plagues in China south of the Yangtse River (Hunan, Chekiang Provinces) have become widespread. As a note of some interest, it may be added that previous to the Sino-Japanese war, bubonic plague had never been known to appear south of the Yangtse River.

1

SECRET

Combined H.Q. Eastern India D.I.S. No. 310
Copy No. 144 - July 43

The Flowering of the Bamboo. From the Southern CHIN HILLS has come a report that a plague of rats seriously damaged TAUNGYA (shifting hill cultivation) crops last year. This apparently insignificant statement may provide a guidance on the availability of bamboo for constructional purposes in the ARAKAN during the next year or two.

For some reason, for which there appears to be no satisfactory explanation, a plague of rats occurs on the ARAKAN YOMAHS at the time of the flowering of the bamboo.

The bamboo has a life period of about 25 years. At the end of this time, it blooms, dies and rots, and new shoots spring from the roots of the old plants. The new shoots grow to maturity in 3 or 4 years, during which period the quality and supply of bamboo are far below normal.

The flowering of the bamboo occurs over a wide tract and spreads very rapidly to neighbouring areas, so that in succeeding localities there is a periodic dearth of this useful plant.

The bamboo last flowered in the LEMRO-KALADAN areas in 1919. The accompanying plague of rats attacked the paddy crops in the fields of MINBYA and MYOHAUNG, as well as in the TAUNGYAS, causing economic distress in the areas affected.

It is reasonable to assume that the flowering of the bamboo which is suspected of having started in the KANPETLET area, on the Eastern ranges of the ARAKAN YOMAHS, will spread to the Western ranges within a year. If this occurs, there will be a shortage of high grade bamboo suitable for temporary bridges in some of the localities of the upper LEMRO-KALADAN areas, if not throughout the whole tract.

Issued at 0830 hrs 21st July 1943.

2

SECRET

Summ. Ec. Int.
USAF 1 Jan 44

HEALTH AND SANITATION

<u>China</u>

A deadly malaria epidemic is sweeping unchecked through Northern Kwangtung Province. Medical authorities have great difficulties in checking this disease because of a lack of quinine and other preventive drugs. At the end of November malaria patients in the city of Shaokuan alone totaled 100,000. Also, it is reported that several cases of small pox have broken out and it is feared a small pox epidemic will follow the malaria epidemic. (J.B. 14 Dec. 43).

16 December 1943

MALARIA AND SMALL POX IN CHINA

Shanghai (December 16, 1943). The epidemics of malaria and smallpox, which are spreading all the time in increasing proportions, in Kwangtung in the north, have caused the death of 100,000 Chinese, according to information from Canton.

The fight against the diseases is difficult due to the lack of medicines. The scarcity of food and of clothing favors the spread of the disease, against which the authorities fight fruitlessly.

NOTE: Translation from Spanish text.

FCC Transcript, April 8, 1943

P41520 Chungking in English at 1100 AM (Wednesday) to North America (Apr.7-43)

/Text/ With the outbreak of a Bubonic Plague last night in/Luangshuan/ (Lung-ch'uan) in Southwestern Chekiang, the Chekiang Provincial Government has taken drastic measures to prevent its spread into other areas. /2 words/ This highway town is virtually shut off from the outside world with /car fueling/ stations /word/ where incoming people are required to take preventative innoculations. Meanwhile the town medical corps has taken local action to drown out infection in affected areas and isolating all persons. /end item/ /BA/

FCCF A344

CHUNGKING IN ENGLISH AT 11:00 AM to North America

(Text) "A cholera epidemic has broken out at Enpei and Wuyuan, two of the largest towns in Western Suiyuan Province, and has already taken a toll of 160 lives.

"The Suiyuan Provincial Government has instructed the magistrate of the two Hsiens to take emergency measures to prevent is spreading.

"Reports state that cholera is also rampert in Peiping and Tientsin where the toll of lives is already heavy."

GD 10/5-1129A

5 October 1943

3.28 July-September 1943, Volume 61, Number 3, PP. 259-263: THE CHINESE MEDICAL JOURNAL: BACTERIAL WARFARE

资料出处： National Archives of the United States, R112, E295A, B11.

内容点评： 本资料来自1943年第3期《中国医学季刊》(总第61号)第259~263页:《细菌战》。文中引用了中国中央卫生署总长金宝善的有关报告。

THE
CHINESE MEDICAL JOURNAL

VOLUME 61 JULY–SEPTEMBER 1943 NUMBER 3

BACTERIAL WARFARE

It is already common knowledge that the Japanese in the conduct of the war in China since 1937 have used every known form of warfare without the least consideration of legality and morality. What surprises one most are the feeble attempts made with some of the weapons, making one believe that they are experimenting on a small scale in order to prepare for extensive operations of similar nature if the experiments should prove successful.

Poison gas has been used repeatedly, but never on an extensive scale. Bacterial warfare has also been attempted and in this field it has been difficult to say how often it has been tried. It is difficult to find evidence of deliberate attempts to produce epidemics of cholera and dysentery, for instance. But in the case of plague the Chinese Government health authorities have definitely proved, with bacteriological methods, that the Japanese air force has several times deliberately attempted to produce epidemics. Happily, there are factors in epidemiology which even ingeniously evil-minded Japanese cannot provide, as a result of which the attempts were attended with very limited success.

We produce here the official statement by Dr. P. Z. King, Director, General of the National Health Administration, on the subject, released for publication in April 1942. The statement covers the first five investigated attempts of the Japanese to produce epidemics of plague in Free China, but since then, on August 30, 1942, a sixth attempt was made in Nanyang in Honan province. Three Japanese planes dropped large quantities of kaoliang (sorghum) and corn which, on bacteriological examination, were found to be contaminated with the bacilli of bubonic plague.

The full text of Dr. King's statement follows:

"Up to the present time the practicability of bacterial warfare has been little known to the public because applicable experimental results, if available, are usually kept a military secret.

"In the past the artifical dissemination of disease germs has been done for military purposes. The pollution of drinking water supplies by the introduction of diseased animals or other infected materials into the wells has been practiced by retreating armies with the intention of causing epidemics of gastro-intestinal infections among the troops in pursuit. Fortunately such water-borne infections can be controlled with relative ease by boiling of all drinking water and disinfection by chemical means.

"Whether or not infectious diseases could be widely and intentionally spread by artifical means with deadly results had not been demonstrated prior to the outbreak of the Sino-Japanese war. However, in the last two years sufficient circumstantial evidence has been gathered to show that the Japanese have been using our people as guinea pigs for experimentation on the practicablity of bacterial warfare. They have tried to produce epidemics of plague in Free China by scattering plague-infected materials from airplanes. The facts thus far collected follow:

"1. On October 29, 1940, bubonic plague for the first time occurred in Ningpo in Chekiang province. The epidemic lasted 34 days and claimed 99 victims. It was reported that on October 27, 1940, Japanese planes raided Ningpo and scattered a considerable quantity of wheat over the port city. Although it was a curious fact to find 'grain from heaven' yet no one at the time seemed to appreciate the enemy's intention and no thorough examination of the grain was made. All the plague victims were local residents. The diagnosis of plague was definitely confirmed by laboratory tests. There was no excessive mortality among rats noticed before the epidemic and, despite careful examination, no exogenous sources of infection could be discovered.

"2. On October 4, 1940, a Japanese plane visited Chuhsien, Chekiang province. After circling over the city it scattered rice and wheat mixed with fleas over the western district of the city. There were many eye-witnesses among whom was a man named Hsu, who collected some grain and dead fleas from the street outside of his own house. He sent them to the local air-raid precautionary corps for transmission to the provincial hygienic laboratory. The laboratory examination result was that 'there were no pathogenic organisms found by bacteriological culture methods.' However, on November 12, 38 days after the Japanese plane's visit, bubonic plague appeared in the same area where the grain and fleas were found in abundance. The epidemic in Chuhsien lasted 24 days, resulting in 21 deaths.

"Available records show bubonic plague never occurred in Chuhsien before. After careful investigation it was believed that the strange visit of the enemy plane was the cause of the epidemic and the transmitting agent was rat fleas, presumably infected with plague and definitely dropped by the enemy plane. As plague is primarily a disease of rodents, the grain was probably used to attract the rats and expose them to the infected fleas mixed therein. It was regrettable that the fleas collected were not properly examined. Owing to deficient laboratory facilities, an animal inoculation test was not performed.

"3. On November 28, 1940, when the plague epidemic in Ningpo and Chuhsien was still in progress, three Japanese planes came to Kinhwa, an important commercial city situated between Ningpo and Chuhsien, and there dropped a large quantity of small granules about the size of shrimp-eggs. These strange objects were collected and examined in a local hospital.

"The granules were more or less round, about one millimeter in diameter, of whitish-yellow, somewhat translucent with a certain amount of glistening reflection from the surface. When brought into contact with water on a glass-slide the granule began to swell to about twice its original size. In a small amount of water in a test tube with some agitation it would break up into whitish flakes and later form a milky suspension. Microscopic examination of these granules revealed the presence of numerous gram-negative bacilli with distinct bipolar staining in some of them and an abundance of involution forms, thus possessing the morphological characteristics of B. Pestis, the positive organism of plague. When cultured in agar medium these gram-negative bacilli showed no growth and because of inadequacy of laboratory facilities animal inoculation tests could not be performed.

"Upon the receipt of such a startling report from Kinhwa the National Health Administration dispatched Dr. W. W. Yung, director of the Department of Epidemic Prevention; Dr. H. M. Jettmar, epidemiologist, formerly of the League of Nation's Epidemic Commission, and other technical experts to investigate the situation. Arriving in Kinhwa early in January, 1941, they examined 26 of these granules and confirmed the previous observations, but inoculation tests performed on guinea pigs by Dr. Jettmar gave negative results. It is difficult to say whether or not the lapse of time and the method of preservation of the granules had something to do with the negative results from the animal inoculation test, which is a crucial test for B. Pestis. At all events no plague occurred in Kinhwa and it indicated that this particular Japanese experiment on bacterial warfare ended in failure.

"4. On November 4, 1941, at about 5 a.m., a lone enemy plane appeared over Changteh, Hunan province, flying very low, the morning being rather misty. Instead of bombs, wheat and rice, pieces of paper, cotton wadding, and some unidentified particles were dropped. After the all-clear signal had been sounded some of these strange gifts from the enemy were collected and sent by the police to a local missionary hospital for examination which revealed the presence of microorganisms reported to resemble B. Pestis.

"On November 11, seven days later, the first clinical case of plague came to notice, followed by five more cases. The diagnosis of bubonic plague was definitely confirmed in one of the six cases in November by bacteriological culture method and animal inoculation test.

"According to the investigation of Dr. W. W. Chen, bacteriologist, who has had special training in plague work in India, and Dr. R. Pollitzer, epidemiologist of the National Health Administration and formerly of the League of Nation's Epidemic Commission, the Changteh plague epidemic was caused by enemy action because of the following strong circumstantial evidence:

"A—That Changteh has never been, as far as is known, afflicted by plague. During previous pandemics and severe epidemics elsewhere in China this part of Hunan (as a matter of fact this part of Central China in general) has never been known to come under the scourge of the disease.

"B—That the present outbreak may have been due to direct contiguous spread from neighboring plague-infected districts is also untenable on epidemiological grounds. Epidemiologically plague spreads along transport routes for grain on which the rats feed. The nearest epidemic center to Changteh is Chuhsien in Chekiang, about 2,000 kilometers away by land or river communication. Furthermore, Changteh being a rice producing district, supplies rice to other districts and does not receive rice from other cities. Besides, all the cases occuring in Changteh were native inhabitants who had not been away from the city or its immediate environs at all.

"C—That all the cases came from the areas within the city where the strange objects dropped by enemy planes were found, and that among the wheat and rice and cotton rags were the most probable included vectors, probably fleas. The fleas were not noticed on the spot because they were not looked for and because the air raid alarm lasted some twelve hours with the result that the fleas must have in the meantime escaped to other hiding places.

"D—That there was no apparent evidence of any excessive rat mortality before and for sometime after the 'aerial incident.' About 200 rats were caught and examined during the months of November and December but no evidence of plague was found. However, toward the end of January and the first part of February of this year, among 78 rats examined there were eighteen with definite plague infection. As plague is primarily a disease of rodents the usual sequence of events is that an epizootic precedes an epidemic but that did not take place in the present case. The infected fleas from the enemy planes must have first attacked men and a little later, the rats.

"E—That all the first six human cases were infected within fifteen days after the 'aerial incident' and that infected fleas are known to be able to survive under suitable conditions for weeks without feeding. The normal incubation period of bubonic plague is three to seven days and may occasionally be prolonged to eight or even fourteen days. The time factor is certainly also a strong circumstantial evidence.

"5. A serious epidemic of plague occurring in Suiyuan, Ningsia and Shensi provinces has recently been reported. From the last week of January this year to date there have been some 600 cases. Those cases were reported in a recent communique from the local military in the northwestern part of the epidemic area. However, considering the fact that plague is known to be enzootic among the native rodents in the Ordos region in Suiyuan one must wait for confirmation of the reports that probably the plague was caused there by enemy action.

"Technical experts, including Dr. Y. N. Yang, Director of the National Health Administration's Northwest Epidemic Prevention Bureau, have been sent there to investigate and help control the epidemic.

"The enumeration of facts thus far collected leads to the conclusion that the Japanese army has attempted bacterial warfare in China. In Chekiang and Hunan they had scattered from the air infective materials and succeeded in causing epidemic outbreaks of plague. Aside from temporary terrorization of the general population in the afflicted areas this inhuman act of our enemy is most condemnable when one realizes that once the disease has taken root in the local rat population it will continue to infect men for many years to come. Fortunately the mode of infection and the method of control of plague are known and it is possible to keep the disease in check by vigorous control measures. Our difficulty at present is the shortage of anti-epidemic supplies required. The recent advance in chemotherapy has given us new drugs that are more or less effective for the treatment of plague cases. These are sulfathiazole and allied sulphonamide compounds which China cannot as yet produce herself.

"For prevention, plague vaccine can be produced in considerable quantities by the National Epidemic Prevention Bureau in Kunming and the Northwest Epidemic Prevention Bureau in Lanchow, provided the raw materials required for vaccine production such as peptone and agar agar are available.

"Rat proofing of all buildings and eradication of rats are fundamental control measures but under war conditions they cannot be satisfactorily carried out.

"If rat poisons such as cyanogas and barium carbonate can be obtained from abroad in large quantities deratization campaigns may be launched in cities where rats are a menace."

JOURNALS OF THE CHINESE MEDICAL ASSOCIATION

Up to December 1941, the Chinese Medical Association published two monthly journals, the National Medical Journal (in Chinese) and the Chinese Medical Journal (in English). The National Medical Journal, which was published in Shanghai, since it was in the Chinese language, was edited primarily for the medical profession in China. The Chinese Medical Journal, which was published in Peiping, aimed to place before the medical world abroad the scientific work of the Chinese medical profession through the medium of the English language. The December 1941 issue of the National Medical Journal was Volume 27, No. 12, while that of the Chinese Medical Journal was Volume 60, No. 12.

The changed war conditions after the attack on Pearl Harbor necessitated the adaptation of these Journals to what are in practice three geographical areas: Free China, Occupied China, and the outside world. Sending of journals from any one of these three areas to either of the other two areas was impossible. It was therefore necessary to undertake the publication of the Journals within each area in accordance with the purposes of the Journals.

The National Medical Journal is being maintained in the form of two editions. The Shanghai edition is continued much as before, as a monthly, the January 1942 issue being Volume 28, No. 1, and this is being circulated among the medical profession in Occupied China. The Chungking edition first appeared as a bi-monthly medical digest in June 1942, continuing in this form for six issues; then in July 1943 it was enlarged into its original size, and included original articles as well as the medical digest.

3.29 14 Sep. 1943: OFFICE OF CENSORSHIP U.S., L.W. 14-9-43, 72, Terminal Mail, AIR, LON 73083/43: DISEASE IN CHINA

资料出处： National Archives of the United States, R112, E295A, B11.

内容点评： 本资料为 1943 年 9 月 14 日美国国家新闻审查处存档情报：中国的疫情。

CONFIDENTIAL

2400.1
26 June 43

Form OC-814 (Rev. 9-43)
OFFICE OF CENSORSHIP
UNITED STATES OF AMERICA

REPRODUCTION OF SUBMISSION FROM FOREIGN CENSORSHIP

L.W. 14-9-43

72
Terminal Mail
AIR

LON 73083/43

C. DOWNWARD (MRS OR MISS)

E.P. MISSION
WUKINGFU, KITYANG,
KWANGTUNG, FREE CHINA

26-6-43

MISS J. GALT. B.A.

PRESBYTERIAN CHURCH OFFICES,
86 TAVISTOCK PLACE,
LONDON.W.C.1
ENGLAND

English

Released

Comment to M/HEALTH
B.B.C.
INF
D.R.E. M.E.W.

HOL T 2/VI 4672 W.E.N. 369 12-9-43

DISEASE IN CHINA

Writer states that this year the CHOLERA Epidemic in KITYANG has begun earlier than usual and is already spreading rapidly. The present unrest due to the approach of Japanese forces, would cause the disease to be much more widespread. It was already in WUKINGFU which usually escaped such diseases.

Owing to the rise in food prices people were less careful about what they ate and in addition to CHOLERA there were other serious intestinal diseases causing distress in that part of the country.

FOR F.T.

2-SD
1-OLLA
2-IE
3-OSS
2-MIS
4-OEW
19-OE
9/24

ENG
MIS
FIN
JAG
MFD
OPD
ORD
PMG
QM
SGO
SSD
TAG
TRN
USW

HD
MDW
NSC
PCD
SC
SDC
WDC

3500 5

SPECIAL NOTICE.—This contains information taken from private communications, and its extremely confidential character must be preserved. It be confided only to those officials whose knowledge of it is necessary to prosecution of the war. In no case should it be widely distributed, or copies made, or in legal proceedings or in any other public way without express consent of the Director of Censorship.

CONFIDENTIAL

3.30　12 Oct. 1943: OFFICE OF CENSORSHIP U.S., Air, CPC 1, Files 3, From: S St. Angela, Catholic Mission, Yuanling, Hunan, China, To: Rev. Mother Estella, Supt. Gen. Grey Sisters Mother House, Pembroke, Ont. : ECONOMIC & MILITARY, Re Conditions in China

资料出处： National Archives of the United States, R112, E295A, B11.

内容点评： 本资料为 1943 年 10 月 12 日美国国家新闻审查处存档湖南沅陵天主教传教士 S. St. Angela 修女予加拿大渥太华 Grey Sisters Mother House Mother Estella 信件，提及当地伤寒、痢疾、霍乱流行猖獗。

CONFIDENTIAL

2400.1

Form OC-314 (Rev. 9-42)
OFFICE OF CENSORSHIP
UNITED STATES OF AMERICA

REPRODUCTION OF SUBMISSION FROM FOREIGN CENSORSHIP CAN. 26366/43

12 Oct. 1943

S. St. Angela
Catholic Mission
Yuanling
Hunan
China.

Rev. Mother Estella
Supt. Gen.
Grey Sisters Mother House
Pembroke,
Ont.

None

None

Oct. 12/43

Air

English

CPC 1
Files 3

Released

None

General

448

Dec. 6/43

Dec. 13/43

DISTRIBUTION
CANADA

ECONOMIC & MILITARY.

Re Conditions in China.

EA 2
Inf 1
Lon 1 M
ND(Army) 1
USDR 1 M
10

EIM/JLT
DEC 11

Relationship: Missionary to Superior.

"Prices are so high that poor people find it hard even to exist. Nearly everyday starving babies are left at the hospital gate..... almost impossible to revive them. Dysentry took children like flies this summer, rich and poor were all infected and in passing by the hospital it took sixteen babies from the nursery..... heavy epidemics of typhus, dysentry, cholera..... There is talk of some priest returning to CHAKIANG but battles still rage.....Cost of living is tremendous. One hundred dollars per day each, barely covers the cost of the direct necessities in food alone. Shoes and clothing are beyond reach. Even to have an old pair re-soled costs two hundred dollars so you can imagine what a new pair would cost......You asked the price of a letter from China. Well for paper and envelopes alone, each one costs seven dollars plus thirteen for stamps. Considering prices, this is reasonable but of course the P.O. is government controlled. ....Kwelin.... is being heavily bombed and several have hit their Mission. We are in perfect peace and the only planes we see are American on their way to and from a bombing......One of the boys...last May.....crashed down near here after an air battle and the sisters fixed his bruises. He came to Yuanling after and the whole town turned out in a big way.....The airmen from a nearby field come down once in a while for a visit."

8500 3

From MIS, Counter Intelligence Group, Censorship Branch.

SPECIAL NOTICE.—This contains information taken from private communications, and its extremely confidential character must be preserved. The in be confided only to those officials whose knowledge of it is necessary to prosecution of the war. In no case should it be widely distributed, or copies made, or the i in legal proceedings or in any other public way without express consent of the Director of Censorship.

BYRO

GPO 16—35803-1

CONFIDENTIAL
CONFIDENTIAL

3.31 27 Nov. 1943: OFFICE OF CENSORSHIP U.S., L.W. 27-11-43, 72, Terminal Mail AIR, LON 405883/43: From: E.W. KENNETH, BRITISH RED CROSS HOSPITAL, CHANGSHA, HUNAN, CHINA, To: MISS G. REES ROBERTS, N. WALES: VIRULENT CHOLERA EPIDEMIC IN CHANGSHA

资料出处：National Archives of the United States, R112, E295A, B11.

内容点评：本资料为 1943 年 11 月 27 日美国国家新闻审查处存档 1943 年 10 月 2 日湖南长沙英国红十字医院 E. W. Kenneth 予北威尔士 G. Rees Roberts 小姐信件，提及长沙霍乱猖獗，所在医院 90% 感染者死亡。

Form OC-314 (Rev. 9-43)
OFFICE OF CENSORSHIP
UNITED STATES OF AMERICA

CONFIDENTIAL

REPRODUCTION OF SUBMISSION FROM FOREIGN CENSORSHIP

2400.1
2 Oct. 1943

D

L.W. 27-11-43

72
Terminal Mail
AIR

ION 405883/43

E.W. KENNETH
BRITISH RED CROSS HOSPITAL,
CHANGSA, HUNAN,
CHINA

2-10-43

MISS G. REES ROBERTS
MOUNT PLEASANT,
CRICCIETH,
N. WALES.

English

Released

Comment to M/HEALTH
D.R.W.

HOL PRI T 8/4 527 C.O.D. 23-11-43

VIRULENT CHOLERA EPIDEMIC IN CHANGSHA

Extract

"since Out Patient Dept. has opened we have many more civilians in. Cholera is abating a little. About 90% of our cases in hospital have died so it has been a virulent infection, though certainly not very widespread."

W D DIST

AAF CB
ACF
BPR
CAD
MAP
PMY
POW
SEB
SSD PCD
TAG SC
TRN SDC
WDC

8500 4

From MIS Intelligence Group, Censorship Branch

SPECIAL NOTICE.—This contains information taken from private communications, and its extremely confidential character must be preserved. be confided only to those officials whose knowledge of it is necessary to prosecution of the war. In no case should it be widely distributed, or copies made, o in legal proceedings or in any other public way without express consent of the Director of Censorship.

CONFIDENTIAL CONFIDENTIAL

3.32 29 Nov. 1943: OFFICE OF CENSORSHIP U.S., I.A. 29.11.43, 72, TERMINAL, Air, LON/SE/213648/43:, From: W. ROY AYTON, METHODIST MISSION, WENCHOW, CHEKIANG, FREE CHINA, To: THE SECRETARIES (REC. H.B.R.) METHODIST MISSIONARY SOCIETY, LONDON N. W. 1.: Plague Spreads in LUNG CHUAN

资料出处： National Archives of the United States, R112, E295A, B11.

内容点评： 本资料为 1943 年 11 月 29 日美国国家新闻审查处存档 1943 年 10 月 16 日浙江温州卫理公会传教士 W. Roy Ayton 予伦敦卫理公会秘书处 REV. H. B. R. 信件，提及浙江龙泉腺鼠疫蔓延。

Ref. made CONFIDENTIAL 2400.1

REPRODUCTION OF SUBMISSION FROM FOREIGN CENSORSHIP

...ERICA 16 Oct. 1943

I.A. 29.11.43.

72.

TERMINAL. LON/SE/213648/43.

Air.

W. ROY AYTON,
METHODIST MISSION,
WENCHOW, CHEKIANG.
FREE CHINA.

THE SECRETARIES (REV. H.B.R.)
METHODIST MISSIONARY SOCIETY,
25, MARYLEBONE ROAD,
LONDON. N.W.1.
English.

Oct. 16th, 1943.

Comment IDA.
Copy FORD.
BBC.
INF.
DRW.

Released.

LONDON. S.E.(F.4.) 471 C.F.for DMM 25.11.43.

SUBJECT:

Unoccupied China.

1. Plague spreads in LUNG CHUAN.
2. Ignorance in country areas of terms of the treaty regarding foreign property.

Extract:
BUBONIC
"BUBONIL plague has been raging at LUNG CHUAN, to the West, but so far it has not appeared here. My wife and children, and HIBBERT, all had to be inoculated against it. Bishop SARGENT of FOOCHOW (Anglican) recently died of it there.

/2.

MIS, EXP, PAY, POW, RB, SXB, VP, ABC, ANT, CDC, EDC, HD, MDW, NSC, PCD, SC, SDC, WDC

FIN, JAG, MPD, OPD, ORD, PMG, QM, SSD, TAG, TRN, USW

8500 2

From MID, Counter Intelligence Group, Censorship Branch

SPECIAL NOTICE.—This contains information taken from private communications, and its extremely confidential character must be preserved. The information must be confided only to those officials whose knowledge of it is necessary to prosecution of the war. In no case should it be widely distributed, or copies made, or the information used in legal proceedings or in any other public way without express consent of the Director of Censorship.

BYRON PRICE,
Director.

CONFIDENTIAL

GPO 16—30800-1

3.33 18 Dec. 1943: OFFICE OF CENSORSHIP U.S., CHINESE INT. WING./00183/43. TRANSIT., INDIAN CENSORSHIP, Letter Dated 14.9.43, From: Mildred (Mrs. Shu Chang Yui.), Mr. M. Tie Ten Quee, National Health Administration, Chungking, To: Charles Chang, Kingston, Jamaica: BACTERIAL WARFARE IN HUNAN

资料出处：National Archives of the United States, R112, E295A, B11.

内容点评：本资料为 1943 年 12 月 18 日美国国家新闻审查处存档 1943 年 9 月 14 日重庆中央卫生署的 Mildred (Mrs. Shu Chang Yui.)、Mr. M. Tie Ten Quee 予牙买加金斯顿 Charles Chang 信件，题目：湖南的细菌战。

UNITED STATES OF AMERICA

REPRODUCTION OF SUBMISSION FROM FOREIGN CENSORSHIP

SECRET

I.A. 18.12.43.
SECRET.

CHINESE INT. WING./00183/43.
TRANSIT.

INDIAN CENSORSHIP.

Intercepted C.I.W. Place: Calcutta. Date: 2.11.43.
Letter Dated: 14.9.43.

This office has no independent confirmation of this. However, Dr. Pollitzer is considered a very reliable source. This office has on file a statement by him that the bubonic plague in Hunan, 1942 and 1943, was caused by the Japanese; because of successful preventative measures it was not widespread.

...harles Chang,
...3, West Street,
...ingston,
...amaica.

Language: ENGLISH.

...ief Censor, India (8)

...EA. BBC. INF.

Extract: Sulphathiazole is used in the treatment of pneumonia and in nearly all septic infections. Now it is the drug needed for threatening plague which the Japs started in Hunan and of which there is danger of becoming a epidemic. We need medical instruments, like forceps for osterical work, rubber gloves, specula for osterical work, opthalmic instruments, haemometers, blood sedimentation tubes, needles, forceps and scissors. I am sure some agreement can be made with the British Government for sending us such drugs and instruments. My husband who is in charge of purchasing drugs for China tells me that there is not a shortage of these suplha drugs in England. Arrangements for purchases from the United States of America may be a bit more difficult due to the difference in currency, but there is no harm in trying.

Dr. Politzer, an Austrian, was sent out here by the League of Nations to work on epidemic prevention. He is a good friend of George and mine and investigated the outbreak in

/Hunan.

8422 1

From MID. – C.I. – Group. Cen. Br

SECRET

UNITED STATES OF AMERICA

REPRODUCTION OF SUBMISSION FROM FOREIGN CENSORSHIP

SECRET

I.A. 18.12.43. CHINESE INT. WING./00183/43.
SECRET. TRANSIT.

INDIAN CENSORSHIP.

Intercepted C.I.W. Place: Calcutta. Date: 2.11.43.
Letter Dated: 14.9.43.

From: Mildred (Mrs. Shu Chang Yui.)
Mr. M. Tie Ten Quee,
National Health Administration,
Chungking.

To: Charles Chang,
53, West Street,
Kingston,
Jamaica.

Postmark: CHUNGKING. and date: 5.10.43. Language: ENGLISH.

ORIGINAL: RELEASED. Distribution: Chief Censor, India (8)

SUBMITTED TO: SUP.(D.M.D.) DRW. MEW. HEA. BBC. INF.
REPORTS G. FORD CAN.

SUBJECT: BACTERIAL WARFARE IN HUNAN.

Extract: Sulphathiazole is used in the treatment of pneumonia and in nearly all septic infections. Now it is the drug needed for threatening plague which the Japs started in Hunan and of which there is danger of becoming a epidemic. We need medical instruments, like forceps for osterical work, rubber gloves, specula for osterical work, opthalmic instruments, haemometers, blood sedimentation tubes, needles, forceps and scissors. I am sure some agreement can be made with the British Government for sending us such drugs and instruments. My husband who is in charge of purchasing drugs for China tells me that there is not a shortage of these suplha drugs in England. Arrangements for purchases from the United States of America may be a bit more difficult due to the difference in currency, but there is no harm in trying.

Dr. Politzer, an Austrian, was sent out here by the the League of Nations to work on epidemic prevention. He is a good friend of George and mine and investigated the outbreak in

/Hunan.

8422 1

From MID. - C.I. - Group. Cen. Br

SECRET

SECRET

-42)
RSHIP
UNITED STATES OF AMERICA

REPRODUCTION OF SUBMISSION FROM FOREIGN CENSORSHIP

-2- CHINESE INT. WING/00183/43.

Hunan. He is the only foreigner in the Wei Sheng Shu (Hygiene Bureau) and his services were retained after he had finished his work on behalf of the League of Nations. He was in charge of investigating the outbreak of plague in Hunan, which started in 1941 de nova, i.e. plague for the first time occurred in this province after the peasants in these parts had seen Japanese planes flying overhead and from these planes there were dropped pieces of cardboard, grain and pieces of cotton wool. The assumption was that the cardboard was a box containing plague fleas. After an incubation period corresponding to the exact time after the Japanese planes dropped the deadly cargoes the infested fleas also found their way to the rats. Dr. Politzer and the other doctors investigating the outbreak are sure that this was the cause of the outbreak and therefore, according to International Law the Japs have again violated this by using bacterial warfare.

The Shanghai Medical College has been evacuated to Koloshan in very beautiful surroundings. There are 220 student men and women. They live in dormitories near the school and their tution books and pocket money, though not much, are given by the Government. Most of the professors from P.U.M.C. and the Shanghai Medical Col ege have also joined the Staff, so that as far as teaching is concerned, they are very fortunate. Dr. James Shen, China's leading surgeon, is the Professor of Surgery. His wife is the Pediatrics Professor. Both are graduates from the U.S.A. There is one English Professor here, Prof. Gordon King, the obstetrics and Gynaecal Professor from the Hongkong University. He is also on the staff. Also one American Professor. Although the buildings are fragile and students lack many of the necessities of life the spirit is really excellent and students are very happy. There are students from Hongkong, Singapore and Shanghai. In fact from all over the world. The National Institute of Health is also at Koloshan. It is subsidised by the Rockfeller Foundation and is doing splendid work in sanitary engineering and research of all kinds. I hope to go to work in the Central Hospital (formerly Shanghai Medical College) after being here for 4-6 months in the Pediatrics Dept.

<u>Censor Comment:</u> Extract as in original.
Chinese Intelligence Wing, 209, Lower Circular Road, Calcutta.
Dated: 2.11.43. No: G/37/59/2419

S.M. CHURN. Capt.,
Actg: O.C. Chinese Intelligence Wing.

SECRET 8422 2

3.34　20 Dec. 1943: OFFICE OF CENSORSHIP U.S., 72 P. H. 20.12 43 TERMINAL Air. LON/414795/43: From: ERIC G. CHIRGWIN, FRIENDS' AMBULANCE UNIT, CHUNGKING. SZECHUAN, FREE CHINA, To: ERIC AND DOROTHY McKIE, LIVERPOOL, ENGLAND: Reference to serious epidemic of bubonic plague in FUKIEN

资料出处： National Archives of the United States, R112, E295A, B11.

内容点评： 本资料为 1943 年 12 月 20 日美国国家新闻审查处存档重庆公谊救护队（Friends' Ambulance Unit）成员 Eric G. Chirgwin 予英国利物浦 Eric McKie 和 Dorothy McKie 信件，提及福建腺鼠疫猖獗。

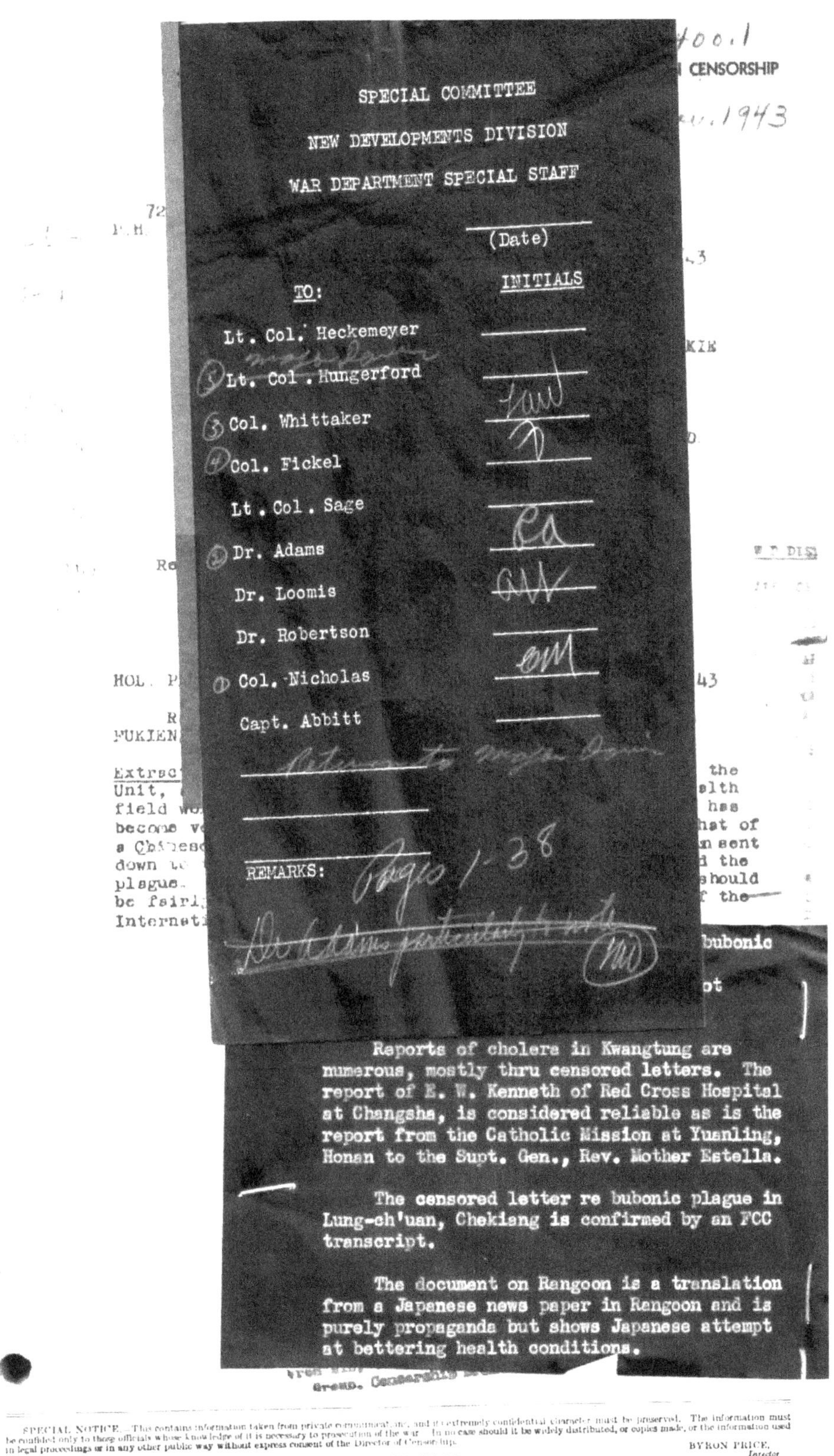

SPECIAL COMMITTEE

NEW DEVELOPMENTS DIVISION

WAR DEPARTMENT SPECIAL STAFF

(Date)

TO: INITIALS

Lt. Col. Heckemeyer

Lt. Col. Hungerford

Col. Whittaker

Col. Fickel

Lt. Col. Sage

Dr. Adams

Dr. Loomis

Dr. Robertson

Col. Nicholas

Capt. Abbitt

REMARKS: Pages 1-38

Reports of cholera in Kwangtung are numerous, mostly thru censored letters. The report of E. W. Kenneth of Red Cross Hospital at Changsha, is considered reliable as is the report from the Catholic Mission at Yuanling, Honan to the Supt. Gen., Rev. Mother Estella.

The censored letter re bubonic plague in Lung-ch'uan, Chekiang is confirmed by an FCC transcript.

The document on Rangoon is a translation from a Japanese news paper in Rangoon and is purely propaganda but shows Japanese attempt at bettering health conditions.

SPECIAL NOTICE.—This contains information taken from private communications, etc., and its extremely confidential character must be preserved. The information must be confided only to those officials whose knowledge of it is necessary to prosecution of the war. In no case should it be widely distributed, or copies made, or the information used in legal proceedings or in any other public way without express consent of the Director of Censorship.

BYRON PRICE, Director

CONFIDENTIAL

2400.1

CONFIDENTIAL

OFFICE OF CENSORSHIP
UNITED STATES OF AMERICA

REPRODUCTION OF SUBMISSION FROM FOREIGN CENSORSHIP

10 Nov. 1943

72
P. H. 20. 12. 43

TERMINAL Air LON/414795/43

ERIC G. CHIRGWIN	ERIC and DOROTHY McKIE
FRIENDS' AMBULANCE UNIT CHUNGKING. SZECHUAN FREE CHINA	"PIPPACOTT" MACHETTS' LANE HUNT'S CROSS LIVERPOOL ENGLAND.
10. 11. 43	English

Comment B. B. C.
" D. R. W.
" CAN.
" HEA.

Released

HOL. PRI. T.4/5 2546 I. K. C. 15. 12. 43

Reference to serious epidemic of bubonic plague in FUKIEN.

Extract "I will be going down with one other member of the Unit, and an Austrian doctor to FUKIEN, to do public health field work, in connection with the bubonic plague which has become very serious down there..... I have just heard that of a Chinese group of public health workers who have... been sent down to the area, eighty percent have already contracted the plague. How far this is true I don't know, though it should be fairly reliable, as I was told it by the Secretary of the International Relief Committee."

This office has confirmation of bubonic plague in Fukien from another source. Meningitis epidemic in Chekiang was not reported to us by any other source.

Reports of cholera in Kwangtung are numerous, mostly thru censored letters. The report of E. W. Kenneth of Red Cross Hospital at Changsha, is considered reliable as is the report from the Catholic Mission at Yuanling, Honan to the Supt. Gen., Rev. Mother Estella.

The censored letter re bubonic plague in Lung-ch'uan, Chekiang is confirmed by an FCC transcript.

The document on Rangoon is a translation from a Japanese news paper in Rangoon and is purely propaganda but shows Japanese attempt at bettering health conditions.

CONFIDENTIAL

2400.1-1

SCJ

Health Conditions in China

7-Dec-1942

a. Hinghwa, Fukien, Free China. (75 mi. SSE of Foochow)

Letter of August 10, 1942.

On May 27, 1942, the writer received his first mail since November, 1941. Five letters dated from December, 1941, to April, 1942.

"It may be that the resistance of the people has been weakened by the years of privation, or that the home-made vaccine is not as effective as the pre-war variety, but whatever the reason the bubonic plague has been very bad this year. And, it is still raging, not seeming to abate as usual with the coming of summer. Even as I write, a letter arrives...saying that there is a case or two...in Futsing."

"At Kio Sauh...with about four hundred deaths in that little town, not one of the pupils died, though three or four had become infected."

The writer also speaks of using local products extensively, such as peanut oil for lamps, charcoal gas to operate ancient model T Ford engines in launches, "Cod" liver oil from local fish, lychee nuts, formerly a delicacy largely exported being used as a food - half as expensive as rice, etc.

b. Futsing, Fukien, Free China. (about half-way bet. Hinghwa & Foochow, on coast.)

Letter of August 6, 1942.

"My secretary-teacher came down with bubonic plague four weeks ago. Fortunately we were able to get enough serum to save him. Now his eldest daughter is down with pneumonia, the most deadly kind, and his two eldest boys with bubonic. It is almost impossible to get serums. 10cc of serum cost $1,200 CN. Each patient should have 100 cc." ($1.00 American equals $18,00 CN.)

c. Tzechung, Szechuan.

Letter of April 8, 1942, rec'd in N.Y. June 8, 1942.

"380 girls in the school; about 65% have trachoma; an abundance of "itch" of extensive proportions; of "athletes foot", and numerous cases of ringworm and other skin deseases. Also hookworm.

A great shortage of trained nurses is mentioned in this and other letters from Tzechung and other places.

Source: From Memo for Colonel Blakeney, subject, "Information from Missionary Sources." Dec. 7, 1942, from Captain ~~Grawford~~, Inf. From letters from China. C.L. Donohugh

CONFIDENTIAL 8500 7

3.35 China Handbook 1937-1943: A Comprehensive Survey of Major Developments in China in Six Years of War, Chapter XVII Public Health and Medicine, Compiled by THE CHINESE MINISTRY OF INFORMATION, New York, THE MACMILLAN COMPANY, 1943

资料出处： National Archives of the United States, R112, E295A, B11.

内容点评： 本资料为中国国民政府主持编写的英文版《战时中华志（1937~1943）》（麦克米伦出版社，纽约，1943）第十七章“公共卫生和医疗”，提及日军在中国的细菌武器攻击。

CHINA HANDBOOK
1937–1943

A Comprehensive Survey of Major Developments in China in Six Years of War

Compiled by
THE CHINESE MINISTRY OF INFORMATION

New York
THE MACMILLAN COMPANY
1943

CHAPTER XVII

PUBLIC HEALTH AND MEDICINE

HISTORY

"The type of medicine practiced in China was quite similar to that of Europe in the pre-scientific era. Philosophical concepts controlled the field, and the ills to which the flesh of man is heir were all related to the universe. Chinese ideas of cosmology were the basis of the theory and art of medicine. Health was dependent upon a proper balance between the two great essences or humors, the *yin* and the *yang*, and the five elements: metal, wood, water, fire and earth. Any disturbance of this delicate balance resulted in disease, and the object of treatment was to restore the equilibrium. Hence, drugs were classified according to their ability to increase or decrease the amount of *yin* or *yang* in the human body, or to bring about a normal correlation among the various elements.

"During the course of centuries an enormous number of substances came to be regarded as possessing medicinal value. Many of these are now known to be worthless, but it is equally certain that many other drugs of real value have been discovered by the Chinese. Although the theory underlying their use was wrong, nevertheless many of the substances themselves are therapeutically useful. Some of these have also been in common use in other parts of the world, some have in recent years been shown to be extremely good remedies, while many others still await systematic study . . . .

"Except for some work by surgeons of the East India Company, the introduction of scientific medicine into China was by medical missionaries. Peter Parker, the first regularly appointed medical missionary, arrived in China in 1834 and began work in Canton a year later. So impressed was Parker with the necessity of training a Chinese medical profession that as early as 1837 he was able to report the admission of three young Chinese students to his hospital for study. Although all through his life Parker pressed for the establishment of a proper medical college in China, it was not until 1866 that a medical school was first opened in connection with the Canton Hospital."*

The history of organized Chinese public health work may be traced to 1902 when the Peiyang Sanitary Department was established. In 1911, the North Manchurian Plague Prevention Service was organized to combat the plague outbreak in North China. Another plague epidemic in 1917 brought into being the National Epidemic Prevention Bureau in Peiping. The administration of health work in the country was, however, vested in the health department of the Ministry of Interior. The department, which was the predecessor of the National Health Administration, was first established in 1911.

(*From :—"Medical Education" by Dr. L. G. Kilborn in *Wartime China as Seen by Westerners*; The China Publishing Co., Chungking, 1942.)

NATIONAL HEALTH ADMINISTRATION

The National Health Administration has been alternately attached to the Ministry of Interior and the Executive Yuan. It was under the Ministry of Interior from April to October, 1927. On November 1, 1927, a Ministry of Health was inaugurated with Mr. Hsueh Tu-pi as minister. He was succeeded by Dr. J. Heng Liu in 1929. In 1931, the ministry was abolished and its work was taken over by the Ministry of Interior with Dr. Liu as the director-general. In 1935, the health administration was placed directly under the Executive Yuan.

At the outbreak of the Sino-Japanese war, a Board of Health was created under the National Military Council to centralize all health and medical activities under its two main divisions: the Army Medical Administration and the National Health Administration. The board was short-lived, for in January, 1938, the Army Medical Administration became affiliated to the Ministry of Military Affairs and the National Health Administration to the Ministry of Interior with Dr. F. C. Yen as director-general. In April, 1940, it had its status raised by coming once again directly under the Executive Yuan. Since then Dr. P. Z. King has been director-general, and Dr. James K. Shen, deputy director-general.

The Administration consists of four departments:

1. Department of General Affairs (director, Mr. S. C. Hsu), which handles documents, correspondence, staff, accounts and publications.

2. Department of Medical Administration (director, Dr. S. Y. Yue), which supervises medical organizations, registers medical personnel and associations, deals with drugs, and compiles and revises the Chinese Pharmacopoeia.

3. Department of Health Organization and Services (director, Dr. C. C. Yen), which promotes local health services, the training of personnel, executes sanitary engineering projects, and is responsible for the examination of food and drink and the improvement of national nutrition.

4. Department of Epidemic Prevention (director, Dr. W. W. Yung), which takes charge of the prevention and control of epidemic and endemic diseases, quarantine, promotion and establishment of anti-epidemic services and supervises the manufacture of biological products.

Subsidiary Organizations

The task of protecting the people against epidemic diseases as well as maintaining the normal health services is undertaken principally through the following subsidiary organizations of the Administration:

The National Institute of Health (director, Dr. C. K. Chu) undertakes research and field demonstrations on various technical problems relating to health. There are two branch institutes, Epidemiological Research Institute and Nutrition Research Institute, and eight departments, public health, experimental medicine, chemistry and materia medica, sanitary engineering, maternity and child health, health education, nursing, and health statistics. Under the Institute is the Public Health Personnel Training Institute in Kweiyang (director, Dr. Yao Hsun-yuan), which trains public health officers, public health nurses and other auxiliary personnel.

The Central Hospital has two branches, one at Chungking (superintendent, Dr. S. C. Wu) and one at Kweiyang (superintendent, Dr. Chung Shih-fan) each with an affiliated school of nursing and a capacity of about 250 beds. Both are equipped with X-ray and modern clinical facilities. There are separate departments for medicine, surgery, gynecology and obstetrics, pediatrics, dermatology, ophthalmology, otolaryngology, dentistry, X-ray, diagnostic laboratory, physico-therapy and pharmacy.

Quarantine Stations carry out the inspection of bus and boat passengers, fumigation of ships and the control of communicable diseases. Preventive inoculations are given at bus stations and wharves against cholera, smallpox, plague, meningitis and diphtheria. In addition to the main station in Chungking and a branch station at Wanhsien above Ichang, temporary ones are established at times of plague and cholera epidemics. Dr. Z. H. Tsok is director of the stations.

Weishengshu (National Health Administration) Anti-Epidemic Corps (director, Dr. W. W. Yung) were first organized in 1938 to meet the increasing need of conducting epidemic prevention, health protection and curative services among the civilians. It has regional offices, anti-epidemic units, isolation hospitals, bacteriological laboratories, sanitary engineering units and supply depots. Their work extends to all provinces in Free China.

Stations for the Treatment of Venereal Diseases were established by the National Health Administration at Enshih (Hupeh), Kweilin (Kwangsi) and Chuhsien (Chekiang). The latter was withdrawn because of the hostilities in Chekiang province in May, 1942.

The Health Commissioner's Office for the Northwest (acting director, Dr. Y. N. Yang) promotes medical and health work in the seven provinces of Shensi, Shansi, Honan, Kansu, Chinghai, Ningsia and Suiyuan. The office maintains a hospital in Lanchow which has a capacity of 120 beds, and is fitted with water supply and central heating systems. The office has a training institute, an experimental health station which maintains an out-patient department and two mobile field units each with a personnel of 20, including four doctors.

Mongolia Health Center (director, Dr. P. N. Song) and Sichang, (director, Dr. Hui C. Chang), Yaan, (director, Dr. Tan Tsu-lieh) and Hweili (director, Chang Tun-jen) Health Centers in Sikang province aim at the development of modern medicine in China's border provinces. Mobile health units were organized to tour outlying districts.

Highway Health Stations were established to render curative and preventive services to travelers, refugees, highway laborers and villagers and to encourage and stimulate the development of health services in various provinces in Free China. By the end of October, 1942, there were 39 stations at important points along different highways, excluding the 16 stations on the Yunnan-Burma highway which had been either wound up or handed over to the local authorities in Yunnan province following the loss of Burma. Each station has a hospital for serious and emergency cases, an outpatient department, and a small diagnostic laboratory.

Emergency Purchasing Committee for Medical Supplies, with Dr. F. Y. Tai as chairman, was organized to relieve any shortage in medical supplies. It was provided with a revolving fund for the purchase and transportation from various sources of essential drugs to be supplied to different medical and health organizations and the general public. To encourage the importation of drugs and supplies for emergency medical relief purposes, the National Health Administration issues duty-free certificates to all pharmacies and medical institutions for such supplies upon request.

The Central Pharmaceutical Manufacturing Company (manager, Dr. T. H. Tang) was formed in the latter part of 1940 to manufacture as many drugs as native raw materials are available therefor. Its capital was subscribed to by government and private sources.

The National Epidemic Prevention Bureau (director, Dr. F. F. Tang) and the Northwest Epidemic Prevention Bureau (Dr. Y. N. Yang) are engaged in research work and the manufacture of biological products. Working under difficult conditions created by the war, the two bureaus have managed to increase their output considerably. Products manufactured include bacterial and virus vaccines, sera and anti-toxins, diagnostic antigens and sera, and toxins and toxoids.

The Narcotics Bureau (director, Dr. C. K. Liang) was established in 1935 in accordance with the international convention held in 1931 for the control of the following ten kinds of narcotics and their preparations: opium, morphine, codeine, dionine, apomorphine hydrochloride, extract cannabis, cocaine, strychnine, eukodal and pantopon. The Bureau operates a factory which is manufacturing tinctures, ampoules, tablets of opium, and its derivatives.

The Surgical Instruments and Hospital Equipment Factory (manager, C. K. Yang) has been making standard surgical instruments, sanitary engineering equipment and artificial limbs. The orthopedic section sends skilled fitters to convalescent camps to fit artificial limbs to disabled soldiers.

Statistical Summary

The following is a statistical summary of the work of the National Health Administration in 1941:

General Affairs

(1) Number of documents handled by the Administration in the year:

Total—43,123:

Received—22,056,

Despatched—21,067.

(2) Laws and regulations promulgated in the year:—52.

(3) Number of staff by the end of the year:—1,899:

M.—1,158, F.—741.

Staff of the Administration proper:—118.

M.—97, F.—21.

(4) Training of public health personnel:

Institutes	Graduated in the Year		Under Training by the End of the Year	
	Classes	Students.	Classes	Students
Kweiyang T. I.	14	234	2	30
Northwest T. I.			6	63

MEDICAL ADMINISTRATION

(5) Medical persons registered in the year :—1,929.

(647 Doctors; 10 dentists; 58 pharmacists; 330 nurses; 506 midwives; 378 dispensers.)

(6) Foreign medical persons registered in the year :—21.
(16 Doctors; 5 nurses.)

(7) Number of licenses issued for patent medicines in the year: 115.

(8) Number of passes issued for free import of emergency relief drugs in the year: 253.

(9) American Red Cross donations distributed through the Administration in the year: Seventeen varieties of drugs and bandages, among which the most used drugs are:

Acetylsalicylic acid	9,181,520 tab.
Quinine bisulphate	10,623,810 tab.
Emetin hydrochloride	21,424 tab.
Boric acid	14,817 lbs.

(10) Most used vaccines distributed to provincial and municipal governments by the Administration in the year:

Cholera vaccine	67,560 bottles
Smallpox vaccine	23,500 dozen

PREVENTIVE AND CURATIVE WORK

(11) Number of patients treated by hospitals in 1941.

HOSPITALS	OUT-PATIENTS		Admitted in Wards	Total
	First Visits	Revisits		
Central H. (Chungking)	12,214	18,989	2,907	34,110
Central H. (Kweiyang)	17,123	37,312	3,363	57,798
1st Northwest H.	9,244	11,100	739	21,083
2nd Northwest H.	11,025	21,472	1,214	33,711
TOTAL	49,606	88,873	8,223	146,702

N.B.—Work of the 1st Northwest Hospital commenced from April, 1941.

(12) Main services rendered by Highway Health Stations, Suburban Health Stations, and Health Centers in 1941

HEALTH STATIONS AND CENTERS	PREVENTIVE INOCULATIONS			PATIENTS TREATED				Deliveries
	Smallpox	Cholera	Typhoid	First Visits	Re-visits	Emergency Calls.	In Wards	
Pingliang HWHS	9,054	10,775	950	8,051	12,211	180	409	128
Tingsi HWHS	27,101	33,396	3,832	12,060	19,585	249	96	201
Hanchung HWHS	10,571	7,971		7,376	9,098	102	218	78
Mienyang HWHS	9,391	15,429	18	20,965	40,082	201	135	264
Neikiang HWHS	5,427	13,256	5,199	18,765	50,672	580	197	161
Pichieh HWHS	4,596	12,639	366	7,146	12,511	97	7	50
Tungtze HWHS	11,777	19,038	1,342	14,270	30,227	694	399	155
Anshun HWHS	11,889	18,155		14,118	17,109	162	181	337
Machangping HWHS	18,525	19,889	4,696	10,691	15,954	226	116	146
Kutsing HWHS	9,042	12,566	496	8,205	9,709	223	788	211
Hwanghsien HWHS	10,700	12,231		9,146	14,675	417	164	248
Kienking HWHS	14,446	19,231		9,413	25,111	8	1	25
Hochih HWHS	7,364	4,446	5,188	30,861	42,117	712	10	174
Mienling HWHS	1,267	344	42	5,710	11,796	83	18	3
Omei HWHS	12	1,178		5,060	7,535	48	82	13
Puling HWHS		1,270		8,064	11,785	297	248	12
Chinmukwan SHS	5,083	4,712	305	10,221	19,727	228	208	156
Lao-in-yen SHS	16,707	13,642	46	13,640	74,761	438	61	209
Jingongpo SHS	667	654	849	4,820	16,935	140	46	39
Manchien SHS	3,528	5,125	1,006	4,255	13,915	113		77
Shemachang SHS	3,711	5,598	456	6,111	11,656	166	37	86
Sanshenmiao SHS	2,992	6,194	555	14,087	28,781	203	108	159
Yunshingchang SHS	4,097	3,983	317	10,034	17,739	31	10	43
Ya-an H. C.	2,689	4,293		7,548	21,126	143	218	49
Hweili H. C.	42			433	701	1	2	2
Sichang H. C.	1,343	2,502		5,620	6,075	29		81
TOTAL	192,021	248,517	25,663	266,670	541,593	5,771	3,759	3,097

N.B.—Work of the Hweili Health Center commenced from November.

ANTI-EPIDEMIC AND QUARANTINE SERVICE

(13) Main services rendered by the Anti-Epidemic Corps in 1941

Preventive Inoculations (persons)		Other Services	
Cholera	252,166	1st visit patients treated	237,146
Typhoid	13,416	Revisit patients treated	373,388
T. and C.	678	Patients treated in wards	345
Smallpox	252,782	Deliveries	510
Plague	38,682	Persons deloused	2,589
Meningitis	837	Pieces of clothing deloused	10,703
Diphtheria	278	Drinking wells disinfected	37,995

(14) A Work done by Quarantine Stations in 1941

STATIONS	Bus Passengers Inspected	Ship Passengers Inspected	Air Passengers Inspected	Tons of Ships Fumigated
Han-I-Yu		76,707	662	36,651
Teng-Yue	447,501			
Maen-Yun Sub-S.	31,438			
Waen-Ting	9,692			
TOTAL	488,631	79,707	662	36,651

(14) B Clinical and preventive work done by Quarantine Stations in 1941

	Teng-Yue	Maen-Yun Sub-S	Waen-Ting	Han-I-Yu	TOTAL
CLINICAL WORK					
1st visit patients	828		2,248		3,076
Revisit patients	752		4,827		5,579
PREVENTIVE INOCULATIONS					
Smallpox	5,324	1,677	1,504	3,907	12,412
Cholera	2,942	517	157	55,251	58,867
Plague	625	5	417		1,047
Dysentery	17				17
Diphtheria	446				446
Meningitis	335				335
T. and C.	389				389

N.B.—(1) Maen-Yun Sub-Station established in July.
(2) Data of Waen-Ting include only November and December.

(15) Patients Treated by Anti-Venereal Diseases Clinics in 1941

PATIENTS	Kweilin	Enshih	Chuhsien	Sian	TOTAL
First visits	694	119	180	227	1,220
Revisits	3,246	642	470	1,049	5,407
TOTAL	3,940	761	650	1,276	6,627

MEDICAL SUPPLIES

(16) Drugs prepared by the Narcotics Bureau in 1941

Narcotics produced in 34 Varieties
Non-Narcotics produced in 61 Varieties
The Main products are:

Narcotics		Non-narcotics	
Dover's powder	355,722 tab.	Tannic acid	261 lb.
Morphine HCl (powder)	9,778 gm.	Ammon. chlor.	1,429 lb.
,, ,, (ampoule)	13,351 bxs.	Fld. ext. glycerrh.	284 lb.
,, ,, (tablet)	552,250 tab.	Bland's pills	90,500 tab.
Cocaine Phosph. (powder)	6,010 gm.	Mag. sulphate	774 lb.
,, ,, (ampoule)	2,522 bxs.	Sodium sulphate	2,106 lb.
,, ,, (tablet)	989,240 tab.	Brown mixture	1,061,956 tab.
Strychnine HCl	184,875 tab.	Aspirin	76,946 tab.

(17) Biological products made by Epidemic Prevention Bureau in 1941

National Epidemic Prevention Bureau's production in 47 Varieties
Northwest Epidemic Prevention Bureau's production in 31 Varieties
The Main products are:

Vaccines, Sera and Anti-toxins	National E. P. B.	Northwest E. P. B.	TOTAL
Cholera	2,613,280 c.c.	1,626,640 c.c.	4,239,920 c.c.
Anti-plague	1,562,290 c.c.	20,000 c.c.	1,582,290 c.c.
Smallpox	1,624,171 cap.		1,624,171 cap.
Dysentery	33,790 c.c.		33,790 c.c.
T. A. B.	30,150 c.c.		30,150 c.c.
T. C.	7,670,080 c.c.	9,973,600 c.c.	17,643,680 c.c.
Anti-tetanus	23,160,000 units	8,203,000 units	31,363,000 units
Anti-anthrax		221,270 c.c.	221,270 c.c.

STATE MEDICINE

China aims to extend a system of organized medical and public health services for the people, the *hsien* (county) health program, which is being incorporated into the new *hsien* system, being one of the means to the end. By this means it is hoped that the services will be within the reach of the rural population. Whenever possible, the National Health Administration helps district health authorities lay a permanent foundation for public health work.

Since the establishment of the Central Field Health Station in 1932, steps have been taken to demonstrate the relative efficiency of the different types of public health services applicable to Chinese communities. Investigation of endemic diseases has also been started. For the training of public health personnel to meet the need of a state medical service, the Public Health Personnel Training Institute was established in 1935. As a step toward the consolidation of national technical organizations, the Central Field Health Station and the Public Health Personnel Training Institute were amalgamated and reorganized into the National Institute of Health in April, 1941. Besides planning, demonstration, and research, the National Institute of Health also assumes the responsibility of the training of senior public health personnel.

The tremendous need for medical personnel in China is being met by training institutes and medical colleges. When the war broke out in July, 1937, there were less than 10,000 qualified doctors and 5,000 qualified nurses in the whole country. By the end of September, 1942, medical personnel registered with the National Health Administration included 11,850 doctors, 794 pharmacists, 322 dentists, 5,770 nurses, 4,971 midwives and 3,983 dispensers.

The National Institute of Health trained 161 senior medical officers in nine classes between January and October, 1942. They included 35 nurses, 97 sanitary inspectors, 9 sanitary overseers, 11 sanitary engineers and 9 medical officers.

Under the Institute are Kweiyang and Lanchow regional training institutes which train junior types of medical personnel. The Kweiyang regional institute, the former Public Health Personnel Training Institute, offered eight courses in 1942, including those for public health officers (six months), public health nurses and midwives (six months), sanitary overseers (eighteen months), sanitary inspectors (one year), laboratory technicians (one year), pharmacists (one year), vital statisticians (six months) and medicial attendants (six months). In 1942, 16 public health officers, 53 public health nurses and midwives, 40 sanitary overseers and 8 laboratory technicians were graduated. Since the establishment of the institute, a total of 1,971 public health workers have been trained, including 512 medical officers, 758 public health nurses, 181 public health midwives, 37 sanitary engineers, 347 sanitary inspectors, 8 public health pharmacists and 128 others.

The training of auxiliary health personnel is conducted by provincial health authorities. By August, 1942, sixteen training institutes were functioning in different places in Free China.

Organized early in 1938 jointly by the Ministries of Military Affairs and Interior, the Emergency Medical Service Training School, now functioning solely under the Ministry of Military Affairs with Dr. Robert Lim as director, has been giving supplementary technical training to the existing personnel in the army medical service. Up to the latter part of 1942, 7,000 had been trained. The training consists of two courses, three-month initial courses and three-month subsequent courses for medical officers in special subjects such as orthopedic surgery, preventive medicine, sanitary engineering, radiology, etc., and for medical subordinates in X-ray, laboratory medicine, sanitation, and nursing.

Beginning in 1941, the school has been offering technical training for new personnel for the army medical service. It consists of two two-year courses for nurses and medical officers to provide nurses for army hospitals and assistant medical officers for regimental and divisional medical units. Field service training is also conducted for officers and men in medical tactics and organizations, including individual, team and formation training covering the operation of all the medical units of an army, while hospital training is given officers and men in clinical routine and hospital service, including practice in the wards, operating room, laboratories, and hospital management.

The school, which is situated in Kweiyang, has five branch schools in different war areas. The important features of training are that methods are standardized, and practical drills and exercises are employed with the minimum of theoretical lectures. The scheme of training is to be extended to each army, as every army sanitary corps and Red Cross unit at the front will carry out a simplified training program for the great mass of junior personnel who cannot leave their work to receive training elsewhere.

Systematic training for all types of personnel has been organized, including promotional training, so that efficiency can be continuously maintained. The final objective is to make available for the civil health service after the war all the army medical personnel not required by the army. To this end, methods taught and used have been coordinated with those employed by the civil health service.

To promote health work in various provinces, the National Health Administration has been giving technical and financial assistance to provincial health authorities. The 1942 health budgets of the various provinces totalled $20,389,469.

Altogether sixteen provincial health departments and one municipal health bureau had been established by August, 1942. Financial assistance was given to Sikang province to expand its health services. Health departments for Shansi and Suiyuan are to be established in 1943.

The promotion of state medicine has been one of the important tasks of the health departments. In 1941, 69 technical workers were sent to fourteen provinces and one municipality. Up to August, 1942, 71 additional technical workers were despatched.

For the purpose of demonstration, subsidies and running expenses were provided for four model county health centers in Kwangsi, Szechwan, Kweichow and Hunan provinces. The subsidies were continued in 1942. In addition, 35 units of ordinary centers and sanitary engineering corps in twelve provinces were subsidized.

Seventy-six health units in the provinces in 1941 received quantities of medical supplies from the National Health Administration, including 158 kinds of drugs, 55 kinds of apparatus, 67,560 bottles of anti-cholera vaccine and 23,500 dozens of tubes of anti-smallpox vaccine. Medical supplies were also distributed to the provinces in 1942. Sanitary engineers were sent to Kwangsi and Szechwan to carry out sanitary engineering projects.

The directors of the health departments in sixteen provinces and the health commissioner of one municipality are:

Szechwan—Dr. C. C. Chen
Kansu—Dr. Yang Shu-hsin
Chinghai—Dr. Hsieh Kang-chieh
Hupeh—Dr. Lu Ching-cheng
Kiangsi—Dr. I. C. Fang
Yunnan—Dr. Joseph An-cheng Miao
Kwangtung—Dr. M. Wong
Chekiang—Dr. Sung Hsu-shang
Shensi—Dr. Yang Hoh-chen
Ningsia—Dr. Pi Tien-min
Honan—Dr. Shih Kuo-fan
Hunan—Dr. W. Chang
Kweichow—Dr. K. F. Yao
Kwangsi—Dr. Wong Wen-yuan
Fukien—Dr. Loh Ti-huan
Anhwei—Dr. Sung Ying-kun.
Chungking—Dr. Wang Tze-hsiang

The National Health Administration's *hsien* (county) health system aims at the promotion of rural health. With the county seat as base, health work is to spread to all corners.

The new system is based on the following principles: To utilize the limited available number of medical workers as the fundamental staff and to train the youths in the villages as the auxiliary working forces; to consider the prevailing diseases and health problems of the people as a whole, with emphasis on preventive measures; to make the services come within the economic power of the people so that with limited funds it will be possible to set up the health organizations on a nation-wide scale.

Through the new system, the health authorities hope to have as many health stations as the post office has branches. It provides for a health center for each county, a health district center for each district, a health station for each town or village, and a health worker for each *pao* (a *pao* consists of six to fifteen *chia*, and each *chia* comprises six to fifteen households).

Coming directly under the county government and concurrently under the supervision of the provincial health department, the county health center will be responsible for the health administration and the promotion of health work in the whole county. Its staff will consist of a county health officer, one to three doctors, one or two public health nurses, two to four midwives, one or two pharmacists, one or two laboratory technicians, two to four sanitary inspectors, one to three clerks, and a number of health workers.

Each county health center will maintain a 20-40 bed hospital, a laboratory and a mobile clinic. It will admit patients sent to it by health centers and stations in districts, towns, and villages under the county. In case of epidemics, a separate ward is to be set up for the isolation and treatment of such cases.

Through the new system, uniformity is being brought into every branch of health work in the country. Standard lists of drugs and medical instruments are distributed among the different grades of county health organizations. Designs of buildings, construction, and lists of equipment and furniture too are standardized.

In 1941, the National Health Administration subsidized the provincial health authorities of Szechwan, Hunan, Kiangsi, Fukien, Chekiang, Yunnan, Kweichow, Kwangtung and Kwangsi in the form of 39 senior medical officers, 3 sanitary engineers, and medical supplies as well as for carrying out sanitary engineering projects for the development of local health organizations. Subsidies for capital and running expenses were provided for four model *hsien* health centers for the purpose of demonstration in addition to 35 ordinary centers.

The following table shows the increase in the number of *hsien* health centers in thirteen provinces during the period 1937 to 1941:

Province	1937	1938	1939	1940	1941
Szechwan			9	47	65
Chekiang	14	61	6	43	60
Kiangsi	83	83	83	81	81
Hunan	6	14	68	75	75
Honan					2
Shensi	8	11	14	43	54
Kansu			5	13	20
Fukien	15	61	62	63	64
Kwangtung			39	60	73
Kwangsi	88	88	99	78	87
Kweichow		33	64	78	76
Hupeh			8	8	17
Yunnan	3	21	37	45	77
Total	217	372	494	634	751

Another project to stimulate the development of the *hsien* health system is the establishment of highway health stations at important points along different highways. The organization, size and composition of staff of such a highway health station approximates that of the permanent *hsien* health center. Housed in uniform buildings with 30-bed wards, an out-patient department and a small diagnostic laboratory, each station undertakes the curative and preventive services over a distance of 100 kilometers, rendering medical service to road workers, travelers, and the people in the district in which it is situated.

Highway stations were first established in 1939 along the northwestern highway extending from Chungking and Chengtu in Szechwan to Lanchow in Kansu. New ones were later established in China's southwestern regions. In cooperation with the Ministry of Communications, seven stations and sixteen mobile units were organized to serve the builders of the Loshan-Sichang highway, linking Szechwan with Sikang, and at present the travelers and the inhabitants of the regions through which the road traverses. In newly developed districts into which government offices and others have moved from congested areas, health stations have also been established.

By the end of 1942, 39 stations were maintained. The stations along the Yunnan-Burma Road were either handed over to the local health authorities or removed after the loss of Burma. The list of highway health stations follows:

Kansu: Tiensui, Pingliang, Chiuchuan, Tingsi, Yungteng; Szechwan: Sinchiao, Mienyang, Omei, Neikiang, Luhsien, Chinmukuan, Nanwenchuan, Chienkiang, Lungtang, Hsuyung, Hsiehmachang, Sanshengmiao, Yunghsin-chang, Hsing-lungchang, Chingkangpo, Laoying-yen; Shensi: Hanchung, Changwu, Hsuanshihpu; Kweichow: Tushan, Tungtze, Anshun, Pichieh, Weining, Annan, Panghsien; Sikang: Fulin, Mienning; Hunan: Chenchi, Huanhsien, Soli; Yunnan: Kutsing, Hsuenwei; Kwangsi: Hochi.

The following is a summary of the more important activities of the highway health stations during the years 1939 to 1941:

Activity	Number 1939	1940	1941
Preventive Inoculations—			
Smallpox	38,511	169,756	192,021
Cholera	194,320	334,716	248,517
Typhoid	9,891	19,681	25,663
Curative Service—			
First visits	120,704	307,182	266,670
Subsequent visits	174,453	533,828	541,593
Emergency calls	3,439	4,965	5,771
Patients admitted to hospital	694	2,399	3,759
Health Service—			
Deliveries	877	3,108	3,092

EPIDEMIC CONTROL

Much of the resources and energies of the National Health Administration is concentrated on the work of epidemic control.

Heading the anti-epidemic forces is the National Health Administration's Anti-Epidemic Corps. With its headquarters in Chungking, the Corps consists of four divisions in charge of four regions, namely, Szechwan-Kweichow-Yunnan; Hunan-Hupeh; Kwangtung-Kwangsi, and Chekiang-Kiangsi-Fukien. Under each division are four mobile medical units, one mobile laboratory unit, one mobile sanitary unit, one isolation hospital and one supply depot. Each anti-epidemic unit is composed of two physicians, four nurses, four dressers, one sanitary inspector, and one clerk, and the unit is capable of breaking up into two sub-units if conditions require. Each diagnostic laboratory, isolation hospital and special sanitary unit is headed respectively by a bacteriologist, a clinician or a sanitary engineer, who with a number of assistants serves as consultant to the mobile units. Each sanitary unit is composed of two sanitary engineers, two sanitary supervisors, two sanitary assistants and three craftsmen.

Formed in 1938, the Corps, besides fighting and controlling epidemics, has rendered special technical service in epidemic areas by providing laboratory and sanitary engineering facilities and has cooperated with public health personnel training centers by providing fields for practical training in communicable disease control methods. It has also collected epidemiological data, initiated special sanitary engineering projects in rural districts and helped local health authorities in controlling endemic diseases such as schistosomiasis and other parasitic infections.

Guarding the health of the troops are army anti-epidemic corps distributed in all war areas, while similar corps have also been organized by provincial health departments.

To bring about closer coordination of all anti-epidemic forces, a Joint Emergency Anti-Epidemic Commission was formed in May, 1940, by the National Health Administration, the Army Medical Administration, the health department of the Board of Supplies and Transport and the Chinese Red Cross Medical Relief Corps. With the establishment of the commission, the report of an outbreak of any disease in the country will reach the leading health organizations simultaneously, and their combined efforts for its control are ensured. Besides maintaining a central epidemiological intelligence service, the commission plans civil and army anti-epidemic programs and publishes handbooks to serve as technical guides for field services.

In addition to a quarantine station in Chungking and a branch at Wanhsien above Ichang, 64 delousing stations have been established, nine of which are mobile in character and under the National Health Administration's Anti-Epidemic Corps, while fourteen are attached to the Administration's highway health stations. The 41 other delousing stations are distributed as follows:

Kansu, 3; Ningsia, 1; Kweichow, 6; Shensi, 7; Szechwan, 3; Kwangsi, 6; Hunan, 3; Hupeh, 2; Kiangsi, 3; Chinghai, 1; Kwangtung, 2; Anhwei, 1; Chekiang, 1; and Yunnan, 2.

Anti-venereal clinics were established at strategic points on national thoroughfares and at places where congregations of troops and laborers were found. The National Health Administration established three, one each in Hupeh, Kwangsi and Chekiang provinces, in 1942. Similar clinics have also been established with the cooperation of local health authorities and medical bodies. The Administration supplies them with drugs, instruments and funds.

Provided raw materials are available in sufficient quantities, Free China is in a position to supply all the biological products required for anti-epidemic work. The National Epidemic Prevention Bureau and the Northwest Epidemic Prevention Bureau, both of the National Health Administration, are supplying the bulk of the vaccines and sera required. The provincial hygienic laboratories of Fukien, Kiangsi, Kwangtung, Kwangsi, and Shensi also produce smallpox, cholera and typhoid vaccines for their own use.

The following table shows some of the important biological products manufactured in the first six months of 1942:

Biological Products	National Epidemic Prevention Bureau	Northwest Epidemic Prevention Bureau
Smallpox vaccine	290,620	600,000
Cholera vaccine	1,901,000	800,000
Cholera, typhoid vaccine	260,000	8,000,000
Typhoid, para-typhoid combined vaccine	110,00	40,000
Plague vaccine	4,849,500	1,200,000
Diphtheria antitoxin	5,707,000	20,000,000
Tetanus antitoxin	7,765,000	..

NOTE:—Smallpox vaccine in capillary tubes other vaccines in c.c.
Diphtheria and tetanus antitoxins in units

Epidemic Outbreaks: In the past several years the following epidemics were found and controlled:

A. Plague

1. Fukien.—Plague has been endemic in Fukien province for more than 40 years and more than 30 *hsien* are known to have been infected at one time or another. In 1937, plague broke out in eighteen *hsien*, claiming about 4,000 lives. The most seriously affected *hsien* were; Weian, Futsing, Putien and Chinkiang. In 1938, sixteen *hsien* were affected with about 300 cases. The epidemic situation was comparatively serious in Yungchun, Putien, Sienyu and Yungan. In 1939, 873 cases were reported in nine *hsien*; in 1940, 466 cases in 23 *hsien*, and in 1941, 626 cases in 21 *hsien*. Between January and June, 1942, 55 cases were reported in eighteen *hsien*.

2. Chekiang.—Plague first broke out in 1938 in Chingyuan, southern Chekiang near the Fukien border, the disease being believed to have spread to Chekiang from northern Fukien. It continued to appear in Chingyuan in 1939 and 1940, but only a small number of cases were reported. In the winter of 1940, for the first time it occurred in Ningpo, eastern Chekiang, and Chuhsien, western Chekiang. Investigation revealed that prior to the outbreak, Japanese planes had dropped rice and wheat grains over the two places. In Ningpo, 97 out of 99 cases were fatal, and in Chuhsien all the 21 cases were fatal. In March, 1941, plague reappeared in Chuhsien, and from March 5 to December 31, there were 166 cases of which 157 were fatal. The rats in Chuhsien were infected, which meant that plague was enzootic among rats and might infect human beings when conditions should so favor. From Chuhsien, the disease spread to Iwu and Tungyang in October, 1941. In Iwu, 145 cases were reported between October and December, 1941, and in Tungyang, there were 71 cases from December, 1941 to the end of May, 1942.

3. Hunan.—Plague for the first time appeared in Changteh, western Hunan, on November 11, 1941, a week after a Japanese plane had dropped grain and cloth wads. Up to the end of December, 1941, there were eight cases, and one more case appeared in January, 1942. In March, the disease reappeared, and between March and July, 31 cases were reported. Plague-infected rats were discovered in Taoyuan in April and May, but no human cases were reported. Taoyuan is 22 kilometers by land and 45 kilometers by water from Changteh. Pneumonic plague broke out in Molinghsiang of Taoyuan *hsien* in May, 1942, resulting in sixteen deaths. It was discovered that a plague patient sneaked out from Changteh, developed pneumonic symptoms and infected his own family and neighbors. By means of strict quarantine, with the assistance of the military, the epidemic was controlled within two weeks.

4. Suiyuan and Ningsia.—Plague has been enzootic in the Ordos region for many years. In the winter of 1941 a pneumonic plague epidemic occurred in Wuyuan, Linho and Tengkow. Later it spread to northern Shensi and Shansi. Toward the end of March, 1941, the epidemic subsided. There were a total of 695 deaths including 540 in Suiyuan, 30 in Ningsia, 99 in Shensi and 26 in Shansi.

5. Kiangsi.—From northern Fukien plague spread to Kwangtse, in eastern Kiangsi bordering Fukien, in the spring of 1941. Excessive mortality among rats was first reported in February and March, and in April human beings were infected. Between April 12 and June 5, 1941, 34 cases were reported. One bubonic plague case—a patient who had escaped from Chuhsien in Chekiang—was found in Shangyao on June 7, 1941. No other case was reported.

6. Kwangtung.—Plague has been endemic on Hainan Island and in the Lienkiang and Suihsi districts for many years. Sporadic cases occurred in 1941 and 1942 in Lienkiang.

7. Yunnan.—Between February and July, 1940, 119 plague cases were reported in Loiwing and Wanting. Plague is known to be endemic in northern Burma and is liable to spread toward the Yunnan border. No cases occurred in 1941 and 1942.

B. Cholera

Cholera broke out in epidemic proportion in the coastal provinces in 1937, when more than 10,000 cases were reported. In 1938, it reappeared in two epidemic centers: in the East River region of Kwangtung province and around Tungting lake in Hunan. It gradually spread to other areas. In all, 167 *hsien* and municipalities in nine provinces were affected. Of a total of 50,043 cases, 13,316 were fatal. In 1939, cholera spread to 278 *hsien* in fifteen provinces, and 34,995 cases were reported. Among the provinces affected were Szechwan, Hunan, Kiangsi, Kweichow, Yunnan, Shensi, Kwangtung, Hupeh, Kwangsi, Fukien, Kansu, Shansi and Chekiang.

In 1940, semi-isolated epidemic outbreaks were reported from the following provinces: (1) Szechwan: A mild winter in 1939 kept the cholera vibrios alive in northern Szechwan, resulting in the outbreak of sporadic cases throughout the spring. In the summer of 1940 the disease broke out in epidemic form again. Altogether ten *hsien* were affected, cases reported almost reaching 40,000. (2) Chekiang: 9,873 cases were reported in 25 *hsien*. (3) Fukien: 4,047 cases were reported in eighteen *hsien*. (4) Hunan: 103 cases were reported in nineteen *hsien*. (5) Kwangtung: 418 cases were reported in four *hsien*.

For the first time since 1937 cholera outbreaks subsided in 1941. In Kwangtung, 265 cases were reported in sixteen *hsien*, while in Hunan, 79 cases were reported in fourteen *hsien*. A few cases were reported in Fukien province.

Between January and September, 1942, 11,951 cases of cholera with 4,576 deaths were reported in 210 *hsien* in twelve provinces and one municipality. The cases did not include those in Chekiang where the figures were not yet compiled.

The epidemic reached its height in July when 4,605 cases and 1,494 deaths were recorded. In September, the cases decreased to 215 with 69 deaths.

The following table shows the cholera situation in the provinces affected:

PROVINCE	Number of *Hsien* Affected	Cases	Deaths	Mortality Percentage
Yunnan	45	4,564	1,875	41.08
Kweichow	26	1,906	355	29.11
Kwangsi	48	3,302	1,453	44.00
Kwangtung	21	420	171	40.71
Hunan	30	1,155	298	25.80
Szechwan	18	279	46	16.48
Kiangsi	10	181	71	39.22
Hupeh	5	108	82	75.92
Chungking City	1	33	25	75.75
Sikang	2	1		
Honan	1	1		
Chekiang	3			
Fukien	1	1		
TOTAL	211	11,951	4,576	38.28

Cholera spread to Kwangsi, Kwangtung and Yunnan from Hongkong and Burma. The disease appeared in Yunnan in May and reached its height in July when 1,623 cases with 448 deaths were recorded.

C. Other Diseases:

Dysentery is most prevalent in China and is an important cause of infant mortality and adult debility. It is, however, considered the least serious because it is common.

Typhus fever and relapsing fever are common among troops and in refugee camps. Delousing stations established in the last few years by the National Health Administration, the Army Medical Administration and the Chinese Red Cross Medical Relief Corps have helped to reduce the total incidence. A serious epidemic occurred in Hupeh in 1941.

Malaria is prevalent south of the Yangtze, especially in Yunnan, Kweichow, and Kwangsi provinces. In 1939, a Yunnan Anti-Malaria Commission was organized, and a second one was formed in Kweichow in 1940. Both commissions are carrying out a systematic control program on a relatively large scale. At the request of the Chinese Government a special medical mission was dispatched by the American Government to take charge of the malaria control work along the projected Yunnan-Burma railway. Assisting the sixteen American members of the mission were nine medical officers, nine sanitary engineers, six entomologists, 15 sanitary supervisors, and 116 sanitary inspectors detailed by the National Health Administration. Active work began in January, 1942, but ended in April owing to the spread of hostilities to Burma.

Diphtheria occurs in epidemic proportions in Kansu and Shensi. In other provinces in Free China, only sporadic cases were reported. Smallpox appears in sporadic form in different provinces.

The following table shows the number of communicable diseases reported in different provinces during 1941 :

Province	Cholera	Typhoid	Dysentery	Typhus Fever	Relapsing Fever	Malaria	Smallpox	Diphtheria	Scarlet Fever	Cerebro-spinal Meningitis	Plague
Chekiang		56	1,889		46	4,464	6	1	1		352
Anhwei		5	55		39	618	158	1			
Kiangsi		848	9,176	100	852	74,368	555	31	3	38	37
Hupeh		669	4,743	190	1,444	12,245	591	10		2	
Hunan	79	534	4,007	71	752	12,173	120	14	4	9	7
Szechwan	3	883	6,917	136	280	32,558	279	224	17	22	
Shansi		65	208	225	638	311	2	7	1		
Honan		3,748	10,963	1,426	2,878	15,323	987	450	511	277	
Shensi		1,413	3,400	1,061	2,874	3,996	122	133	109	36	
Kansu		423	1,283	283	422	308	200	913	39	4	
Fukien	5	335	1,524	30	277	15,102	1,774	22	3	328	626
Kwangtung	265	2,409	25,744	495	195	73,850	3,168	84	26	141	85
Kwangsi		1,452	19,365	185	440	54,932	3,220	202	61	90	
Yunnan		571	6,121	108	528	29,159	328	36	60	48	
Kweichow		375	4,894	108	285	20 708	282	70	33	44	
Sikang		560	267	420	344	1,087	6	12			
Suiyuan		125	272	21	88	59	4	20	3		39
Ningsia		747	860	362	426	60	169	152	9	1	
Total	352	15,218	101,686	6,320	12,808	351,431	11,966	2,382	880	1,040	1,146

Bacterial Warfare

Dr. P. Z. King's statement released on April 9, 1942, and reports submitted by Chinese and foreign medical experts definitely prove that at least on five occasions Japan resorted to bacterial warfare in China.

Yet a sixth attempt was made on the morning of August 30, 1942, when three Japanese planes dropped a large quantity of "kaoliang" and corn in Nanyang, in Honan province. The grain was analyzed by local medical offices and found to contain bubonic plague bacteria.

The first Japanese attempt was made on October 27, 1940, when a quantity of wheat was dropped by Japanese planes over Ningpo. An epidemic broke out soon afterward and lasted 34 days, claiming 99 victims. Diagnosis of plague was definitely confirmed in laboratory tests. On October 4, 1940, a Japanese plane scattered rice and wheat and fleas over Chuhsien, Chekiang. Bubonic plague appeared 38 days later, causing 21 deaths. Kinhwa was attacked by three Japanese planes on November 28, 1940, when a large quantity of translucent granules like shrimp-eggs were dropped. Microscopic examination revealed the presence of plague bacilli though no epidemic resulted. On November 4, 1941, a Japanese plane visited Changteh, western Hunan, dropping rice, paper, and cotton wads on which bacilli were found. Later nine cases of plague were reported. Numerous circumstantial evidence, including infected rats, proved beyond doubt the origin of the epidemic. Lastly, a serious attack of plague broke out in Suiyuan, Ningsia, and Shensi. Six hundred cases were reported. A communique from local military authorities stated that a large number of sick rodents was set free by the enemy there.

The full text of Dr. King's statement reads as follows:

"Up to the present time the practicability of bacterial warfare has been little known to the public because applicable experimental results, if available, are usually kept a military secret.

"In the past the artificial dissemination of disease germs has been done for military purposes. The pollution of drinking water supplies by the introduction of diseased animals or other infected materials into the wells has been practiced by retreating armies with the intention of causing epidemics of gastro-intestinal infections among the troops in pursuit. Fortunately such water-borne infections can be controlled with relative ease by boiling of all drinking water and disinfection by chemical means.

"Whether or not infectious diseases could be widely and intentionally spread by artificial means with deadly results had not been demonstrated prior to the outbreak of the Sino-Japanese war. However, in the last two years sufficient circumstantial evidence has been gathered to show that the Japanese have been using our people as guinea pigs for experimentation on the practicability of bacterial warfare. They have tried to produce epidemics of plague in Free China by scattering plague-infected materials from airplanes. The facts thus far collected follow:

"1. On October 29, 1940, bubonic plague for the first time occurred in Ningpo in Chekiang province. The epidemic lasted 34 days and claimed 99 victims. It was reported that on October 27, 1940, Japanese planes raided Ningpo and scattered a considerable quantity of wheat over the port city. Although it was a curious fact to find 'grain from heaven' yet no one at the time seemed to appreciate the enemy's intention and no thorough examination of the grain was made. All the plague victims were local residents. The diagnosis of plague was definitely confirmed by laboratory tests. There was no excessive mortality among rats noticed before the epidemic and, despite careful examination, no exogenous sources of infection could be discovered.

"2. On October 4, 1940, a Japanese plane visited Chuhsien, Chekiang province. After circling over the city it scattered rice and wheat mixed with fleas over the western district of the city. There were many eye-witnesses among whom was a man named Hsu, who collected some grain and dead fleas from the street outside of his own house. He sent them to the local air-raid precautionary corps for transmission to the provincial hygienic laboratory. The laboratory examination result was that 'there were no pathogenic organisms found by bacteriological culture methods.' However, on November 12, 38 days after the Japanese plane's visit, bubonic plague appeared in the same area where the grain and fleas were found in abundance. The epidemic in Chuhsien lasted 24 days, resulting in 21 deaths.

"Available records show bubonic plague never occurred in Chuhsien before. After careful investigation it was believed that the strange visit of the enemy plane was the cause of the epidemic and the transmitting agent was rat fleas, presumably infected with plague and definitely dropped by the enemy plane. As plague is primarily a disease of rodents, the grain was probably used to attract the rats and expose them to the infected fleas mixed therein. It was regrettable that the fleas collected were not properly examined. Owing to deficient laboratory facilities, an animal inoculation test was not performed.

"3. On November 28, 1940, when the plague epidemic in Ningpo and Chuhsien was still in progress, three Japanese planes came to Kinhwa, an important commercial city situated between Ningpo and Chuhsien, and there dropped a large quantity of small granules about the size of shrimp-eggs. These strange objects were collected and examined in a local hospital.

"The granules were more or less round, about one millimeter in diameter, of whitish-yellow, somewhat translucent with a certain amount of glistening reflection from the surface. When brought into contact with a drop of water on a glass slide the granule began to swell to about twice its original size. In a small amount of water in a test tube with some agitation it would break up into whitish flakes and later form a milky suspension. Microscopic examination of these granules revealed the presence of numerous gram-negative bacilli with distinct bipolar staining in some of them and an abundance of involution forms, thus possessing the morphological characteristics of B. Pestis, the positive organism of plague. When cultured in agar medium these gram-negative bacilli showed no growth and because of inadequacy of laboratory facilities animal inoculation tests could not be performed.

"Upon the receipt of such a startling report from Kinhwa the National Health Administration dispatched Dr. W. W. Yung, director of the Department of Epidemic Prevention; Dr. H. M. Jettmar, epidemiologist, formerly of the League of Nation's Epidemic Commission, and other technical experts to investigate the situation. Arriving in Kinhwa early in January, 1941, they examined 26 of these granules and confirmed the previous observations, but inoculation tests performed on guinea pigs by Dr. Jettmar gave negative results. It is difficult to say whether or not the lapse of time and the method of preservation of the granules had something to do with the negative results from the animal inoculation test, which is a crucial test for B. Pestis. At all events no plague occurred in Kinhwa and it indicated that this particular Japanese experiment on bacterial warfare ended in failure.

"4. On November 4, 1941, at about 5 a.m., a lone enemy plane appeared over Changteh, Hunan province, flying very low, the morning being rather misty. Instead of bombs, wheat and rice, pieces of paper, cotton wadding, and some unidentified particles were dropped. After the all-clear signal had been sounded some of these strange gifts from the enemy were collected and sent by the police to a local missionary hospital for examination which revealed the presence of micro-organisms reported to resemble B. Pestis.

"On November 11, seven days later, the first clinical case of plague came to notice, followed by five more cases. The diagnosis of bubonic plague was definitely confirmed in one of the six cases in November by bacteriological culture method and animal inoculation test.

"According to the investigation of Dr. W. W. Chen, bacteriologist, who has had special training in plague work in India, and Dr. R. Pollitzer, epidemiologist of the National Health Administration and formerly of the League of Nation's Epidemic Commission, the Changteh plague epidemic was caused by enemy action because of the following strong circumstantial evidence:

"A—That Changteh has never been, as far as is known, afflicted by plague. During previous pandemics and severe epidemics elsewhere in China this part of Hunan (as a matter of fact this part of Central China in general) has never been known to come under the scourge of the disease.

"B—That the present outbreak may have been due to direct contiguous spread from neighboring plague-infected districts is also untenable on epidemiological grounds. Epidemiologically plague spreads along transport routes for grain on which the rats feed. The nearest epidemic center to Changteh is Chuhsien in Chekiang, about 2,000 kilometers away by land or river communication. Furthermore, Changteh being a rice producing district, supplies rice to other districts and does not receive rice from other cities. Besides, all the cases occurring in Changteh were native inhabitants who had not been away from the city or its immediate environs at all.

"C—That all the cases came from the areas within the city where the strange objects dropped by enemy planes were found, and that among the wheat and rice and cotton rags were the most probable included vectors, probably fleas. The fleas were not noticed on the spot because they were not looked for and because the air raid alarm lasted some twelve hours with the result that the fleas must have in the meantime escaped to other hiding places.

"D—That there was no apparent evidence of any excessive rat mortality before and for sometime after the 'aerial incident.' About 200 rats were caught and examined during the months of November and December but no evidence of plague was found. However, toward the end of January and the first part of February of this year, among 78 rats examined there were eighteen with definite plague infection. As plague is primarily a disease of rodents the usual sequence of events is that an epizootic precedes an epidemic but that did not take place in the present case. The infected fleas from the enemy planes must have first attacked men and a little later, the rats.

"E—That all the first six human cases were infected within fifteen days after the 'aerial incident' and that infected fleas are known to be able to survive under suitable conditions for weeks without feeding. The normal incubation period of bubonic plague is three to seven days and may occasionally be prolonged to eight or even fourteen days. The time factor is certainly also a strong circumstantial evidence.

"5. A serious epidemic of plague occurring in Suiyuan, Ningsia and Shensi provinces has recently been reported. From the last week of January this year to date there have been some 600 cases. Those cases were reported in a recent communique from the local military in the northwestern part of the epidemic area. However, considering the fact that plague is known to be enzootic among the native rodents in the Ordos region in Suiyuan one must wait for confirmation of the reports that probably the plague was caused there by enemy action.

"Technical experts, including Dr. Y. N. Yang, Director of the National Health Administration's Northwest Epidemic Prevention Bureau, have been sent there to investigate and help control the epidemic.

"The enumeration of facts thus far collected leads to the conclusion that the Japanese army has attempted bacterial warfare in China. In Chekiang and Hunan they had scattered from the air infective materials and succeeded in causing epidemic outbreaks of plague. Aside from temporary terrorization of the general population in the afflicted areas this inhuman act of our enemy is most condemnable when one realizes that once the disease has taken root in the local rat population it will continue to infect men for many years to come. Fortunately the mode of infection and the method of control of plague are known and it is possible to keep the disease in check by vigorous control measures. Our difficulty at present is the shortage of anti-epidemic supplies required. The recent advance in chemotherapy has given us new drugs that are more or less effective for the treatment of plague cases. These are sulfathiazole and allied sulphonamide compounds which China cannot as yet produce herself.

"For prevention, plague vaccine can be produced in considerable quantities by the National Epidemic Prevention Bureau in Kunming and the Northwest Epidemic Prevention Bureau in Lanchow, provided the raw materials required for vaccine production such as peptone and agar agar are available.

"Rat proofing of all buildings and eradication of rats are fundamental control measures but under war conditions they cannot be satisfactorily carried out.

"If rat poisons such as cyanogas and barium carbonate can be obtained from abroad in large quantities deratization campaigns may be launched in cities where rats are a menace."

Improvement of Nutrition

One of the wartime health activities aims at the improvement of nutrition. The National Institute of Health did the following dietary surveys and nutritional studies in 1941:

Dr. C. F. Wang formulated an "egg yolk-legume mixture" to take the place of milk or milk powder. Feeding experiments on a 15-day old baby with the new mixture was tried for 60 consecutive days. The results were found to be very favorable and promising.

A study of nutritional values between biscuits made with white flour and those made with mixed cereals resulted in the preparation of mixed cereal biscuits by the department to advertise their nutritional value.

A manual was prepared on improved cooking methods and suggested recipes using various cereal meals, sweet potatoes and other products of high nutritional value.

Dietary studies were made of the workmen, the staff members and their families of the National Health Administration in the department's survey of the diets of public functionaries during wartime. The results of these studies seem to indicate that there existed protein and vitamin C deficiency in all the three groups. With the exception of the third group there seems to be a general lack of sufficient total calories and vitamin A. In all three diets there is no indication of the shortage of any of the essential minerals.

Four kinds of booklets on nutrition were written and published for general distribution. Free copies of these were sent to schools, libraries and public organizations.

A series of investigations were made on human vitamin C nutrition. The daily vitamin C requirement of healthy Chinese adults was found to be 0.70-0.76 mg. per kg. of body weight. The requirement of vitamin C of both children and lactating women is higher than adult. 1.0-1.6 mg. of vitamin C per kg. per day would be required in such cases. Investigations were made into plasma vitamin C content of 108 residents in Kweiyang, Kweichow province, and into the effect of cooking on the total ascorbic acid content of vegetables. It was found that considerable amount of vitamin C is destroyed by improper methods of cooking such as frying, steaming as well as by the use of copper vessels for cooking vegetables.

The Nutrition Promotion Committee was organized in December, 1940, with the following nine government officials on its presidium: Dr. H. H. Kung, Vice-President of the Executive Yuan and Minister of Finance; Mr. Chen Li-fu, Minister of Education; Dr. Wong Wen-hao, Minister of Economic Affairs; Admiral Shen Hung-lieh, Minister of Agriculture and Forestry; Mr. Ku Cheng-kang, Minister of Social Affairs; Dr. P. Z. King, Director-General of the National Health Administration; Mr. Chen Chi-tsai, Controller-General; Dr. K. C. Wu, former Mayor of Chungking and now Vice-Minister of Foreign Affairs, and Mr. Kang Hsin-ju, Chairman of the Chungking Provisional Political Council.

In one of the publicity campaigns sponsored by the Committee in Chungking in September, 1942, the National Health Administration displayed models, charts, maps, and diagrams, giving details of a healthy diet, and of the contents and nutritive value of all kinds of common food. The Ministry of Social Affairs and the National New Life Movement Association participated in the exhibition. The preparation and cooking of inexpensive and yet nutritive dishes were demonstrated.

The following chart, dealing with the nutritive value of China's staple food, attracted wide attention:

Food	*Fats*	*Protein*	*Starch*	*Phosphorus*	*Iron*	*Vitamins*
Unpolished wheat	2	12	74	XX	XX	XXX
Unpolished rice	1	8	76	XX	XX	XXX
flour	1	11	77	X	X	0
Polished rice	0	7	79	X	X	0

As a demonstration of the right food combination, the Committee on one occasion treated hundreds of guests to a model dinner. The menu consisted of:

	Vitamins					*Phosphorus*	*Iron*	*Calcium*	*Calories*
	A	*B*	*C*	*D*	*E*				
1. Soup	X	XX			X	XXX	X	X	36
2. Cabbage & Liver	XXX	XX	XXX	X	XX	XXX	XXX	X	88
3. Cabbage & Pork	X	XX			XX	XXX	X	X	210
4. Beancurd	X					X	X	XX	60
5. Salted Beef	X	X	X	X	XX	XXX	XX	X	278
6. Salted Cabbage		XX	XXX		XX	X	XX	X	48
7. Rice with Beans	X	XX			X	XXX	XX	X	446
8. Green Bean Soup	X	XX			X	XXX	XX	X	66
9. Vita-cake	X	XX			X	XXX	X	X	91
10. Vita-beanmilk	X	XX			X	XXX	X	X	186

(The Sign X indicates the percentage of vitamins A,B,C,D,E and of other contents. According to a footnote on the menu, the human body needs 2,400 calories daily.)

As a preliminary step toward the improvement of nutrition for the Chinese army, a comprehensive research was made to obtain actual food and nutrition conditions of Chinese soldiers in general as well as to prepare a standardized list of minimum diet and nutrition requirements for the reference of the various armed forces of China.

The study, lasting seven months, used as subjects of the experimentation and research privates of two companies, each of 127 men, who were divided into an experimental group and a control group.

The study was divided into three periods of investigation and examination, experimentation, and confirmation. Those in the experimental group were given a modified diet prepared under strict supervision for a period of 75 days. After that both groups were put on this improved diet for another 45 days, duration of the last period of confirmation.

Prior to the research, soldiers of the two companies daily consumed on the average 772.80 grams of rice, 6.50 grams of oil, 9.60 grams of meat, 308.90 grams of vegetables, 15 grams of soy bean, 8.40 grams of salt, 4.40 grams of other seasoning matters, and 1.06 grams of miscellaneous items. These foods were calculated to yield about 3,100 calories of heat per day.

The improved diet, yielding approximately 3,400 calories of heat daily, gives each soldier every day the following: 822.30 grams of rice, 11.40 grams of flour, 15.50 grams of oil, 29.60 grams of meat including animal blood, 150 grams of vegetables (approximately 80 grams of which were leaves and 70 grams roots), 68.80 grams of soy bean and bean products (29.90 grams of which were soy bean), 10.20 grams of salt, and 7.30 grams of other food substances.

In weight, physical endurance as well as general health the soldiers experimented on showed marked improvement after they were given the improved diet. After 75 days of experimentation during which the modified diet was used, the weight of soldiers in the experimental group increased on the average from 114.68±1.17 pounds to 121.77±1.04 pounds, giving an average increase of 7.03±1.56 pounds for each soldier. This goes to prove the defect of the original diet and also the effects of nutritional improvement on body weight.

At the end of the experimentation period the average weight of the control group was 116.36±1.15 pounds, having no apparent increase over the pre-examination average weight of 115.35 ±1.29 pounds. However, after the confirmation period the control group's average weight shot up to 121.41±1.41 pounds, registering a per capita increase of 5.02±1.90 pounds over the weight before the improved diet was given this group of soldiers.

Based on the data of their studies, the research workers drew up a suggested standardized diet list which requires a minimum of:

Total heat yield 3,400 calories—

Protein	80	grams
Fat	30	,,
Carbohydrate	660	,,
Calcium	0.64	,,
Phosphorous	1.32	,,
Iron	0.01	,,

To get these food contents each soldier should consume per day at least 823 grams of coarse rice, 16 grams of oil, for cooking, 30 grams of meat (including blood, liver and egg), 68 grams of bean products (chiefly soy bean), 150 grams of vegetables (the amount of root vegetables not to exceed leaf vegetables), 10 grams of salt, 5 grams of other seasoning matters, and 20 grams of other things.

MEDICAL SUPPLIES

The number of drug factories in Free China is estimated at 40, the majority being small in size. Much of the chemicals is produced on a small scale, while many of the reagents needed are still made by laboratory methods or are in the experimental stage.

Among the difficulties encountered by the drug manufacturers are lack of trained personnel and shortage in workable materials. Coal distillation is still in an embryonic stage. There are no efficient systems of refrigeration and of vacuum distillation. In the absence of essentials, such as acid resisting steel, suitable containers, specified machinery and tools, the manufacturers have learned to improve and improvise where necessary or possible in order to produce whatever they can.

Free China has sufficient ordinary inorganic substance. The National Health Administration has been acting as coordinator between manufacturers and the government organizations controlling the needed raw materials. Other assistance the health authorities have given includes technical advice and subsidies. In this way it is hoped that efficiency and production of the factories may be stimulated and the quality of the products improved.

Essential medical supplies, which cannot be made in China or which are produced in too small quantities to meet the demands, are imported by an official committee for general distribution to allay any fear of a drug famine and to maintain drug prices at an equitable level.

Among the drugs which are being manufactured in Free China in fairly large quantities are:

Acidum Boricum	Acidum Tannicum	Aether
Albumini Tannas	Ammonii Chloridum	Argenti Nitras
Bismuth Compounds	Blaud's Tablets	Brown Mixture Tablets
Calamina	Calcii Chloridum	Calcii Lactas
Calx Chlorinata	Camphor	Carbo Animalis
Chloroformum	Cupri Citras	Cupri Sulphas
Dextrosum	Dobell's Tablets	Ferri et Ammonii Citras
Hydrargyri Oxidum Flavum	Hydrargyri Perchloridum	Hydrargyri Subchloridum
Hydrargyrum Ammoniatum	Liq. Ammoniae Fortis	Magnesii Oxidum
Magnessi Carbonas	Magnesii Sulphas	Menthol
Oleum Ricini	Oleum Terebinthinae	Pix Pini
Plumbi Acetas	Potassa Sulphurata	Oleum Menthae
Potassii Chloras	Potassii Citras	Sapo Millis
Serum Anti-diphthericum	Serum Anti-dysentericum	Serum Anti-meningococcus
Serum Anti-plague	Serum Tetanicum	Sodii Bicarbonas
Sodii Chloridum	Sodii Sulphas	Spiritus Aetheris Nitrosi
Sulphur	Tab. Gentianae et Rhei Co.	Tab. Santon. et Hydrarg. Subchlor.
Tinctura Benzoin Co.*	Talcum	Zinci Sulphas
Acidum Citricum	Acidum Hydrochloricum	Acidum Sulphuricum
Arseni Trioxidum	Ferri Perchloridum	Ferri Sulphas
Ferrum Reductum	Sodii Poras	Sodii Hydroxide
Cotton Absorbent	Gauze Absorbent	

*Benzoin must be imported.

Among the drugs which can be partially supplied by Chinese factories are:

Aethylis Chloridum	Antimonii et Potassii Tartras*	Argento-Porteinum Forte (Portargol)
Argento-Proteinum Mite (Argyrol)	Atropinae Sulphas	Chloralis Hydras
Digitalis	Clycerinum	Potassii Permagnas
Sodii Bromidum	Sodii Thiosulphas	Zinci Oxidum
Acidum Aceticum Glaciale	Acidum Lacticum	

*Tartaric acid must be imported.

While it is impossible to give a complete list of all the manufacturing plants and the exact quantity and variety of their products, the following list of some of the best known manufacturing institutions with descriptions of a few of them will give a partial idea of what is being undertaken toward meeting the tremendous demand.

MANUFACTURING INSTITUTIONS	MAIN PRODUCTS
National Epidemic Prevention Bureau (under the National Health Administration). Kansu, and Yunnan.	The chief source of the supply of the nation's anti-toxins and epidemic preventives; also, a number of common medicines from native drugs.
National Central Narcotics Bureau, Szechwan.	Narcotics and non-narcotics.
China Pharmaceutical Manufacturing Company, Szechwan.	Pharmaceutical preparations (official and non-official) mostly from native crude drugs.
China Drug Co., Ltd., Szechwan.	Pharmaceutical preparations.
The New Asia Chemical Works, Ltd., Szechwan.	Ampoules, chemicals and specialties.
West China Chemical and Pharmaceutical Industries, Kansu.	Absorbent cotton and gauze, chemicals and pharmaceutical preparations.
Scientific Apparatus Manufacturing Co., Szechwan.	Scientific apparatus for hospitals, schools, etc.
The Wood Dry Distillation Co., Szechwan.	Acetic acid, alcohol, etc.
The Golden Sea Chemical Research Institute, Szechwan.	Gallic acid and its derivatives.
Northwest Chemical Works, Kansu.	Pharmaceutical preparations, absorbent cotton and absorbent gauze.
New China Chemical Works, Szechwan.	Chemicals.
The Kunming Chemical Factory, Yunnan (a joint enterprise of merchants and the Ministry of Economic Affairs).	Chemicals, etc.
The Yungli Sulphuric Acid Factory, Szechwan.	The annual output was estimated some time ago at 100,000 barrels of sulphuric acid.
Two other sulphuric acid manufacturing plants with a working capital of about NC $1,000,000 each also operate in Szechwan.	
The Central Pharmaceutical Manufacturing Co., Chungking and Chengtu.	This institution was organized in 1940, with three main departments, namely:—Research, Manufacturing, Business. It produces principally pure chemicals and basic drugs, about 95 per cent of which are made from native raw materials. The value of chemicals and drugs produced monthly is NC $800,000 and $1,000,000.
The Pharmacist Friends Laboratories, Szechwan.	Chemicals, pharmaceutical preparations and specialties.

With a view to achieving self-sufficiency in medical supplies and simplifying the question of supply and demand, the National Health Administration, after much deliberation, has listed 104 kinds of drugs as essentials, in addition to ten kinds of special drugs and nine kinds of biological products, all of which are regarded as sufficient to meet the general demands. Of the number, 80 per cent can be made in China. Medical practitioners have been advised by the Administration to prescribe whenever possible only the listed drugs. The list follows:

A. ORDINARY DRUGS

Acetphenetidinum (Phenacetin)	Acidum Acetylsalicylicum (Aspirin)	Acidum Boricum
Acidum Hydrochloricum Dilutum	Acidum Salicylicum	Acidum Tannicum
Adrenalinum	Aether	Albumini Tannas
Alcohol	Allum	Alumen

Ammonni Chloridum	Amylum	Antimonii of Potassii Tartras or Antimonii et Sodii Tartras
Apomorphinae Hydrochloridum	Argenti Nitras	Argento-Profeinum Forte (Protargol)
Arseni Trioxidum	Atropinae Sulphas	Aurentii Amari Cortex
Barbitalum	Benzoinum	Bismuthi Subcarbonas
Bismuthi Subgallas	Bismuthi et Sodii Tartras	Caffeina
Calamina	Calcii Carbonas Praecipitatus or Creta Praeparata	Calcii Chloridum
Calcii Lactas	Calx	Calx Chlorinata
Camphorae	Carbo Activatus or Carbo Animalis	Chloralis Hydras
Chloroformum	Cocainaee Hydrochloridum	Codeinae Phosphas
Coptis	Cresol	Cupri Sulphas
Digitalis	Emetinae Hydrochloridum	Ephedra
Ephedrinae Hydrochloridum	Ergota	Ferri Sulphas
Galla	Gentiana	Glucosum
Glycerinum	Glycyrrhizae	Hydrargyri Oxidum Flavum
Hydrargyri Perchloridum	Hydrargyri Subchloridum	Hydrargyrum
Hydrargyrum Ammoniatum	Iodoformum	Iodum
Kaolinum	Magnesii Carponas	Magnesii Sulphas
Menthol	Pharbitis	Phenol
Pituitarium Posterium	Pix Pini	Plumbi Acetas
Polygala	Potassii Acetas	Potassii Iodidum
Potassii Permanganas	Procainae Hydrochloridum	Morphinae Hydrochloridum
Neoarsphenamina	Nux Vomica	Oleum Eucalypti
Oleum Hydnocarpae	Oleum Menthae	Oleum Ricini
Oleum	Oleum Terebinthinae	Opium
Paraffinum Molle (Vaseline)	Quininae Bisulphas (or Sulphas)	Quininae Dihydrochloridum
Rheum	Santoninum	Sodii Bicarbonas
Sodii Boras (Borax)	Sodii Bromidum	Sodii Chloridum
Sodii Citras	Sodii Salicylas	Sodii Sulphas
Sodii Thiosulphas	Stramonium	Sulphur Sublimatum
Talcum Purificatum	Thymol	Trinitrinum
Zinci Oxidum	Zinci Sulphas	

B. Special Drugs

Chiniofonum (Yatren)	Thiaminae Chloridum	Insulinum
Physostigminae Salicylas	Quininae Aethylcargonas	Sulfanilamidum
Sulfathiazolum	Plasmoquininae Tab.	Thyroideum
	Mersalylum (Salyrgan)	

C. Biological Products

Antitoxinum Diphthericum	Antitoxinum Tetanicum	Toxoidum Diphthericum
Toxidum Tetanicum	Vaccinum Cholerae	Vaccinum Cholerae et Typho-Paratyphosum
Vaccinum Rabies	Vaccinum Typho-Paratyphosum	Vaccinum Variolae

The manufacture of surgical instruments, hospital equipment and artificial limbs has been handicapped by shortage of necessary machines and tools, raw materials and skilled workmen. Two government factories in Szechwan are working overtime to meet the demand which has proved to be out of all proportions to those of prewar years.

Removed from Nanking to Szechwan, the Surgical Instrument and Hospital Equipment Factory of the National Health Administration has been manufacturing since March, 1938, surgical instruments and equipment, field operating tables, collapsible stretchers, portable field shower baths, Thomas splints and artificial limbs for use in army hospitals. Its output was increased from 9,924 articles in 1939 to over 48,000 in 1941.

The Military Sanitary Equipment Factory of the Ministry of Military Affairs is producing a total of 13,000 pieces of surgical instruments and hospital supplies in addition to between 400 to 500 artificial limbs a month. The factory's products consist of more than 300 kinds of instruments, ten kinds of artificial limbs and twenty kinds of hospital supplies. If the plant is required to produce only one kind of instrument, the output can be increased to 40,000 articles a month, or about 500,000 a year. Its artificial limbs section sends trained technicians to army hospitals to take measurements and make plaster moulds for disabled soldiers.

Established in July, 1940, the plant has several types of old machines collected in interior China, one being converted into instrument-making service from its original can-stamping purpose. Lien Jui-chi, German-trained pharmacist, is the director of the factory, while Wang Yun-hsuan, trained at Technische-Hochschule zu Berlin, is the chief engineer.

The orthopedic center in Kweiyang also produces orthopedic appliances, such as splints, crutches and artificial limbs.

First with a revolving fund of $1,000,000 and later reinforced by £168,000 British export credits, the National Health Administration through its Emergency Purchasing Committee for Medical Supplies has been supplying essential drugs to medical and health organizations and the general public at cost.

In the first year after its inauguration in November, 1939, the committee purchased 2,091 packages of medical supplies, and in 1940, 1,839 packages besides 48 cases of cotton and gauze from local factories. Purchases were limited to local plants in 1941, when altogether $2,040,132 worth of drugs and medical supplies were sold to 222 units. Between January and June, 1942, 360 packages were bought from local drug plants. Arrangements were made by the end of July for the importation of 20 tons of medical supplies from India.

The Committee maintains two agencies to facilitate transportation and two sales offices and two dispensaries in Chungking. Sales were made in seventeen Free China provinces.

Dr. F. Y. Tai is chairman of the committee, the other members being S. C. Hsu, Dr. S. Y. Yue, Dr. Hsu Shih-chin and S. S. Kung. Dr. C. Y. Shu is the general secretary. An advisory technical committee for medical supplies to China was organized with Dr. P. Z. King, director-general of the National Health Administration, as chairman.

OLD STYLE MEDICAL PRACTITIONERS

The Old Style Medical Practitioners Committee of the National Health Administration supervises and registers Chinese medicine institutions and organizations; determines the qualifications of herb doctors and supervises their practice; deals with matters concerning the training of old style medical personnel; examines patent herb medicine and supervises herb stores; examines and compiles publications on old style medicine, and administers general affairs relating to old style medicine.

No accurate statistics are available as to the number of old style medical practitioners in the whole of China, but it is estimated to be more than 100,000 persons. Up to October, 1942, at least 5,130 herb doctors were registered with the National Health Administration. Herb doctors may register with provincial and municipal authorities, but the final examination of their qualifications is done by the Committee. Between October, 1941 and August, 1942, herb doctors passed totalled 798, including 389 doctors registered with the Szechwan provincial government, 37 with the Kweichow provincial government, 152 with the Kiangsi provincial government, 100 with the Anhwei provincial government and 120 with the Fukien provincial government.

The Committee has issued certificates to 27 practitioners in war zones and abroad.

Patent herb medicines examined by the Committee between October, 1941 and August, 1942 totalled 99.

Publications on Chinese medicine examined by the Committee in the same period numbered eight.

Herb doctors' associations established in the period number 35, and herb store unions 89.

Books on herbs and on the practice of old style medicine published in the same period numbered three.

Dr. Chen Yu is the chairman of the Committee, and members of the standing committee are: Doctors Peng Yang-kuang, Chang Chieh-chai, Yao Feng Huang, and Chang You-chih.

Hospitals in China

No accurate statistics on hospitals and hospital beds in Free China are available as the difficulty in communications and the removals of institutions resulting from the constant shifting of fighting zones have left gaps in surveys of an extensive nature, and have caused delays and omissions in the collection of reports from various places.

General and special hospitals maintained by provincial and municipal governments at the end of 1941 numbered 43. The number of beds in 34 of them was 2,038. With the increase in the number of *hsien* health centers, more hospital wards have been made available to the public. The *hsien* health system requires each center to maintain a 20 to 40-bed hospital. By the end of 1941, 751 centers had been established in thirteen provinces.

Attempts to obtain accurate and complete numbers of private and mission hospitals in Free China have been equally unsuccessful. Reports reaching the National Health Administration put the number of such hospitals at the end of 1941 at 237 in fourteen provinces with a total of 6,326 beds. The figures are known to have fallen far short of the actual number of hospitals existing in Free China. Some of the hospitals known in operation were found missing from the lists, while in certain cases, figures of hospitals and hospital beds have not yet been received in Chungking. The tables given below were based on reports received by the National Health Administration.

Number of Hospitals, Laboratories and Health Centers Maintained by Municipal and Provincial Governments at the End of 1941

Municipality & Provinces	General Hospital	Special Hospital	Laboratory	Health Centers
Chungking	3	1	0	0
Szechwan	0	2	0	65
Chekiang	0	0	1	60
Kiangsi	1	2	1	81
Hupeh	1	0	0	17
Hunan	1	0	1	75
Honan	1	2	1	2
Shensi	0	1	2	54
Kansu	1	0	0	20
Chinghai	1	0	0	0
Fukien	2	1	1	64
Kwangtung	1	3	1	73
Kwangsi	11	0	1	87
Yunnan	2	2	1	77
Kweichow	2	1	1	76
Ningsia	1	0	0	0
Total	28	15	11	751

Number of Private and Mission Hospitals in China at the End of 1941

Municipality & Provinces	Hospitals	Beds	Municipality & Provinces	Hospitals	Beds
Chungking	5	325	Kwangtung	4	104
Szechwan	23	664	Kwangsi	10	367
Chekiang	56	1,298	Kweichow	1	57
Anhwei	6	94	Kansu	8	212
Kiangsi	7	356	Honan	32	437
Hupeh	4	136	Chinghai	1	15
Hunan	36	1,536	Yunnan*		
Shansi	1	5	Fukien*		
Shensi	43	720	Sikang*		
			Suiyuan*		

Total number of hospitals: 237, and beds 6,326

*Figures unavailable

To make the best possible use of existing hospital facilities throughout the country, the Chinese Government has provided subsidies through the National Health Administration for non-governmental hospitals to enable them to treat wounded or sick soldiers and refugees.

The funds available for such subsidies amount to $100,000 a month; and the scheme of hospital subsidies has been in effect with slight modifications since the outbreak of hostilities in 1937. The hospitals are subsidized on the basis of monthly returns giving the number of wounded or sick soldiers and refugees treated at a daily rate of $2 per inpatient and 40 cents per outpatient visit. Besides such cash subsidies, grants of medical supplies are provided.

A total of 80 hospitals with a bed capacity of 4,000 in Free China came within the scope of this scheme in 1942. The subsidies ranged from $600 to $1,800 a month for each hospital Of the $100,000, 40 per cent was in cash, while 60 per cent in medical supplies.

Three orthopedic centers are treating wounded soldiers and civilian air raid casualties, and at the same time, additional technical personnel are being trained there to start orthopedic work in other parts of China so that the number of deformities may be substantially reduced. All the three centers are attached to the Emergency Medical Service Training Schools of the Ministry of Military Affairs.

The first center, with 200 beds, forms part of the 1,000-bed training hospital and school at Kweiyang. Equipment to the value of £2,000 was provided by the British Orthopedic Society, while the British Fund for Relief of Distressed in China gave HK $2,000 for the maintenance of the center for the first six months.

The Kweiyang center operates a workshop to provide artificial limbs. Vocational training along useful lines is given convalescent patients.

The two branch centers, each with a capacity of between 50 and 70 beds, are attached to training schools, one at Paocheng, Shensi, and the other at Tungan, Hunan.

Conscription of Personnel

Graduates of medical colleges, dentistry, and nursing schools, with the exception of fifteen per cent of them who might work in their original schools, have been required since 1942 to join army and civil medical service. The distribution of the 85 per cent of medical graduates was as follows: 40 per cent to the Army Medical Administration, 30 per cent to the National Health Administration, and 15 per cent to the Red Cross Medical Relief Commission. Half of the graduates of midwifery schools were required to work in the National Health Administration. The distribution of the graduates among the three services was to be decided by drawing lots at the schools.

Graduation certificates, according to the regulations promulgated on May 5, 1942, will be awarded the students upon completion of one year's service with either of the three organizations. The schools are required to send the names of graduates to the Ministry of Education and the Wartime Medical Personnel Conscription Committee for reference. Conscripted graduates are required to join the assigned service three months after graduation. Traveling, board and lodging expenses of the conscripted personnel are paid by the organizations they join.

Conscription of medical personnel was first enforced in 1939, when 284 doctors and 10 pharmacists were called to government medical service. One hundred medical practitioners in several provinces and 281 graduates of army medical schools were likewise asked to enlist.

Judicial Medicine

Judicial medicine was first listed on the curriculum of the Peking Medical College and the provincial medical colleges of Chekiang and Kiangsu in 1915. In 1930, the Peking Medical College, then changed to Medical School of Peiping University, opened a special course for such studies. Not until 1934, by a decree of the Ministry of Education, did judicial medicine become one of the required subjects in medical colleges.

Following the establishment of the Judicial Physicians' Training Institute in 1932 in Chenju, near Shanghai, doctors were enlisted for a two-year special course, one and a half year in study, and half a year for practice. In 1935, 20 doctors were graduated and appointed to courts in different provinces. In September the same year, an institute for judicial medicine was established under the medical college of Peiping University. In Chenju, 20 additional doctors were trained between 1936 and 1937.

Following the outbreak of the war, the two institutes moved to Chungking where they were merged into one. Dr. Lynn Ge, trained at Berlin University, who first headed the Chenju institute, was the director of the one in Peiping. Dr. Sung Kwei-fang, French returned student, was the director of the Chenju institute.

ARMY MEDICAL SERVICE

The army medical service is maintained by four organizations. Though under separate command they run as the component parts of one integral administration, each having its specific duties. The organizations come under the armies, the medical department of the Board of Supplies and Transport of the National Military Council, the Army Medical Administration and the Central Wounded Soldiers Administration of the Ministry of Military Affairs.

Army medical units serve at the front, clearing the combat zone, rendering first aid and emergency treatment and evacuating the casualties to collecting and dressing stations and the divisional field hospital.

The medical department of the Board of Supplies and Transport receives wounded soldiers from army medical units, takes care of them while in transit and transports them to army hospitals in the rear. Under its direction are receiving stations and field hospitals which are organized by the Army Medical Administration and assigned to the medical department along lines of communication. For the transportation of the wounded, the medical department has at its disposal stretcher-bearer units, motor ambulances, hospital trains and hospital boats.

Besides organizing receiving stations and field hospitals, the Army Medical Administration maintains base hospitals in the rear, surgical hospitals and hospitals for special cases.

Cured soldiers are sent to the convalescent hostels organized by the Central Wounded Soldiers Administration. Able-bodied ones are given a short period of refresher-training prior to return to active service. The disabled and crippled are given relief.

The army medical service is organized as follows:

(1) Formations belonging to armies at the front:

(*a*) Regimental—company bearers (transport unit); battalion headquarters medical section (first aid); regimental headquarters medical section (first aid); regimental medical transport unit.

(*b*) Divisional—divisional headquarters medical section (command); divisional medical transport unit; divisional field hospital.

(*c*) Army—army headquarters medical section (command); army hospital and army field hospital.

(*d*) Group Army—group army headquarters medical department (first aid).

The units are under orders of their respective military commanders and operate independently without any unified direct technical control.

(2) Formations along lines of communication:

In roadless area—

(*a*) Transport units—ambulance corps; stretcher-bearers units; stretcher-bearers regiments.

(*b*) Transit accommodation—food and rest stations; collecting stations.

(*c*) Hospitalization—evacuation hospitals.

In highway area—

(*a*) Transport units—ambulance trains; motor ambulance convoys; ambulance boats.

(*b*) Transit accommodation—food and rest stations; collecting stations.

(*c*) Hospitalization—evacuation hospitals.

(*d*) Supplies—medical supplies depots.

(*e*) Clothing—stores for clothing.

(*f*) Anti-epidemic service—sanitary corps.

The units in a roadless area are under the command of the medical section of the quartermaster-general's headquarters attached to a group army, while those in a highway area are commanded by the medical section of the quartermaster-general's headquarters attached to a war area command. The section attached to a group army comes under the control of the one attached to the war area command, and the latter section in turn is under the medical department of the Board of Supplies and Transport.

(3) Formations belonging to the Army Medical Administration:

(a) Transport units (between hospitals in the rear)—motor ambulance convoys; boat ambulance convoys.

(b) Hospitalization and treatment—severely-wounded for hospitals; for base hospitals; army medical hospitals.

(c) Operating teams—surgical operating team.

(d) Medical and general supplies—medical supplies depots; general supplies depots.

Cases sent to the rear are taken care of by the above formations which are controlled by the Army Medical Administration through its sub-offices.

(4) Formations belonging to the Central Wounded Soldiers Administration:

(a) Receiving stations—overflow transit accommodation.

(b) Convalescent hostels.

(c) Disabled soldiers' hostels.

(d) Honor regiments.

(e) Hostels for Class A disabled soldiers.

Army Medical Administration

The Army Medical Administration has a sub-office in each province which directs army medical service of the rear zones and maintains all medical units except those belonging to the troops and the Central Wounded Soldiers Administration. In addition, it is responsible for the technical supervision of all army medical services, training of army medical personnel, anti-epidemic services and the provision of medical supplies.

The units functioning along lines of communication and the staff of the medical sections attached to a group army and a war area command from the director downwards are appointed by the Army Medical Administration. Although they are under the command of the director of the medical department of the Board of Supplies and Transport they are maintained in respect of pay, expenses and supplies, by the Army Medical Administration.

The Administration is organized as follows:

Director-General: Dr. C. T. Loo; Deputy Director-General: Dr. Hsu Sei-ling.

First Department, in charge of personnel and pay. Director: Dr. S. L. Hsu;

Second Department, responsible for medical units, and discipline of the wounded. Director: Dr. P. L. Chu;

Third Department, in charge of health and sanitation matters and also the training of medical personnel. Director: Dr. Mo-sheng Li.

The Administration has a staff of 19,087 persons, of whom 11,668 are medical personnel, while the remaining 7,419 persons belong to the clerical staff. The staff of the Administration proper consists of 81 medical and 295 other personnel, totalling 376 persons.

The Administration maintains more than 300 hospitals providing 233,500 beds. Altogether 35,000 persons are enlisted with the army medical service. They are sent from time to time to the Emergency Medical Service Training School and its branches, and the Army Medical College, for advanced training.

The Central Wounded Soldiers Administration appoints officers to various army hospitals, while the Board of Political Training of the National Military Council sends supervisors to give political training to convalescent soldiers.

The Administration also maintains an inspector-general's department to examine health matters among troops, military organizations, army medical schools, and the Administration's subsidiary organizations. A purchasing committee (secretary: Pucheng P. Chen) looks after the problem of medical supplies. Tablets, tinctures, ampoules, and a limited quantity of simple drugs are supplied by its sanitary depot, while the Military Sanitary Equipment Factory manufactures surgical instruments and artificial limbs. The number of articles manufactured is estimated at 13,500 a month. A separate plant produces a certain amount of absorbent cotton and gauze.

Six hundred and seventy-two doctors and other senior medical personnel are graduated each year from the Army Medical College, while each of its two branch schools supplies 120 doctors a year.

Established in 1902 in Tientsin, the college now functions in Kweichow province. Up to the present, 1,742 doctors and senior medical officers have been graduated. Generalissimo

Chiang Kai-shek is the president of the college, while Dr. Cheng Chien is the dean.

The first branch college, with Dr. Teng Shu-tung as the director, is located in Sian, Shensi province. Up to the present, 131 doctors and senior medical officers have been graduated. The second branch carries on in Kunming. Dr. Ching Ling-pa is the director.

Under the supervision of the college is a unit of reserve medical officers in Kweilin, where refresher courses are available for medical officers, and junior medical officers are being trained. Organized in 1937, the unit has supplied the army medical service with 3,629 well-trained officers. About 840 officers are graduated from the unit every year. There are two sub-units, one in Sian and the other in Shaoyang, Hunan province. The two sub-units were established in 1941, and up to the present, 686 officers have been graduated.

Field training for all classes of personnel is given by the Emergency Medical Service Training School and its five branch schools. Details are given in the section entitled "State Medicine." The directors of the five branch schools are Drs. Chen Tao, Lim Ching-pang, Thomas Ma, Peng Ta-mu and Lin Ching-cheng.

Cholera in southwestern China and the bubonic plague in Chekiang and Hunan in the past two years little affected the health of the Chinese troops. Preventive measures, including wholesale inoculations, by anti-epidemic corps in war areas proved effective.

When the outbreak of bubonic plague was first reported, preventive advice was circularized among the troops with instructions to follow the suggestions. Pamphlets giving rudimentary knowledge on general health and sanitation are widely distributed from time to time.

Anti-epidemic corps are found in every war area. Besides giving inoculations they carry out sanitary engineering projects, build delousing stations, sterilize drinking water and clean troop centers of stagnant and dirty water and refuse.

There are altogether eleven army anti-epidemic corps each of which is composed of 66 medical officers, sanitary engineers, and technicians, besides a group of assistants. Each corps is divided into three units which may function in different areas. Altogether 1,100 medical personnel and assistants are enlisted in the corps.

Between January and November, 1942, 1,539,931 officers and men were vaccinated against smallpox, while anti-cholera and anti-typhoid inoculations were given 1,735,034 officers and men.

The most common diseases among the troops are dysentery and malaria, while typhoid and relapsing fever come next in prevalence.

Stations for Wounded Soldiers

Seventeen main service corps, composed of 3,000 men, are maintaining 408 stations in fourteen provinces to receive wounded soldiers in transit. The first five corps directing 120 receiving stations belong to the Christian Service Council for Wounded Soldiers of which Dr. H. H. Kung, Vice-President of the Executive Yuan and Minister of Finance, is chairman. The Board of Supplies and Transport of the National Military Council has in the field seven corps directing 168 receiving stations, while the National War Relief Association maintains the remaining five corps in charge of 120 receiving stations.

The service for wounded soldiers in transit was first started by the three cooperating organizations in September, 1938, when the battle for the defense of the Wuhan area became critical. Villagers were evacuating from both sides of the highways adjacent to the war fronts. As a result, wounded men from the front lines found it extremely difficult to get food and water. As an experiment, 20 receiving stations, one every three miles, were established along the highways linking the three provinces of Hunan, Hupeh and Kiangsi. Their service proving satisfactory, more stations were set up.

Each station is staffed by six men—an officer-in-charge, two assistants and three staff members. Most of them have had special training for their work.

Housed in temples or other available buildings, the stations provide water, food and shelter to the wounded soldiers. Here their wounds are redressed and their clothes washed and deloused. For the heavily wounded, stretcher-bearers are secured for the next lap of the journey until they can reach a base hospital.

Central Wounded Soldiers Administration

The Central Wounded Soldiers Administration runs hostels for disabled soldiers, has organized 77 wounded soldiers' cooperatives and established two agricultural villages for the crippled. The handicraft section of 19 hostels affords employment to the inmates.

Working on farms are two groups numbering 9,213 persons. Farmland cultivated totals 29,337 mow, while a much bigger area measuring 291,811 mow is being developed. The soldiers have planted 455,000 tung trees, 30,000,000 tea trees and 20,000 pine trees. Crops reaped by them includes 13,329 piculs of rice, 300,800 catties of potatoes and 2,800 piculs of peanuts.

To supplement the work of the administration, which is a component part of the Chinese army medical service, a separate bureau was established last September to give employment to disabled soldiers. Branches will be established in every province. Through the bureau, 6,000 soldiers have been sent to the Ministry of Agriculture and Forestry to engage in farming. The bureau operates a farm and two factories.

The administration, which has branches in various provinces in Free China, is staffed by more than 500 army officers. At communication centers, stations have been established to take care of the wounded in transit.

The administration maintains receiving stations, convalescent hostels, disabled soldiers' hostels, and hostels for Class A disabled soldiers, besides organizing honor regiments. There are altogether 13 administration offices, 21 branch offices, and 26 sub-offices distributed in war zones.

Chinese Red Cross

The National Red Cross Society of China was founded in 1904, Mr. D. F. Shen, a prominent Shanghai resident, being one of the promoters. The Society later became an affiliated member of the International Red Cross Committee at Geneva.

By an order of the Executive Yuan, the Society was reorganized in February, 1943. Generalissimo Chiang Kai-shek was made honorary chairman; Dr. Chiang Mon-lin, President of National Peking University, chairman; Dr. T. V. Soong, Tai Chi-tao, General Shang Chen, Wang Hsiao-lai, and Dr. Wong Wen-hao, members of the executive committee of the board of directors. The honorary vice-chairmen are Madame Chiang Kai-shek, Tai Chi-tao, Dr. H. H. Kung, Dr. T. V. Soong, General Wu Te-chen, Dr. C. T. Wang, and Yu Ya-ching.

Dr. L. S. Woo, Harvard Medical School, 1918, was appointed director of the medical relief corps, Dr. P. C. Nyi, Johns Hopkins Medical School, 1922, assistant director, and Dr. Robert Lim of Edinburgh University, general adviser. Dr. Woo was made concurrently secretary-general of the Chinese Red Cross.

The head office, located in Chungking, has three departments. The first department is in charge of clerical work, general business, transportation, and personnel; the second department, of publications, statistics, and extension work; and the third department, of nursing, supplies, and medical services. There is also a department of accounting which audits all the accounts of the head office as well as of its subsidiary organizations.

Since the outbreak af the Sino-Japanese war, the Society has concentrated its efforts on the relief of wounded and sick soldiers, civilians, and refugees.

The following will sum up various activities of the Society in wartime:

Described as the "power house" of the Society, the Medical Relief Corps, under the administration of the Medical Relief Commission, did 7,197 surgical operations on wounded soldiers besides treating 324,554 civilians in clinics set up by the corps.

The following statistics show the number of cases undertaken by the corps in the first half year of 1942:

Surgical operations	7,197 cases
Reduction of fractures	2,598 „
X-ray examinations	3,645 „
Special diets	66,767 „
Immunizations	420,036 „
Medical cases	143,744 „;

Organized at the end of 1937 after the fall of Nanking to take care of the wounded and sick, the corps maintains two branches of field work: medical units and truck-ambulance convoys. The headquarters of the corps, located in Kweiyang, has three departments: medical, general administration and accounting, all working under the direction of the director-general and his two assistant directors.

The medical units are assigned to work in field and base hospitals as well as in dressing and receiving stations along the main lines of transportation. With the exception of the X-ray and laboratory units, they all perform threefold functions: curative, nursing, and preventive. The units assigned to a particular line constitute a group, while several groups in a war zone or a defined area constitute a division. There are seven divisions, forty groups and one hundred units.

A geographical study of these units shows that they extend to 54 *hsien* in twelve provinces: Kweichow, Shensi, Honan, Hupeh, Chekiang, Fukien, Kiangsi, Hunan, Kwangtung, Kwangsi, Yunnan, and Szechwan. At one time, units were also sent to Burma and India to serve the Chinese Expeditionary Force.

Each of these units has, in general, one doctor, two nurses, one nursing or sanitary assistant, in addition to four or six stretcher-bearers. Most of the units set up clinics to look after the health of the civilian population.

The truck-ambulance convoys transport wounded soldiers, medical supplies and personnel. The scope of the service often extends much farther beyond the needs of the corps. It has not only helped military, civil, and mission hospitals, army and civil health services, and local relief committees in transporting their own medical supplies and personnel, but has also brought to them large quantities of Red Cross medical supplies.

The convoys are stationed at four key cities: Kunming, Chungking, Hengyang and Kweiyang. The following table shows distribution of convoys and vehicles, and line of operation:

Location of Station	No. of Convoys	No. of Vehicles	Line of Operation
Chungking	2	14	Chungking-Chengtu-Paocheng-Lanchow
Kunming	2	14	Hsiakwan-Kunming-Kweiyang
Kweiyang	2	14	Kweiyang-Chinchengkiang-Kweiyang-Chikiang
Hengyang	2	14	Hengyang-Taiho-Nanping

To provide repairing services and to keep the vehicles in the best possible running condition, a repair shop is maintained at Kweiyang. In addition, mechanics are assigned to work with the transport stations to handle simple jobs of adjusting and repairing.

Serving civilians in interior provinces, the Society began organizing medical corps in 1940. Beginning with eight units, the number was increased by the end of September, 1942, to five groups and 23 units distributed in Szechwan, Yunnan, Kweichow, Kwangtung, Kwangsi, Hunan, Kiangsi and Fukien. One unit is stationed in Kweichow in a camp for war prisoners. The services rendered by the corps up to June, 1942, were:

Patients Treated:	
First Visits	109,904
Preventive Inoculations:	
Smallpox	40,914
Cholera and Typhoid	108,329

Following the outbreak of the Pacific War, the medical corps aided Chinese refugees returning to China by way of Kwangtung and Yunnan. The corps also helped combat the cholera epidemic in the southwestern provinces by giving inoculations to the populace in affected areas.

One general clinic, two medical units, one isolation hospital, and one general hospital are maintained by the Society for medical relief in Chungking. Ambulance services are provided air-raid victims.

The general clinic, established in the New Life Model Center in the city, consists of six departments: medicine, surgery, gynecology, pediatrics, X-ray, and clinical laboratory. Patients are treated free of charge except those requiring extended treatment or laboratory examination who are charged a small registration fee. Drugs are given to all patients without charge. The clinic has been in operation for a year and treats from 600 to 800 patients a day.

Far away from the busy centers of the city, an isolation hospital has been built on the south bank of the Yangtze. At present it has 50 beds, but if necessary the bed capacity may be expanded. It is also prepared to take care of air-raid and emergency cases.

The general hospital, situated some twenty kilometers from the city, has nine departments: medicine, surgery, gynecology and obstetrics, pediatrics, skin and venereal diseases, eye-ear-nose-throat, dentistry, and physical therapy. Of its 200 beds, 150 are assigned to third class patients who get all their medicines and medical care free but pay nominal sums for their food.

The Society began maintaining a hospital for Chungking's bombing victims and the poor after the disastrous raids of May 3 and 4, 1939. Situated on the outskirts of the city, the hospital, with 50 beds, was twice bombed in August, 1941. The new hospital, construction of which began early in 1942, is situated further away from the city.

The supply depots, of which there are twelve distributed in eight provinces, are maintained to store, prepare and issue medical equipment and supplies. They work in close relation with the medical units and the truck-ambulance convoys.

The central depot, under the direct administration of the head office, consists of three divisions: drugs, chemicals, and instruments. There is, in addition, a production division which prepares or purifies certain local materials to replace imports. Sodium chloride, sodium sulphate, copper sulphate, plaster of paris, etc., can now be provided in reasonable quantities.

The central depot packs supplies in standard packages to be distributed to its branch depots and sub-depots for the use of medical units, clinics, and hospitals. A standard supply list has been prepared to give information as to what equipment, drugs, dressings, etc., are available, and must be maintained for the work in the field. Large quantities of supplies are also issued to other military, civil, and relief organizations.

The local chapters of the Red Cross are organized purely on the basis of voluntary service. There were 512 chapters scattered throughout the country before the war. At present, only 74 maintain contact with the head office. Szechwan heads the list with 34 chapters, Hunan and Kwangtung six each, Honan five, Yunnan and Fukien four each, Shensi and Kwangsi three each, Kweichow and Hupeh two each, Kiangsi, Chekiang, Kansu, Shantung and Anhwei one each. The chapters have been operating altogether 31 hospitals, 63 clinics, and 37 medical units.

The services of the Society are maintained by more than 2,000 medical and non-medical men and women, and its monthly running expenses amount to $1,500,000. The work has been made possible through assistance from organizations and individuals in China and abroad and from the Central Government. Prominent among the contributors are the American Red Cross, the British Government, the Australian Red Cross, the New Zealand Red Cross, and the Indian Government.

Chinese in the Netherlands East Indies were by far the chief contributors of funds, quinine, and foodstuffs. The Chinese population throughout Java, Sumatra, Dutch Borneo, Celebes, Bali, and Flores contributed generously until the Pacific War broke out. Western friends and Chinese in the United States have donated most of the ambulances and medical supplies used by the Red Cross.

3.36　1 Nov. 1943: MEMORANDUM FOR GENERAL SIMMONS, R. C. JACOBS, JR., Col., G-2

资料出处： National Archives of the United States, R112, E295A, B11.

内容点评： 本资料为1943年11月1日情报部，R. C. Jacobs，Jr. 上校向Simmons将军提交的备忘录：日军要求腾冲南—缅甸—云南地区居民上交活鼠。

SECRET

By authority A. C. of S., G-2
Date 1 Nov 43 (RC)
Initials

WAR DEPARTMENT
WAR DEPARTMENT GENERAL STAFF
MILITARY INTELLIGENCE DIVISION G-2
WASHINGTON

1 November 1943.

MEMORANDUM FOR GENERAL SIMMONS:

From the party you visited in Stilwell's area, I have received request to forward you the following:

> Possible B.W. activity is indicated by a report from a Chinese source that the Japanese have requested that each family in the area Teng Chung - Burma - Yunan furnish three living mice. Medical personnel are there alerted for plague. Possible C.W.S. activity indicated by reported establishment by Japanese of two gas factories south of Hanku Railroad Station near Tientsin. Subject factories could make chlorine, this being a salt producing area. Friendly reporter states he will take no action but will continue observation and report.

Mr. J. P. Marquand has been notified as above.

R. C. Jacobs

R. C. JACOBS, JR.,
Colonel, General Staff,
Executive Officer, G-2.

SECRET

3.37 16 Jun. 1944: JOINT COMMITTEE ON NEW WEAPONS AND EQUIPMENT MEMORANDUM FOR INFORMATION NO. 16, NOTES CONCERNING BIOLOGICAL WARFARE

资料出处：National Archives of the United States, R112, E295A, B11.

内容点评：本资料为美国新型武器装备联合委员会1944年6月16日情报备忘录16号，内容关于细菌战。

S E C R E T COPY NO. 2

16 June 1944

JOINT COMMITTEE ON NEW WEAPONS AND EQUIPMENT

MEMORANDUM FOR INFORMATION NO. 16

NOTES CONCERNING BIOLOGICAL WARFARE

Note by the Secretary

1. The Enclosure, obtained in conference with Mr. George Merck, 15 June 1944, is forwarded as of interest to the Committee. The current Japanese intelligence is of particular interest.

EDWIN COX,
Secretary.

S E C R E T

E N C L O S U R E

NOTES CONCERNING BIOLOGICAL WARFARE

1. Organization.

a. A change in organization is being effected. The committee of the War Research Service will be inactivated, and a War Department Committee formed with the equivalent mission and close coordination with the Chemical Warfare Service. Major General S. G. Henry and Major General W. D. Styer will serve with Mr. George Merck.

(1) Mr. George Merck will be an assistant in the Office of the Secretary of War.

(2) Mr. J. P. Marquand will continue as an assistant to Mr. Merck for intelligence.

(3) Lieut. Commander Sarles will continue with this Committee as Naval Liaison Officer.

Physically, with the exception of Mr. Merck, the Committee offices will remain in its present location.

2. Current Intelligence.

a. First direct information of Japanese biological warfare.

(1) In the checking of Pacific Theatre G-2 files, by Lieut. Colonel H. I. Cole, Chemical Warfare Service, two instances of captured Japanese documents revealed biological warfare information. Both were diaries of air pilots. In both instances the diarist listed Japanese bacillus bombs and their classification as Mark ~~II~~ 1. These data were apparently training notes. Reports were from different areas and

-1-

SECRET

were dated 2 May 1944 and 28 May 1944.

(2) Copies of the reports are being obtained.

b. Dr. C. B. Ellis, of a recent British Scientific Mission, states to Mr. J. P. Marquand that he had positive knowledge of German use of bacterial warfare agents against captured Poles.

c. Lieut. Colonel Moore, USA, Liaison Officer of this committee formerly in London is in transit to Rome to develop information from Italian sources on bacterial warfare.

3. Difficulties this committee is experiencing are:

a. Classification of subject matter. Downgrading of subject matter is essential in order that committee may operate.

b. Intelligence -- there is need for:

(1) Personnel to evaluate in field.

(2) Promptness and speed in forwarding intelligence and information - example, Japanese Mark ~~IX~~ 7 Bombs.

(3) Full interchange of information with United Kingdom.

(4) Field representation on adequate level.

c. Policy - a broad overall policy is necessary.

d. The assistance of the Joint New Weapons Committee was requested in overcoming these obstacles.

-2-

3.38 5 Sep. 1944: Paraphrased Extract from Cable Received C. C., 14th Air Force, Kunming, China (CM-In-4314 of 5 September 44)

资料出处：National Archives of the United States, R112, E295A, B11.

内容点评：本资料为 1944 年 9 月 5 日美军情报部门的昆明第十四航空队来电摘要：数日前日军飞机于福清投下羽毛，疑为细菌攻击，正在检验。

SECRET

Paraphrased extract from Cable received C.G., 14th Air Force, Kunming, China. (CM-IN-4814 of 5 September 44)

* * * * * * *

Chinese afraid that unloading of feathers by Japs over Futsing few days ago may imply beginning of biological warfare. Feathers are undergoing analysis.

* * * * * * *

G-2 Comment: The efficacy of this method of bacteria distribution cannot be stated. This is the first report on such a method. Psittacosis virus especially would lend itself to dissemination by this method. A cable request for a report of the analysis has been sent.

SECRET

3.39 2 Oct. 1944: MILITARY ATTACHE REPORT, No. 10,127, Japan-biological Warfare Miscellaneous Items

资料出处： National Archives of the United States, R112, E295A, B11.

内容点评： 本资料为 1944 年 10 月 2 日美国驻华大使馆武官发自重庆的报告，题目：关于日本细菌战的零星情报。

SECRET

ENCLOSURES

COPY NO. ______ (For Record Section only)

12089

JICA/CBI REPORT

MILITARY INTELLIGENCE DIVISION W. D. G. S.

MILITARY ATTACHE REPORT (Country reported on)

Subject Japan - Biological Warfare - Miscellaneous Items (Brief descriptive title) I. G. No.

From MA. Chungking Report No. 10,127 Date 2 October 19

Source and degree of reliability: Chinese.

Evaluation: C-3.

SUMMARY.—Here enter careful summary of report, containing substance succinctly stated; include important facts, names, places, dates, etc.

Of interest to the Biological Section, Chemical Warfare service are the following items:

(1) A report from Nanking concerning the movement of one thousand white rats infected with plague from Shanghai to Nanking. Several Chinese army medical corps personnel believe this movement was for routine experimental purposes.

(2) A report from a chemist concerning conditions in Peking relative to medical supplies and quarantine control.

(3) A report from a doctor who departed from Peking about five months ago concerning immunization of Japanese soldiers.

(4) A report from a former staff member of the Peking Union Medical College concerning conditions at the college.

NOTE: This document contains information affecting the national defense of the United States within the meaning of the Espionage Act, 50 U. S. C., 31 and 32, as amended. Its transmission or the revelation of its contents in any manner to an unauthorized person is prohibited by law. It may not be reproduced in whole or in part, by other than War Dep't Agencies, except by permission of the A C of S, G-2, W. D G. S.

DAVID R. [illegible],
Major, Cavalry,
CinC, JICA/CBI Br., APO 879.

GEORGE E. ARMSTRONG,
Colonel, Medical Corps,
Asst. Theater Surgeon

JLRC; JICA, APO 885; G-2, ME.

Distribution by originator

Routing space below for use in M. I. D. The section indicating the distribution will place a check mark in the lower part of the recipients' box in case one copy only is to go to him, or will indicate the number of copies in case more than one should be sent. The message center of the Intelligence Branch will draw a circle around the box of the recipient to which the particular copy is to go.

AGF	AAF	ASF	AC of S G-2	Chief IG	Eur.-Afr.	Far East	N. Amer.	Air	Dissem.	AIC	FLBR	OSS
MA Sec.	CIC	Rec. Sec.	ONI	BEW	CWS	ENG.	OPD	QRC	Sig.	State	QMG	

MIS 69446
Sci - 5
Lib - 1
HQAAF - 1
CWS - 2
Med - 2
ONI - 3
OSS - 2

Enclosures:

SECRET

WAR DEPARTMENT
O.C.S.17 (2nd Rev.)

S E C R E T

Biological Section, Chemical Warfare Service Miscellaneous Intelligence.

1. A paraphrase of a radio received through the U. S. Naval channels, 22 September 1944:

"Informant in Nanking, with C-3 rating, reports white rats, numbering one thousand (1000), infected with plague, sent recently to Nanking from Shanghai in an effort by Nips to infect Chinese troops. This is similiar report of some four months ago regarding coastal region. Recent reports from Wenchow, Nancheng, and Foochow show increased evidence of plague. Your medical personnel should investigate in your area and inform us."

a. During conference with Chinese army medical officers on 28 September, the subject of plague was brought up very casually. They volunteered the information that they had recently received a report from a non-professional source announcing the arrival of 1000 white mice in Nanking. They believe the Japanese are operating an experimental bacteriological laboratory in Nanking, probably in the "lab" buildings formerly occupied by the Chinese National Health Administration. It was their opinion that the 1000 white mice were shipped there for routine experimental purposes.

b. It is the opinion of the Chinese, concurred in by this office, that an attempt by the Japanese to spread plague would be through the dissemination of infected fleas rather than by infected mice or rats. The latter would die before they had accomplished their mission. Also white mice or rats, turned loose on the populace, would immediately become objects of suspicion to the Chinese.

c. In view of the above, this office does not attach much importance to the report.

2. A report from a middle age Chinese chemist, a former professor of a school in Peking, who brought his family out in April or May of 1944, contains the information:

a. All drug houses in Peking were called upon to produce as much caffeine as possible. It was being made into small pills.

b. All used tea leaves were bought from teahouses and reported that they were dried and fed to horses.

c. The Japs were stupid in quarantine enforcements of a cholera epidemic in Peking, setting up a Chinese quarantine unit with one Jap officer at each gate. One family had to wash feet, baggage, and food (bread) in a phenol solution.

d. The sale of quinine to civilians was stopped suddenly last January before which it was easily obtainable in all drug stores.

3. Remarks of a M.D., who formerly lived in Peking until five months ago but is now in Free China.

a. Japanese have something else for malaria besides quinine, but it is not known what it is or how good it is.

b. The Jap medical service is apparently quite well supplied with drugs of all kinds.

c. Soldiers are immunized against typhoid, smallpox, cholera, tetanus, and maybe plague. Did not know of immunization against typhus, scrub typhus, or any other endemic diseases of this region. He was sure they were the subject of experimental study and limited use but would not say more.

From: JICA/CBI Br., Chungking. Report No. 11037 SECRET 2 October 1944

DRG/Wl Page 2

d. He thinks the Japs have a good sanitary system both for their troops and for civilians as soon as they move into a new community. Their quarantine of civilians in the event of communicable disease is rigidly enforced.

e. Japanese-made drugs are readily available at reasonable prices in drug stores. Sulfadiazine is not available but other sulfa drugs can easily be purchased at reasonable prices.

4. A former staff member of the Peking Union Medical College, who has now been in Free China for four months, reports:

a. The library is intact and available for use of Chinese professors of Peking Medical College by pass.

b. The hospital is used as a base hospital for Japanese army officers.

c. The preclinical buildings have been converted into 'Army epidemic prevention service,' who apparently do sanitary bacteriological and research.

d. The animal house has been changed to accommodate more monkeys. They also used vinca pigs.

e. The nurses home (Oliver Jones Hall) was used as detention quarters for persons arrested by Military Police, and Lockheart Hall as a branch office for Military Police.

f. All of the above buildings are guarded by armed soldiers.

g. The Yin Compound is the home of the Japanese Officer (Commandant).

h. enham Hall is used as a dormitory for Japanese civilian workers.

i. The South and North compounds are used for homes for officers and civilians.

j. Civilians are required to carry a card showing the date of smallpox

3.40 3 Oct. 1944: Paraphrase of CM-in-1877, Secret SGO No. 51230, dated 2 Oct. 1944, From CG US Army Forces Pacific Ocean Areas, Ft. Shafter, TH, To War Department. Richardson to Surgeon General's Office, Attn: Lt. Col. G. W. Anderson

资料出处： National Archives of the United States, R112, E295A, B11.

内容点评： 本资料为 1944 年 10 月 3 日美军太平洋部队 Richardson 发送陆军部军医总长办公室 G.W. Anderson 中校的秘密情报：感染鼠疫老鼠从上海运往南京；南昌、福州、温州鼠疫蔓延更烈。

/jc

SECRET

3 October 1944

Paraphrase of CM-IN-1877, Secret SGO No. 51230, dated 2 October 1944, From CG US Army Forces Pacific Ocean Areas, Ft. Shafter, TH, To War Department. Richardson to Surgeon General's Office, Attn: Lt.Col. G. W. Anderson.

Paraphrase — According to statement of agent in Nanking the recent transfer of thousand rats with plague from Shanghai to Nanking is reported in radiogram 221340 September from COMNAVGROUP China to COMINCH. Plague reported at a higher rate from Nancheng Foochow and Wenchow in recent past. Reliability of report rated as C 3.

cc: Gen. Bayne-Jones
Dr. Hudson
Lt. Col. Anderson ✓

OCT 3 1944

Col. Anderson!
Gen. Bayne-Jones signed log sheet in form and
Dr. Hudson's absence indicating no action necessary.
[illegible]

SECRET

3.41 16 Oct. 1944: MEMORANDUM FOR MAJ. GEN. WILHELM D. STYER (Thru Chief, Intelligence Division, ASF), HOWARD I. COLE, Lt. Col. C.W.S. Chief, Intelligence Branch, Special Project Divisions

资料出处： National Archives of the United States, R112, E295A, B11.

内容点评： 本资料为1944年10月16日美军特别项目局情报科主任、化学战部队中校 Howard I. Cole 提交 Wilhelm D. Styer 少将备忘录：据缴获的日军机密文件，日军有谋略部队编制，并提及撒播细菌。

SECRET

ARMY SERVICE FORCES
OFFICE CHIEF OF CHEMICAL WARFARE SERVICE
WASHINGTON 25, D. C.

LWF/bjc

In reply refer to:
(16 Oct 44)

16 October 1944.

MEMORANDUM FOR MAJ. GEN. WILHELM D. STYER (Thru Chief, Intelligence Division, ASF)

Information has just been received from the Southwest Pacific that a Japanese document captured at Morotai, 24 September 1944, classified secret issued by E 33rd Force, dated 1944 and belonging to 2nd Lt. Heriuchi, "NI" Force, contained details of the organization, functions and equipment of "Raiding Diversionary Unit". The following statement is quoted:

"Great results can be obtained by contaminating their food and drink in kitchen by bacterial strategy."

Comment: Complete translation is being requested. It is possible that this type of unit is similar to the one mentioned in cable CFB 22692, 16 September 1944, from Chungking, China: a five man patrol, the leader carries a bottle of "germs" and a can of phosphorus paint; carbine or a light machine gun carried by two men, the remaining two carry bolo knives and rope.

Several other captured documents indicate that this type of sabotage has been envisaged by the Japanese since, at least, 1941.

HOWARD I. COLE
Lt. Colonel, C. W. S.
Chief, Intelligence Branch
Special Projects Division

W. D., A. G. O.
Form No. 0115-A
2 March 1944

HEADQUARTERS ARMY SERVICE FORCES
MEMO ROUTING SLIP

SECRET

To the following in order indicated:

GPO 16—38689-1

	(Name or title)	(Organization)	(Building and room)	(Initials) / (Date)
1	General Styer			
2				
3				

Noted in office of C.G.A.S.F.

Return to

From J. M. ROAMER
Colonel, G. S. C.
Director of Intelligence

16 Oct 44 (Date)
(Telephone)

SECURITY CLASSIFICATION NOT REGRADED
REVIEW FOR SEC ARMY BY TAG PER 013

SECRET

LWF/bjo

16 October 1944.

(16 Oct 44)

MEMORANDUM FOR MAJ. GEN. WILHELM D. STYER (Thru Chief, Intelligence Division, ASF)

Information has just been received from the Southwest Pacific that a Japanese document captured at Morotai, 24 September 1944, classified secret issued by E 33rd Force, dated 1944 and belonging to 2nd Lt. Heriuchi, "NI" Force, contained details of the organization, functions and equipment of "Raiding Diversionary Unit". The following statement is quoted:

"Great results can be obtained by contaminating their food and drink in kitchen by bacterial strategy."

Comment: Complete translation is being requested. It is possible that this type of unit is similar to the one mentioned in cable CFB 22692, 16 September 1944, from Chungking, China: a five man patrol, the leader carries a bottle of "germs" and a can of phosphorus paint; carbine or a light machine gun carried by two men, the remaining two carry bolo knives and rope.

Several other captured documents indicate that this type of sabotage has been envisaged by the Japanese since, at least, 1941.

HOWARD I. COLE
Lt. Colonel, C. W. S.
Chief, Intelligence Branch
Special Projects Division

SECRET

3.42 3 Nov. 1944: MILITARY ATTACHE REPORT, No. 10,325, Medical Intelligence - Fukien

资料出处： National Archives of the United States, R112, E295A, B11.

内容点评： 本资料为1944年11月3日美国驻重庆大使馆武官提交美国陆军部军事情报局报告，题目：福建卫生情报。提及福州鼠疫疫情。

RESTRICTED
(Classification)

ENCLOSURES

COPY NO. ______ (For Record Section only)

REP. 28 Nov. 1944
Auth [illegible]
No. of copies 12

JICA/CBI REPORT TRB:

MILITARY INTELLIGENCE DIVISION, W. D. G. S.

MILITARY ATTACHE REPORT CHINA (Country reported on)

Subject: Medical Intelligence - Fukien (Brief descriptive title) I. G. No. ______

From MA Chungking Report No. [illegible]325 Date 3 November 1944

Source and degree of reliability: Chinese Doctor
Evaluation: B-2

NOTE: This document contains information affecting the national defense of the United States within the meaning of the Espionage Act, 50 U. S. C., 31 and 32, as amended. Its transmission or the revelation of its contents in any manner to an unauthorized person is prohibited by law. It may not be reproduced in whole or in part, by other than War Dep't Agencies, except by permission of the A C of S, G-2, W. D. G. S.

SUMMARY.—Here enter careful summary of report, containing substance succinctly stated; include important facts, names, places, dates, etc.

The following information was obtained during an interview with a Chinese doctor on 17 October 1944. Source, age 34, received his M.D. in 1934 from the Peking University Medical College. Lt. Col. John E. Tripp, Sn C, states that he is an authority in his subject, having had one year of research work at the Rockefeller Laboratories, Princeton, N.J., and one year of research at Columbia Medical College, N.Y., and having published numerous articles. The source made the following observations in Foochow between 3 July 1944 and 12 August 1944.

Plague. The incidence, which was reported high in 1943, said to be 10,000 cases in Fuchow, is much lower in 1944. During 5 weeks of observation in this city, searching for cases of plague, he saw only 25 cases, including 21 bubonic, 3 septicemic, 1 pneumonic. The progression of plague spread is usually in the direction of rice transport, from inland toward the coast, but in 1944 the opposite direction of spread was noted, cause undetermined. Furthermore, in 1944 cases appeared in many new areas not previously affected by plague. The Results of scientific investigations are that sulfadiazine, if given within 2 days of the start of symptoms, causes 100% recovery. If given later the recovery is less rapid and less certain. The method of protection expected to be used by the Japanese is compulsory immunization. Other diseases in Fuchow. Malaria. Many cases, both tertian and estivo-autumnal types, were present. Dengue fever. A small number of cases were present in 1943. Relapsing fever. The number of cases has been increasing. Cholera. Many proven cases occurred.

ROBERT L. CAVENAUGH,
Major, Medical Corps,
Asst. Theater Surgeon,
USAF/CBI.

JICA, JICA, APO 885; G-2, FE; JICA, APO 465 (2) (one for XX Bomber Command); JICA, APO 627

MIS 81544

*Socio-1
Sci-1
Lib-1
HQAAF-1
Med-1
Int Div-1
ONI-3
OSS-2

Distribution by originator

Routing space below for use in M. I. D. The section indicating the distribution will place a check mark in the lower part of the recipients' box in case one copy only is to go to him, or will indicate the number of copies in case more than one should be sent. The message center of the Intelligence Branch will draw a circle around the box of the recipient to which the particular copy is to go.

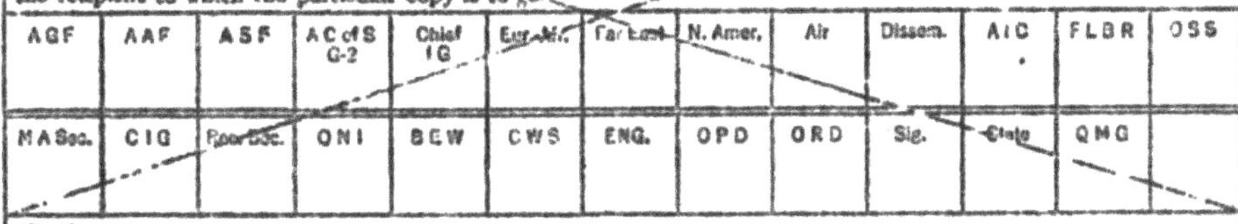

AGF	AAF	ASF	AC of S G-2	Chief IG	Eur.-Af.	Far East	N. Amer.	Air	Dissem.	AIC	FLBR	OSS
MA Sec.	CIG	Poor Sec.	ONI	BEW	CWS	ENG.	OPD	ORD	Sig.	State	QMG	

Enclosures:

RESTRICTED
RESTRICTED

WAR DEPARTMENT
O.C.S.17 (2nd Rev.)

3.43 17 Nov. 1944: AG 381 (17 Nov. 44) B, Bacterial Warfare, TO: the Chief of Staff, FROM: R. B. LOWRY, 1st Lt., A.G.D., Asst Adjutant General

资料出处：National Archives of the United States, R112, E295A, B11.

内容点评：本资料为 1944 年 11 月 17 日美军副官助理、中尉 R. B. Lowry 向美军总参谋长提交的报告，题目：细菌战。称据日军战俘，日军防疫给水部队在“新京”进行细菌战实验。

Fickel
III f

SEC #2 CRET

Date 27 Nov. 1944

GENERAL HEA
SOUTHWEST

Subject Bacterial Warfare

17 Nov. 1944

AG 381 (17 Nov 44) B

DISSEMINATION

SUBJECT: Bacterial Warfare.

TO : The Chief of Staff, Washington, D. C.
(Attention: A.C. of S., G-2)

In accordance with War Department radio WX 67454, 20 July 1944, the following information is submitted:

"Prisoner of War (100249), Superior Private, member of 41 Mountain Artillery Regiment, 41 Division,captured YAKAMUL, NEW GUINEA, 19 August 1944, states that while at Palau in October 1943, he heard from a soldier with whom he wasworking that bacterial warfare experiments were being carried out at HSINKING, MANCHURIA, by the water pruification unit, He heard that on one ocassion, a gas was sprayed from the air and when it was first released it looked like a fog but gradually faded away. During experiment, gelatin, in trays were set out and later checked to see results as to amount of bacteria falling on that area and the rapidity of spreading. There were also experiments on diseases for horses being carried out. These were glanders and an unidentified."

For the Commander-in-Chief:

R. B. LOWRY,
1st Lt., A.G.D.,
Asst Adjutant General.

G-2 Comment:

This report corroberates previous reports (Extract from ATIS-SWPA No. 1487, Item 2- 14588-G, 5 Oct. 44; ATIS SWPA Serial No. 600, 16 Sept 44; Letter Hq SWPA - AG 381 (6 Oct. 44) B; Cables CM IN 1700, 2 Aug 44 and CM IN 22315, 24 Aug 44) that BW experiments have been carried out in Manchuria. Maj. Gen. ISHII, Shiro, has been mentioned in connection with these experiments as well as with water purification work. HSINKING (Changchun) is approximately 150 miles Southwest of HARBIN, MANCHURIA.

SECRET

NOV 22 1944

SECRET

GENERAL HEADQUARTERS
SOUTHWEST PACIFIC AREA

AG 381 (17 Nov 44) B

APO 500
17 Nov 1944

SUBJECT: Bacterial Warfare.

TO : The Chief of Staff, Washington, D. C.
(Attention: A.C. of S., G-2)

In accordance with War Department radio WX 67454, 20 July 1944, the following information is submitted:

"Prisoner of War (100249), Superior Private, member of 41 Mountain Artillery Regiment, 41 Division, captured YAKAMUL, NEW GUINEA, 19 August 1944, states that while at Palau in October 1943, he heard from a soldier with whom he wasworking that bacterial warfare experiments were being carried out at HSINKING, MANCHURIA, by the water pruification unit, He heard that on one ocassion, a gas was sprayed from the air and when it was first released it looked like a fog but gradually faded away. During experiment, gelatin, in trays were set out and later checked to see results as to amount of bacteria falling on that area and the rapidity of spreading. There were also experiments on diseases for horses being carried out. These were glanders and an unidentified."

For the Commander-in-Chief:

R. B. LOWRY,
1st Lt., A.G.D.,
Asst Adjutant General.

G-2 Comment:

This report corroberates previous reports (Extract from ATIS-SWPA No. 1487, Item 2- 14588-G, 5 Oct. 44; ATIS SWPA Serial No. 600, 16 Sept 44; Letter Hq SWPA - AG 381 (6 Oct. 44) B; Cables CM IN 1700, 2 Aug 44 and CM IN 22315, 24 Aug 44) that BW experiments have been carried out in Manchuria. Maj. Gen. ISHII, Shiro, has been mentioned in connection with these experiments as well as with water purification work. HSINKING (Changchun) is approximately 150 miles Southwest of HARBIN, MANCHURIA.

SECRET

3.44 28 Nov. 1944: AG 385 (28 Nov. 44) B, Bacterial Warfare, TO: The Chief of Staff, FROM: R. B. LOWRY, 1st Lt., A.G.D., Asst Adjutant General

资料出处：National Archives of the United States, R112, E295A, B11.

内容点评：本资料为 1944 年 11 月 28 日美军副官助理 R. B. Lowry 向美军总参谋长提交的报告，题目：细菌战——缴获的日军文件内容。

SECRET

GENERAL HEADQUARTERS
SOUTHWEST PACIFIC AREA

Rear Echelon,
A.P.O. 500,
28 Nov. 1944.

AG 385 (28 Nov 44)B

SUBJECT: Bacterial Warfare.

TO : The Chief of Staff, Washington, D. C.
(Attention: A. C. of S., G-2).

In accordance with War Department radio No. WX 67454 dated 20 July 1944, the following information is submitted:

16 Div HQ Intelligence Report No 27, 12 Oct 44, entitled: "Intelligence Report Concerning Bacillus Tactics in the THAILAND-BURMA Area (SHOBU Report 12 Oct 44)" is as follows:

(1) "During the middle part of September in the THAILAND BURMA Area it was confirmed that cholera bacilli were found in a yellow liquid filled ampoule of 20 cubic cm capacity which the natives picked up. The natives claimed that they were dropped from enemy planes. Many other similar incidents were reported. Taking into consideration the unexpected prevalence of cholera in the THAILAND BURMA Area the enemy is suspected of bacillus operations."

(2) "Even in the THAILAND Area plague carrying rats appeared during the latter part of September and approximately 100 rats were captured by the 7th. (No case reported among troops). In reference to the 1st article those diseases were probably dropped in conjunction with the THAILAND BURMA air operations."

(3) "When an epidemic breaks out following the ever increasing air operations it is necessary to make detailed reports of the situation and take strict precautionary measures against the enemy's bacillus operations." (From XXIV Corps ATIS Adv Ech translation of document captured DAGAMI, LEYTE, P.I., 7 Nov 44; XXIVCAET No 7, p 12).

For the Commander-in-Chief:

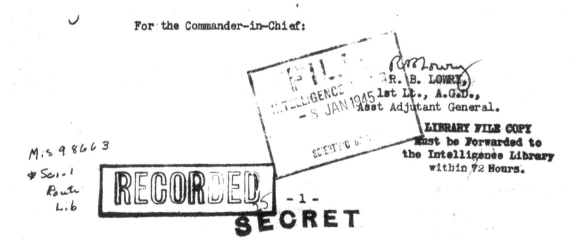

R. B. Lowry
R. B. LOWRY,
1st Lt., A.G.D.,
Asst Adjutant General.

SECRET

3.45 30 Nov. 1944: MILITARY ATTACHE REPORT, No. 1237, BACTERIAL WARFARE, 0402 LEE Q. WASSER, Col., A.C., Military Air Attache

资料出处： National Archives of the United States, R112, E295A, B11.

内容点评： 本资料为 1944 年 11 月 30 日美国驻华大使馆武官、空军上校 Lee Q. Wasser 提交的情报报告，题目：细菌战。提及日本人命令青岛伪政府警察局，让居民上交活鼠；日军可能利用老鼠散布鼠疫。

CONFIDENTIAL

ENCLOSURES

COPY NO.

26 DEC 1944

BW

Col. Anderson's file

MILITARY INTELLIGENCE DIVISION W. D. G. S.

MILITARY ATTACHE REPORT JAPAN
(Country reported on)

Subject BACTERIAL WARFARE I. G. No.
(Brief descriptive title)

From M. A. A. China Report No. 1237 Date 30 November, 1944

Source and degree of reliability:
Chinese G-2

Rated: C - 3

SUMMARY.— Here enter careful summary of report, containing substance succinctly stated; include important facts, names, places, dates, etc.

SCIENTIFIC

Report dated 28 November, 1944, states that "the puppet municipal government" and police bureau of TSINGTAO (120:19/36:04) received an order recently from the Japanese to have one live rat submitted by every three (3) of the local population, under the pretext of using the rats for medical necessities and for the making of furcoats for airmen. The rats are supposed to be used for the manufacture of bubonic vaccine and anti-bubonic serum. The local population are being pressed for same.

Comment:

This might be an indication that Japanese would use these rats to infect them with bubonic plague and turn them loose to infect desired areas.

0402 LEE Q. WASSER,
Colonel, A.C.
Military Air Attache.

NOTE: This document contains information affecting the national defense of the United States within the meaning of the Espionage Act, 50 U. S. C., 31 and 32, as amended. Its transmission or the revelation of its contents in any manner to an unauthorized person is prohibited by law. It may not be reproduced in whole or in part, by other than War Dep't Agencies, except by permission of the A C of S, G-2, W. D. G. S.

MIS 92086

*Sci-3
Lib-1
HQAAF-1
CIS-1
Med-1
OWI-3
CFS-2
FEA-1

LQW:cw

Distribution by originator: JICA APO 627; G-2 HQ AF APO 879; JICA Br APO 879; JICA APO 885; JICA APO 465 (2) (One for XX Bomber Cmd); File.

Routing space below for use in M. I. D. The section indicating the distribution will place a check mark in the lower part of the recipients' box in case one copy only is to go to him, or will indicate the number of copies in case more than one should be sent. The message center of the Intelligence Branch will draw a circle around the box of the recipient to which the particular copy is to go.

AGF	AAF	ASF	AC of S G-2	Chief IG	Eur.-Afr.	Far East	N. Amer.	Air	Dissem.	AIC	FLBR	OSS
MA Sec.	CIG	Rec. Sec.	ONI	BEW	CWS	ENG.	OPD	ORD	Sig.	State	QMG	

Enclosures:

None

CONFIDENTIAL

WAR DEPARTMENT
O.C.S.17 (2nd Rev.)

3.46 2 Jan. 1945: TECHNICAL INTELLIGENCE BULLETIN (NO. 2) BIOLOGICAL WARFARE, E.H. JULIAN, Lt. Col. Inf. T.I. Coord

资料出处：National Archives of the United States, R112, E295A, B11.

内容点评：本资料为 1945 年 1 月 2 日美军技术情报部门技术情报助理 E. H. Julian 中校提交的技术情报简报第 2 号，题目：细菌战。

RESTRICTED

HEADQUARTERS EIGHTH ARMY
Office of the AC of S., G-2
TECHNICAL INTELLIGENCE SECTION
APO 343

2 January 1945

TECHNICAL INTELLIGENCE BULLETIN)

NO. 2)

BIOLOGICAL WARFARE

1. Biological Warfare may be defined as the employment of bacterial and toxic agents, other than war gasses, to produce death or disease in man, plant, or animal.

2. Due to his steady deterioration, the enemy may in desparation, resort to Biological Warfare. It is imperative that all intelligence, medical, and other officers be alert to possible methods of attack, and be able to recognize presumptive evidence of it's contemplated or attempted use.

3. The Japanese attempted to spread Bubonic Plague in China by dropping packets of rice and fleas, mixed with wisps of cotton rag contaminated with the plague microbe, from low flying aircraft. This attempt against the Chinese (1941) was reported partially successful. Present data indicate that this type of disease spreading is a possibility.

4. From information available, Biological Warfare may be made by a mass tactical, or external attack such as the Japanese used in China, or by sabotage (pollution of water systems etc.). The following could be taken to indicate enemy intentions in this respect:

a. The appearance of specialized troops in strategic areas, such as certain types of chemical and engineer troops trained in biological methods, for otherwise unexplained purposes.

b. Unusual types and amounts of special equipment such as:

(1) Delousing units.
(2) Field laboratories.
(3) Field autoclaves.
(4) New type artillery and mortar shells and bombs.
(5) Unusual types of innoculations. (Taken from personal records, paybooks, medical tests etc. of enemy personnel).

RESTRICTED

RESTRICTED

(6) New issues of gas masks or decontamination clothing.
(7) Instruction of line troops in Biological Warfare.
(8) New techniques or equipment for projecting smoke or mists by aircraft or artillery.
(9) Flasks, ampules, gelatinuous masses, refuse, food particles, or containers for animals dropped from aircraft.
(10) Unusual taste of food, water supplies, or other beverages, or the sudden reduction or disappearance of the residual chlorine in water supply.
(11) Appearance of a disease in a previously noninfected area which cannot be accounted for by normal means of transmission.
(12) Numerous unexplained deaths in a given area.
(13) Abnormal deaths or decrease in the rat population in a given area.

5. Agents that appear most likely to be used have never less than a two hour lag between contact and the first outward appearances of symptoms; however it may extend to days. It is desired that all intelligence officers be alerted to the possibilities of Biological Warfare. Whenever physical evidence is found, the nearest laboratory equipped to conduct examination should be utilized. Such material should be treated as contaminated.

6. All information or exhibits collected should be promptly reported and sent, through G-2 channels, to the Assistant Chief of Staff, G-2 War Department General Staff, Washington D. C.

For the AC of S., G-2:

E.H. JULIAN
Lt. Col. Inf.
T.I. Coord.

RESTRICTED

3.47 2 Jan. 1945: BW, TO: Lt. Col. M. Moses, WDGS, MIS, Washington 25, D. C. FROM: GAYLORD W. ANDERSON, Lt. Col., Medical Corps

资料出处： National Archives of the United States, R112, E295A, B11.

内容点评： 本资料为 1945 年 1 月 2 日美军卫生部队中校 Gaylord W. Anderson 向陆军部军事情报局中校 M. Moses 提交的报告，题目：细菌战。提及日军文件等显示，日军可能实施炭疽菌攻击，必须取得日军炭疽疫苗。

SECRET

ALL COMMUNICATIONS SHOULD BE ADDRESSED TO "THE SURGEON GENERAL, U. S. ARMY, WASHINGTON 25, D. C."

SAVE

ARMY SERVICE FORCES
OFFICE OF THE SURGEON GENERAL
WASHINGTON 25, D. C.

IN REPLY REFER TO SPMDI

GWA/abh

L-JAPAN 0402 -

2 January 1945

96709

4150
1P2C

SUBJECT: BW

TO: Lieut. Colonel M. Moses, WDGS, MIS, Washington 25, D. C.

1. Attention is directed to recent Japanese documents regarding anthrax and study of terrain from standpoint of bacillus tactics. These documents coupled with previous report on bacillus bombs and the recovery of a bottle of anthrax K vaccine adjusted for human use make a logical part of a pattern suggesting possible attempts to spread anthrax. This organism, which may stay alive in the soil for as long as 25 years, would lend itself to use in a bomb which could be charged long in advance of use. The Japanese are doubtless aware of the German studies during the '30's in which sheep on an island off the coast of Spain were infected with anthrax spread by shells fired from a warship. It is logical to believe that anthrax is one of the organisms that the Japanese are considering and is a very probable component of the Mark 7 bomb. It is highly desirable that attempts to obtain Japanese anthrax vaccine be renewed. If such vaccine is recovered, it should be sent by courier to this office for examination at the Army Medical School. Samples of blood serum should be obtained from any survivors of the group for whom the antianthrax injections were ordered.

For The Surgeon General:

Gaylord W. Anderson
GAYLORD W. ANDERSON
Lieut. Colonel, Medical Corps

MIS 96709
+ Sci-2
Route
Lib

(25)

SECRET

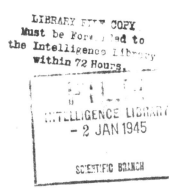

3.48 RY OF BW INTELLIGENCE 8 NOV. 1944 TO 15 JAN. 1945, HOWARD I. COLE, Lt. Col., C.W.S., Chief, Intelligence Branch, Special Projects Division

资料出处： National Archives of the United States, R112, E295A, B11.

内容点评： 本资料为美军特别项目局情报科主任、化学战部队中校 Howard I. Cole 提交的 1944 年 11 月 8 日至 1945 年 1 月 15 日细菌战情报报告。

SECRET

RY OF BW INTELLIGENCE 8 NOVEMBER 1944 TO 15 JANUARY 1945

1. This report is supplemental to the report submitted to the US BW Comittee under date of 8 November 1944.

Germany

2. Information was offered by a German POW, who deserted to the Americans, concerning tunnels constructed by him at Deblin, Poland; Goslar, Harz; Munich; Wipperfurth and one in Norway. He stated that they were heavily guarded during construction. He was later informed by a Dr. Toll that they were to be used for the storage of bacteria which could be used for war purposes, either by spraying from airplanes or by contamination of water supplies.

Comment: These targets will be investigated when uncovered. Due to the intensive bombing of Germany it would be necessary for the Germans to provide storage facilities of this nature if large quantities of BW agents were on hand.

3. Interesting information has just been received from our agents in the Strasburg area. The laboratories and letter file of Dr. E. Haagen, previously mentioned as being connected with German BW activities, were captured, together with some of his staff, although Dr. Haagen himself escaped. Dr. Haagen is an authority on virus diseases and worked at the Rockefeller Institute in 1932 on yellow fever virus (par. 8, SPPIR No. 5, 16 October 1944). The laboratories at the Hygiene Institute of Strasburg University were evidently mostly concerned with virus work and the preparation of antigens for active immunization. The diseases under study were influenza, typhus, epidemic hepatitus and yellow fever. No direct evidence was found connecting the work with BW activities.

The laboratories at Fort Fransecky (formerly the Maginot Ft. Ney) were equipped to carry on fundamental research on BW problems although no proof was obtained that BW agents were under investigation. On the other hand certain things remain unexplained:

a. The location in an isolated, well-guarded place of bacteriological laboratories for Dr. Haagen when he had similar facilities available in nearby Strasburg.

b. The destruction by fire of certain of the laboratories and preparations for the destruction of others.

c. The presence of three gas-tight chambers suitable for gas or BW experiments.

d. Evidence that experimental work was carried on by Dr. Haagen using inmates from concentration camps such as the one at Natzweiler, 30 miles southwest of Strasburg. A gas chamber similar to the one at Fort Fransecky was found outside the enclosure of the Natzweiler Camp.

SECRET

Haagen's files disclosed valuable information concerning the military research organization of Germany, and that medical experimental work involving human subjects was being conducted through the SS, and under Haagen's supervision, in concentration camps near Strasbourg. The investigation is being continued.

Japan

4. During this period a number of reports indicate that the Japanese have thoroughly considered BW from both the offensive and defensive view point.

5. A recent reference to a Japanese anthrax K vaccine as well as a reference to study of terrain from the standpoint of bacillus tactics and an order to a Japanese Unit captured on Leyte stating "Anti-anthrax injections will be given tomorrow" lends added significance to their previously mentioned "bacillus bomb". Although the filling of the bomb is still unknown, anthrax might well be one of the agents used especially if the Japanese have an anthrax vaccine for their own troops. On the other hand the anthrax vaccine might be used only to protect those troops handling horses or cattle.

6. A report by a POW of an incident which occurred during the Chekiang campaign of 1942 remains unconfirmed. The purpose of the campaign was to wipe out three airfields which the Japanese believed had been used by the Doolittle raiders. POW asserts that BW agents were spread by the Japanese from airplanes equipped with four electric refrigerators filled with test tubes containing cholera, typhoid and dysentery germs. The Japanese over ran the area in which the BW attack was made and POW states that as a result they had more than 1700 dead, chiefly from cholera. He states that he saw these statistics at the Headquarters of Water Supply and Purification at Nanking. POW, a former medical student, is credited by the interrogators as being very intelligent and sincere.

7. Several large Japanese balloons capable of carrying loads of 450 pounds have landed in the Western United States. The purpose of these balloons is not yet clear, but one of the more likely ones is to ~~automatically~~ spread causative agents of animal or human diseases directly or by releasing infected insects or animals. BW teams and kits for collection of samples have been set up and preparations for adequate study of all specimens have been made. One team is at present on the Pacific coast. A sample of snow taken at the location of one balloon landing has so far given negative results for pathogenic organisms. It is planned to have several BW teams (2 Persons each) strategically located so that quick access to future balloons will be possible. Since balloons of this type could be sent over in large numbers they represent a possible BW menace to the Western United States.

Howard I. Cole
HOWARD I. COLE
Lt. Colonel, C.W.S.
Chief, Intelligence Branch
Special Projects Division

SECRET

3.49 20 Jan. 1945: Nr. 23754, From: US Military Attache, Chungking, China, To: War Department

资料出处：National Archives of the United States, R112, E295A, B11.

内容点评：本资料为 1945 年 1 月 20 日重庆美国大使馆武官向美陆军部发送的电文：日军将于我前线与后方散布细菌，作为报复手段；12 月中旬，大阪化学研究所生产的细菌运达上海。

WAR DEPARTMENT
CLASSIFIED MESSAGE CENTER
INCOMING CLASSIFIED MESSAGE

SECRET IVI

From: US Military Attache, Chungking, China

To: War Department

Nr: 23754 20 January 1945

To MILID 23754 from Wasser from DePass signed Wedemeyer.

Coming from Sino G-2 with rating C-3 as result of infliction casualties on puppets and Japanese at Hankou and Shanghai by Allied planes Commanding General Jap Forces in China General Okamura conferred with Jap Air Force Commander in China Lt General Tsukawaro Shimoyama (3rd Japanese Flying Division Commander concurrently) also conferred with Cmdr Japanese Naval Fleets on China waters Admiral Kondo.

Spreading of bacteria at both our front and rear air bases as retaliatory measure also to increase strength of their air forces in China. Information that follows possible vaccine for enemy forces:

Chinese G-2 reported shipment of malaria Bubonic plague, typhoid, tuberculosis bacteria produced chemical research institute Osaka, middle December transported to Shanghai. For use in various places bacteria will be sent secretly soon.

End

470.6 (Japan) F

ACTION: G-2

INFO : CG AAF, OPD, Log

CM-IN-20271 (21 Jan 45) DTG 200908Z m/m

SECRET 59849

S.G.O. No.

SECRET

COPY NO. 51

THE MAKING OF AN EXACT COPY OF THIS MESSAGE IS FORBIDDEN

3.50 31 Jan. (1945): HEADQUARTERS US FORCES CHINA THEATRE OSS, FROM: HELLIWELL FOR HEPPNER, TO: 154 FOR KNOLLENBERG

资料出处：National Archives of the United States, R112, E295A, B11.

内容点评：本资料为1945年1月31日美军中国战区司令部战略情报局Helliwell情报，提及日本大阪化学研究所生产伤寒鼠疫菌，计划用飞机撒播美军集中地区；12月15日，第一批装载细菌飞机运达上海。

HEADQUARTERS
US FORCES CHINA THEATRE
OFFICE OF STRATEGIC SERVICES
APO 879.

FROM: HELLIWELL FOR HEPPNER 31 JAN

TO ; 154 FOR KNOLLENBERG

AS A RETALIATORY MEASURE AGAINST THE AMERICAN AIR FORCE ATTACKS, THE OSAKA CHEMICAL RESEARCH INSTITUTE IS MAKING TYPHOID AND BLACK PLAGUE GERMS. THE PLAN IS TO SCATTER THESE GERMS BY PLANES IN THE AREAS WHERE AMERICANS ARE CONCENTRATED. THE FIRST CONSIGNMEMMENT OF SUCH GERMS CAME BY PLANE ON DECEMBER 15 FROM OSAKA TO SHANGHAI. EVERY EFFORT IS BEING MADE TO OBTAIN ADDITIONAL INFORMATION OF THE ABOVE NATURE.

3.51 23 Jan. 1945: INTELLIGENCE REPORT, FROM: 6TH SERVICE COM AND DISTRICT NO. 3: Dr. Gerald Laiser Downie, Missionary Physician: Health and Sanitation, Nanping, Fukien Province

资料出处： National Archives of the United States, R112, E295A, B11.

内容点评： 本资料为 1945 年 1 月 23 日美军收到的教会医生 Dr. Gerald Laiser Downie 情报报告，题目：福建省南平的公共卫生。

I. G. File No. 53 CONFIDENTIAL

Report No. 2194

CLASSIFICATION

Enclosures

Copy No.

INTELLIGENCE REPORT

FOR GENERAL USE BY ANY U.S. INTELLIGENCE AGENCY

From SIXTH SERVICE COMMAND, DISTRICT NO. 3 Date 23 January 1945

Source Dr. Gerald Leiser Downie, Missionary Physician Eval. B.O.

Area Reported On Nanping, (Yenping) Province, Fukien Province. Subject Health and Sanitation China.

Reference (Directive, correspondence, previous report, etc., if applicable.)

SUMMARY: Enter careful summary of report, containing substance succinctly stated. Answer questions where, when, what, etc., how many, and give date of event. In a final one sentence paragraph give significance. Begin text on page 2.

Report is divided as follows:

1. Information Concerning Source.

2. Health and Sanitation at Nanping (Yenping), in Fukien Province-China. City of 80,000 population, one-hundred per cent (100%) Chinese.

A. Public Health Organization.

B. Medical Facilities and Personnel.

C. Disease Control and Sanitation.

NOTE: This document contains information affecting the national defense of the United States within the meaning of the Espionage Act, 50 U. S. C., 31 and 32, as amended. Its transmission or the revelation of its contents in any manner to an unauthorized person is prohibited by law. It may not be reproduced in whole or in part, by other than War Dep't Agencies, except by permission of the A C of S, G-2, W. D. G. S.

DECLASSIFIED E.O. 12065, Sec. 3-402 NND 574-5 BY WHLewis NARS, Date 4/8/80

RLS/kp

BW-FE

Distribution by Originator

MIS Serial No. 103953

MIS Distribution

Socio 2
Acute
Lib
Sci 1
SOAAF 2
Med 1
Int Div 1
ONI 3

Distribution of Enclosures

none

CONFIDENTIAL

FORM 6517
3RD REV.

CONFIDENTIAL

1. Information Concerning Source.

Dr. Gerald Loiser Downie, born Mount Ayr, Iowa - 20 July 1903. Missionary physician in Nanping, China, from September 1932, to May 1937, and from November 1938 to April 1944.

Dr. Downie is at present on the staff of Wesley Memorial Hospital, 250 East Superior Street, Chicago, Illinois. Phone, Delaware 6500. His residence is 541 East Court Street, Kankakee, Illinois.

The Garrison Commander, Li Lien-Yeng, at Foochow (the port city, one hundred and forty (140) miles southeast of Nanping) was personal friend of Dr. Downie as was Francis Cheng, or Cheng Sho-Cheng, the local provincial youth corps, director at Nanping.

Dr. Downie is doing special work at Wesley Memorial Hospital and is glad to give any further information he might have of interest to the War Department, although it is believed the enclosed report covers all pertinent information.

2. Nanping (Yenping) China. Health and Sanitation.

A. (1) "Community health program is largely set up in community hospitals and clinics and is the best of all the programs in this area," statement by Dr. Downie. The chief health officer of the town of Nanping, is the community hospital superintendent, appointed by the local magistrate with provincial approval.

Community hospitals take no in-patients but do a clinic practice for poorer patients who come to them. They are responsible for a large part of the preventive medicine that is done in the community.

5302.0100.

(2) A special agency engaged in a strong health program is the National Epidemic Prevention Bureau. In 19[illegible] this bureau sent an anti-plague unit to Nanping City which was made headquarters for a province wide anti-campaign. (Nanping is one of the few endemic foci for bubonic plague in the province.) They produce vaccines and direct their use in epidemic prevention.

The Community-Provincial health programs handle school health, pre and post natal care, a mid-wifery school, and a preventive medical school.

5302.0400.

B. (1) The Provincial Hospital has about forty (40) beds and takes the wealthier type of patients. They have a large out patient department with about four hundred (400) patients per day.

5303.0100.

(2) Staff of ten (10) doctors and their surgeon is a graduate of Hunan-Yale School. Also one medical out of senior members of their staff is trained in Japan.

5303.0300.

C. Disease control and sanitation other than that practiced by the National Epidemic Prevention Bureau's anti-bubonic plague are:-

(1) An attempt is being made to eliminate rats and rat fleas. There is no control exercised over mosquitoes. There is no scarlet fever and no yellow fever in the district although there are numerous cases of plague, malaria, and tuberculosis. Dissentery and venereal diseases are very common.

5304.0300.

(2) The source of their drinking water is from wells, rivers, and creeks. They are all contaminated. They have a crude running water system, mostly through long bamboo pipes.

CONFIDENTIAL

C O N F I D E N T I A L

- 2 -

CONFIDENTIAL

343

(3) In isolated cases attempts have been made to purify water by chemicals, but all water consumed by humans should be boiled.

5304.0603.

(4) Sewerage is carried right through town in buckets. Some is dumped into the river, but most is kept for fertilizer.

5304.0601.

Dr. Downie stated that Dr. R. Pollitzer, the National Epidemic Bureau Plague Advisor, is convinced that on one and possibly two occasions, the Japanese have dropped plague infected fleas in this area of Free China. These small valleys produce a great deal of rice.

5304.0300.

Prepared by:

Ross L. Stockman
ROSS L. STOCKMAN,
Captain, C. M. P.

J. D. Krisor
J. D. Krisor,
1st Lt., C. M. P.

Reviewed and approved for transmittal to the Director of Intelligence, Army Service Forces:

RALPH S. MOYER
1st Lt, MAC
Asst. Chief, Foreign Section
Intelligence Section
Security and Intelligence Division
Headquarters, Sixth Service Command

CONFIDENTIAL

3.52 28 Jan. 1945: Intelligence Notes #1

资料出处：National Archives of the United States, R112, E295A, B11.

内容点评：本资料为 1945 年 1 月 28 日美军收获情报：1943 年春，日军在江西北部投下染鼠疫菌稻米；1943 年 11 月，日军下令云南西部腾冲百姓收集 1800 只活鼠。

Intelligence notes #1

Rated B-2 & in R&A files KMG

Dated Jan 28, 1945

HQ 202 file

Jap. dropped plague infected rice in Northern Kiangsi in Spring 1943

In Nov 1943 Jap. ordered population of Teng-Chung in western Yunnan to collect 1,800 live rats. Military developments prevented Jap. from exploiting whatever their intentions had been.

3.53　3 Mar. 1945: Bacteriological Warfare, To: ASFRTS, From: Chief, SI, OSS, CT, PAUL L. S. HELLIWELL Lt. Col. F. A., Chief, SI, Oss, CT

资料出处： National Archives of the United States, R112, E295A, B11.

内容点评： 本资料为 1945 年 3 月 3 日美军中国战区战略情报局科学情报部门主任 Paul L. S. Helliwell 中校的报告，题目：细菌战。

TOP SECRET

51-001-303
File

HEADQUARTERS
OFFICE OF STRATEGIC SERVICES CHINA THEATER
SI BRANCH

APO 627
3 March 1945

To : AGFRTS

From: Chief, SI, OSS,CT

Subj: Bacteriological Warfare

1. Request is made that you instruct agents operating in Shanghai to attempt to find out what activities are being carried on by the Shanghai Natural Science Committee, formerly located in Shanghai between Hongkew Park and 3068-3494 Road near 1131-6839-1653 Station. This committee may also have offices on the western part of Route Joseph Frelupt.

2. This agency is suspected of preparing bacteriological warfare, and top priority is to be given to this request.

PAUL L. E. HELLIWELL
Lt. Colonel, F. A.
Chief, SI, OSS, CT

PLEH/oc

TOP SECRET

3.54　8 Mar. 1945: Further Report on Epidemic Germs as a War Weapon, JOSEPH K. DICKEY, Col., GSC, AC of S, G-2

资料出处：National Archives of the United States, R112, E295A, B11.

内容点评：本资料为 1945 年 3 月 8 日美军情报部参谋长助理、参谋团上校 Joseph K. Dickey 提交的中国战区的报告，题目：关于以流行病菌为武器的进一步报告。

S E C R E T

HEADQUARTERS
UNITED STATES FORCES
CHINA THEATER

A.P.O. 879
8 March 1945.

SUBJECT: Further Report On Epedemic Germs as a War Weapon.

6217
5

TO : Ass't Chief of Staff, G-2, War Dept General Staff, Washington, D.C.
Theater Surgeon, U.S. Forces, China Theater, APO 627.
Chemical Warfare Officer, U.S. Forces, China Theater, APO 627.
JAG, U.S. Forces, China Theater, APO 879 (Attention: Major WEST).

1. The following report, dated 3 March 1945 is from OSS, APO 879 forwarded for your information.

2. The information is dated 25 February, 1945, and was obtained secretly from sources in the SHANGHAI Japanese Army Headquarters by a Chinese agent. The report is rated B-3.

"1. Bacteriological warfare is expected to be used as a last resort in industrial areas of YUNNAN, KWANGSI, HUNAN, KWEICHOW, and SZECHWAN Provinces, particularly allied airfield areas, and at the battle fronts. (See Note.)

2. If and when such an attack is carried out, it is expected that dissemination will be on a large scale.

3. Dissemination is expected to be by aerial bombs and/or by spraying in the form of liquid or powder from planes.

4. Bombs are made in an Osaka chemical laboratory.

5. The powder and liquid forms are manufactured jointly by the Japanese TOYEN (T'ung-jen in Chinese) (同仁)(Together Benevolent, or Together Love) association, Central China Branch, and by the SHANGHAI Natural Science Committee, formerly located in SHANGHAI between HONGKEW PARK and CHIANG-WAN (江湾) (Kiangwan) Road near T'ien-t'ung-tu (天通庵) station. These operate under the guise of the production of medicines from glucose-D, from which, by a process of reduction, there is derived a ferment termed enzyme which is used in the culture of bacteria.

6. The Science Study Committee, which applies most of its time to studies of bacteria, is located in the western part of Route Joseph Freluft.

7. To enable the bacteria to be cultured under the proper conditions, laboratories have also been set up in the Yangtze Valley, so it appears likely that there is a plant in KIUKIANG. (This was reported in YS/C[illegible] [illegible]0, 1944.)

8. Plague, cholera, typhoid, and malaria are [illegible] subject of research.

S E C R E T

129569-1

R E T

Ltr, Hqs, USF, CT, Subj: Further Rept on Epodemic Germs as a War Weapon dtd 8 Mar 45.

---

9. Bacteria bombs arrived in SHANGHAI in the latter part of January from Osaka, and were stored in the HONGKEW District in SHANGHAI.

NOTES:

1. This report was made in answer to direct questions.

2. The message had "particularly allied AIAXUC and airfield areas." We have not been able to decide what the AIAXUC means."

Joseph K. Dickey
JOSEPH K. DICKEY
Colonel, GSC
AC of S, G-2.

- 2 -

S E C R E T

129-69-2

3.55 13 Mar. 1945: Report No R-237-Ch-45, Japanese B. W. Activities, From: JICA/CT Br., Kunming, China

资料出处： National Archives of the United States, R112, E295A, B11.

内容点评： 本资料为1945年3月13日美军化学战部队少校 James R. Geddes 自昆明美国联合情报部中国战区局递交的报告，题目：日本的细菌战活动。

6 April 194[illegible]
Classification chan[illegible]
to Secret by author[illegible]
the A. C. of S., G-[illegible]
BID O[illegible] W.[illegible]
Col. [illegible]

~~TOP SECRET~~

~~SECRET~~ [illegible] BRANCH REPORT

Country reported on: CENTRAL CHINA (OCCUPIED).

Subject: Japanese B.W. Activities.

From: JICA/CT Br., Kunming, China. Report No. R-237-CH-45 13 March 1945

Source: Chinese Agent of OSS Reference: JICA CK 10127, 2 Oct 44, MAA, China [illegible] 30 Nov 44, OSS KM Y-2167, 9 Dec 44, OSS, Ch 26-[illegible] 19 Jan 45.

Evaluation: B-3 (by source).

Summary:

1. B.W. is expected to be used by the Japanese as a last resort in thickly populated industrial areas in YUNAN, KWANGSI, KWEICHOW, [illegible], and HUNAN against allied concentrations, airfields and on the battle fronts in the form of aerial bombs and liquid and/or powder aerial sprays.

2. Bombs are made in an OSAKA chemical laboratory.

3. The powder and liquid are made by:
   a. Jap 0681-0058 Association.
   b. Shanghai Natural Science Committee - which was formerly located between Hongkew Park and 3068-3494 Road near 1131-6639-1653 Station, operating under the guise of the production of medicines by fermentation of glucose with enzymes but which were used in the culture of bacteria. The Science Study Committee is applying most of its time to bacteria study and is located in the western part of Route Joseph Frelupt (R.N. in French concession).

4. To acclimate the bacteria, laboratories have been set up in the Yangtze valley (R.N. no locations stated), and it appears likely there is one in CHIU CHIANG (九江) (E11603, N2943), Kiangsi province.

5. Plague, cholera, typhoid and malaria serums are under research.

6. Bacteria bombs arrived in SHANGHAI from OSAKA in late January and were stored in the Hongkew district.

COMMENT: See page 2.

NOTE: This document contains information affecting the national defense of the United States within the meaning of the Espionage Act, 50 U. S. C., 31 and 32, as amended. Its transmission or the revelation of its contents in any manner to an unauthorized person is prohibited by law. It may not be reproduced in whole or in part, by other than War Dep't Agencies, except by permission of the A C of S, G-2, WDGS.

7109 JAMES R. GEDDES,
Major, C.W.S.

Approved & Forwarded

ROBERT G. STOUT
Major, Inf.
Acting Exec. Officer

MIS 139166 (Sci Br)
MSci 4
Route
Lib
G-2 ETOUSA/Sci 3
CWS/Sci 2
~~Med/Sci 1~~
NDD/Sci 1
OSW/Sci 1
OSRD/Sci 1

Distribution: JIA C; OC-CWS; G-2, CT; Cml. Of., 14th AF; Cml. Of., A.L.C.; Cml. Of. IBT; File (2).

~~SECRET~~

~~TOP SECRET~~

NPH

SECRET

TOP SECRET

COMMENTS TO JICA RE ... R-237-CH-45.

SECRET

Comments of Colonel John Wood, M.C., head of the OWS mission, with Chemical Office, China Theater.

Concerning the sera listed in (5), it is pertinent to consider the latest scientific information on:

MALARIA: Man can be infected only by the bite of an infected mosquito or by an injection of infected malaria blood with a hypodermic syringe. It is a scie... impossibility to spread disease by means of a powder or liquid dispersed in bacterial bomb. The Japs cannot improve upon the natural conditions already existing in the areas mentioned for the spread of malaria.

CHOLERA and TYPHOID: These are filth diseases, spread from man to man by human excreta in water or food. Flying or crawling insects, particularly house flies may spread the bacteria from human excreta to food or water, but to get the di... man must eat the infected food or drink the infected water. Man may also get these diseases by soiling his hands with the excreta of a human case and transferring the bacteria to his mouth.

These diseases are widely endemic in China and all unboiled water or unco... food is a potential source. So long as the boiling of drinking water and the cooking of foods, as normally practiced in China by Americans and Chinese ali... is observed, these diseases are not apt to spread. In the massive overcrowdi... which occurs in Chinese towns during an evacuation when filth and human excreta are everywhere and flies are rampant, these and the dysenteries usually appear and spread naturally, often in epidemic form. This is due to a breakdown of ... rules of sanitation.

These are delicate organisms, readily killed by heat, sunlight or drying ... air. They can be prepared in living virulent form as a powder only by drying ... high vacuum under conditions difficult to attain on any practical scale. The dried bacteria die off rapidly when the vacuum is broken and air reaches them. In liquid culture they are sticky and adhere to any surface they touch and can... fly about as a dust to be inhaled or swallowed by man until they are dry. But drying in air or exposure to sunlight rapidly kills them, and so they cannot b... practically disseminated to man in this manner. The detonation of a bomb would probably destroy a high percentage of these organisms, either in powder or li... form.

Unless they are employed as sabotage agents to infect water or food, which has already been prepared, cooled and considered safe by the user, it is diffi... to see how the Japanese can increase the potential threat of these diseases which is constantly present in the areas mentioned.

PLAGUE: This is a disease of man, rat and a few other mammals (eg. the ground squirrel). It is usually spread from rat to rat and from rat to man by the bites of infected rat fleas. The pneumonic form of plague can be spread dire... from man to man by the inhalation of infected droplets breathed out from plag... infected lungs. It is endemic in many parts of China and can be spread to oth... where there is a dense rat population.

The bacteria themselves are delicate and cannot be practically dissemin... in a bomb to infect man directly for the reasons stated above for cholera and typhoid.

Report from JICA Kunming, China. Report No. R-237-CH-45. 13 March 19..

JRG/wk Page

SECRET

TOP SECRET

SECRET

SECRET

The dropping of plague infected fleas from airplanes is a possibility, but the spread of plague from this source will still depend upon the biological conditions existing in the area into which they are dropped. For plague to spread there must be a dense rat population and a close cohabitation of man and rat. The chances of starting a plague epidemic of any military importance by this method are believed be small.

It is also possible to drop plague infected rats, infested with fleas, from airplanes. Again the spread of plague will depend upon biological conditions in the area, as expressed above, and the chances of deterring military operations by this means are equally small.

The method of disseminating plague which probably offers the greatest chance of success is to inject the bacteria directly into man, using a living virulent culture and a hypodermic syringe, and to disperse these infected men among centers of population. Pneumonic cases are certain to develop among these men and spread without the necessity of a dense rat population and close association between rat and man. Japanese could accomplish this, since it is their custom to compel Chinese laborers to work for them in occupied territory. Chinese evacuees usually migrate rather [illegible] to towns or cities where the chance of spreading plague is greatest. This method [illegible] be useful in leaving plague infected centers behind <u>if the Japs are planning to [illegible]</u> but it would be pointless for them to introduce plague into an area they intend to occupy.

COMMENTS OF THE THEATER SURGEON, CHINA THEATER.

I agree with the comments made on the attached document. I believe that there [illegible] little likelihood of the Japanese using any of the organisms mentioned in this report. However, this office will insure that American personnel will have ample protection against diseases mentioned.

Report JICA Kunming, China. Report No. R-237-CH-45 13 March [illegible]

JRG/wk

SECRET

TOP SECRET

SECRET

3.56　19 Mar. 1945: Further Report on Epidemic Germs as a War Weapon, RICHARD H. AGNEW, Lt. Col, GSC, Act'g AC of S, G-2

资料出处：National Archives of the United States, R112, E295A, B11.

内容点评：本资料为 1945 年 3 月 19 日美军情报部参谋长助理、参谋团中校 Richard H. Agnew 提交的中国战区的报告，题目：关于以流行病菌为武器的进一步报告。

SECRET

HEADQUARTERS
UNITED STATES FORCES
CHINA THEATER

A.P.O. 879
19 March 1945.

SUBJECT: Further Report On Epidemic Germs as a War Weapon.

TO : Ass't Chief of Staff, G-2, War Dept General Staff, Washington, D.C.
Theater Surgeon, U.S. Forces, China Theater, APO 627.
Chemical Warfare Officer, U.S. Forces, China Theater, APO 627.
JAG, U.S. Forces, China Theater, APO 879 (Attention: Major WEST).

1. The following report, dated 3 March 1945 is from OSS, APO 879 forwarded for your information.

"1. In response to the request contained in Reference (b) for more information on the subject of the possible use of epidemic germs by the Japanese, the following information is forwarded. It was received from a Chinese Special Agent in a report dated 1 March 1945.

2. The bacterial bombs which were shipped to SHANGHAI from OSAKA in December and January were later sent to HAN-K'OU, where they are intended for use in war zones in the provinces of Yunnan, Kweichow, Szechwan, Kwangsi, and Hunan. The report also stated that the bacteria would be scattered over industrial areas in cities in these provinces.

3. The bombs are said to include four different kinds of germs; namely, typhoid, cholera, bubonic plague, and malaria. (Both Chinese reports dealing with this subject of bacteriological warfare which have been received by this activity have included malaria germs as one of the types of bacteria to be spread by aerial bombs. Inasmuch as it is not possible to spread malaria in this manner, no mention was made of malaria germs in Reference (a). It is included here in an effort to arrive at a proper evaluation of the information contained in these reports.)

4. The bombs are made by the OSAKA Chemical Research Institute and the germs are cultivated in the SHANGHAI Tungyen Club, Central China Branch (上海同仁會華中支部) and the Natural Science Research Institute.

5. The germs are to be disseminated by aerial bombs containing either powders or solutions. The report also states that trials will be made "in accordance with the suitable breeding quality of the germs." (This may mean that the Japs will try out a small quantity of each type of germ in order to determine the most suitable medium of dissemination.)"

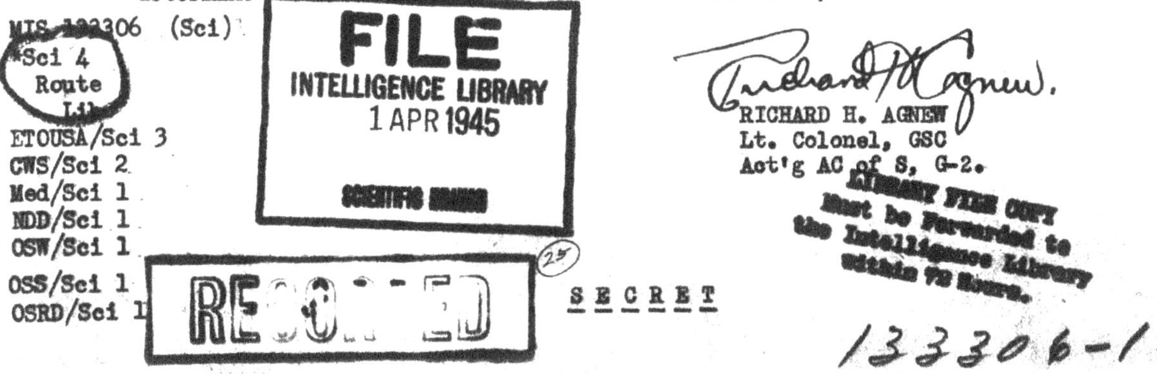

MIS 133306 (Sci)
Sci 4
Route
Lib
ETOUSA/Sci 3
CWS/Sci 2
Med/Sci 1
NDD/Sci 1
OSW/Sci 1
OSS/Sci 1
OSRD/Sci 1

RICHARD H. AGNEW
Lt. Colonel, GSC
Act'g AC of S, G-2.

SECRET

133306-1

3.57 20 Mar. 1945: Bacteriological Warfare, TO: Col. Richard P. Heppner, Hdq. USAF CBI, FROM: Col. H. W. Dix

资料出处： National Archives of the United States, R112, E295A, B11.

内容点评： 本资料为1945年3月20日美军上校H. W. Dix提交美空军司令部Richard P. Heppner上校的报告，题目：细菌战。

SECRET

TO 278
YLA-223

20 March 1945

TO : Col. Richard P. Heppner
Hdq. USAF CBI
APO 627, c/c Postmaster
San Francisco, California

FROM : Colonel H. W. Dix HWD

SUBJECT : Bacteriological Warfare

Inclosed is a short summary of the present status of Japanese biological warfare preparations, and our intelligence needs in this field. There is included a set of suggested questions, originally intended for interrogation of PW, but also indicative of the type of material that can be asked of individuals contacted ahead of the lines.

There is also included a list of indicators; this list can be given to agents, and should be of value as providing a means for the agent to examine economic, manufacturing, and transportation phases of a region, and draw conclusions therefrom, as to whether active preparation for biological warfare is going on.

There has been considerable indoctrination of army medical and intelligence officers in the Far East on what to look for as indications of Japanese BW activities, and how to handle any intelligence coming to light. There has been less indoctrination of naval personnel, although some has been attempted. It is believed, however, that our sources will prove of more value than will military or naval sources, because of the nature of the subject. Presumably, the Japanese will make every effort to avoid information of projected use of BW agents filtering forward to the lines where it might be obtained by us, at least until the last possible moment prior to its actual use.

Mr. J. D. Hitch is being sent to China for us, and is well briefed on this topic. He will undoubtedly discuss it further with various individuals in that theater.

SECRET

SECRET

X0272
YLA-223

JAPANESE BIOLOGICAL WARFARE

Various reports from Japanese sources indicate considerable interest in Biological Warfare, not only as a means of sabotage, but also regarding its use, or possible use on a fairly large scale against large concentrations of people, both military and civilian. It is evident that the Japanese have a special experimental bomb generally listed as being the Mark 7 Bacillus Bomb, weight of which is usually given as 1 kg. Experimental work and field trials have been reported at HARBIN (PINGKIANG) and HSINLING (CHANGCHUN) in Manchiria. Water Supply and Purification Departments and Units are -- in some instances -- said to be closely connected with Biological Warfare. (This is said to be particularly true of the Department in NANKING.) Some Diversionary Raiding parties, "Commando" Units and Saboteurs have received directions on the use of bacteria. Special note is made of the recommendation that they should use bacteria of such diseases as are already present so as not to arouse undue suspicion. An Engineer Manual on Raiding suggests the releasing of bacteria in reservoirs. One document even notes a study of terrain from the standpoint of "Bacillus Tactics". Some troops have apparently been immunized against anthrax. BW agents are reported to have been released by plane in the CHEKIANG Campaign in 1942. Maj. Gen. ISHII, Shiro is often mentioned in connection with BW. Bacteria or viruses of the following diseases are often mentioned: typhoid, cholera, dysentery, plague, tuberculosis, anthrax, Japanese B encephalitis, etc.

More information is particularly desired on Biological Warfare Research, Experimental and Development centers, munitions being developed and manufactured, manufacturing centers, storage centers, actual diseases under investigation, methods of use and units likely to use BW, Bw tactics, reason for anthrax immunization, and personnel connected with BW in any manner.

SECRET

SECRET

BIOLOGICAL WARFARE

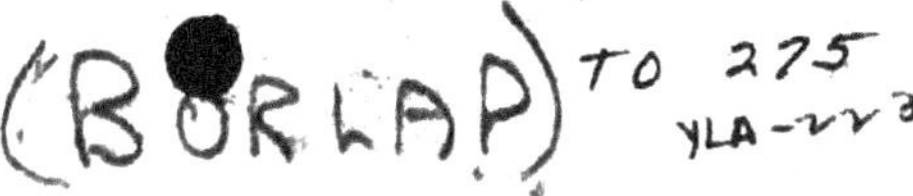

1. Have you ever been given any instructions in the use of bacteria as a warfare agent?

2. By whom?

3. When?

4. To what groups were these instructions given?

5. About what bacteria were you taught?

6. How were you taught to use them?

7. How were they to be made available to you?

8. Under what circumstances were you instructed to use them?

9. What were you told as to their probable effect?

10. What precautions were you taught as to their use - or handling?

11. Were you taught anything about protecting yourself when, and if you use them?

12. Have you ever heard of a bacterial bomb or bacillus bomb?

13. What is in the bomb?

14. Where is the bomb made?

15. Where are the bacteria for use in the bomb grown?

16. Where is the bomb filled?

17. When is it filled?

18. Does the bomb come to you all ready for use?

19. How is the bomb stored?

20. Have you ever seen the bomb used?

21. If so, under what circumstances?

22. Have you had any practice exercises with the bomb?

23. What did you do to protect yourself?

24. How soon after it is used did you go into the area where it hit?

25. Did you take any precautions when you went into the area?

26. What was the effect of the bomb?

SECRET

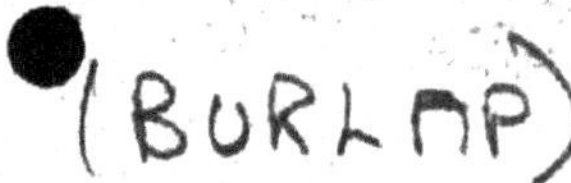

27. Against what was it used?

28. Against what can it be used?

29. When using it, do you have to take into consideration weather conditions?

30. Where were the trials conducted?

31. What units of the Military are responsible for the use of the bombs -- Army, Navy, or Air?

32. Can you describe the bomb? Any markings - color, or colored strips?

33. Who would give you orders to use it.

34. How do you plant to evaluate the results of the use of these bombs?

35. Are you required to make any special report on the effectiveness of the bomb?

36. If so, what kind of report and to whom?

37. Are there any other types of bombs, shells or other means of spreading bacteria?

38. If so - what?

(Obtain answers to all questions regarding bombs - also with respect to other means of bacterial warfare.)

39. Have you ever been told that the enemy would use -- or had used bacteria or poisons as a means of warfare?

40. If so, who told you?

41. When?

42. What Bacteria or Poisons did he say had been used?

43. When?

44. How was it used?

45. Did it have any effect?

46. What effect?

47. What were you told as to the likelihood that the enemy would use bacteria?

48. Were you taught any means of protecting yourself if the enemy should use bacteria?

49. Were the civilians given any instructions as to protection against the use of bacteria, either as a weapon or as a method of sabotage?

~~50. Have the civilians been given any instructions as to protection against the~~

SECRET

SECRET
- 3 -

ught anything about methods you could use to determine whether or not the enemy was using bacteria?

51. What instructions have you been given regarding protection of your drinking water supply?

52. Have you been taught any means of testing your drinking water?

53. What have you been taught as to protection of your food supply?

54. Have you ever heard of any research being carried on with respect to the use of bacteria in warfare?

55. If so - who told you?

56. When?

57. Where is this research going on?

58. Who is doing it?

59. What particular bacteria or poisons are being studied?

60. What supplies (raw products) are used by these laboratories?

61. What experimental animals are being used?

62. In great quantities?

63. What methods of spreading bacteria or other agents - are being studied?

64. What individual is responsible for this research?

65. Have you ever heard of Maj. Gen. IISHI, Shiro?

66. Have studies been made of the use of bacteria against animals?

67. Have studies been made of the use of bacteria or other agents to destroy crops?

68. Do you know of anyone who has been immunized against anthrax?

69. Why?

70. What kind of Anthrax vaccine was used and who makes the vaccine?

71. How many injections are given?

72. At what intervals?

73. How long does the immunization last?

74. What provisions are made for re-vaccination?

75. Is it any good?

SECRET

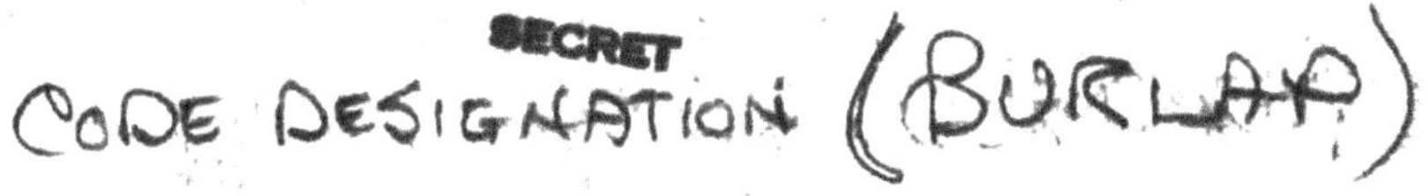

More comprehensive indicators which it is less harmful to publicize:

1. Are there any hatcheries which receive eggs but do not produce a comparable number of chicks for market? Are there any unusual uses of eggs or chicks?

2. Are there any important consumers of caseins from the dairy industry or digested proteins of any kind?

3. Are there any factories using "steep water" (the by-product of slaughter houses)? What dispostion is made of this material?

4. Are there any biological material manufacturers who have increased their orders for eggs, caseins, digested proteins or "steep water" within the last few years, or any other manufacturers who have suddenly started using these materials?

Much of these raw materials can be checked through the transportation papers and waybills, receipts, etc.

CODE DESIGNATION

(BURLAP)

3.58 27 Mar. 1945: Plague in North Hunan, China, Statement made from memory, Dr. Phillips F. Greene, Superintendent of the Hsiang Ya Hospital, Changsha, China

资料出处： National Archives of the United States, R112, E295A, B11.

内容点评： 本资料为 1945 年 3 月 27 日长沙湘雅医院院长 Phillips F. Greene 博士关于中国湖南北部鼠疫流行的回忆。

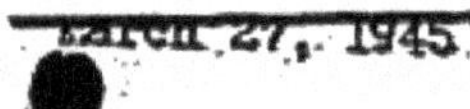

Statement made from memory, Dr. Phillips F. Greene, Superintendent of the Hsiang Ya Hospital, Changsha, China

Plague in North Hunan, China

North Hunan between the Yangtzee and the Yuan Rivers had had the of being an endemic area for plague during the last three centuries. D the nineteenth century there are said to have been three outbreaks of e proportion. One of them involving a fairly extended area. I am told it occured about the year 1880. Occasional sporadic cases have been report until about 1900. From then on this area was said to be free.

In 1939 we had rumors that there had been several cases North of Chang. In 1940 near the city of Tauyuan, there were two well localized areas in which Bubonic Plague developed there with a total of about 40 known cases and several deaths. One of these areas was a refugee camp, largely from people from the costal areas. The second area was the nearest village to the camp. In 1941, in December there were a few cases. In this same region in 1942 a third epidemic of small proportion broke out. I had a chance to talk with the Public Health Director stationed at Tauyuan who had himself seen upwards to twenty cases. They occured in two families not far from the area involved in 1940. Of these there were five deaths and two post mortem examinations showed undoubted plague. Both pneumonic and bubonic forms were present. Though only two of the cases were pneumonic. At the same time it was reported large numbers of rats were found dead in the open. About two weeks later there was a similar smaller outbreak in the city of Changteh. This same Public Health Officer was able to trace the connection between the Tauyuan cases and those at Changteh.

Our best guess was that the origin of these cases was the refugees from Fukien had re-introduced plague into Northern Hunan. But as we had many such refugees in other parts of Hunan without outbreaks of plague among them, I felt unwilling to set aside the possibility of a local recrudescence.

I believe it was this outbreak at Changteh which was given rather large publicity as due to dropping of infected fleas from airplanes by the Japanese. In the light of the above information it seems to us quite unlikely. Moreover in reviewing the whole matter later with the National Public Health Authorities at Chungking, I found they also were inclined to doubt that the Japanese had been directly connected with these cases.

3.59 6 Apr. 1945: TO 146, FROM: Technical Section, Col. H. W. Dix

资料出处：National Archives of the United States, R112, E295A, B11.

内容点评：本资料为 1945 年 4 月 6 日技术部上校 H. W. Dix 报告的 3 月 21 日情报：日军下令从桂林基地出发，沿 Ledo Road 撒播细菌，攻击地区为云南、密支那、八莫一带。

OFFICE OF STRATEGIC SERVICES
TECHNICAL INTELLIGENCE

6 April 1945
T0146

FROM: Technical Section
Colonel H. W. Dix

A recent cable, evaluation C-3, with information dated 21 March states that orders have been issued by the Japanese War Ministry that germs are to be disseminated by plane along the Ledo Road; the areas especially mentioned are Yunaan, Myitkyina and Bhamo areas. The method by which they will be disseminated from the plane is not known but the operations are to proceed from a base at Kwalein. It is understood that typhoid, diptheria and cholera are to be used.

SMS:as

cc: Lt. Comdr. W. B. Sarles
Lt. Col. Howard I. Cole, CWS
Maj. Frederick A. Voigt (6 copies)

3.60 9 Apr. 1945: Further Report on Epidemic Germs as a War Weapon, RICHARD H. AGNEW, Lt. Col, GSC, Exec. to AC of S, G-2

资料出处：National Archives of the United States, R112, E295A, B11.

内容点评：本资料为 1945 年 4 月 9 日情报部执行参谋长助理、参谋团中校 Richard H. Agnew 提交陆军参谋部情报部参谋长助理的报告，题目：关于以流行病菌为武器的进一步报告。日军下令沿 Ledo Road 散布细菌，特别针对云南、八莫、密支那地区，散布细菌为霍乱、伤寒、白喉、疟疾；用飞机撒播，以桂林为基地。未说明疟疾散布手段。

S E C R E T

RIP 0142911

HEADQUARTERS
UNITED STATES FORCES
CHINA THEATER

A.P.O. 879
9 April 1945.

6217
2C

SUBJECT: Further Report on Epidemic Germs as a War Weapon.

TO : Ass't Chief of Staff, G-2, War Department General Staff, Washington, D. C.
Theater Surgeon, U.S. Forces, China Theater, A.P.O. 627.
Chemical Warfare Officer, A.P.O. 627.
JAG, U.S. Forces, China Theater, A.P.O. 879 (Attn: Major West).

1. In response to the request contained in Reference (b) for more information on the subject of the possible use of epidemic germs by the Japanese, the following information is forwarded. Source is rated usually reliable and information possibly true. In substance, the report is as follows:

> Order has been given to disseminate germs along Ledo Road and especially the Yunnan-Bhamo and Myitkyina areas. Germ diseases to be disseminated are cholera, typhoid, diphtheria, and malaria.
>
> Airplanes will be used, bomb or spray not indicated, time not indicated, but Kweilin will be used as the headquarters. The Japanese War Ministry gave orders for the dissemination.

2. No indication was given on how malaria would be spread as above named method of dissemination is not believed possible.

RICHARD H. AGNEW
Lt. Colonel, GSC
Exec. to AC of S, G-2.

MIS 142911
(SCI Br)

*Sci-5
Route
Lib
CWS/Sci-2
Med/Sci-1
OSW/SCI-1
NDD/SCI-1
OSS/SCI-1
OSRD/Sci-1
ETOUSA/SCI-3

S E C R E T

142911-1

3.61　19 Apr. 1945: JICAN/CT Br. Kunming, China, CENTRAL CHINA (OCCUPIED) -Bacteriological Warfare Breeding of Viri., 7109 James R. Geddes , Maj., C. W. S

资料出处： National Archives of the United States, R112, E295A, B11.

内容点评： 本资料为 1945 年 4 月 19 日美军化学战部队少校 James R. Geddes 发自昆明的报告，内容有关细菌战。

SECRET

~~SECRET~~ JICA/CT

JICA SN R-416-CH-45

From JICA/CT Br. at Kunming, China Date 19 April, 1945

Reference JICA/CT R-237-CH-45, R-404-CH-45, R-415-CH-45.
(For identification with previous reports)

Source OSS Radio of 17 April 1945 Evaluation As noted.
(A-1 to F-0 etc.)

BID #0402.0000

Subject CENTRAL CHINA (OCCUPIED) - Bacteriological Warfare, Breeding of Viri.
(Nation reported on) (Main title as per index guide)
(Subtitles) (Make separate report for each title)

Brief.—(Here enter careful summary of report, containing substance succinctly stated; include important facts, names, places, dates, etc.)

Transmitted herewith is a report that there is a Japanese laboratory in SHANG HAI which is reported to be breeding cholera, typhoid and plague bacteria.

A Japanese hospital near the city of CHIA HSING (Kashing) (嘉 兴) (E12045, N3046) is reported to be making "death dealing" poison fluid for use in streams and lakes.

The head of the CWS mission in China gives his opinion that the activity is incorrectly reported and improbable.

7109 JAMES R. GEDDES,
Major, C.W.S.

Approved and forwarded:

CARL S. GRAYBEAL,
Colonel, G.S.C.,
Chief, JICA/CIB/SEA.

NOTE: This document contains information affecting the national defense of the United States within the meaning of the Espionage Act, 50 U.S.C., 31 and 32, as amended. Its transmission or the revelation of its contents in any manner to an unauthorized person is prohibited by law. It may not be reproduced in whole or in part, by other than War Department agencies, except by permission of A. C. of S., G-2, W.D.G.S.

Distribution by Originator: JIABC; [redacted]; G-2, CT, APO 879 (2); OC, CWS; Cml. Of., 14th A.F., APO 627; Cml. Of., A.S.C., APO 671; Cml. Of., IBT, APO 885; File. ~~SECRET~~
(Space above this line to be filled in by JICA)

JICA SN

Army

Navy

AAF

OSS

FEA

OWI

MIS 150237 (Sci Lr)
*Sci-4
Route
Lib
CWS/SCI-2
~~MED/SCI-1~~
CSW/SCI-1
ONI/SCI-3
OSS/SCI-1
OSRD/SCI-1

Encls to all cop:

JICA-1

SECRET

Bacteriological Warfare **SECRET**

Evaluation: B-3 by Source.

A recheck of the information given in JICA/CT R-237-CH-45 by another source states that a branch laboratory of the CENTRAL CHINA CHEMICAL ASSOCIATION (Universal Sympathy Society) is located near Hongkew Park in the city of SHANG HAI (上 海) (E12130, N3114), Kiangsu Province and that the branch laboratory is breeding cholera, typhoid and plague bacteria.

Evaluation: C-3 by Source.

Source states that Japanese hospital outside the East gate of the city of CHIA HSING (Kashing) (嘉 興) (E12045, N3046) at a place called KAO CHIA AN is making "death dealing" poison fluid for use in streams and lakes. Further information on the subject is being requested.

COMMENT BY THE HEAD OF THE C.S MISSION

Immunization against cholera and typhoid of Japanese troops and the civilian population in much of Japanese Occupied China is well known to be a routine procedure. (From a study of immunization certificates (R-404-CH-45), and interrogation of refugees and Japanese prisoners of war.) Recently the Japanese have begun immunization of their troops against plague as a protective measure, because they have encountered plague in the civilian population of occupied Chinese towns. (Reference: JICA/CT R-415-CH- of 18 April 1945.)

Large amounts of vaccine would be required to accomplish these immunizations. It is believed to be more likely that the facilities of the Hongkew Park laboratory are devoted to the preparation of such vaccines rather than that they are being employed for offensive bacteriological warfare. The opinion has previously been expressed by this officer that cholera and typhoid bacteria are not suitable BW agents, and could be employed only by sabotage methods. (Reference: Comments to JICA/CT R-237-CH-45.)

No opinion can be expressed regarding the "death dealing poison fluid for use in streams and lakes", said to be prepared at KAO CHIA AN, for the lack of specific information at this time. However, there are heat stable drugs and chemicals more suitable for such purpose than living bacteria (eg., diisopropyl fluorophosphate, sodium fluoroacetate, tris-beta-chloroetyhlaminehydrochloride, etc.).

BW INFORMATION

COMMITTEE COMMENT:

We concurr in the above comment.

From: JICA/CT Dr., Kunming, China.　　R-416-CH-45　　19 April 1945

JRG/wk　　Page 2.

SECRET

3.62　21 Apr. 45: HEADQUARTERS US FORCES CHINA THEATRE OFFICE OF STRATEGIC SERVICES, FROM: HELLIWELL, TO: 154, BIRD AND DICKEY, TOLEDO

资料出处： National Archives of the United States, R112, E295A, B11.

内容点评： 本资料为美军中国战区司令部战略情报局 Helliwell 1945 年 4 月 21 日情报报告。参见 3.61，1945 年 4 月 19 日化学战部队少校 James R. Geddes 的报告。

HEADQUARTERS
US FORCES CHINA THEATRE
OFFICE OF STRATEGIC SERVICES
A P O 879.

~~SECRET CONTROL~~

FROM: HELLIWELL DATE: 21 APR 45

TO : 154, BIRD AND DICKEY TOLEDO

PARN YOKE YOKE ZERO ZERO SIX ZERO DISTRIBUTION ONE TWO PARN REFERENCE OUR 215 OF THREE MARCH AND OUR 985 OF FIVE APRIL. RECHECK THRU ANOTHER SOURCE ON LABORATORY LOCATED NEAR HONGKEW PART (Park) IN SHANGHAI IDENTIFIES LABORATORY AS BRANCH LABORATORY OF CENTRAL CHINA CHEMICAL ASSOCIATION PARN ANOTHER NAME BEING UNIVERSAL SYMPATHY SOCIETY PARN BREEDING CHOLERA TYPHOID AND PLAGUE BACTERIA. SOURCE MICHIGAN SUBSOURCE START BAKER THREE. SOURCE MICHIGAN SUBSOURCE EVART RATED CHARLIE THREE STATES JAP HOSPITAL OUTSIDE EAST GATE KASHING CITY (30-47, 120-45) AT PLACE CALLED KOA CHIA WAN RPT KOA CHIA WAN CLAIMS JAPS ARE MAKING DEATH DEALING POISON FLUID FOR USE IN STREAMS AND LAKES. ON THE LATTER WE ARE ASKING FURTHER INFO.

3.63　1 May 1945: Summary, Laboratories, Toledo

资料出处：National Archives of the United States, R112, E295A, B11.

内容点评：本资料为 1945 年 5 月 1 日美军情报中心情报汇编：日本细菌战实验机构与有关人员。

page 1

Toledo

Laboratories Summary, May 1, 1945

Shinkyo (Hsinking) - Reference TO-299 of Mar. 27, 1945.

(A) Army Hospital - about ½ mile east of RR on N. side Koan Highway.

(B) Army Hospital - for contagious diseases - about 7/8 mile E of RR. on S. side of Koan Highway. (3/8 mile E. of (A)).

(C) Medical Lab. - Research lab. - joint enterprise of Manch. Gov't & Shinkyo Univ. - about 3 3/8 miles E of RR. on S. side of Koan Highway. (2½ miles E. of (B)).

(D) Army Medical Officers School - Orientation courses given for Medical Officers.

(E) Hygiene & Water Purification Department (Boekikyusui Bu) Under Maj.-Gen. Ishii, Shiro - All experimental results coordinated here.

Harbin - Reference TO-299 of Mar., 1945

(F) Bacteriological Experimental Center (Saikin Kenkyu Sho)
Under Maj. Gen. Ishii, Shiro
Secret experiments - findings never published for general assimilation - no civilian personnel.

(G) Hygiene & Water Purification Dep't (Boekikyusui Bu).
One of main H.&W.P.D. of Kwantung Army.
Collects & evaluates results of Biological experiments.
Close liason with (F) & might even be same as (F).

page 2
Toledo

Laboratories, cont'd Summary, May 1, 1945

Tokyo - Reference TO-299 of Mar, 1945

(H) Large medical research lab. (Name unknown)
Located at Shirokane-Cho, Shiba-Ku
Joint enterprise of Jap. Govt & Imperial University
Probably supervises manufacture of serums & vaccines in Tokyo district

(J) Technical Center ? (Gijutsu Sho)
Exact location unknown.
Possibly engaged in biological experiments.

Osaka - Reference - Cable, Jan 31, 1944 to Washington.

(K) Osaka Chemical Research Institute.
Making Typhoid & Black Plague germs.
on Dec 15, 1944 made first shipment to Shanghai (sent by plane).

Shanghai Reference letter Mar. 3, 1945, LtCol H to AGFRTS

(L) Shanghai Natural Science Committee
Formerly located between Hongkew Park & 3068-3494 Road near 1131-6639-1653 station
May have offices on western part of Route Joseph Frelupt.
Suspected of preparing BW

Page 3
Toledo

Laboratories, contd Summary, May 5, 1945

(L) cont'd Reference Cable Apr. 21, 1945 To Washington.

(L) now identified as branch lab. of Central China Chemical Association (or Universal Sympathy Society)

Breeding cholera, typhoid + plague bacteria. (B-3)

(M) Japanese Hospital – near Shanghai

located outside east gate Kashing City (30-47, 120-45)

at place called Koa Chia Wan

"making poison fluid for use in streams + wells" (C-3)

Page 1
Toledo

Personalities

Reference TO-299 of Mar., 1945

Maj. Gen Ishii, Shiro

Organizer of Hygiene + Water Purification Dept CG Bacteriological Experimental Center and of the H.&W. P. Dept, Kwantung Army, 1943

Decorated for development of water purification machine.

Lt. Gen. Kambayashi

CG Jap. Army Medical Corps, 1943

Lt. Gen Karizuka (Kajizuka)

CG Jap. Army Medical Corps, Kwantung Army, 1943

3.64 8 May 1945: JICA SN R-489-CH-45, BID #0812-0402: CWS INTELLIGENCE MISSION IN CHINA-STATUS REPORT NO. 2. 1 MAY 1945

资料出处： National Archives of the United States, R112, E295A, B11.

内容点评： 本资料为 1945 年 5 月 8 日美国化学战部队中国调查团的情况报告第 2 号（1945 年 5 月 1 日），为缅甸曼德勒缴获日军防疫服检验报告。

26 MAY 1945

SECRET JICA/CHINA

JICA SN B-489-CH-45 BID #0812 - - 0402

From JICA/CHINA at Kunming, China Date 8 May 1945

Reference

(For identification with previous reports)

Source Personal observation and conferences with Chinese General Officers, US Army officers, and missionaries. Evaluation C-3 (A-1 to F-0 etc.)

Subject CWS INTELLIGENCE MISSION IN CHINA - STATUS REPORT NO. 2, 1 MAY 1945.

(Nation reported on) (Subtitles) (Main title as per Index guide) (Make separate report for each title)

Brief—(Here enter careful summary of report, containing substance succinctly stated; include important facts, names, places, dates, etc.)

1. The four field teams of the mission departed Kunming on 9 February by motor vehicle and arrived at their field bases as follows:
   - Team 2 arrived Poseh, Kwangsi, 18 February 1945
   - Team 3 arrived Hsian, Shensi, 10 March 1945.
   - Team 4 arrived Lao-ho-k'ou, Hupeh, 11 March 1945.
   - Team 5 arrived Chih-chiang, Hunan, 25 February 1945.

2. Between 9 February and 9 March, Team 1 toured the Kwangsi front, as far as Tien-tung (also called P'ing-ma); the Hunan front, as far as Sha-wan; and visited the CCC Central Command at Kweiyang, Kweichow. Conferences were held with responsible American and Chinese Commanders and with a few missionaries, in these areas and at points enroute.

3. Satisfactory arrangements have been completed for effective operations of Teams 2 and 5 in their respective areas.

4. No U.S. Army officer interviewed had ever witnessed Japanese employment of war gases, or seen a Chinese gas casualty.

5. Most of the Chinese Commanders had received reports from subordinates of Japanese use of gas, chiefly tear and sneeze (vomiting) gas, but few had made any first-hand observations.

6. No one interviewed had ever witnessed Japanese attempts to employ BW, and only two had ever heard of such an attempt.

Forwarded:

HAROLD E. PRIDE,
Colonel, C.A.C.,
Chief, JICA/CHINA.

JOHN R. WOOD, O-17821,
Colonel, Medical Corps,
Commanding CWS Mission.

NOTE: This document contains information affecting the national defense of the United States within the meaning of the Espionage Act, 50 U.S.C., 31 and 32, as amended. Its transmission or the revelation of its contents in any manner to an unauthorized person is prohibited. It may not be reproduced in whole or in part, by other than War Dep't Agencies, except by permission of the A.C. of S., G-2, W.D.G.S.

Distribution by Originator: JIARO;OC, CWS; G-2, CT (2); Cml O, CT; G-2, CCC; File

(Space above this line to be filled in by JICA)

JICA SN

Army

Navy

AAF

OSS

FEA

MIS 157184
Mil-2
*Sci-2
Route
Lib
HQAAF-2
CWS-2
Med-1
ONI-3
OSS-2

JICA-1

SECRET

SECRET

REAR ECHELON
HEADQUARTERS CHINA THEATER
APO 627, c/o POSTMASTER, NEW YORK, N. Y.

NOTE: This document contains information affecting the national defense of the United States within the meaning of the Espionage Act, 50 U. S. C., 31 and 32, as amended. Its transmission or the revelation of its contents in any manner to an unauthorized person is prohibited by law. It may not be reproduced in whole or in part, by other than War Dep't Agencies, except by permission of the A C of S, G-2, W. D. G. S.

OSS INTELLIGENCE MISSION IN CHINA
STATUS REPORT NO. 2
1 May 1945

COPY NO. 1

0 MAY 1945

SECRET SECRET JICA China

JICA SN B-538-CH-45

From JICA/CHINA at Kunming. Date 8 May, 1945

Reference None

(For identification with previous reports)

Source U.S. Army Officer with CWS Mission Evaluation A-2.

(A-1 to F-O etc.)

BID/D503.0800

Subject JAPAN - Examination of Captured Japanese "Anti-Disease Suit"

(Nation reported on) (Subtitles) (Main title as per index guide) (Make separate report for each title)

Brief.—(Here enter careful summary of report, containing substance succinctly stated; include important facts, names, places, dates, etc.)

The officer was called to the EBIS/CWS office in Chabua, Assam on 17 April 1945 to participate in an investigation of captured Japanese equipment suspected of being BW material. The captured equipment found at Fort Dufferin, Mandalay consisted principally of (1) "anti-disease suit", found in a (2)"Water Purification Chest, #67" with many miscellaneous items - smocks, gloves, canvas bag, filters, apron, carrying bag, cellophane and tissue paper, manual on autopsy procedure, liquid pump, gauze, box of ampoules, etc.

The impermeable "anti-disease suit" made of light weight, rubberized silk, is of the coverall type with zipper front and neck draw strings. Boots and hood of the same material, and heavy rubber gloves complete the suit. The suit gives complete coverage of the body with freedom of movement, but the impermeability of the material limits the wearing of the suit for more than a few minutes. The lightness of the material prevents wearing the suit for rough work or out of doors. Tests indicate the suit is not satisfactory as a protective garment against chemical warfare vesicant agents.

It is the opinion of the investigating officer that the "anti-disease suit" does not afford any specific evidence of enemy intentions with regard to offensive use of BW.

7109 JAMES R. GEDDES,
Major, C.W.S.

Approved and forwarded:

HAROLD E. PRIDE,
Colonel, C.A.C.,
Chief, JICA/China.

Exec — Prof —
JSS — Med —
SBJ — NP —
ESF — Surg —
Gen — Econ —

Distribution by Originator: JICRC; G-2, CT, APO 879 (2); OC, CWS; CWS Mission, China; EBIS/CWS, IBT, APO 629; Theа. Surg., IBT, via Chem. Of., IBT, APO 885; File.

(Space above this line to be filled in by JICA) SECRET

JICA SN Ind Cont MIS-159221 Incls
Army Nutr Stat. Econ-2 Econ-1
Navy Civ Route Route
AAF M & P M & P
OSS Lib Lib
FEA HQAAF-1 HQAAF-1
OWL CWS-2 Med-2
Med-2 ONI-1
ONI-3

Initials and Return to Intelligence
NOT to next office checked

JICA-1

SECRET

SECRET

ABSTRACT

A. Summary

Pursuant to paragraph 12, SO 106, Rear Echelon Headquarters, USF/CT, the undersigned proceeded from Kunming, China to Chabua, India on 17 April 1945 for the purpose of participating in a special investigation of a captured Japanese rubberized silk (anti-disease) suit. The investigation was conducted at the EEIS Laboratories in Chabua, India in conjunction with Major J.F. Danser, Colonel Karl Lundeberg and Major M.S. Schott. The material which had been captured at Fort Duffern, Mandalay, Burma on 20 March 1945 and forwarded to Chabua, India by EEIS field teams included such articles as metal petri dishes, a folding microscope and a Water Purification Unit chest and vaccines.

B. Conclusions

As a result of this examination the following pertinent facts are evident.

a) The rubberized silk garment is designed to give unusually complete protection to an individual working with highly infectious material. (eg., in performing autopsies on plague victims).

b) The suit would not prevent the inhalation of bacteria suspended in the air but would give unusually complete protection to the body surfaces.

c) The suit is not designed for protection against war gases.

d) The impermeability of the suit makes its wearing for long periods of time or at high work rates impractical, especially in the tropical environment in which it was captured.

e) The material of which the suit is made is not durable enough to permit it to be used for rough work.

f) Neither the suit nor any of the items studied lend any evidence that they were designed primarily for BW purposes.

g) The suit is issued to "Water Purification Units".

h) Water Purification Units are charged with the control of outbreaks of epidemic diseases such as plague and on one occasion are reported to have examined ampoules said to have contained cholera germs and suspected of being a BW episode initiated by the Allies in Burma.

C. Recommendations

a) It is recommended that the items, with this report be forwarded to CG, C.W.S, Washington, D.C.

b) It is further recommended that the source from which this material was obtained be further explored by a competent officer in an effort to gain more complete information and that every effort be made to collect information in regard to T.O.'s, T.E.'s and activities of Japanese Water Purification Units.

INTRODUCTION

Pursuant to paragraph 12, SO 106, Rear Echelon Headquarters, USF/CT, dated 17 April 1945 the undersigned proceeded by air on 17 April 1945 from Kunming, Yunnan, China to Chabua, India for the purpose of participating in a special investigation of a rubberized protective garment, petri dishes and container, microscope, field chest and vaccines.

After arriving at Chabua at 0030 hours on 18 April 1945 the undersigned contacted at 0830 hours Major James R. Danser, S.-C., Chief of Laboratory, EEIS, Colonel Karl Lundeberg, M.C., Chief, Preventive Medicine Division, Office of the Surgeon, IBT, and Major M.S. Schott, C.W.S., Executive Officer, Office of the Theater Chemical Officer, IBT. These Officers had conducted an examination of the above mentioned equipment from 14 April to 17 April 1945. The material was discussed with Colonel Lundeberg and Major Schott who requested this officer to make an independent examination of the equipment.

From: JICA/CHINA, Kunming, R-538-CH-45 8 May 1945

JRG/wk SECRET Page 2.

SECRET

During the examination conducted on 18 and 19 April 1945 further contacts were made with Major J.P. Conlan, Commanding Officer, 45th Chemical Laboratory and Major J.L. Arbogast, MC, Assistant Chief, 9th General Medical Laboratory. During the examination all of the items were carefully examined and a detailed description of the pertinent items was written.

CIRCUMSTANCES SURROUNDING CAPTURE OF ITEMS AND EXAMINATION

The items under examination were captured when Fort Dufferin, Mandalay fell on 20 March 1945. The items were found inside the fort in conjunction with stores of medical and laboratory supplies by representatives of SEIS. Before the arrival of the SEIS representatives, the British had gone through the captured equipment extracting instruments and equipment of various types. Because of this fact the contents of the chest containing one of five listed anti-disease suits are probably not the items originally packed in the chest. The Petri Dish container with Petri Dishes was found in the same storeroom with the chest containing the anti-disease suit but this Petri Dish container was not in the chest. No cultures of any type were found inside the storeroom or the fort itself. The only culture media found in this storeroom were tubes and tablets used in the preparation of Endo Media. Also found in this storeroom but not in conjunction with the chest were bottles of various types of vaccines.

The anti-disease suit in its carrying case was found in the chest in conjunction with many miscellaneous items. A small book was found in this chest whose title translation is "Direction Book for Pathological Anatomy". This is a brief manual with descriptions and illustrations of autopsy procedures. It contained directions for the autopsy surgeons working with bodies that had died from infectious diseases and specified that the person performing the autopsy should wear a hood, mouth piece, eye shield and rubber boots.

In a radiogram to Director of Intelligence ASF on 31 March 1945, Major Danser described "One protective rubber suit consisting of hood with large rectangular window, a light rubber silk lined suit, rubber shoes and leg covers, rubber gloves, found in Surgical Kit". On 9 April Major Danser received a letter from Lt. Colonel Leeds, Director of [illegible], subject "Japanese Biological Warfare". Lt. Colonel Leeds requested all offices to familiarize themselves with the WD letter and also requested Major Danser to re-examine the garments previously mentioned to determine whether they could be used in BW, and advised Major Danser to inform in case the suspicions were aroused.

Major Danser and Major Arbogast re-examined the light weight rubberized silk suit and on 10 April sent a radio to G-2, Delhi giving more complete descriptions of the suit and an opinion that the suit was designed primarily for work with viruses or bacilla. The radio further stated that the hood contained a multiple flap apparently designed to hold a pad saturated chemically or medically to prevent wearer from becoming contaminated with the agent. The radio further contained information about 400 aluminum Petri Dishes apparently designed for the field growth of cultures, microscope, books, phamplets on mosquitoes, other pests and viruses. No mention of any cultures was made in this radio.

On 14 April 1945 Colonel K.R. Lundeberg, MC and Major Schott from Delhi arrived at the SEIS Laboratories, APO 629 to conduct a special examination of the above mentioned equipment. Samples of the rubberized silk suit were submitted to the 45th Chemical Laboratory for examination. This Laboratory reported, "It is concluded that this clothing was not designed primarily to offer protection against any of the CW vesicants".

As a result of the examination by Col. Lundeberg and Major Schott, the following conclusions were listed in their report.

1. This suit is an item which would give unusually complete protection against particulate matter in the presence of infectious agents.

2. It would be of no value as a protection against war gases. This was demostrated in penetration tests by the 45th Chemical Laboratory.

3. This suit would be very useful for autopsy purposes dealing with virulent and infectious diseases and tissues but appears to be more elaborate than ordinary autopsy work requires.

From: JICA/CHINA, Kunming. R-538-CH-45 8 May 1945

JRG/wk SECRET Page 3.

SECRET

SECRET

4. Due to its impermeability, this suit could not be worn for a great length of time in high temperatures.
5. This suit is too fragile to be used for rough work.
6. Neither the suit or any other items examined have any significance that would that would indicate offensive intentions on the part of the enemy.
7. There is no specific indication that any of the items listed in "Contents of Chest as Found" (page 4 of this report) were intended primarily for B. purposes.

DESCRIPTION OF THE CHEST

"Water Purification Section, Doctors, 67 7/10, Decontamination Section".

The heavy chest, constructed of wood, reinforced with painted sheet metal has red crosses on both sides and on the back. The top, front and back of the chest are further reinforced by strips of wood. Cloth covered, rope carrying handles are attached to either end of the chest and two leather straps with buckles wrap around the chest. Outside dimensions of the chest are 28 3/4" long by 14" wide by 16" high. A latch for a padlock is located at the center of the top and upper center of the front side of the chest. The top is attached to the chest by two metal hinges. Inside the top of the chest is a pocket with two leather straps and buckles 15" long and 6" wide constructed from white canvas. Otherwise the lining of the chest is smooth, brown painted wood. A white card, 7¼" by 10" with Japanese characters printed with black ink is attached by means of four brads to the right inside top of the lid. The characters have been translated, "Water Purification Chest No. 67". Chest contents: leather strap (small 2); long rubber boots, 5 pairs; anti-disease clothing, 5 sets (literal; against disease clothing, tools).

On the top of the lid in bold Japanese characters is an inscription in black paint translation of which reads: "Water Purification Section Doctors 67 7/10 Decontamination Section".

CONTENTS OF CHEST AS FOUND

1. One double breasted, heavy green, cotton smock type coat with taped sleeves. This coat is similar to a laboratory coat.
2. One white flannel smock having the appearance of a bed jacket. Translation of characters on smock: "Use outside of homeland, small size".
3. One white rubber apron with large bib reaching to neck. This is made of heavy rubber and is probably an autopsy apron. Translation of characters on apron; "rubber apron, physicians use".
4. One collapsable bucket, canvas. Translation of characters on bucket: "canvas water bag, inspected, manufactured 1940".
5. One white cotton smock, physicians. No markings; appears to be an operating gown.
6. One pocket filter. Porcelain, probably for water purification and similar to our diatomaceous earth items. Translation of characters on filter: "Pocket filter made in KYOTO".
7. One metal, candle type filter. Translation of characters on filter: "NGK - portable filter instrument, Model FA 27, Japan, Special Porcelain Manufacturing Company, NAGOYA".
8. One long handled (20") surgical tool which could be used as a crushing instrument and somewhat resembles a gut clamp. Use unknown.
9. One heavy metal mallet. Seems to be a part of the item listed above.
10. One pair cotton khaki work gloves.
11. One large linen sheet of coarse unbleached linen.
12. One large khaki canvas carrying bag with leather straps designed to be worn on the back. On the back of the top covering flap is a red cross with white background. This covers two large side pockets. It was in one of these pockets that the one rubberized silk suit was found. A check of the fit of the anti-disease suit and its carrying case in the canvas carrying bag by Major Danser leads him to believe that no more than two anti-disease suits could be place in the bag.

From: JICA/CHINA, Kunming. R-538-CH-45 8 May 1945

JRG/wk  Page 4.

SECRET

SECRET

The large carrying bag (photo #1) is constructed of different material and its mode of design is totally different from the carrying case for the suit. The undersigned is of the opinion that this large carrying bag was not designed to carry the anti-disease suit and the findings of the suit in the bag was coincidental.

On the back of the bag are two small pockets with flaps covering thin tops which are held in place with buckles and leather straps. Stamped on the inside of these two flaps are Japanese characters. Translation of characters on flap: "1941 inspected". Characters on left pocket flap: "Tincture of iodine, 200 gms., Methyl alcohol, 100 gms., Alcohol, 500 gms." Characters on right pocket flap: "Long pinches (forceps) puller 1; flashlight 2; thermometer 2; knife 1; screw tourniquet 2; detention tourniquet 2; rubber gloves 1 pr; scissors for various uses 1 pr; sterilization kit for hand 1; pinches 1; none of these items were found except for one pair of scissors.

13. One heavy leather apron; appears to be a horse shoeing apron. Translation of characters: "Inspected May 1938, Medical Supply Depot".

14. Map of Bengal in Japanese.

15. One piece of heavy brown oiled paper.

16. One large package of celophane or pliofilm. 40 to 50 sheets about one yard square and 1/1000" thickness.

17. One large package of heavy, glazed, tough tissue paper.

18. One piece rubber tubing (black), about 6 feet long. This is of good grade black rubber and is 3/8" in diameter.

19. One gasoline burner.

20. One sheet of trigometric drawings. Appears to be students sheet of mathematical problems.

21. One pair of scissors.

22. One cloth bag with metal parts.

23. One white cotton smock (ward type doctor's jacket). Translation of characters on smock: "Fatigue smock (small) Model 40, made 1943, white".

24. One manual on autopsy procedure. Translation of characters on cover: "Direction Book for Pathological Anatomy, Army Medical Corps, printed 20 November 1933, issued 25 November 1933".

25. Two rubber hoses in a cloth bag. Translation of characters on cloth bag: "Two syphons, enema instruments, Takimato manufactured".

26. One metal pump. Translation of characters on pump: "Instrument for pumping liquid medical compounds".

27. One package gauze. Translation of characters on package: "Sterilized gauze, 55 gms., made January 1942, Army Sanitary Supply Main Depot".

28. One package of gauze. Translation of characters on package: "Package gauze, made August 1943".

29. One package of absorbent cotton. Translation of characters on package: "Package Absorbent Cotton, 100 gms., made August 1941".

30. One box vials containing four ampoules of what may be a calcium preparation. Translation of characters on box: "Inspect solution for soft, weak bone symptoms. Contents: a sol 5, Central China Field Material Depot. Veterinary Material Depot".

31. One "anti-disease suit".

The above listed items are obviously not the intended contents of the chest. It is the opinion of this officer that 5 sets of the "anti-disease suit" and 5 pairs of rubber boots would fill the chest and make a compact chest.

DESCRIPTION OF ANTI-DISEASE SUIT

The captured Japanese dark gray, pliable, light weight, rubberized silk impermeable suit consisting of two boots, coverall type garment with zipper front with neck draw strings and a pair of heavy type rubber gloves, which comes packed in a heavy canvas carrying case. The suit, which shows no evidence of previous use, has been termed from translations of Japanese characters on the chest in which it was found, "Anti-disease Suit". There are no markings or characters on any part of the garment or on its carrying case.

From: JICA/CHINA, Kunming. R-538-CH-45 8 May 1945

JRG/wk SECRET Page 5.

SECRET

SECRET

Carrying case (photo 2) - Single layer, heavy khaki canvas with canvas carrying handle attached to folding top by means of metal rings, brads and metal ring holders. The top is reinforced with a piece of soft metal sewn into top between two pieces of canvas. This soft thin metal reinforcement measures 1" wide by 9½" long and to it the carrying handle, metal rings and ring holders are attached by means of four metal brads. The top is fastened to the front side of the case by means of two leather straps and buckles which are sewn to the case. The margins of the folding top are rimmed with leather khaki cloth to prevent raveling. The case measures 14" by 7½" by 4".

Gloves - The pair of rubber gloves are made of heavy weight rubber of a good grade. They are grayish brown in color and the size corresponds approximately to the U.S. standard size 6. These gloves are comparable to gloves, post mortem, rubber, issued by the U.S. Army Medical Department (photo #3).

Boots - The boots are of a light weight rubberized silk and measure 20" long and 8" wide (flat surface). The seams, sewn in the front and back, are sealed by a second layer of rubberized silk 5/8" wide which is cemented over the inner side of the seam by means of rubber cement. The sole of the boot is of the same light weight, pliable rubberized silk and is sewn to the margins of the leggin position of the boot. Peculiarly this seam is not reinforced with a second layer of silk. Sewn to the top of the back side of each boot is a cloth "tie string". This tie string is 3/8" wide and 50" long. (photo #3).

Hood - The hood, constructed of the same thin, pliable, rubberized silk material, is constructed to completely cover the head, neck and shoulders. Sewn to the front of the neck margin is a cloth tie string 3/8" wide and 60" long. The hood is constructed from five pieces of rubberized silk which serves as front, back, two sides, and shoulder sections. The margins of the section are folded under and seamed together by means of single stitch seam made with silk thread. All seams are sealed with a 5/8" wide strip of rubberized silk glued to the inner side by means of rubber cement.

Adequate vision is provided for by means of a pliable, transparent plastic strip 4½" by 3¼". This is sewn into the opening in the front face piece of the hood, by means of a double stitch through a two layer folded strip or rubberized silk around the outer margin of the visor, the plastic visor and the margin of the visor opening of the hood. The seam is sealed by means of a 5/8" wide strip of rubberized silk glued to the inner side by means of a rubberized cement.

Air outlets and inlets for breathing are provided for by means of six (6) metal rimmed round openings 3/8" in diameter. The metal openings stamped in as brads, are arranged in upper and lower rows of three each in the fashion demonstrated below.

0 0 0
0 0 0

These openings are covered by a loose flap of four layers of rubberized silk 5¼" wide by 3" long. The upper margin to this flap hangs from and is sewn to the lower margin of the plastic visor. The lower margin of the flap may be snapped over the six openings by means of two metal snaps at either corner, thus leaving the lower and side margins between the flap and the hood open. The flap itself is constructed of two double layers of rubberized silk. The margins of each double layer are sewn separately. In the inner layer are placed twelve round openings arranged in two rows of six openings each. The openings, which measure ¼" in diameter are rimmed with metal brads. The outer layer is without openings and the two lower corners of each layer are secured together by means of the female position of the metal snaps, leaving the two sides and the lower margins of the flap open.

The shoulder section of the hood is 10" wide allowing it to fit well over the shoulders, chest and back. When the neck tie string is secured the action of breathing causes the hood to balloon out on expiration and collapse on inspiration. (Photos #4, #5 and #6).

Suit - The suit is of a "coverall" type made from a single layer of rubberized silk with an inner flap behind a zipper closure of the entire front of the garment. This flap of two layers of rubberized silk is 5½" wide and is secured by a snap at the top over the left shoulder and at the mid position by a snap attached to a small "wrap around" strap 7½" long. The entire right margin of the flap is sewn to the front of

From: JICA/CHINA, Kunming. R-538-CH-45 8 May 1945

JRG/wk SECRET

SECRET

SECRET

the garment. There are snaps at both wrist openings, above which the sleeve is open for 5". There is a waist belt of two layers of rubberized silk 1 3/8" wide which is sewn to the back of the garment and may be secured in front by means of a buckle and metal brad eyelets in the belt. The leg openings are secured by a tie string 25½" long. At the neck the collar, ~~is~~ constructed of a 4" wide double layer of rubberized silk, is fastened in front by means of a metal hook and eyelet. All seams are single stiched and are sealed by a second layer of rubberized silk 5/8" wide which is cemented over the inner side of the seams by means of a rubber cement. (Photos #7, man with suit, #8, #9 and #10).

DISCUSSION

The suit is designed to give unusually complete coverage to the entire body in the presence of virulent infectious agents. It is well constructed and every effort has been made to seal up all openings except those for breathing. The pliability of the materials renders the wearer remarkable freedom of movement; however, the heavy gloves would make delicate work with the hands rather difficult. This type of glove is used by some western pathologists in the performance of autopsies.

The impermeability of the material and the sealing of all openings including the stitching makes any prolonged wearing of the garment impractical. The fact that the saturated warm air of expiration causes the hood to balloon out, thus exposing the head and upper portion of the neck of the wearer to this saturated warm air, makes the hood uncomfortable to wear and markedly shortens the time during which the garment may be worn. Considerable discomfort and sweating is caused by wearing the hood under resting conditions for a period of as short as ten minutes in a warm climate. The lightness in weight and durability of the material would seem to make rough or out of door wearing of the garment impractical.

The flap over the breathing openings below the visor has been the subject of considerable discussion; however, it does not seem likely that it would be practical to place any type of filter or filter material in or over this flap. There is no means by which any type of gas mask could be worn by the wearer. Particulate matter such as bacteria suspended in the air, could freely pass through the breathing openings in the hood and be inhaled in the act of respiration. Any type of surgeon's mask or cloth filters even if placed in or over the flap would only partially eliminate the inhalation of particulate matter suspended in the air. This statement is based on classified experimental work conducted by this officer.

It seems probable that this garment has been designed to be worn by individuals conducting autopsies on men and/or on animals which have died from a highly virulent infectious disease such as plague. The garment would give excellent protection against splattered blood. It is of interest to note that plague has been prevalent in the area from which this garment was captured. The garment is issued to Water Purification Units.

It is the opinion of this officer that the garment does not afford any specific evidence of enemy intentions about the offensive use of B.W. The suit is not satisfactory for use as a protective garment against chemical warfare vesicant agents as indicated by tests made by the 45th Chemical Laboratory.

A copy of the 45th Chemical Laboratory Company letter (copied from Major Danser's file) regarding the testing of the anti-disease suit.

45th Chemical Laboratory Company
Intermediate General Depot No. 2
S.O.S.

AC/evr
APO 629
17 April 1945

SUBJECT: C.W. Protection of Japanese Clothing

TO : Commanding Officer, CWLB, CWRF, IBT, APO 629.

1. Samples of light weight Japanese rubberized clothing consisting of full length

From: JICA/CHINA, Kunming. R-538-CH-45 8 May 1945

JRG/wk SECRET Page 7.

SECRET

SECRET

suit, leggings, hood, and rubber gloves were delivered to this unit 14 April 1945 for test to determine its protective value against vesicant agents.

2. Tests against mustard, lewisite and nitrogen mustard (HN-2) were conducted in the static Diffusion Box for Impermeable materials at a temperature of 30°C./1°, with agents of greater than 95% purity. The results are summarized below:

CLOTHING	AGENTS		
	H	L	HN-2
suit	2 minutes	45 seconds	5 minutes
gloves	31 minutes	42 minutes	30 minutes

3. Protective value of the clothing against any of the agents is considered negligible, since comparable material of U.S. manufacture offers a minimum protection of 60 minutes when designated for vesicant protection. The protective value of the gloves is adequate for use against vesicants and compares favorably with light weight gloves of U.S. manufacture designed for this purpose.

4. It is concluded that this clothing was not designed primarily to offer protection against any of the CW vesicants.

s/ William F. Conlan
WILLIAM F. CONLAN,
Major, C.W.S.,
Commanding.

Particular attention is drawn to the statement in paragraph 4 of the above letter.

JOHN . ADAMS, JR.,
Major, C.C.,
CWS Team #2.

From: JICA/CHINA, Kunming. R-538-CH-45 8 May 1945

JRG/wk SECRET Page 8.

SECRET

159221 I

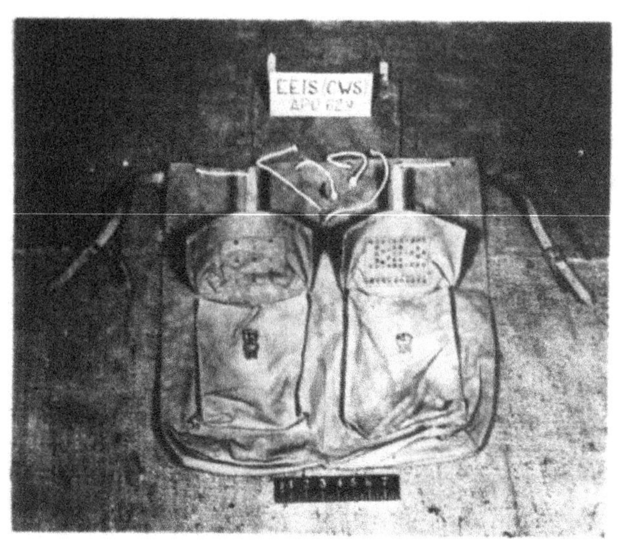

159221 2

159221 3

159221 4

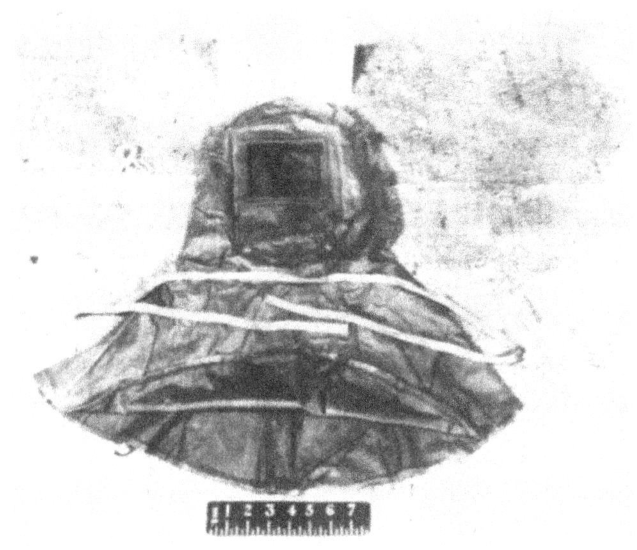

159221 5

159221 6

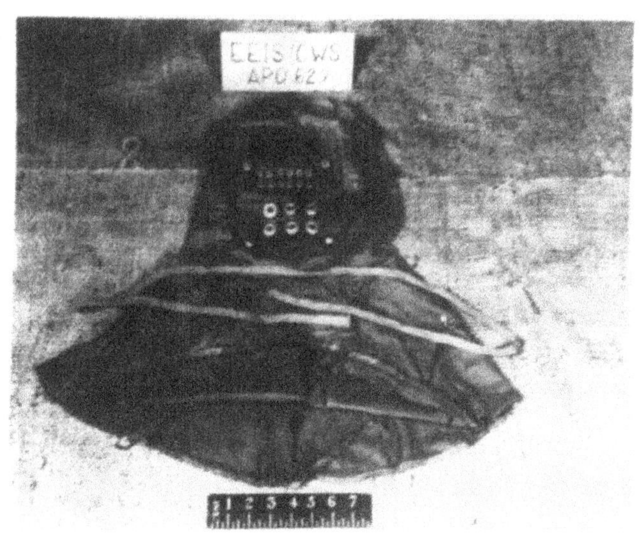

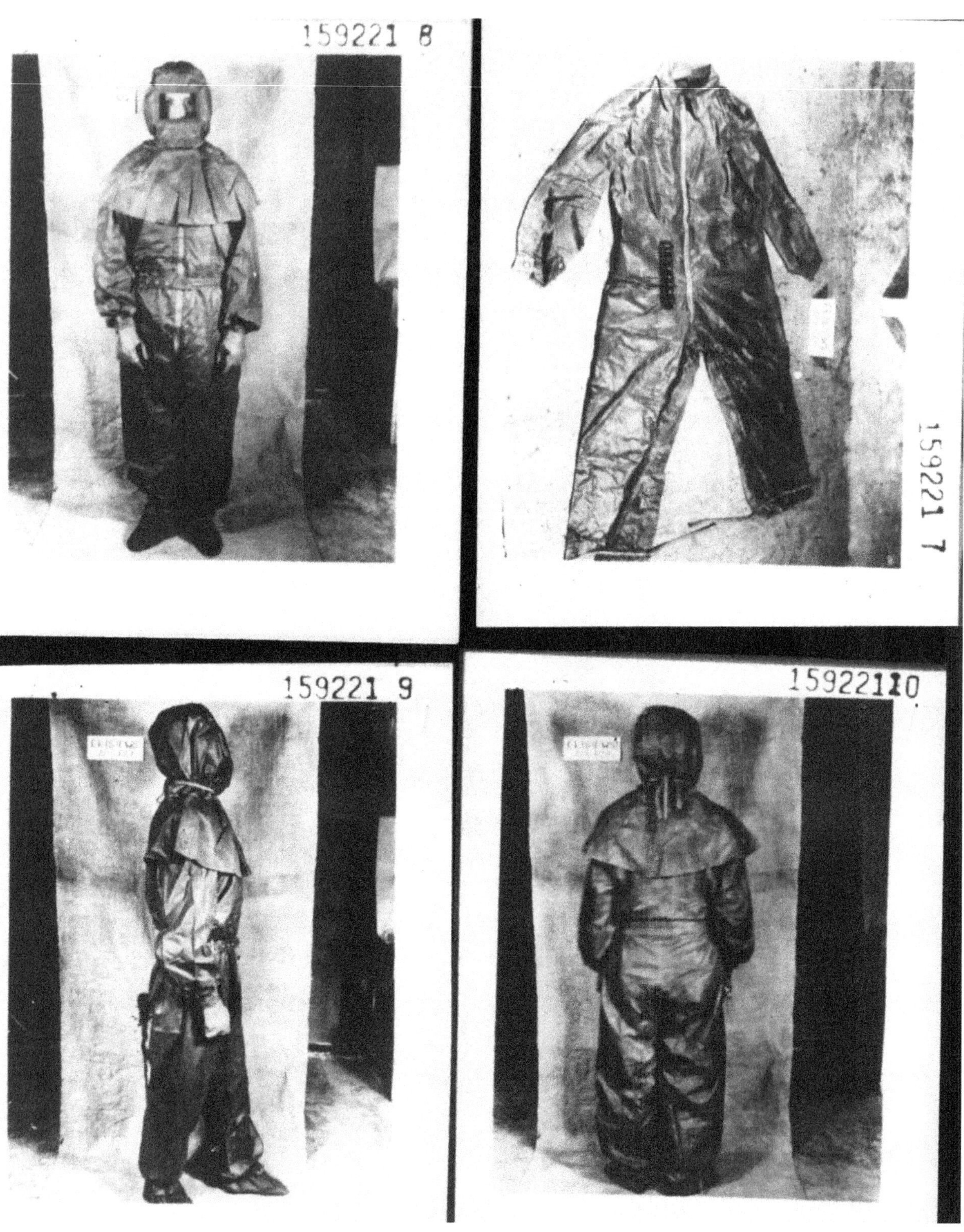
159221 8
159221 7
159221 9
15922110

3.65 12 May 1945: Transmittal of BIO/6822 Report: JAPAN AND BIOLOGICAL WARFARE, To: A C of S, G-2, War Dept. From: H. K. CALVERT, Major, F.A., Assistant to the Military Attache

资料出处：National Archives of the United States, R112, E295A, B11.

内容点评：本资料为 1945 年 5 月 12 日美国驻伦敦大使馆武官助理 H. K. Calvert 少校提交美国陆军部情报部参谋长助理的报告，题目：日本与细菌战。

AMERICAN EMBASSY
OFFICE OF THE MILITARY ATTACHÉ
1, GROSVENOR SQUARE, W. 1
LONDON, ENGLAND

12 May 1945

Subject: Transmittal of BIO/6822 Report.

To : A C of S, G-2, War Dept., Washington, D. C.
Attn: Col. W. M. Adams, Supervisor of Source Control, MIS.

1. Forwarded herewith one copy of BIO/6822 appreciation of "Japan and Biological Warfare" received from Dr. Fildes, of B.W.I.C.

2. Discussion of this paper is on the agenda for the next B.W.I.C. meeting. Any alteration in conclusions drawn therefrom will be forwarded.

For the Military Attache:

H. K. Calvert
H. K. CALVERT
Major, F.A.
Assistant to the Military Attache.

Incl:
As listed above.

MR MERCK (OSW) – 1
LT COL COLE (CWS) - 1
" " ANDERSON (SGO) - 1
SCIENTIFIC DR - 7

SECRET

Bio. 6822

JAPAN AND BIOLOGICAL WARFARE

The volume of evidence emanating from Far Eastern sources and implying Japanese interest and preparedness in biological warfare is very much greater and more specific than that involving Germany. As one might expect, however, emphasis is placed more on methods involving sabotage by individual operators (poisoning of wells, food stuffs etc.) than on orthodox means such as the design of weapons dispersing bacteria for the attack of large groups of people at one time.

Our knowledge of Japanese activities and intentions in this field of warfare is derived from a number of sources, of which the most conclusive are captured documents and interrogation of prisoners of war. Allegations by members of the Allied Nations and rumours collected by Intelligence frequently complicate the picture in view of the impossibility of assessing their true value.

In the Appendix an attempt has been made to collect and collate all relevant items bearing upon the subject, information being grouped under the following headings:

1. Japanese intentions.
   (a) Captured and other documents relating to B.W. Defence.
   (b) Captured and other documents relating to B.W. Offence.

2. Japanese B.W. Research.
   (a) Tokyo and other research laboratories.
   (b) General Ishii and the Water Supply and Purification Department.

3. Weapons.
   (a) Bacillus Bombs.
   (b) Balloons.

4. Allegations of use of B.W.
   (a) Allies accuse Japan.
   (b) Japanese accuse Allies.
   (c) Japanese admissions.

5. Miscellaneous.

As a result of this general review of Japanese intentions we may conclude that:

1. Japan is aware of some of the potentialities of the weapon though we are ignorant of the degree of experimental work which she has expended upon it.

2. Her interest lies more in the potentialities of sabotage than on more orthodox methods. For this reason she has framed and circulated widely, defensive instructions calling attention to the danger and stressing preventive measures.

3. Japan's offensive intentions are clearly implied in her widely circulated instructions to certain of her troops to disseminate disease by sabotage methods.

4. A number of allusions to a Mark 7 bacillus bomb in captured documents may imply her intention to resort, should the need arise, to more orthodox methods. Since in one instance the "bomb" is described as made of glass, it is possible, however, that it is a non-explosive variety designed for contaminating foodstuffs, water etc. by sabotage methods. This supposition is strengthened by the notes appended to the description of the bomb, that it is for use in market places, in springs, and for the contamination of men and animals. No bomb itself has yet been captured.

5. Allegations by the United Nations against Japan are meagre and inconclusive. Those incidents which have been capable of being assessed have been found to be non-proven.

6. On the other hand allegations by Japan against the Allies are more numerous. Her allegations are concerned almost entirely with sabotage and fifth column activities. Their number imply that Japan is endeavouring to build up a case to justify her resort to biological warfare. Certain statements of prisoners of war admit that she has resorted to this method of warfare in at least four instances, by dropping bacteria from aircraft. But these admissions are unproven.

J.F.S. STONE.

Biology Section,
Porton.
27th April, 1945.

- 3 -

APPENDIX

JAPAN AND B.W.

---

1. Japanese B.W. Intentions.

(a) Captured and other documents relating to B.W. Defence.

(i) "Commentary on International Law regarding Chemical and Bacterial Warfare" with a foreword by the Vice Minister of the Navy, Yamamoto, dated May 1937. This document was captured at Finschafen and received in New Guinea on 20.10.43. It summarizes and reviews the general provisions concerning both types of warfare contained in various treaties from the St. Petersburg Proclamation to the League of Nations Disarmament Conference. It does not mention Japanese intentions. (ATIS Enemy Publication No. 209, 6.10.44).

(ii) Document No. 12893 captured in Hollandia on 22.5.44. entitled "Method of using simplified poison tester set" and issued 30.9.42. This states that the Allies frequently and secretly perform sabotage by putting poison or pathogenic bacteria into food and wells. The method of using the testing set is described. (ATIS Enemy Pub. No. 197, 1.10.44). Somewhat similar instructions were captured at Wakde (ATIS Bull. No.1391, quoted in SPPIR No. 5, 16.10.44).

(iii) ATIS report No. 1376 contains a translation of a 'most secret' Japanese document dated 31.8.41 entitled "Supply Service in relation to Bacterial Warfare - Kuantung Army Intendence Department".

It shows that the Japanese Army envisaged the possibility of B.W. as early as 1941. Possible B.W. agents listed are typhoid, para-typhoid, dysentery and cholera by mouth; typhus, plague and malaria by insects; anthrax by contact with diseased animals or by sabotage.

Both sabotage and tactical use are mentioned as methods. The latter include dropping from aircraft, by methods involving principles of gas projection, and by letting loose infected insects.

Preventive measures include immunization and careful supervision of food, animals and sanitation; also precautions on buying and cooking of food and treatment of fodder (SPPIR No. 4, 16.8.44).

(iv) Mimeographed pamphlet entitled "The Truth about B.W." undated but captured at Cape Gloucester on 26.12.43. This reviews B.W. in general and alleged B.W. incidents in the 1914-1918 European War. It alleges that the Russians have a well advanced B.W. experimental station at Vladivostok, and cites incidents which implicate China in 1937 (see below under Allegations 4(b)(i)). It considers the reasons why B.W. has not started in the

Russo-German war and compares B.W. with C.W. It concludes with a consideration of defensive measures designed mainly to combat dissemination of disease by sabotage methods (ATIS No. 1162).

This is a straightforward account from the point of view of defence but there is nothing in the paper to suggest that the author has any particular knowledge of the subject.

(v) On 10.8.43 the Tokyo Mainichi reported a "Strategic Manoeuvre" held in Tokyo the preceding day for air defence practice with soldiers and civilians participating. The exercise included the supposition that pathogenic bacteria had been broadcast in the vicinity of a water purifying plant (JICA/CBI Rep. No.10310, 26.10.44).

(vi) A Japanese report on measures for prevention of contagious disease in 1943 classified 'secret'. The instructions envisage the dissemination of bacteria and poisons by the Allies (ATIS Bull. No. 1495, 8.10.44).

(vii) Cyclostyled document in the file of Nagayama, Butai, marked 'very secret', and captured 29.7.44. It is titled "Directions regarding enemy use of bacteria and poisons". B.W. is defined and possible methods of disseminating bacteria, mostly by sabotage, are described. Likely bacteria are listed and alleged examples of incidents quoted. Whilst it is stated these methods may be carried out by Allied agents, civilians in Allied employ, and by infiltrating patrols (c.f.1(b)(iv) and (v) below) it is also recognised that bombs containing bacteria may be dropped from aircraft. Defensive measures are considered (SEATIC Trans. Rep. No. 43, 30.9.44).

(viii) Mimeographed pamphlet "Service Regulations for Water Purifying Unit", undated and issued by Harbin, Kamo Force Purification Section, Hailar Branch.

The Water Purifying Section is made up of a headquarters and various squads, the organization being motorized. It consists of:

Headquarters
Epidemic Prevention Reconnaissance Patrol
Epidemic Prevention Pathogen Testing Squad
Poison Detecting and Water Examination Squad
Disinfection and Medical Examination Squad
Water Purification Squad
Water Supplying Squad
Maintenance and Materials Squad
Battle Field and Guidance Squad
Battle Field Research Squad.

The duties of each squad are closely defined. The unit, the regulations state, follows the front line troops and is under the command of the division to which it is attached. They are responsible for collecting intelligence reports on Allies' use of bacterial and poison warfare, reconnoitering water supplies, testing materials for pathogenic organisms, carrying out epidemic

-5-

- 3 -

prevention duties, detecting poisons and examining water physically and chemically. They are also responsible for disinfection of personnel, material and water, carrying out medical examinations and post-mortems, and supervising epidemic control. Other duties include supply of pure water, research on preventive measures against bacteria, poisons, bullets, heat, cold and malnutrition; also fire fighting. (ATIS Bull. No.1487, 5.10.44).

These regulations should be compared with the statements of prisoners of war formerly of the Water Supply and Purification Department, which indicate that the unit is also concerned with offensive activities (see 2(b)(v) and (vi) below).

(ix) Circular captured in the Kalemyo area on 24.11.44 entitled "Counter Measures against Bacteriological Warfare" addressed to unit commanders and independent platoon commanders. It states: "Recently there have been sporadic local epidemics of dysentery, cholera and cattle plague in the defence areas of Tatsu and Kiku Heidans. Owing to the change in the war situation we can no longer discount the possibility of enemy schemes to use bacteria and poisons. Units will take steps to discover the cause of present outbreaks....... Henceforth special efforts will be made to obtain information concerning the enemy's plans for bacteriological warfare". (SE ASIA Trans. Rep. No. 72, 3.1.45).

(x) Bound mimeographed file entitled "Interrogation of Prisoners of War" undated. Under handling of Ps.W. occurs "4. Warning on divestment of camouflage. Because fifth columnists do not throw off their camouflage, care must be taken against infiltration. Especially guard against the infiltration of victims of contagious diseases and of fifth columnists with bacteria" (ATIS-SWPA Enemy Pub. No.255, 25.12.44).

<u>Comment</u>: From the above reports it is clear that Japan is aware of the sabotage potentialities of B.W., and has issued necessary instructions to combat the danger.

(b) <u>Captured and other documents relating to B.W. Offence.</u>

(i) Document No. 14798 captured in Hollandia on 25.4.44. is a handwritten notebook concerning intelligence and fifth column activities in total war, undated, writer and unit not stated. The contents are presumably copied from a manual.

The collection of intelligence is considered an integral part of fifth column activities, which are defined. A suitable organization is described and general rules for subversive duties outlined. Actual methods for use against the person and against property are listed, and these include the use of pathogenic bacteria, harmful insects and poisons. (ATIS Enemy Pub. No. 271, 7.1.45).

- 6 -

(ii) "Manual on Raiding", Army Engineer School, dated April 1944, is presumed to have been captured on Saipan. The copy belonged to Kaminari 3200 Butai. Under "Execution of an Attack, Section I - Infiltration Manoeuvres" occurs "Reservoirs - Destroy the dam (sluice). Water pipes - try to destroy them at several places and at points where the damage will not easily be discovered. Another plan is to release bacteria" (CINCPAC-CINCPOA Trans. No.15, 17.1.45).

(iii) Another document captured in Hollandia on 25.4.44 consists of 27 pages of handwitten notes, undated, owner and unit unknown, concerning demolitions and sabotage, from which it appears that the Japanese are teaching and are prepared to use sabotage methods which include bacterial agents.

Thus bacteria are noted for destroying food. Also: "2. Note: It is important that the enemy does not find out your scheme.

(a) Arson: Wind, light. Spontaneous combustion scheme.

(b) Bacteria: In fish and vegetable markets and kitchens use a contagious disease which has been prevalent.

Warehouses:
2. Contaminate food with bacteria.

Destruction of Watersheds:
2. Spread bacteria around the watershed.

Cutting off water supply:
2. Bacteria is futile because of chlorine disinfection".
(ATIS Rep. No.249, 20.12.44.)

(iv) A bound mimeographed file entitled "NI Raiding Diversionary Tactics" classified 'secret' was captured at Morotai on 24.9.44. It was issued by E 33rd Force, dated 1944, and belonged to 2nd Lt. Horiuchi, NI Force. This document gives details of the organization, functions and equipment of the "Raiding Diversionary Unit". It contains the following: "Great results can be obtained by contaminating their food and drink in kitchen by bacterial strategy". (AG 381, 6.10.44).

(v) Document concerning the organization, equipment and duties of a "Five Man Raiding Party", captured in the Lungling region probably in early September 1944. The equipment listed appears to be normal until one arrives at that separately listed under <u>Infiltration Equipment</u>, the commander of the party being responsible for carrying the following:

"Luminous compass
Flashlight (with coloured lenses)
Watch
Climbing irons
Handflags

- 5 -

Special sword-stick
Luminous paint
Rope - 30 metres
Bacteria - if necessary"

(JICA SN 9502, 21.11.44)

A photostat of the original document has been checked and the words "if necessary bacteria" are unquestionably present.

(vi) "Extract of KAKI Operation Order ..... containing information collecting plan for Northern Leyte Defense Unit ..... Thirteen pages (fully translated by XXIV CAE, Translation II AE 194, Item 134). "Special characteristics of terrain from the standpoint of bacillus tactics. Field sanitation, and sanitation in regard to animals used by the Army". (AG 385, 12.12.44).

These two groups of words are not sentences and have no meaning unless they are assumed to be headings of sections. In the latter event the details of the sections should make clear the meaning of the headings, but they are not given.

(vii) 27 loose handwritten sheets containing notes on counter-intelligence, espionage and fifth column activity, undated, owner and unit not stated. Captured at Mongado, Luzon. The following occurs in the document: "C. Mass Fifth Column Work.

1. Poison - Community wells, springs.

2. Bacteria:
   a. Transport of uncultured bacteria.
   b. Culture of bacteria.
   c. Dissemination by airplane.
   d. Will be disseminated by avoiding sunlight - powdered form.
   e. Wells, rivers, springs, market goods.
   f. Prevent their theft.
   g. Prevent transport of uncultured bacteria.
   h. If not kept in the house during daylight, they are ineffective and they should be inspected from this standpoint.

(ATIS-SWPA Trans. No. 75, 27.2.45).

(viii) For details of captured documents relating to the Mark 7 Bacillus Bomb see below under 3 (a). Other captured documents containing accusations against the Allies of the use of B.W. are considered below under 4 (b).

Comment: These documents indicate that the Japanese are teaching and organizing sabotage by B.W. methods. Emphasis is laid on individual dissemination of bacteria for contaminating foodstuffs etc.

2. Japanese B.W. Research

(a) Tokyo and other research laboratories.

P.W. statement (JA 149359, 2nd Lt., Medical Officer). "So that the Jap Army would be prepared for taking counter measures if bacteria warfare were used by the enemy, research into B.W. was being conducted at laboratories attached to Jap universities. P.W. stated that all the universities had research laboratories for normal research and these were also being used for B.W. investigations. The principal one was the Infectious Diseases Research Laboratory at Tokyo. P.W. said that he knew no details as to how bacteria would be used in war because it was a closely guarded secret in Japan. He thought it would be spread by airplanes and guns. Although the Chinese had contaminated wells with bacteria, the Japanese had not retaliated because they were meeting with sufficient success against the Chinese without using this form of warfare." (ATIS-SWPA I.R. No.539, 29.8.44)

Another P.W. was told by a Jap officer that Japan was experimenting with bombs containing germs, the experimental station being supposed to be near Tokyo (SPPIR No. 5, 16.10.44).

Comment: Laboratories in towns would be suitable for manufacturing small quantities of cultures but would not be suitable for field experimental work.

(b) Major Gen. Ishii and the Water Supply and Purification Dept.

A number of P.W. statements referring to experiments carried out in Manchuria with Bacillus Bombs etc., under Maj. Gen. Ishii have been received; also on the activities of the Water Purification Unit. Specific references to the existence of a Bacillus Bomb are noted below under 3 (a)

(i) P.W. (JA 147935), while working in the Bacteriology Dept. of Chuzan University at Canton in 1941, heard that Gen. Ishii was conducting experiments with bacillus bombs at the branch of the Army Medical College at Harbin, Manchuria. Previously Ishii had been head of the Laboratory Section of the Army Medical College at Tokyo. In 1935 Ishii had invented a water purifier (ATIS I.R. No. 449, 16.9.44).

(ii) P.W. (1st Lt. of C Hospital) had heard of Gen. Ishii and his bacteriological work about 13 years ago and thought he was still doing this work. He thought water purification was the main objective of Ishii's experiments (ATIS IR 465, 17.9.44).

(iii) P.W. (JA 148282, Lt. Col. Pharmacist) is said to confirm the statement of P.W. (JA 147935) that experiments were carried out by Ishii at Harbin on a bacillus bomb. P.W. could give no further information as the subject was classified secret. He stated that Ishii's unit was known as "Ishii's Force" (AG 381 (6.10.44)B)

(iv) P.W. (100249, Private) stated that in 1943 he heard that B.W. experiments were being carried out at Hsinking in Manchuria, by the Water Purification Unit. He heard that on one occasion a gas was sprayed from the air and when it was first released it looked like a fog but gradually faded away. During the experiment gelatine in trays was

- 9 -

set out and later checked to see results as to the amount of bacteria falling on that area, and the rapidity of spreading. There were also experiments on diseases for horses which included glanders. (AG 381 (17.11.44)B).

(v) P.W. (No. 229), Lance Cpl. in the Water Supply and Purification Depts. at Nanking (Headquarters) and Kiukiang (Branch), was a graduate of the Med. Coll. of Nagoya Imperial University and was by profession an X-ray specialist. He has supplied a considerable amount of information on the organization and activities of the Water Supply and Purification Departments. Under the latter may be noted:

"2. Sanitation Section (Epidemic Prevention Section)

C. Cultivation of Bacteria. The principle categories of bacteria cultivated are cholera, typhus and dysentery bacilli. Large quantities of animals (guinea-pigs, rats etc.) were used for experiments in the section access to which was strictly forbidden to all unauthorized personnel.

5. Physico-chemical laboratory.

b. Manufacture poisons and drugs (purpose not known).

6. A nursery or garden is attached to the Physico-chemical Section in Nanking. This is located adjacent to the building housing the Water Supply Purification Dept. H.Q. In it are cultivated poisonous (alkaloid) plants. Area about 4000 sq. yds."

P.W. described in detail the 4 sizes of water filtration plant used by the Japanese Army and supposedly invented by Maj. Gen. Ishii (JICA No. 10595, 6.12.44).

Further information from the same P.W. is contained in SINTIC Item No. 213. Relevant details follow:-

(1) To P.W.'s knowledge, bacteria cultivated in Nanking are cholera, typhus and dysentery: experiments with plague were under way in 1944.

(2) Vaccines manufactured are "Yonshu Kongo - " (a mixture of para-typhoid A, B, dysentery and cholera, called "Quadruple mixture", and others (not specified). Quantity produced is sufficient for Japanese Army in Central China as well as among civilians in the area.

(3) The building in Nanking where the vaccines are made is shown on sketch (not reproduced).

(4) Raw materials used are agar-agar, eggs, meat extracts, casein, animal blood, glucose, maltose and powdered liver. Animals used include cows horses, rabbits, goats, guinea pigs, mice, geese and marmots (?)

(5) Effluent from building is somewhat yellowish in colour and has the odour of putrid fish; it is mixed with waste steam and then disposed of into the sewer.

(6) Individuals working in the building where bacteria are cultivated wear rubber gloves and simple nose-mouth masks. They "disinfect" before leaving. Every three months they are required to take pills which contain immunizing agents and are a substitute for injections. (Exact nature not known).

(7) Access to second and upper floors of building permitted only to Japanese Army officers and warrant officers who have special permits. Certain specially qualified civilians also work there; some of them are former Army surgeons and many of them high ranking officers.

(8) The Water Supply etc., Branch at Kiukiang had a research department cultivating bacteria, but on a small scale only. P.W. thinks other branches may have similar sections. Vaccines for the Army in North China are made at Peiping.

(9) P.W. stated that Japanese soldiers as a rule have no knowledge of use of bacteria by their army. There is a standing order forbidding troops and civilians attached to the Department to mention their work, and normally members of various departments do not know each other. P.W. believes that in case of a B.W. attack by the Japanese army, possibly only commanders of divisions and independent units near the affected area would be notified, and such knowledge would be withheld from other officers and from all troops.

(10) When Japanese troops overran an area in which a B.W. attack had been made during the Chekiang campaign in 1942, casualties upward from 10,000 resulted within a very brief period of time. Diseases were particularly cholera, but also dysentery and plague. Victims were usually rushed to hospitals in rear, particularly to the Hangchow Army Hospital, but cholera victims, usually being treated too late, mostly died. Statistics, which P.W. saw at Nanking, showed more than 1,700 dead, chiefly from cholera. But P.W. believes that actual deaths were higher "it being a common practice to pare down unpleasant figures".

(11) P.W. believes incubation period in case of cholera infection was about a day; 3-4 days for typhus, and about 10 days for para-typhoid. Infection resulted mainly from drinking water, but also from food.

(12) The bacteria used in the Chekiang campaign were produced at Nanking. They were spread from special aircraft attached to the Water Supply etc. Dept. at Nanking. This H.Q. has three special aircraft attached to it which are stationed at the airfield in front of the Department's H.Q. The plane or planes for the Chekiang bacteria attack took off from there.

/13.

(13) P.W. was not certain how the bacteria were dropped. He has heard that for attacks the planes carry four electric refrigerators filled with test tubes containing bacteria, there being "tens of thousands" of tubes in the plane.

(14) Other Water Supply etc. Depts. in China also have special planes attached to them; in 1943 a total of six planes were said to be attached to these departments in China. They are apparently small (reconnaissance type?) planes and they always fly under fighter escort.

<u>Interrogator's note</u>: P.W. himself, being an N.C.O. did not work in the Research Dept. of the Water Supply etc., H.Q. ..... His information is based on statistics and reports he saw whilst assigned to another department of the said H.Q., and to a small degree on observations and "general knowledge within the H.Q." .....

(vi) According to a report by a Chinese soldier, formerly with the Japanese Department of Epidemic Defence and Water Supply Branch at Kiukiang, who has now returned to the Chinese side, the mission of that department at the present time is to prepare disease serums and cultures. During the first period of the Chekiang-Kiangsi battle the enemy spread cultures of typhoid, cholera and dysentery by plane in the pools and streams along the important communication lines between Kinhwa and Lan-ch'i. The hope was to infect soldiers and civilians and thus weaken Allied fighting strength (OSS A-47271, 9.12.44).

<u>Comment:</u> There appears to be no doubt that General Ishii has been concerned with the normal duties of an army hygienist, for instance, control of water supplies and manufacture of vaccines (see (b)(v) to para. (9)). There are, however, statements from P.W.'s that he has experimented with "Bacillus Bombs" and spraying bacteria from the air. This latter technique is stated to have been in operational use resulting in the loss of over 1700 men of his own side. It is impossible to evaluate this evidence, but in general it would seem improbable that an officer in charge of normal hygiene precautions would be concerned to any important degree with offensive B.W. activities.

A captured document "Service Regulations for Water Purification Unit" issued by the Harbin Kamo Force Purification Section has already been noted (see 1(a) (viii) above); the document itself in no way implies offensive activities though it stresses the defensive aspects of B.W. Remarks on the alleged Chekiang incident will be found under 4 (c) below.

3. <u>Weapons</u>

(a) <u>Bacillus Bombs</u>.

Certain vague references to bacillus bomb experiments by Gen. Ishii have already been noted (see 2(b)(i) and (iii) above). P.W. Kitagawa Nobutaka has stated that he heard rumours that research

- 10 -

on dropping bacteria in bombs is being carried out in Japan though he has not seen any equipment or apparatus (SPPIR No. 5, 16.10.44) A report that 30,000 bombs containing typhus, diphtheria and plague were transported from Japan to China (SPPIR No.2, 13.5.44), became translated into shells in a captured message from a Japanese garrison commander (SEATIC Trans. Rep. No.9, 31.1.44, quoted in SPPIR No.4, 15.8.44). The same report appeared in the Chinese press with the addition that 2 bottles of liquid germs were found inside an unexploded bomb dropped on a mountain near Kosanche (SPPIR No. 5, 16.10.44). It is probable that these bombs were in reality C.W. weapons since it has been stated that they were produced at the Osaka Chemical Works.

On the other hand a P.W. (Shigeru Yamacuichi) of the Japanese Naval Air Force captured on 4.8.44 has listed the bombs used by the Air Force. Under special duty bombs he noted "No.1 germ or bacterial bomb 1 kg.". At the same time he insisted that such bombs have not been produced by Japan since further research is necessary (CINCPAC-CINCPOA IR No. 93, 4.12.44).

More concrete evidence of the existence or projected design of a B.W. bomb, and confirming Yamacuichi's statement, is contained in a number of captured documents, derived mostly, it would appear from lectures on ordnance in general. These documents consist of lists of bombs designed for the purposes noted. Photostat copies of four of the original Japanese documents have been received and translations of the relevant passages checked. These are:

(i) JICPOA Item No. 8438, 2.5.44. Notebook of Yamashita Otakichi. "Special Bomb Mark 7 - green purple grey purple - Bacillus Bomb - for special circumstances".

(ii) JICPOA Item No. 8306, 28.5.44. Notebook of Akiraji Watanabe. "Special Bomb Mark 7 - Market places of cities, places where there are springs, for the infection of men and horses (Bacillus). Example - Air Arsenal Type 13 Experimental 1 kg. Mark 7".

(iii) JICPOA Item No. 5753, 19.5.44. In a list of bombs the Mark 7 bomb is mentioned with the note "Bacteria for scattering in market places", under the heading 60 kg. (which may be a mistake as all other reports refer to a 1 kg. bomb).

(iv) JICPOA Item No. 8713. Again the Mark 7 special bomb is noted as "1 kg. bacillus glass bomb". The mention of glass (in Japanese kana, garasu) is of interest.

Comment: So far no bomb containing bacteria has been captured. We are therefore ignorant whether the bomb is an explosive type for producing bacterial aerosols or merely a glass 'bomb' for scattering the contents over foodstuffs etc. in markets and kitchens, for sabotage purposes.

(b) **Balloons.**

Several large Japanese balloons capable of carrying loads up to 450 lb. have landed in the Western United States and Canada. The purpose of these is not yet clear but it has been suggested in view of their small carrying capacity that they might be used for spreading animal or human diseases. They are under active examination (MI 10/4215, 20.2.45 and SPPIR No.7, 7.2.45). A "General Report number one on Free Balloons and Related Incidents"

- 13 -

has been issued by the U.S.A. War Dept. dated 29.1.45.

By 19.2.45 some hundreds of these balloons are stated to have landed in North America, some travelling as far inland as Ohio. Few have been recovered intact but four have so far had receptacles containing an unidentified powder. No conclusions have yet been reached (C.W. III, 19.2.45).

4. Allegations.

(a) Allies accuse Japan.

(i) Chinese alleged that Japanese dropped from aircraft plague infected grain etc. during 1940 on Chii-hsien, Ningpo and Kinghwa, all in Chekiang province, and that cases of bubonic plague resulted. The evidence was not conclusive (MI 10/B/MS/115, 6.6.42). A similar allegation that Japanese aircraft dropped sundry infected articles on Changteh in Hunan province on 4.11.41 (MI 10/B/3398, 28.4.42) was assessed on the evidence available as non-proven (BWIC Periodic Summary No.1, 7.9.44).

(ii) On 10.4.40 an unconfirmed report stated that the Japanese General Staff stationed in China had established in Hankow a Central China Expeditionary Force bacteria/gas Research Bureau for training Japanese soldiers. General Watanabe was appointed superintendent of research (CX/37431/IIIa/W.2321, 7.7.40). On 5.2.41 it was stated that reliable information indicated that the Japanese had a B.W. battalion attached to each of two C.W. regiments and had trained over 2000 paratroops (JIS 21, page 10, 8.1.43).

(iii) A report dated 2.10.42 stated that three Japanese aircraft flying over the Nanyang district in Honan dropped large quantities of cholera infected cereals (MI 10, 3.3.43). This recalls an extract from an intercepted letter dated 28.1.42 which claimed that bottles of starved fleas infected with plague, old rags and food were dropped on Hunan province to the consternation of Chungking (MI 10/B/MS/102, 2.5.42); as also a vague report that cobweb like material was dropped over Anhwei province, cases of meningitis subsequently occurring (SF 53/8/46/Blc, 18.4.42.)

(iv) Kweilin Intelligence Summary No. 50 of 26.4.44 reported that according to recent arrivals from Peiping, the hospital of the Peking Union Med. Coll. had been taken over by the Japanese and converted into a "Virus Cultivation Centre". The report added that the Japanese had assembled a large crowd of beggars for the purpose of lice breeding and had ordered the inhabitants to collect flies and rats. Captured Japanese health orders indicate, however, that these were normal sanitary precautions, the natives being encouraged to catch rats etc. for which they were paid. (SEATIC Trans. Nos. 17 and 18). This has been confirmed by Dr. Grant (MA New Delhi Rep. No. 1853, 19.6.44), and by a former member of the staff who has stated that the hospital is being used as a base hospital for Japanese Army officers. The army epidemic prevention service is doing sanitary and bacteriological research there (JICA/CBI Rep. No. 10127,

2.10.44 quoted in SPPIR No. 6, 15.12.44).

(v) Chinese intelligence reports dated 20.1.45 stated that the Japanese High Command have been studying the possibility of spreading bacteria at both our front and rear air bases. It further reports a shipment of malaria, plague, typhus and tuberculosis bacteria, supposedly produced at the Chemical Research Institute, Osaka, to Shanghai during December 1944 (SPPIR No.7, 7.2.45). This report recalls the alleged shipment of 30,000 bacteria bombs from the same chemical works (see 3(a) above), and may be considered of the rumour type only.

(b) Japanese accuse Allies.

(i) In a captured document already noted (see 1(a)(iv) above) the Japanese alleged that the Chinese endeavoured to stop the advance of their army to Nanking by scattering cholera in the wells in the summer of 1937; that a Japanese soldier in the vicinity of Kiating in the winter of 1937 found a glass bottled filled with glanders bacteria floating down a creek; that Russian biologists were labouring to produce several billion fleas per day for B.W. purposes; that the white races were introducing respiratory and venereal diseases into Japan as a long term strategy; and that in the northern province of Hsingan anthrax was deliberately spread by Europeans (ATIS No.1162).

(ii) Certain allegations are contained in the captured document entitled "Directions regarding enemy use of Bacteria and Poisons" noted above (1(a)(vii)). Thus it is claimed that in 1938 during the siege of Hankow the Chinese polluted with cholera the only source of water supply in Kiu Kiang city; officers and men of the Imperial Army succumbed. Again in Mukden city it was found that melons in the market were contaminated with cholera. Also that during operations in Burma it was found that wells in the city of Prome had been polluted with cholera germs by British Indian troops. Further, that the 'nose ulcer' prevalent amongst horses in Manchuria is strong evidence of the Allies' schemes (SEATIC Trans. Rep. No. 43, 30.9.44).

(iii) ATIS Research Rep. No. 84, 24.7.44, quoted in SPPIR No.4 of 15.8.44 lists a number of allegations obtained from a captured file of counter intelligence instructions dated 30.9.41. Here the Japanese accuse the Russians of using B.W. by sabotage methods, the following being a summary:

Upon outbreak of war between Japan and Russia, the Soviet Union's Consul-General at Harbin will immediately order his underground agents in important cities in Manchukuo to spread typhus germs among the Japanese military, in urban areas, factories, schools etc., as well as among individuals and animals.

An outbreak of cholera in a village in Tokuto was ascribed to a bandit invasion, the cholera bacilli being discovered in five wells in the village.

At Shankuli a bottle of anthrax germs was discovered among the personal effects of Soviet Union spies who committed suicide after they were surrounded.

Further, a bound file of mimeographed charts belonging to a Japanese medical officer are stated to have been used to accuse the Chinese of poisoning wells, food, liquor, etc. One chart is stated to give 68 instances of the Chinese using poisonous substances against the Japanese from the beginning of the China Incident to May 1942.

(iv) In a captured Japanese military bulletin is the following note dated 9.11.43: "Recently an attempt was made to poison soldiers travelling in a train by throwing poison into the water tank. This occurred in Legaspi Station (on Luzon Island). Drinking water other than from one's own canteen is prohibited". A U.S.A. comment on this refers to the fact that the Philippine guerrillas have been operating constantly in the Philippines during the Japanese regime (ATIS Bull. No. 1678, 4.1.45, quoted in SPPIR No.7, 21.2.45).

(v) P.W. (JA 149359), medical officer, stated that although the Chinese had contaminated wells with bacteria, the Japanese had not retaliated because they were meeting with sufficient success (AG 385, 16.10.44).

(vi) A bound mimeographed file of Japanese Intelligence notes captured at Leyte in the Philippines on 7.11.44, and dated 12.10.44, states that in September in the Burma area it was confirmed that cholera bacilli were found in 20cc. ampoules which the natives picked up claiming that they had been dropped from Allied aircraft. In view of the unexpected prevalence of cholera cases in the area the Japanese suspect the Allies of carrying out bacterial fifth column activities. The Japanese report also states that in the Thailand area plague carrying rats appeared during the latter part of September and approximately 100 rats were exterminated by the 7th. The report goes on to say that these two incidents must be related and that the diseases were probably dropped in conjunction with the Thailand-Burma operations. The last part of the report contains the following warning: "When an epidemic breaks out following the ever increasing air operations it is necessary to make detailed reports of the situation and take strict precautionary measures against the enemy's bacterial 5th Column activities". (ATIS - SWPA Bull. No.1638, 20.12.44).

The suggestions in this file are reminiscent of the somewhat vague insinuations in the captured document from Kalenyo noted above (1(a)(ix)).

(c) Japanese admissions.

The statement and interrogation of P.W. (No.229) has already been given (2(b)(v)) referring to the alleged B.W. attack by the Japanese during the Chekiang campaign in 1942 and in which they themselves suffered a large number of casualties. If this really

- 16 -

took place it seems surprising that confirmation is not more adequate.

The admission of the Chinese soldier, formerly a member of the Japanese Water Supply Branch at Kiukiang also noted above (2(b)(vi)) probably refers to the same incident. It will be recalled that he stated that during the first period of the Chekiang-Kiangsi battle, the Japanese spread cultures of typhoid, cholera and dysentery by plane in the pools and streams along the communication lines between Kinhwa and Lan-ch'i.

Further interrogation of P.W. (No.229) and of another P.W. (No.230), a Lance Cpl. captured in December 1943 in Hunan and who participated in the Chekiang-Kiangsi campaign of 1942, elicited the following information on known instances of the Japanese use of B.W., the bacteria in each instance being dropped from aircraft.

Campaign.	Date	Location	Bacteria used.
Chekiang-Kiangsi	May 1942	Kiangsi Province	Typhus
" "	"	Shanghsiao	Dysentery
" "	"	Kinhwa, Chekiang	Typhus, Cholera and Dysentery.
Changte	Nov.1943	Changte, Hunan	Cholera.

(JICA No.10596, 4.12.44).

5. **Miscellaneous.**

(i) "Medical Intelligence reports the finding of anthrax K vaccine of a dosage apparently intended for humans rather than animals in Japanese medical supplies found in the Sarmi-Maffin area" (SPPIR No. 5, 16.10.44).

(ii) A captured mimeographed file of bulletins belonging to I company 20th Infantry Regiment contained a bulletin dated 20th January "Anti-anthrax injections will be given tomorrow" (AG. 381 (18.12.44)B).

Comment: It has been suggested that these two reports taken together may imply Japan's intention to use anthrax as a B.W. agent against man. Since, however, no vaccine suitable for man is known, it is extremely doubtful whether this is the intention. The Japanese have stressed the B.W. use of anthrax against cattle and horses and have in fact stated that the Allies have used this agent against their animals (see 1(a)(iii) and 4(b)(i) above). It would seem therefore more likely that these reports refer to the health and care of animals for which vaccines are suitable.

3.66 6 Jun. 1945: Jap High Command Meets (From OSS, Wash, DC Intel Dissemination #A-56750); 21 May 1945: Kempei B. W. Agents (From WD G-2 Rpt A-208)

资料出处： National Archives of the United States, R112, E295A, B11.

内容点评： 本资料为 1945 年 6 月 6 日美军战略情报局情报，题目：日本高级指挥官会面；以及 1945 年 5 月 21 日美国陆军部情报部情报，题目：宪兵细菌武器。据 1944 年 7 月 23 日塞班岛俘获日本宪兵战俘，实施细菌战为日本宪兵职能，野战中，宪兵部队特别调查队奉命雇用特工散布细菌。

JAP HIGH COMMAND MEETS.

(From OSS, Wash, DC Intel Dissemination
A-56750, 6 June 1945 - C-3 Reliability)

At a meeting of the Japanese High Command on 20 April 1945 which Prime Minister SUZUKI attended, the following decisions were reached:

a) The main forces are to be moved from KARAFUTO and HOKKAIDO to KYUSHU.

b) General Shunroku HATA, the joint commander with General SUGIYAMA of all forces in JAPAN, is to be sent to inspect KYUSHU.

c) All reserves are to be called into service.

d) A part of the People's Volunteer Corps is to be called for immediate service.

e) The Combined Fleet is to be reorganized.

f) The troops in CHINA are to be ordered not to enlarge their present holdings and to confine any actions to local engagements.

Following a regular cabinet meeting on 27 April 1945, a conference was held by the High Command. The following decisions are among those made:

a) Part of the naval planes now under production will be given to the Army.

b) In time of emergency, the navy in the Southern Regions and CHINA must accept the orders of the commander of the army forces in the area of joint operations.

It has been learned that these decisions have been accepted by the Navy authorities, who guarantee that the Army-Navy friction will cease.

On 4 April 1945, high ranking officers of the Army and Navy were called together at NANKING, for a secret conference to consider continental operations. At the conference it was decided to send an urgent message to TOKYO requesting the reinforcement of the air forces at NANKING and SHANGHAI, as at present the strength is insufficient for battle.

On 17 April, a conference was held in NANKING which was attended by General OKAMURA, Yasuji, CG China Expeditionary Forces, Admiral KONDO, Nobutake, the commander of the China Fleet, and TANI, Masayuki, the Jap ambassador to NANKING. The following decisions were agreed upon:

a) Move the capital of the puppet government to North CHINA from NANKING if necessary, and merge the North CHINA puppet government with the NANKING puppet government.

b) The puppet regime may continue to maintain partial adminis-

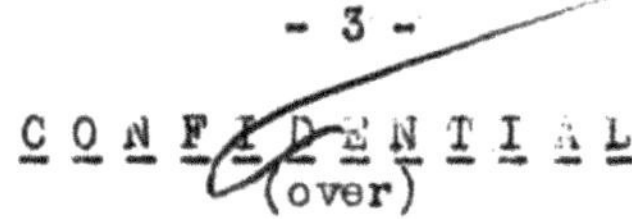

- 3 -

C O N F I D E N T I A L
(over)

JAP HIGH COMMAND MEETS (CONT'D)

trative privileges, but only on the condition that this does not unfavorably affect the Jap military situation in CHINA.

c) Seek ways and means to arrive at peace terms with CHINA.

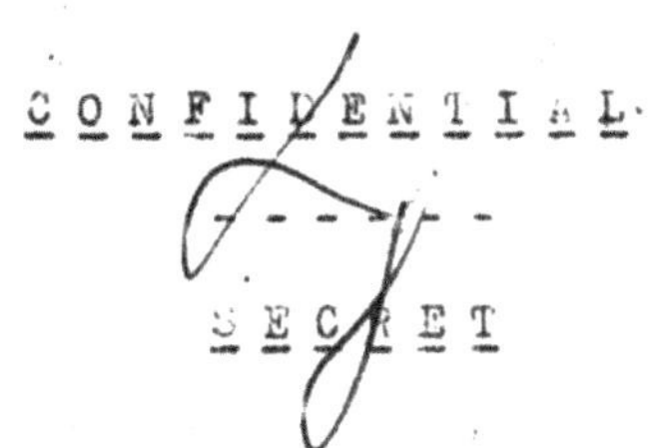

KEMPEI B.W. AGENTS

(From WD G-2 Rpt A-208, 21 May 45)

A sergeant in the Kempei, captured 23 July 1944 on SAIPAN, had the following comments to make regarding Jap use of BW when interrogated in the United States in April 1945.

Bacteriological warfare is a function of the Kempei. At the school for Kempei in TOKYO, the function was studied and experimental research was carried on under the supervision of medical officers. In the field, the Special Investigation Section of Kempei Units (in collaboration with the Tokumu Kikan) was charged with the responsibility of hiring special agents who were called upon to spread bacteria. (P/W's information regarding this function was based on hearsay). He thought that airplanes and balloons might be used for this purpose, but seemed more certain that agents would be more effective means of spreading germs, such as typhoid, typhus, cholera, bubonic plague, meningitis, meningial encephalitis, bacillary dysentery, small-pox, paratyphoid. Food and meat poisoning, he thought, were also possibilities in Bacteriological Warfare but the details of such a procedure were not known to him. In general he referred to this type of warfare as "defensive only." (WD states P/W was cooperative and information given is considered reliable.)

- 4 -

SECRET

3.67 12 Jun. 1945: INTELLIGENCE REPORT, Translation of Japanese Documents on BW, From MIS. War Department, ALSOS Mission

资料出处： National Archives of the United States, R112, E295A, B11.

内容点评： 本资料为 1945 年 6 月 12 日美国陆军部军事情报局 ALSOS MISSION 有关细菌战的德国官方文件和报告，内容为日本陆军军医学校北条圆了提供德方的论文《关于细菌战》。共 32 页，缺第 29 页。

Enclosures
Copy No.

INTELLIGENCE REPORT

FOR GENERAL USE BY ANY U.S. INTELLIGENCE AGENCY

From MIS. War Department, ALSOS Mission, Washington, D. C. (Agency or Officer / Station) Date 12 June 1945

Source Capt. Wm. Cromartie, MC, AUS; Lt. J. W. Hofer, MC-USNR Eval.

Area Reported On Germany Subject Translation of Japanese Documents on BW

Reference Official German Documents and Reports on BW. H-H/168 dated 24 May 45 (Directive, correspondence, previous report, etc., if applicable.)

SUMMARY: Enter careful summary of report, containing substance succinctly stated. Answer questions where, when, what, how, how many, and give date of event. In a final one sentence paragraph give significance. Begin text on page 2.

MARK FOR THE READING PANEL

In addition to any other distribution of this report, War Department directive requires that copies must go to the following as a minimum:

O.S.R.D. (Office of Field Service)
O.N.I. (Office Coordinator of Research and Development)
Director of Intelligence, ASF
Chief, Scientific Branch, MIS

NOTE: This document contains information affecting the national defense of the United States within the meaning of the Espionage Act, 50 U. S. C., 31 and 32, as amended. Its transmission or the revelation of its contents in any manner to an unauthorized person is prohibited by law. It may not be reproduced in whole or in part, by other than War Dep't Agencies, except by permission of the A C of S, G-2, W. D. G. S.

Distribution by Originator:

MIS Serial No. 167588 (Sci Br)

MIS Distribution

*Sci 5
Route
Lib
Foreign Br (ALSOS) 15
HQAAF 1
G-2 China/S ci 1
G-2 SWPA/Sci 1
G-2 POA/Sci 1
G-2 India-Burma/Sci 1
CWS/Sci 2
Med/Sci 1

Int Div 1
OSW/Sci 1
NDD/Sci 1
ONI 1
OSRD/Sci 1

Distribution of Enclosures

With all copies

UNCLASSIFIED

FORM OCS17
3RD REV.

SECRET
CLASSIFICATION

HEADQUARTERS
EUROPEAN THEATER OF OPERATIONS
UNITED STATES ARMY
ALSOS MISSION
APO 887

REF: C-H/300

SUBJECT: Translation of Japanese Documents on BW

Foreword to Translations on Japanese BW:

Among the records obtained from Professor Kliewe as described in an earlier report (Official German Documents and Reports on BW. H-H/168 dated 24 May 45) was a folder containing information about Japanese BW.

One large document was entitled "About Bacteriological Warfare." This document was presented to Professor Kliewe late in 1942 by Dr. Hoyzo, of the Japanese Embassy in Berlin, for Professor Kliewe's study and evaluation. After extensive study Professor Kliewe submitted a list of sixteen questions to the Japanese physician (attached to document). These remained unanswered.

According to Professor Kliewe there was no liaison between the German and Japanese governments in the study of bacterial warfare. They distrusted one another. While Professor Kliewe had no knowledge of the activities of the Japanese in experimental bacterial warfare, he considered this report to be different from anything he had seen previously and he thought it was probably based on experimental studies.

To the reader it will be evident that the sentences and paragraphs lack good construction. Professor Kliewe made many corrections in the original text and the corrected document was used in the translation.

Lt. J. W. Hofer, MC-USNR

5a JAPAN "Ja"

No. 124		About the bacteriological attack of the Chinese army in the Japanese--Chinese conflict (Oberfeldarzt T. Hoyzo, to Army Medical School).
No. 125		About bacteriological warfare (Dr. Enryo Hojo).
No. 25/41	A Foreign Defense I H. A. No. 366/3.41	Regarding Far East--China Plan.
No. 126/41		Copy. Memorandum about alleged bacteriological warfare of the Japanese against the Chinese.
No. 127	Wig III c	Regarding result of evaluation of Serial No. VIII 1007047 plan.
No. 128/43	STU (Wi G IIIc) ...../43g	Plan. Regarding bacteriological warfare.
No. 24/41	A Foreign Defense I H. A. No. 3252	Copy. Regarding Far East--Japan--Bacteriological warfare. Report (?) by Mann.
No. 129/43	Army High Command SU 214/43 g, staff March 5, 43	Regarding bacteriological warfare. Military report, Tokio.
----	----	Invisible weapons, by Dr. Lims.
----	Reich Geographical Inst.	The danger of bacteriological warfare.

COPY Berlin, 3 November 1944

Reich Institute for Geography
Literature - Evaluation.

"El Gran Diario"
(Republic San Salvador)
of 29 June 1944

"The danger of bacteriological warfare"
Rather than suffer a terrible defeat
the axis powers may possibly resort to
microbes as a last resort for war.
By Dr. Juli Cantals for El Gran Diario.

New York, 23 June 1944

In short extracts we report about those deadly rockets which the Germans are firing at England. They are some sort of a toy from the laboratory, the military effects of which are of very small importance and which are mainly directed against the civilian population. It seems the only weapon left to the axis powers by now are the use of gases containing sickness-germs. I do not believe that these gases are already such a useful weapon that they could be used by the Allies to blockade Germany and Japan in short order. As regards the use of gassing with bacteria, it is perhaps a tactical mistake made by the Japanese with respect to war department.

The microbes in the Orient.

The possibility to use bacteria at the fighting front has always been far away from the minds of the military men who have studied this problem. A book, published by the Publishing Co. of Barday Newman, "Japan's secret weapon" has practically disappeared from the public eye. It states that the Japanese have been using bacteria as a weapon for a long time. The author insists that malaria and other sicknesses are factors which the Japanese are keeping ready for the purpose of infecting their enemies. The sicknesses which they are in the habit of causing are, for example, cerebral paralysis (encephacilitis letargica) and infantile paralysis. It is true that the Japanese have worked very diligently on the discovery of these sicknesses; the first one who discovered this bacillus was the famous Noghuchi, who was gaining fame at the Rockefeller Institute for a long time.

The Chinese are the guinea-pigs for India.

Such experiments have been performed in China. Newman asserts that the Japanese have used bacteria against the Chinese in at least five campaigns. The author mentions an official document from the Chinese government-office (April 1942) in which the use of microbes by the Japanese is being certified. The plague-blister occurs for the first time in the province Chekiamg after an attack by the Japanese. In this district large wheat and rice infections also occur, the origin of which cannot be explained. Before the battle of Pearl Harbor an unending number of curious small pieces of paper and cotton was raining down on Changteh; an examination showed them to contain plague bacilli.

Bacteriological warfare is a weapon hard to handle.

Nobody knows of the events which take place in today's laboratories. Up to now bacteriological warfare has been a two-edged sword which could turn against the attacker after arrival at the enemy. The 1922 disarmament conference at Washington created a commission of international character to study this problem.

Officially
Oberstabsarzt

Berlin, 4 March 1943

Army High Command
Army General Staff/attache' -- Dept. (VIII)
Nr. 337/43 top-secret

2 copies

1. Copy: Army medical inspectorate
2. Copy: Original

1. Copy for hand acts

Top-Secret

No. 129/43

Reference: Nr. 213D/43 secret General army office/army medical (Wi G III c) inspectorate

Nr. 337/43 top-secret Attache' -- Dept. (VIII)

Regarding: Bacteriological warfare :Army High Command--Army medical inspectorate :No. 214/43 top-secret :5 March 1943

Military attache' Tokio reports under Nr. 36/43 secret of 1 March 1943:

"According to Japanese General Staff the time -- assertion is pulled out of thin air. Here until now no bacteriological warfare from any side."

By order of

COPY

Secret!

Foreign Office (?) / Defense
Nr. 3252/241 Defense l. g. Defense IHt

Berlin, 25 Feb. 1941

No. 24/41

To

Foreign Armies East
Army medical inspectorate
Inspectorate of chemical warfare troops
General of chemical warfare troops, with commander-in-chief of the army
Wa Z5

Regarding Far East -- Japan -- Bacteriological Warfare.

Agent reports:

"It is generally known in Japan that experiments are being performed for waging war with bacteria. The agent did not learn where this is happening nor how far these experiments have progressed. The Japanese are speaking especially of plague bacilli used by the Russians in the Russo-Japanese incidents and in Finland.

The agent then mixed up the purely military studies -- which are being pursued to a limited extent--with the civil medical service; he pointed out that there was no serum at hand during a recent plague-case in Hsinking."

Hand-written note:

It is known that the Russians have worked in this field. Statements about Japan completely credible.
5 March RS

By order of

signed

SECRET

Original   Berlin, 11 February 1943

Army Medical Inspectorate   No. 128/43
(Vi G III c) . . . . . /43g   Secret

Oberkriegsarzt Prof. Kliewe

Regarding: Bacteriological Warfare

To

Army General Staff/Attache' Dept.

It is hereby requested to ask the Japanese for further information as to the truthfulness of the report that plague bacilli have been used in the Chinese city of Tschangteh (see attached article "Invisible Weapon" in "Time of 9 March 1942).

Point of view of army medical inspectorate:

In the Japanese article "About bacteriological warfare" Oberfeldarzt Dr. med. Enryo Hojo writes "so it seems to us that the negative opinion of Prof. Juergens about the effects of bacteriological warfare is perhaps a diligent attempt to keep his country's preparations for bacteriological warfare a secret" (Prof. Juergens was German committee representative at the League of Nations). In the same article there is the statement: "I, too, have to consider the effects of bacteriological warfare as certain .... one has to pursue one's studies diligently and has to solve unclear questions." It follows without a doubt from those few quotations that Dr. Hojo favors bacteriological warfare; because of the fact that the article was handed to the army medical inspectorate in the presence of a representative of the Japanese legation, it has to be assumed that the article reflects the opinion of the Japanese armed forces. Because of the type of treatment accorded the subject it has to be concluded that the Japanese have worked zealously on the problem of using bacteria. The article gave data about the length of life of the various types of bacteria on the outside; about the effects of the bacteriological attack; about the methods of attack; the attack-targets; about the equipment for bacteriological warfare (exact data about the quantity resp. number of nutritive media, instruments and apparatus necessary for the production of certain quantities of bacteria and for the attack equipment).

Now it has been stated in the report of the high command of the armed forces, dated 25 July 1941, that the Japanese have waged bacteriological warfare against the troops of the Tschunking government with great success. Foreign Office (?), Defense IHt (Nr. 366/3.41y) reports from an agent indicate that the Japanese have used plague-bacteria powder and fine, dried, infected grains in Far-East-China. The Japanese themselves have suffered repeatedly from the successful use on the Chinese of cholera--, typhoid-- and dysentery -- agent; the Japanese also knew of the preparations of the Russians.

It is certain that under these conditions the Japanese have not looked on idly. On the contrary, everything points to the fact that they too, have been actively engaged in the matter. Dr. Hojo writes in his paper that "In the method to allow infected insects to fall in streams, plague carrying fleas are sprayed by releasing them from a plane in streams; they have to be intermingled with numerous

- 6 -

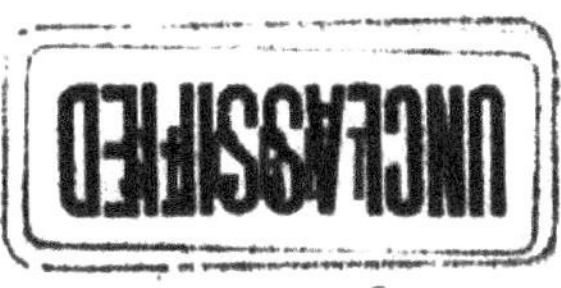

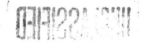

little pieces of cloth or cotton in order to decrease possibility of mixing (?) during descent." He writes furthermore "Plague bacilli can live in wheat for 18 days" (probably meant are rice grains). It is extraordinary that the article in "Time" gives the same method of attack (scattered rice grains and cotton shreds) as the one stated by Dr. Hojo in his unpublished paper. One may therefore assume with certainty that the Japanese have used plague bacilli against the Chinese in a field experiment, especially since the Chinese, too, have used such materials against Japanese troops.

By order of

Wi G

Chief I III IIIc

Penciled Note:

"Time" 9 March 1942.

The Japanese have been reported to have used plague bacilli at Tschangteh. Military expert Fletcher Pratt relates the matter. The Japanese dropped rice grains and cotton shreds from planes. One week later 6 cases of plague had occurred. For 10 (20?) generations no plague had been observed in this locality. Even the chairman of the Chinese Red Cross caught an artificial infection.

RS

Wi g IIIc No. 127

Regarding: Result of Evaluation, serial wr. VIII 1007047

For artificial infection of smallpox only liquid or dried pus from pustules of smallpox patients can be considered. The conditions under which the infectious material has to be used, however, are so difficult (rub into the skin or wounds, dispersing of powders of dust, etc) that merely because of them one has to decline the assertion that a person was present in the following of the Japanese diplomats who committed acts of sabotage.

The assertion is probably enemy propaganda.

RS, 28 October

Copy No. 126/41

Report of high command of the armed forces, dated 25 July 1941, states that the Japanese have waged bacteriological warfare against troops of the Tschungking government with great success.

Original

Army Medical Inspectorate No. 25/41

Military Medical Academy
Hyg. bact. Institute
Dept. Oberkriegsarzt
Prof. Dr. Kliewe
Regarding: Far East -- China

Berlin NW 40, 16 March 1941
35 Scharnhorst Street
41 65 71

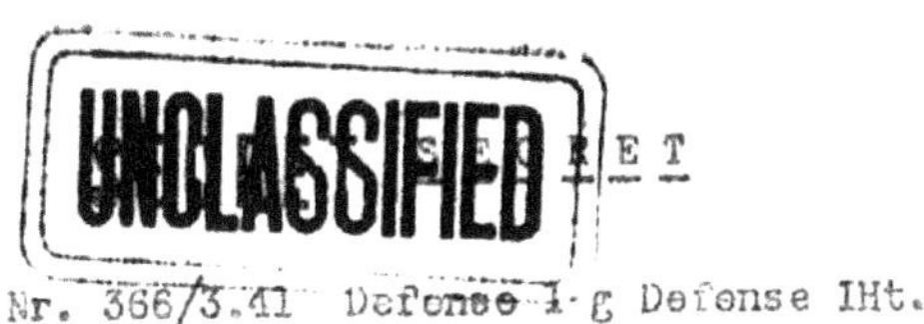

S E C R E T

Nr. 366/3.41 Defense I-g Defense IHt.

Even though the possibility that the Japanese are using plague bacilli as a weapon against the Chinese cannot be denied, the report of the agent still cannot be correct. For plague can hardly be caused by dried plague bacteria powder or dry, fine grains; if dry, the germs perish within 2 hours to a few days. If one considers that for the production of the usable powder, for the packing, the shipment, etc., one needs about 2 to 3 days, then one can hardly assume that live bactéria would get to their destination. Furthermore, various atmospheric conditions such as lighting, change of dryness and dampness, etc, are able to harm the germs especially badly and fast.

As another argument against the assumption that plague bacilli have been sprayed in this case one has, as already mentioned in the attached report, that 1) plague is indigenous to China, 2) the Chinese military authorities have not used the matter for propaganda purposes, 3) the Japanese would bring themselves into danger.

No. 124

About Bacteriological attack of the Chinese army during the Japanese -- China Conflict.

by

Oberfeldarzt Dr. med. E. Hozyo at the military medical academy.

In the year 1940.

-8-

In the year 1941.

No. 125

ABOUT BACTERIOLOGICAL WARFARE

by

Lt. Col. (med.) Enryo Hojo

to the

Army Medical School

ABOUT BACTERIOLOGICAL WARFARE

Contents

SECRET ~~SECRET~~

PREFACE

Bacteriological warfare is a new type of warfare, which uses as its weapons the pathogenic microbes and which attempts to utilize communicable diseases as means for war.

It is possible to wage this bacteriological warfare both in time of war and in time of peace; one can imagine that in peace-time communicable diseases are spread by sending spies into a certain assumed enemy ---- country. Thereby the country's inhabitants, domestic animals, agricultural products would be devastated.

In the 1925 disarmament conference of the League of Nations it was decided upon suggestion of specialists to prohibit use of bacteria such as poison gas, in war; these specialists were thinking of the dangerous effect of bacteriological warfare upon any nation. They referred the following proposal to the special committee for chemical and bacteriological weapons; namely, the waging of bacteriological warfare is to be strictly prohibited.

The representatives of 42 countries, including those of England, U. S., France, Russia, Germany, Italy, Japan, Finland, took part in this agreement.

But, if in spite of this agreement a state desired to make secret preparations for bacteriological warfare or if it attempted a bacteriological attack, it could hardly be supervised and hindered. That is the case because in the presence of persons afflicted with communicable diseases germs may be obtained at any time; furthermore, every laboratory receives pathogenic germs because of bacteriological studies and because of production of the various vaccines. Growing of bacteriological cultures for that purpose is not prohibited but is furthered. It is known to us that there were many cases of accidental and sudden epidemics in the history of war--history of communicable diseases.

Should these epidemics be repeated in future times, it would be very hard and almost impossible to decide whether their causes are natural or artificial germs retraceable to bacteriological warfare.

It is questionable whether in the case of a nation fighting for its honor such an idea of justice as propounded by the League of Nations will be upheld or not. In the case of a victorious enemy such a moral agreement might possibly be only a dead letter.

It is unknown to me (?), whether Japan at present is making preparations for bacteriological warfare or not; I believe, however, that under the present circumstances every state should certainly work on the prevention of epidemics.

Each and every state will take effective and strict precautionary measures against a bacteriological attack as long as exact information (?) as to how the enemy is going to use bacteria in time of war is not available. Should an enemy attack us with all sorts of bacterial agents, then it would be definitely necessary to have effective precautionary measures and thereby reduce the damage to a minimum.

It is undoubtedly true, however, that one cannot take the best possible precautionary measures without a thorough understanding of the methods employed by the enemy in a bacteriological attack.

SECRET S E C R E T

I should like to give my opinion about bacteriological warfare and precautionary measures against it. I have conjectured upon bacteriological methods which an assumed enemy-country might use and I have added to that our present knowledge of precautionary measures against communicable diseases.

The Types of Bacterial Agents Usable for Attack

It may be remembered that according to our knowledge of bacteriology and quite a bit of literature, in which bacteriological warfare is being mentioned, the following bacterial agents might be used in the attack phase of bacteriological warfare.

1. Agents which exert pathogenic influences on the human body and which may cause epidemics, especially in the Army.

2. Agents which exert pathogenic influences on animals and which may cause epidemics, especially in the case of animals used by the Army.

3. Agents which exert pathogenic influences on plants and which may destroy particularly grain and vegetables.

In every case the purpose of bacteriological attack is to reduce enemy armies and to cause confusion in the enemy homeland. It is therefore clear that the unexpected and explosive epidemic or exterminating large-scale infection is to be expected rather than the diffuse endemic.

It is evident that bacteria to be utilized for attack should be chosen with that purpose in mind; they should be easily obtainable and should be easily produced in large quantities. The following bacteria might be considered:

1. Agents for the human body-Vibrio cholerae, Bacillus dysenteriae, Bacillus paratyphosa, Febris melitensis (Malta-fever), Bacillus pestis, Bacterium tularense (Tularaemia), Bacillus typhosus, Yellow Fever.

2. Agents for animals - Anthrax, Glanders, Pleuropneumonia, Foot and Mouth Disease.

3. Agents for plants - "Uredinales" (plant pathogens ?) for wheat, potato-rot, Bacillus aroideae, Bacterium beticola for potatoes and others.

If it is desired to use the agents mentioned above as weapons, then the most important factors regarding their practical value are their productive capacity, resistance on the outside, ways of infection, germ carriers, conditions of immunity. Their important points are as follows:

a. Vibrio cholerae

Productive capacity--As a rule it is easily possible to produce on a large scale on agar. Culture medium is also usable but the fluid medium contains the antivirus. The cholera germs in the media develop within a certain threshhold and the germs are hard to obtain in case concentrated solution (fluidity?) is needed. The facts mentioned above possibly made culture media appear unfit as weapons.

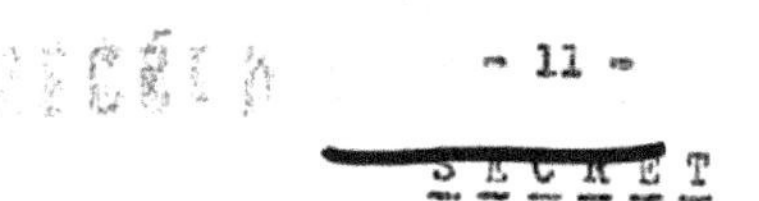

SECRET S E C R E T

SECRET

S E C R E T

Resistance on the outside--1 to 3 days in dirty water. A few weeks in running and salt water, 2 to 3 months in sterilized tap water. 1 to 3 days in the ground. Usually 1 to 3 days, somtimes as many as 30 days in defecation. 1 to 2 days if dry. Ways of infection--It is only possible to consider infection through the mouth.

Germ Carriers--Defecation and vomitus of sick and germ carriers; also substances soiled by them, such as flies, water, fish, vegetables, fruit, etc.

Conditions of immunity--Vaccination is effective for from 6 to 12 months. We have few good results from serum therapy.

b. Bacillus dysenteriae

Productive capacity--As a rule it is easily possible to produce on a large scale on agar. Culture media cannot be recommended for the same reason as with Vibrio cholerae.

Resistance on the outside--We should like to mention the weaker resisting Schiga--Kruse bacilli. 2 to 6 days in running and salt water. A few months in the wet ground. 2 to 3 days in defecation, approximately one week on garments. Approximately 10 days on fruit and vegetables. Approximately 30 minutes in the direct rays of the sun (during summer).

Ways of infection--It is only possible to consider infection through the mouth.

Germ Carriers--Defecation of sick and germ carriers; also substances soiled by them such as flies, water, vegetables, fruit and other drinks.

Conditions of immunity--Vaccination is effective for from 6 to 12 months.

Immunization through the mouth does not have a very noticeable effect. We have few good results from serum therapy.

c. Bacillus typhosus

Productive capacity--As a rule it is easily possible to produce on a large scale on agar. Culture media are not to be recommended for the same reason that applied for Vibrio cholerae.

Resistance on the outside--1 week in waste water, A few months in tap water. 5 to 10 days in running water. 1 to 3 months in the ground. 3 months in ice, 1 to 4 months in defecation. A few days on vegetables and fruit. 3 months on garments (military garments). A few months if dry (in a room). Approximately 2 hours under the direct rays of the sun (on agar).

Ways of infection--In most cases infection through the mouth; but to a certain extent infection through air and in a few cases infection through the skin can be taken into account.

Germ Carriers--Defecation, urine, excrements of sick and those soiled by them; fly, vegetables, fruit, and other drinks.

Conditions of immunity--Vaccination is effective for from 6 to 12 months. We have few good results for serum therapy.

d. Bacillus paratyphosus

- 12 -

S E C R E T

SECRET

S E C R E T

Productive capacity--The same as that of Bacillus typhosus.

Resistance on the outside--For weeks in waste water. 6 to 7 months in tap water. 2 to 3 months in well water. Approximately 1 month on vegetables and fruit. Strength of resistance if dry (?). Approximately half a year in dried germ film (at room temperature). Approximately 2 years in dried defecation.

Ways of infection-- In most cases infection through mouth, but infection through air may also be considered.

Germ Carriers--The same as those of Bacillus typhosus.

e. Bacillus melitensis (Malta Fever)

Productive capacity--It is possible fairly easily to produce in large scale production.

Resistance on the outside--Approximately 1 week in tap water. Approximately 2 months in sterilized water. Approximately 20 days in milk. Approximately 6 days in defecation and urine. 1 to 3 months on garments. For months in dried germ film (at room temperature).

Ways of infection--Infections are traceable to mouth, air, skin (incase of a wound).

Germ Carriers--Sick men and animals, and those soiled by their excretions, defecation, urine, milk. Many cases are infected by means of food and drinks, especially by goatmilk.

Conditions of immunity--Vaccination is used for prevention and healing. Effect of serum therapy is scanty, but recently Sulfonamid has been used to advantage.

f. Bacterium pestis

Productive capacity--As a rule it is easily possible to produce in large quantities on the agar. Addition of the vitimin factor or of Glutamic Acid Sodium Prolin as an activator is effective for mass productions. It is also possible to use the plague-carrying rat and fleas. It is not possible to obtain these rats and fleas in large quantities faster than bacteria; if, however, preparations taking a long time should be made, then their large-scale multiplication will be easy.

Resistance on the outside--5 to 20 days in tap water. 2 months in the ground. 18 days in grain. Six to twenty-four days in animal cadavers (at room temperature). Thirty days in the buried animal cadaver (packed in a case). Twenty days in the fester of bubonic plague. Ten to 16 days in the excretion of lung plague. Two days in the defecation of the plague - carrying rat (at room temperature). Weak resistance if dry; less than 24 hours on garments. 4 to 7 days in dried fester or innards of infected animals. 1 to 4 hours on cover glass in the rays of the sun. 18 hours on cotton and hemp fabrics. It can live 12 to 24 days in the cold at 0° to 20° below zero.

Ways of infection--Mostly infection by air, eye, and skin (in case of a wound); infection through the mouth has been shown, however.

Germ Carrier--Sick and their excretions (vomitus, fester, saliva, defecation, urine); those soiled by them; house, garment, tools, etc. The most important germ carrier is the flea which sucks the blood of the sick and of infected animals.

SECRET S E C R E T

Conditions of immunity--Vaccination is effective for approximately 6 to 12 months. Serum therapy can also be used to advantage. According to the latest reports Sulfonamid is also effective for healing purposes.

g. Bacterium tularense

Productive capacity--Unfavorable development on agar; one can produce fairly easily in large quantities on egg yolk medium or blood dextrose nutritive medium.

Resistance on the outside--3 to 4 weeks in the glucose medium (at room temperature). 5 days in the innards of a sick animal at room temperature, 14 days in a refrigerated room (below 0°C). Weak resistance if dry; 2 to 3 days on silk thread in dried air (at room temperature). Alive for 2 hours in nutritive medium in the direct rays of the sun.

Ways of infection--Infections by skin, mouth, air can be proven, hence the germ is advantageous for attack.

Germ Carriers--Excretions of patients and sick animals and those by them.

h. Bacterium tuberculosis

Productive capacity--It can be grown fairly easily in large quantities in a medium of glycerine agar.

Resistance on the outside--70 to 150 days in tap water. 48 days in the rotten animal cadaver. Sometimes it is possible to show a few bacilli 3 years after burial of the human body; 175 days in the buried animal cadaver. A few months in the drying house. Alive for 2 to 3 months in a wet and dark place.

Ways of infection--Infections through the air, skin, mouth are known to us.

Conditions of immunity--B.C.G. and A.O. vaccine which were supposed to give immunity with really poisonous live bacilli, and Tuberculin are effective according to report.

i. Corynebacterium diphtheriae

Productive Capacity--These bacteria may be produced in large quantities fairly easily in the Loeffler nutritive medium or in the glycerine-agar nutritive medium. The somewhat varying virulence of the bacilli is very much worth noticing.

Resistance on the outside--Approximately 3 months in dry (at room temperature). 5 months in pseudomembrane. If these bacteria are squirted into small droplets they remain alive for 1 to 2 days under indirect rays of the sun.

Ways of infection--Infection by way of the mouth; mostly the mucous membrane of the upper windpipe and sometimes other mucous membranes and the skin are infected.

Germ Carriers--Excretion, saliva and secretion (furnishes ?) the seat of the germ from sick and germ carriers (literal translation?).

Conditions of Immunity--Antitoxin is effective as a preventive measure. Immunization serum therapy is known to be effective.

j. Rabies

Productive Capacity--This agent is the filterable virus.

SECRET

S E C R E T

After infecting many dogs and rabbits with street virus and thereby making them sick, this virus may be obtained in large quantities from their brains and spines.

Resistance on the outside--This virus is sensitive to heat, its dying-out process being sped up by heating to 90°. It has stronger resistance against cold, however; it retains its virulence for approximately 1 month in the damp location at 10°below zero.

Weak resistance to drying--Pasteur proved great diminution of the virulence upon exposure to dried air (at room temperature) for 10 days.

Means of Infection--Wound by biting and contact by licking on the part of sick dogs cause infections.

Germ Carriers--Saliva of sick dogs.

Conditions of Immunity--Protective vaccination is known to be effective.

k. Typhus Fever

Conditions for Producing--This virus is Rickettsia prowazeki, is carried as known by the louse, hence for bacteriological attack one must produce lice in especial quantity and let them suck the blood of the sick. Louse contains the greatest amount of exciting agent (virus) in 5 to 7 days after sucking the blood of the patient. That the louse carrying the virus imparts the exciting agent to its nits has been proved. However, the mass production for bacteriological attack is somewhat difficult.

Resistance in the Outside World--Resistance of this virus is finally louse resistance, so I would like to mention the resistance of the louse.

Developed louse and nit are (remain?) alive 3 to 4 days long at 4° to 7° below zero. 24 hours (developed louse), 28 hours (nit) in water. 15 minutes (developed louse), 60 minutes (nit) at 60°.

Germ Carrier--Louse alone.

Immunity Conditions--Serum from man and animals, fallen sick, and active immunization by infected louse, are effective.

Effective vaccine is obtained from Rickettsia and organ-culture. Serum from the patient who has recovered is moreover effective for preventive injection.

l. Yellow Fever

Several yellow fever research workers such as Reed, Caroll and Agramonte (1901) expressed the idea that the exciting agent was a filterable virus and was transmitted by Aedes aegypti. Several authors later showed irregular tendencies of this virus, but in 1928 Stokes succeeded in infecting Macacus Rhesus and proved according to his work, that it was a filterable virus.

This pestilence is now restricted to South Africa and South America, however, where Aedes aegypti is found, the pestilence may break out; in Europe it is not always to be found, but one could in 1921 find 20,000 cases in Barcelona and in 1857 in Lisbon 7000 cases.

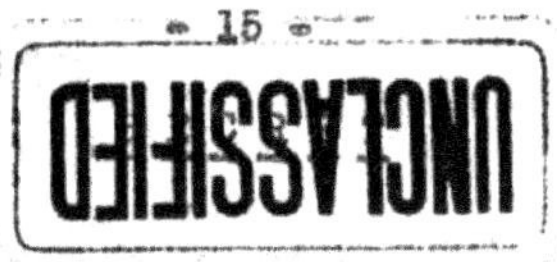

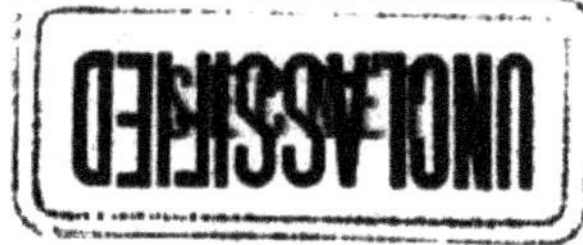

S E C R E T

The transmission of the germ from mosquito to man endures 12 days after blood sucking (poor construction; incubation period apparently meant).

This virus undergoes a certain change in the body of the mosquito and the mosquito egg too receives the virus.

This virus can be vaccinated one generation after another with mouse brain and guinea pig brain.

Production Conditions--For producing the virus one raises Aedes aegypti in quantity and allows them to suck the blood of Macacus Rhesus sick with the disease.

Resistance--When one cools the liver of the sick animal, pulverized in a vacuum desiccator, one can maintain the virulence for a long time. By refrigerating the liver itself the virulence does not diminish in 2 to 3 weeks. When one heats the virus for 5 minutes at 55°C, the virulence diminished very greatly.

Germ Carriers--Sick animals are in addition to Macacus rhesus, Macacus innus and Nemestrimus.

Aedes aegypti which sucks on these sick animals and patients, is the lone germ carrier.

Conditions of Immunity--Immunization through the first infection. According to reports the tissue-culture of the mouse fixation virus and of this virus is effective as a vaccine.

m. Bacillus anthracis

Productive Capacity--This bacillus grows sufficiently in any nutritive medium and may be produced very easily in large quantities. For preservation of the spores one likes to use spore-agar nutritive media.

Resistance on the Outside--Vegetating form of these bacilli is nearly the same as those of ther bacteria without spores. Strength of spore resistance is known to us all; under dry conditions it is alive for 20 to 30 years at room temperature.

Ways of infection--Infection through mouth and skin (wound) have already been proven. According to reports; infection through the windpipe is present as anthrax pneumonia.

Although this germ is an animal-epidemic germ, its effect on the human body in bacteriological use is notable.

Germ Carriers--Secretions of sick animals and seats of germs, and fodder infected by them.

Conditions of Immunity--Immunization with live germs, the poison being eliminated by the high-temperature method of culture, is of advantage. Immunization serum is used with effect.

n. Bacillus mallei

Productive Capacity--As a rule it can be produced in large quantities in the agar nutritive medium.

Resistance on the Outside--Approximately 2 months in water. With respect to direct rays of the sun and drying it is usually weaker than other bacteria.

- 16 -

S E C R E T

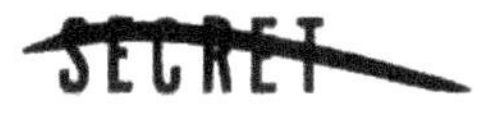

Ways of Infection--Infections by means of skin and air have been proven. Although this germ is also an animal epidemic germ, it has effects on the human body. In case of a bacteriological attack one should look out for human beings.

Germ Carriers--According to Reports vaccination with live germs, the poison having been eliminated, is effective.

o. The Foot and Mouth Disease

Productive Capacity--This germ is a filterable virus; artificial breeding is possible now. Therefore blood, defecation, urine, secretions as the focus of infection by the germs in the sick animals have to be utilized for bacteriological attack.

Resistance--It is possible to keep the virus without diminution of its virulence in the membrane as the germ focus for 5 days if placed in a reagent flask. In a refrigerated room it can be kept for 3 to 4 months.

Ways of Infection--Infections through skin and mouth have already been proven.

Germ Carriers--The seat of secretion of the germs, defecation, urine, milk of the sick animal.

Conditions of Immunity--Active immunization with serum of the sick animal is effective.

p. Tylenchus tritici

It is a species of the Nematoda which makes wheat unfruitful by sponging upon its seed buds.

q. Puccinia glumarum

It reduces the harvest of barley, wheat, rye by sponging upon the leaves of these plants. It may easily be grown in large quantities.

r. Tilletia tritici

It sponges upon the spicule of wheat, making it unfruitful and converting it to black spicule; thereby it falls to the ground and infects the new wheat the next year. Infection cannot be caused by breeding; the attack materials have to be multiplied in the particular wheat field. (?)

s. Phytophthoria infestans

It is a species of Pero osporoceae; it causes potato-leaves to become colored grey and to perish. This germ-thread invades the rootstock and infects the strength of the organism.

Large-scale breeding is easy.

A few other bacteria besides the agents mentioned above can be utilized as bacteriological weapons. Among all the agents causing epidemics in armies and population, however, it seems to us that these are the ones most easily obtainable in large quantities.

As yet I have not written about particular properties (?) of

the agents causing disease, especially about the virulence of the culture-germ. Consequently I should like to mention various points which are common to every germ with regard to improvement and preservation of its virulence.

It is known that the virulence of the agents is usually stronger in the beginning of their isolation from patients or sick animals. It is to be noted, however, that even among them this is sometimes not the case, ability to infect being absent. One should choose strains of normal biological and immunological properties.

In the strain which is kept for a long time the virulence is often weakened considerably. For intensification of the virulence one usually use experimental animals. If the given agents is able ti infect the animal (i.e., B. pestis, B. anthracis, B. mallei) the virulence can be increased through animal passage.

Bacteria as B. dysenteriae and V. cholerae to which animals are insensitive, raise the virulence for the experimental animal treated by animal passage; ability to infect the human body can hardly be increased, however.

This is also true in the case of many filterable viruses.

Our experiments have shown that "Astitijagar", "Hirnblei", Eggyolk-Agar are excellent as nutritive media as regards preservation of the virulence.

The Effects of the Bacteriological Attack

According to earlier literature a few investigators of bacteriological warfare had varying opinions about the bacteriological attack. One negates its effects; another one thinks of it as the most effective and cheapest method of attack; a third one insists that under present circumstances the effects cannot be determined.

Professor Juergens is perhaps the representative of those who negate the effects of the bacteriological attack.

Professor Juergens conceded the possibility of large-scale production of bacteria and their distribution among armies and population. He insisted, however, that by distribution alone one could not cause epidemics according to a certain purpose and plan. Therefore, he reasoned, it was impossible to cause indigenous (or native) infection, the purpose of which is the infection of the population.

Dysentery caused by bacilli is, for example, a terrible epidemic both in time of peace and in time of war. In past wars especially during sieges, dysentery epidemics used to break out in both besieging and defending armies, thereby placing both armies in danger (?). But existence of B. dysenteriae does not necessarily mean a spreading of the epidemic. Despite the occurrence of cases of dysentery along the whole front in the first world war, a large epidemic never broke out; it was always stopped effectively. It follows that the epidemic can cause a large-scale infection only if the conditions necessary for infection are present.

This is the case with V. cholerae. During the first world war many cases of cholera occurred among prisoners of war in bivouac in Danzig. Despite the fact that V. cholerae was shown to be present in the water of the district they were living in, the cholera epidemic did

not spread to the inhabitants of the district but remained alone with the bivouacking prisoners of war. Therefore the distribution or presence of bacterial agents may often cause infection but it does not exert a deciding influence on epidemics. The deciding influence (?) are conditions such as sensitivity of the human being for these agents, seasons of the year, etc.

Although infection has to take place in order to spread bacteria, occurrence of infection in itself does not necessarily mean an outbreak of an epidemic. The conditions necessary for an epidemic are, in fact, still unknown to us; an epidemic does not occur without infection, however.

So Professor Juergens contends that one need not be afraid of the effects of bacteriological warfare because spreading of the artificial agent does not always cause an epidemic.

The development of today's bacteriology allowed the furtherance of knowledge about every agent; the preventive measures showed fast progress and effective vaccinations were made. Means for fighting epidemics became, therefore, excellent.

Even if the terrible B. pestis or spotted typhus louse were spread in Germany at present, an epidemic would not break out. The conditions for infection are not present among civilized nations; the Professor therefore concludes that no special measures are necessary with reference to bacteriological warfare except preservation of health and good conditions of living.

Other specialists who recognize the effects of the bacteriological attack criticize the above mentioned opinion of Juergens as follows:

Professor Juergens does not deny absolutely that infection is indispensable for the spreading of an epidemic (?); but he does look at the matter too lightly (?).

If for a few days large quantities of intestinal mesenteric agents are put into the water supply and if inhabitants and the army are allowed to drink from it, then, perhaps, many sicknesses will occur. This large-scale infection equals in its result a widely-spread epidemic. Prof. Juergens does not mention this large-scale infection; with regard to bacteriological warfare it is of the greatest importance, however.

Nobody can guarantee that in case of artificial spreading of the bacterial agents large-scale infections will result. With regard to the possibility of infection one can notice many cases in the war history of humanity where in time of war large epidemics appeared even without a planned spreading of the germs. Even if that is disregarded, who can guarantee that this spreading is not always in agreement with every sort of condition for infection. (?)

So it seems to us that Juergens' denying opinion about the effect of bacteriological warfare, is perhaps a diligent attempt to keep his country's preparations for it a secret.

As already mentioned I have written a review of the denying and affirming opinion. The opinions of the specialists given in the special committee for chemical and bacteriological warfare at the 1927 disarmament conference of the League of Nations are as follows: bacteriological warfare is still a puzzle to us. One can only guess at the conditions allowing it to be waged, at the methods of waging it, and at the preventive measures against it. One knows about the existence of the pertinent explosive epidemics and one has data about natural forms of all epidemics. But one knows nothing about the effects of artificial infection on humans and animals.

Since the materials (and data?) at hand were hardly sufficient to judge the magnitude and importance of the possibility of bacteriological warfare, it was simply reported that the effects of bacteriological warfare were uncertain.

I, too, have to consider the effects of bacteriological warfare as certain. But it would be too hasty a step to deny these effects as Prof. Juergens did; conditions for infection are still in the dark and cannot be influenced by artificial treatments (theoretical discussions ?). One has to keep at one's studies diligently and solve undear questions.

Professor Trillat at the Pasteur Institute has been making an interesting study of the air-infection of chicken cholera since 1914. He makes clear that germ life in air depends upon pressure, temperature, humidity, electricity in the air, In 1930 he reported a connection between meteorological conditions and air-infection of chicken cholera; he particularly pointed out there are meteorological conditions for epidemic infection (?).

The epidemiological conditions which Prof. Juergens regarded as not clear are now being investigated by many research men

It is clear that in future times the (results ?) are going to be used for bacteriological warfare. In case a nation should find out these unclear epidemiological conditions for some agent and use them to best advantage, it could be victor in a bacteriological war.

Besides that I should think that it is too much to state that special preventive measures are not needed. One's life depends upon the present progressive hugiene and bacteriology.

Regardless how well the fight against epidemics is being pursued and regardless how much vaccines are being used, their power is limited. Bacause it is possible to spread a large quantity of poisonous agents I cannot believe that one would not be infected by one (?).

In case an air-raid shelter is built to withstand a 100 kg. bomb it would hardly withstand a 1000 kg. one. An air-raid shelter designed for a 1000 kg. bomb would likewise not be able to withstand a 2000-3000 kg. bomb and would be destroyed.

To speak about operational effects of bacteriological warfare, which would need just that, is premature, in order to judge its effects many questions remain to be solved; one may perhaps imagine, though, that secretly every nation is working on the solution of these questions.

Consequently we consider it wise to work on these questions on the one hand and on the other hand to take all sorts of preventive steps, guessing at all possible methods of attack for all agents.

The Anticipated Methods of Attack

The methods to be used for spreading the above mentioned agents among the enemy and causing epidemics should be chosen with reference to aims of the attack, species of agents for attack, methods of propagation of the agents.

With regard to a synopsis of the life of the agents, especially their resistance and their infection of humans, one finds the following methods:

(A) The method to allow to fall in streams (sprays ?)

(B) The artillery explosive method.
(C) The method to allow to drop.
(D) The method to allow to remain behind in case of retreat.
(E) The method to have spies spread the germs.

Following I should like to give my private opinion about the five methods mentioned above.

(A) The method to allow to fall in streams (sprays ?). This is the method in which the bacteria are usually transported by airplane and allowed to fall into the target by means of special apparatus.

(a) The method to allow the germ suspension to fall in streams (sprays ?). In case it is desired to have germ showers and have people and animals inhale the germs directly, especially large spray-diffusers are needed.

This method is suited for agents such as B. pestis, B. tularense, B. tuberculosis, B. diphtheriae, B. mallei, B. anthracis. This method has the disadvantage, however, of requiring dangerously low flying for a concentrated attack (?); also, the showers turn into a heavy fine fog (?).

With spraying at an altitude it is hard for the germs to reach their target because of the too slow velocity of descent; this is especially true in case of wind (?). If the germs are allowed to remain in the air for long they may die off and become ineffective.

Bacteria such as V. cholerae, B. dysenteriae, B. typhosus, Febris melitensis mainly infect fodder and water supplies and cause secondary infection through the mouth.

If possible, these bacteria should be used in a concentrated germ suspension; after mixture of the suspension with various effective nutritive media it should be allowed to fall in streams (sprays ?) and infect the target.

The larger the specific gravity of the germ solution the shorter will be the time of descent and consequently the better will be the accuracy. Therefore one can operate at flight height (?). Besides that, of course, one will use it especially for a purpose (?).

(b) The method to allow the dried and pulverized bacteria to fall in streams (sprays ?).

The agents with resistance against drying out (B. typhosus, B. tuberculosis, B. diphtheria, anthrax spores, agents for plants), mixed with starch or sand, may be allowed to fall in streams (sprays ?)--for this method special apparatus is necessary.

(c) The method to allow ampules with bacteria to fall in streams (sprays ?).

In this method the particular germ suspension is filled into many breakable ampules; these are then allowed to drop from an airplane, break, and spread. This method will be of use with regard to treatment of the agents and technique of spraying.

(d) The method to allow infected insects to fall in streams (sprays?).

In this method plague carrying fleas and typhus carrying lice are spread by allowing them to fall in streams from planes.

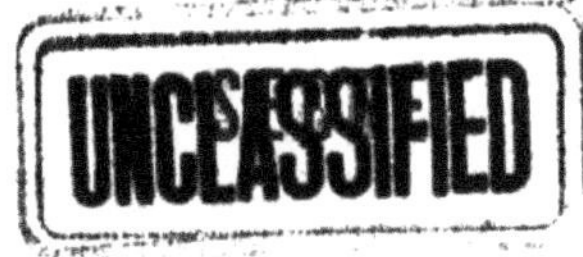

SECRET S E C R E T

They have to be intermingled with numerous little pieces of cloth or cotton fabrics in order to diminish the stirring-up (?) during descent.

(e) The method to allow the tissue of the infected animal or excretion and secretion of patients to fall in streams (sprays ?).

It is possible to spray the following in suspension from a plane in accord with the concentrated germ--suspension method: The ground tissues of those which carry the unbreedable agents, such as the viruses of rabies, the foot and mouth disease, etc; the ground innards of animals which have died from anthrax or glanders, and the bacterial agents carried by cholera, typhoid, dysentery patients.

(B) The artillery explosive method. In this method the bacterial agents are fired into the targets in special bombs or cannon balls.

(a) The Bomb. This method is usable with agents being able to resist explosions. In order to spray these agents over a large area the bombs should explode about 100 m to 50 m above the target.

To make this bomb of porcelain or glass is effective for the existence of the agents (?); it will hardly be a dummy because it will break easily during descent. With a diminished quantity of powder it is also possible to spray such insects as plague carrying fleas by this method, in the hope that they will not die out (?).

(b) The Bombardment. A target can be bombarded with gas bombs, many bacterial agents being squeezed in instead of poisonous gases. In that way the agents are sprayed and opportunity for infection exists.

These germ-suspensions should be made in concentrated and mucous consistency; gelative, gum-arabic or chicken eggs should be added in order that the germ will not be killed off during the explosion.

(C) The method to allow infected animals and insects to fall. The following should be put into appropriate containers, flown by plane and brought into the target by parachute; mice infected with plague; dogs and flies infected with rabies; those having been allowed to suck the blood of yellow fever patients; and others. The containers should be designed in such a way as to open by themselves upon landing.

(D) The method to allow bacterial agents to remain behind in case of retreat. The method consists of infecting all articles of possible use to the enemy with bacterial agents. This method is very easily carried out and is very useful.

(E) The method to have spies spread the germs. This method consists of having spies transport the germs secretly and having them spread them in useful localities in the enemy country, starting epidemics there. The design of the germ containers has to be considered carefully.

As a supplement to the work of spies dropping from a plane has to be taken into account. A combination of the anticipated methods of attack with the ways of infection is mainly the following (?).

The Assumed Operation

I have already mentioned the effects of bacteriological weapons and their anticipated methods of attack. Now one has to consider very carefully the use of this bacteriological weapon in an operation.

- 22 -

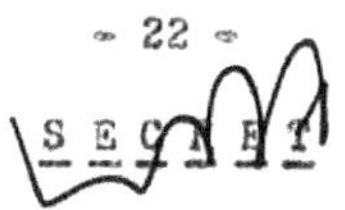

SECRET S E C R E T

According to the properties bacteriological weapons should really have the same infectious effects on both friend and enemy. Unless these weapons are used carefully they may infect the friend who has sprayed them. For operational use of bacterial weapons one has, therefore, to know exactly the types of infection and their effects, especially the correlation of the season and locality with particular epidemics; one has to select targets not endangering the friend, and has to choose appropriate weapons and methods of attack (?).

Mainly the following targets of the bacteriological attack may be imagined:

(a) Army	(e) Water supply
(b) Rear area	(f) Factory
(c) Fortress	(g) Breeding animals
(d) Town	(h) Agrarian product.

(A) It is possible to make a bacteriological attack upon an army which is close to our own (?). In case the friendly army is supposed to occupy the enemy's former positions, bacteriological weapons can be used only sparingly. But wherever a line of battle develops and the enemy position is strong, bacteria which the friendly army can easily fight, such as these causing intestinal infection, should be used.

If one has to retreat, the above mentioned method of leaving bacteria agents behind in case of retreat should be thoroughly applied. Plague-carrying mice, plague-carrying fleas, yellow fever-carrying flies are let loose in houses; strong doses of cholerae, B. typhosis, B. dysenteriae, B. melitensis are put into remaining fodder, tapwater, well-water. It is especially important to get B. botulinus into canned goods so that their contents will not change. This method of leaving bacterial agents behind is very useful because the enemy is hardly able to detect it.

B. anthracis and B. mallei should be sprinkled into horse fodder. During the Japanese-Chinese incident the Chinese army used to apply this method frequently, embarrassing the Japanese army in the beginning. When we advanced toward Shianhai the Chinese army sprayed V. cholerae and B. dysenteriae into appropriate wells at every retreat; it was possible to show that V. cholerae had been sprayed so heavily into one well that the well water seemed to be a germ suspension. At the battle near Jyuukian many cases of cholera occurred among the inhabitants and the Japanese army after the Chinese army had fled. In well water near the locality where these cases occurred, V. cholerae was proven to be present; at the same time numerous fragments of an ampule with bacteria used by the Chinese army were found. This represented definite proof of the bacteriological work of the Chinese army.

(B) In case of attack upon rear areas their military installations, army, inhabitants, etc., should be attacked with all methods; supply to the battle line should be stopped. This is useful to the operation.

(C) In case of attack upon a fortress, in particular upon an isolated fortress, the bacteriological attack is very useful; every type of bacterial agent and all methods of attack are usable.

(D) In case of attack upon a city such agents as those causing infection through air or skin should be utilized. Hygienic appliances (and methods ?) are being developed in many cities; agents which cause infection through the mouth are easily controlled and their effect is perhaps small. It is naturally useful for the operation to have epidemics break out in towns of military or political--economic importance, thus disturbing the enemy's methods of supply (?).

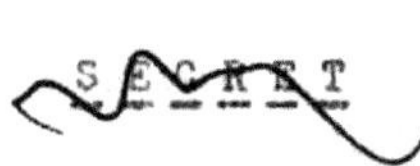

SECRET S E C R E T

(E) Water supply of tap water should be the best target of the bacteriological attack. Bacterial agents particular to water, such as V. cholerae, B. dysenteriae are naturally used.

(F) It seems to us that the first target among factories are the military ones; later targets are factories making other products. With regard to the actual operation it is naturally useful to have epidemics break out among the workers in the most important factories of the enemy country, thereby stopping their work. On the other hand the attack is perhaps effective because it exerts influence upon trade and economy of the nation and because it diminishes the nation's power. In case of attack upon factories it is very useful to have spies infect food being imported into that area with bacterial agents working through the mouth.

(G) Breeding animals and agrarian products. Breeding animals can be attacked fairly easily with B. anthracis and B. mallei and agrarian products with every type of plant agent; the methods of attack used are to allow to fall in streams or the method of utilizing spies.

I have already mentioned the attack--targets during an operation. I have also mentioned that with regard to bacteriological weapons many unclear points remain. It is not always possible to cause large epidemics to break out by spraying in small quantities; in that case only spraying in large quantities can cause a large-scale infection (?).

It follows that attacks with small quantities repeated a hundred times are inferior to a few attacks with large quantities. If we launch a bacteriological attack we have to count on an avenging attack by the enemy stronger than our own. It is evident that shelter (and precautionary measures against such an attack ?) have to be completed. At the same time he (the enemy?) is bound to realize that he has to attack and destroy enemy factories producing bacteriological warfare agents.

The Protective Measures Against Bacteriological Warfare

As regards protective measures against bacteriological warfare, the aims of control of epidemics which have been taken into account up to now should remain unchanged; those include prevention of virus importation, destruction of the bacterial agent, restricting the manners of infection, carrying through of individual preventive measures. Up to now every sort of preventive measure has been taken against the natural infection. In case of an attack with bacteriological weapons where every sort of infectious agent, the propagation of which might be outside all contemplation, would be sprayed everywhere, the methods of epidemic control carried through up till now might not any more fit the purpose. I should like to mention my private opinion about preventive measures against bacteriological warfare.

1. As regards prevention of virus importation, protection against plane attack is of the utmost importance; that is the case because in bacteriological warfare the spraying method by plane mentioned above would be likely to be used most often. From the point of view of control of epidemics, air superiority is absolutely necessary.

One must not only concentrate all of one s power on the stricter control of epidemics and enforcement of the quarantive, but also has to concentrate on plugging-up the hold of agent-spraying by spies; this is particularly necessary in localities liable to become targets of a bacteriological attack, such as military positions, fodder store-fouses, water supply.

- 24 -

SECRET

S E C R E T

SECRET S E C R E T

Furthermore it is perhaps a very useful precautionary measure to destroy the bacteriological strong points of the enemy; these include factories producing bacteriological warfare agents, bacteriological institutes, bacteriological field laboratories.

2. Regarding the destruction of the bacterial agent it is very important to find in short order the places under attack and the types of agents used; a complete disinfection has to be carried through at once. Improvement of every sort of the arrangement for disinfection is absolutely necessary, especially for the people in and behind the lines of battle.

It is evident that the bacteriological field laboratories on the battle field should be charged with the detection of bacterial agents and with disinfection; but even in the rear areas every military and civil organization having bacteriological laboratories has to be given the assignment mentioned above. In times of peace the assigned territories (?) should be divided. In a locality under attack timely and suited measures have to be taken, such as separation from other places and closing down of traffic; this should be enforced until disinfection has been completed according to the properties of the agents.

In places where the target of the bacteriological attack is easily recognizable, such as water supply, factories producing foodstuffs and their storehouses, the hygienic supervision has to be increased; timely investigation and disinfection have to be carried through thoroughly.

3. Regarding restriction of the manners of infection one has to equip special shelters (such as air-raid shelters) and find safety there. If necessary, these shelters have to be built air-tight; their ventilating apparatus requires an air-purifier (especially disinfection). Anti-mouse, anti-fly, anti-gnat (?) devices have to be completed, of course.

On the battle field one has to prohibit the utilization of water supplies and food-stuffs left behind by the enemy, unless the bacteriological field laboratories have investigated them first. It may very well be expected that losses through bacteriological weapons will decrease as hygienic measures progress; therefore military and civilians have to be indoctrinated with the known facts about bacteriological warfare, especially precautionary measures, hygiene, and epidemic control.

4. Regarding individual precautionary measures the vaccination is perhaps extremely effective and reliable. It is true that one frequently runs into epidemics whose effects have not as yet been recognized exactly. One does recognize, however, the effects of preventive measures against some epidemics, in particular (?) against the ones assumed above as the bacteriological weapons; these effects are recognized, whether they are active immunity, passive immunity, or mixed immunity. As the types of bacteriological weapons increase the types of vaccinations will likewise increase; eventually the necessity (?) to use all these vaccinations will become annoying to us. Simplification of vaccinations, such as measures involving mixed immunity are certainly a question urgently requiring investigation.

Besides administering vaccinations, anti-germ masks and anti-germ garments will have to be distributed for defense. According to our experiments the gas masks and anti-germ garments are effective mainly against poison gas; however, we were also able to definitely recognize their effects against bacteria. In that respect one, therefore, does not need to prepare oneself doubly.

Furthermore it is very necessary and useful that with regard to defense against bacteriological warfare everybody look out for his hygiene; everybody should further his health to remove sensitivity for every sort of epidemic (?).

Equipment for Bacteriological Warfare

Above I have shown in outline form a possibility for realization of bacteriological warfare. The sort of equipment needed for it is interesting to everybody. Presuming furthermore that this equipment is necessary for realization of bacteriological warfare, I should like to give my private opinion in outline form (?) about necessary equipment.

(A) Productive equipment.

As has already been mentioned, the aim of bacteriological warfare is large-scale infection through large-scale spraying of the bacterial agents. It is generally known that the power of multiplying of bacteria is very large; so it seems to us that large-scale production of bacteria is easy. However, if used as weapons, a suitable quantity can hardly be bred in reagent bottles. If, for example, it were desired to have 1 ton of live typhoid bacilli for airplane spraying on nutritive agar, then the following large rooms, various instruments, and personnel would be needed. Large reagent bottles - - - - - -

20,000,000 bottles, a necessary quantity (?) of 50 mg of live culture per 1 bottle.

Metal baskets as containers for the reagent bottles - 2000,000,0 (200,000 ?) baskets, 100 bottles per 1 basket.

Nutritive agar - 4000,000,000 cc, but 20 cc of laboratory (space ?) necessary for 1 (cc ?) of nutritive agar.

Large high pressure - sterilization instruments -- 400 instruments; one sterilizes 400 baskets at one time and does this five times each per day.

Large incubators - - - 200 incubators, 1000 baskets per 1 incubator.

Drying chambers - - 800 drying chembers; one sterilizes 50 baskets at one time and does this five times each per day.

For vaccination (und Auskratzung) necessary personnel - - 10,000 personnel (abertäglich 20 Körbe auf den Kopf).

Necessary working space - - Approximately 30,000 square meters, working space of personnel and store rooms for instruments being included.

The things listed above are only part of the necessities; one would actually need many more instruments and personnel. Whether one can prepare so many instruments, personnel, and large working space for the production of 1 ton of live bacteria is questionable; it is impossible with the old laboratory procedure.

In that respect the following mechanization and simplification should be thought out; mass production processes for nutritive media, mass vaccination (and Auskratzungs) processes, chambers and instruments for mass culture, sterilization processes.

SECRET S E C R E T

It will be hard to multiply in large quantities and infect insects such as fleas, lice, bugs, gnats, and animals such as mice and dogs, -- it is very important to find simplifications for these processes.

(B) Equipment for attack.

Since I already have mentioned the assumed (?) methods for a bacteriological attack, I should here only like to enumerate the articles necessary for the attack.

(a) Spraying apparatus, plane to be equipped with it. Apparatus for germ fog, concentrated germ suspension, dried germ powder, insects, ampules with germs, etc.

(b) Bombs. With sensitive fuse, insensitive fuse, set fuse, air pressure fuse, etc.

(c) Parachutes. For animals, insects, etc.

(d) Cannon balls (shells ?). For concentrated germ suspension, dried germ powder, etc.

(e) Materials for spies. One has to think daily of fruit, foodstuffs, and other materials.

(C) Protective equipment.

I have already mentioned preventive measures against germs. Here I should only like to mention the following questions important for the carrying-out of bacteriological warfare.

(1) Mass shelters

(a) Completed public shelters (air raid shelters). As already mentioned, the air raid shelter has to be equipped with apparatus able to make it completely airtight. For ventilation there are air-purifiers (especially disinfection apparatus).

(b) Selection of the leaders for epidemic control. In case of bacteriological attack there are many cases where proof for the attack is hardly found. This is especially the case if the attack is made cunningly. In order to detect it early and initiate preventive measures, bacteriologists have to be made systematic and authorized supervisors and leaders in epidemic control.

(c) Groups with suited (suitable?) personnel should be formed on battle fields as well as in capitals and neighborhood communities, in order to investigate and fight epidemics. These groups should be given the mission to investigate bacteriological attack a gents and to fight epidemics.

(d) Enlargement of public disinfection facilities. It cannot be predicted how often cases needing disinfection will multiply with realization of bacteriological warfare. Disinfection facilities have to have enough room to be on the safe side in that respect.

(2) Individual protective measures

SECRET S E C R E T

(a) Larger application and execution of vaccination. One should produce beforehand every type of bacteriological agent in laboratories of every locality (?).

(b) Equipment of safety garment and anti-germ mask. They should protect everybody against poison gas, too.

Resources for Preparation for Bacteriological Warfare.

I have already presented in outline form the defensive measures and the necessary equipment for bacteriological warfare. Here I should like to write about the resources which have to be taken into account if it is desired to carry out bacteriological warfare as mentioned.

For preparation of bacteriological warfare one needs the above mentioned planes, cannons, spraying apparatus, special bombs and cannon balls, etc. Besides that one needs inland resources such as materials for investigation of germ cultures and for disinfection.

Since particularly the resources for mass production of germ cultures might suddenly be cut off, they have to be stored in sufficient quantity in time of peace.

If one wants to figure on the culture materials necessary for the production of 1 ton of B. typhosus and on the necessary daily quantity of vaccine suspension (?), one will need the quantities enumerated below;

Culture materials for the production of 1 ton of B. typhosus.

Agar - - - - - - - - - - - - - - - -	10,200 kg
Bouillon - - - - - - - - - - - - - - -	3,400 kg
Peptone - - - - - - - - - - - - - - -	3,400 kg
Table salt - - - - - - - - - - - - - -	170 kg
Caustic soda - - - - - - - - - - - - -	150 kg

Since the purpose of bacteriological warfare is mass infection through large-scale spraying of the bacterial agents, a yes or no as to the possibility of mass production is perhaps the deciding factor in this type of warfare. Mass production of the agents depends undoubtedly upon the resources of nutritive media available. Although at present basic investigative problems of bacteriological warfare are still in dispute, it is impossible to foresee at what time an enemy might use his new weapons against us.

If one is thinking of bacteriological warfare, even if only in terms of a possible plan (?), one should prepare resources for it with diligence.

SECRET

No. 124

A few proofs for bacteriological attacks carried out by the Chinese army.

1) Cases of spreading of bacteria by the Chinese army which are confirmed by the Japanese army (?).

Before retreating the Chinese army has frequently sprayed bacterial agents into wells, tap water, foodstuffs, etc, with intent to cause epidemics in the Japanese army.

Japanese medical troops have verified many cases of spraying of bacteria; the table below gives a summary of such cases.

Time	Locality	Places sprayed	Verified bacterial agents
Aug-Oct 1937	Vicinity of Shanghai	Well, 4 places	V. cholerae
October 1937	Vicinity of Shanghai	Well, 1 place	B. typhoid
Nov. 1938	Vicinity of Taiso	Creek	B. anthracis
Jan. 1938	Sowcho	Well	B. typhoid
Jan. 1938	Nanking	Water basin	B. anthracis & B. typhoid
May 1938	Jyochu	Water melon	V. cholerae
July 1938	Tynkian	Well	V. cholerae
Nov. 1938	Kantong	Tap water reservoir	B typhoid & paratyphoid
June 1939	Unchan	Well	V. cholerae
August 1939	Shinscho	Well	V. cholerae

The spraying of bacteria performed by the Chinese army in case of retreat may be proven as shown above; one can assume that there are many more cases besides the ones mentioned there.

Although the Japanese army has always considered control of epidemics many cases of epidemics have nevertheless occurred.

2) About ampules for spraying of bacteria which were found on a Chinese spy.

When the Japanese army occupied the vicinity of Shanghai in 1937, a Chinese spy with bacteria-ampules as shown in the following figures was captured. This spy was captured in a Japanese occupation - territory; he confessed that he had received orders to spray bacterial agents into wells, foodstuffs, etc., for the Japanese army.

This ampule is the one made of brown glass (diameter appr. 1.5 cm, height appr. 2.5 cm); it contains about 2 cc of suspension, similar to a bouillon-culture suspension.

They were all grown and tested; various types of live agents, as shown in the following figures, were shown to be present.

3) A definite proof that the Chinese army has sprayed V. cholerae into wells.

Immediately after the Japanese army had occupied Tyukian in 1938, cholera occurred in the Japanese army and among remaining inhabitants. An investigation by the Japanese field laboratory proved

- 30 -

that V. cholerae was present in well water near the place of occurrence of the cases. After drainage of the well ampule splinters as shown in the following figure (Feb. 3) were found at its bottom.

This is exactly the same ampule as had previously been found on the Chinese spy.

What has been said definitely proves that the Chinese have used bacteria as a weapon.

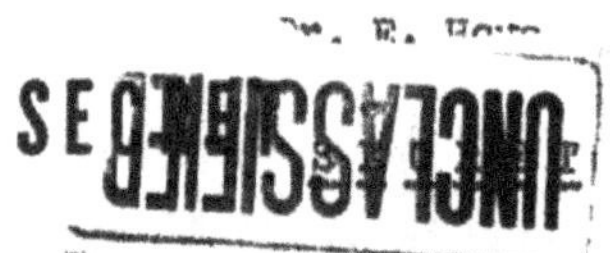

Questions (by Kliewe) about the essay "Bacteriological War" by Dr. E. Hoyo

1. For what purpose was the essay written? To whom else was it shown?

2. *P. 21, (A): What is meant by "the method of releasing in streams"?

3. P. 21, (a): Are the germs to be released in the form of rain dispersals or in the form of clouds (as aerial brine)?
Are there special additional substances for the conservation of the germs? Is distilled water, NaCl solution, or bouillon used as solvent?

4. P. 22: How large are the drops formed when germ solutions are released? At what heights are the releases made, and under what atmospheric conditions? Are there any experimental data available?

5. P. 22, (C): What is meant by "releasing pulverized bacteria in streams?

6. P. 22, (c): How large are the ampules for the bacterial solutions, and what is their shape?

7. P. 23, (B): Would the germs released in bombs or shells not be killed by the heat of explosion?

8. P. 23, (b): Are the bombs which are filled with bacterial solutions coated with rust resisting material (glass, varnish, etc.)?

9. P. 24, (c): How can you shoot disease agents (tetanus, gas-gangrene, melitensis, tularemia, plague) from a rifle?

10. P. 24, (C): Are the containers used for dropping animals by parachute made of glass or metal?

11. Is it of greater advantage to spread plague bacilli by means of infected fleas or infected rats?

12. P. 30: How can you be sure when the enemy has disseminated germs? How do you prove the existence of germs in the air?

13. P. 31, 3: How are the trenches to be disinfected? Can vapors of formaldehyde be used?

14. Are masks a protection against viruses?

15. Do the Russians, Chinese, or Americans have mass production factories of bacteria? What germs are manufactured, and where are those factories?

16. Has Japan established mass defense stations (AA trenches with disinfecting apparatus, organization of troops for the examination of germs and the combating of epidemics), or are they merely planned? Why are no animal disease agents mentioned?

* T.N. - Page numbers listed above refer to original document.

3.68 29 Jun. 1945: CHINA: PLAGUE OUTBREAK IN AREA SOUTH OF T'ENG-CH'UNG, SOUTHWEST YUNAN, JUNE 1944 - JANUARY 1945, Chinese Doctor, Representative of the Chinese National Health Administration

资料出处：National Archives of the United States, R112, E295A, B11.

内容点评：本资料为 1945 年 6 月 29 日美军中国战区收到的中国中央卫生署医生报告，题目：1944 年 6 月至 1945 年 1 月云南西南部腾冲南部地区鼠疫的爆发流行。

-CH-45   ETD #5301.0300 (218) 177985

TNA   At: Kunming, China   Date: 29 June 1945

Reference: JICA/Ch[illegible] May 45   Evaluation: C-2

Source: Chinese doctor, representative of the Chinese National Health Administration.

7152 Subject: CHINA: PLAGUE OUTBREAK IN AREA SOUTH OF T'ENG-CH'UNG, SOUTHWEST YUNNAN: June 1944 - January 1945

Transmitted herewith is a report of a plague outbreak in Southwest Yunnan in the Burma Road area during June 1944 to mid-January 1945. It was prepared by Dr. Y. N. Yang of the Chinese N. H. A. (National Health Administration) who had been loaned to direct the investigation and control of this outbreak. Dr. Yang was formerly Commissioner of Fukien Provincial Plague Prevention Bureau and is also the Director of the N.W. E.P.B. (Northwest Epidemic Prevention Bureau) located at LAN-CHOW, Kansu. The report was made available by the Chief Surgeon, China Theater.

Plague has occurred in this section of Southwest China for many years and during the pandemic of 1894-96 approximately 20,000 deaths due to plague were reported for this area. In 1943, during September and October, a serious epidemic of unknown number of cases occurred in the T'ALUNGCHUAN area. From February through May 1944 another outbreak occurred in the same section and 148 deaths are known to have resulted. In June 1944 plague was introduced into LAN-TUNG, one of 50 some odd villages in the LO PU SZU CHUANG (罗卜思庄) (E98-10, N24-37) rice-growing section south of T'ENG-CH'UNG (腾冲) (E-98-29, N25-01). During July and August 138 cases with 105 deaths were recorded from 10 of the LO PU SZU CHUANG villages. The disease spread northward to CHI-[illegible]U-CHI and CHE-[illegible]AO and during July and August, 26 cases with 14 deaths were reported from those two towns. Again the disease spread northward; by November it appeared in NAN-TIEN (南甸)(E-98-20, N24-49) where from 9 November 1944 to 9 January 1945, 102 cases with 23 deaths occurred. Dead rats were found in all of the towns where human plague cases occurred.

Paragraph 3 gives an analysis of the NAN-TIEN cases. 59% of the cases had received plague vaccine and many had been treated with serum and sulfa drugs thus the fatality rates were lower among this group. The analysis gives the distribution of the cases according to age groups, according to location of the "bubo", according to whether or not plague vaccine had been given and gives the case fatality rates in relation to the type of treatment used. The fatality rates were much higher in the older age groups, in those not having had plague vaccine and amongst those having had inadequate treatment. The results obtained in this small series of cases indicates the effectiveness of plague vaccine.

Excellent descriptions of the homes and living conditions which have enabled plague to become endemic in the area are presented in Par 4. A discussion of preparatory preventative work is also given. Par 5 offers suggestions for future anti-plague work. The importance of cooperation between the groups working in the area is emphasized. To eliminate plague from this area would require much time, personnel, equipment, and funds which are not now available. The best that can be hoped for at this time is an adequate plague control program. The report is valuable and since the Burma Road passes through this plague endemic area it is most important that the disease be controlled. Two maps and five tables are included in the report.

MIS 177985   Incl:
              With all copies.

Socio 1
Sci 2
Route
Ldh
Spec Br 1
HQAAF 2
CWS 2
Med 2
Int Div 1
CSW 1
CNT 3
OSS 2

7152 PAUL [illegible] SLATER,
Lt. Col. [illegible]

Approved and Forwarded:

HAROLD [illegible],
Colonel, C.A.C.

[illegible] MACDONALD,
Commander, USNR.

DISTRIBUTION: JIAMC; Chief Surgeon, [illegible], Surgeon/USS; Surgeon/SOS*; Surgeon JICA file (2); [illegible]
*thru Surgeon/14th AF & CO, [illegible] /thru Surgeon/CTC / CCC

RESTRICTED RESTRICTED

A PRELIMINARY REPORT ON AN OUTBREAK OF PLAGUE IN THE AREA SOUTH OF T'ENG-CH'UNG PREPARED BY DR. Y. N. YANG AND SUBMITTED BY HIM AT KUNMING, YUNNAN, 18 January 1945

1. Circumstances Leading to the Survey.

On the 23rd of December 1944 I was informed of an outbreak of plague around T'ENG-CH'UNG area by Dr. Claude Forkner and Maj. Mouton, Dr. C. H. Hwang (黄祯祥) and Dr. L. S. Chu (朱亮威). I was given permission to proceed to Kunming from Chungking by air on 29 December 1944. After reaching Kunming conferences were held with representatives of the U. S. Army Medical Department, Yunnan Provincial Health Administration, the National Epidemic Prevention Bureau and the Friends Ambulance Unit. On the 31st of December 1944 we flew to T'ENG-CH'UNG. Two days were spent there in enlisting military and civil support. The trip from T'ENG-CH'UNG to NAN-TIEN was made on horseback on 3 January 1945. The services of the following organizations were co-ordinated upon arrival: Dr. T. C. Ma and Dr. Y. C. Li representing the Yunnan Provincial Health Administration; Captain Rouderbough of the liaison office of the 198th Division, Chinese Army; a team of workers of Friends Ambulance Unit attached to the 198th Division. Furthermore Dr. Peter Roads and two foreign nurses (Miss Briggs and Miss King) from the Friends Ambulance Unit joined us. Mr. C. T. Koo (過基同) a sanitary engineer of the National Health Administration flew from Chungking to T'ENG-CH'UNG in two stages. Dr. P. H. Teng, formerly of the Fukien Provincial Plague Prevention Bureau and Dr. C. C. Wang joined the NAN-TIEN team of workers on the 9th of January. The workers left behind for further work are: In NAN-TIEN: Dr. P. H. Teng, Dr. L. S. Chu from the National Institute of Health, Mr. C. T. Koo of the Sanitary Corps, Chungking, Dr. C. C. Wang especially engaged by the Plague Committee, Dr. Roads, Friends Ambulance Unit, Mr. D. Stafford, Friends Ambulance Unit, Mr. M. Tai, Yunnan Provincial Health Administration, Dr. Y. C. Li, Yunnan Provincial Health Administration. In T'ENG-CH'UNG: Dr. T. C. Ma, Yunnan Provincial Health Administration and Dr. Y. Chi, of the same organization. Dr. P. H. Teng will be in charge of the affairs set-up from the time of the departure of Dr. Y. N. Yang.

The Epidemic of Bubonic Plague in the T'ENG-CH'UNG Area.

At a conference attended by 35 residents and senior dignitaries I was told that at the time of the world pandemic in 1894-96, the following areas and cities were visited by plague. More than 20,000 people succumbed to the disease in the YIN-KIANG (盈江), BHAMO (八莫), NAN-TIEN (南甸), LUNG-CHUAN (龍川), LUNG-LING (龍陵) and PAO-SHAN (保山) Areas.

Drs. Robertson, Jettmar and F. F. T'ang also carried out plague work in 1939.

Dr. Y. C. Li of the Yunnan Provincial Health Administration made a trip south as far as TA-LUNG-CHUAN (大龍川) and found that an epidemic of bubonic plague had broken out in TA-LUNG-CHUAN in September and October 1943. (See Map Appendix I). There is no record available of the actual number of cases. From February to May 1944, it was known that 142 deaths had been reported. LUNG-CHUAN (龍川) is about 2 days walk from the Burma border, and has a population of about 1,000 homes. The natives there said that plague epidemic used to break out every year in districts at the Burma border.

From TA-LUNG-CHUAN northward, an outbreak of bubonic plague was reported in LO PU SHIH CH'UAN (羅卜司莊) from July to September 1944. (See Maps Appendix I and II). This is about two days walk from TA-LUNG-CHUAN. Between these two places no plague cases have been reported except one unverified case in SHAN MU LUNG (杉木龍). The story goes that a trader came back from TA-LUNG-CHUAN to MAN TUNG (蛮東), a village in LO PU SHIH CH'UAN, in the latter part of June 1944, was taken ill with symptoms of bubonic plague and died a few days later. Dead rats were, however, found in the village one month before appearance of the first human case. In the months of July and August there were altogether 50 cases of bubonic plague in MAN TUNG with 35 deaths. Early in July, a woman in HSIAO HUNG PO (小紅坡) came down with this disease after a visit to MAN TUNG. Since then 23 more cases were reported in HSIAO HUNG PO in July and August. Here again dead rats were found about one month before the outbreak amongst the human population. LO PU SHIH CH'UAN consists of 48 villages in the valley, where the road leading to T'ENG-CH'UNG passes,

From: JICA/CAIMA, Kunming. R-673-CI-45 29 June 1945

PRS/rew Page 2 RESTRICTED

RESTRICTED

RESTRICTED

and four villages up in the hills. Of the 48 villages in the valley, plague cases were reported in 10 villages--including the two just mentioned--namely NA MENG (那猛) 9 cases and all died; HSIAO HUNG PO 24 cases with 14 deaths; LI SO (里索) 28 cases with 24 deaths; HSIAO WAN (小碗) 9 cases all died; HU TUNG (户东) 5 cases all died; CHI (CHE) MAO (遮帽) 6 cases with 4 deaths; CHIN MENG (金猛) 2 cases both died; LAN TUNG 50 cases with 35 deaths; WANG CHAO (望着) 3 cases all died. Dead rats were found where human cases occurred. In TA SHU CHAI (大树寨) dead rats were found but no human cases were reported. Of the four villages on the hills, only two cases, all recorded, ... were reported from village KUO CHIA CHAI (郭家寨) (See Map Appendix A-1 and 2).

In districts north of LO TU SHIH CHUAN 20 cases of bubonic plague with 11 deaths were reported from CHI MU CHAI (杞木寨) in July and August of last year. Dead rats were also found there. However, no dead rats nor human cases were found in LIANG HO (梁河). In CHE TAO (遮岛) where the chief of the tribesmen resides there were 6 cases with 3 deaths occurred in December. Dead rats too were found in that place. In NAN-TIEN (南甸) there occurred a very severe epidemic in November-December 1944. Since the medical corps of the 198th Division as well as the epidemic prevention units of the Yunnan Provincial Health Administration (YPHA) were there at that time, more detailed records of the epidemic were available, which will be described presently.

No case of bubonic plague had been reported north of NAN-TIEN last year. Dead rats were however found in YU-HSIEN village (雨伞) in SHANG MING LANG (上明朗) about 10 kilometers southwest of TENG-CH'UNG. In a smear made from the spleen of a dead rat found in this place by the YPHA unit, bacilli morphologically similar to B. Pestis were found. In January this year appearances of dead rats were reported from HSIN HSIA PA (新沙坝) 4 kilometers north of NAN-TIEN. Dead rats were secured for study and controlled fumugation was carried out. This will be described later in the report.

The occurrence of a plague epidemic around T'ENG-CH'UNG area was mentioned in the reports from Headquarters, Chinese Expeditionary Forces district commissioner (专员) and Magistrate of T'ENG-CH'UNG early in October 1944. Acting on these reports the YPHA sent a group of three doctors and one sanitarian, headed by Dr. Ma to the plague area. This group left Kunming on October 25th and arrived in T'ENG-CH'UNG on November 8th. A Committee for Plague Prevention was organized at T'ENG-CH'UNG. Representatives of Hq, Chinese Expeditionary Forces, 54th Army, 198th Division, Magistrate of T'ENG-CH'UNG, Burma Road Engineers, Friends Ambulance Unit, and YPHA participated. In the meeting held on December 13th, the following two resolutions were made:

a. Three traffic inspection stations to be set up at KAN CHIEH CHAI (甘蔗寨), SHANG MING LANG, and LAN PU CHAI (囊浦寨) respectively by the medical officers of the 54th Army.

b. Prophylactic innoculations and treatment of patients to be carried out by the YPHA units.

Following the decision of the Committee, two traffic inspection stations at KAN CHIEH CHAI and SHANG MING LANG were actually set up. Persons coming from the plague area were detained at the stations for a period of 10 days and given anti-plague innoculations. It was originally decided that rice for military use on its way to T'ENG-CH'UNG must be stopped at these stations, spread out in the sunshine for several hours, put into new sacks and transported to T'ENG-CH'UNG by men and horses from plague-free areas or by trucks. However these measures for rice inspection had never been carried out. The above two inspection stations were abolished after about two weeks of their existence because the medical officers in charge of these two stations belonged to the 594th Regiment and moved with their regiment to another place at the end of December. The inspection station at LAN PU CHAI was never established.

3. Clinical Data on the NAN-TIEN Cases.

According to the natives, no cases of bubonic plague had ever occurred in NAN-TIEN before the present outbreak. At the beginning of November 1944 many dead rats (1,000 to 2,000) were found. From a dead rat Dr. John Wilks of the Friends Ambulance Unit found bacilli morphologically identical with B. Pestis. The first human case occurred on November 9t

From: JICA/CBI.A, Kunming. R-673-CH-45 177985 RESTRICTED 3

FWS/rew Page 3

RESTRICTED RESTRICTED

From that date up to January 9th, 1945 102 cases (including both proven and doubtful cases) with 23 deaths were reported. Included in this number were 6 cases with one death among the soldiers and officers of the 198th Division. Among those 102 cases, 54 are males and 48 females. Appendix III Table I shows the distribution of the cases in the different age groups. It will be seen that more than half of the cases occurred in children and young adults (below 20). It is interesting to note that relatively more deaths occurred among older people (above 30) as shown by a higher case mortality rate among the latter age groups. Analysis of the data concerning the localization of the bubo is given in Table II. The percentage of cervical buboes (20.6%) seems to be higher as compared with similar data in other epidemics Table III shows that among the 102 cases, 29 were not innoculated, 69 received one to four innoculations of plague vaccine prepared by the Northwest Epidemic Prevention Bureau and the Northeast Epidemic Prevention Bureau (the soldiers as well as a few civilians were innoculated with Cutter's vaccine), and four cases with no records concerning their prophylactic innoculations. Table IV also shows that the case mortality rate is 41% among the non-innoculated as compared with 19.0%, 13.6%, 12.5% and 0% among the groups receiving 1,2, 3 or 4 innoculations. This speaks favorably for the efficacy of the plague vaccine prepared in our laboratories.

As to the treatment of patients, in districts south of NAN-TIEN where the cases occurred in July, August and September last year practically all the cases received no treatment except Chinese herbal medicines. At NAN-TIEN where the YPHA workers and the medical corps attached to the 198th Division were stationed sulfa drugs as well as anti-plague serum were well supplied and freely prescribed for patients. A temporary plague hospital with 12 beds was set up by the YPHA in a temple near NAN-TIEN on December 13th. However, they found no patients willing to be admitted. This hospital was later turned over to the medical corps of the 198th Division. A tent was sent up in the temple to be used tentatively as an isolation ward for plague patients. The 6 patients from the army as well as 7 civilian patients have so far been admitted. Other plague patients were taken care of in the homes. The attending doctors were impressed by the mildness of most of the cases. Very few fulminating of comatose cases were seen and no septicemic or pneumonic cases were reported. The patients were treated with sulfathiazole, sulfadiazine and anti-plague serum prepared by the NEPB or sulfa drugs plus serum. The results are given in Table IV. Deaths occurred in 64.3% of the untreated cases as contrasted with lower mortality rate among treated cases. No opinion could be given regarding the relative merits of the different methods of treatment as patients were treated in their homes. The higher mortality rate in groups treated with both sulfa drug and serum is probably due to the fact that the more serious type of cases were treated in this way.

4. Description of Living Conditions and Preparatory Preventative work.

Improvement of Sanitary Conditions: NAN-TIEN with a population of 1,000 (200 houses) is located 90 li (45 kms) south and west of T'ENG-CH'UNG City and between it and LUNG-CHUAN which is 200 li southwestward from NAN-TIEN, there is a wide valley along the banks of the TA YING CHIANG (大盈江). Rice is cultivated in this wide area; therefore the population is composed mainly of farmers, the majority of them are native tribes (白夷人) who reside mostly either in the adjoining hills or south of the NAN-TIEN village. At least 100,000 people inhabit this region and are distributed over 70 villages. Rice from this region is supplied to the places north of T'ENG-CH'UNG. This village of NAN-TIEN is 3,000 feet above sea level whereas T'ENG-CH'UNG is 5,000 feet above sea level. The monsoon seasons begin from May to September. The inter-monsoon period is dry and relatively warm.

Mode of Living: There are few large families living in one premise. Even in their living quarters domestic animals like chickens, pigs, horses and dogs are placed very intimately. Straw, hay, rubbish and garbage are strewn all over the house. The bed consists of single board with a straw matress on top. Underneath the bed there are also receptacles and oddities. The bedroom is totally dark and without a single window or other opening and so even in the broad daylight it is entirely dim. No chimney is found in the combined kitchen and parlor and therefore during the cooking hours the smoke is present within the house. Rice flour is milled inside the premises and the paraphenalia also adorns the premises. Remains of food and food particles are left back for animals consumption. Horse manure and discharges from the domestic animals are seen in most houses. Apart from their farming, the male members do not have other occupations and are as a rule lazy and inactive, whilst the women folk keep less indoors as evidenced on market days. Bound feet are still present for females over 30 years old but the men do not wear shoes as a rule.

Rat Infestation: Due to the excessive number of deaths by the epizootic amongst the rat population during the last three months (which accounted for at least 10-20 dead rats per house during the period) live rats are few but evidence of their presence is still abundant. Permanent rat harbourages are found which might come up to 3 or 3 per room in the corners between the wall and floor. Temporary harbourages seem to exist in old furniture, straw heaps and drawers of ancestral worship benches. Judging by the number of dead rats and the harbourages found, it would seem that the infestation of rats were very great.

Construction of Dwellings: Houses here are very low and almost entirely one-storied. The exterior walls are of mud or of earth-brick. Partitions divide the rooms. The foundation is of rubble less than two feet above the ground and extending but a few inches under the ground. The roof is tiled and a few are made of thatch without ceiling inside. The floor is usually of mud. The bed rooms have no windows. No private well is found in the homes. In close proximity to their bedrooms are the latrines, (squat type) kitchen and quarters for animals, even horses. There is no drainage, hence the floor is constantly wet. Rice is stored in matting enclosures, some in non-rat-proof wooden godowns. Yards are small and only occupy one fifth of the total floor area.

Housing Conditions: The houses and the partitioned rooms are grouped together, one adjoining the other. They are dark, wet and ill-ventilated. The kitchen and all the available floor space is occupied either by receptacles or animals. Due to the poor housing conditions, it has been decided to take the following measures for the improvement of sanitary conditions.

General Cleaning up Campaign: A general cleaning up campaign had been carried out on the 15th of January. Legs of the members of the inspection squads were smeared with a 5% solution of DDT dissolved in gasoline and vegetable oil. Every year from now on two dates will be set aside for this purpose -- March 15th and November 15th. The people were asked to take all movable furniture and articles out of the house for a full day of sunning. All refuse and garbage was burned and the whole cleaned up, and sprayed with lime (altogether [illegible],000 catties were used). Sixty-six soldiers from the 198th Division were trained to enforce the cleaning up and to check up. The normal habitat of the rat was therefore disturbed and conditions for their existence rendered intolerable. Rat holes were sealed, dust around corners were swept away to give place to a layer of lime to prevent fleas from breeding in great numbers.

Opening of Windows: Etc: Advice had previously been given and a time limit set for windows to be opened in the homes and rooms. At least one window had to be opened (area of window at least 1/10th the total floor area). By this means, in sleeping quarters, conditions for flea infestation are made unfavorable. This minimizes the danger of infection which most likely takes place through the fleas biting the victims in bed. The people were taught to construct the drainage from the inside of the house in such a way as to block the entrance of the R. Norvigicus from coming in through the drains from outside premises. Plans are borne in mind to initiate the construction of public incenerators and the householders are being taught regarding garbage disposal for the ultimate use of manure.

Public Talks: At a meeting of representatives from the MAU CHA and CHU a public talk was given on the rat-flea-human chain, the ways of rat and flea infestation and the methods of spread of the epidemic.

Cyanogas Fumigation of Infected Houses and Villages: Since the thorough fumigation of the houses and villages where dead rats were found is an important step this was undertaken. On my arrival I found that the epidemic was dying down. The supply of cyanogas was received at MAN-TIEN on January 12th. Control fumigation in MAN-TIEN was not carried out but was carried out in one important military premises and formerly infected houses. Fumigation with cyanogas was carried out in SIN SHA P. (新沙坝) 2 kilometers north of MAN-TIEN where dead rats had been found. Three houses (15 rooms) were inspected, and 32 rat holes were fumigated and blocked. The work of fumigation in areas which had been infected and in places where dead rats had been found will be systematically continued.

177985

From: CBGA China Theater, Kunming. R-673-CH-45 29 June 1945

PHS rcw Page 5

RESTRICTED

RESTRICTED

Preparation of Rat and Flea Indices Survey: A sample of the Indian Wandor cage trap was brought down from Chungking to have 50 of them reproduced in Kunming. The U.S. Army has been approached for a similar number from India. Before the arrival of cyanogas, it was considered unsafe to handle fleas from dead rats, but since the consignment came, 5 fleas all X. Cheopis were recovered fro 7 rats, 3 of which were R. Tattus and 4 were R. Norvegicus. This survey of rat and flea indices will be systematically continued. Autopsies performed on the dead rats showed morphologically plague-like bacilli from the smear of the spleen. A guinea pig innoculation was performed. The result of this experiment is not known as yet. The above work is carried on for two reasons: (a) To determine the existence of plague flea X. Cheopis and (b) For training future staff for permanent work on rat and flea indices survey. Equally important is work on meteorological records. As no hygrometer is available here, a request to supply this was made to the U.S. Army, and after its arrival daily records of meteorological findings should at least be systematically carried on for one complete year. A laboratory equipped with a dissecting microscope is now operating in the temple where the isolation hospital should have been.

Establishment of Rice Control Station: It is well known that plague will not be carried over by the plague patient to a contact, even if fleas should be present on his body. The danger of spreading the disease in this manner to other places is unlikely. It is my opinion that the plausible reason for the spread of this epidemic to other areas is due to the transportation of infected fleas carried by rice. Since this epidemic area is rich in rice, and is handling the supply of the majority of rice for the military, therefore I feel that it is of paramount importance to establish a rice control station at the point, (in this case T'ENG-CH'UNG) through which all the rice carried from the endemic area is transported to PAO-SHAN. After a visit to PAO-SHAN where I had a conference with Marshal Wei, it was decided to establish a rice control station in T'ENG-CH'UNG. This barrier will have a lime surface ground (underneath with a mixture of lime, clay and sand) which could deal with 30,000 catties of rice per day. Exposure to the sun in winter will take one day, but with strong summer sunlight it will take only two hours to treat a thin layer of rice. Four members (at present only 2) of the Yunnan Provincial Health Administration were assigned to take charge of this work. The 54th Army on the instructions of Marshal Wei, will assign a group of soldiers for the station. The "hsien" authorities will be responsible to send 4 employed laborers to work in the station. A subsidy will be given for the board of the soldiers and laborers. The "hsien" authorities will also be approached to contribute half of the cost of construction of the surface ground and a small hut to house the laborers. A request for the loan of another tent will be made to the U.S. Army authorities. Check-ups will be made along the roads to avoid possible evaders of the control scheme.

Anti-Plague Innoculations: Plague vaccine used came from the following sources: (a) North Epidemic Prevention Bureau of 1,000 million bacilli per cc-300 bottles of 40 cc each; (b) Northwest Epidemic Prevention Bureau of 1,000 million bacilli per cc-696 bottles of 40 cc each. During July and August, cases had been noticed in the valley and reports were sent up to the high command which resulted in the provincial authorities dispatching anti-epidemic units here. The innoculation campaign was started on November 13th by the YPHA units. All the vaccine made by the NWEPB was used up. Then vaccine from the NEPB was used. Finally the NWEPB was again used. Before this campaign began, the 198th Division had received Cutter vaccine (2,000 million bacilli per cc) from the U.S. Army and all the soldiers of this division were vaccinated with this vaccine. A number of civilians in NAN-TIEN had also been innoculated with this vaccine before the first case of plague was seen. Workers from the YPHA units were split up into 3 groups: (a) The first group worked in villages between LUNG-CHUAN (大龍川) and LO PU SHIH CHUAN (羅卜司莊); (b) The second group in the NAN-TIEN area; (c) The third group in T'ENG-CH'UNG area. The number of persons vaccinated is shown in Appendix III, Table V. 470 bottles of vaccine were given by Dr. Ma of the YPHA to Dr. Liang of the BRE for the Burma Road laborers (11,133 laborers were vaccinated with this lot of vaccine). As seen from Table V altogether, 20,573 persons were vaccinated (including the Burma Road laborers), 58% received one dose; 42% received 2 doses while those in the NAN-TIEN area received 3 doses. At present there are 2,400 x 40 cc bottles and still available for future use.

From: JICA/CHINA, Kunming | R-673-CH-45 | 29 June 1945

PMJ/rew | Page 6 | 17708 RESTRICTED

RESTRICTED

RESTRICTED

5. Recommendations for Future Plan of Anti-Plague Campaign.

Yunnan Province, the southwestern gateway into China, has always had a place in the history of plague in the country, and throughout the centuries especially during the late '90s and during the first two decades of the twentieth century, plague has taken innumerable toll of human lives. With the opening of the Burma Road with consequent increase in traffic, epidemiologists have always been on the qui vive for major outbreak of the "Yang Tze Ping" (痒子病), which is the local name for a group of diseases with enlargment of the lymphatic glands and fever. It includes also t.b. glands and enlargement of glands from septic foci. The people here also know that "Yang-tze-ping" comes out in epidemic form. It is most important that measures be adopted for future plague work in western Yunnan.

A service should be set up with the following duties. The one-time quarantine station, called the Tengchung Quarantine Station, which existed for some time before the enemy occupation, could once more come into being or a new medical relief and preventative unit under the "Wei Sheng Shu" be established. Before the re-opening of the Burma Road, this quarantine station should confine its activities to anti-plague work, and despite its name, need not necessarily be in T'ENG-CH'UNG itself. For practical purposes PAO-SHAN (保山) or LUNG-LING (龍陵) might be preferred. If the station is placed in one of the three places then the other two will have to have sub-stations. In addition LANG SHIH (芒市) might also have a sub-station for similar work. Besides this project, special funds must be appropriated for anti-plague work by the government. Alternatively a composite unit i.e. medical relief and preventive unit, could be put into three divisional units. Within these divisional units, two specific units, namely sanitary and laboratory, must be incorporated. Similarly special funds must be provided for anti-plague work in addition to its regular running budget. Whether the quarantine station or the medical relief and preventive unit is set up, ample facilities must be at hand for transportation for field work. If either of the organizations is set up, it must be under the direct auspices of the National Government, because it may assume inter-provincial and even international importance.

Any attempt at anti-plague work must have continuity and stability. It is essential therefore that the National Government, keeping in mind the importance of the Burma Road, should have this far-sighted policy.

It is my considered opinion that the task of eradicating the reservoir of plague in an endemic area is a gigantic one, especially during war time. Trained personnel, funds, and much needed supplies must be directed for use in places of urgent military value. While engaged in the task of localising the epidemic, more attention must be given to preventing its spread to other important areas.

It is generally known now that the Burma Road Engineers are gathering in force and numbers for the imminent re-opening of the road to traffic, and so I feel that this important strip of China's soil must be free from plague. In short small field units should be placed at the stopping points of motor traffic along the road. With increased military activity and civilian migration along the road, one cannot ignore the danger; public health workers attached to the Allied Command are all agreed that permanent steps must be undertaken to prevent the possibility of a wide-spread plague epidemic along the Burma Road. It is futile to concentrate only on the epidemic areas which are not the strategic centers of traffic and besides the population in these areas is not dense. Small field units could however be dispatched at any time from the nearest divisional unit in case of a threatened epidemic in any village within the endemic area. Therefore ample supplies for curative purposes must be stocked in the divisional units.

A mobile hospital unit should be provided so that it could be dispatched to the epidemic spot, for the isolation and treatment of cases. This unit should be equipped as follows:

a. 3 tents
b. 20 beds with bedding, bed pans, urinals and drinking cups etc.
c. Clinical instruments, such as syringes, thermometers, infusion sets, etc.
d. Drugs-sulfa drugs, anti-plague serum, etc.
e. Routine hospital stationery such as temperature charts, history and laboratory sheets etc.

From: JICA/CHINA, Kunming. R-673-CH-45

Whatever organization might be set up, the following important work must be done.

a. Further inquiries of plague history in the southwest part of Yunnan Province.
b. Rat and Flea Surveys and meteorological recordings.
c. Training of personnel in field and laboratory work.
d. Improving of sanitary conditions and proofing (ratproofing) measures.

Further Inquiries of Plague History in Yunnan: Inquiries into the history of the present epidemic lead me to think that one could delve more deeply into the epidemiological background of other towns even up to the border towns of both China and Burma. That area from PAO-SHAN southwestwards to LUNG-LING, MANG SHIH (芒市), CHE FANG (遮放), WAN-TING (畹町), then westwards to NAMKAM (南坎) and BHAMO (八莫) should respectively occupy the attention of the epidemiologists. The following places must be surveyed; PAO-SHAN, T'ENG-CH'UNG, towards MYITKYINA with a strip of land extending down to MENG KUNG (孟拱). Valuable information might be obtained of places deep inside Burmese territory. Inquiries regarding the history of plague should be made in the following manner: (1) Year of epidemic. (2) Duration of epidemic, (3) Area of epidemic. (4) Number of cases, (5) Number of deaths, (6) Method of spread of epidemic, (7) Whether dead rats found previous to epidemic, (8) Seasonal incidence, (9) Rate of rat infestation, (10) Source of rice and other important food stuffs, (11) Method of rice transportation, (12) Communication between epidemic area and neighboring parts. (13) Mode of living, (14) Housing conditions, (15) Sanitary conditions, (16) Incidence of pneumonic plague cases.

Training of Personnel: For workers engaged in plague work, special training must be given. The type of personnel needed for this work is listed below: (1) Clinicians who are familiar with plague (2) Sanitary engineers who are conversant with methods of fumigation, rat-proofing, food control measures, and sewage disposal (3) Sanitarians to act as assistants to sanitary engineers. (4) Fumigators. (5) Laboratory technicians who must understand the entomology of fleas and rats in addition to ordinary laboratory methods. They must also carry out meteorological recording.

Schedule of training: A training class must be organized in the headquarters of the anti-plague work for two years. One sanitary engineer, six sanitarians, twenty fumigators, two laboratory technicians, and two student technicians must be trained. Sanitarians must be qualified sanitary inspectors with special training in rat-proofing, fumigation, and other anti-plague measures for one or two months. Fumigators must be local high school graduates with training in general sanitation and fumigation for 2 months. Two qualified technicians with one months training in the entomology, meteorological recording technique. Two student lab technicians, high school graduates, training for 2 months.

Instructors for the above training class will be seconded from the National Institute of Health, NHEPB, and NEPB. Instructors should bring with them such material, specimens, and instruments [illegible] as are required for teaching purposes from their own institutions (on a loan basis if they cannot be spared). Special training funds for this purpose might be obtained from the American Bureau for Medical Aid to China. Representatives from the Chinese and U.S. Armies, YFMA, FAU, etc. should also come for training in special technique associated with plague prevention.

Rat and Flea Surveys and Meteorological Recordings: Two centers in the endemic areas which are easily accessible should be chosen for rat and flea survey and meteorological recordings. At present MAN-TIEN (or T'ENG-CH'UNG) and MANG SHIH (or LUNG-LING) are suitable for this purpose. Each of the two lab stations must have the following: (1) One set dissecting microscope and one set microscope with oil immersion; (2) Two thermometers; (3) One hygrometer (sling hygrometer preferred); (4) Fifty Wander pattern cage traps. Two cyanogas dusters (foot pumps) (6) One complete set each of post-mortem and entomological instruments. (7) A supply of necessary indicators, stains, chemicals, and laboratory diagnostic sets such as haemometers, haemocytometers, glassware, etc.

From: JICA/CHINA, Kunming. R-673-CH-45 17795 29 June 1945

PMS/rew Page 8

The personnel will consist of one lab technician, one student technician, one sanitarian, two local employees to act as fumigators. Trapping must be done daily with 50 traps, fleas collected from rats trapped and identified. From the result of trapping and identification, rat index-number of rats trapped. Flea index is obtained by calculating the average number of fleas per rat, specific flea index-by calculating the number of specific fleas per rat. ______ Daily and monthly mean temperatures must be recorded daily. Daily and monthly mean relative humidity and saturation deficiency in inches of mercury must be obtained under fixed conditions. All the rats trapped must be autopsied. Smears must be made in suspicious cases. In case of many dead rats, cultural and animal examinations should be performed.

Sanitary improvements and Rat-Proofing: At least two independent mobile units must be organized by the quarantine station of the medical relief and preventive unit for work along the strategic points on the Burma Road. Food and grain shops, hotels and restaurants, ought to be constantly inspected and sanitary changes enforced. Trapping and poisoning campaigns must be carried out as infestation rate mounts higher. Any permanent rat harbourage must be treated with cyanogas and blocked properly. Conditions for temporary harbourages must be removed. Regulations should be drafted and enforced to guide house construction with rat proofing ideas incorporated in the buildings. These mobile units will be charged with the responsibility of dealing with all traffic centers by stages so that the whole area could be covered. The work of these mobile units should be checked up repreatedly by inspectors from headquarters. Rat eradication and mass innoculations should be enforced in the vicinity of the Burma Road where there is infection with plague. Quarantine inspection and control of rice transportation should be carried out if necessary.

6. Remarks.

A loan of CNC $5,000,000 was made through Dr. McClure (FAU) and Commissioner [illegible]o (YPHA) from a merchant of T'ENG-CH'UNG. It is understood that as soon as funds are available either from the government or foreign contributions, this sum should be refunded. (I now hear that British Red Cross has contributed 1,500,000 and Canadian Red Cross 3,500,000 to make up this amount). I recommend that a sum not less than CNC $10,000,000 should be appropriated for the initial expenses of establishing the whole scheme. Until the U.S. Army and the FAU became actively interested in the work no supplies or equipment were available in T'ENG-CH'UNG area; but all supplies have arrived through the help of the U.S. Army, especially transport facilities for the personnel and supplies were readily given by the U.S. Army. In order to carry out the future plan, transportation and supplies are absolutely essential. During the time of war, it would be difficult for the government to cope with the situation without the active assistance of the U.S. Army. Therefore it would seem desirable to arrange with the U.S. Army to assign a sanitary officer for anti-plague work, and to co-ordinate all the services in this region, and the adjoining areas.

From: JICA/CHINA, Kunming　　R-673-CH-45　　29 June 1945

RLS/rew　　Page 9

RESTRICTED

APPENDIX III

TABLE I

DISTRIBUTION OF PLAGUE CASES AMONG DIFFERENT AGE GROUPS (JICA/CHINA Rpt R-673-CH-4

Age	Cases	Per cent	Death	Case Mortality Rate
1-10	34	33.3%	4	11.8%
11-20	23	25.5%	2	8.7%
21-30	13	12.8%	2	15.4%
31-40	16	15.7%	7	43.8%
41-50	6	5.9%	3	50.0%
51-60	3	2.9%	3	100.0%
Over 60	5	4.9%	2	40.0%
No record	2	1.9%	0	0
TOTALS	102	100.0%	23	22.5%

TABLE II

CLASSIFICATION OF CASES ACCORDING TO LOCALIZATION OF BUBO

Bubo	Cases	Per cent	Male	Per cent	Female	Per cent
Inguinal	31	30.4%	17	31.5%	14	29.2%
Femoral	5	4.9%	3	5.5%	2	4.2%
Popliteal	2	2.0%	1	1.8%	1	2.1%
Axillary	11	10.8%	5	9.3%	[illegible]	12.5%
Epitrochlear	1	1.0%	1	1.8%	0	0
Cervical	21	20.6%	[illegible]	14.8%	13	27.1%
No record	31	30.4%	19	35.2%	12	25.0%
TOTALS	102	100.0%	54	100.0%	48	100.0%

TABLE III

MORTALITY AMONG INNOCULATED AND NON-INNOCULATED CASES

Innoculation	Cases	Deaths	Case Mortality Rate
No innoculations	29	12	41.4%
1	21	4	19.0%
2	22	3	13.6%
3	24	3	12.5%
4	2	0	0
No record	4	1	25.0%
TOTALS	102	23	22.5%

TABLE IV

RESULT OF TREATMENT OF PLAGUE PATIENTS

Treatment	Cases	Deaths	CASE MORTALITY RATE
No treatment	14	9	64.3%
Sulfathiozol	40	8	20.0%
Sulfadiazine	27	1	3.7%
Serum	6	0	0
Serum & sulfathiazole	2	1	[illegible]
Serum & sulfadiazine	13	4	[illegible]
TOTALS	[illegible]	[illegible]	[illegible]

RESTRICTED

RESTRICTED

TABLE V

TABLE SHOWING ANTI-PLAGUE INOCULATIONS

NAME OF PLACE						
Chinese	English	Population	No. of Houses	Total Vaccinated	1 injection	2 injections
和顺乡	HO CHUN SHAN	10,000/		388	388	
[illegible]和乡	CHUNG HO SHAN	8,000/		1,612	1,200	412
[illegible]乡	YEE LO SHAN	6,000/		450	362	86
[illegible]街	T'ENG CH'UNG	10,000		3,544	1,182	2,363
[illegible]镇	CHENG POU CHIN	10,000		279	279	
[illegible]	YOU SHUNG RIN	5,000	1,000	1,400	1,300	100
[illegible]街	CHOW PAR KAI	4,000		799	799	
[illegible]乡	LING LUNG SHAN	4,000		1,817	987	830
[illegible]水乡	CHING SHE SHAN	7,000		120	120	
[illegible]柳乡	SHAR PAR SHAN	7,000		562	562	
[illegible]乡	HO SUI SHAN	10,000		2,650	1,057	1,593
[illegible]甸	NAN TIEN	989		1,254	640	612
[illegible]司庄	LO POO SHI CHANG					
[illegible]家寨	KO CHAR CHAI	200		241	91	150
[illegible]	CHE TAO	1,500		805	425	380
[illegible]	WAR LEN	225	40-50	395	195	200
[illegible]坡	SI HONG PO	275	50-60	95	37	58
[illegible]	LUN TUNG	2,000		358	162	196
[illegible]树寨	DA SHE CHAI	150/	30/	255	135	120
[illegible]	LEI KOK CHAI				40	45
[illegible]寨	CHE LOOK CHAI	4,000/	800/	200	115	
[illegible]	TE PING TIEN	105	21-	23	9	14
[illegible]川	LO KWONG	200/	40/	90	90	
[illegible]寨	LA CHAR CHAI	125/	25/	47	19	28
[illegible]	LUN LING	50/	10/	36	12	24
[illegible]	HON YIEN	50/	10/	35	19	16
[illegible]	CHANG PAR	60/	12/	25	11	14
木老	MO LAO	100/	20/	97	41	56
鸡头坡	CHE TAO PO	130/	26/	[illegible]	28	40
遮福	CHE HO	250/	50/	153	71	82
户那	HO NA	425/	85/	43	18	25
梁河	LIANG HO	2,500/	500/			
大厰	TA CHENG			125	125	
上大厰	SHAN TA CHENG			39	39	
鄒家寨	CHO CHAR CHAI			160	160	
下鄒家寨	SHAR CHO CHAR CHAI			35	35	
永安寨	WING AN CHAI			154	154	
陇川(城子)	RON CHUAN	5,000/		357	357	
杉木笼	SA MO ROG	300/		501	245	256
新老沙坝	SIN LAO SHA PAI	250/	50/	128	128	
	TOTAL	99,884/		19,390	11,687	7,703
保密公路	PAN SHAN MICHINA RD.			1,183	288	895

Percentage of people having one injection: 58.21%

Percentage of people having two injections: 41.79%

Percentage of people vaccinated (excluding the 1,183 of the mobile units of the 保密公路 19.41%

In some of the places the number of people vaccinated is greater than the population. In such cases it may be assumed that some of the people vaccinated did not belong to those places.

Total number of people vaccinated (including those of the mobile units of the 保密公路 20,573.

From: JICA/CHINA, Kunming. R-673-CH-45 29 June 1945

PLS/rew Page 11

177985 RESTRICTED

3.69 5 Dec. 1945: Final Report of the Committee for the Technical and Scientific Investigation of Japanese Activities in Medical Sciences, TO: The Chief Surgeon, GHQ, AFPAC, APO 500, Manila, W. S. Moore, Lt. Col., Medical Corps, Chairman

资料出处： National Archives of the United States, R112, E295A, B11.

内容点评： 本资料为1945年12月5日美军卫生部队中校W. S. Moore提交驻马尼拉美军太平洋部队总司令部军医部部长的报告，题目：科学技术调查委员会关于日本医学领域活动的最终报告。该文件少附件A、B、C、D。

GENERAL HEADQUARTERS
UNITED STATES ARMY FORCES, PACIFIC
OFFICE OF THE CHIEF SURGEON
(Advance Echelon)

0239072

5 December 45

TO: The Chief Surgeon, GHQ, AFPAC, APO 500, Manila

THRU: The Chief Surgeon, Adv. Ech., Tokyo

INFO: The Surgeon General, Washington, D.C.

SUBJECT: Final report of The Committee for the Technical and Scientific Investigation of Japanese Activities in Medical Sciences.

1. This committee was established at Manila by Order No. 640 of the Chief Surgeon's Office, GHQ, AFPAC, APO 500, dated 22 August 45, with the expectation of benefiting from independent Japanese research and development in the field of medicine and thus gaining in the overall knowledge in this science. The delegated functions of the committee were:

a. Examine and evaluate such Japanese installations and personalities associated with the medical sciences as may be practical during the occupation.

b. Correlate the activities of the medical section of the Enemy Equipment Intelligence Units attached to the armies.

c. Engage in the investigation of such other phases of Japanese Medical activities as may be directed by the Chief Surgeon.

2. The Committee arrived in Japan in two sections. One came with an Eighth Army unit (42nd General Hospital) to Yokohama, arriving at the same time as the advanced echelon of GHQ, and the other approximately a month later, with the Sixth Army (135th Medical Group) to Wakayama, then to Tokyo. The committee operated as a section of the Chief Surgeon's Office, Adv. Ech., Tokyo.

3. The plan for carrying out the investigation, as set up at Manila, was changed through force of circumstances and through prescribed procedure developing from the peaceful occupation and general cooperation from Japanese officials. The method of investigation that developed was, in general, as follows: Activities of the committee followed command channels, keeping in touch with the surgeons of the various echelons. Full cooperation was received from each. Official liaison channels were utilized in dealing with the Japanese. In many cases the Japanese Central Liaison Office, on request through G-2 Japanese Liaison, made available a representative to facilitated arrangements.

II.

4. In the above manner, over the past 3 months, every city of importance in medical education and every first class medical institution associated with research and developments in Japan, was visited. The heads of the institutions and professors of their departments were interrogated. Reprints and manuscripts were secured to supplement information gained during the interrogation. It is believed that a complete screening of Japanese Medicine for new developments and methods was accomplished

5. A vast amount of literature and information concerning all sorts of medical activity over the past 20 years became subject to examination. This forced the committee to become a "screening" rather than an "investigating" agency. During the screening procedure, new developments, original research since 1940, unfamiliar procedures and theories evolved, and literature produced since 1940, were sought.

6. Through necessity, imposed by the scope of the mission, the committee accepted statements and reports from persons interrogated which it was unable to examine and properly evaluate. Many claims, some of them of definite scientific interest, were made by the Japanese. These claims, though not accepted as factual have been reported in the periodic reports. They were considered of interest and reported with that in view.

7. During the investigation other agencies, with somewhat similar interests, began their activities. These activities were coordinated with those of the committee as far as was possible. Information secured by the committee was made available to other agencies, when it seemed to be of primary interest of the other agency and to be reported upon by that agency. Thus, matters pertaining to Aviation Medicine were turned over to ATIC, FEAF; those pertaining to BW, to the BW office, AFPAC; those of naval interest, to NavTechJap, SCAP, including research projects report from the Naval Medical College; those concerning the Atomic Bomb to the Atomic Bomb Survey; Technical Intelligence to G-2, AFPAC; and the Chairman acted as medical member of the Scientific Intelligence Survey.

8. Staff supervision of Medical Technical Intelligence was exercised through G-2, AFPAC. Plans, for the completion of technical intelligence coverage of Japan, were implemented.

9. The screening of Japanese Medical Activities in the Home Islands, with the exception of certain "Class B" institutions, which are considered of little consequence, is now completed, and such has been reported upon.

10. Attached, as Appendix "A", is a complete list of reports on institutions and special subjects. Attached, as Appendix "B", is a list of individuals whose activities have been examined. As Appendix "C", is a list of items of interest, with reference to sections of the report, and Appendix "D" is a list of institutions screened.

III.

11. Composition of the Committee was as follows:

Lt. Col. William S. Moore, M.C.
Lt. Col. James A. French, M.C.
Lt. Col. Dan Tucker, M.C.
Maj. Ray E. Trussell, M.C.
Maj. Theodore G. Anderson, SnC.
Maj. Arthur Stull, SnC.
Maj. Charles L. Leckor, M.A.C.
Capt. John E. Tobie, SnC.
Capt. Edgar J. LaLonde, M.A.C.

W. S. MOORE
Lt. Col., Medical Corps
Chairman

Index "A" - Reports listed under Institutions.
Index "B" - Persons whose activities have been examined, listed alphabetically and by geographical areas.
Index "C" - List of Items of Interest
Index "D" - Alphabetical list of Institutions screened.

Distribution:

Chief Surgeon, GHQ, AFPAC, Manila......3 copies
Surgeon General, Washington, D.C.......5 Info copies
A C of S, G-2, GHQ, AFPAC..............7 " "
Economic & Scientific Section, SCAP....1 " "
Public Health & Welfare, SCAP..........3 " "
NavTechJap - Comdr. Ayres..............2 " "
ATIG, FEAF - Capt. Castor..............1 " "
U.S.S.B.S., Medical Section............1 " "